This volume of specially commissioned essays takes as its theme the legacy of Rome in Carolingian culture in eighth- and ninth-century Europe. The authors, all leading scholars in the field, examine the 'Carolingian Renaissance', political theory, the teaching of grammar, Latin and German literature, thought, the writing of history, script and book production, art and music. Each chapter therefore addresses the theme of the legacy of Rome from the vantage point of a particular specialism, incorporates the author's own new research and provides an introduction to the study of each subject.

In every respect the essays demonstrate the creation of firm cultural foundations and the inauguration of a long period of intellectual and artistic creativity. Besides the emulation of Rome, the Carolingians made many remarkable innovations in all aspects of cultural life. Rather than focusing on 'renewal', as has usually been done, this book stresses the vigorous use of a rich heritage to create something new and distinctively Carolingian that provided the bedrock for the subsequent development of medieval European culture.

Carolingian culture: emulation and innovation

Carolingian culture: emulation and innovation

Edited by
ROSAMOND McKITTERICK
Reader in Early Medieval European History,
University of Cambridge

Published by the Press Syndicate of the University of Cambridge
The Pitt Building, Trumpington Street, Cambridge CB2 1RP
40 West 20th Street, New York, NY 10011–4211, USA
10 Stamford Road, Oakleigh, Victoria 3166, Australia

First published 1994

Printed in Great Britain at the University Press, Cambridge

A catalogue record for this book is available from the British Library

Library of Congress cataloguing in publication data

Carolingian culture: emulation and innovation / edited by Rosamond McKitterick.
p. cm.
Includes index.
ISBN 0 521 40524 6
1. Carolingians. 2. Learning and scholarship – History – Medieval, 500–1500. 3. Civilization. Medieval – Roman influences. 4. Culture diffusion – Europe. 5. Art, Carolingian. 6. Arts – Europe.
I. McKitterick, Rosamond.
DC70.C34 1993
944′.014 – dc20 92–36984 CIP

ISBN 0 521 40524 6 hardback
ISBN 0 521 40586 6 paperback

CE

IN MEMORIAM

Bernhard Bischoff
1906–1991

Contents

Select bibliographies for chapters 1–10 are to be found at the ends of these chapters.

Plates

Between pp. 78 and 79

Contributors

Giles Brown	Westminster School, London
Cyril Edwards	Lecturer in German, Goldsmiths' College, University of London
Mary Garrison	Research Fellow, Christ's College, Cambridge
George Henderson	Professor of Medieval Art, University of Cambridge and Fellow of Downing College
Matthew Innes	Peterhouse, Cambridge
Vivien Law	Fellow of Sidney Sussex College, Cambridge
Rosamond McKitterick	Reader in Early Medieval European History, University of Cambridge and Fellow of Newnham College
John Marenbon	Fellow of Trinity College, Cambridge
Janet L. Nelson	Professor of History, King's College, University of London
Susan Rankin	Lecturer in Music, University of Cambridge and Fellow of Emmanuel College

Preface

This book began life as a course of lectures in the History Faculty in Cambridge for final-year undergraduates taking the Specified Subject: 'Rome's heirs: the Germanic kingdoms of western Europe 476–987'. Each lecturer addressed the question of the legacy of Rome within the context of his or her own particular speciality, and on the basis of his or her own original research. It was remarkable how much in accord our emphases and conclusions were, firstly, on the degree of emulation of Rome and the classical past, and, secondly, concerning innovation and new, pioneering developments, in so many different aspects of Carolingian culture. There remain, nevertheless, areas that could not be considered fully in the compass of this book, the most obvious being law, liturgy and hagiography, saints' cults and relics. I am very grateful to all the contributors in this volume for having been willing to expand their lectures on the central topics that have been discussed in the papers as they are presented here. In particular, our thanks are due to Janet Nelson (and Cambridge University Press), for allowing us to print a specially revised version of a chapter originally published in the *Cambridge History of Medieval Political Thought*, and to Cyril Edwards who wrote his chapter specially for this volume, without having been part of the original lecture series. I should like to thank most warmly William Davies of Cambridge University Press whose idea it was that the lecture course should be transformed into a book and who has been a constant source of encouragement and support; Sheila Willson of the Faculty of History in Cambridge, who cheerfully typed Janet Nelson's paper according to an entirely different set of conventions for this book; and Susan Rankin and Matthew Innes for their critical comments and suggestions. Above all, I am indebted to the undergraduates over the past five years who have taken the 'Rome's heirs' paper and provided an invaluable, and apparently inexhaustible, supply of stimulating comments, questions and enthusiasm. In more ways than they may realise, this book is theirs.

Rosamond McKitterick

Acknowledgements

For permission to reproduce illustrations from manuscripts or carved ivories in their possession we are grateful to the following:

Antwerp, Plantin-Moretus Museum
Bernard Quaritch Ltd
Cambridge, The Master and Fellows of Corpus Christi College
Cambridge, The Syndics of The Fitzwilliam Museum
Laon, Bibliothèque Municipale
London, British Library
London, The Board of Trustees of The Victoria and Albert Museum
Munich, Bayerische Staatsbibliothek
Oxford, Bodleian Library
Paris, Bibliothèque Nationale
Rome, Biblioteca Apostolica Vaticana
St Gallen, Stiftsbibliothek
Stuttgart, Württembergische Landesbibliothek

Abbreviations

AASS	Acta sanctorum (Antwerp, 1643–)
AASS OSB	Acta sanctorum, Ordo sancti Benedicti, ed. L. d'Achery and J. Mabillon (Paris, 1668–1701)
Annales ESC	*Annales: Economies, Sociétés, Civilisations*
BAR	British Archaeological Reports
Bischoff, *MS* I,II,III	B. Bischoff, *Mittelalterliche Studien. Ausgewählte Aufsätze zur Schriftkunde und Literaturgeschichte* I (Stuttgart, 1966), II (Stuttgart, 1967), III (Stuttgart, 1981)
BL	London, British Library
BN	Paris, Bibliothèque Nationale
CCSL	Corpus christianorum, Series latina
CCSL (CM)	Corpus christianorum, Series latina, Continuatio medievalis
Charlemagne's Heir	*Charlemagne's Heir: New Perspectives on the Reign of Louis the Pious*, ed. P. Godman and R. Collins (Oxford, 1990)
ChLA	Albert Bruckner and Robert Marichal, *Chartae latinae antiquiores. Facsimile Edition of the Latin Charters Prior to the Ninth Century* I– (Olten, Lausanne, 1954–)
CLA	E. A. Lowe, *Codices latini antiquiores. A Palaeographical Guide to Latin Manuscripts Prior to the Ninth Century* I–XI plus Supplement (Oxford, 1935–71)
CSEL	Corpus scriptorum ecclesiasticorum latinorum
DA	*Deutsches Archiv für Erforschung des Mittelalters*
EHR	*English Historical Review*

EME	*Early Medieval Europe*
GL	*Grammatici latini*, ed. H. Keil, 8 vols. (Leipzig, 1955–80)
Godman, *Poetry*	*Poetry of the Carolingian Renaissance*, ed. P. Godman (London, 1985)
Karl der Grosse	*Karl der Grosse, Lebenswerk und Nachleben*, ed. W. Braunfels (Düsseldorf, 1965) I *Persönlichkeit und Geschichte*, ed. H. Beumann II *Das geistige Leben*, ed. B. Bischoff III *Karolingische Kunst*, ed. W. Braunfels and H. Schnitzler IV *Das Nachleben*, ed. W. Braunfels and P. E. Schramm
McKitterick, *Carolingians*	*The Carolingians and the Written Word* (Cambridge, 1989)
MGH	Monumenta germaniae historica
MGH AA	MGH Auctores antiquissimi
MGH Cap.	MGH Capitularia
MGH Cap. episc.	MGH Capitularia episcoporum
MGH Conc.	MGH Concilia
MGH Dip.	MGH Diplomata
MGH Dip. Kar.	MGH Diplomata Karolinorum
MGH Epp.	MGH Epistolae
MGH Epp. Sel.	MGH Epistolae selectae in usum scholarum
MGH Fontes	MGH Fontes iuris germanici antiqui in usum scholarum ex monumentis germaniae historicis separatim editi
MGH Form.	MGH Formulae merowingici et Karolini aevi
MGH Leges nat. germ.	MGH Leges nationum germanicarum
MGH Lib. Mem.	MGH Libri memoriales *and* Libri memoriales et necrologia, nova series
MGH Nec. Germ.	MGH Necrologia germaniae
MGH Poet.	MGH Poetae latini aevi Karolini
MGH SRG	MGH Scriptores rerum germanicarum in usum scholarum saec. VI–IX
MGH SRL	MGH Scriptores rerum langobardarum et italicarum
MGH SRM	MGH Scriptores rerum merovingicarum
MGH SS	MGH Scriptores
Munich Cgm	Munich, Bayerische Staatsbibliothek, Codex germanicus monacensis
Munich Clm	Munich, Bayerische Staatsbibliothek, Codiex latinus monacensis

PL	Patrologia latina, ed. J.-P. Migne
Rau, *Quellen*	*Quellen zur karolingischen Reichsgeschichte* I–III, ed. R. Rau (Darmstadt, 1974, 1972, 1975)
Settimane	*Settimane di studio del centro italiano di studi sull'alto medioevo*
TCBS	*Transactions of the Cambridge Bibliographical Society*
TLS	*The Times Literary Supplement*
TRHS	*Transactions of the Royal Historical Society*
Uses of Literacy	*The Uses of Literacy in Early Medieval Europe* ed. R. McKitterick (Cambridge, 1990)
Vat.	Biblioteca Apostolica Vaticana
ZfdA	*Zeitschrift für deutsches Altertum*

References to the Psalms are according to the Latin Vulgate.

I

Introduction: the Carolingian Renaissance

Giles Brown

The origins of the Carolingian Renaissance

The 'Carolingian Renaissance' may be defined as the revival of learning in conjunction with a movement to reform (to 'correct') both the institutions of the Church and the lives of the Christian peoples living under Carolingian rule. The ideal was by no means new: it was implicit within the pastoral responsibility of Christian ministers of every rank, and, from the time of Constantine onwards, within that of the Christian ruler also, the *minister Dei*. The Christian soul relied ultimately for its *reformatio* or *renovatio* on divine grace, but *correctio, emendatio*, by the relevant authorities was important in order to create the context in which that divine grace could operate since human will alone could not be relied upon.

In the pagan period the emperor, as *pontifex maximus*, had already been held 'responsible for the religious well-being of his subjects and answerable to the deity for their transgressions'; but from the fourth century onwards 'the monarch's duties towards God assumed an unprecedented seriousness'. Eusebius of Caesarea identified the task of Constantine as one of renovation and purification, of 'cleansing all the filth of godless error from His kingdom on earth'; he was 'the good shepherd', 'the teacher of knowledge about God'.[1] Here in the fourth century, as later in the eighth, there is a perception of the close link between the revival of learning and wisdom and the revival of morals, an idea that Christian Rome indeed took over from its pagan predecessor. Aponius, early in the fifth century, held that the function of the ruler ('vicegerent of God on earth, head of the Christian people') was to reform the 'body of the Church to its pristine purity'.[2] The Civil Code of Justinian (527–34) shows up very

[1] J. Procopé, 'Greek and Roman political theory', in: *The Cambridge History of Medieval Political Thought*, ed. J. Burns (Cambridge, 1988) pp. 21–36 at pp. 27, 32 and 34. Also G. Ladner, *The Idea of Reform: Its Impact on Christian Thought and Action in the Age of the Fathers* (Cambridge, Mass., 1959) pp. 41 (n.9), 119–23.

[2] Ladner, *Idea of Reform*, p. 131 n.66.

clearly the responsibilities of the emperor towards his Christian people. Here the emperor underlines his commitment, in general terms, to 'correct what is necessary', and in the preface to 'Novel' 6 voices his commitment to ensure the purity of both religious doctrine and clerical morals.[3] At the end of the century Pope Gregory the Great could, as a matter of course, use the word *rector* to describe both secular and ecclesiastical rulers, thus underlining starkly the pastoral responsibilities of the former.[4] Gregory was especially fond of lecturing kings (and bishops) on their duties.

Evidence for the application of the 'Christian reform idea' in practice, for efforts to give substance, via conversion, pastoral care, education and preaching, to the ideal of a Christian society, is most plentiful for the Frankish kingdoms under Merovingian rule from the late sixth century onwards, and for the Visigothic kingdom of Spain and the Anglo-Saxon kingdoms of Britain in the seventh century, when, indeed, everywhere in western Europe 'kings move into an ecclesiastical atmosphere'.[5] The influence of Roman practice is plainly discernible, but so too, increasingly, is that of the Old Testament, indicated by the frequent references to paradigmatic figures of kingship like David and Solomon. Among the Franks and the Anglo-Saxons at least, the idea of a barbarian *gens* as the New Israel was already gaining ground. The anointing of Visigothic kings from 672 suggests a similar process at work in Visigothic Spain. Isidore of Seville, for whom kingship was a *praesulatus* for the ruling of the people, recognised that the kingdom and its rulers, both royal and ecclesiastical, as in other *membra Christi* in Gaul, Italy and elsewhere, would be judged by God according to how effectively and how efficiently He saw that the faith had been preached. A king was 'useful' in so far as he established the 'norms of correct living' (*norma recte vivendi*) in his laws: 'he who does not correct does not rule', he wrote. The rapid and widespread dissemination of Isidore's works in the later seventh and early eighth centuries indicates how much others, both in Spain and outside, shared his sense of priorities. If the superficially impressive culture of seventh-century Visigothic Spain was, in reality, merely 'the culture of a few great bishops and abbots and an occasional lay noble', at least they recognised that the way forward, the prospects for effective reform, lay with educated clerics and more of them.[6] What they managed to achieve before the eclipse of their kingdom and its culture is less clear. This was a path that Charlemagne was to tread more energetically and, apparently, with greater success. What is important for our present purposes is that the Visigothic kings with the help of their bishops, in the interests of political unity and the Christian *utilitas* of their

[3] P. Stein, 'Roman law', in: *Medieval Political Thought*, ed. Burns, pp. 42–6; G. Ladner, 'Gregory the Great and Gregory VII: a comparison of their concepts of renewal', *Viator* 4 (1973) pp. 1–26 at pp. 24–6.

[4] R. Markus, 'The Latin fathers', in: *Medieval Political Thought*, ed. Burns, pp. 92–122 at pp. 119–20.

[5] J. M. Wallace-Hadrill, *Early Germanic Kingship in England and on the Continent* (Oxford, 1971), p. 47.

[6] B. Bischoff, 'Die europäische Verbreitung der Werke Isidors von Sevilla', in: *Isidoriana* (León, 1961) pp. 317–44, reprinted in Bischoff, *MS* I, pp. 171–94, and J. N. Hillgarth, 'Popular religion in Visigothic Spain', in: *Visigothic Spain: New Approaches*, ed. E. James (Oxford, 1980) pp. 1–60 at p. 18.

people, promoted religious reform in a manner that in important respects anticipates that of the Carolingians.

In the religious culture of the 'Northumbrian Golden Age' of the late seventh and early eighth centuries in England, as exemplified in the writings of Bede, we meet the same concerns: an exclusive interest in learning that was relevant and useful, a dependence on patristic authority, a commitment to furnish an educated and disciplined clergy as the means to correct the lives of the population at large. Among his contemporaries there is also an evident concern for correct Latinity, both in speech and writing, and a desire to reform liturgical practices in line with those in use in Rome. Bede's ideals may have had limited application in the eighth-century Anglo-Saxon kingdoms but they had considerable impact in Francia, both through the rapid dissemination of his writings there in the generation after his death by Anglo-Saxon missionaries and through the person of Alcuin, a key figure at the court of Charlemagne from the early 780s. Like Isidore of Seville, Bede believed that the unity of a people was grounded in its religion: this idea also was to have an important place in the Carolingian reforms. In short, these reforms, when they begin, are moving along lines already mapped out by the Visigoths and the Anglo-Saxons.

In Gaul, as in Spain, the culture of the late Roman world, and its educational tradition, survived more or less intact into the seventh century when episcopal schools were still functioning, Church councils continued to debate religious doctrine, theological works continued to be written, and when there is still fairly widespread evidence of literacy of some kind amongst kings and the lay aristocracy, not least in the continued use of the written word in business of all kinds, a fact only now being fully appreciated.[7] Pope Gregory the Great's famous letter condemning Bishop Desiderius of Cahors for lecturing on classical texts says as much about how the onus for preserving classical learning had fallen into the hands of the Church as about Gregory's own attitude to secular learning ('the same lips cannot sing the praises of Love and the praises of Christ').[8] As the seventh century opened it is clear not only that episcopal schools continued to function but also that classical learning, albeit in the service of religious education, could still find a place in them.

It is for these reasons, and because of a new understanding of Christian culture in the British Isles in the seventh century and its export to the continent in the wake of missionaries and *peregrini*, that many historians have come to question seriously the traditional view of the period 630–780 as a dark age in Europe; and by extension, necessarily, the concept of a 'Carolingian Renaissance'. The implication is that there was no Carolingian Renaissance, at least not in Charlemagne's time, because there was no long dark night which preceded it.

It is instructive to see the Carolingian revival of learning in these terms and

[7] See McKitterick, *Carolingians*, pp. 2–3 and 23–4, with many references to recent research, and I. N. Wood, 'Administration, law and culture in Merovingian Gaul', in: *Uses of Literacy*, pp. 63–81.

[8] Ep. xi, 34, MGH Epp. II, p. 303, lines 14–15.

Charlemagne's role in the movement as a whole needs to be kept in proportion. There are clear elements of cultural continuity in Francia over the period 650–750; the recent *La Neustrie* exhibition mounted in Rouen, the two volumes published in the *Beihefte der Francia* series under the same title, and the publication of the relevant volumes in the *Chartae latinae antiquiores* series have emphasised how strong these elements were.[9] It has been suggested that if there are, after about 700, no more legal documents or judgements issued in the name of the Merovingians, and very few *diplomata*, this has as much to do with the collapse of royal government as the collapse of learning.[10] Certainly there are centres, like the monastery of Corbie near Amiens, for example, where, from the testimony of the surviving manuscripts and their scripts, there is evidence of just such continuity.[11] The steady evolution of minuscule scripts, and other calligraphic techniques, at monasteries such as Corbie and Luxeuil, and elsewhere, from *ca* 700 onwards certainly argues for a decent, organised, level of literary and scribal activity in these centres.[12]

The influence of the *Annales* school is clearly evident in this interpretation of events, with emphasis placed on substructural developments of *la longue durée*. For all its merits, however, revisionism of this kind runs the risk of overemphasising continuity at the expense of change; and of failing to acknowledge the depths of the nadir to which learning and the welfare of the Church had sunk across the Frankish territories as a whole in the late seventh and early eighth centuries. Isolated pockets, or *foyers*, of culture may indeed be discerned here and there, but overall the picture is bleak: the (limited) activity of these centres apart, there is little evidence either of the copying of manuscripts or of the composition of new works of any kind. The evidence for cultural activity on any significant scale in the Frankish monasteries and episcopal churches of the late Merovingian period is simply not there; and what evidence there is, in the form of manuscripts copied at this time, is notoriously difficult to interpret: very few eighth-century manuscripts can be dated with any precision or located to a particular centre with any reasonable degree of certainty. The arguments in favour of significant continuity in the sphere of cultural activity over the period 650–750 in Gaul rest on very uncertain foundations.

The abbey of St Denis may serve as an example. The evidence for literary activity here, at the greatest of all Neustrian houses, greater even than Corbie in terms of wealth and status, in the first half of the eighth century is confidently asserted by Riché principally on the basis of three assumptions: firstly that the historical source known as the *Liber historiae francorum* was put together here in

9 P. Perrin, and L.-C. Feffer, *La Neustrie* (Rouen, 1985) and *La Neustrie. Les Pays au nord de la Loire de 650 à 850*, ed. H. Atsma, Beihefte der Francia 16, 2 vols. (Sigmaringen, 1989), especially the papers by Vezin, McKitterick and Riché. See also *ChLA*, vols. XIII–XIV, XVII–XIX, ed. H. Atsma and J. Vezin (Zurich, 1981–7).

10 J. Nelson, 'Literacy in Carolingian government', in: *Uses of Literacy*, pp. 258–96 at p. 261.

11 D. Ganz, 'Corbie and Neustrian monastic culture, 661–849', in: *La Neustrie*, ed. Atsma, II, pp. 339–48.

12 See McKitterick, below, chapter 8, pp. 221–47.

the late 720s, secondly that the young Pippin III was sent to be educated here by his father Charles Martel, and thirdly that a sacramentary was written and illuminated here during Pippin's reign.[13] In fact recent opinion locates the origin of the *Liber* rather at Soissons (Notre-Dame? St Médard?).[14] Pippin's 'education' at St Denis is deduced from his own testimony that he was *enotritus* (sic: *nutritus*) here, and that *ab sua infantia* he had seen the monks extracting tolls and taxes from merchants coming to the October fair.[15] Subsequently there is no sign of this education; there is no evidence that Pippin could either read or write nor as mayor did he take a personal initiative in promoting learning at his court. The abbey of St Denis was a favoured royal residence; there was a palace here (rebuilt by Abbot Fardulf for Charlemagne) where Pippin's wife Bertrada evidently spent much time.[16] The word *nutritus* here may refer simply to an awareness on Pippin's part that the saint had sustained him, both materially and spiritually: what he has in mind is the time he spent at St Denis as a boy rather than any education received of whatever kind whilst he was there. The origin of the eighth-century Gelasian Sacramentary referred to by Riché (Vat. Reg. lat. 316) is now thought to be either Chelles or Jouarre, not St Denis.[17] Other evidence cited is as tenuous: it is very unlikely that the *passion anonyme* of St Denis cited by Riché (the so-called *Post beatam ac gloriosam*) was written before the last quarter of the eighth century.[18] There is no evidence that the magnificent late-antique half-uncial manuscripts of Vergil and St Hilary of Poitiers were at St Denis before Charlemagne's reign. In fact there is no concrete evidence of manuscript copying at St Denis before the reign of Abbot Fardulf (792–804), although a royal diploma of December 774 (not actually discussed by Riché) grants valuable woodland and hunting rights to the monks 'for the covering of books'.[19] This hardly seems enough to justify the description of the abbey in the first half of the eighth century as a great centre of learning. The potential and resources of other institutions cited as *foyers* of culture at this period seem to be exaggerated in like fashion, with too much weight being placed on the available evidence. It may be that the declining number of royal documents in the late Merovingian period in Francia must be attributable first and foremost to the decline of royal power as Janet Nelson suggests; but the few royal charters that we possess from the first half of the eighth century are very

[13] P. Riché, *Education and Culture in the Barbarian West, Sixth through Eighth Centuries*, trans. J. J. Contreni (Columbia, S. C., 1976) pp. 442–3 and P. Riché, *Écoles et enseignement dans l'haut moyen âge, fin du Ve siècle – milieu du XIe siècle* (2nd edn Paris, 1989) p. 66

[14] R. Gerberding, *The Rise of the Carolingians and the Liber Historiae Francorum* (Oxford, 1987) pp. 146–59 (St Médard?) and J. Nelson, *TLS*, 11–17 March 1988, p. 286 (Notre Dame?).

[15] MGH Dip. Kar. I, no. 8, line 7, p. 13 (29 July 755) and no. 12, line 2, p. 18 (30 October 759).

[16] *Miracula sancti Dionysii* I, c. 16, ed. J. Mabillon, AASS OSB, saec. III, pars. 2, p. 348 and Fardulf, MGH Poet. I, pp. 353, 408–10.

[17] See R. McKitterick, 'Nuns' scriptoria in Francia and England in the eighth century', *Francia* 19/1 (1992) pp. 1–35.

[18] See G. Brown, 'Politics and patronage at the abbey of St Denis (814–98): the rise of a royal patron saint', unpublished D. Phil. thesis (Oxford, 1990) pp. 230–44, 281.

[19] MGH Dip. Kar. I, no. 87, line 35, p. 126.

inferior productions, both in terms of Latinity and scribal technique, to those of the preceding or succeeding periods.

The extent to which cultural activity was maintained, and widely diffused, in the churches of late Merovingian Gaul is therefore debatable. What is clear, however, is that the 'Christian reform idea', and the Christian culture which was characteristic of it, were not inventions of the Carolingian Renaissance since this culture is already evident in Visigothic Spain and in Anglo-Saxon England in the wake of conversion during the seventh century. It had also taken firm root in Merovingian Gaul. Merovingian kings, at least until the mid-seventh century, were concerned about the *correctio* of their people as a series of edicts makes clear.[20] What these surviving edicts show, and we may assume that there were once more of them, is that the Merovingian kings, in public at least, were committed to shaping a Christian society pleasing to God, where the clergy lived disciplined lives according to the dictates of canon law, and where the laity, abandoning all vestiges of their pagan past, held fast to the moral standards of the Christian faith; against a background of peace, discipline and just laws, all were to prosper together, pleasing God and working out their salvation. This is the kind of all-embracing social programme associated with the Carolingians, and in particular with Charlemagne; the frequent use of fundamental concepts like *emendatio*, *admonitio* and above all *correctio* is common to both. The only difference seems to be that the Carolingians pursued the ideal with more purpose, more success and greater resources. In the absence of more source material the Merovingian reform effort, in its scope and impact, is hard to assess. But what can be said of it is this: if the Carolingian reforms, and the ideals behind them, were anticipated in late Roman imperial practice, in Visigothic Spain and in Anglo-Saxon England, it is above all from the effort of their Merovingian predecessors, themselves conscious of the norms of Christian Roman rulership, that the Carolingian programme seems to draw inspiration.

The canons of the councils of the Merovingian Church held in the same period show how the institutions of the Church and the lives of the clergy were to be reformed so as to further these aims. There survive from the period 511–*ca* 680 the records (partial or complete) of more than twenty councils in which more than one province of the Church of Gaul was represented; besides that the records of two provincial councils and one (only) diocesan synod. From these we know that efforts were made to establish a Church hierarchy, to secure the rights of metropolitan bishops over their diocesans, and the supervisory rights of these diocesans over their priests and abbots, to ensure the appointment of educated clergy, to safeguard their economic welfare and to discipline their conduct, to regulate the lives of monks, to provide some uniformity in liturgical matters. As for the laity, efforts were made to suppress their pagan practices and

20 MGH Cap. I, no. 2, pp. 2–3; no. 5, pp. 11–12; no. 7, p. 15; no. 8, p. 18; no. 9, pp. 20–2.

to ensure worship on Sunday rather than Thursday ('Jove's Day'), to make the payment of tithe obligatory, to regularise marriage according to the dictates of canon law. Once again these are all concerns which anticipate Carolingian practice.

This is true also of another feature which requires special emphasis, namely the desire to regulate norms of practice and behaviour so as to accord more closely with Roman practice. Roman influence was particularly marked in the southern province of Arles during the time of Bishop Caesarius, papal vicar; but veneration for the Church of Rome is apparent across Merovingian Gaul as a whole. Church dedications to Sts Peter and Paul far outnumber those to native saints, particularly in the seventh century: the majority of the new monastic foundations of the period were dedicated to these Roman martyrs even if the cult of a local saint quickly came to have greater prominence. Merovingian councils acknowledged Rome's right to pronounce on doctrinal matters, and by the seventh century were advocating the division of episcopal revenues according to the Roman pattern. Roman influence on the liturgy of the Frankish churches was strong but not uniform, a patchwork of local variations giving rise to that 'fruitful confusion so characteristic of Merovingian liturgy'.[21] The spread of the Rule of St Benedict in seventh-century Gaul is surely to be related likewise to its links with Rome and Pope Gregory the Great.

Thus a council held at Autun (663–675) could enjoin that all monks followed the Rule of St Benedict.[22] The eighth-century popes rightly calculated that they could depend on the Franks and their Carolingian mayors because, as Pope Gregory II (715–31) put it, they venerated St Peter as if he were a god on earth.[23] 'In other words, it was not from the Anglo-Saxons that the Franks learnt about the cult of St Peter and the primacy of Rome.'[24]

The councils of the Merovingian Church have much to say about the problem of persisting pagan practices after the official conversion of the Franks under Clovis at the turn of the fifth and sixth centuries. The Church had to contend with a pattern of customs and tradition engrained over centuries. 'You will never uproot our customs', St Eligius was rudely told; 'we will go on with our rituals forever ... No man will ever be able to stop us doing what we love and what we have done for so long.'[25] Even among the Roman population vestiges of pagan ritual still endured in the middle of the eighth century, a state

21 J. M. Wallace-Hadrill, *The Frankish Church* (Oxford, 1983) pp. 118–19.
22 MGH Conc. I, p. 22, line 16.
23 Letter of Gregory II to the Emperor Leo III, ed. J. Gouillard, 'Aux origines de l'iconoclasme: le témoignage de Grégoire II', in *Centre de recherche d'histoire et civilisation byzantines, Paris, Travaux et mémoires* 3 (1968) 243–307 at p. 297, line 261.
24 Wallace-Hadrill, *Frankish Church*, p. 113.
25 *Vita Eligii*, II, c. 20, MGH SRM IV, pp. 711–12, trans. P. Fouracre, 'The work of Audoenus of Rouen and Eligius of Noyon in extending episcopal influence from the town to the country in seventh-century Neustria', in: *The Church in Town and Countryside*, ed. D. Baker, Studies in Church History 16 (Oxford, 1979) pp. 77–91 at p. 82.

of affairs that greatly concerned St Boniface.[26] Eligius was operating around Noyon in the 660s. Thereafter the situation was unlikely to improve. From around this time the Frankish Church ceased to convene in council; at least no records survive to indicate that it did. In 742 Boniface claimed to be reliably informed by 'old men' that the Franks 'have not held a council for more than eighty years', nor had an archbishop, 'nor have they established or restored in any place the canons of the Church', and that *ecclesiastica religio* had been completely neglected for fifty or sixty years.[27] The evidence indicates that the Frankish Church suffered greatly as a result of the collapse of Merovingian power. In the first place it was the king who guaranteed the existence of the Church as an independent body with the institution of the immunity. Broadly speaking the right of immunity gave churches, both monasteries and bishoprics, the right to govern their own affairs independently of the local lay official, the count. The system depended entirely on the king to uphold it, abbots and bishops being given access to appeal directly to the king if their immunity were being encroached upon. The inability of the central power to guarantee the immune status of churches opened the door to the loss of their lands and revenues, to secularisation, with offices held by laymen and lands given over to the support of an armed following, a process which could threaten the very existence of a church. The Frankish Church ceased to hold synods and councils, and ceased to have a consciousness of itself as an independent institution, at the same time as it ceased to be one. The struggle for mastery between the Carolingians and their rivals, now given free reign in the absence of a royal authority to keep it in check, encouraged the wholesale alienation of church lands to support *milites*. Without lands a monastic community was forced to disperse, and a bishop was denied the means to support diocesan organisation and activity, in short the work of *correctio*. Few resources remained for the production of books. Charters and diplomas attest that the standard of written Latin had sunk to an alarming level. Against this background, and with so few indications that manuscripts continued to be copied and new works composed, it would seem unwise to place much emphasis on the continuity of learning and cultural activity over this period.

Some qualifications must of course be made to this generally gloomy picture. There were many variations within this overall pattern. Some parts of Gaul suffered more than most, notably Aquitaine, subject firstly to Moslem invasion then Carolingian reconquest and subjugation: here long gaps in the episcopal lists indicate that from the 720s the Aquitainian Church had practically ceased to exist. In the north some churches were less affected than others: magnates no less than kings required the intercession of saints as well as the support of soldiers and

[26] Boniface to Pope Zacharias, Ep. 50, ed. M. Tangl, *Die Briefe des heiligen Bonifatius und Lullus*, MGH Epp. Sel. I (Hanover, 1916) p. 84.

[27] Ibid., p. 82; Eng. trans. C. H. Talbot, *The Anglo-Saxon Missionaries in Germany* (2nd edn London, 1981) no. 27, p. 99.

a favoured church might be spared for that reason. A monastery close to the Carolingians, Echternach for example, appears to have got off lightly. Here manuscripts continued to be copied.[28] An important Neustrian shrine like that of St Denis where Charles Martel was buried and his son Pippin *enotritus* may also have been favourably treated. On the other hand churches occupied by opponents of Carolingian domination, for example the Burgundian episcopal church of Auxerre and its neighbours, appear to have been systematically stripped of their possessions with the aim of emasculating resistance. There was also a difference between regularised alienation (often *pro verbo regis*) for which (in theory) a rent was to be paid, and outright despoliation. The former could even be justified according to contemporary standards (if not those of the ninth century): thus Carloman I, ruling as mayor in 742 or 743, explained that ecclesiastical lands had been redistributed 'on account of the imminent wars and persecutions of other peoples all around us'.[29] The Carolingian mayors were also patrons of the Church in the sense that they supported missionary work in Alemannia, in the German lands east of the Rhine, and on the lower reaches of the Rhine and Maas rivers, in Frisia and Toxandria. In this they had taken over a responsibility exercised by earlier Merovingian kings such as Dagobert I. It was another way in which, as *principes*, they came to exercise the function of royalty long before they acquired the name of it. There were political as well as spiritual rewards to be gained here; the extension and consolidation of the Christian faith among the Germans, the Alemannians and the Frisians went hand in hand with the extension and consolidation of Frankish political authority in these regions, the latter two conscious of their traditions of semi-independent rule under native dukes who had successfully cast off Frankish overlordship as Merovingian rule became more remote. Missionary work could only be effective if backed up by military force as St Boniface, in a letter to Bishop Daniel of Winchester, made clear: 'without the patronage of the Frankish prince I can neither govern the faithful of the Church nor protect the priests, clerics, monks and nuns of God, nor can I forbid the practice of heathen rites and the worship of idols in Germany without his orders and the fear he inspires'.[30] The reality was that conversion took place at the point of a sword, as St Lebuin, in the later eighth century, sought to impress upon the Saxons: 'if you are not willing to become adherents of God ... there is a king in the neighbouring land who will enter your land, conquer and devastate it'.[31] Missionaries who trusted too exclusively in the power of the Gospel were inclined to fail.

Many of the leading figures in this missionary work from the late seventh century onwards were Anglo-Saxons, who like an earlier ascetic and reformer St Columbanus, the Irishman, took to heart God's command to Abraham to go

[28] R. McKitterick, 'The diffusion of Insular culture in Neustria between 650 and 850: the implications of the manuscript evidence', in: *La Neustrie*, ed. Atsma, II, pp. 395–432 at pp. 422–9.

[29] Capitulary of Leptinnes, MGH Cap. I, no. 11, c. 2, p. 28.

[30] Boniface, Ep. 63, ed. Tangl, *Briefe*, p. 130; Eng. trans. Talbot, *Anglo-Saxon Missionaries*, no. 30, p. 117.

[31] *Vita Lebuini antiqua* c. 6, MGH SS XXX, p. 794.

forth from his native land and kindred.[32] Foremost of these were Sts Willibrord, or 'Clement' (died 739), and Winfryth, better known by his adopted Roman name of Boniface (died 753). Willibrord worked among the Frisians from Utrecht, as St Amand had done before him in the 630s; here Boniface joined him in 716 before moving away to work east of the Rhine in Hesse and Thuringia where he established sees at Buraburg, Erfurt, Würzburg and (later) Eichstätt. With the death of Charles Martel and the accession of his two sons Pippin III and Carloman I in 741, Boniface embarked upon a new stage of his career, namely the reform of the Frankish Church and its institutions.

The Carolingian reform movement may be said to begin in 742 or 743 with the first of Carloman's councils. But reform had its roots in the missionary work of the preceding generations on the peripheries of the Frankish realm, in which monastic units had played an important role. In reality missionary work and church reform were closely linked, not least because, as missionaries frequently complained, it was singularly inappropriate that the morality of Christians living in Francia should compare so unfavourably with those of the pagans among whom they worked. The reform movement also drew inspiration from earlier Merovingian practice, and from the widespread patronage of monasticism which had been so marked a feature of the seventh century and in which the Frankish aristocracy, both secular and ecclesiastical, had been centrally involved. In short, reform of the Frankish Church was bound to begin again once royal (or mayoral) authority had managed to reassert itself.

The role of the Irish in the seventh-century expansion of Frankish monasticism, and that of the Anglo-Saxons both in the missionary activity on the edges of the Frankish territories, and in the subsequent reform programme within them, were both important; but they must not be overstated. Many of Columbanus' 'Irish' followers are now thought in fact to have been Franks (St Gall, for example), subsequently labelled as such when it became fashionable to equate Irish origin with extreme asceticism or sanctity. The cult of St Peter was already widely established in Francia and Germany. However, it is likely that Boniface, albeit working within an established tradition and with the full backing of the Carolingian mayors, was in some measure responsible for the close alignment of the Frankish Church, and its rulers, with Rome, which is so characteristic a feature of the eighth century.[33] Willibrord and, in particular, Boniface certainly kept in close touch with Rome during the course of their work, and had their authority confirmed by titles, and insignia, conferred on them in Rome; though this can only have been with the approval, perhaps even the active encouragement, of their Carolingian (and Bavarian) masters. For its part there are indications that the papacy was taking a greater interest in the spread of the Christian faith north of the Alps, in a *universalis gentium confessio*, from the seventh century

32 Jonas of Bobbio, *Vita Columbani*, I, 4–5, MGH SRM IV, p. 71.

33 T. Reuter, 'St Boniface and Europe', in: *The Greatest Englishman. Essays on St Boniface and the Church at Crediton*, ed. T. Reuter (Exeter, 1980) pp. 69–94 at pp. 85–6.

onwards; this, as well as the growing Lombard threat and the problems of the Byzantines, both political and doctrinal, would be bound to sharpen papal interest in the rise of Carolingian power. The interests of the papacy and the Carolingians, for the most part, fitted supremely well together.

The Insular contribution to the development of learning in the Frankish territories of the seventh and eighth centuries is also important.[34] Perhaps as many as twenty texts, pagan as well as Christian, owe a crucial stage of their transmission in the Frankish lands to Insular contributions.[35] The manuscript evidence is instructive in other ways: forms of script, methods of manuscript preparation and a variety of scribal habits in punctuation (much valued by the Anglo-Saxons) and abbreviation indicate that a significant proportion of the manuscripts which survive from this period, 650–800, were copied either by Anglo-Saxon or Irish personnel, or by Frankish scribes trained in the Insular tradition. This trend is as apparent in manuscripts associated with Neustria as it is in those associated with monastic scriptoria in the German lands where the presence of Anglo-Saxon scribes is the more explicable. Thereafter Insular scribal habits decline somewhat as the revival of Roman practices increases.[36] But we can say, without exaggeration, that in a variety of ways the contribution of the Irish and the Anglo-Saxons to the early phases of the Carolingian Renaissance was highly significant.

The reform of the Frankish Church under the Carolingians

By 741 the Frankish Church was ripe for reform. The bleak assessment of the state of the Frankish Church in the early 740s given by St Boniface in his letters must be taken seriously, even when all allowances have been made for regional variations (the problems in the German lands are likely to have been worse) and political antagonisms. According to Boniface the reputation of Frankish clergy, bishops and priests, as adulterers was notorious. Because no councils had been held for such a long time, Pope Zacharias said, 'many who call themselves priests hardly know what the priesthood is'.[37] Shortly after the death of his father Carloman I instructed Boniface to convene a synod because, says Boniface in a letter to the pope, he wanted 'to correct and emend (*corrigere et emendare*) ecclesiastical discipline' which, 'for a long time' had suffered neglect.[38] The outcome, in either 742 or 743 was a council known as the *Concilium germanicum*, presided over by St Boniface. This was followed shortly after by a second

[34] On what follows see McKitterick, 'Diffusion', pp. 395–432.

[35] Ibid., pp. 400–3.

[36] B. Bischoff, *Latin Palaeography. Antiquity and the Middle Ages* (Cambridge, 1990), pp. 17, 22, 26–7, 39, 60, 65 and 81; also R. McKitterick, 'Anglo-Saxon missionaries in Germany: reflections on the manuscript evidence', *TCBS* 9 (1989) pp. 291–329.

[37] Boniface, Epp. 50, 51 and 63, ed. Tangl, *Briefe*, pp. 80–92, 129–32; Eng. trans. Talbot, *Anglo-Saxon Missionaries*, nos. 27, 28 and 30, pp. 99–106.

[38] Boniface, Ep. 50, ed. Tangl, *Briefe*, p. 82.

council held at Leptinnes (or Les Estinnes) in 744, also convoked by Carloman, and a third, in the same year, summoned by his brother Pippin at Soissons for the Neustrian lands under his control. Both date and content make it clear that the brothers were here working in partnership. The concern of all three councils was that the Church should function 'according to the canons'. Both rulers ordained that henceforth synods were to be held annually, in Carloman's territory under the aegis of Boniface, *qui est missus sancti Petri*.[39] If these annual synods were held there is no sign of them, a salutary reminder that these beginnings were modest, and that what these early Carolingian councils really amount to are statements not of achievement but of intent. The degenerate state of the Frankish Church in Carloman's kingdom is highlighted by the fact that so few bishops were called upon to attend: only seven, for example, attended the *Concilium germanicum*, at least three of whom (the bishops of Buraburg, Würzburg and Eichstätt) were Boniface's disciples; of the others perhaps only Regenfrid of Cologne was a Frank. We must assume that Boniface considered the other bishops in Carloman's territories to be useless to the work of reform. In Neustria things were better: as many as twenty-seven (unnamed) bishops attended Pippin's council at Soissons. The focus at these gatherings was squarely on the Church and its reform: 'so that the resolutions of the canons and the laws of the Church may be restored and the Christian religion emended'. It was to be de-secularised and reconstituted as an independent and distinctive institution: clerics were to live and dress distinctively, not carrying arms; above all they were to be celibate. It was vital that they set a good moral example. Both monks and nuns were to observe the Rule of St Benedict, at least in Carloman's territory. They were to have enough land to fulfil their vocation but were entitled to no more: the surplus should be rented out (in a controlled fashion) to support *milites*. Candidates for the priesthood, and bishoprics, should be examined by a synod to ensure they were not ignorant. Priests were to be subject to bishops. Both were to ensure *diligenter* that pagan practices were outlawed and heresies suppressed. Carloman, at Leptinnes, maintained that in ordering the suppression of paganism he was continuing what his father had started. Here the fundamental aim was spelt out: 'so that the Christian people may achieve salvation'. The reform of the Church was the precondition for the salvation of the people. Laymen must not fornicate, nor swear false oaths; they must look after the Church of God: counts (or *graviones*) were to co-operate with bishops in their pastoral work; indeed they were urged to see themselves as office-holders with a key role to play: they were protectors of the Church. At Soissons the role of secular authority is forcefully stressed: the prince (*princeps*) and his counts, as well as his bishops, are ready to discipline anyone who disregards this decree. Here, too, there is a conception of the different orders (*ordines* of the Christian

39 *Concilium germanicum* c. 1, MGH Cap. I, no. 10, p. 25; Capitulary of Soissons, c. 2, MGH Cap. I, no. 12, p. 29.

society, an idea that figures prominently in the imperial legislation of Charlemagne and Louis the Pious.[40]

Already in the 740s then we meet the concerns that will animate subsequent Carolingian legislation: the regulation of marriage according to the demands of the Church, ecclesiastical discipline, order and hierarchy, a commitment to an educated priesthood, uniformity of religious observance (for example in the stipulation that the Benedictine Rule alone was to be observed in monasteries), the suppression of pagan practices, and above all a determination to organise life, in every department, according to canon law. The programme, in its overall aim and in the stated means to achieve it, is no different in substance from that set down in the edicts of earlier Merovingian rulers. The Carolingian reform initiative owes as much to native Frankish tradition as it does to Anglo-Saxon influence.

One other issue must be stressed, namely the restoration of the wealth that had been stolen from the Church in the previous generations. If the church was to be de-secularised it needed to be independent of lay control, and for this it needed independent means. From his correspondence we know that Boniface envisaged wholesale restitution of church lands; we know too that Carloman and Pippin resisted this: it could not be done without distraining the *milites* (warriors) on whom Carolingian authority relied. But at Leptinnes and Soissons it was stipulated that the Church was to be 'consoled' for its losses according to its needs; beyond that surplus wealth was to be given over *in adiutorium exercitus nostri* (that is, for military purposes, at least 'for a little while', says Carloman) but the Church's proprietary right to it was to be recognised by the payment of a rent.[41] To what extent this principle was put into practice at this point must be doubtful: the reiteration of the injunction time and time again by eighth- and ninth-century councils that this rent, ninths and tenths (*nona et decima*), was to be paid suggests that it was difficult to enforce. Moreover settlements of this sort required detailed surveys of ecclesiastical property of the kind that became possible only in the next generation. Nevertheless the principle that underlay it, enunciated here for the first time at the councils of Soissons and Leptinnes, known as apportionment (*divisio*), namely that because of pressing secular needs churches were entitled only to that proportion of their landed resources necessary for the proper fulfilment of their function, was one that was to have an important future in the Carolingian period.

In 747 another council was held, probably in the aftermath of Carloman's departure for Rome, and covering both territories now united under the rule of Pippin. No formal record of its proceedings has survived; but it is referred to by Boniface in a letter to Archbishop Cuthbert.[42] Evidently it covered the same

[40] See *Concilium germanicum*, preface and cc. 1–5, 7 and 10, MGH Cap. I. no. 10, pp. 25–6; Capitulary of Soissons, cc. 2–4, 6–9, *ibid.*, no. 12, pp. 29–30; Capitulary of Leptinnes, cc. 1–2 ibid., no. 11, pp. 27–8.
[41] Capitulary of Leptinnes c. 2, ibid., p. 28; Soissons c. 3, ibid., p. 29.
[42] MGH Conc. II.i, no. 6(A), pp. 45–8; Eng. trans. Talbot, *Anglo-Saxon Missionaries*, no. 35, pp. 129–34.

ground as the previous councils but, at least on some points, in more detail. More significant is the fact that all the attendant bishops swore in writing 'that in all things we shall obey the orders of St Peter . . . to these declarations we have all agreed and subscribed, and we have forwarded them to the shrine of St Peter'. This amounted to a formal profession of unity with Rome under the jurisdiction of St Peter; that at least is how it appeared to Pope Zacharias who congratulated the Frankish bishops on joining with *nostrae societati in uno pastorali ovili*.[43] All shared one lord in St Peter, the 'prince of the Apostles'. The procedure adhered to by the Carolingian reformers reflected this state of affairs: they proceeded to renew pre-existing *regulae et canones*, and when in doubt turned to Rome. As Pope Zacharias himself neatly expressed it: 'we have no right to teach anything except the traditions of the Fathers, but if some new situation arises through the wiles of the devil and no solution is suggested in the provisions of the Church canons, do not hesitate to refer the matter to us'.[44] Papal letters of the period, preserved in the later *Codex Carolinus*, show indeed the extent to which both rulers had looked to Rome for guidance. We know, for example, that at about this time Pippin received from Pope Zacharias manuscripts of canon law (part of the collection put together by Dionysius Exiguus which Charlemagne was to receive in its entirety in 774) to assist in the organisation of the Christian society.[45] These letters also show the extent to which Pippin was acting and planning independently of Boniface. Pippin's closest counsellors in the business of reform were both Franks, namely Chrodegang, bishop of Metz from 742, who was to succeed Boniface as papal legate in Francia, and Fulrad, abbot of St Denis from 749 or 750. Both had close ties with Rome, and exploited this privilege to acquire from there books and relics. The translation to Francia of relics of Roman saints, now as later, was construed by contemporaries as an integral and important part of the drive to centre and focus the Frankish Church on Rome. In time it was a vital part of the notion that (Christian) Rome had been reborn or revived in Francia.

In 751 Pippin was crowned king of the Franks, and anointed; he became thereafter king by the grace of God (*rex Dei gratia*). The use of this title served to highlight the fact that the royal office was a *ministerium* but in essence this was what it had always been. However, it suited the Carolingians, for political reasons, to stress that their kingship, which was neither hallowed by blood nor grounded in tradition, derived its authority from God and St Peter. Pippin had been chosen, it was argued, because he was useful for furthering the interests of the Church: these included not only the defence of the Roman Church against Lombard aggression and the expansion of the frontiers of Catholic Christianity (centred on Rome), but also the *correctio* of the Frankish people and their allies.

43 MGH Conc. II.i, pp. 48–50 at p. 49 (Letter of Zacharias, May 748).

44 Boniface, Epp. 51, ed. Tangl, *Briefe*, p. 91–2; Eng. trans. Talbot, *Anglo-Saxon Missionaries*, no. 28, p. 106.

45 *Codex Carolinus* no. 3, ed. W. Gundlach, MGH Epp. III, pp. 476–657 at pp. 479–87. See also MGH Conc. II.i, p. 31.

Self-interest and idealism fitted compactly together. Reform may have been in the Carolingian interest but that does not mean that it was not sincerely and conscientiously pursued.

With Chrodegang at the helm, the papal alliance consolidated by a second anointing at St Denis in 754, and a king marked out and consecrated by God, the series of reforming councils was continued with conventions held at Ver in 755, Verberie in 756, Compiègne in 757, and Attigny in 760 or 762.[46] The business at Verberie and Compiègne was almost exclusively concerned with the proper regulations for marriage; here the lead was taken by George, bishop of Ostia, the papal legate. The concerns of the synod of Ver were wider-ranging, reflecting those of the earlier reform councils of the 740s: here the focus was on clerical discipline and the clergy's responsibility to correct and emend, not only the laity but each other. The preface to the text of the proceedings celebrates the advent of a new 'golden age' of reform under Carolingian rule. A vision of a Christian society and the harmonious working of its parts is emerging. Metropolitans, bishops, priests, monks and canons all have duties; monks and canons, here distinguished for the first time in the Frankish world, must follow their respective Rules or *ordines*. Priests too have an *ordo*, or code of conduct fitting to their station and function. At Gentilly in 767 some kind of formal debate was staged between the rival Roman (iconophile) and Byzantine (iconoclast) parties on the question of images in the presence of the king. Two years later twelve Frankish bishops, described as 'most expert and erudite', joined thirty-nine Italian bishops in debating the same issue in a synod convened by the new pope, Stephen III, in Rome.[47] Their erudition may have been exaggerated but the participation both here and at Gentilly of Frankish clergy in doctrinal debate is an indication of the progress that the reform movement had made during the course of Pippin's rule. At Attigny in 760–2 the forty-four assembled bishops and abbots had bound themselves together in a confraternity of prayer, a concrete indication of growing confidence and self-awareness.[48]

After Pope Stephen's visit to Francia in 753–4, and Pippin's formal anointing at St Denis, a concerted effort was made to reform the liturgy of the Frankish Church in accordance with Roman practices. Many contemporary sources bear witness to such an initiative; and Charlemagne too explicitly acknowledged that his work in this field was but a continuation of his father's.[49] In about 760 Pope Paul I reported that he had despatched to the Frankish court a group of liturgical texts: an *antiphonale*, a *responsale* and an *horologium nocturnale*.[50] Two of the leading figures in this work of reform were Chrodegang of Metz (also the author of a *regula* for canons based on that of St Augustine) and Pippin's own

[46] MGH Cap. I, nos. 14–16 and 106, pp. 33–41, 221–2.

[47] MGH Conc. II.i, no. 14, pp. 74–92, especially p. 74, line 24 and p. 75.

[48] Ibid., no. 13, pp. 72–3, on which see O. G. Oexle and K. Schmid, 'Voraussetzungen und Wirkung des Gebetsbundes von Attigny', *Francia* 2 (1974) pp. 71–121.

[49] See, for example, the *Admonitio generalis* (789) c. 80, MGH Cap. I, p. 61.

[50] *Codex Carolinus*, no. 24, ed. Gundlach, MGH Epp. III, p. 529.

half-brother, Remedius (or Remigius) of Rouen who set up schools of chant run by Roman personnel, or Frankish personnel trained at Rome, at their episcopal churches. The liturgy in question was enshrined chiefly in a type of sacramentary known as the 'Gelasian of the eighth century', cobbled together from various elements, not all of which in fact were Roman, by someone close to Pippin's court (perhaps at Flavigny under Abbot Manasses), and a deliberate, if limited, effort seems to have been made to copy texts of this type for general use. The ultimate aim was to introduce into the Frankish churches, hitherto attached to variant liturgical customs – some Roman, some Frankish (or 'Gallican') – one uniform, standard liturgy which conformed more closely to contemporary Roman practices. The initiative was to be continued by Charlemagne. To some extent this liturgical reform was reflected in contemporary architectural projects, for example at St Denis where Fulrad, a man with close Roman ties, was abbot, at Metz, Chrodegang's own see, and at Lorsch, his own foundation.

Pippin's reform of the Church thus aimed at the correction of morals, the restoration of ecclesiastical discipline, the establishment of a Church hierarchy, the uniformity of religious observance in accordance with Roman practice. These were the objectives; but how far were they achieved? The consensus of opinion among scholars is that real progress on all these fronts was only made by Charlemagne and after him by his son Louis the Pious. What Pippin had achieved above all was the availability of material resources. If any religious house found that it could not fulfil its function (its *ordo*) then the bishops were to examine the case and report the matter to the king who would emend the situation.[51] In 765, in the wake of a famine which was construed as divine chastisement, Pippin reminded his bishops in a circular letter, in no uncertain terms, that all men were to pay tithes (as the Israelites had done) 'whether they like it or not'.[52] By such means was the material welfare of the Church guaranteed. Without resources nothing could have been achieved. It would never do to underestimate the significance of the material base on which the Carolingian Renaissance and its achievement rested.

For their part both Charlemagne and his son Louis the Pious were ready to acknowledge that their work for the reform of the Church was only a continuation of Pippin's. Initially Charlemagne was more concerned with neutralising what he perceived as a threat from his brother Carloman; but his destruction of the Saxon cult-site at the Irminsul in 772 recounted in the Royal Frankish Annals, must be seen in the context of a desire to suppress paganism as well as a desire to acquire plunder and booty. His campaign into Italy in 773–4, and his successful annexation of the Lombard kingdom, similarly must be seen first and foremost as an indication of his commitment to take over his father's responsibility for protecting the Roman Church, a responsibility which indeed

[51] MGH Cap. I, no. 14, c. 6, p. 34.
[52] Ibid., no. 17, p. 42.

he had shared since his anointing at the hands of Pope Stephen in 754. At Easter of the year 774 in Rome Charlemagne received from the pope a complete text of the collection of canon law put together in the early sixth century by Dionysius Exiguus, augmented with subsequent additions, and known as the *Dionysio-Hadriana* on account of this gift. The reception of this text by the Frankish ruler, undoubtedly with great publicity, indicates that a further programme of reform was envisaged.

The first fruits of such a programme are apparent within five years. In 779 Charlemagne promulgated his first significant piece of legislation, the so-called 'Capitulary of Herstal'. The themes of the capitulary are at once familiar: order, authority and obedience to it 'according to canon law', justice and morality. Clerics must be subject to their bishops, bishops to their archbishops, all are reminded of their duty to 'emend and correct'. A cleric from one diocese cannot move to another; all must pay tithes and these the bishop will control. Monasteries must follow rules. Other provisions show a determination to eradicate perjury, and to have courts dispensing justice.[53] Evidently this capitulary was regarded as an important document, a copy of which, moreover, was kept at court, for later capitularies often refer to it.

Ten years later, in 789, follows a greater piece of legislation, the so-called *Admonitio generalis*. Here we have eighty-two clauses compared to the twenty-three of the Herstal capitulary, the first fifty-nine of which draw extensively from the *Dionysio-Hadriana*. However 'it was no mere re-issue of these canonical regulations for the clergy, but a considered and careful re-use of a selection of... [those] most relevant to the situation in the Frankish Church at the end of the eighth century'.[54] The text as a whole is well constructed, preceded by a lengthy preamble or preface, well written, and laced with biblical quotations: in short it testifies to the significant increase in the level of culture and learning at Charlemagne's court which we know from other sources to have taken place in the 780s.

It has been said that the *Admonitio* 'contains the most complete statement of all the proposals [of Charlemagne] for the reform of the Church and its ministers and for the education of the people'.[55] The preface states clearly that Charlemagne's fundamental responsibility as ruler is the salvation of the people. This is to be achieved by *admonitio* (hence the title given to the text); 'they must be admonished, exhorted and if necessary compelled' to observe the 'canonical prohibitions', the 'ancient institutes of universal councils'. The enterprise is a joint one shared by the bishops and their king whose *missi* will be despatched to assist them in the work of 'correcting those things which need correcting'. 'For we read in the Books of Kings how the holy Josiah strove to recall the kingdom

[53] Ibid., no. 20, cc. 1, 3, 7, 10 and 21, pp. 47–9, 51.

[54] Ibid., no. 22, pp. 52–62; R. McKitterick, *The Frankish Church and the Carolingian Reforms, 789–895* (London, 1977) pp. 1–8 at p. 4.

[55] McKitterick, *Frankish Church*, p. 1.

given to him by God to the worship of true religion, by visitation, by correction, by admonition', and 'it is incumbent upon us always, and in every way, to follow the *exempla sanctorum*'.[56] The Franks then under their anointed kings were the New Israel, as a succession of popes had been keen to stress. This idea of a Christian people following in the footsteps of the Israelites of the Old Testament was not a new one. But the notion of the Franks as a chosen people, a *gens sancta*, marked by divine favour and prepared for a providential mission, was naturally fostered by the triumph of Carolingian arms over successive generations and over fearsome pagan peoples like the Arabs and the Saxons. Thus here in the *Admonitio* the king was 'considering . . . the abundant favour of Christ the king towards us and our people'. There were other exempla of rulership in mind here besides those of the Old Testament: in the stress on the royal duty of *correctio* there are clear echoes, conscious or otherwise, of late Roman Imperial edicts.

In the *Admonitio* we have firstly, as before, a strong emphasis on obedience, hierarchy and order within the structure of the Church, and proper discipline according to canon law. In addition, however, there is a detailed discussion of the function of the priesthood, a function now considered to be of utmost significance. Priests, as befits their holy function, are to live exemplary lives; their faith is to be 'diligently examined' by their bishops, and they must not be ignorant of the 'institutes of the holy canons'.[57] The bishops are to oversee their priests' correct celebration of the mass, their correct administration of baptism, their correct singing of psalms and the *gloria* (*cc.* 6–7, 70). Bishops themselves must not 'dare to innovate' (*c.* 8). Neither should priests introduce anything 'new and uncanonical' into their preaching; rather they must preach 'rightly and honestly' and the bishops must see to this too (*c.* 2). Preaching (*praedicatio*) is now seen as a prime function of the clergy, for Christ himself is the 'great preacher' (*magnus praedicator*). The king here lays down what they are to preach: the Lord's Prayer, the Creed, stressing the nature of the Trinity, the meaning of the Incarnation, the threat of judgement and the promise of resurrection, warnings against mortal sins (here listed); also they are to 'admonish' the people about the need to love God and their neighbour, about faith and hope, humility and patience, chastity and continence, goodness and compassion (*cc.* 32, 61, 82). The Christian faith, its essential message of love – *Deus caritas est* (*c.* 61) – and redemption as well as its moral precepts, is to be preached *diligenter* and to *omni populo*. The clergy are also to set down, and monitor, clear moral guidelines: avarice, usury, bestiality, homicide, theft, homosexuality, corrupt judicial processes, perjury are all condemned, as are sorcery, augury, unknown angels, 'false martyrs and uncertain shrines' and other pagan practices (*Deo exercrabilis*) like praying at trees, stones or springs.[58] Clear directions are given as to what work

56 MGH Cap. I, pp. 53–4; Eng. trans. P. D. King, *Charlemagne: Translated Sources* (Kendal, 1987) p. 209.

57 MGH Cap. I, no. 22, cc. 26, 72, 2, 70 and 55 respectively, pp. 56, 59–60, 54, 59 and 57.

58 Ibid. (on preaching), cc. 5, 33, 39, 49, 67–8, 63–4, pp. 54, 56–9: and (augury etc.) cc. 18, 65, 16, 42, pp. 55–6, 58–9.

can and cannot be done on Sundays; children are to honour their parents (*cc.* 69, 81). Concern for the clergy's function of *praedicatio* is from now on a consistent theme of royal legislation. A letter of Charlemagne's dating from the period 801–10, for example, addressed to Bishop Gerbald of Liège though probably in fact the only extant copy of a circular letter sent out to all bishops, explains to him what he and his clergy are to preach and reminds him that 'often in our councils and assemblies we have drawn your attention to preaching in the Church'.[59] Subsequently Charlemagne was to set down in law that it was the responsibility of god-parents to teach to the young the Creed and the Lord's prayer as well as Christian moral standards.[60]

According to the *Admonitio* of 789, 'peace, concord and unanimity' among the whole Christian people are thus to be fostered by the Christian virtues outlined above, for these bind the Christian society together and create an environment in which salvation may be won. For 'nothing is pleasing to God without peace' (*c.* 62). Conversely the *corpus Christi* is rent asunder by sin. These moral themes, emphasising virtue as the means to unity, reappear constantly in Charlemagne's legislation, especially in the years afater 800, and in that of Louis the Pious also.

These prescriptions presuppose one vital requirement: that the parish clergy, from whom so much is now expected, are educated in Christian doctrine, and possess not only decent copies of the key Christian texts – biblical, canonical, penitential and liturgical – but also the literacy to use them. Here in the *Admonitio generalis* we run up against the key role of learning and literacy in the programme of reform. In clause 72 it is enjoined that both monasteries and cathedral churches should set up schools to teach the psalms, musical notation, singing, computation and grammar. This is no humanistic programme of education. It is not expressly stated who these *pueri* are but evidently they are destined for careers in the Church. The needs of the liturgy are uppermost in the king's mind. This is clear from what follows. Monks and clerics are instructed to 'correct properly the catholic books', and the reason given here is crucial to understanding the role of learning in the work of reform, and consequently the very nature of the Carolingian Renaissance: 'for often, although people wish to pray to God in the proper fashion, they yet pray improperly because of uncorrected books'. The text then runs on: 'and do not allow your boys to corrupt the books when they copy them; and if it is necessary to copy the gospel, psalter or missal, let men of full age do the copying, and with great diligence'. Faulty, corrupt texts (it is implied) are not only displeasing to God and cause him not to answer prayers; they also foment heretical beliefs. Key Christian texts may therefore be copied only by experienced scribes. The Roman Cassiodorus, writing in Ostrogothic Italy, had placed similar emphasis on the

[59] MGH Cap. I, no. 122, p. 241.

[60] *Capitulare generale* (813) c. 29, ed. H. Mordek and G. Schmitz, 'Neue Kapitularien und Kapitulariensammlungen', *DA* 43 (1987) pp. 361–489 at p. 421.

careful copying of manuscripts at his community of Vivarium for identical reasons.[61] The logic is this. The suppression of heresy and the triumph of orthodoxy require uniformity of faith. This depends upon uniformity of observance. Both of these depend upon corrected texts and the widespread availability of them. It is acknowledged, therefore, that the programme of reform depends upon the availability of such texts, and thus upon the availability of trained, learned scribes. We see clearly in the *Admonitio* how learning was understood as the servant of reform and not vice versa, as a means to an end and not as an end in itself.

Similar principles are enunciated in the other key text concerning the revival of learning under Charlemagne, namely his letter to Abbot Baugulf of Fulda, known as the *Epistola de litteris colendis* ('Letter on the cultivation of learning').[62] The letter, although undated, can be closely related to clause 72 of the *Admonitio* just discussed, and thus datable to the same period, the late 780s or 790s. It is argued that the letter was in fact a circular which Charlemagne intended every bishop and abbot to receive. Here Charlemagne, having consulted his advisers, states that, besides their duty of following the religious life according to their profession, these ecclesiastical communities also have a responsibility to provide tuition in the study of letters to all in the community who are able to learn. Learning is pleasing to God, and the ideal monk is the learned monk who speaks well: 'those who seek to please God by correct living ought to please him also by correct speaking' since, according to scripture: 'by thy words thou shalt be justified, and by thy words thou shalt be condemned' (Matthew 12:37). Thus reform is needed here because, as Charlemagne notes in another context: 'no-one finds salvation unless they please God'. Education is important for the clergy because 'knowing comes before doing'. If faith is the key to understanding, understanding, it is here argued, is the key to faith.

Christian learning is thus of crucial importance for monks, nuns and canons. In the first place their correct Latinity, in speech or writing, is pleasing to God. Secondly it unlocks for them the mysteries of the scriptures in the Latin Bible and enables them to make proper and effective use of biblical handbooks or commentaries. Thirdly they are less likely to fall into doctrinal error. All this enhances their prospects of salvation. There could be no clearer statement of the close link between relevant learning and Christian reform. The correct Latinity of Carolingian clergy was important for another reason. Their prayers were considered to be vital for the prosperity of the *regnum* both in war and peace. If intercession were to be efficacious, both the Latinity of the participants and the texts that they used had to be correct, principally because of the notion that the Church straddled both heaven and earth, and that angels and men participated in

[61] Cassiodorus, *Institutiones* I, 30.i, ed. R. A. B. Mynors, *Cassiodori senatoris institutiones* (Oxford, 1937) pp. 75–6.

[62] MGH Cap. I, no. 29, pp. 78–9 and P. Lehmann, 'Fuldaer Studien', *Sitzungsberichte der bayerischen Akademie der Wissenschaften, phil.-hist. Kl.* (1927) pp. 3–13; Eng. trans. King, *Charlemagne*, pp. 232–3.

a single liturgy at the same time. Thus the demand for a uniform liturgy based on Roman practice (linked to which was the desire to make all monastic houses conform to the Rule of St Benedict), and also the necessity for accurate time-keeping (*computus*).

In the *Admonitio generalis* Charlemagne had confirmed what his father had instituted, namely that 'all the clergy ... are to learn the Roman chant thoroughly and that it is to be employed throughout the office, night and day, in the correct form, in conformity with what our father of blessed memory, King Pippin, strove to bring to pass when he abolished the Gallican chant for the sake of unanimity with the apostolic see and the peaceful harmony of God's holy Church', affirming explicitly that Roman practice was to be followed regarding the kiss of peace and the reading of the names of those to be commemorated during the mass (cc. 53–4, 80). Subsequent legislation reiterates these demands, either in general or in particular terms. Bishops were constantly reminded, as in the *Admonitio*, to oversee their priests, and particularly their celebration of the liturgy, presumably to ensure not only that it was 'correct' but also that it was Roman. The evidence suggests that Charlemagne's churchmen responded to his directive. Archbishop Arn of Salzburg for example, in his provincial council at Rispach in 798, ordered his suffragans to ensure that every priest had a good copy of the appropriate sacramentary, that they could read and understood the scriptures, and that they could celebrate the liturgy 'according to the tradition of the Roman Church'. They were to set up schools, under the direction of a 'teacher learned in the Roman tradition' for this purpose. Other bishops, it seems, were likewise busy ensuring that their priests were taught the liturgy 'according to the practice of Rome'.[63]

Charlemagne's commitment to introducing a uniform liturgy in the territories under his rule went further than simply legislating for it. Sometime in the 780s he had commissioned from Paul the Deacon, a Lombard scholar then resident at his court, a homiliary, or lectionary, containing readings culled from the Fathers for use in the night office. A circular letter addressed 'to the religious lectors' authorises Paul's homiliary for general use on the grounds that existing texts of the kind were inappropriate and strewn with errors.[64] According to the manuscript evidence, Paul's homiliary (or rather Charlemagne's effort to popularise it) was a success. In 787 the king took advantage of a visit to Monte Cassino to ask the monks for a careful copy of the manuscript of St Benedict's Rule which the abbey preserved as an autograph of the saint himself, a text which, to judge by an extant Carolingian copy (St Gall MS 914), does indeed seem to have been a purer version than any in circulation in Francia at that time.[65] This initiative can also be related to Charlemagne's concern for one standard, uniform liturgy.

63 MGH Cap. I, no. 116, c. 4, p. 234: also no. 117, c. 9, p. 235; McKitterick, *Frankish Church*, p. 135. Council of Rispach, MGH Conc. II.i, no. 22 (C), cc. 4–5, p. 198.

64 MGH Cap. I, no, 30, pp. 80–1.

65 MGH Epp. III, pp. 519–24.

A few years earlier the king had asked Pope Hadrian, again via Paul the Deacon, for a pure, authentic copy of the sacramentary reputedly 'put in order by Pope Gregory'.[66] What the pope in fact sent was a type of Gregorian sacramentary known, through its association with him, as the *Hadrianum*: but it was not the 'pure, authentic' exemplum asked for, nor was it suitable for Frankish use in its received form; nor was it, being at least a hundred years old, even representative of current Roman practice. Nevertheless its putative association with Gregory the Great ensured that it was kept with honour at court, in the *bibliothecae cubiculus*, as one of a series of 'authentic texts' available for copy, along with Paul the Deacon's homiliary, the Cassinese copy of the Benedictine Rule, and the *Dionysio-Hadriana* canon law manuscript received in 774. In due course, early in the ninth century, a supplement together with a preface (known from its opening as the *Hucusque*) were added to it by Benedict of Aniane (not Alcuin as was previously thought) in order to render this text suitable for Frankish use; at the same time the author corrected the grammatical faults of the text to accord with improved Carolingian taste. Whether or not Benedict (if it were he) was commissioned to draw up his supplement by either Charlemagne or Louis the Pious is unclear. Certainly it did not enjoy wide currency before Louis' reign. Even then it never became a standard, uniform text: certainly both the *Hadrianum* and Benedict's supplement were extensively copied in ninth-century Francia but the copying was 'far more varied and "irregular" than the familiar picture of Carolingian standardization would suggest', and more especially other kinds of sacramentary, notably the 'Gelasian of the eighth century', evidently remained in use.[67] Thus Charlemagne too failed in his aim of introducing one standard liturgy into Francia. The initiative was continued in the next reign, by Helisacher, Louis' archchancellor, and Amalarius of Metz, but again with only limited success.

To this concern for a standard, correct liturgy can also be related Charlemagne's sponsorship of Bible reform. Eighth-century Francia used several different Latin translations of the Bible in varying manuscript traditions, many of which were seriously vitiated by omissions and corruptions. Against this background, and given both the unique importance of Holy Writ and the emphasis being placed on liturgical conformity, biblical reform and the acquisition of a standard, 'authentic' text was an indispensable need. Careful copying of the kind envisaged in the *Admonitio* of 789 was no more than a partial solution to the problem. There is no evidence of any initiative undertaken by Pippin III to reform the Bible; but Charlemagne seems to have taken the matter in hand relatively early in his reign, probably in the 780s. His circular letter addressed 'to the religious lectors', referred to above, authorising the use of Paul the Deacon's

[66] Ibid., p. 626. See C. Vogel, *Medieval Liturgy. An Introduction to the Sources* (Washington D.C., 1986) pp. 79–81, 123–4.

[67] D. Bullough and A. Harting-Correa, 'Texts, chant and the chapel of Louis the Pious', in: *Charlemagne's Heir*, pp. 489–508 at p. 494 (with n.16); also McKitterick, *Frankish Church*, pp. 133–5 and Vogel, *Medieval Liturgy*, p. 92.

homiliary, claims that he has already (indeed 'long ago') ensured the correction of both Old and New Testaments. The letter can only be roughly dated to the period 786–800, but whatever its date 'long ago' seems something of an exaggeration. In fact Bible reform was taken in hand by several institutions and individuals in the last quarter of the eighth century, including Corbie (under Abbot Maurdramnus), Metz (under Bishop Angilramn, the king's court chaplain), at Orleans (under Theodulf) and pre-eminently by Alcuin at Tours. According to Thegan this concern still preoccupied the emperor's mind as the reign drew to its close.[68] Alcuin is known to have sent a presentation copy of his bible to Charlemagne on the occasion of his imperial coronation in Rome on Christmas Day 800.[69] Subsequently Tours was busy providing texts of Alcuin's bible for other churches, many lavishly illustrated. Despite its worth and popularity, however, Alcuin's text continued to co-exist with its rivals rather than replace them. Once again correction was easier to achieve than uniformity. It is hard to see how significantly more could have been achieved by the Carolingian reformers given the conditions under which they worked.

The imperial coronation of 800 brought about no substantial change to the objectives or content of the reform programme. Whatever one chooses to make of this coronation and its significance, it remains the logical consequence of what had gone before rather than a point of new departure. The emperor's responsibility for his Christian people was no different from that of the Christian king. What we can say, however, is that the imperial coronation gave further impetus to the reform programme, enhancing Charles' sense of his *ministerium* just as the elevation to kingship, and the administration of unction, had enhanced his father's.

The events of 802 bear this out. In that year, the Lorsch annalist reports, 'the Lord Charles Caesar stayed quietly at the palace of Aachen with the Franks; there was no campaign'.[70] This suggests that discussions were going on about the implications of imperial rule. The same source says that in October Charlemagne held a gathering of bishops, priests and deacons 'and there caused to be read to them all the canons'. Abbots and monks were given a recitation of the Benedictine Rule. In each case the readings were followed by detailed discussion and exposition. What followed was, in the words of the annalist, 'a command (*iussio*) of general application to . . . the entire clergy, that as clerics they were to live in accordance with the canons, each in his own station . . . as the holy fathers laid down; and that they were to correct in accordance with the precepts of the canons whatever faults or shortcomings might appear in the clergy or the people; and that they were to have corrected in accordance with the Rule of St Benedict whatever might be done in monasteries or among monks in contravention of that same Rule . . . '

[68] Thegan, *Vita Hludowici imperatoris* c. 7, MGH SS II, p. 592.
[69] MGH Epp. IV, no. 261, p. 419.
[70] MGH SS I, p. 38; Eng. trans. King, *Charlemagne*, pp. 144–5.

In fact 'general orders' of this kind, the *Capitulare missorum generale* and *Capitularia missorum specialia*, had already gone out. Shortly after Easter the new emperor had despatched his *missi*, now chosen from the *optimates*, to all parts of the empire.[71] They were asked to look into a variety of issues, most of which had been the king's concern in earlier capitularies. In particular they were urged to ensure that effective justice was available to all, especially to the *pauperiores*, and to find out if bishops, abbots, counts and vassals were living in *concordia et amicitia* with each other. In general their brief was to discover if the various parts of Charles' empire were functioning properly and in harmony:

> all men, in accordance with God's command, are to live in an entirely just manner, with just judgement, and everybody is to be admonished (*admonere*) to persist wholeheartedly in his way of life and calling (*in suo proposito vel professione*): canons are to observe the canonical life in full . . . ; nuns are to maintain their way of life under diligent supervision; laymen and members of the secular clergy are to keep their laws properly without wicked fraud; and all are to live in perfect charity and peace (*in caritate et pace perfecte*) one with another.

Here there is a clear conception of a Christian society where each category of person has a definable code of conduct (*ordo*, *professio*, *propositum*), and an obligation to live by it. Monks, nuns and canons must follow their rules, clerics must abide by the canons. Laymen must avoid sin and vice, venerate the Church, protect the poor and live in charity with one another; the emperor wants to know 'above all how each is striving to keep himself in God's service (*in sancto Dei servitio*). All are to take a new oath of loyalty to Charles as emperor, an oath which not only binds them to fidelity to him but also lays upon them the obligation to behave like true Christians: 'Concerning the fidelity to be promised to the lord emperor ... all should know that oath to contain the following meaning within it: first, that everybody is personally to strive, to the best of his understanding and ability, to maintain himself fully in God's command and his own promise.' This is because, although it is the emperor's obligation to correct his people, he 'cannot himself provide the necessary care and discipline for each man individually'. Those who depart from their *professio* displease both God and emperor at the same time. In other words the purpose of the oath is to impress upon the people that disloyalty to their God is also disloyalty to their ruler – and, by implication, vice versa.

This vision of the Christian society and its parts can be traced in the legislation of Charles' father Pippin but here, in the aftermath of the imperial coronation, it appears in its most developed form to date. The same idea can be traced in the writings of Boniface, one of the architects of Pippin's legislation. 'There is one faith in the Church', he wrote, 'but different ranks, all having their own obligations', probably with his eye on similar words of St Paul in I Cor-

[71] MGH Cap. I, nos. 33 (Programmatic Capitulary; Eng. trans. here from King, *Charlemagne*, pp. 234, 242) and 34, pp. 91–102; see also MGH SS I, p. 38 (s.a. 802).

inthians.[72] The stress placed by the Carolingians upon the duties and responsibilities of the 'order of laymen' is a distinctive feature of their programme of *correctio*, and one which distinguishes it from similar reform initiatives undertaken in the late Roman world, in Visigothic Spain and Merovingian Gaul: as Alcuin said, Christ had entrusted talents of money to all of whatever station, not just to bishops and priests.[73] But the idea of a Christian society embracing all social orders working in harmony together, animated by peace and justice, was not new. Its chief theorist was St Augustine, and it is for this reason that the Carolingian reform programme has been described as an example of 'l'Augustinisme politique'.[74] In his *De ordine*, Augustine had written: 'order (*ordo*) is that which if we follow it in our lives will lead us to God'.[75] Given the underlying aim of Carolingian rulership, namely the salvation of the people, then the preoccupation with *ordo* and *ordines* is easy to comprehend. Earthly order reflected heavenly order; God's Church was functioning properly only if, in its organisation, its habits and its worship (hence once more the desire for a uniform, Roman liturgy), it reflected heavenly practice. Thus the deposition of the last Merovingian could be justified by the 'Royal Frankish annalist' *ut non conturbaretur ordo*. It is no coincidence that one of the writers who most fascinated Charles the Bald and his court was the Pseudo-Dionysius with his exposition of the hierarchies of heaven and earth; nor is it surprising if Einhard thought it appropriate for his hero to have found 'great pleasure in the books of St Augustine and especially in those which are called "The City of God"'.[76]

Other directives from the period 801–14 underline Charlemagne's concern that his people should faithfully serve God in their respective *ordines*. These were years in which Charles' *missi* were especially active. It was this same concern which animated the two great reform councils convened at Aachen by Louis the Pious in August 816 and July 817.[77] Monks, canons and nuns were all to follow prescribed *ordines* or *regulae*, here set out at great length and after much discussion, as in 802. All the indications are that a determined effort was made to enforce these prescriptions, certainly that monks should follow the Rule of St Benedict (as revised and modified at Aachen) and no other; but once more the drive for uniformity was, it seems, only partially successful.

Another significant piece of legislation drafted by Louis and his advisers is the so-called *Admonitio* (or *Ordinatio*) of 823–5.[78] Its importance is underlined by the fact that (according to the manuscript evidence) it was evidently designed to

72 Sermo ix, PL 89, col. 860B–C; compare I Cor. 2:12.
73 MGH Epp. IV, no. 111, p. 160.
74 H.-X. Arquillière, *L'Augustinisme politique. Essai sur la formation des théories politiques du moyen âge* (Paris, 1934) pp. 105–21, 152–4.
75 *De ordine* I, 9, 27 ed. P. Knoll, CSEL 63 (Vienna, 1922) p. 139, lines 11–12.
76 Einhard, *Vita Karoli* c. 24, ed. L. Halphen, *Eginhard, vie de Charlemagne*, (Paris, 1981) p. 72; Eng. trans. L. Thorpe, *Two Lives of Charlemagne* (London, 1969) p. 78.
77 MGH Conc. II.i, nos. 39–40, pp. 307–466; MGH Cap. I, no. 170, pp. 343–9. K. Hallinger, *Corpus consuetudinum monasticarum* I (Siegburg, 1963) pp. 433–563.
78 MGH Cap. I, no. 150, pp. 303–7, 414–19.

circulate together with Charlemagne's *Admonitio generalis* of 789, and some other material, in a collection put together by a man close to Louis' court, Abbot Ansegisus of St Wandrille. Here in this second great *Admonitio* Church and state are defined as one and the same (*c.* 1). Three *capitula* are described as being of paramount importance: that all look after the defence and the *honor* of the Church and its officers, that all live in peace, and that justice prevails everywhere in all things (*c.* 2). The regnal duty is to admonish, to correct and to emend; but this is a *ministerium* in which all share, each in their own *ordo*: thus Louis is the *admonitor*, but his subjects are his *adiutores*, a notion with evident constitutional implications (*cc.* 1, 3). Subsequently each 'order' in turn is reminded of its responsibilities, defined as they have been in earlier capitularies. Bishops, for example, must support schools 'to teach and instruct the sons and ministers of the church' (*c.* 5). Counts must be not only the *adiutores* of the ruler and sponsors of the Church; they are also to be 'guardians of the people' dispensing justice equally and looking after the poor (*c.* 6). Laymen in general must show due respect for the Church and its preaching (*c.* 7). There is much talk of the *communis utilitas* (e.g. *c.* 13). One of those who helped to draft this impressive piece of legislation was Bishop Jonas of Orleans. Other writings of his reveal the extent to which he shared this view of the Church as a *corpus Christi* in which each member had a role to play, a *regula*: the ruler had to correct what needed correcting, the layman had to uphold justice and to defend the peace of the Church with arms, monks must seek quiet in order to pray, bishops (and priests) were to superintend all the rest, correcting them where necessary *ad lineam rectitudinis*.[79] A highly developed view of the Christian society, its parts and their responsibilities is emerging.

The capitularies record the attempts made by the Carolingians to regulate the structure and behaviour of the Christian society entrusted to them by God. At the same time related efforts were made, particularly after 800, to codify, complement and amend the customary laws of the Franks and of the other peoples under Carolingian rule. This was all part of the royal duty of *correctio et emendatio*; but it also evoked the imperial tradition of Constantine, Theodosius II and Justinian. The aspect of these emperors' activity which most impressed the Carolingians was their law-making, in short their work of *correctio*. Thus Bishop Freculf of Lisieux, writing a 'World history' for the young Charles the Bald in the 830s, described Theodosius II, the codifier of Roman law, as 'a man necessary for restoring the state', who 'corrected many laws, and added to them . . . Whatever laws he saw in the city to be pernicious or redundant . . . he authorised to be removed; and he saw to it that whatever laws were necessary to help the state were added.'[80] Einhard reports how Charlemagne tried to live up to the imperial tradition:

[79] Jonas of Orleans, *De institutione regia* c. 8, ed. J. Reviron, *Les Idées politico-religieuse d'un évêque du IXe siècle: Jonas d'Orléans et son De institutione regia* (Paris, 1930) p. 158; *Vita secunda sancti Hucberti*, AASS, Nov. I, col. 817B–C.

[80] *Chronicon* III, 27, PL 106, col. 1226.

> Now that he was emperor, he discovered that there were many defects in the legal system of his own people ... He gave much thought to how he could best fill the gaps, reconcile the discrepancies, correct the errors and rewrite the laws which were ill-expressed. None of this was ever finished; he added a few sections, but even these remained incomplete. What he did do was to have collected together and committed to writing the laws of all the nations under his jurisdiction which still remained unrecorded.[81]

Einhard's testimony is confirmed by the Lorsch annalist who in his entry for the year 802 records how Charlemagne 'assembled the dukes, counts and the rest of the Christian people, together with men skilled in the laws, and had all the laws in his realm read out, each man's law expounded to him and emended wherever necessary, and the emended law written down'.[82]

The manuscript evidence bears witness also to the scale of Charlemagne's effort, for the version of the *Lex Salica* associated with the reform effort of 802 as described above by the Lorsch annalist, the so-called 'K' version, survives in a very large number of ninth-century copies, indicating widespread circulation. Capitulary legislation confirms the statement of the Lorsch annalist to the effect that Charlemagne intended his *iudices*, namely the counts and their representatives, to consult legal written texts in the course of their everyday business; and the manuscript evidence suggests that such texts, containing not just the *Lex Salica* but other legal material besides, were widely disseminated.[83] On at least five occasions between 816 and 820 Louis the Pious followed Charlemagne in making further amendments and additions to the law-codes of his people. Recent research has indicated that his court made successful efforts to distribute copies of these changes throughout the empire: many of the manuscripts containing these texts can be traced to a scriptorium linked with Abbot Fredegisus, Louis the Pious' archchancellor.[84] A well-known property dispute between the abbeys of Fleury and St Denis in the 820s proves that such amendments were being taken account of, and adhered to, very soon after their promulgation.[85]

There is little doubt that the written word was used extensively in the business of Carolingian government. But it did not replace the spoken word, nor was it intended that it should. If Carolingian counts were expected to keep and use their capitularies and law-codes they were also, it seems, expected to know them by heart.[86] The revival of learning not only provided priests who could read and write and scribes to copy the manuscripts they needed for their work in the field. It meant also that greater use could be made of the written word in government: rulers could count on scribes being available to copy

[81] Einhard, *Vita Karoli* c. 29, ed. Halphen, pp. 80–2; Eng. trans., Thorpe, *Two Lives*, p. 81.
[82] MGH SS I, p. 38; Eng. trans., King, *Charlemagne*, p. 145.
[83] McKitterick, *Carolingians*, pp. 40–4.
[84] Ibid., pp. 58–9.
[85] G. Schmitz, 'The capitulary legislation of Louis the Pious', in: *Charlemagne's Heir*, pp. 425–36 at pp. 433–4.
[86] *Capitula a missis dominicis ad comites directa* (801–13), MGH Cap. I, no. 85, p. 184 and *Responsio misso cuidam data* (801–14), cc. 2 and 4, ibid., no. 58, p. 145.

injunctions (either at court or, more likely, in the household of a bishop or the *mallus* of a count) and at least a basic measure of literacy on the part of those who were to receive them. Once again the interests of Church and royalty dovetailed neatly together. Louis the Pious may have turned a deaf ear to the plea of Agobard of Lyons that he should unite his subjects under one secular law-code, but as Christians sharing one Bible and one canon law they were already integrated into one *corpus Christi*.[87] This integration is now seen as one of the major achievements of Louis' reign. Ironically it came about just at the time when the empire, as a political unit, was breaking up to accommodate dynastic rivalries, but it ensured that the notion of empire and a sense of Frankish unity, remained vital and meaningful for at least another half-century.

Learning and scholarship in the Carolingian Renaissance

The role of Charlemagne

In his *Admonitio* of 789 and his circular letter *De litteris colendis* Charlemagne urges his prelates to supervise the restoration of learning in the dioceses and monasteries in order to further the work of reform. The 'letter to the religious lectors' (786 – 800), another circular directive, likewise underlines the role of learning in this context.[88] Here the king says that in order to improve the state of his Church he has taken steps to revive learning, hitherto practically defunct; and to this end he has encouraged those with the necessary skills in the business of teaching the liberal arts to others. This seems to refer to an invitation to scholars to attend his court and to make it a centre of learning. No doubt the needs of the reform movement were in the king's mind; but the patronage of learning at court served to enhance his dignity by linking him with late Roman and earlier Merovingian practice.[89] For ninth-century writers it was axiomatic that Charlemagne had indeed revived learning after a long period of neglect; modern opinion, however, regards the king's own statement here that he found the study of letters 'almost obliterated because of the neglect of his predecessors' as too sweeping and exaggerated. Nevertheless it remains true that it is only from the time of Charlemagne's reign that we have firm evidence of activity in ecclesiastical scriptoria on a significant and widespread basis.[90] His patronage of learning at court certainly entitled him to claim, as he does in the 'letter to the religious lectors', that he has led the way by example.

The development of Charlemagne's court as a centre of learning seems to postdate the annexation of the Lombard kingdom in 774, and the two events are commonly linked. Nothing is more likely, certainly, than that the acquisition of

87 Agobard, *Liber adversus legem Gundobaldi*, PL 104, col. 115.
88 MGH Cap. I, no. 30, pp. 80–1; Eng. trans. King, *Charlemagne*, p. 208.
89 Emphasised, for example, by H. Fichtenau, *The Carolingian Empire* (Oxford, 1957), p. 91.
90 B. Bischoff, 'Panorama der Handschriftenüberlieferung aus der Zeit Karls des Grossen', Bischoff, *MS* III, pp. 5–38.

a second kingdom should have encouraged the patrician of the Romans to act in a way which identified him more closely with late Roman traditions. The Lombard rulers had had some kind of resident palace complex at Pavia, as Charlemagne was later to have at Aachen, where it seems men of learning could be found.[91] From 774 we find a group of scholars from outside Francia converging on Charlemagne's court as it became clear that he not only enjoyed divine favour but also, and increasingly, great wealth. One of the first was the Italian Paulinus, the leading religious poet of Charlemagne's reign, and, moreover, a teacher of grammar. Subsequently Charlemagne appointed him patriarch of Aquileia (north-east of Venice), the foremost ecclesiastical post in the Lombard kingdom. Peter of Pisa, formerly an important figure at the court of the Lombard king Desiderius, also arrived at Charlemagne's court very shortly after 774.[92] Einhard tells us that he taught grammar to Charlemagne himself; we know too that he wrote a manual on the subject, based largely on the *Ars minor* of Donatus.[93] At least two other Peters, both Italians and presumably valued for their learning, were also at Charlemagne's court at this period, being rewarded at a later date with the bishoprics of Pavia and Verdun.

All these may have come willingly from Italy to Charlemagne's court; others, for example the Lombard Fardulf, abbot of St Denis from 792 or 793, came originally as hostages. Fardulf may also have been a man of learning because the scriptorium of St Denis was certainly very active under his charge, developing a house style of its own. Another hostage was the brother of Paul the Deacon. Paul himself travelled to the Frankish court shortly after 776 to plead for his brother's release. Once there, he too stayed. Paul, like Peter of Pisa, had formerly been an important literary figure in the circle around the court of King Desiderius. A poem composed by him in 763 indeed honoured Adalperga's husband, Arichis of Benevento,[94] with the assertion that he was 'almost the only prince of our age to hold the palm of wisdom'. It may be that the spoils of Charlemagne's conquest included not only scholars and poets but also books, since the beautiful and much-vaunted manuscript art associated with Charlemagne's court evidently derives to some extent from Greco-Roman models, especially that of the Aachen period after 794, in particular the art of the so-called 'Coronation Gospels' now in Vienna and the Gospels preserved in the cathedral treasury at Aachen. What we know of eighth-century church building and decoration in Italy suggests that antique cultural traditions remained strong here; it is thus not surprising if, after 774, we find Charlemagne behaving in a more self-consciously Roman way. The first of these court manuscripts, as remarkable for their

[91] D. Bullough, 'Urban change in early medieval Italy: the example of Pavia', *Papers of the British School at Rome* 34 (1966) pp. 82–131, especially pp. 94–102.

[92] D. Bullough, '*Aula renovata*: the Carolingian court before the Aachen palace', *Proceedings of the British Academy* 71 (1985) pp. 267–301 at pp. 279 (with n.1), 284–5, reprinted D. Bullough, *Carolingian Renewal: Sources and Heritage* (Manchester, 1991) pp. 123–60.

[93] Einhard, *Vita Karoli* c. 25, ed. Halphen, p. 74.

[94] Not Desiderius as Godman mistakenly assumed. *Carmina* 2, ed. K. Neff, *Die Gedichte des Paulus Diaconus*, Quellen und Untersuchungen zur lateinischen philologie des Mittelalters (Munich, 1908) p. 12.

lavish use of purple and gold as for the quality of their workmanship, was written for the king shortly after 781, a magnificent illustrated Gospel lectionary written mostly in uncial ('Roman letters'), but with some pages in caroline minuscule script, by one Godescalc.[95] The dedicatory verses to the manuscript emphasise the richness of the materials used in its production as befitting the status of the gospel text; similar principles underlie Charlemagne's own emphasis on the careful copying and emendation of biblical texts.[96]

Godescalc's verses also celebrate Charlemagne's great enthusiasm for learning.[97] The same point was emphasised by Adam, abbot of the monastery of Masmünster, who in 780 had made a copy of the grammar of Diomedes at Charlemagne's request.[98] Adam's work, taken in conjunction with the grammatical interests of men like Peter of Pisa and Paulinus, suggests that some kind of grammatical instruction, in other words, teaching, was taking place at Charlemagne's court in the late 770s. A letter written in 799 refers explicitly to Peter's teaching of grammar at court.[99] Further evidence for the study of grammar, and indeed of other components of the liberal arts curriculum, at Charlemagne's court is furnished by Paul the Deacon's despatch to the king of his reworking of Festus' grammatical work, 'On the significance of words', and the presence here, by 791, of a text like 'The ten categories', a fourth-century introduction to the concepts and terminology of Aristotelian logic.[100]

Italians were not the only migrants to Charlemagne's court even if, at least in the 770s, they had the highest profile. Already in the later 770s Beornrad, an Anglo-Saxon, appears at Charlemagne's court; the king's valuation of him is indicated by his gift firstly of the abbacy of Echternach (a house with a strong Anglo-Saxon link going back to its founder Willibrord) and subsequently the archbishopric of Sens. Another Anglo-Saxon, Cathwulf, was also close to the king on the evidence of his letter of advice written *ca* 775.[101] In 781 Charlemagne met Alcuin, not for the first time, at Parma in northern Italy and engaged him in his service.[102] Others recruited from the British Isles to teach, to learn, or simply to add lustre now included Joseph the Deacon, Cadac-Andreas, Candidus, Dungal – an expert in astronomy, a key subject of the *quadrivium* – and Dicuil (either of whom is to be identified with *Hibernicus exul*).

Like Peter and Paulinus, Alcuin was a teacher. His activity and expertise in

95 Fine illustrations in F. Mütherich, 'Die Buchmalerei am Hofe Karls des Grossen', in: *Karl der Grosse* III, pp. 9–53 between pp. 32 and 33.

96 See Henderson, chapter 9 below, pp. 248–73.

97 MGH Poet. I, p. 94, esp. line 7.

98 Ibid., p. 93.

99 MGH Epp. IV, p. 285. A splendid copy of Peter's grammar, Brussels, Bibliothèque Royale II. 2572 (CLA X, 1553) may have belonged to the king himself. On grammar, see Law, chapter 3 below, pp. 88–110.

100 MGH Epp. IV, p. 508, and see Marenbon, chapter 6 below, pp. 171–92.

101 MGH Epp. IV, pp. 501–5.

102 *Vita Alcuini* c. 9, MGH SS XV.i, p. 190. See D. Bullough, '*Albuinus deliciosus Karoli regis*: Alcuin of York and the shaping of the early Carolingian court', in: *Institutionen, Kultur und Gesellschaft im Mittelalter. Festschrift für Josef Fleckenstein zu seinem 65. Geburtstag*, ed. L. Fenske, W. Rosener and T. Zotz (Sigmaringen, 1984) pp. 73–92.

this field is underscored firstly by the fact that among his works, written either at court or subsequently at Tours, are an *Ars grammatica*, a *De dialectica*, a *De orthographia* ('On spelling'), and a *De rhetorica*; and secondly by the fact that almost every significant scholar of the next generation was apparently taught by him at some stage (as Notker noted), although whether at court or at Tours after 794 is rarely clear.[103] We may deduce, therefore, that the emphasis at court, in the 770s and 780s, was on instruction. In the words of Angilbert, writing in the 790s, 'David (i.e. Charlemagne) wishes to have wise-minded teachers to lend distinction and fame to every discipline at his court.'[104]

But who was taught at court, and precisely in what context, is less clear. What exactly did Alcuin have in mind when he referred to the king's *scola palatii*?[105] References abound certainly to the teaching of boys (*pueri*) at court.[106] Angilbert, the future lay abbot of St Riquier, was evidently one such *puer*, and Fredegisus, Alcuin's compatriot, another. For the instruction of these boys, who were being lined up for careers in royal administration, we may assume that there was formal tuition in a *scola*, perhaps affiliated to the royal chapel, and perhaps located (before 794) at Herstal, a favoured residence. This was no more than a Merovingian king such as Dagobert I had provided. Whether the *scola*, as an organised institution, amounted to anything more exalted than that, given the itinerant nature of Charlemagne's court before the Aachen period began in 794, by which time the scholars and *magistri grammatici* who had given it lustre in the later 770s and 780s had dispersed, is questionable. Alcuin's title of *magister* seems to have been honorific rather than formal or official since he continued to employ it after he had left the court. Certainly he described the court as an academy; but this must be seen in the context of the efforts made by courtiers such as he and Theodulf to flatter the king by exaggerating his own intellectual and academic expertise, undoubtedly with the aim of presenting him as a latter-day Solomon presiding over a court whose ruling virtue was Christian *sapientia*. The court could certainly be the scene for set-piece debate, with prepared texts, on special occasions such as the meetings convened to discuss images (*ca* 790–2), Adoptianism (800), and *computus* (809). It is evident, moreover, that much informed discussion on various aspects of learning also took place at Charlemagne's court on a regular but less formal basis. To Alcuin and others the gathering of such a learned circle constituted a 'school' where his own position was, at least for a while, pre-eminent and where other courtiers, such as Riculf who left in 787 to become archbishop of Mainz, could be seen as his *discipuli*.[107] But this was *ad hoc* rather than institutionalised debate. Just as the

103 *Gesta Karoli* I, c. 2, ed. H. Haefele, MGH SRG (Berlin, 1959) p. 3; also K.-F. Werner, '*Hludovicus Augustus*: gouverner l'empire chrétien – idées et réalités', in *Charlemagne's Heir*, pp. 3–123 at pp. 38–9 n.124.

104 Eng. trans., Godman, *Poetry*, pp. 114–15.

105 Alcuin, *Disputatio de arte rhetorica* c. 35, ed. W. Howell, *The Rhetoric of Alcuin and Charlemagne. A Translation with an Introduction, the Latin text and Notes* (London, 1941) p. 128, line 938.

106 For example, MGH Epp. IV, pp. 285, 518 and Notker, *Gesta Karoli* c. 1, ed. Haefele, MGH SRG n.s. 12 (Munich, 1959) p. 2.

107 MGH Epp. IV, no. 13, p. 39, line 7.

projection of a unified, cohesive group of court poets is an illusion, so too, it seems, is the portrayal of an institutionalised 'court academy' or 'palace school'.

Even if he is no longer seen as the 'head of Charlemagne's palace school', or the inventor and propagator of Caroline minuscule script, Alcuin remains one of the key figures at court and one of the foremost architects of the reform movement. His prominent role in the drafting of documents such as the *Admonitio generalis* (789) and the *Epistola de litteris colendis* has been strongly advocated.[108] Sentiments similar to those outlined in these two texts regarding the importance of careful copying and correct orthography for the proper performance of the liturgy are to be found in other writings of Alcuin's, particularly in his *De orthographia* where detailed guidance is given on such matters. Alcuin was not alone in these concerns, and his role in the direction of affairs must not be exaggerated; nevertheless it remains true that his master Charlemagne presided over the crucial phase in the process whereby Carolingian Latin was reformed to accord more closely with classical models, even if improvements in this field are already detectable under Pippin.[109]

Alcuin's other writings also show the extent to which learning was directed to serve the interests of reform: these include biblical commentaries, saints' lives, moral writings on the Virtues and the Vices and on the Soul, and works on the Trinity and against Adoptianism. He worked closely within the reform tradition as mapped out by Bede, his inspiration.[110] After 796 Alcuin worked not at court but at Tours, a transfer which implies neither lessening of favour nor a reduction of interest in or appreciation of his qualities on the part of the king. Instead it can be seen as part of a wider pattern whereby the court scholars, both masters and pupils, were despatched to fructify the branches of the Frankish church. Thus many churches over which former court scholars presided became important centres of Christian learning and book production at this time, as envisaged by the *Epistola de litteris colendis*. These included Lorsch (Ricbod and Adalung), St Martin's Tours (Alcuin), St Riquier (Angilbert), St Amand and Salzburg (Arn), St Wandrille (Einhard) and Lyons (Leidrad), to which may perhaps be added also St Denis (Fardulf), and Fleury, Orleans and St Aignan (Theodulf of Orleans). It seems clear that these scholars worked to order. Alcuin wrote to assure Charlemagne that 'in accordance with your instructions I am attempting to administer to some here at St Martin's the honey of holy scripture; others I would like to intoxicate with the pure wine of holy wisdom; others I feed with the fruits of grammatical subtleties; to others I teach astronomy'.[111] The accent is very firmly on relevant, Christian learning: 'above

108 L. Wallach, *Alcuin and Charlemagne* (2nd edn Ithaca, N.Y., 1968) pp. 198–226 and Bullough, '*Aula renovata*', p. 284.

109 See *Latin and the Romance languages in the early Middle Ages*, ed. R. Wright (London, 1991) for full references.

110 A. Thacker, 'Bede's ideal of reform', in: *Ideal and Reality in Frankish and Anglo-Saxon Society. Studies Presented to J. M. Wallace-Hadrill*, ed. P. Wormald (Oxford, 1983) pp. 130–53, especially pp. 151–3.

111 MGH Epp IV, pp. 176–7.

all else', he says, 'I am trying to train them to be useful to the holy Church ...' Similarly Leidrad, appointed by Charlemagne to the see of Lyons in the 790s (the exact date is unclear) wrote a long letter to the king reporting on the progress that he had made in restoring the ecclesiastical communities in his diocese, male and female, and in the setting up of schools for the training of scribes and clergy.[112] Just as *missi dominici*, after 802, were expected to report on their work to the king in writing so too, it seems, were prelates expected to keep in touch on the progress of reform. Here, as elsewhere one feels the driving thrust of Charlemagne himself behind the work of reform.

With the court scholars went books. It is thought likely that in around 780 Charlemagne sent out a general request for books, on the evidence of verses at the head of a Commentary on Genesis by Wigbod to the effect that Charlemagne, by his decree, had brought together books from many lands.[113] In other words a concerted attempt to build up a court library was being made. The overriding concern seems to have been to acquire 'authentic', in other words uncorrupt, texts that could either be copied at court or borrowed for copying elsewhere. Charlemagne's court library included a fine collection of pagan as well as Christian Latin authors. A list of books in a Berlin manuscript (Diez B. Sant. 66), which has been linked with Peter of Pisa, is thought to record only some of those pagan texts available at Charlemagne's court. The authors listed include Lucan (*Civil War*), Terence (*Andria* and *Eunuchus*), Statius (his epic poem *Thebaid*), Claudian (poems), Juvenal (*Satires*), Tibullus (poems), Horace (*Ars poetica*), Martial (*Epigrams*), Cicero (*Prosecutions of Catiline and Verre*) and Sallust (parts of both *The Catiline Conspiracy* and *The History of the Jugurthine War*). The fact that some of these texts reappear at Lorsch, Corbie, Tours or Fleury in the next generation suggests that copies were taken there by court scholars like Ricbod, Adalhard (Charlemagne's cousin), Alcuin and Theodulf, appointed abbots of Lorsch, Corbie, St Martin's and Fleury respectively by the king. Given the Merovingian evidence, the interest shown in such authors at Charlemagne's court constitutes a marked revival. Likewise the series of illustrated Gospel Books made at Charles' court were distributed around the major churches of the empire, the last of them apparently to St Médard at Soissons by Louis the Pious in 827.[114] The plan, it seems, was that the court should constitute the source for the revival of relevant learning in the churches of the kingdom; and the evidence does indeed suggest that Charlemagne's court played a key role, as a source of both scholars and manuscripts, in the early phases of the revival of learning. By such means what began as a renaissance that was, to some degree, centrally planned, came to take on a momentum of its own.

112 A. Coville, *Recherches sur l'histoire de Lyon* (Paris, 1928) pp. 283–7.

113 On this and what follows see B. Bischoff, 'Die Hofbibliothek Karls des Grossen', in: *Karl der Grosse* II, pp. 42–62, especially pp. 45–6 and 57–61, reprinted in a revised version in Bischoff, *MS* III, pp. 149–70. See also McKitterick chapter 8, below, pp. 221–47.

114 See McKitterick, 'Royal patronage of culture in the Frankish kingdoms under the Carolingians: motives and consequences', *Settimane* 39 (Spoleto, 1992) pp. 93–129.

The nature of Carolingian culture

The activities of scholars, rising standards of Latinity and increasing levels of literacy, not only in the Church but also in the lay community, at least in its upper echelons, all testify, if indirectly, to the effective functioning of Carolingian schools, and thus to the success of the initiative to revive learning as set out in clause 72 of the *Admonitio generalis* and the *Epistola de litteris colendis*. So also does the very large number of manuscripts which survive from the ninth century. For the first eight hundred years of the Christian era some 1,800 western manuscripts or fragments of manuscripts remain, while over 7,000 survive from the ninth century alone. It may be argued that Carolingian manuscripts are more likely to be preserved than those of preceding centuries on account of their improved Latinity, better texts, more consistent orthography and punctuation, and clearer script, but this still remains a staggering contrast. Moreover these manuscripts were highly costly to produce.[115] The greatest contribution made by the Carolingian rulers to the revival of learning in their territories was thus less in legislating for it than in guaranteeing the Church's enjoyment of the requisite material resources in the face of various conflicting interests and pressures.

The contents of these manuscripts make it abundantly clear that the revival of learning, as reaffirmed at the Synod of Savonnières (859), was aimed at cultivating that 'useful learning, both divine and humane, through which the fruit of God's church may be increased'.[116] Learning was to serve God and the work of reform. Thus biblical and liturgical texts predominate, followed by biblical commentaries, usually patristic but also those of more recent or contemporary authors, saints' lives and canon law. *Florilegia* and *compendia* of all kinds of information thought useful or relevant abound, many of which bear witness to the level of effort invested in providing parish priests with the tools essential to their task of *correctio*; there are also glossaries, word-lists and various encyclopaedias. A wide variety of schoolbooks, grammatical texts to the fore, are also extant, providing further evidence of the functioning of Carolingian schools.[117]

Ninth-century book-lists and library catalogues likewise record the overwhelming preponderance of religious over secular learning.[118] The best-documented libraries are those of the Alemannian monasteries of St Gall and Reichenau, both renowned centres of learning in this period. A mid-ninth-century catalogue from St Gall lists nearly 400 manuscripts, interspersed among

115 McKitterick, *Carolingians*, pp. 153–64.

116 MGH Conc. III, p. 478.

117 One such manuscript is discussed in detail by R. McKitterick, 'A ninth-century schoolbook from the Loire valley: Phillipps MS 16308', *Scriptorium* 30 (1976) pp. 225–31.

118 G. Becker, *Catalogi bibliothecarum antiqui* (Bonn, 1886) and P. Lehmann, *Mittelalterliche bibliothekskataloge Deutschlands und der Schweiz I Die Bistümer Konstanz und Chur* (Munich, 1918); see also McKitterick, *Carolingians*, pp. 169–210.

which are only four pagan classical authors: Vergil, Servius, Justinus and Josephus (thrice). Included in this list (no. 288) are some *capitula Caroli imperatoris* bound together with *glossae* from Genesis, Exodus, Leviticus, Numbers, Deuteronomy, Joshua, Judges, Ruth and Kings, a reminder that Carolingian capitularies and Old Testament law were seen as stemming from one tradition.[119] Of the sixty-seven books which Hartmut the librarian of the house acquired during the reign of Abbot Grimald (841–72), only five contained the works of pagan authors: Josephus again (thrice), Festus Pompeius and a *Gesta Alexandri*. Abbot Grimald's private book collection comprised thirty-five books, including one volume of Vergil's poetry and Vegetius' *Art of War*; the remainder (with one exception) were all religious texts. A book-list from Reichenau, dated 821 or 822, numbers over 400 manuscripts.[120] The only pagan classical authors represented are Vergil and Josephus (twice each). In addition there is a Latin translation of pseudo-Dares Phrygius on the fall of Troy and a treatise *De architectura*. Another list from the same monastery, datable to the second half of the ninth century, is more forthcoming.[121] Here, among 384 books, we find more pagan classical texts: Macrobius, Chalcidius, Vegetius, Aristotle's *Categories* (in translation), Claudian, Festus Pompeius, Seneca, Sallust and Ovid (*Metamorphoses* and *Art of Loving*).

The number of classical texts of the pagan period in the Carolingian libraries of St Gall and Reichenau was thus a very insignificant part of the whole. The pattern is repeated elsewhere. Of the fifty-odd manuscripts that can be associated with Carolingian St Denis, for example, all but four contain works of exclusively Christian learning, the exceptions being Josephus, Vegetius' *De re militari* and some medical texts.[122] Likewise an inventory of books from St Riquier, dated 831, contains over 500 titles in 256 manuscripts and only a handful of pagan authors: the ubiquitous Vergil, Josephus and the grammarians, also Cicero, Pliny and again some medical writings.[123] Other monasteries such as Lorsch, Corbie, Fulda and Fleury had more significant holdings of classical authors, as of course did Charlemagne's palace library.[124] We do not know whether lists of this kind represented the sum total of books in a given library. Our knowledge of the holdings at Fleury encourages circumspection: here one ninth-century book-list contains mostly theological works while another from the next century is almost entirely made up of pagan authors. But the pattern is

119 Lehmann, *Mittelalterliche Bibliothekskataloge*, pp. 71–84 at pp. 82–4

120 Ibid., pp. 240–52.

121 Ibid., pp. 262–8.

122 D. Nebbiai dalla Guarda, *La Bibliothèque de l'abbaye de Saint-Denis en France du IXe au XVIIIe siècle* (Paris, 1985) pp. 289–317.

123 Hariulf, *Chronicon Centulense* III, c. 3, ed. F. Lot, *Chronique de l'abbaye de Saint-Riquier Ve siècle–1104* (Paris, 1894) pp. 88–94

124 L. D. Reynolds and N. G. Wilson, *Scribes and Scholars. A Guide to the Transmission of Greek and Latin Literature* (3rd edn Oxford, 1991) pp. 97–101. B. Bischoff, 'Hadoard and the classical manuscripts from Corbie', in: *Didascaliae. Studies in Honor of Anselm M. Albareda*, ed. S. Prete (New York, 1961) pp. 39–57, revised German version in Bischoff, *MS* I, pp. 49–63; D. Ganz, *Corbie in the Carolingian Renaissance*, Beihefte der Francia 20 (Sigmaringen, 1990) pp. 93–7.

clear: the focus of interest was primarily, and almost exclusively, on Christian learning, and especially on that of the patristic period, of the fourth and fifth centuries. Thus a ninth-century catalogue from Lorsch contains close to 600 titles arranged in sixty-three sections, no fewer than eighteen of which are devoted to Augustine and six to Jerome.[125] Similarly an early ninth-century list from Fulda or one of its dependencies lists 110 titles of which thirty-six are works by Jerome. The Reichenau list of 821 or 822 is especially interesting because the texts are noted according to a rough hierarchy of importance. Listed first are the thirty-five biblical manuscripts. Then come the commentaries on the Bible listed according to author: Augustine first (twenty-eight manuscripts), then Jerome (twenty-eight), Gregory (nineteen), and a handful by other writers. Then follow eighteen manuscripts containing lives of the early saints of the Church. Next come the abbey's collection of 137 liturgical texts: fifty-eight sacramentaries, fifty Psalters, twelve lectionaries, and ten antiphonaries. After this are listed various works by authors of the fourth to eighth centuries, homiliaries, manuscripts of canon law, monastic rules, more saints' lives and grammars (ten in all). A similar scheme is apparent in the contemporary St Riquier inventory, except here Jerome (twenty-two manuscripts) precedes Augustine (twenty-nine manuscripts).[126] The number of books may not seem very large by modern standards. But whatever the total number what is certain is that libraries were much better stocked in the ninth century than they had been in the eighth.

The texts used in the Carolingian schools as schoolbooks for those learning to read, texts which survive in considerable numbers, underline this emphasis on relevant Christian learning, an emphasis which the Carolingian era, as we have seen, took over from those which preceded it. For the most part they were texts written between the fourth and sixth centuries, focused primarily on the Bible, in an effort to provide a distinctly Christian educational tradition, but preserving, and thus teaching to their readers, the literary values and standards of that pagan Roman culture. Such texts included Avitus of Vienne's poem on the Creation, Juvencus' verse conflation of the four Gospel stories, Sedulius' 'Easter story', in prose and verse versions, which contained Old and New Testament passages relating to Christ's coming and Resurrection, Arator's epic which told the story of the Acts of the Apostles, Defensor of Ligugé's *Liber scintillarum*, a collection of extracts from the Old and New Testaments, and Paulinus of Nola's verse paraphrase of the Psalms. The aim of those late Roman authors, as Sedulius explicitly stated, was to render accessible the substance of the classical poetic tradition for the delectation and instruction of readers in an acceptably Christian guise.[127] Other popular texts focused on moral virtues, for example Prudentius' *Psychomachia*, an account of a pitched battle fought between the

[125] B. Bischoff, *Lorsch im Spiegel seiner Handschriften* (Munich, 1974) pp. 18–28.
[126] On these libraries see McKitterick, *Carolingians*, pp. 179–82 and her references.
[127] Ed. J. Heumer, CSEL 24 (Vienna, 1891) pp. 4–5.

virtues and the vices, and the *Disticha Catonis*, a collection of sayings and aphorisms. Such texts as the above appear constantly in the library catalogues and book-lists of the Carolingian period.

With this solid grounding in Christian culture, and fortified by the memorisation of key parts of the Bible such as the Psalms, the student then proceeded to study the seven liberal arts, firstly the *trivium*, namely more grammar together with rhetoric and dialectic or logic, then the *quadrivium* – arithmetic, geometry, music and astronomy. The key textbooks here were those of Isidore of Seville, namely his *Etymologies* and his *De natura rerum*, and Martianus Capella's *On the Marriage of Mercury and Philology* in which the sevenfold structure of the liberal arts was set out, followed by Augustine's *De doctrina christiana* and Cassiodorus' *Institutiones* (part II). By no means were all the *artes liberales* considered to be of equal use, however. The study of grammar (in particular), rhetoric and dialectic were considered essential tools in unlocking the meaning of the Bible, and revealing the divine will.[128] For scripture, as Cassiodorus observed, is 'succinct in its definitions, beautiful in its ornaments, outstanding in the propriety of its usage, skilful in contriving syllogisms, sparkling in its use of every technical skill'.[129] Here again, in the emphasis placed on grammatical studies, the Carolingians were closely aligning themselves with late Roman traditions of learning. *Grammatica* meant more than simply learning to write: 'the art of grammar', wrote Marius Victorinus, citing Varro, 'which we call literature (*litteratura*), is the science of the things said by poets, historians and orators; its principal functions are: to read, to write, to understand and to prove'.[130] The Christian exegetical tradition, from Origen and Augustine and taken further by Gregory the Great and Bede, held that every word of the Bible was of profound significance and capable of interpretation on several levels: the literal, the allegorical, the anagogical and the moral (or tropological). These various levels of meaning were, to Gregory the Great, 'bright green plants' to be picked and chewed by exposition. Knowledge of these ancient disciplines was also vital if proper use was to be made of the patristic commentaries which, according to Cassiodorus, constituted the rungs on Jacob's ladder by which the human soul might ascend to heaven.[131] New texts for teaching the *trivium* were provided by Carolingian scholars like Alcuin. By contrast study of the *quadrivium* was limited. Arithmetic was learned in the context of *computus*, music as a means to augment the impact of the liturgy, astronomy as a means to detect the providential plan in the movement of the planets, and geometry hardly at all since it was difficult to apply usefully in the context of Christian learning. This had been the case at least since the decline of the public schools in Gaul and Italy in the late sixth and early seventh centuries. What is immediately obvious at

[128] See Law, chapter 3, below, pp. 88–107.

[129] *Expositio psalmorum*, preface c. 15, CCSL 97 (Turnhout, 1958) p. 19, lines 50–3; Eng. trans. G. Evans, *The Thought of Gregory the Great* (Cambridge, 1986) p. 34.

[130] *Ars grammatica*, I, 6–7, ed. I. Mariotti, *Marii Victorini Ars grammatica* (Florence, 1967), pp. 65–6.

[131] *Institutiones* I preface c. 2, ed. Mynors, p. 4, lines 6–8.

every turn, and requires emphasis, is that the culture of the Carolingian Renaissance was firmly grounded in, and grafted onto, that religious culture which had taken shape in the late Roman world of the fifth and sixth centuries, and continued to develop in the seventh century in Merovingian Gaul, Visigothic Spain and Anglo-Saxon England. What was achieved by the Carolingians was the vigorous renewal of this tradition, the reformation of a Latin religious culture that was to form the bedrock of the civilisation of the Latin west down to the sixteenth century and beyond.

The Carolingians' attitude toward pagan Latin learning conformed similarly to that enshrined in this tradition. Where possible pagan culture could be given a Christian gloss; where not it might be tolerated because it was useful. Thus to Hraban Maur 'the useful elements in the secular poets are so much grist to the human mill: what is not useful we wipe from our minds, and that applies above all to any mention of the heathen gods or of love'. Similarly Hadoard of Corbie, the ninth-century scholar, recalls how he had feared to read authors whom he knew to be outside the Christian enclosure and whose souls languished in outer darkness; yet he acknowledged that their works contained hidden treasure or, using a classical metaphor, base metal that could, by Christians such as himself, be turned to gold.[132] Pagan authors, moreover, contained much practical knowledge that was worth having: Vitruvius on architecture, Vegetius on war, Palladius on plants, Pliny on the natural world, Galen on medicine were all texts which were copied in the Carolingian period. Other texts might be enjoyed for special reasons: Vergil's *Aeneid*, for example, on account of its epic format and the martial prowess of its hero, and because it was from the Trojans, the seed of Aeneas, that the Franks traced their descent; Josephus' *Histories* because they focused on the Jewish people, the *gens sancta* whose mantle the Franks had assumed; and also Cicero's writings because he had been lavishly praised, and used as a source for Christian philosophy, by St Augustine.

It is clear from a variety of sources, however, that pagan texts could be read with pleasure as well as profit in the Carolingian period, and that there was some degree of interest in many facets of the pagan Roman past among the educated elite, not least in the pagan myths themselves. It was, of course, customary to deride and condemn such interest; but the warnings delivered by such as Bede, Alcuin, Hraban, Hadoard, Paschasius Radbert, Lupus of Ferrières, Paul Albarus and Notker against the dangers faced by the Christian soul acquainted with the pagan tradition must be seen to some degree merely as a form of literary cliché inherited from the patristic culture which the Carolingians strove so hard to recreate. Thus, to his hagiographer, it was appropriate that Alcuin should have been admonished in a dream for his love of Vergil as Jerome had been for his love of Cicero.[133] In short the attitude of the Carolingians towards pagan Latin

132 Hraban Maur, *De institutione clericorum* III, 16, PL 107, col. 394; Hadoard, MGH Poet. II, p. 685, especially lines 93–4.

133 *Vita Alcuini*, MGH SS XV.1, p. 185; Jerome, *Epistolae* XXII, 29, PL 22, col. 416.

learning was no less ambivalent than that of the fathers themselves. Evidently Charlemagne's court poets, Alcuin included, were well acquainted with the work of their pagan counterparts; and the significant holding of classical writings at Charlemagne's court has already been referred to. Ninth-century Carolingian scholars may have derived the greater part of their classical learning from anthologies, or second-hand from the Christian writers of the fourth, fifth and sixth centuries; but interest in the authors of pagan Rome remained alive. Even if these authors were not studied for their own sake, their works were recopied where time, resources and occasion allowed, and it is clear that some scholars at least, for example Lupus of Ferrières or Heiric of Auxerre, were sufficiently interested, and had the opportunity, to read a number of these works in their entirety. The pagan Roman Empire was as much part of the providential plan as the Incarnation, and for this reason, besides its utility, its learning might be preserved. Moreover this learning bestowed dignity upon those who had knowledge of it as also upon the ruler – *rex francorum et langobardorum ac patricius romanorum* – who sponsored its preservation at his court.

Accordingly, although pagan classical texts held only a very limited place in the framework of Carolingian studies, this was sufficient to ensure that a substantial part of the classical heritage was preserved and passed on to medieval Europe. The Carolingian period witnessed a revival of interest in this heritage which, although modest, was nevertheless vital for its preservation. By 900, as a result of careful Carolingian copying in a script that was clear, and offset by disciplined orthography and punctuation, authors such as Vergil, Horace, Lucan, Juvenal, Persius, Terence, Statius, Cicero (philosophical works), Sallust, Pliny the Elder, Justinus and Vitruvius were assured of survival. Works of Seneca, Quintilian, Martial and Suetonius were available but rare and for the most part incomplete; those of Plautus, Lucretius, Livy, Pliny the Younger, Ovid, Tacitus, Columella, Petronius and Ammianus Marcellinus rarer still. The survival of other works balanced on a knife edge: the poems of Tibullus, Catullus and Propertius, and some works of Tacitus and Livy, for example, were barely preserved, some in a single manuscript only. This serves as a reminder not to exaggerate this interest in, and appreciation of, pagan classical literature, even at the court of Charlemagne. Significantly, before Adam of Masmünster presented his copy of Diomedes' grammar to Charlemagne in around 780 he had taken care to remove many quotations from pagan authors.[134] Like Bede's, this was a Christian society concerned primarily with saving souls through preaching, pastoral work or prayer; in this context pagan learning and literature was at best only of limited, secondary importance as the library catalogues and book-lists of the period already discussed make plain.

We have only to look at the work of Carolingian scholars to appreciate the force of this statement. Alcuin's writings, exclusively concerned as they are with

[134] Bischoff, 'Hofbibliothek Karls', p. 45 with n.19.

'useful', Christian learning, have already been referred to. His pupil Hraban Maur was perhaps the best-respected of Carolingian scholars, and for this reason the range and character of his work is worth looking at in some detail. In the first place he was prolific, his surviving works filling no fewer than six large volumes of Migne's Patrologia latina. Before 806 he had been a pupil of Alcuin, probably at Tours, who it seems gave him the nickname of Maurus, the name of St Benedict's favourite pupil; thereafter he returned to Fulda where he became abbot in 822, before becoming archbishop of Mainz in 847. He died in 856. Even more than Alcuin's, his writings clearly demonstrate the extent to which learning was valued for its usefulness and relevance in advancing the objectives of Christian society.

In the first place much of it was focused on the Bible. He composed commentaries on no less than twenty of its books, commentaries which were evidently highly valued and widely read: his commentary on Matthew alone survives in over 70 copies, at least fifteen of which date from the ninth century.[135] In his choice of books it is clear, as Le Maître has stressed, that Hraban saw himself as the disciple of Bede and Alcuin, completing a project that they had begun, namely, to provide a contemporary commentary on the scriptures based upon patristic wisdom, but updating that wisdom and rendering it the more familiar and the more accessible to a contemporary audience.

It is here, in the context of biblical exegesis, that the Anglo-Saxon contribution to the religious culture of the Carolingian Renaissance is most clearly apparent. Like those of Bede and Alcuin, the greater part of Hraban's commentaries are composed of quotations from relevant works of Augustine, Gregory, Origen and others: they exemplify what is known as the *catena* (or chain) method of biblical commentry. In this he, like Bede and Alcuin, did not intend to deceive: his sources were for the most part clearly acknowledged by marginal annotation, as were his own ideas with the initial 'M' (for Maurus), and he urged copyists to respect these annotations as an integral, and indispensable, part of the textual apparatus. In short he claimed, deliberately choosing the words of Bede, that he had been 'solicitous throughout lest I should be said to have stolen the words of greater men and to have put them together as if they were my own'.[136] The aim was to provide a dossier of patristic authority on every word and phrase of the Bible, one that would elucidate for the average student, without the means, the intellectual resources or the time to consult the Fathers at first hand, the various levels of meaning inherent in Holy Writ: the literal or historical, the allegorical, the moral or tropological and the anagogical or spiritual.[137] His sense of mission was to ransack the storehouse of Christian learning, and thereby to render it and its wisdom, the highest form of know-

[135] P. Le Maître, 'Les Méthodes exégetiques de Raban Maur', in: *Haut moyen âge. Culture, éducation et société: études offerts à Pierre Riché* (Paris, 1990) pp. 343–52 at p. 343 n.1.

[136] MGH Epp. V, p. 389; Eng. trans. G. Constable, 'Forgery and plagiarism in the middle ages', *Archiv für Diplomatik* 29 (1983) pp. 1–41 at p. 28.

[137] Le Maître, 'Raban Maur', p. 344, citing Hraban's *In Jeremiam*, PL 111, cols. 793–4, and p. 346.

ledge, more readily accessible to a Carolingian audience. He 'bent over backwards in the effort not to be original', to be a faithful mouthpiece for what others better qualified than he had already said, as he himself stressed in the preface to his commentary on Ezechiel: 'it seems to me healthier to lean upon the doctrines of the holy Fathers . . . than improperly to offer my own'.[138] Here, as in the search for 'authentic texts' at the court of Charlemagne, is the aim of returning *ad fontes*, of drawing Christian wisdom from the source in all its purity, 'because the better water is the coldest water of the spring, and the better for drinking than the streams wandering here and there through the steep hills of the mountains and fields, disturbed by animals, beasts and pigs'.[139] In the ambition to make tradition and authority the norm of contemporary living, we touch the essential meaning of the Carolingian *renovatio*.

In fact Hraban's commentaries, like those of Alcuin and especially Bede before him, contain a sizeable element of originality, on occasion (for example in his Matthew commentary) his own contribution amounting to nearly 50 per cent of the whole. Moreover these compilations are sensibly and intelligently arranged, all carefully integrated into a credible and coherent whole, and 'bearing the impress of the writer's own mind and personality'.[140] To this extent they constitute 'original' works of scholarship. Other Carolingian commentators such as Paschasius Radbert, Angelomus of Luxeuil and Christian of Stavelot, selecting their material and varying their approach to meet the requirements of their particular audiences, worked in the same way with greater or lesser degrees of success, as indeed did contemporary compilers of handbooks, dossiers and *florilegia* of all kinds, containing both Christian and secular learning, produced for a variety of purposes in accordance with contemporary tastes and needs. Like Isidore, Hraban showed especial reverence for *pater Augustinus*.[141] Thus learning, for Hraban and others, was the acquisition of pre-existing knowledge, not original thought. Those who strayed too far from the tradition, such as Amalarius, Claudius of Turin, Gottschalk and John Scottus Eriugena, were liable to find themselves in hot water, accused of *superbia* or worse. What this approach demanded was that its exponents should be phenomenally well read in the writings of the fathers, for which the prerequisite in turn was a well-stocked library and many busy scribes to provide for it. This point is well made by Alcuin in a letter to Charlemagne regarding the tracts he had commissioned from his scholars in the attack against Adoptianism: 'if the writings agree in their defence of the faith, we can see that one spirit speaks through the lips and hearts of all; but if any difference is found, let it be seen who

138 R. McKitterick, *The Frankish Kingdoms under the Carolingians, 751–987* (London, 1983) p. 202. The preface to the Ezechiel commentary (PL 110, col. 498A–B) is cited by Constable, 'Forgery and plagiarism', p. 29.

139 *Alcuini epistolae*, appendix 2, MGH Epp. IV p. 486, discussed by N. Hathaway, '*Compilatio*: from plagiarism to compiling', *Viator* 20 (1989) pp. 19–44 at p. 29.

140 M. L. W. Laistner, 'Some early medieval commentaries on the Old Testament' in *The Intellectual Heritage of the Early Middle Ages. Selected Essays by M. L. W. Laistner*, ed. C. Starr (Ithaca, N.Y., 1957) pp. 181–201 at p. 182; also Le Maître, 'Raban Maur', p. 352.

141 MGH Epp. V, pp. 402, 457.

has the greater authority in scripture and the Fathers'.[142] Hraban's biblical commentaries, in their method and expertise, are thus as instructive of Carolingian scholarship, its methods and its limitations, as the testimony of the surviving manuscripts and book-lists.

Hraban's other works largely follow the same derivative path. His *De institutione clericorum* closely follows Augustine's *De doctrina christiana*, but here he rearranges the whole, excising some bits and adding material from Cassiodorus, Isidore and Bede. Similarly his scientific treatise *De rerum naturis* (or *De universo*) is essentially a reworking of Isidore's *Etymologies*, indispensable as an 'encyclopaedia of the knowledge necessary for the understanding of the scriptures'.[143] The *De rerum naturis* shows how all knowledge was Christianised. The universe, the stars in the heavens, the earth and its creatures, had all been shaped by the divine will and thus bore its mark. Traces of the divine nature thus remained hidden in the natural world, but in forms of meaning that could be unlocked by the use of allegory and symbol. The rationale of Hraban's work, as of Isidore's, was that the origin and meaning of the names given to natural objects were a guide to their essential nature, and thus also to the divinity hidden within them. The mystical symbolism of these objects was thus what mattered, not the objects themselves. Scientific knowledge, like other branches of learning, was thus relevant only in so far as it pertained to the Christian faith and its significance.

Hraban's work, characteristic of Carolingian scholarship then in so many ways, is thus essentially derivative, self-consciously so. It may be uninspiring to the modern reader in consequence. But to follow *vestigia patrum*, as Bede put it, and to render patristic wisdom accessible to the present, was the accepted, and cherished, aim of early medieval scholarship. All shared in one body of knowledge, one Truth, to which all had access, upon which all might draw, and consequently which any might appropriate. One must appreciate what it was that Hraban and his contemporaries were trying to do: namely to provide the practical tools by which their Christian society might be corrected, reformed, renewed and therefore saved in the shortest possible time. The biblical commentaries apart, almost all Hraban's other works are intended for use in the practical context of pastoral care and underline the extent, once again, to which the uses and resources of learning were directed towards the needs of reform. The ultimate compliment was paid to Hraban (and to himself) by his master Lothar I who is reported to have said: 'Just as God gave my predecessors Jerome, Augustine and Ambrose, so he has given me Hraban.'[144]

Hraban wrote several of his biblical commentaries for friends, for example Hilduin of St Denis (Louis the Pious' archchaplain), Gerward of Lorsch (the

142 MGH Epp. IV, no. 149, p. 244, lines 7–11; Eng. trans. S. Allott, *Alcuin. His Life and Letters* (York, 1974) p. 96.

143 D. Moran, *The Philosophy of John Scottus Eriugena. A Study of Idealism in the Middle Ages* (Cambridge, Mass., 1989) p. 12 and Le Maitre, 'Raban Maur', p. 345.

144 MGH Epp. V, p. 504, line 3.

court librarian), and Bishop Freculf of Lisieux, sending them texts of the finished product.[145] Such a friendship network, with widespread ramifications, as the record of Hraban's correspondence makes clear, was by no means exceptional. All the evidence shows that both men and manuscripts moved freely about the empire; and this intercourse between Carolingian churches, fostered alike by ties of confraternity (formal prayer arrangements between churches) and by the frequent meetings of bishops and abbots, and their retinues, at court, synod and council, is one of the most important aspects of intellectual life in the Carolingian period.[146] Lupus, abbot of Ferrières between 841 and 862, is the most striking illustration of what has been termed 'the gregariousness of Carolingian scholarship', and of the importance of connections, both personal and institutional, for the cultivation of learning.[147] Our source here is his outstanding letter collection. Several letters refer to the lending of books; others ask, or dispense, advice on a variety of academic points, many concerning the *correctio* of grammar or pronunciation.[148] Books are exchanged not merely for reading but also for copying. It was above all through this kind of co-operative exchange, both of views and manuscripts, that the Carolingian Renaissance proceeded.

Several of the texts referred to in these letters are pagan classical texts. It is evident, moreover, that Lupus and his friends sought not just to acquire such texts, but to acquire the best corrected, least corrupt texts. This characteristic Carolingian concern with correct, authentic texts, evident at the court of Charlemagne, and applied first of all to Christian learning, especially to the Bible and the liturgy, was also, we see, being applied to classical learning by Lupus and his friends. We can see Lupus in particular collecting many different variant manuscripts of a given text in order to compare and collate them so as to arrive at the most correct, most authentic version possible. He and his friends thus played an important part in ensuring that good classical texts survived into the modern period. Their attentions are focused not only on the classical writings best known to ninth-century audiences, for example those of Cicero or Vergil, but also on lesser-known authors such as Sallust, Caesar, Martial and Suetonius.

The circle of friends who shared Lupus' enthusiasm for all aspects of classical learning, however, was not a large one; first and foremost he himself was a scholar of Christian learning. His extant writings include, for example, theological works on the nature of the Eucharist and on predestination, on the meaning and function of kingship in a Christian society, and several saints' lives. He also drafted some conciliar legislation for Charles the Bald. His letters remind us that the pagan classics certainly did appeal to a learned elite among

145 MGH Epp. V, pp. 389, 402–3.
146 McKitterick, *Frankish Kingdoms*, pp. 210–12.
147 Ibid., p. 211.
148 Lupus of Ferrières, Epp. nos. 1, 4–5, 8–9, 35, 53, 65, 69, 79–80, 87, 95, 100–1, 108, 124, ed. L. Levillain, *Loup de Ferrières. Correspondance*, 2 vols. (Paris, 1964).

ninth-century Carolingian churchmen, as they had to some at Charlemagne's court, and that they were certainly thought worthy of preservation: but they remained at best an undercurrent in Carolingian learning, removed from the mainstream of effort and interest.

Conclusion

From what has been said already it will be clear that the revival of learning which is so prominent a feature of Charlemagne's reign did not end with his death in 814, despite the witness of Einhard, Walafrid and Lupus to that effect; neither did it end with the break-up of the empire in 840, nor in 877 with the death of Charles the Bald. Wherever one looks there is continuity through the ninth century and beyond.[149] This is especially true in the east where Ottonian culture is but late Carolingian culture under another name, and only less so in the west where the growth of tenth-century monastic reform, based on the monasteries of Cluny, Fleury, Gorze and Brogne, is plainly a sucker from the plant of its Carolingian counterpart. To emphasise the continuity between the ninth and tenth centuries, however, is not to deny that the Church faced very grave problems at this time. Foremost among these was the decline of royal power and authority resulting, as in the later Merovingian period, in the loss of church lands and, to some extent, secularisation of the Church itself as abbacies and bishoprics were filled by men whose outlook, dress and behaviour were secular rather than religious. The loss of lands could mean that schools closed, copying ceased, and even that communities dispersed. The availability of material resources was the crucial prerequisite for the pursuit of learning, and this the Carolingian kings, from Pippin III to Charles the Bald, broadly speaking had ensured. It was military success in the first place that had enabled them to do this: much of the wealth which provided for the Carolingian Renaissance was plunder and tribute from conquered lands. If learning declined in the late ninth and early tenth centuries it was largely because central authority could no longer guarantee the Church's enjoyment of its material resources in the face of lay encroachment. The weakening of central authority, and the political fragmentation of society concomitant with this, also made it more difficult for churches and individuals to maintain the links with others which had sponsored the fruitful interchange and exchange of manuscripts and personnel upon which so much of ninth-century scholarship and copying had depended.

Patronage of the Church in any form is an investment: laymen patronised churches because they expected a return, either spiritual, or temporal, in the form of greater control over that church and its resources. The Carolingian Renaissance may be seen as an exercise in patronage on a grand scale by the

149 See select bibliography at the end of this chapter.

Carolingian rulers. Church lands could be relied upon to provide the *milites* upon whom Carolingian power and authority depended. The Church was also a medium through which their territories could be more effectively controlled. Only through the Church, its institutions, and its laws, could disparate populations, with different languages and law-codes, be integrated and administered. The royal interest is an essential and integral part of the Carolingian Renaissance, whether construed as the reform of society according to Christian norms or simply as a revival of learning, and crucial to understanding why this development took place at all. The Carolingians were faced with two principal problems: not only how to bind together and govern disparate and far-flung territories, but also simply how best to consolidate and legitimise their newly acquired royal authority. In such circumstances it is easy to see the attraction of the idea that God's destiny for them was to construct, with papal backing, a unified Christian society held together by the Christian virtue of obedience. The position of the Carolingian rulers, oath-breakers and usurpers, could thus be fortified by an unction which signified that God's favour and choice had fallen upon them. Rulers drawn from outside an ancient royal kindred could be seen to lack fortitude. As anointed kings set over a Christian society they were both God's elect and God's representatives: rebellion against their authority thus became rebellion also against God. Obedience to the dictates of the faith and obedience to the ruler whose divinely appointed task was to institute those dictates by law could be made to seem indistinguishable.

Education and learning were conceived as being vital to the success of the enterprise of moral *correctio*. Here too there were important implications for royal authority. Classicising tendencies in both art and literature, and notably in court poetry, served to enhance the ruler's prestige by associating him with late Roman imperial traditions; and government was more efficient, and more Roman, if articulated and conducted in writing as well as in speech. Recent research has very clearly underlined the extent to which writing was employed in Carolingian government, especially from the time of Louis the Pious onwards. Thus the Latin language could be employed in secular administration, as well as in the liturgy, to bind together subject peoples who spoke different tongues.[150]

The needs of government are thus an important factor in understanding the Carolingian Renaissance and its causes. An even larger one is Carolingian military success. In the first place it created a vast amount of wealth, a large proportion of which was given over to the Church in the form of a thank offering. Secondly, with the exception of Anglo-Saxon England and the kingdom of the Asturias, it created the reality of a unified Christendom against which the ideal could be matched. Thirdly it brought the Franks into closer contact with both Italy and Spain and the richness of their cultural traditions.

150 McKitterick, *Carolingians*, and Nelson, 'Literacy in Carolingian government'.

Fourthly, Carolingian military triumphs, particularly over feared pagan opponents like the Saxons and the Avars, stimulated and advanced the Franks' self-confident belief in themselves as a chosen people, the New Israel, with a mission to promote the Christian faith much as a similar experience had earlier inspired the Visigoths. To the Carolingians the triumph of arms indicated that God had a special destiny in store for them. But what? The answer that they and their advisers came up with was Christian *reformatio*. This entailed both a revival of Christian learning and a further development of it, drawing on patristic tradition and feeding on more recent cultural developments worked out in Visigothic Spain, Anglo-Saxon England and Merovingian Gaul: *Roma renascens*. The Frankish Church, for its part, remained confident in the healing, revivifying powers of the Holy Spirit to create all things anew: 'Behold, a new spring has come ... the seasons are joyously renewed according to the eternal laws'.[151]

Select bibliography

The concept of the Carolingian Renaissance

A. Guerreau-Jalabert, 'La "Renaissance carolingienne": modèles culturels, usages linguistiques et structures sociales', *Bibliothèque de l'Ecole des Chartes* 139 (1981) pp. 5–35

P. Lehmann, 'Das Problem der karolingische Renaissance', *Settimane* 1 (Spoleto, 1954) pp. 310–57

J. L. Nelson, 'On the limits of the Carolingian Renaissance', in: *Renaissance and Renewal in Christian History*, ed. D. Baker, Studies in Church History 14 (Oxford, 1977) pp. 41–59, reprinted in J. L. Nelson, *Politics and Ritual in Early Medieval Europe* (London, 1986) pp. 49–68

E. Patzelt, 'L'Essor carolingien. Simples réflexions sur un sujet classique', *Revue des Sciences Religieuses* 41 (1967) pp. 109–28

Die karolingische Renaissance (Graz, 1965)

P. E. Schramm, *Kaiser, Rom und Renovatio*, 4th edn (Darmstadt, 1984)

'Karl der Grosse: Denkart und Grundauffassungen – Die von ihm bewirkte "correctio" (nicht "Renaissance")', *Historische Zeitschrift* 198 (1964) pp. 306–45

W. Treadgold (ed.) *Renaissances before the Renaissance. Cultural Revivals of Late Antiquity and the Middle Ages* (Stanford, CA, 1984), especially J. J. Contreni, 'The Carolingian Renaissance', pp. 59–74, 184–91, 213–16

G. Trompf, 'The concept of the Carolingian Renaissance', *Journal of the History of Ideas* 34 (1973) pp. 3–26

W. Ullmann, *The Carolingian Renaissance and the Idea of Kingship* (London, 1967)

151 Theodulf of Orleans, 'On the court', trans. Godman, *Poetry*, pp. 152–3: 'Ver venit ecce novum ... En renovatur ovans aeternis legibus annus.'

Background

The late Roman and Visigothic inheritance

R. Bezzola, *Les Origines et la formation de littérature courtoise en Occident* (Paris, 1944)
R. Bolgar, *The Classical Heritage and its Beneficiaries* (Cambridge, 1954)
J. Burns (ed.), *The Cambridge History of Medieval Political Thought* (Cambridge, 1988)
P. Courcelle, *Les Lettres grecques en Occident de Macrobe à Cassiodore* (Paris, 1945)
J. Fontaine, *Isidore de Séville et la culture classique dans l'Espagne wisigothique* (Paris, 1959)
M. Gibson (ed.), *Boethius: His Life, Thought and Influence* (Oxford, 1981)
P. D. King, *Law and Society in Visigothic Spain* (Cambridge, 1972)
G. Ladner, *The Idea of Reform: Its Impact on Christian Thought and Action in the Age of the Fathers* (Cambridge, Mass., 1959)
R. McKitterick (ed.), *Uses of Literacy*
H. Marrou, *A History of Education in Antiquity* (New York, 1956)
F. Raby, *A History of Christian Latin Poetry* (Oxford, 1927)
A History of Secular Latin Poetry, 2 vols. (Oxford, 1934)

Merovingian Francia

H. Atsma (ed.), *La Neustrie. Les Pays au nord de la Loire, 650 à 850*, 2 vols., Beihefte der Francia, 16 (Sigmaringen, 1989)
H. Beck, *The Pastoral Care of Souls in South East Gaul in the Sixth Century* (Rome, 1950)
H. Clarke and M. Brennan (eds.), *Columbanus and Merovingian Monasticism*, BAR Supplementary Reports, International Series (Oxford, 1981)
P. Fouracre, 'The work of Audoenus of Rouen and Eligius of Noyon in extending episcopal influence from the town to the country in seventh century Neustria', in *The Church in Town and Countryside*, ed. D. Baker, Studies in Church History 16 (Oxford, 1979) pp. 77–91
D. Ganz, 'Bureaucratic shorthand and Merovingian learning', in: *Ideal and Reality in Frankish and Anglo-Saxon Society: Studies Presented to J. M. Wallace-Hadrill*, ed. P. Wormald (Oxford, 1983) pp. 58–75
'Corbie and Neustrian monastic culture', in: *La Neustrie*, ed. Atsma, II, pp. 339–48
E. James, *The Origins of France* (London, 1982)
R. McKitterick, 'The diffusion of insular culture in Neustria between 650 and 850: the implications of the manuscript evidence', in: *La Neustrie*, ed. Atsma, II, pp. 395–432
'The scriptoria of Merovingian Gaul', in: *Columbanus*, ed. Clarke and Brennan, pp. 173–207
O. Pontal, *Histoire des conciles mérovingiens* (Paris, 1989)
F. Prinz, *Frühes Mönchtum im Frankenreich* (Munich, 1965)
P. Riché, 'Les Centres de culture en Neustrie de 650 à 750', in: *La Neustrie*, ed. Atsma, II, pp. 297–307.
Écoles et enseignement dans le haut moyen âge (Paris, 1979)
Education and Culture in the Barbarian West, Sixth through Eighth Centuries (trans. J. J. Contreni, Columbia, S.C., 1976)
'L'Instruction des laïcs en Gaule mérovingienne au VIIe siècle', *Settimane* 5 (Spoleto, 1957) pp. 873–88, repr. in *Instruction et vie religieuse*
Instruction et vie religieuse (London, 1981)

J. Vezin, 'Les Scriptoria de Neustrie, 650–850', in: *La Neustrie*, ed. Atsma, II, pp. 307–18

J. M. Wallace-Hadrill, 'A background to Boniface's mission', in: *England before the Conquest*, ed. P. C. Clemoes and K. Hughes (Cambridge, 1971) pp. 35–48, repr. in: *Early Medieval History* (Oxford, 1976) pp. 138–54

Early Germanic Kingship in England and on the Continent (Oxford, 1971)

The Frankish Church (Oxford, 1983)

K.-F. Werner, 'Le Rôle de l'aristocratie dans la christianisation du nord-est de la Gaule', *Revue d'Histoire de l'Église de France* 63 (1976) pp. 45–73, repr. in idem, *Structures politiques du monde franc (VIe–XIIe. siècles)* (London, 1979)

I. Wood, 'Administration, law and culture in Merovingian Gaul', in: *Uses of Literacy*, pp. 63–81

The Anglo-Saxons

M. Coens, 'St Boniface et sa mission historique d'après quelques auteurs récents', *Analecta Bollandiana* 73 (1955) pp. 462–95

W. Levison, *England and the Continent in the Eighth Century* (Oxford, 1946)

R. McKitterick, 'Anglo-Saxon missionaries in Germany: reflections on the manuscript evidence', *TCBS* 9 (1989) pp. 281–329

H. Mayr-Harting, *The Coming of Christianity to Anglo-Saxon England*, 3rd edn (London, 1991)

The Greatest Englishman. Essays on St. Boniface and the Church at Crediton, ed. T. Reuter (Exeter, 1980)

Sankt Bonifatius Gedenkgabe (Fulda, 1954)

T. Schieffer, *Angelsachsen und Franken* (Mainz, 1950)

Winfrid-Bonifatius und die christliche Grundlegung Europas (Freiburg, 1954)

A. Thacker, 'Bede's ideal of reform', in: *Ideal and Reality in Frankish and Anglo-Saxon Society. Studies Presented to J. M. Wallace-Hadrill*, ed. P. Wormald (Oxford, 1983), pp. 130–53.

The Carolingian Reforms

W. Braunfels (ed.) *Karl der Grosse. Lebenswerk und Nachleben*, 4 vols. (Düsseldorf, 1965)

D. Bullough, *The Age of Charlemagne* (London, 1965)

D. Bullough and A. Harting-Corrêa, 'Texts, chant and the chapel of Louis the Pious', in: *Charlemagne's Heir*, pp. 489–508

G. Constable, *Monastic Tithes from their Origins to the Twelfth Century* (Cambridge, 1964)

'*Nona et decima*. An aspect of Carolingian economy', *Speculum* 35 (1960) pp. 224–50

C. de Clercq, *La Législation religieuse franque*, 2 vols. (Louvain–Paris–Antwerp, 1935–58)

J. Deshusses, 'Le "Supplément" au sacramentaire grégorien: Alcuin ou St Benoit d'Aniane?', *Archiv für Liturgiewissenschaft* 9 (1965) pp. 48–71

G. Devailly, 'La pastorale en Gaule au IXe siècle', *Revue d'histoire de l'Église de France* 59 (1973) pp. 23–54

A. Dierkens, 'La Christianisation des campagnes de l'Empire de Louis le Pieux: L'exemple du diocèse de Liège sous l'épiscopat de Walcaud', in: *Charlemagne's Heir*, pp. 309–31

S. Dulcy, *La Règle de St Benoit d'Aniane et la réforme monastique à l'époque carolingienne* (Nancy, 1935)

E. Ewig, 'Beobachtungen zur Entwicklung der fränkischen Reichskirke unter Chrodegang von Metz', *Frühmittelalterliche Studien* 2 (1968) pp. 67–77
B. Fischer, 'Bibletext und Bibelreform unter Karl der Grosse', in: *Karl der Grosse* II, pp. 156–216
F.-L. Ganshof, *The Carolingians and the Frankish Monarchy* (London, 1971)
O. Guillot, 'Une *ordinatio* méconnue', in: *Charlemagne's Heir*, pp. 455–86
R. Kottje, 'Einheit und Vielfalt des kirchlichen Lebens in der Karolingerzeit', *Zeitschrift für Kirchengeschichte* 76 (1965) pp. 323–42
G. W. H. Lampe (ed.), *The Cambridge History of the Bible*, II (Cambridge, 1969)
E. Lesne, *Histoire de la propriété ecclésiastique en France* (Lille, 1910–40)
R. McKitterick, *The Frankish Church and the Carolingian Reforms, 789–895* (London, 1977)
H. Mordek, '*Dionysio-Hadriana* und *Vetus gallica*, historisch geordnetes und systematisches Kirchenrecht am Hofe Karls des Grossen', *Zeitschrift der Savigny Stiftung für Rechtsgeschichte* (kanon. Abt.) 55 (1969) pp. 39–63
Kirchenrecht und Reform in Frankenreich. Die 'Collectio vetus gallica', die älteste systematische Kanonensammlung des Fränkischen Gallien (Berlin, 1975)
'Recently discovered capitulary texts belonging to the legislation of Louis the Pious', in: *Charlemagne's Heir*, pp. 437–53
H. Mordek, and G. Schmitz, 'Neue Kapitularien und Kapitulariensammlungen, *DA* 43 (1987) pp. 361–439
B. Moreton, *The Eighth Century Gelasian Sacramentary* (Oxford, 1976)
J. L. Nelson, 'Making ends meet: wealth and poverty in the Carolingian church', in: *The Church and Wealth*, ed. W. J. Sheils, Studies in Church History 24 (Oxford, 1987) pp. 25–35.
Politics and Ritual in Early Medieval Europe (London, 1986)
O. G. Oexle, *Forschungen zu monastischen und geistlichen Gemeinschaften im westfränkischen Reich* (Munich, 1978)
P. Riché, 'La Pastorale populaire en occident, VIe–XIe siècles', in: *Histoire vécue du peuple chrétien*, ed. J. Delumeau (Toulouse, 1979) I, pp. 195–221
St Chrodegang. Communications présentées au colloque tenu à Metz à l'occasion du douzième centenaire de sa mort (Metz, 1967)
G. Schmitz, 'The capitulary legislation of Louis the Pious', in: *Charlemagne's Heir*, pp. 425–36
P. Schmitz, *Histoire de l'ordre de St Benoit*, I (Maredsous, 1948)
'L'Influence de St Benoit d'Aniane et l'histoire de l'ordre de St Benoit', *Settimane* 4 (Spoleto, 1957) pp. 401–15
J. Semmler, 'Benedictus II: Una regula – una consuetudo', in: *Benedictine Culture 750–1050*, ed. W. Lourdaux and D. Verhulst (Louvain, 1983) pp. 1–49
'Die Beschlüsse des Aachener Konzils im Jahr 816', *Zeitschrift für Kirchengeschichte*, 74 (1963) pp. 15–82
'Corvey und Herford in der benediktinischen Reformbewegung des 9. Jh.', *Frühmittelalterliche Studien* 4 (1970) pp. 289–319
'Karl der Grosse und das fränkische Mönchtum', in: *Karl der Grosse*, II, pp. 255–89
'Pippin III und die fränkische Kloster', *Francia* 3 (1975) pp. 88–146
'Reichsidee und karolingische Gesetzgebung bei Ludwigs dem Frommen', *Zeitschrift für Kirchengeschichte*, 71 (1960) pp. 37–65
'Studien zur *Supplex libellus* und zur anianischen Reform in Fulda', *Zeitschrift für Kirchengeschichte* 69 (1958) pp. 269–98

'Zur Überlieferung der monastischen Gesetzgebung Ludwigs des Fromen', *DA* 16 (1960) pp. 309–88

J. Semmler and A. Verhulst, 'Les Statuts d'Adalhard de Corbie de l'an 822', *Le Moyen Age*, 78 (1962) pp. 91–123, 233–69

C. Vogel, *Medieval Liturgy: An Introduction to the Sources* (Washington D.C., 1986)

Literature and learning

C. H. Beeson, *Lupus of Ferrières as Scribe and Text Critic* (Cambridge, Mass., 1930)

B. Bischoff, 'Hadoard and the classical manuscripts from Corbie', in: *Didascaliae. Studies in Honor of Anselm M. Albareda*, ed. S. Prete (New York, 1961), pp. 39–57

'Die Hofbibliothek Karls des Grossen', in: *Karl der Grosse*, II, pp. 42–62, repr. in: Bischoff, *MS* III, pp. 149–70

'Die Hofbibliothek unter Ludwig dem Frommen', in: *Medieval Learning and Literature. Essays presented to R. W. Hunt*, ed. J. Alexander and M. Gibson, (Oxford, 1976) pp. 3–22, repr. in: Bischoff, *MS* III, pp. 171–86

Latin Palaeography. Antiquity and the Middle Ages (Cambridge, 1990)

'Panorama der Handschriftüberlieferung aus der Zeit Karls des Grossen', in: *Karl der Grosse*, II, pp. 233–54, repr. in: Bischoff, *MS* III, pp. 5–38

F. Brunhölzl, 'Die Bildungsauftrag der Hofschule', in: *Karl der Grosse*, II, pp. 28–41

Geschichte der lateinischen Literatur des Mittelalters. I. Von Cassiodor bis zum Ausklang der karolingischen Erneuerung (Munich, 1975)

D. Bullough, '*Albuinus deliciosus Karoli regis*. Alcuin of York and the shaping of the early Carolingian court', in: *Institutionen, Kultur und Gesellschaft im Mittelalter*. Festschrift für J. Fleckenstein zu seinem 65. Geburtstag, ed. L. Fenske, W. Rösener, T. Zotz (Sigmaringen, 1984) pp. 73–92

'Alcuin and the kingdom of heaven: liturgy, theology and the Carolingian age', in: *Carolingian Essays*, ed. U.-R. Blumenthal (Washington, 1983) pp. 1–6

'*Aula renovata*: the Carolingian court before the Aachen palace', *Proceedings of the British Academy* 71 (1985) pp. 267–301, reprinted in D. Bullough, *Carolingian Renewal: Sources and Heritage* (Manchester, 1992)

J. J. Contreni, *The Cathedral School of Laon from 850 to 930, Its Manuscripts and Masters* (Munich, 1978)

J. Devisse, *Hincmar, Archévêque de Reims (845–82)*, 3 vols. (Geneva, 1975)

D. Ganz, *Corbie in the Carolingian Renaissance*, Beihefte der Francia 20 (Sigmaringen, 1990)

R. Gariépy, 'Lupus, Carolingian scribe and critic', in *Medieval Studies* 30 (1968) pp. 90–105

M. Gibson, 'Boethius in the Carolingian schools', in *Transactions of the Royal Historical Society* 32 (1982) pp. 43–56

M. L. W. Laistner, 'The revival of Greek in western Europe in the Carolingian age', *History* (1924) pp. 177–87

Thought and Letters in Western Europe, AD 500–900 (London, 1931)

H. Liebeschutz, 'Theodulf of Orleans and the problem of the Carolingian Renaissance', in: *F. Saxl. A Volume of Memorial Essays*, ed. D. Gordon (London, 1957), pp. 77–92

R. McKitterick, *The Carolingians and the Written Word* (Cambridge, 1989)

'Charles the Bald and his library. The patronage of learning', *The English Historical Review* 95 (1980) pp. 28–47

'Nuns' scriptoria in Francia and England in the eighth century', *Francia* 19/I (1992) pp. 1–35

'The Palace school of Charles the Bald', in: *Charles the Bald, Court and Kingdom*, ed. J. L. Nelson and M. T. Gibson, 2nd edn (Aldershot, 1990) 326–39

'Royal patronage of culture in the Frankish kingdoms under the Carolingians: motives and consequences', *Settimane* 39 (Spoleto, 1992), pp. 93–129

L. Reynolds, and N. Wilson, *Scribes and Scholars. A Guide to the Transmission of Greek and Latin Literature*, 3rd edn (Oxford, 1991)

P. Riché, *Instruction et vie religieuse dans le haut moyen âge* (London, 1981)

2

Kingship and empire in the Carolingian world

Janet L. Nelson

The Carolingian period saw the consolidation of ideas about rulership which had been taking shape in the early medieval west since Christian Late Antiquity.[1] In the eighth century, significant Spanish and Insular contributions were incorporated into the mainstream of western political thought,[2] and in the ninth and tenth centuries that mainstream in turn irrigated new political formations in northern and central Europe. Between the eighth century and the tenth, an expanding Latin Christendom was dominated first by the Frankish Empire, then by states that succeeded to or were profoundly influenced by it. The creation of the Frankish Empire strengthened in the short run the traditional elements in barbarian kingship, successful leadership of the people (*gens*) in wars of conquest and plunder bringing Frankish domination of other *gentes*. Hence the hegemonial idea of empire, of the emperor ruling many peoples and realms, arose directly from the political experience of the eighth-century west. In the longer run power devolved to kingdoms that proved durable, without a gentile identity or an economic base in plunder and tribute. This brought new formulations of the realm as a territorial and sociological entity, the aristocracy sharing power and responsibility with the king. The idea of empire detached from its gentile anchorage acquired Roman-Christian universality.

In the eighth century the Frankish kings Pippin and Charlemagne successfully mobilised two elites, the higher clergy of the Frankish Church and the Frankish aristocracy. Power-sharing was built into the fabric of the Carolingian Empire though it was masked at first by a community of interest that evoked a chorus of praise for rulers evidently possessed of divine approval. Second thoughts were voiced in the ninth century when the stabilising of internal and external frontiers engendered fiercer competition for power within kingdoms. Some churchmen

[1] See select bibliography at the end of this chapter.

[2] Contributions from Spain and the British Isles: H. H. Anton, *Fürstenspiegel und Herrscherethos in der Karolingerzeit*, Bonner Historische Forschungen 32 (Bonn, 1968) pp. 55–74, 103–7; S. Reynolds, *Kingdoms and Communities in Western Europe, 900–1300* (Oxford, 1984), chapters 1 and 8, illuminate kingship in this period.

now clarified and qualified the terms of their support for kings and emperors, while aristocratic groupings formed by and around royal regimes recalled ideas of rights and of consent which could justify restraints on, and even resistance to, royal power.

In the latter part of the period, more intensive economic exploitation made possible new concentrations of resources in the hands of magnates, lay and clerical, and also of kings. So closely were church resources enmeshed in the structure of kingdoms that few ecclesiastics, especially if they sought reform, could part company with kings for long, though clerical protests were sometimes lodged against royal oppression. But it was the reaction of lay aristocrats against 'tyranny' that stimulated the clearer, more widespread articulation of ideas of collective resistance and of representation of political communities. The Carolingian period is therefore doubly crucial: in the legitimisation of kingship and empire, and in the working-out of critiques of power. Theocracy thrived: but so did the seeds of constitutionalism.

The relationship of ideas to reality is a general problem in the history of political thought. Peculiar to the earlier Middle Ages, however, is the difficulty with so much of the material of answering such basic questions as: who wrote it and for what audience? Is it a public work in the sense of expressing the 'official line' of the regime? Or is it a private work revealing the opinions of an individual or coterie? To take an example: the Donation of Constantine is an eighth-century forgery that purports to convey the transfer of imperial power and privileges to the pope and his entourage. Assessment of its significance in terms of its contemporary impact depends on whether it is identified as a papal document produced in 753 to justify Pope Stephen II's summoning of the Franks into Italy to protect the lands of St Peter, in disregard of Byzantine claims to authority,[3] or alternatively as a 'literary divertissement' produced in the late 750s or 760s by a Lateran cleric[4] to elevate Rome at the expense of Ravenna. Further, the circumstances of its production, whatever these were, have to be distinguished from the motives of the Frankish clergy who in the ninth century incorporated the text into a collection of canons designed to buttress ecclesiastical property-rights. Ideological content may vary with context. The fact that medieval writers, often with polemical purpose, used and re-used 'authorities' like the Donation with blithe unconsciousness of anachronism makes it especially important – and difficult – for modern historians to avoid this pitfall. Finally there is the problem of assessing how far a writer's view or concept was shared by his or her contemporaries. For instance, Agobard of Lyons' suggestion that the emperor Louis the Pious should impose one law on all the peoples of

[3] W. Ullmann, *The Growth of Papal Government in the Middle Ages*, 2nd edn (London, 1962), pp. 58–61, 74–86.

[4] P. Ourliac, 'Review of Fuhrmann 1972–4', *Francia* 8 (1980) p. 790. See also below, pp. 69–70.

his empire is interesting but quite unrepresentative[5] (as well as impractical!). It has seemed best in a general survey to concentrate mainly on texts that have a normative character or seem to present some fairly widely held viewpoint for their period. But it has to be admitted that sheer scarcity of evidence sometimes makes representativeness hard to gauge.

Carolingian kingship

In tracing the development of ideas about kingship, 750 is a more defensible starting point than most periodisations of history. In that year envoys were sent from Francia to Pope Zacharias to ask him whether or not it was good that there should be kings in Francia at that time who lacked royal power. Pope Zacharias told Pippin that it would be better to call king the man who had power than the man who was still there without royal power. So that order might not be disturbed, he ordered through apostolic authority that Pippin be made king.

Thus the Royal Frankish Annals produced at the court of Pippin's son Charlemagne some forty years after these events.[6] A strictly contemporary writer, commissioned by Pippin's own uncle, simply notes that 'an embassy was sent to the apostolic see' and that 'on receipt of the pope's official reply', Pippin 'by the election of all the Franks to the throne of the kingdom, by the consecration of bishops and by the subjection of the lay magnates, together with the queen Bertrada, as the rules of ancient tradition require was elevated into the kingdom'.[7] Whatever form previous royal inaugurations had taken, the novelty here was certainly the 'consecration', the anointing of Pippin by bishops – a novelty which it is obviously tempting to link with the pope's 'reply'.[8] Fritz Kern, probably the most influential of modern commentators on medieval political thought, did make this link, and drew far-reaching conclusions from these events. Hitherto, he inferred, the Franks' 'primitive beliefs', their 'superstitious aversion ... from parting with a phantom-like dynasty', had permitted Merovingian kings without power to succeed one another for over a century. The appeal to the pope in 750 meant the replacement of Germanic kin-right by 'Christian principles', of supernatural sanctification drawn from 'old pagan mythical roots' by an equally supernatural but Christian sanctification. Pippin's anointing, for Kern, signified a 'great revolution'.[9] For Henri Pirenne, it signalled the transition from the late-antique to the medieval world, from a still

[5] J. L. Nelson, 'On the Limits of the Carolingian Renaissance', *Studies in Church History* 14 (1977) p. 63. For the general problem of ideas and contexts: N. Staubach, 'Germanisches Königtum und lateinische Literatur', *Frühmittelalterliche Studien* 17 (1983) pp. 7–8.

[6] *Annales regni francorum* s.a. 749, ed. Rau, *Quellen* I, p. 8.

[7] Continuator of Fredegar, c. 33. ed. J. M. Wallace-Hadrill, *The Fourth Book of the Chronicle of Fredegar and its Continuations* (London, 1960) p. 102.

[8] J. Jarnut, 'Wer hat Pippin 751 zum König gesalbt?', *Frühmittelalterliche Studien* 16 (1982), pp. 54–7.

[9] F. Kern, *Kingship and Law in the Middle Ages* (Oxford, 1954), pp. 20–2, 25, 66–7. The quotations in the text are from the translation by Chrimes 1939, pp. 13, 16, 21, 35.

basically secular Merovingian kingship to the ecclesiastically conditioned rule of Carolingians 'by the grace of God'.[10]

There is too much evidence of the Christianisation of Merovingian kingship and of the Frankish aristocracy in the seventh and early eighth centuries[11] for Kern's 'revolution' to carry conviction. What is really striking about 750–1 is the coincidence of Frankish clerical interests with lay aristocratic interests and of both of those with the interests of the papacy. Pippin invoked papal approval 'with the consent of the Franks'. There was no question of alternative or competing types of legitimation when the pope approved what the Franks, with Pippin, had in fact already decided.[12] Pippin's installation as king demonstrated what dissension amongst the Franks had been obscuring for some time before 750: the gentile basis of Frankish kingship. Pippin's constituency was the *gens francorum*, already in the generation before 750 learning to see itself as a chosen people, a new Israel.[13] Its thought-world was shaped by the Old Testament Books of Exodus and Deuteronomy. The Children of Israel had had a special relationship with the Almighty, who had promised them that their kings, when they got them, would be chosen by Him 'out of the number of your brothers' (Deuteronomy 17:15). Only in the light of this identification with Israel was it apposite for Frankish priests to be anointed like Aaron (as they were already some decades before 750) or for a Frankish king to be anointed as Samuel anointed David.[14] The religious legitimation of Pippin depended on a prior and equally religious legitimation of the Franks. This theme, rather than their own individual consecrations, was what Pippin and Charlemagne sought to cultivate and to play on in the years after 750. Pippin's reissue of *Lex Salica*, the law of the *gens*, was accompanied by a paean of praise to the God-beloved Franks.[15] The Royal Frankish Annals report the victories not of Charlemagne alone but of 'the Franks, with God's help',[16] and the oaths of the conquered Saxons 'to maintain Christianity and faithfulness to King Charles and his sons and the Franks'.[17] Liturgical acclamations for Charlemagne and his family, the *Laudes regiae*, also have invocations for 'all the judges and the whole army of the Franks'.[18]

The new intimacy of this linking of the Franks with their ruling dynasty emerges equally clearly from the papal correspondence of the period. In a letter of 747 to Pippin, Mayor of the Palace, and 'all the magnates (*principes*) in the

10 H. Pirenne, *Mohammed and Charlemagne* (London, 1939) pp. 265–74.

11 E. Ewig, 'Zum christlichen Königsgedanken im Frühmittelalter', in: *Das Königtum*, Vorträge und Forschungen 3 (Sigmaringen, 1956) pp. 7–73; P. Riché, 'L'Enseignement et la culture des laïcs dans l'Occident pré-carolingien', *Settimane* 19 (Spoleto, 1972), pp. 231–53.

12 W. Affeldt, 'Untersuchungen zur Königserhebung Pippins', *Frühmittelalterliche Studien* 14 (1980) pp. 95–187.

13 Ewig, 'Zum christlichen Königsgedanken', pp. 42–5.

14 J. L. Nelson, 'Inauguration rituals', in: *Early Medieval Kingship*, ed. P. Sawyer and I. N. Wood (Leeds, 1977), pp. 50–71 at pp. 56–8.

15 *Lex Salica*, 100-Titel Text, ed. K. A. Eckhardt, MGH Leges nat. germ. IV.ii (Hanover, 1969), pp. 6–8.

16 *Annales regni francorum* s.a. 773, 776, 783.

17 *Ibid.*, s.a. 777.

18 E. H. Kantorowicz, *Laudes Regiae. A Study in Liturgical Acclamations and Medieval Ruler Worship*, University of California Publications in History 33, 2nd edn (Berkeley, 1958) pp. 15, 43.

region of the Franks', Pope Zacharias acknowledged that in Francia, as in contemporary Rome, a warrior aristocracy held the key to the Church's well-being.[19] The form of Zacharias' response in 751 may have been influenced by Augustinian notions of cosmic order,[20] but its substance was a shrewd assessment of the realities of power in Francia and their relevance to papal interests. Zacharias' successor Stephen II invoked 'the utility of your patron St Peter' when he appealed to all the chiefs (*duces*) of the Frankish *gens* to help King Pippin.[21] This papal utilitarianism meant the mobilising not only of Frankish kingship but also of Frankish consent. When the needs of St Peter – that is, the need to defend claims to territory in central Italy – drove Stephen II to cross the Alps in winter to seek Frankish aid, he forged links not only (through a new consecration) between himself and Pippin and his sons, but between St Peter and the Frankish aristocracy. To them as well as to the royal family, 'St Peter' appealed as his 'adoptive sons'. Just as God called the Israelites 'his peculiar people', so Stephen's successor Paul I (757–67) enrolled the Franks as 'St Peter's peculiar people', calling them, in words St Peter himself was believed to have used for the Christian community, 'a holy tribe, a royal priesthood'.[22]

Less dominant in papal appeals, but no less resonant in Frankish ears, were the notes of lordship and patronage. Paul I reminded Pippin of 'the faithful kings [of Israel] who in days of old pleased God'.[23] Pippin too was cast as a faithful king who would please his patron St Peter. Faithfulness for the Franks immediately evoked the service of youth (*puer*, *vassus*) to the old man (*senior*), a service first and foremost military. Physical power was the prime qualification for those who served. Again, Frankish and papal views coincided. Annals written *ca* 805 to glorify the Carolingians castigated the fecklessness (*desidia*) of the Merovingians and praised the toughness and stamina (*strenuitas*) of the new leaders under whom the Franks had re-established their power over other peoples.[24] In the 830s Einhard, Charlemagne's biographer, drew a dramatic (and perhaps ironic) contrast between the symbolic senescence of the last Merovingian and the youthful vitality of Charles Martel and Pippin.[25] Also *ca* 830 a historian of the Franks imagined a conversation at the Frankish court between the last

19 *Codex Carolinus*, ed. W. Gundlach, MGH Epp. III (Hanover, 1892) no. 3, p. 480.

20 H. Büttner, 'An den Anfangen des abendländischen Staatsgedankens: die Königserhebung Pippins' in: *Das Königtum*, Vorträge und Forschungen 3 (Sigmaringen, 1956), pp. 155–67 at pp. 160–1.

21 *Codex Carolinus*, ed. W. Gundlach, MGH Epp. III (Hanover, 1892), no. 5, p. 488: 'utilitas fautoris vestri, beati apostolorum principis Petri'.

22 *Ibid.*, nos. 10, p. 501 and 39, p. 552. See A. Angenendt, 'Das geistliche Bundnis der Päpste mit den Karolingern', *Historisches Jahrbuch* 100 (1980) pp. 40–63, idem, '*Rex et sacerdos*. Zur Genese der Königssalbung', in *Tradition als historische Kraft*, ed. N. Kamp and J. Wollasch (Berlin, 1982), pp. 109–10. Historical context: T. F. X. Noble, *The Republic of St Peter. The Birth of the Papal State, 680–825* (Philadelphia, 1984) chapters 2 and 3.

23 *Codex Carolinus*, ed. W. Gundlach, MGH Epp. III (Hanover, 1892), no. 42, p. 555.

24 The so-called *Annales Mettenses*: I. Haselbach, *Aufstieg und Herrschaft der Karlinger in der Darstellung der sogenannten Annales Mettenses Priores*, Historische Studien 412 (Hamburg, 1970), pp. 171–2, 178–9.

25 Einhard, *Vita Karoli Magni*, ed. O. Holder-Egger, MGH SS rer. Germ. i.u.s. 25 (Hanover, 1911), trans. L. Thorpe (Harmondsworth, 1969) p. 3: the Merovingian had only the *inane regis vocabulum*, Charles Martel and Pippin had *et opes et potentia regni*.

Merovingian and Pope Stephen II (sic!) in which the king explained his inability to give military help: '"Don't you see, Father, that I lack both the power and the dignity of a king?" The pope agreed ... and turning to Prince Pippin said: "On St Peter's authority I order you to tonsure this man and send him into a monastery. How can he hold a land? He is useful neither to himself nor to others!"' In context, this is clearly a usefulness gauged in terms of benefits to king, Franks and St Peter alike.[26]

Though they were aware that past societies, including ancient Israel and until recently the Saxons, had managed with the rule of judges or nobles,[27] Carolingian writers of contemporary history saw kingship as the basic political form in their own world. Christianity was no necessary qualification. The emir of Cordoba was a king, so were the Muslim ruler of Barcelona and the Bulgar khan.[28] Archbishop Hincmar of Rheims in a learned treatise distinguished between kings and tyrants, between legitimate and illegitimate ways of assuming power, between rulers directly instituted by God to promote justice and 'usurpers' permitted by God to punish sin – while insisting, with St Paul, that all power was divinely authorised and hence to be obeyed.[29] Wearing another hat, as annalist, Hincmar recognised that the sustained support of a sizeable faction of the aristocracy in a particular region was what in fact made a king, both in the sense of installing him and of supplying him with the means to rule.[30] Other annalists reflect a similar contemporary pragmatism. When two rivals for the kingship of the Wilzi brought their case before a Frankish assembly, Louis the Pious had no difficulty in recognising as king the man favoured by the 'will of the people' (*voluntas gentis*), that is, with greater support among the leading men of the Wilzi.[31] Horic 'king of the Danes' was the man to whom Carolingian kings could appeal to make a wayward Danish warlord (*dux*) disgorge what he had plundered from the Franks.[32] When the *Colodici* were beaten by the Franks and their king killed, another king had to be 'hurriedly made' so that the Franks could take from him 'oaths, hostages and much of their land'.[33]

A royal blessing-prayer, *Prospice* ('Look down'), provides an epitome of Frankish expectations of their king in the time of Charlemagne when the prayer was used, and probably composed.[34] It also sets out ideas of kingship which

[26] 'Reversusque ad principem Pipinum aiebat: "Ex auctoritate Sancti Petri tibi praecipio: tonde hunc et destina in monasterium; ut quid terram occupat? nec sibi nec aliis utilis est".' See E. Peters, *The Shadow King. Rex Inutilis in Medieval Law and Literature, 751–1327* (New Haven, 1970) pp. 53–4.

[27] *Vita Lebuini antiqua*, ed. A. Hofmeister, MGH SS XXX. ii (Hanover, 1934), cc. 4–6, pp. 793–4.

[28] *Annales Bertiniani* ed. G. Waitz, MGH SRG (Hanover, 1964) and F. Grat, J. Vielliard and S. Clémencet, (Paris, 1964)' Eng. trans. J. L. Nelson, *The Annals of St Bertin* (Manchester 1991) s.a. 847, p. 53; Ermold, *In honorem Hludowici*, line 638, p. 50; *Annales Bertiniani* trans. Nelson *Annals* s.a. 866, p. 133.

[29] Hincmar of Rheims, *De divortio Lotharii regis et Tetbergae reginae*, PL 125: 619–772, col. 758, and *De regis persona* cols. 834–6. See Anton, *Fürstenspiegel*, pp. 295–7.

[30] *Annales Bertiniani*, trans. Nelson, *Annals*, s.a. 873, pp. 189–90.

[31] *Annales regni francorum*, Eng. trans. B. Scholz, *Carolingian Chronicles* (Ann Arbor, 1970), s.a. 823, p. 160.

[32] *Annales Bertiniani*, trans. Nelson, *Annals*, s.a. 847, pp. 54–5. Compare *MGH Cap.* II, no. 204, p. 70.

[33] *Annales Bertiniani*, trans. Nelson *Annals*, s.a. 839, p. 35.

[34] C. A. Bouman, *Sacring and Crowning. The Development of the Latin Ritual for the Anointing of Kings and the Coronation of an Emperor before the Eleventh Century* (Djakarta and Groningen, 1957), pp. 7, 40, 90–4; E. Ewig, 'Zum christlichen Königsgedanken, p. 45.

were to remain standard throughout the Middle Ages and beyond, for the prayer was incorporated into the rite of royal consecration early in the Carolingian period and thence passed into general use in the kingdoms of the Latin west.[35]

> Look down, Omnipotent God, with serene eyes on this most glorious king. As Thou didst bless Abraham, Isaac and Jacob, so deign to irrigate and bathe him by Thy potency with abundant blessings of spiritual grace with all its fullness. Grant him from the dew of heaven and the fatness of earth abundance of corn, wine and oil and a wealth of all fruits from the generous store of divine gifts, through long years; so that, while he is reigning, there may be healthiness of bodies in the fatherland, and peace may be unbroken in the realm, and the glorious dignity of the royal palace may shine before the eyes of all with the greatest splendour of royal power and be seen to be glittering and bright as if filled with the utmost splendour by the greatest light.
>
> Grant him Omnipotent God, to be a most mighty protector of the fatherland, and a comforter of churches and holy monasteries with the greatest piety of royal munificence, and to be the mightiest of kings, triumphing over his enemies so as to crush rebels and heathen nations; and may he be very terrible to his enemies with the utmost strength of royal potency.
>
> Also may he be generous and loveable and pious to the magnates and the outstanding leaders and the faithful men of his realm, that he may be feared and loved by all.
>
> Also may kings come forth from his loins through successions of future times to rule this whole realm. And after glorious and happy times in this present life, may he be worthy to have eternal joys in perpetual blessedness.[36]

The repeated use of the terms *potentia* and *potestas* here shows that the invocation of divine omnipotence to sustain royal potency is no mere liturgical cliché but conveys the central political idea of the Carolingian period: power came from God. The king acted as his deputy in securing justice and peace for the Christian people. Authors of 'Mirrors of princes', treatises of royal instruc-

35 E. S. Dewick, ed., *The Coronation Book of Charles V of France*, Henry Bradshaw Society 16 (London, 1899), cols. 23–4; Bouman, *Sacring and Crowning*, pp. 90, 107–8. *Prospice* was also included in imperial consecration-rites from the middle of the tenth century: below p. 79.

36 'Prospice omnipotens deus hunc gloriosissimum regem serenis obtutibus, sicut benedixisti Abraham, Isaac et Iacob, sic illum largis benedictionibus spiritalis gratiae cum omni plenitudine potentia irrigare atque perfundere dignare. Tribue ei de rore caeli et de pinguedine terrae abundantiam frumenti, vini et olei et omnium frugum opulentia ex largitate muneris divini longa per tempora, ut illo regnante sit sanitas corporum in patria et pax inviolata sit in regno, et dignitas gloriosa regalis palatii maximae splendore regiae potestatis oculis omnium fulgeat luce clarissima coruscare atque splendere quasi splendissima fulgora maximo perfusa lumine videantur. Tribue ei, omnipotens deus, ut sit fortissimus protector patriae et consolator ecclesiarum atque coenobiorum sanctorum maxima cum pietate regalis munificentiae, atque et sit fortissimus regum, triumphator hostium ad opprimendum rebelles et paganas nationes, sitque inimicis suis satis terribilis proxima fortitudine regalis potentiae. Optimatibus quoque atque praecelsis proceribusque ac fidelibus sui regni sit munificus et amabilis et pius, et ab omnibus timeatur atque diligatur. Reges quoque de lumbis eius per successiones temporum futurorum egrediantur hoc regnum regere totum. Et post gloriosa tempora atque felicia praesentis vitae, gaudia sempiterna in perpetua beatitudine habere mereatur.' Compare Bouman, *Sacring and Crowning*, p. 91. The Old Testament references are to Gen. 27:28 and Ps. 4:8.

tion, concentrated not on the gap between incumbent and office, between merely human ruler and God, but on the bridging of that gap through divine grace. Few scriptural tags were oftener quoted than Proverbs 21:1 – 'The heart of the king is in the hand of the Lord.'[37] *Prospice* stressed the effects of divine action confidently asserted to ensue – the outpouring of blessings – rather than priestly mediation. Just as God had acted through the patriarchs to give Israel food, health and peace, so he would act through the consecrated king of the Franks. Other regal benedictions invoke a series of Old Testament judges and kings renowned for their success in war and wisdom in judgement. David and Solomon were favourite models in 'Mirrors of princes'.[38]

The Frankish realm can be classed in Weber's sense as a patrimonial regime in which power legitimised as divinely ordained was exercised as the ruler's personal authority like a father's over his household.[39] The Frankish kingdom was a family concern, in which royal kin had a special stake.[40] They resided with the king, his wife and children in a palace that was also home and school for young aristocrats, a great household which regularly expanded when assemblies gathered there, to embrace the political realm as it were in a single huge family. Frankish writers, all too aware of the tensions in close kinship, were especially attracted by the image of the court as a place of peace where 'all dissensions and discords were to be suppressed'.[41] *Prospice* highlights the splendour of the palace – a sacred space likened by poets to Solomon's Temple and seen as prefiguring the heavenly Jerusalem.[42] One Carolingian court poet, Ermold, described an Easter Day procession at the palace:

> Each in his rank hastens to obey the royal commands.
> One man runs, another stays: one goes this way, another that . . .
> Preceded by the elders, followed by the younger men,
> With magnates surrounding you, you come, revered king.
> . . . As the sun illuminates the earth with his rays . . .

37 Anton, *Fürstenspiegel*, pp. 357–62. Compare Pippin's diploma of 762, MGH, Dip. Kar. I, no. 16, p. 22: 'divina nobis providentia in solium regni unxisse manifestum est . . . et . . . reges ex Deo regnant nobisque gentes et regna pro sua misericordia ad gubernandum commisit'. See H. Fichtenau, *Arenga*, Mitteilungen des Instituts für Österreichische Geschichtsforschung, Erganzungsband 18 (Cologne and Vienna, 1957) p. 143.

38 J. M. Wallace-Hadrill, 'The *Via Regia* of the Carolingian age', in: *Trends in Medieval Political Thought*, ed. B. Smalley (Oxford, 1965); Anton, *Fürstenspiegel*, pp. 419–36; Regal benedictions: Bouman, *Sacring and Crowning*, pp. 191–2.

39 M. Weber, *Economy and Society. An Outline of Interpretative Sociology*, ed. G. Roth, and C. Wittich, 2 vols. (Berkeley, 1978) vol. I, pp. 231–41, vol. II, pp. 1006–110. See also J. Fried, 'Der karolingische Herrschaftsverband im 9. Jh. zwischen "Kirche" und "Königshaus"', *Historische Zeitschrift* 2345 (1982) pp. 18–27.

40 See J. L. Nelson 'Public "Histories" and private history in the work of Nithard', *Speculum* 60 (1985), pp. 251–93 at pp. 269–71.

41 Council of Paris (829), c. 91, MGH Conc. II, p. 678: 'Ubi igitur omnes dissensiones et discordiae dirimendae et omnis malitia imperiali auctoritate est comprimenda, necesse est ut quod in aliis corrigere decernit, in ea [i.e. sacra domu] minime reperitur.' Peace as cosmic order: R. Bonnaud-Delamare, *L'Idée de paix à l'époque carolingienne* (Paris, 1939). *Familiaritas* at assemblies: J. L. Nelson, 'Legislation and consensus in the reign of Charles the Bald', in: *Ideal and Reality in Frankish and Anglo-Saxon Society. Studies Presented to J. M. Wallace-Hadrill*, ed. P. Wormald (Oxford, 1983) pp. 202–28 at p. 220.

42 P. Riché, 'Les Représentations du palais dans les textes littéraires du haut moyen âge', *Francia* 4 (1976) pp. 161–71 at pp. 167–9.

Signalling joy to trees, crops, sailors,
So the king in his coming brings joy to his people.[43]

Royal biographers chose to locate their heroes in the setting of the household, where arrangements for the hunt or the dining-table symbolised their authority.[44] It was thought essential that the ruler maintain right relations within the royal family itself. The divine injunction in Deuteronomy 14:17, 'Let [the king] not have more than one wife', quoted by learned churchmen to Charlemagne and Louis the Pious,[45] had special relevance when all politics were 'palace, even family politics',[46] and the ambitions of successive royal wives and their offspring could throw kingdoms into confusion. Archbishop Agobard of Lyons justified the rebellion of his patron Lothar against his father the emperor by invoking his duty to restore and purify the palace that evildoers had made a brothel.[47] The programme of rectification (*correctio*) proposed by ecclesiastical reformers and eagerly taken up by Charlemagne and his successors was in effect a transposition to the realm as a whole of the ruler's personal and domestic good order. It was the more necessary for Lothar II, whose domestic affairs were notoriously *dis*ordered, to be advised that a good king did the job of ruling (*regendi ministerium*) in three ways: 'by ruling first himself, second his own wife and children and the members of his household, third the people committed to him'.[48]

Carolingian clerical theorists used the Church as a model of an ordered society: in this sense the realm, and the king's job, were contained within the Church.[49] But in terms of practical politics, the Church was part of the realm, and the king's obligation to safeguard it an essential part of his patrimonial role. The clergy and monks, unarmed, were like widows and orphans in need of protection.[50] The Carolingians involved the resources and personnel of the Church much more closely in their regime than any previous medieval rulers had done.[51] The author of *Prospice* observed the rewards of 'royal munificence'.

43 Ermold, *Carmen in honorem Pippini regis*, in E. Faral (ed.), *Poème sur Louis le Pieux et épîtres au roi Pépin* (Paris, 1932), I, lines 18–32, p. 204.

44 Ermold, *In honorem Hludowici*, in E. Faral (ed.), *Poème sur Louis le Pieux et épîtres au roi Pépin* (Paris, 1932), lines 2338–503, pp. 178–90; Notker the Stammerer, *Gesta Karoli*, ed. H. F. Haefele, MGH SS rer. germ. n.s. 13, trans. L. Thorpe (Harmondsworth, 1959), I, c. II, p. 16, c. 30, p. 41, II, c. 6, pp. 54–7, c. 8, pp. 59–61.

45 Cathwulf, MGH Epp. IV, p. 503; Council of Paris (829), c. 55, MGH Conc. II, p. 649.

46 P. Stafford, *Queens, Concubines, and Dowagers. The King's Wife in the Early Middle Ages* (London, 1983), chapter 4.

47 Agobard, of Lyons, *Opera*, PL 104: 29–251. *Libri duo pro filiis et contra Iudith uxorem Ludovici Pii*, ed. G. Waitz, MGH SS XV, pp. 274–9 at p. 275.

48 Sedulius Scottus, *Liber de rectoribus christianis*, ed. S. Hellmann, Quellen und Untersuchungen zur lateinischen Philologie des Mittelalters I, 1 (Munich, 1906), c. 5, p. 34: 'primo se ipsum ... secundo uxorem propriam et liberos suosque domesticos, tertio populum sibi commissum'.

49 Fried, 'Karolingische Herrschaftsverband', and compare pp. 66–7 below.

50 See J. Devisse, *Hincmar, Archévêque de Reims 845–882*, 3 vols. (Geneva, 1975–6) I, pp. 500–2; G. Duby, *Les Trois Ordres ou l'imaginaire du féodalisme* (Paris, 1978) p. 224.

51 F. L. Ganshof, 'L'Église et le pouvoir royal dans la monarchie franque sous Pépin III et Charlemagne', *Settimane* 7 (Spoleto, 1960); Eng. trans. F. L. Ganshof, *The Carolingians and the Frankish Monarchy* (London, 1971) chapter 11; F. Prinz, *Klerus und Krieg im früheren Mittelalter*, Monographien zur Geschichte des Mittelalters 2 (Stuttgart, 1971).

But the king believed his power to depend on the Church's preservation of the Faith.[52] When the papacy itself seemed to waver in its response to the Byzantine court's excessive veneration of icons, Charlemagne had his leading theologian Theodulf in the *Libri Carolini* remind the pope of the orthodoxy for which Rome stood. Justifying his implied rebuke, Charlemagne told the pope that the Church had been 'committed for us for ruling'.[53] In 747 Pope Zacharias had set out in a letter to the Franks and their leader a division of labour between those who fought and the clergy who prayed for their victory.[54] In 796, Alcuin on Charlemagne's behalf quoted this back at Pope Leo III: 'Our job is the defence of the Church and the fortification of the Faith; yours to aid our warfare by prayer.'[55] But the Church owed more than prayer alone. In bracketing royal 'comfort of churches and monasteries' with royal triumph over rebels and heathens, *Prospice* hinted at the military service owed, and faithfully performed by the Church to the Carolingians.[56]

The model of Christian rulership elaborated in 'Mirrors of princes' was projected mainly for kings themselves. But the evangelising Carolingian Church aimed at the minds (as well as the souls) of the laity at large. It preached lordship, using the same language for political and religious obligation. 'Faith' (*fides*) meant both Christian belief and the bond between lord and man.[57] The Book of Psalms, the textbook of Carolingian spirituality, could be read as a manifesto of divine Lordship. Christ was presented as lord of a warrior-retinue.[58] Fidelity in political contexts acquired strong Christian overtones. In addressing his documents, Pippin identified his own faithful men with God's: *fideles dei et regis*.[59] Charlemagne hammered the point home when he imposed faithfulness in both kinds on the conquered Saxons.[60] In the middle of the ninth century the Frankish noblewoman Dhuoda urged both on her son as he joined the king's military retinue.[61]

The great household as an image of order and purity, and the ordered hierarchy of personal service within it, were political ideas that corresponded to

52 A. Waas, 'Karls des Grossen Frommigkeit', *Historische Zeitschrift* 203 (1966) pp. 265–79.

53 MGH Conc. II, Supplement, p. 2: 'nobis [i.e. Charlemagne, using the royal 'we'] quibus in huius saeculi procellosis fluctibus [ecclesia] ad regendum commissa est'. See J. M. Wallace-Hadrill, *The Frankish Church* (Oxford, 1983) pp. 219–22.

54 See n. 19 above.

55 *Codex Carolinus*. Ed. W. Gundlach, MGH Epp. III (Hanover, 1892), no. 93, pp. 137–8: 'Nostrum est secundum auxilium divinae pietatis sanctam undique Christi ecclesiam ab incursu paganorum et ab infidelium devastatione armis defendere foris, et intus catholicae fidei agnitione munire. Vestrum est, sanctissime pater, elevatis ad Deum cum Moyse manibus nostram adiuvare militiam, quatenus vobis intercedentibus . . . populus christianus super inimicos . . . semper habeat victoriam.'

56 J. L. Nelson, 'The Church's military service in the ninth century: a contemporary comparative view?', in: *The Church and War*, ed. W. J. Sheils, Studies in Church History 20 (1983) pp. 15–30.

57 F. Graus, The stress of W. Schlesinger, *Beiträge zur deutschen Verfassungsgeschichte des Mittelalters*, 2 vols. (Berlin, 1963) pp. 296–334, on the Germanic background is compatible with Graus' insistence on the ideological role of the Carolingian Church. Compare D. Green, *The Carolingian Lord* (Cambridge, 1965) pp. 216–32.

58 See below pp. 74–5 and n.131.

59 H. Helbig, 'Fideles Dei et regis', *Archiv für Kirchengeschichte* 33 (1951) pp. 275–306.

60 MGH Cap. I, no. 26, pp. 68–70.

61 Dhuoda, ed. P. Riché, *Le Manuel de Dhuoda* (Paris, 1975) III, cc. 4, 5, pp. 148–59.

social realities and were constantly reinforced by experience. Peasants who journeyed to palaces to seek royal protection against lordly violence[62] perceived the king as a mighty overlord who could uphold the free status of the humble. Enthroned, flanked by his counsellors and warrior-retinue, in a hall adorned with depictions of his ancestors' achievements, the Carolingian ruler was a commanding yet approachable figure.[63] The members of the aristocracy who sustained his regime were in regular contact with the court. Dhuoda, familiar with both palace and noble household, saw parallels between them. Much could be learned, she told her son as he went off to the palace, from the discussions that go on 'in a big house such as that one'. 'When you are grown up, organise your own household in lawful ranks and effectively. And [meanwhile] ... carry out all your tasks in public affairs in due order, and faithfully.'[64] Faithfulness, which bound the faithful man to his lord, provided Dhuoda with a model for the relationship of wife to husband, of child to father – and of those who served to the king.[65]

When the author of *Prospice* mentioned royal 'piety', in precisely this context, he had in mind a political as well as a moral virtue, manifested, with 'generosity' and 'lovableness', in the distribution of wealth and the delegation of power over men. This piety was the return for faithful service.[66] Charlemagne, like his Merovingian predecessors, wanted all the men in his realm to swear fidelity to him. In 802 he added to the oath the phrase: '[faithful] as a man ought in right (*per drictum*) to be faithful to his lord'.[67] This heralded no constitutional change, no shift (as sometimes alleged) from 'sovereignty' to 'contractual' authority, no watering-down of 'subjects' obligations'.[68] Classical, or modern, legal categories imposed on the early Middle Ages can mislead. The relationship between Frankish king and aristocracy had been based all along on mutual, personal, service and mutual advantage: there was no break here with Merovingian tradition. With the words 'in right', Charlemagne signalled faithfulness as deep-rooted in contemporaries' values.[69] He invoked it, not through conceptual

62 G. Tessier, *Recueil des actes de Charles II le Chauve, 3 vols.* (Paris, 1943–55), ii, no. 228, pp. 7–9. Compare C. Wickham, *Early Medieval Italy. Central Power and Local Society 400–1000* (London, 1982) pp. 109–12.

63 Ermold, *In honorem Hludowici*, in E. Faral (ed.) *Poème sur Louis le Pieux et épîtres au roi Pépin* (Paris, 1932), lines 2148–63, p. 164, describes the *gesta paterna* depicted at Ingelheim. It is uncertain how far reality was designed to correspond to manuscript-image, and how far genre-bound image reflected contemporary (as distinct from late-antique) ideology: D. Bullough, '*Imagines Regum* and their significance in the early medieval west', in: *Studies in Memory of David Talbot Rice*, ed. Giles Robertson and George Henderson (Edinburgh, 1975) pp. 252–3.

64 Dhuoda, ed. Riché, III, c. 9, p. 170; x, c. 3, pp. 346–8.

65 J. Wollasch, 'Eine adlige Familie des frühen Mittelalters', *Archiv für Kulturgeschichte* 39 (1959) pp. 150–88.

66 R. Schieffer, 'Ludwig "der Fromme". Zur Entstehung eines Karlingischen Herrscherbeinamens', *Frühmittelalterliche Studien* 16 (1982) pp. 58–73. See also I. Haselbach, *Aufstieg und Herrschaft der Karlinger in der Darstellung der sogenannten Annales Mettenses Priores*, Historische Studien 412 (Hamburg, 1970) pp. 153–8.

67 MGH Cap. I, no. 34, p. 101: 'sicut per drictum debet esse homo domino suo'.

68 H. Brunner, *Deutsche Rechtsgeschichte*, 2 vols., 2nd edn (Leipzig, 1928), vol. II, p. 82; F. L. Ganshof, *The Carolingians and the Frankish Monarchy* (London, 1971) pp. 117–18. Useful on historiography but over-legalistic on oath-formulae: C. E. Odegaard, 'Carolingian oaths of fidelity', *Speculum* 16 (1941) pp. 284–96.

69 J. Niermeyer, *Mediae latinitatis lexicon minus* (London, 1976), s.v. *directum*. Merovingian background to *fidelitas*: M. Lemosse, 'La Lèse-Majesté dans la monarchie franque', *Revue de moyen âge latin* 2 (1946) pp. 13–16.

muddle – the king was a lord like no other – but to clarify and intensify for each of his people a sense of what was owed to the king. Entirely apt therefore was the usual collective designation of the Carolingian aristocracy: the *fideles*, the faithful men. By contrast, the notion of the subject was never really at home in Carolingian political thought.[70] It practically never occurs in the capitularies that record the deliberations of king and aristocracy in assemblies. Similarly the Roman law concept of treason (*laesa majestas, lèse majesté*) was a learned gloss sometimes imposed on individual acts of faithlessness.[71] The near-contemporary account of the Royal Frankish Annals has Tassilo duke of the Bavarians condemned in 788 as 'not having kept his faith', but the revised text of the Annals presents this, a generation later, as treason. Tassilo's faithlessness had taken two forms: he had seduced away the loyalty of others among the king's vassals, and he had instructed his own men to swear Charlemagne false oaths.[72] The king's piety towards the faithful required the turning of wrath on Tassilo. The face of the king, now familiar now terrible, resembled the face of the Lord.

Few medieval writers cared to recall that the Lord had not originally planned for Israel to be ruled by kings. Many noted the Lord's preference, once Israel's kingship had been set up, for hereditary succession. Only such wicked kings as Jeroboam and Ahab had been divinely punished by the extinction of their lines. Pippin clearly intended to found a dynasty, for his wife, apparently unlike Merovingian queens, received some form of consecration alongside her husband.[73] This ritual practice, later adopted elsewhere in Latin Christendom, can probably be linked with a preference for filial, rather than fraternal, succession.[74] But though eldest sons often received a preferential share, the Carolingian king, like his Merovingian predecessors, partitioned his realm between the queen's sons. In the eighth century, as already in the seventh, such divisions were far from arbitrary, however, for the building-blocks, the *regna*, from which composite 'imperial realms' were constructed, were not themselves divisible. Paternal acquisitions meant shares for more sons: Charlemagne provided for two sons in this way. But his eldest son by Queen Hildigard was designated to inherit the whole patrimony of Francia[75] – a plan that probably resulted from a combin-

[70] Verbs denoting 'being subject' (less often the noun) appear as borrowings from scriptural or patristic texts: e.g. Rom. 13; Gregory the Great, *Moralia* xxi, 23, PL 76, col. 203, or as echoes of Roman law, canon law or liturgy. Isidore's notion of *subjectis prodesse*: Anton, *Fürstenspiegel*, p. 365 n.40.

[71] Lemosse, 'La Lèse-Majesté', pp. 16–18.

[72] *Annales regni francorum* ed. Kurze, MGH SRG 6; Eng. trans. B. Scholz, *Carolingian Chronicles* (Ann Arbor, 197), s.a. 788, p. 80.

[73] See n. 7 above, where 'ancient tradition' refers to 'elevation' (enthronement), not to the queen's participation in it: J. L. Nelson 'Inauguration rituals', in *Early Medieval Kingship*, ed. I. Sawyer and I. N. Wood (Leeds, 1977) pp. 53, 57–8. But *Codex Carolinus*, ed. W. Gundlach, MGH Epp. III (Hanover, 1892), no. 11, p. 505, implies a consecration of Bertrada in 754, even if the so-called *Clausula de unctione Pippini* cannot be accepted as near-contemporary evidence for either 754 or 751. The final section of *Prospice*, above, p. 58, stresses hereditary succession.

[74] P. Stafford, 'The King's wife in Wessex 800–1066', *Past and Present* 91 (1981) pp. 3–27 at pp. 10–12, 16–18.

[75] P. Classen, 'Karl der Grosse und die Thronfolge im Frankenreich', in: *Festschrift für H. Heimpel*, II (Berlin, 1972); E. Ewig, 'Überlegungen zu den Merowingischen und Karolingischen Teilungen', *Settimane* 27 (Spoleto, 1981) pp. 225–53.

ation of the eldest son's ambitions with the interest of some Frankish magnates in keeping their patrimonies as far as possible under a single royal lord. In the next generation, rival fraternal ambitions were supported by nobles who gave priority to their interests in particular regions: in 843 a three-way division of Francia created the cores of three kingdoms at the Treaty of Verdun.[76]

These partitions, treating the realm as the personal property of the ruler and his heirs, have been seen as characteristic of patrimonial authority. Though Hincmar of Rheims was familiar with seventh-century Spanish legislation in which the resources of the Crown had been clearly distinguished from the ruler's private holdings,[77] he never made any such distinction in the Carolingians' case. If the term *res publica* could be used by ninth-century writers to denote simply the fisc,[78] then arguably it lacked its classical meaning of the state. It has been argued, further, that a 'true' concept of office is equally elusive in the Carolingian period.[79] Where the Visigoths had defined monarchy as an institution in terms borrowed from late Roman law, a whiff of the household clung to the Carolingian notion of 'ministry' (*ministerium*), royal or otherwise, as personal service. In the absence of a clear distinction between office and incumbent, a king could be judged only as an individual, as father or lord. This was what happened to Louis the Pious, deprived of power by rebellious sons and their supporters in 833. The rebels' propagandist, Agobard, could only pronounce this a divine judgement and Louis a confessed sinner on whom public penance could be imposed.[80] Conversely Hraban Maur, who remained loyal to Louis, countered with appeals to filial duty and scriptural precept: 'The powers that be are ordained of God' (Romans 13:1).[81] Subsequent Carolingian conflicts evoked similar appeals, as when Hincmar reminded Louis the German, invading his brother's kingdom in 858: 'Thou shalt not touch the Lord's anointed' (Psalms 104:15).[82]

Another major limitation of Carolingian political thought has been identified in the concept of law as an individual 'subjective' possession, for this too allegedly forestalled any awareness of the *res publica*, the state, transcending private interests. When Charles the Bald in 843 stated his willingness 'to keep for each his due law', he abdicated, on this view, the prime function of the state in defining the law. Kern, for instance, posed stark alternatives: on the one hand, strong central government making and enforcing unified 'objective' statute law, on the other, a multiplicity of 'subjective' rights tending towards anarchy.[83]

76 P. Classen, 'Die Verträge von Verdun und Coulaines 843 als politischen Grundlagen des Westfränkischen Reiches', *Historische Zeitschrift* 196 (1963) pp. 1–35; Nelson, 'Public *Histories* and private history'.

77 Compare J. L. Nelson 'Kingship, law and liturgy in the political thought of Hincmar of Rheims', *English Historical Review* 92 (1977), pp. 241–79 at p. 254 n.1.

78 Fried, 'Karolingische Herrschaftsverband', pp. 11–16.

79 *Ibid.*, pp. 29–33.

80 Nelson, 'Kingship, law and liturgy', pp. 243–4.

81 MGH Epp. V pp. 406–7.

82 MGH Cap. II, no. 297, p. 440.

83 F. Kern, 'Recht und Verfassung im Mittelalter', *Historische Zeitschrift* 24 (1919) pp. 58–60 (F. Kern, *Kingship and Law in the Middle Ages* (Oxford, 1954) pp. 192–4); Fried, 'Karolingische Herrschaftsverband'

Since Charles the Bald has often been blamed for the Carolingian Empire's lurch to the bad, it is worth noting that Charlemagne too had wished to keep for each his law, and promised to 'make amends' to anyone against whose law royal agents had taken action.[84] But this only underlines the point that the notion of law as right was important throughout the Carolingian period. A man was entitled to judgement according to customary procedures with due account taken of individual rank and status.

The limitations of Carolingian political thought, its hesitations, inconsistencies and shortcomings of expression, are very obvious. Yet to deny the ninth century any idea of the state or of public office is to throw out the baby with the bathwater. Political thought is embodied not only in theories but in contemporaries' *ad hoc* responses to political problems and to perceived discrepancies between ideals and realities. From the ninth century, such responses are preserved in the capitularies produced by Carolingian rulers and those who gave them counsel. So, for instance, the careful delineation of frontiers in ninth-century partitions shows that kingdoms were thought of as possessing territorial definitions and integrity. Royal control over the coinage and over fortifications was asserted throughout the whole territory. Rulers threatened, and sometimes imposed, sanctions on recalcitrant or rebellious nobles: public humiliation, withdrawal of high office, confiscation not only of benefices but of patrimonies or allods. In the exercise of criminal justice, the king claimed the right to send agents into areas under landlords' jurisdiction (immunities) to apprehend malefactors, and all faithful men had to swear to aid in such action. This oath signalled and reinforced the free man's obligations but did not create them. 'All, without any excuse, must come to the defence of the fatherland.'[85] That liability arose, not from the holding of a benefice, or from personal commitment to the royal lord, but from residence in the realm.[86] Even if central power was mediated in practice through the aristocracy, it was exercised through institutions – courts, musters of the host – vested with public authority. The Carolingian regime rested on regalian rights and its own capacity to maintain public

p. 17 with n.66. Charles the Bald's statement in 843: MGH Cap. II, no. 254, p. 255: 'Legem vero unicuique competentem ... in omni dignitate et ordine favente Deo me observaturum perdono.' See also Nelson, 'Kingship, law and liturgy', p. 255. E. Magnou-Nortier, *Foi et fidelité: recherches sur l'évolution des liens personnels chez les Francs du VIIe au IXe siècle* (Toulouse, 1976) pp. 103–8 is a valuable corrective.

[84] MGH Cap. I, no. 25, p. 67: 'Explicare debent ipsi missi qualiter domni regi dictum est, quod multi se conplangunt legem non habere conservatam, et quia omnino voluntas domni regis est ut unusquisque homo suam legem pleniter habeat conservata; et si alicui contra legem factum est, non est voluntas nec sua iussio.'

[85] Some examples from the capitularies of Charles the Bald: MGH Cap. II, no. 251, pp. 193–5 (division of 870); no. 273 (Pîtres 869), cc. 8–24, pp. 314–29 (coinage), section C, c. I, p. 328 (fortifications), c. 21, p. 319 (public humiliation), c. 18, p. 317 (royal agents empowered to enter immunities), c. 27, p. 322 (defence of fatherland); no. 260 (Servias 854), c. 13, p. 274 (oaths to denounce criminals); no. 242 (Coblenz 860), p. 158 (withdrawal of high office, confiscation of allods); no. 274 (Tusey 865), c. 13, p. 331 (summons to host). These capitularies draw on those of Charlemagne and especially of Louis the Pious, but also contain significant additions. General comments: J. L. Nelson, 'The rites of the conqueror', *Proceedings of the Battle Conference* 4 (1982) pp. 117–32, 210–21; eadem, 'Legislation and Consensus'.

[86] Compare T. N. Bisson, 'The problem of feudal monarchy: Aragon, Catalonia, and France', *Speculum* 53 (1978) pp. 464–5, 467–9, 477–8.

order. The Church's prayer that 'peace may be unbroken in the realm' was combined with a realistic perception that this outcome depended on royal 'abundance' and 'wealth'.

It is often claimed that royal authority failed in the ninth century because external attacks could only be met effectively by local resistance and this forced a devolution of power into the hands of the aristocracy.[87] Further, this political shift was allegedly reflected in ideas of consensus and of constraints on rulers, for instance through a new stress on the elective basis of kingship.[88] In such reconstructions, neither the history nor the history of thought is wholly convincing. External challenge evoked, on the whole, more vigorous exercise of central authority.[89] Ideas of consensus were not new but traditional, not anti-royal but linked to specific expectations of kingship. If these ideas and expectations were articulated more clearly in the ninth century, this was in part a response to a new, potentially oppressive, royal vigour.

Hincmar of Rheims, the leading elaborator and recorder of west Frankish royal consecration-rites in the ninth century, set down the functions of kingship in a promise required of the king before his consecration.[90] Given the clear parallel with episcopal ordination, and the availability of Pope Gelasius' statements on the divine dispensation of a 'two-fold ruling of the world', it became possible for Hincmar both to model an idea of kingly office on a pre-existent idea of episcopal office and to link the bishops' role as consecrators with their superior dignity in terms of Gelasius' distinction between royal power and priestly authority. Hence, just as the bishop undertook before his ordination to keep the canons of the Church, so the king before his inauguration had to promise 'to keep the laws and statutes for the people committed by God's mercy to me to rule'. The form and context of this royal promise implied that human agents would be able to guarantee the king's fulfilment of this commitment by checking on his conformity to law. Moreover, where previous clerical theorists had been unable to project the Church's authority beyond spiritual responsibility for the king as an individual Christian, Hincmar could assert the bishops' jurisdiction over the king's conduct of an office to which they had consecrated him. These ideas, infrequently and hesitantly as Hincmar expressed them – he never explicitly claimed the competence to depose a king – are nevertheless remarkable attempts at an effective critique of secular rulership. No less remark-

87 M. Bloch, *La Société féodale*, II (Paris, 1940) pp. 173–5; Eng. trans., *Feudal Society* (London 1961) pp. 395–6; J. Dhondt, *Etudes sur la naissance des principautés territoriales en France (IXe–XIe siècle)* (Ghent, 1948), pp. 38–9.

88 W. Schlesinger, 'Kaisertum und Reichsteiling. Zur *Divisio regnorum* von 806', in: *Festgabe für Hans Herzfeld*, repr. in W.Schlesinger, *Beiträge zur deutschen Verfassungsgeschichte des Mittelalters*, 2 vols. (Berlin, 1963) pp. 132–8.

89 K.-U. Jäschke, *Burgenbau und Landesverteidigung um 900* (Sigmaringen, 1975).

90 M. David, *La Souveraineté et les limites juridiques du pouvoir monarchique du IXe au XVe siècle* (Paris, 1954) pp. 120–30; K. F. Morrison, *The Two Kingdoms. Ecclesiology in Carolingian Political Thought* (Princeton, 1964) pp. 201–6; Nelson 'Kingship, law and liturgy'.

able is the insistence of the ageing Hincmar, dealing now with young and inexperienced kings, that the realm be ruled through counsel with the leading men, lay and clerical: only through consensus thus maintained could faction be avoided.[91]

The layman Nithard, writing his 'Histories' between 841 and 843, showed similar concerns though his emphasis was on the role of the lay aristocracy. The public good should take priority over private interests. Nithard denounced those who misused public resources for personal advantage; he also recorded with approval an episcopal denunciation of a ruler (Lothar) who lacked both 'knowledge of how to govern the commonwealth' (*scientia gubernandi rem publicam*) and 'good will in his government' (*bona voluntas in sua gubernatione*).[92] Through detailed description of contemporary politics, Nithard showed how the Franks could help their kings keep the 'royal road'. Shared counsels produced a collective judgement as to what was both fair and feasible. By following such counsels, a king could assure his faithful men's support. But they in turn had a sanction against a king who reneged on such an agreed course of action. At Strasbourg in 842 the two Carolingian kings Charles the Bald and Louis the German promised each other to maintain a common front against their brother Lothar until he should come to terms. Their oaths were sworn before their faithful men – 'in your sight'. Each king in pursuit 'of the common advantage' summoned his men to act as guarantors of the royal commitment: 'If I forswear this oath I swear to my brother, I release each and every one of you from the oath you have sworn to me.' Further to underscore this point, the faithful men themselves took an oath: 'If my lord breaks his oath, while his brother keeps his ... I shall give him no aid against his brother.'[93] Though the releasing from oath would be on an individual basis, the assumption clearly was that all the faithful men would coincide in their judgements on the king's conduct, hence would undertake concerted action to check the king. The significance of this was not that faithfulness was conditional – it had always been so – but that the faithful men of each kingdom were being treated as a collectivity and were committed to uphold a specific condition on which the common interest depended.

Other near-contemporary evidence from the west Frankish kingdom as it emerged from the Treaty of Verdun shows efforts being made to find appropriate terms to express the group-consciousness of the faithful men. The meeting at Coulaines in November 843 had west Frankish magnates, lay and

91 Nelson, 'The rites of the conqueror', pp. 117–32, 210–21; 'Legislation and consensus'.

92 Nithard, *Historiarum libri IV*, ed. with French trans. by P. Lauer, *Histoire des fils de Louis le Pieux* (Paris, 1926); Eng. trans. B. Scholz, *Carolingian Chronicles* (Ann Arbor, 1970), IV, I, p. 118. Compare ibid., I, 3, III, 2, IV, 6, pp. 10, 84, 142.

93 Nithard, *Historiarum libri IV*, III, 5, pp. 102–8. Nithard uses the classical terms *plebs* and *populus*. Compare *Annales Bertiniani*, trans. Nelson, *Annals* s.a. 842, p. 40: 'Fideles populi partis utriusque pari se iuramento constrinxerunt ut, uter eorundem fratrum adversus alterum sinistri quippiam moliretur, relicto prorsus auctore discidii, omnes sese ad servatorem fraternitatis amicitiaeque converterent.' On the oaths see Roger Wright, *Late Latin and Early Romance in Spain and Carolingian France* (Liverpool, 1982) pp. 122–6.

ecclesiastical, coming together 'into one thing' (*in unum*) and making an agreement (*convenientia*) to which the king then lent his backing. At Meersen in 851, the *convenientia* was said to be made by the three brother-kings and their faithful men; any individual of either category who breached the agreement was to be forced into conformity by all the rest, kings and faithful men alike. In 856 the word *pactum* was used of the similar understanding between Charles the Bald and his faithful men. If one of the latter violated the agreement, he was to be subject to a series of penalties culminating in exile from 'our collective association' (*a nostra omnium societate*). If the king breached the agreement in respect of any individual, he was to be brought back into accord with 'right reason' by the faithful men, lay and ecclesiastical together, 'none abandoning his peer'. What touched one by implication touched all the faithful men. In 857 the group was identified by a new collective noun: *bar(o)natus*.[94]

Almost exactly contemporary is the appeal of west Frankish rebels to the east Frankish King Louis to come and 'liberate them from the tyranny' of Charles. Louis, as a Carolingian and Charles' elder brother, was termed 'legitimate lord'. Charles was said to 'rage against his own people', his promises and oaths no longer to command any trust. The appeal was brought by envoys claiming to speak for the 'people'.[95] Faithful men might unite to reject their king on other grounds than tyranny: withdrawal of fidelity was justified if a king neglected the functions of his rank and title (*honor et nomen*). Military and political failure could cause a Carolingian to be abandoned as 'useless'.[96]

In all these cases from the middle of the ninth century, literate men seem to be striving to articulate the relationship between the king and his constituency. Classical terms jostle with the language of fidelity. The outcome is close to contract theory and a right of resistance. This burst of creativity arose from efforts to resolve an unusual prolonged period of tension in the west Frankish kingdom. It was possible only because political thought for laymen as well as clergy was on the agenda of Carolingian reformers. Thus contestation took place against a background of collaboration between king and aristocracy at an ideological as well as a practical level. In *The Government of the Palace*, Hincmar described the shaping of counsel at assemblies where the king met with 'the generality of the aristocracy as a whole' (*generalitas universorum maiorum*).[97] The

[94] MGH Cap. II, no. 254; no. 205, c. 8, pp. 73–4; no. 262, c. 10, p. 281; 'ut nullus suum parem dimittat ut contra suam legem et rectam rationem et iustum iudicium, etiamsi voluerit, quod absit, rex noster alicui facere non possit'; no. 268, p. 295 (*adnuntiatio Karoli*).

[95] *Annales Fuldenses*. Ed. F. Kurze, MGH SRG 7; Eng. trans T. Reuter, *The Annals of Fulda* (Manchester, 1992) s.a. 858, pp. 49–50.

[96] *Annales Bertiniani*, trans. Nelson, *Annals*, s.a. 848, p. 55: Pippin II of Aquitaine abandoned for *desidia* and *inertia*: s.a. 862, p. 87: Charles of Provence abandoned (but not definitively) as *inutilis* and *inconveniens regio honore et nomini*. See also Peters, *The Shadow King*, pp. 47–80.

[97] Hincmar of Rheims, *De regis persona et regio ministerio*, PL 125 cols. 833–56; *De divortio Lotharii regis et Tetbergae reginae*, PL 125, cols. 619–772; *De ordine palatii*, ed. T. Gross, and R. Schieffer, MGH Fontes III (Hanover, 1980). Eng. trans. D. Herlihy, *A History of Feudalism* (London, 1970), c. 29, pp. 84–5. J. Hannig, *Consensus Fidelium. Frühfeudale Interpretationen des Verhältnisses von Königtum und Adel am Beispiel des Frankenreiches*, Monographien zur Geschichte des Mittelalters 27 (Stuttgart, 1982) p. 199: '*Consensus*

reality of consensus politics was expressed in the capitularies' invocations of consent, consultation, counsel and aid, and in references to common welfare and public utility as the ends in view. The co-operation of king and faithful men in law-making and judgement-finding was grounded in shared convictions as to what constituted justice, reasonable treatment and fair dues, as well as in shared interest in social order. Participation in power at the centre, not just in the localities, made faithful men, laymen and higher clergy alike, more self-conscious political actors and keepers of the peace. Their *societias* foreshadowed the community of the realm.

The Roman Empire contained many dependent *regna*: this was enough of a commonplace to be included in Isidore's *Etymologies*.[98] At the beginning of the seventh century, the author of a little treatise on official posts excised Romanity from this hegemonial conception, defining an emperor as a ruler over kings. Carl Erdmann termed this a 'Rome-free' imperial idea.[99] For Alcuin the word *empire* (*imperium*) could mean overlordship of a number of different *gentes* 'divided by language and separated by race according to their ancestors' names'. Alcuin was impressed by the capacity to impose peace of hegemons (past and present) in Britain.[100] The Frankish author of the early ninth-century *Paderborn Epic* was just as impressed by Charlemagne: 'a king [who] excelled kings on the summit of empire'.[101] Universality had been the hallmark of the Roman Empire, and then also of the Christian Church that grew within it. When imperial power lapsed in the west, learned men came to terms with barbarian regimes, and elaborated conceptions of Christian kingship.[102] But the equation of Romanity with Christendom remained fossilised in the Church's liturgy: 'Have mercy, O God, on the sins of thy people, ... that the secure liberty of the Roman name may always exult in thy devotion'. In the eighth century Frankish clergy substituted 'Frankish' for 'Roman' in this and similar prayers.[103] The Continua-

fidelium is, so to speak, the "complementary concept" to the Christian ideal of kingship' ('der "Komplementärbegriff" zum christlichen Königsideal').

98 The best surveys of ideas of empire from the ninth to the twelfth centuries are K. F. Werner, 'L'Empire carolingien et le saint empire', in: *Le Concept d'empire*, ed. M. Duverger (Paris, 1980). Still useful: G. Barraclough, *The Mediaeval Empire, Ideal and Reality* (London, 1950).

99 Dating and genre: P. E. Schramm, *Der König von Frankreich. Das Wesen der Monarchie vom 9. zum 16. Jahrhundert*, 2nd edn (Cologne and Vienna, 1960). *Kaiser, Könige und Päpste*, 4 vols., (Stuttgart, 1968), vol. I, pp. 120–7.

100 Alcuin, *The Bishops, Kings and Saints of York*, ed. and trans. by P. Godman (Oxford, 1982) pp. 42–3, and Godman's comments ibid., pp. lxxxvii–xciii. See also F. L. Ganshof, *The Imperial Coronation of Charlemagne. Theories and Facts*, The David Murray Lecture no. 16 (Glasgow, 1949), reprinted in Ganshof, *Carolingians*.

101 MGH Poet. I, line 86, p. 368: 'imperii ... rex culmine reges / excellit'. This poem is also known as *Karolus magnus et Leo papa*.

102 M. Reydellet, *La Royauté dans la littérature latine de Sidoine Apollinaire à Isidore de Séville* (Rome, 1981).

103 *Gelasian Sacramentary*, no. 1503, p. 217: 'populi tui, quaesumus, omnipotens deus, propitiare peccatis ... ut romani nominis secura libertas in tua devocione semper exultet'; and ibid., nos. 1480, 1488 and 1496, pp. 214–6. Compare *Missale francorum*, ed. L. C. Mohlberg, Rerum ecclesiasticarum documenta, Series maior, Fontes II (Rome, 1957), pp. 20–1, altering to *regni francorum nominis*, etc. See G. Tellenbach, 'Römischer und christlicher Reichsgedanke in der Liturgie des frühen Mittelalters', *Heidelberger Akademie der Wissenschaften, philosoph.–historische Klasse, Sitzungsberichte* (Heidelberg, 1934/5), and p. 61 and comments pp. 20–2.

tor of Fredegar imagined the pope contemplating secession from the authority of the emperor in Constantinople and turning instead to the Franks.[104] No less imaginatively, a Roman cleric *ca* 760, drawing on the hagiographical legend of Pope Silvester, concocted the Donation of Constantine in which the fourth-century emperor transferred his authority and privileges in the west to the pope, who, in baptising him, had also cured him of leprosy. Though echoes of the Constantine legend occasionally resounded in papal letters, the Donation itself was not used, and had almost certainly never been conceived, as documentary support for papal imperialism in the later eighth century. (Only by a quirk of fate, having got into a Frankish canon law collection in the ninth century as a proof-text for the inviolability of ecclesiastical property against lay encroachment, did the Donation return with this collection to Rome in the eleventh century, to be put to new uses by Gregorian reformers.)[105] The Donation may have scored points in the centuries-old rivalry between Rome and Ravenna. But it was not designed to meet the papacy's increasingly desperate need for an ideological as well as a practical solution to the problem of political order in and around Rome. The eighth-century Republic of St Peter was a bold but abortive experiment.[106] Charlemagne's patriciate of the Romans turned out not to commit him to act effectively to protect the pope. *Faute de mieux*, Leo III would have to call into being a new, western, Roman empire when the old one failed him.

On Christmas Day 800 the two ideas of empire, Rome-free and Rome-centred, briefly intersected in the coronation of Charlemagne by Leo III in Rome. According to Einhard, Charlemagne used to say that 'if he had known beforehand the pope's plan, he would never have entered the church',[107] Leo's plan was to provide himself and his Roman clergy and people with a replica of the too-distant empire in Constantinople: hence the imitation of Byzantine ritual.[108] The Franks had other ideas. For them Charlemagne was an emperor but not a specifically Roman one; he owed his title not to papal coronation but to an acknowledgement of his power by the peoples he ruled. A Frankish annalist wrote that he 'assumed the title of Empire in accordance with the will of God and at the request of all his Christian people'.[109] Charlemagne's imperial seal was inscribed *Renovatio romani imperii*, but this was a renovation that could be conducted far from the city of Rome itself. The *rex francorum* fought shy of the pope's attempt to involve him in a similarly personal relationship with the

[104] Continuator of Fredegar, c. 22, ed. Wallace-Hadrill, p. 96.

[105] Exemplary edition (as *Constitutum Constantini*), origin and early history: H. Fuhrmann, 'Konstantinische Schenkung und Sylvesterlegende in neuer Sicht', *Deutsches Archiv* 15 (1959), 1966; later incorporation in the pseudo-Isidorian collection and subsequent use: idem 1972–4. See also pp. 245–6 below.

[106] Noble, *Republic of St Peter*.

[107] Einhard, *Vita Karoli* ed. O. Holder-Egger. MGH SRG XXV (Hanover, 1911), Eng. trans. Thorpe, *Two Lives*, c. 28, p. 32: 'Quo tempore imperatoris et augusti nomen accepit. Quod primo in tantum aversatus est ut adfirmaret se eo die . . . ecclesiam non intraturum si pontificis consilium praescire poteusset.'

[108] Schramm, *Der König von Frankreich*; idem, *Kaiser, Könige und Päpste*, I, pp. 215–63.

[109] *Annales Laureshamenses*, MGH SS I: 19–39, p. 37: 'iustum eis [i.e. the assembled clergy and Frankish aristocracy] esse videbatur ut ipse cum deo adiutorio et universo christiano populo petente ipsum nomen [i.e. imperatoris] haberet'.

people of Rome. Charlemagne never used the title 'emperor of the Romans': instead he 'steered the Roman Empire' from Aachen.[110]

In 806, when Charlemagne took counsel with the Franks and envisaged the succession of his son Charles to an undivided patrimony in Francia, with his two younger sons Pippin and Louis retaining the acquired realms (which they had ruled nominally since 781) of Italy and Aquitaine, he made a breach with Frankish royal custom which corresponded to the new-found role of the Franks as an imperial people and of Francia as the seat of empire.[111] The young Charles had probably been destined to succeed to the imperial title; but he and Pippin predeceased their father. In 813 at Aachen, only four months before his own death, Charlemagne named and crowned Louis co-emperor. The inscription of Louis' seal, *renovatio regni francorum*, highlighted the Frankish basis of this imperial realm, and the succession project agreed between Louis and his sons in 817 preserved, as in 806, the unity of Francia, with Louis' eldest son Lothar being crowned co-emperor with the approval of the Franks. The drafter(s) of the document specifying these arrangements put a new stress on the religious legitimacy of the empire, adducing a divine preference for unity which chimed well with Louis' concern to inhibit divisive aristocratic factionalism focusing around Lothar.[112] Growing tension between the co-emperors in the early 820s was eased in the short run when Louis sent Lothar to make an imperial kingdom of Italy. This enabled the pope to reassert the reference of the imperial title to the protectorship of Rome: Paschal I recrowned Lothar as emperor and sought renewed guarantees for papal security.[113] For the next century or so, the imperial title swung between a specific, local meaning (Lothar's heir Louis II was known to contemporary west Franks as 'emperor of Italy')[114] and a wider connotation recalling Charlemagne and the Frankish-imperial tradition. The resumption in 843 of royal custom in the division of Francia between Louis the Pious' sons, the territorial limitations of emperor's powers, and the papacy's consistent pursuit of its local interests resulted in an empire confined *de facto* to Italy. Papal efforts to recast emperorship as a papal gift[115] foundered with the collapse of papal power in Rome in the late ninth century. Churchmen tended to be preoccupied with politics at the level of the kingdom, and the idea of empire, like the collective responsibility of Carolingian brother-kings for the

110 P. Classen, '*Romanum gubernans imperium:* zur Vorgeschichte der Kaisertitulatur Karls des Grossen', *DA* 9 (1951) pp. 103–21. Charlemagne's seal: Schramm, *Kaiser, Könige und Päpste*, I, pp. 274–84.

111 P. Classen, 'Karl der Grosse und die Thronfolge im Frankenreich' in: *Festschrift für H. Heimpel*, II, (Berlin, 1972). Further dimensions of the 806 text: W. Schlesinger, 'Kaisertum und Reichsteilung. Zur *Divisio regnorum* von 806', in: *Festgabe für Hans Herzfeld*, repr. in W. Schlesinger *Beiträge zue deutschen Verfassungsgeschichte des Mittelalters*, 2 vols. (Berlin, 1963). Text translated in H. Loyn and J. Percival, *The Reign of Charlemagne* (London, 1975) pp. 91–6.

112 Religious aspects of imperial ideals of Louis and his advisers: T. F. X. Noble, 'The Monastic Ideal as a Model for Empire: The Case of Louis the Pious', *Revue Bénédictine* 86 (1976) pp. 235–50. P. Classen 'Karl der Grosse und die Thronfolge', argues for continuity between 806 and 817. Eng. trans Brian Pullan, *Sources for the History of Medieval Europe* (Oxford, 1966) pp. 38–42.

113 *Annales regni francorum* s.a. 823; Eng. trans. Scholz, *Carolingian Chronicles*, pp. 160–1.

114 *Annales Bertiniani*, s.a. 860, 863, trans. Nelson, *Annals*, pp. 83, 96, 97.

115 On the significance of John VIII's pontificate see Ullmann, *Growth of Papal Government*, pp. 219–25.

one Church, came to mean little to the aged Hincmar.[116] It had been resurrected to legitimise Frankish imperialism. Frankish divisions made it hard to sustain. For its substance had always been the oneness of the Frankish people: there were many *regna* and several kings, but only one *regnum francorum*. In 881, Hincmar felt himself to be in a kingdom that was only a 'small bit' (*particula*) of that *regnum*.[117]

Yet two other dimensions of the Carolingian imperial revival ensured that the idea of empire survived the divisions of the ninth century. First, the Franks' political success brought to the spokesmen of Latin Christendom a new sense of separateness from the world of the Greeks, Byzantium. The *Libri Carolini* denied authority in the west to those 'kings' in Constantinople who had usurped the imperial title that belonged to Christ alone.[118] Charlemagne once having become (somewhat inconsistently) an emperor himself claimed parity with his 'brother' in the east and gained Byzantine recognition of his title in 812. Later, parity was no longer enough. Ermold turned against Constantinople the very symbol of cultural superiority she had once directed to the west: the organ. Constantine V had sent one to Pippin in 757 and much impressed the Franks. Seventy years later Louis the Pious had one made for him at Aachen, thereby, according to Ermold, taking away from Constantinople her 'chief glory': 'Maybe it will be a sign that they [the Greeks] should bow their necks to the Franks.'[119] In 871 a letter written on behalf of the Emperor Louis II told the emperor in Constantinople that the 'Greeks' had lost the empire of the Romans because of their heretical opinions: that empire had been transferred to the Franks 'by virtue of our orthodoxy'.[120] A Frankish court, to which came embassies and gifts from subordinate peoples and from the east, was an apt vantage point for the spatial dimension of the Latin-Christian idea of empire.

For the second dimension, that of time, the vantage point was the monastery. At St Gall, Notker the Stammerer pondered Daniel's prophecy of the four monarchies and concluded that the contemporary Frankish Empire, reunited as Notker wrote under Charles the Fat, was the last of these and destined to last till the end of time.[121] Notker's faith could overcome such obstacles as Charles the Fat's personal failings or the fragmentation of the empire in 888. Similarly in the tenth century, when that fragmentation had become permanent, Adso of Montierender affirmed the continuance of the Roman Empire under 'the kings of the Franks' whose efforts held off the coming of Antichrist.[122] Both Notker and

116 U. Penndorf, *Das Problem der 'Reichseinheitsidee' nach der Teilung von Verdun (843)*, Münchener Beiträge zur Mediävistik und Renaissance-Forschung 20 (Munich, 1974) pp. 77–90.

117 Council of St Macre, Fismes, c. 8, PL 125, col. 1085. On plurality of *regna* see K. F. Werner, 'La genèse des duchés en France et en Allemagne', *Settimane* 27 (1981) pp. 175–207; *Regnum francorum*: P. Classen, Comments in discussion of Werner 1981, ibid., pp. 209–12.

118 MGH Conc. II, Supplement, pp. 3, 5, 16–17.

119 Ermold, *In honorem Hludowici*, lines 2520–9, p. 192. Arrival of Byzantine organ: *Annales regni francorum* s.a. 757; Eng. trans. Scholz, p. 14.

120 MGH Epp. VII, p. 385.

121 H.-W. Goetz, *Strukturen der spätkarolingischen Epoche im Spiegel der Vorstellungen eines zeitgenössischen Mönchs* (Bonn, 1981).

122 B. Schneidmüller, *Karolingische Tradition und frühes französisches Königtum* (Wiesbaden, 1979) pp. 61–4).

Adso were monks writing for rulers. 'The Christian idea of empire . . . was a powerful force in the middle ages, influential in the minds and actions of many kings and emperors', wrote Geoffrey Barraclough, . . . 'But we shall simply pile up confusion if we attempt to identify it with the historical empire in the west, or indeed with any other empire of this world.'[123] Because eschatology shaped the monastic world-view and because monks shaped so much of recorded medieval thought, it was the eschatological dimension that gave the idea of empire its extraordinary capacity to withstand the repeated shocks of confrontation with dissonant political realities.

Carolingian legacies

The west Frankish realm

The rapid weakening of west Frankish kingship towards the close of the ninth century led to a reinforcing of the theocratic central prop of Carolingian political thought. Hincmar's successor Fulk of Rheims flirted with elective kingship, arguing in the disputed succession of 888 that his candidate, as a tried warleader, was more 'suitable' than a nine-year-old claimant.[124] But there were risks in putting too much stress on meritocratic criteria. The problem diagnosed by the historian Regino of Prüm was not shortage but excess of quality among the Frankish magnates leading to 'emulation and mutual ruin'.[125] Hence a heavy reinvestment by churchmen in the rights of heirship and blood when royal authority seemed to offer the only defence against the privatisation of ecclesiastical resources. Though the see of Rheims suffered more than most from this threat in the tenth century, its claim to possess the holy oil brought from heaven for Clovis' baptism became a powerful myth legitimising both west Frankish kingship and Rheims prerogatives.[126] From Hincmar's time onwards, consecration was indispensable for west Frankish kings in the sense that none dispensed with it.[127] The drawing of a parallel between the king and Christ the Anointed One was encouraged by the 'uncompromisingly Christocentric' monastic piety of the period.[128] A west Frankish royal *ordo* of *ca* 900 invoked 'Christ anointed

[123] G. Barraclough, *The Mediaeval Empire, Ideal and Reality* (London, 1950) p. 26.

[124] Flodoard, *Historia Remensis Ecclesiae*, ed. I. Heller and G. Waitz, MGH SS XIII (Hanover, 1881) IV, c. 5, p. 563: 'Karolus adhuc admodum corpore simul et scientia parvulus existebat nec regni gubernaculis idoneus erat.'

[125] Regino of Prüm, *Chronicon*, ed. F. Kurze, MGH SRG L, s.a. 888, p. 129: '[Wars arose] non quia principes Francorum deessent, qui nobilitate, fortitudine et sapientia regnis imperare possent, sed quia inter ipsos aequalitas generositatis, dignitatis ac potentiae discordiam augebat, nemine tantum ceteros precellente, ut eius dominio relinqui se submittere dignarentur. Multos enim idoneos principes ad regni gubernacula moderanda Francia genuisset, nisi fortuna eos aemulatione virtutis in pernitiem mutuam armasset.' Despite classical echoes, the idea of suitability here is clearly contemporary.

[126] Hincmar first made the claim, in 869: MGH Cap. II, no. 276, p. 340.

[127] Schramm, *Der König von Frankreich*, pp. 62–4, 145–7.

[128] E. H. Kantorowicz, '*Deus per naturam, Deus per gratiam:* a note on mediaeval political theology', *Harvard Theological Review* 4 (1982), pp. 253–77. Idem, *The King's Two Bodies. A Study in Medieval Political Theology* (Princeton, 1957) pp. 61, 78.

by the oil of exultation above His fellows'. The same rite's coronation prayer enjoined that the king 'believe himself to bear the name and deputyship of Christ', while at the enthronement, Christ was requested as 'mediator of God and man' to 'strengthen on this throne of the realm [the king] as mediator of clergy and people'.[129] These prayers should not be pressed for a precise legalistic meaning: they assert the Church's traditional view of the divine origin, and responsibilities, of kingship. The apt ritual complement to anointing and coronation is the bishops' girding-on of the king's sword for use 'in ejecting the Church's enemies and caring for the realm and protecting the fortresses of God'.[130]

As in liturgy so in vernacular literature the late ninth century was notably productive. Even if only indirectly, lay attitudes to kingship seem to be reflected here. The monk Otfrid probably wrote for lay aristocrats as well as fellow monks when he presented Christ as a war leader dying to save his faithful men, hence snatching victory from death.[131] The *Ludwigslied* written in 881 to celebrate the victory of a Frankish king over the Vikings in that year was perhaps a learned monastic pastiche of a living oral tradition of secular poetry, but could surely have been relished outside as well as inside the 'fortresses of God'. It establishes King Louis' credentials:

> The Lord gave him manhood, a lordly following,
> A throne in Francia – long may he hold it!

Before battle is joined Louis promises his men:

> Who here in hero's strength does God's will
> I shall reward if he comes away safe:
> If he dies in battle I shall reward his kin . . .
> Song was sung, battle begun.
> Blood shone in cheeks as the Franks played.

And the poem ends:

> Well being to you Louis, king blessed in war![132]

The *chansons de geste* survive only from two centuries later, but since they took shape around episodes in Carolingian history they are arguably another part of this Carolingian legacy.[133] The *Song of Roland* in its extant form of *ca* 1100

129 Crowning-prayer: '[Christus] cuius nomen vicemque gestare rex crederis'; sword-prayer: '[Salvator] cuius typum geris in nomine'; enthronement-prayer: 'quatinus mediator Dei et hominum te mediatorem cleri et plebis in hoc regni solio confirmet et in regnum eternum secum regnare faciat'. Co-rulership in heaven: Schramm, *Kaiser, Könige und Päpste*, I, pp. 79–85; compare the image of ruler as servant: R. Deshman, 'The exalted servant: the ruler theology of the prayer book of Charles the Bald', *Viator* 11 (1980), pp. 385–417.

130 'Erdmann' Ordo: Schramm, *Kaiser, Könige und Päpste*, II, pp. 218.

131 R. McKitterick, *The Frankish Church and the Carolingian Reforms, 789–895* (London, 1977) pp. 198–203; Wallace-Hadrill, *The Frankish Church*, pp. 385–7: one copy of Otfrid's work was addressed to Louis the German.

132 *Ludwigslied*, lines 5–6, 39–41, 48–9, 57, pp. 25–7: for discussion see Edwards, chapter 5 below, pp. 158–61.

133 R. Louis, 'L'Epopée française et Carolingienne', *Coloquios de Roncesvalles 1955* (Saragossa, 1956) pp. 327–460.

stressed royal war leadership all the more fervently for being able to blend it with the crusading theme of Christian warfare against Muslims. But the ruler who fights God's battles under his orders bears the true Carolingian stamp. His is also a traditional authority in another sense. The *Song of Roland* first depicts the silver-bearded Charlemagne not on the battlefield but in an orchard surrounded by noble peers sitting on white carpets. The politics of counsel and consent are playing out in this setting:

> Beneath a pine straightway the king is gone
> And calls his barons to council thereupon:
> By French advice what'er he does is done.[134]

What is striking in the main *chanson* tradition is the continued centripetal pull of kingship for the aristocracy: here, faithfulness though owed in principle to any lord was focused overwhelmingly on the king. The word 'betrayal' (*trahison*) acquired the sense of a uniquely heinous crime against the king or his officers. 'Treason was a dominant, even compulsory, motif in the *chansons*.'[135] Hence though Roland's Charlemagne is an archetypical patrimonial figure, he is also representative of a public power whose claims override those of private vengeance. If there are clear continuities with Carolingian ideas of royal responsibility for the peace of the realm, there are also parallels with the Roman law concept of *majestas* invoked by learned men from the early eleventh century onwards to defend royal or princely authority.

Given the role of the *chansons* as a medium of cultural values in the tenth, eleventh and early twelfth centuries, it becomes unsurprising that the diminishing scope of royal power left kingship unimpugned as a source of legitimation for the power of others. The idea that all authority, and specifically high justice, depended ultimately on delegation from the king was nurtured by magnates whose own position was often threatened from below.[136] The princes of the west Frankish kingdom might not have recognised themselves in R. W. Southern's thumbnail sketch as 'shockingly unconsecrated and dumb'.[137] For they symbolically claimed their share in the king's consecration by linking their power to his, whether through participating in his ritual inauguration, or else by using titles that proclaimed them still the 'ministers' of the king, offerers of faith and counsel, sharers in royal virtues.[138] As Carolingian traditions were cultivated equally assiduously by the later Carolingian kings and by their Robertian rivals in the century following 888, the idea of the west Frankish realm became detached from a particular dynasty.[139] Further, it could be plausibly recon-

[134] Eng. trans. D. Sayers, *The Song of Roland* (Harmondsworth, 1957).

[135] M. Jones, '"Bons Bretons et bons Francoys": the language and meaning of treason in later medieval France', *TRHS* 5th series, 32 (1982) pp. 93–6.

[136] K. F. Werner, 'Königtum und Fürstentum im französischen 12. Jahrhundert', Vorträge und Forschungen 12 (Sigmaringen, 1968), pp. 177–225; Eng. trans., *The Medieval Nobility*, ed. T. Reuter (Amsterdam, Oxford and New York, 1979).

[137] R. W. Southern, *The Making of the Middle Ages* (London, 1953) p. 99.

[138] Werner, 'Königtum und Fürstentum'.

[139] Schneidmüller, *Karolingische Tradition*.

structed as an imperial realm once territorial princes had laid claim to provincial authority in Normandy, Aquitaine, Gothia, Burgundy.[140] The Rheims cleric Richer at the close of the tenth century described the 'princes of the Gauls' assembled in 987 to choose between a Carolingian claimant, Charles of Lorraine, and Hugh Capet, duke of Francia. Hugh was the choice of 'Gauls, Bretons, Danes, Aquitainians, Goths, Spaniards and Gascons'[141] – wishful thinking on Richer's part since only northern princes were in fact involved, but clearly an attempt to make Hugh's 'empire' coextensive with the old west Frankish realm. Equally revealing is the reason given for the princes' rejection of the Carolingian claimant: 'he had not been horrified to serve a foreign king', that is, Otto III. What is being asserted here is the separate identity of 'Gaul' as against the Ottonian realm 'across the Rhine'. For Richer as for other contemporaries, the continuance of twin Frankish kingdoms, eastern and western, had become an anachronism. Around the turn of the tenth/eleventh centuries, the westerners came to monopolise the 'Frankish' label for their own kingdom.[142] A final significant point is made when Richer says that the princes rejected Charles of Lorraine because 'he had married a wife who, being of the knightly class, was not his equal'. Here is the reflection of the high nobility's consciousness of themselves as 'peers' who could intermarry with and rule with the king's family.[143] It was this group whom Richer referred to as the 'princes' or 'primates' that in fact as well as in theory underwrote the nascent French kingdom.

The weak early Capetian kings could gain little mileage from Carolingian traditions of royal warleadership. The monk Helgaud of the royally patronised house of Fleury made a virtue of necessity when he presented in his life of Robert the Pious a pacific, protective royal father and almsgiver: and an image of royal sanctity.[144] When Bishop Adalbero of Laon urged Robert to restore law and order by collaborating with his bishops, he recommended the skills of the orator, exploiting that word's double meaning of pray-er and public-speaker.[145] Robert, swaying God and man, might have been cast as a perfect mediator. A

140 K. F. Werner, 'Königtum und Fürstentum im französischen 12. Jht,' Eng. trans. T. Reuter, *The Medieval Nobility* (Oxford, 1978) pp. 137–202; Schneidmüller, *Karolingische Tradition* pp. 185–93.

141 Richer, *Historiarum libri* IV, ed. G. Waitz, MGH SRG (Hanover 1877) and R. Latouche ed. and (Fr.) trans, *Richer histoire de France* (888–995) (Paris, 1967), IV, cc. 11–12, pp. 132–3; once the *principes Galliarum* are assembled, 'dux [Hugo] omnium consensu in regnum promovetur . . ., Gallis, Brittannis, Dahis, Aquitanis, Gothis, Hispanis, Wasconibus rex . . . prerogatur. Stipatus itaque regnorum principibus, more regio decreta fecit legesque condidit, felici successu omnia ordinans atque distribuens.'

142 Ibid., pp. 133: Archbishop Adalbero of Rheims sways the assembly against the Carolingian Charles of Lorraine: 'Quid dignum Karolo conferri potest, quem fides non regit, torpor enervat, postremo qui tanta capitis imminutione hebuit, et externo regi servire non horruerit?' Francia as the western Frankish realm, hence France: K. F. Werner, 'Das hochmittelalterliche Imperium im politischen Bewusstsein Frankreichs (10–12 Jhdts)', *Historische Zeitschrift* 200 (1965) pp. 1–60, at pp. 10–13; J. Ehlers, 'Karolingische Tradition und Frühes Nationalbewusstsein in Frankreich', *Francia* 4 (1976) pp. 213–35 at pp. 224–7.

143 Richer, *Historiarum libri IV*, ed. Latouche, IV, c. II, p. 133: 'uxorem de militari ordine sibi imparem duxdrit'.

144 C. Carozzi, 'Le roi et la liturgie chez Helgaud de Fleury', *Hagiographie, cultures, et sociétés IVe–XIIe siècles* (Paris, 1981) pp. 417–32.

145 Duby, *Les trois ordres*, pp. 64–5.

century later, with Capetian kings becoming more active and more powerful, Abbot Suger of St Denis could fuse the full range of Carolingian traditions with contemporary themes, presenting Louis VI as a paladin of Christian warfare, defending the Church against tyrannical castellans and his realm against an aggressor from across the Rhine.[146] At his royal inauguration, the young Louis, 'his sword of secular knighthood put aside, had girded on him an ecclesiastical sword, to wreak vengeance on malefactors'.[147] In avenging the murder of his vassal the Flemish count, Louis shed blood by which Flanders was 'washed white as if rebaptised': again a Christocentric image beloved of monastic writers but appealing at the same time to the audience of the *chansons* (a genre also cultivated at St Denis).[148] In Suger's hands, the cult of monarchy was depersonalised and the Crown was on the way to becoming the symbol of the 'realm of France' – a consummation devoutly wished by the monks of St Denis, custodians of the regalia but not of Clovis' heaven-sent oil.

The east Frankish realm

The Ottonians' kingdom was a direct heir of the Carolingian Empire and its image was constructed by men steeped in Carolingian traditions. Widukind, writing his *Deeds of the Saxons* in the late 960s in the royal abbey of Corvey, linked the Ottonians with the Saxon *gens* just as Einhard had linked the Carolingians with the destiny of the Franks. Otto I, like Charlemagne, was an overlord of *gentes*. It was the dukes as leaders of the *gentes* who symbolically sustained Otto by serving him at his coronation feast. Widukind saw no incongruity in describing, first, Otto's enthronement outside the church by 'dukes and warriors', second, his consecration inside by bishops.[149] The *virtus* Widukind saw in the Ottonians could be appreciated by warriors and bishops alike. It impressed the learned monk as a kind of muscular Christianity: there is nothing that need suggest ancient Germanic notions of sacred kingship.[150] The first Ottonian, Henry I, sacrificed territory to acquire the potent relic of the Holy Lance.[151] He may have (though Widukind does not say so) declined anointing by the archbishop of Mainz on the grounds that 'it was enough to be designated and declared king', that is, designated by his predecessor and declared by aristocratic support.[152] Henry's preference has more to do with Carolingian traditionalism (ninth-century east Frankish Carolingians were not anointed)

[146] Ibid., pp. 277–81.
[147] Suger, *Vie de Louis VI le Gros*, ed. H. Waquet (Paris, 1929) p. 86.
[148] Ibid., p. 250.
[149] Einhard, *Vita Karoli*, c. 7, saw Franks and Saxons united as one *populus* in Christianity.
[150] K. L. Leyser, *Rule and Conflict in an Early Medieval Society. Ottonian Saxony* (London, 1979) pp. 77–82.
[151] Ibid., p. 88.
[152] *Vita Udalrici*, MGH SS IV, p. 389, a late tenth-century text. See M. Bloch, *Les Rois thaumaturges: Etude sur le caractère surnaturel attribué à la puissance royale particulièrement en France et en Angleterre* (Strasbourg, 1924) pp. 472–3 (Eng. trans. 1973, pp. 270–1).

than with resisting Christian charisma in the name of Germanic *Heil*.[153] By *ca* 960 some east Frankish liturgist(s), probably at Mainz, conflated an earlier east Frankish rite with a west Frankish one to produce the most splendid royal *ordo* of the early Middle Ages.[154] Here the king was said to become a 'sharer in the ministry' of his consecrators. They were 'pastors and rectors of souls *in interioribus*' he was 'strenuous defender of the Church against its enemies *in exterioribus*'[155] a partnership in the Gelasian tradition.

The court artists of the later Ottonians and Salians, like those of the Carolingians in the generations after Charlemagne, increasingly stressed the king's majesty and nearness to God.[156] Ritual linked him more publicly with the aristocracy of the *gentes* when, following his inauguration, he rode around the component *regna* of the realm to receive their recognition.[157] For the king's sacrality, as Karl Leyser has pointed out, was an evolving thing, a function of aristocratic as well as of royal needs. The king's judging – his allocation of wealth and power, reward and punishment, peace and wrath – was the 'force of cohesion' that kept the realm together.[158] Hence the extended itineraries of the later Ottonians had political as well as symbolic significance.

Some German historians have claimed that 'a principle of the indivisibility of the realm' came into being in the tenth century.[159] Though this is only an inference from a sequence of undivided successions resulting from dynastic accident, the fact that in 1024 when the Ottonian line ended Conrad II was elected to an undivided realm suggests at least a preference (if not a principle) on the part of the electors, that is, the bishops and lay magnates. From this a political idea could emerge. In his *Deeds of Conrad*, Wipo, one of Conrad's chaplains, described the dangers that in 1024 beset the commonwealth (*res publica*): it was the dowager empress and 'eminent men', clerical and lay, who steered the fatherland (*patria*) safely into harbour.[160] Like Carolingian scholars in similar circumstances, Wipo drew on his classical reading to voice anew a 'transpersonal idea of the state'. When the citizens of Pavia, hearing of Henry II's death, destroyed the royal palace there, on the grounds that there was no longer a king who owned it, Conrad countered their argument by distin-

153 W. Schlesinger, 'Kaisertum und Reichsteilung. Zur *Divisio regnorum* von 806', in: *Festgabe für Hans Herzfeld*, repr. in Schlesinger, *Beitrage zur deutchen Verfassungsgeschichte des Mittelalters*, 2 vols. (Berlin, 1963) p. 160.

154 *Pontificale romano-germanicum*, ed. C. Vogel and R. Elze, 2 vols. Studi e Testi 226 (Rome, 1963), I, pp. 246–59.

155 Coronation-prayer, ibid., p. 257.

156 E. H. Kantorowicz, *The King's Two Bodies. A Study in Medieval Political Theology* (Princeton, 1957) pp. 61–78; R. Deshman, '*Christus rex et magi reges*: kingship and Christology in Ottonian and Anglo-Saxon art', *Frühmittelalterliche Studien* 10 (1976) pp. 375–405.

157 R. Schmidt, 'Königsumritt und Huldigung in ottonisch-salischer Zeit', Vorträge und Forschungen 6 (Sigmaringen, 1961).

158 Leyser, *Rule and Conflict*, pp. 104–5; idem, *Medieval Germany and its Neighbours, 900–1250* (London, 1982) pp. 94–6.

159 But compare J. B. Gillingham, *The Kingdom of Germany in the High Middle Ages* (London, 1971) pp. 9–10.

160 Wipo, *Gesta Chuonradi*, ed. H. Bresslau, MGH SRG LXI (Hanover, 1915), c. 1, p. 9; Eng. trans., T. E. Mommsen and K. F. Morrison, *Imperial Lives and Letters of the Eleventh Century*, Records of Civilisation: Texts and Studies LXVII (New York, 1962) p. 57–8.

1 *Exhortatio ad plebem christianam*, Munich, Clm 6244, fols. 144v–145r, s.ix ^{in}., from southern Bavaria.

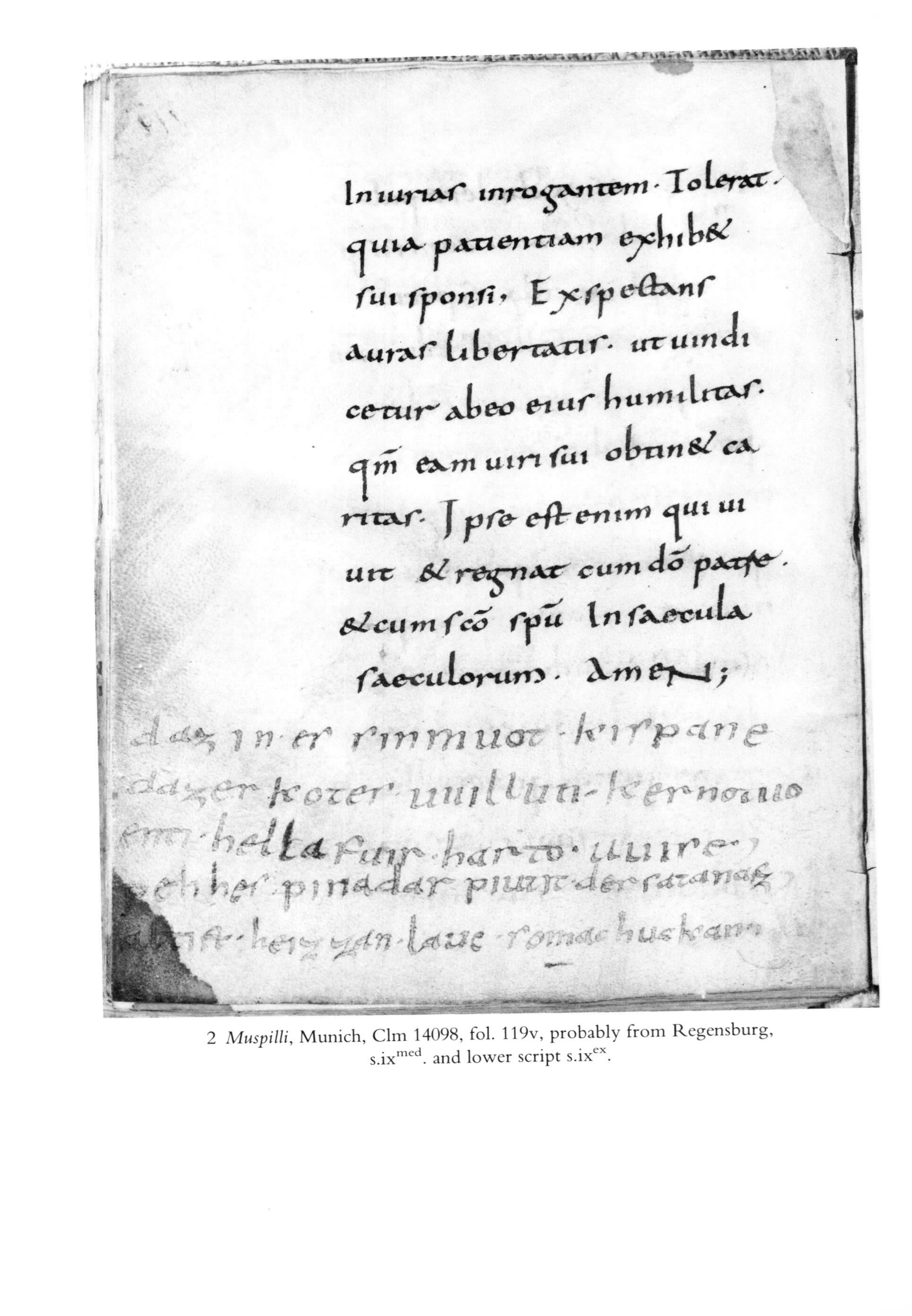

2 *Muspilli*, Munich, Clm 14098, fol. 119v, probably from Regensburg, s.ix^{med}. and lower script s.ix^{ex}.

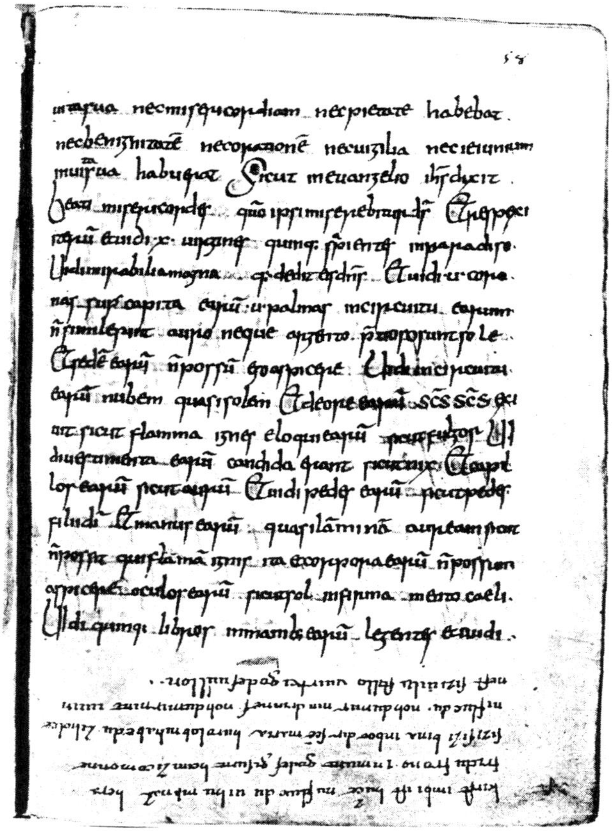

3 *Lorsch Bee Charm*, written upside down in the lower margin of Vat. pal. lat. 220, fol. 58 (s.ix^{in}., Middle Rhine, Insular minuscule), epitomising the relationship between Latin and the vernacular in Carolingian Germany. The manuscript, a collection of sermons, was by 900 at Lorsch where marginalia were added in the tenth century.

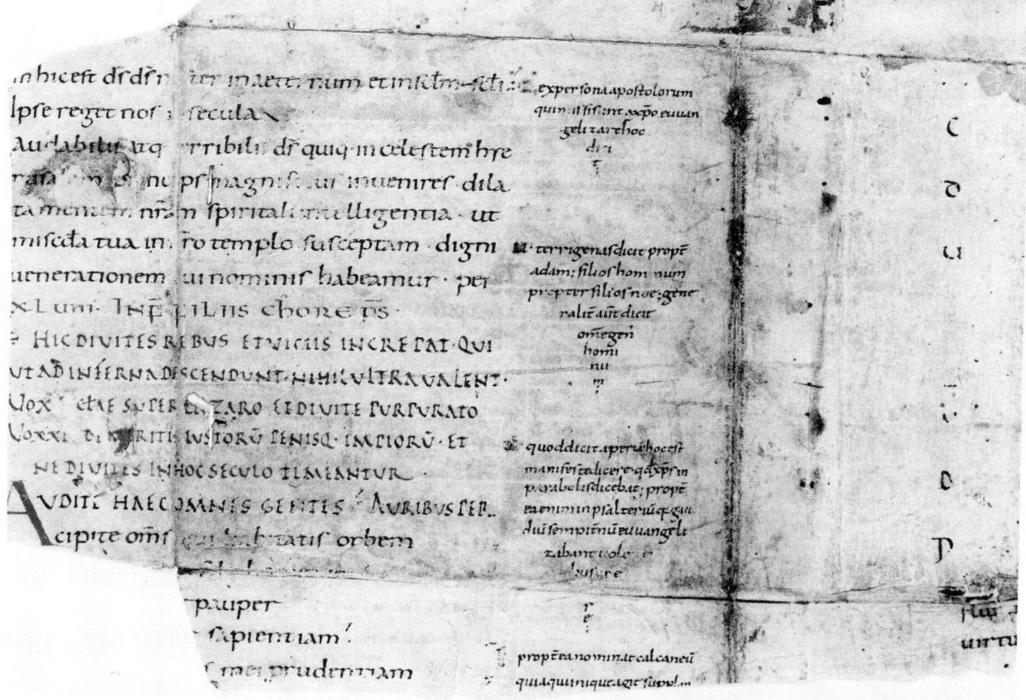

4 Bernard Quaritch Ltd, glossed Psalter fragment, written in caroline minuscule with uncial headings, s.ix^{2}, N. Italy.

34

monachi diuina reuelatione rep(er)tum alexandriam p(er)ducit(ur) et in
eccl(esi)a sc(ı) iohis baptiste humatur V DCCLXXIII

Iustinian(us) minor reg(nat) ann(is) XI. narsis patricius postqua(m) sub iustiniano
augusto totilane(m) regem gothoru(m) in italia superauit · sophie augus
te iustiniani coniugis minis p(er)territus longobardos a pannoniis in
uitauit. eosq(ue) in italia(m) introducit · hac tempestate leuuigildus rex
gothoru(m) quasdam hispaniae regiones sibi rebelles in potestate(m) sui
regni superando redegit quinq(ue) milia DCCLXXX

Tiberius reg(nat) ann(is) VII · Goti p(er) hermenegildum leuuigildi regis fi
lium bifarie diuisi mutua cede uastantur V DCCCI

Mauricius reg(nat) ann(is) XXI · sueui a leuuigildo rege obtenti · gotis subi
ciuntur · Gothi p(er) richaredo principe intendente ad fidem catholica(m)
reuertuntur · hoc temp(o)r(e) s(an)c(tu)s gregorius romae ep(iscopu)s insignis celebrat(ur) ·
Eodem etiam temp(o)r(e) auares aduersum romanos dimicantes auro
magisq(ue) ferro pelluntur V DCCC VIIII

Focas reg(nat) ann(is) VIII · iste seditione militari imp(erato)r effect(us) mauricium
aug(ustum) nobilumq(ue) multos interfec(it) · hui(us) temp(o)r(e) p(ra)sini et beneti p(er) oriente(m)
et aegyptu(m) ciuile bellum faciunt · ac sese mutua cede p(ro)sternunt · p(ro)
lia quoq(ue) p(er)saru(m) grauissima aduersum rem publica(m) excitant(ur) · a q(ui)
b(us) romani fortiter debellati plurimas prouincias · et ipsam hiero
solimam amiserunt V DCCCCXIIII

Eraclius dehinc quinto agit anno imperium · sisebot(us) gothoru(m) glo
riosissimus princeps in hispania plurimas romane militiae urbes
sibi bellando subiecit · et iudeos sui regni subditos ad xp(ist)i fidem
conuertit

Sunt igitur ab initio mundi usq(ue) in era(m) p(rae)sentem V DCCCCXIIII ·
Hoc e(st) in anno quinto imperii aeraclii · et quarto religiosissimi
principis sisebuti · Residuum s(e)c(u)li tempus humane naturae inuesti

5 BN lat. 1863, fol. 34r, caroline minuscule from Rheims, s.ix[ex].

6 BN lat. 2296, fol. 7r. A Sacramentary from St Amand, written in early caroline minuscule, with uncial headings and large capitals to set out the text, s.viii/ix.

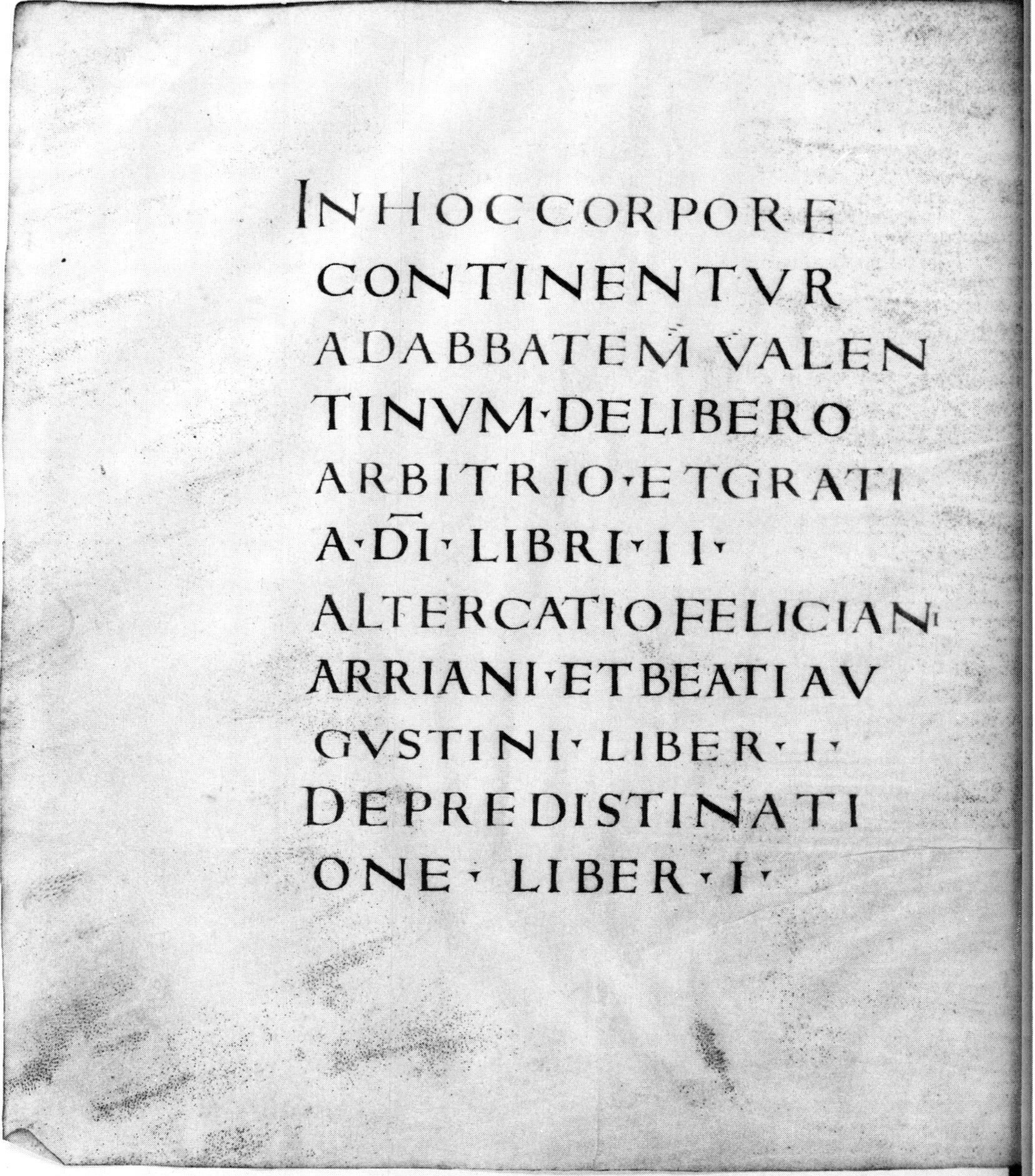
INHOCCORPORE
CONTINENTVR
ADABBATEM VALEN
TINVM·DELIBERO
ARBITRIO·ETGRATI
A·D̄I·LIBRI·II·
ALTERCATIOFELICIANI
ARRIANI·ETBEATIAV
GVSTINI·LIBER·I·
DEPREDISTINATI
ONE·LIBER·I·

7 BN lat. 974, fol. 6v. St Amand square capitals, s.ix^{1}.

8 Trier, east elevation, imperial baths.

9 Cambridge, Fitzwilliam Museum, Ivory M.11/1904.

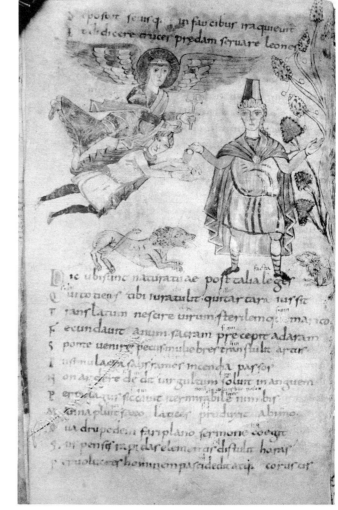

10 *Carmen paschale*, Antwerp, Plantin Museum.

11 London, Victoria and Albert Museum, Ivory (from Metz).

12 Aachen Cathedral, lion mask door handle.

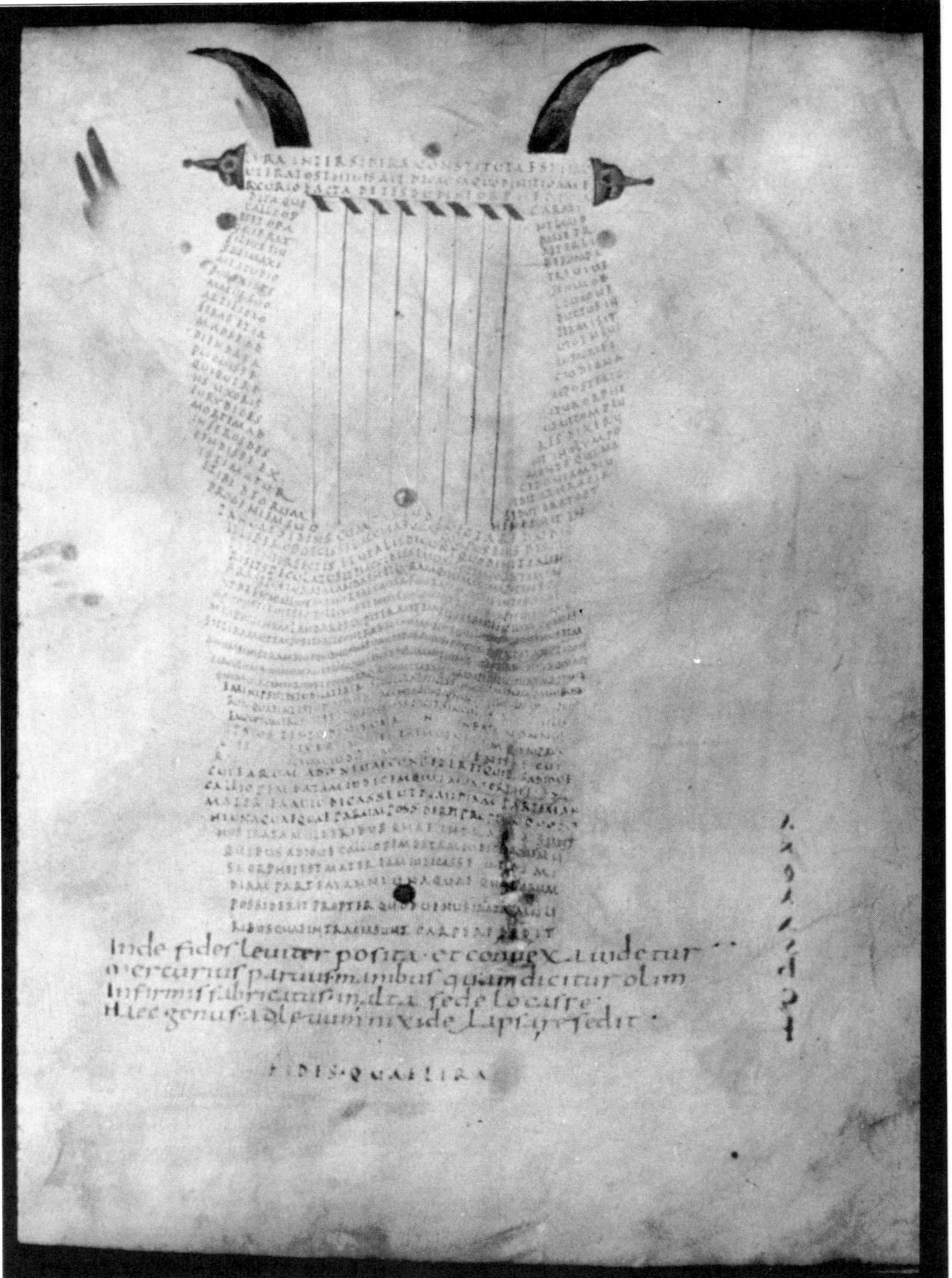

13 London, BL Harley 647, fol. 5r.

61.

Inclinabo in parabolam aurem meam
aperiam in psalterio propositionem meam
Cur timebo in die mala
iniquitas calcanei mei circumdabit me
Qui confidunt in uirtute sua
& in multitudine diuitiarū suarū gloriant(ur)
Frater non redemit · redimet homo
non dabit dō placationem suam
Et pretium redemptionis animae suae
& laborabit in aeternū & uiuet adhuc in finē
Non uidebit interitum cum uiderit
sapientes morientes
simul insipiens & stultus peribunt
Et relinquent alienis diuitias suas
& sepulchra eorū domus illorum in aeternum
Tabernacula eorum in progenie & progenie
uocauerunt nomina sua in terris suis
Et homo cum in honore esset non intellexit
comparatus est iumentis insipientibus
& similis factus est illis

14 Psalm 48, Stuttgart, Württembergische Landesbibliothek, Biblia fol. 23, written and illustrated at St Germain des Prés *ca* 820.

15 Douce Psalter, Oxford, Bodleian Library, Douce 59, written and illustrated at Rheims, s.ix^{2}.

16 Cambridge, Fitzwilliam Museum M.12/1904 (detail).

17 Cambridge, Fitzwilliam Museum M.12/1904.

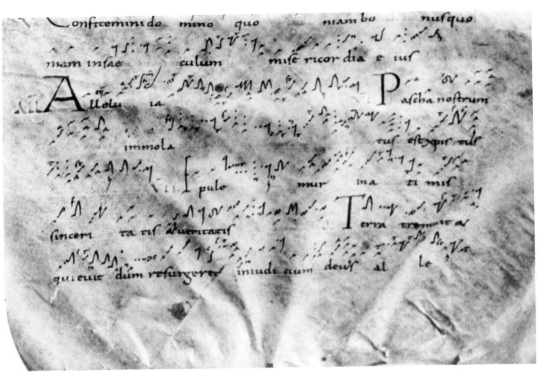

18 French notation, Laon, Bibliothèque Municipale 239, fol. 52r (detail).

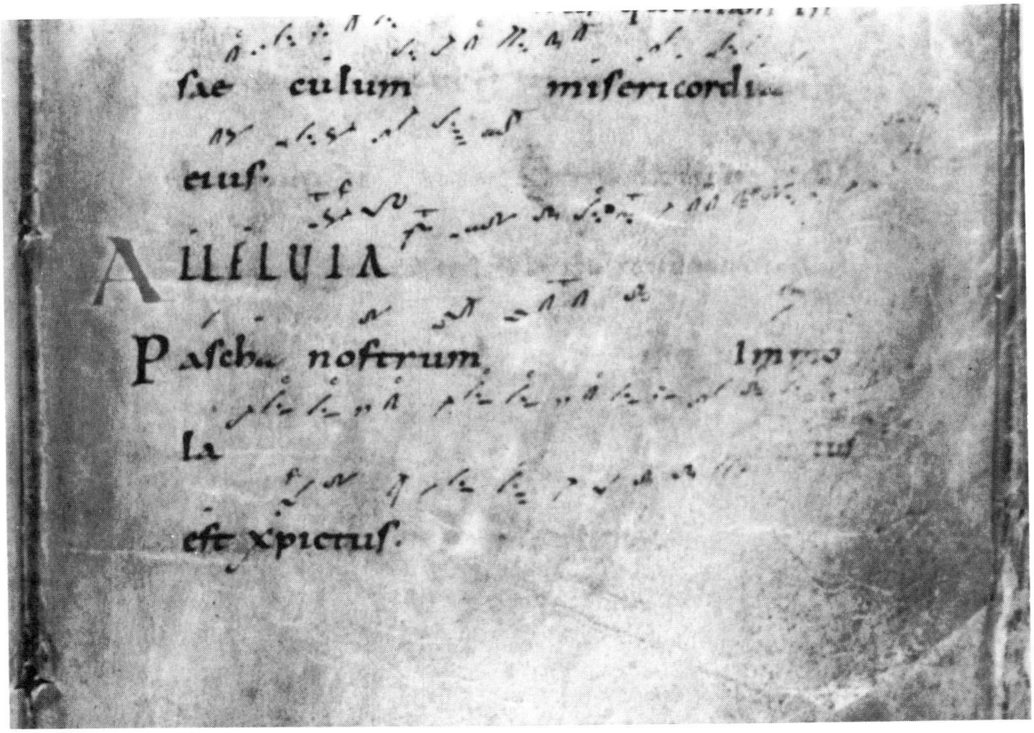

19 St Gall notation, St Gall, Stiftsbibliothek 359, fol. 107r (detail).

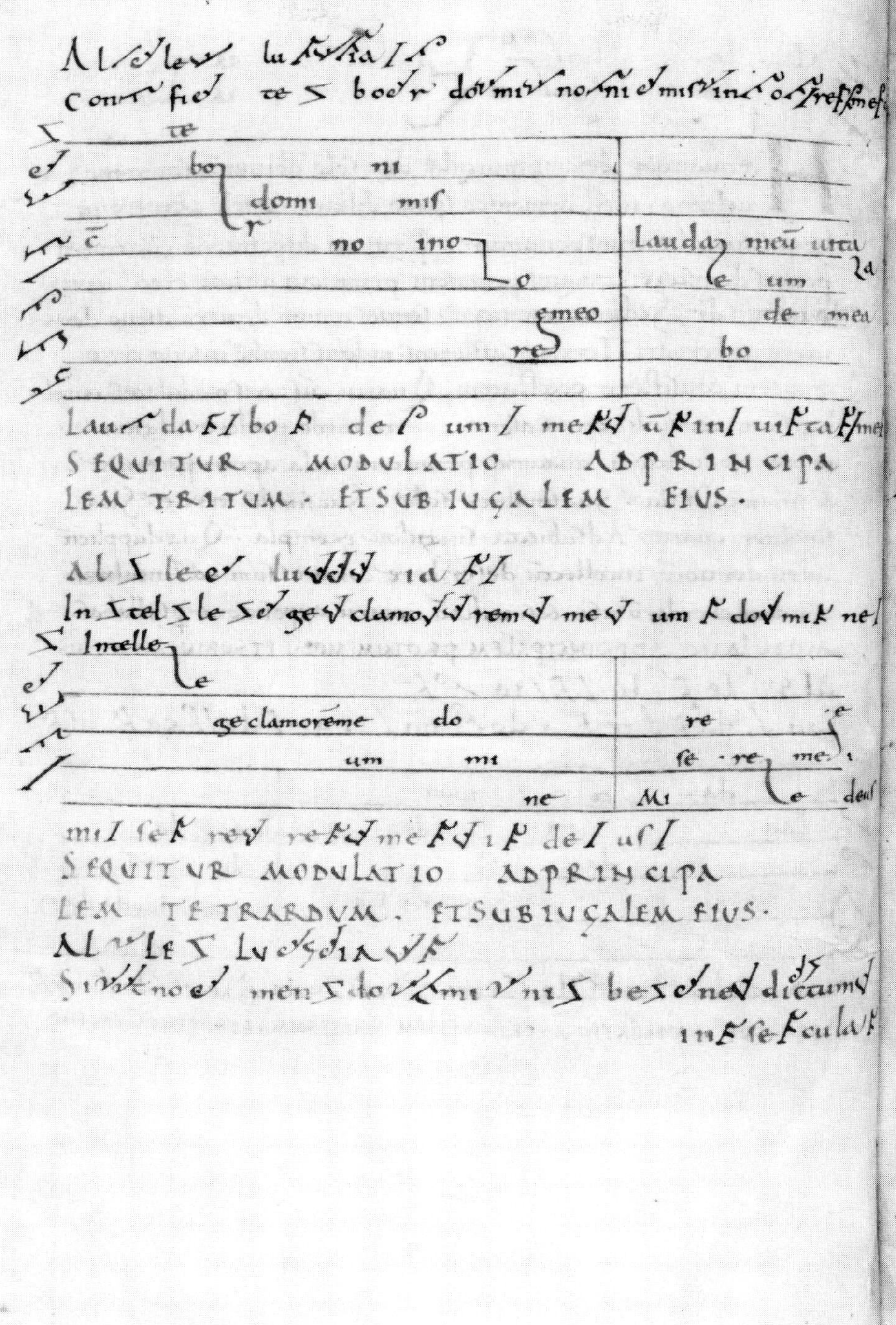

20 Diagram from the *Musica enchiriadis*, Cambridge, Corpus Christi College 260, fol. 6r.

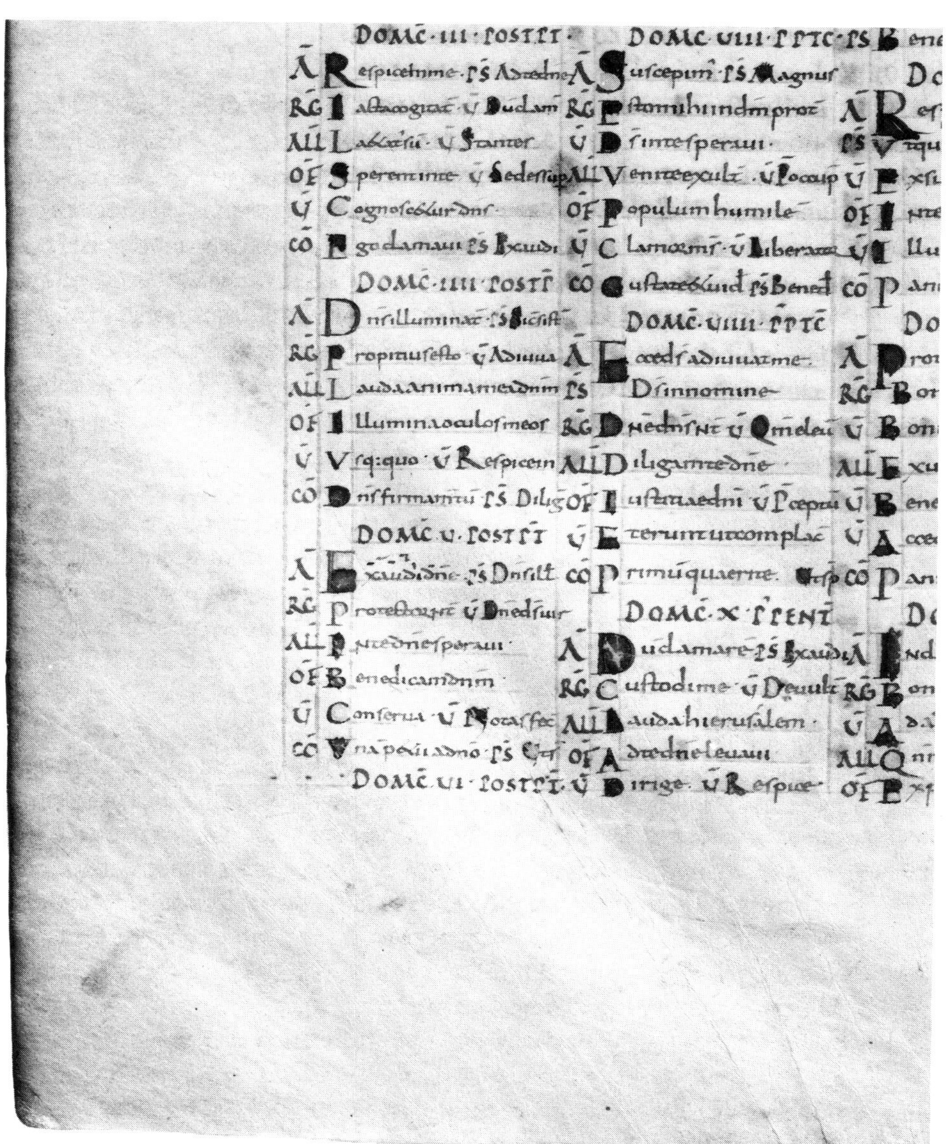

21 *Incipits* of mass chants, BN lat. 2291, fol. 14v (detail), written at St Amand, s.ix$^{3/4}$.

guishing between 'the house of the king' and 'a royal house': 'Even if the king is dead, the kingdom has remained.'[161] The appeal to public laws may have made sense to an Italian audience. North of the Alps the 'transpersonal idea' needed another anchorage. But it was not yet associated with nationhood. Conrad's *regnum* consisted of several *regna*, and its 'archthrone' was at Aachen. Wipo quoted a saying: 'The saddle of Conrad has the stirrup of Charles.' The tendency of those whom Wipo called the 'Latin Franks' to monopolise the label 'Frankish' did not provoke Wipo to seek a new label for Conrad's kingdom.[162] Kings were, as ever, conservative in their titulature. But later in the eleventh century the term *regnum teutonicorum* appeared more often in annalists' work. Significantly, it suggests language as a defining characteristic. It had first been used by Italians, apparently to express hostility to 'foreign' rule. Later it could express Gregorians' determination to confine the Salian kings north of the Alps. German historians, eager to find the origins of Germany, have taken it as evidence of nascent national consciousness on the part of the 'German' aristocracy, noting that it is used by the same writers who seem convinced that 'responsibility for the realm is borne not by the king alone but by the magnates along with the king'.[163] The conviction itself was not new: gentile identities were giving ground before a sense of the realm as a territory, but that too continued Carolingian political traditions.

Again as in Charlemagne's time, the hegemonial character of Ottonian kingship evoked a revived Rome-free idea of empire. According to Widukind, Henry I was an 'emperor of many peoples', while Otto I was acclaimed emperor after his victory at the Lechfeld (his later coronation by the pope was unmentioned by Widukind).[164] At Mainz *ca* 960 clergy copied out an imperial consecration-rite entirely derived from royal *ordines* (hence including the prayer *Prospice*): an imperial realm was an empire *secundum occidentales*.[165] Then Otto followed Charlemagne in extending his authority into Italy. This brought him to Rome, where Otto, like Charlemagne, was crowned by the pope. But the Ottonians' empire became more firmly Rome-bound than Charlemagne's. Bishop Liutprand of Cremona saw Otto in the line of Constantine and Justinian, appointed by God to establish peace in this world. Returning from an embassy to Constantinople in 968, Liutprand denounced the ritual technology of the 'Greeks' as empty form: the substance of true Roman emperorship now lay in

[161] Ibid., c. 7, p. 30: '"Si rex periit, regnum remansit . . . Aedes publicae fuerant, non privatae."' 'Transpersonal idea': H. Beumann, 'Zur Entwicklung transpersonaler Staatsvorstellungen', in *Das Königtum*, Vorträge und Forschungen 3 (Sigmaringen, 1956) pp. 185–244. The idea was evidently not shared by the Pavians.

[162] Wipo, *Gesta Chuonradi*, ed. H. Bresslau. MGH SRG LXI (Hanover, 1915), cc. 1, 6, pp. 12, 28–9 (trans., Mommsen and Morrison, *Imperial Lives and Letters of the Eleventh Century*, pp. 60, 72).

[163] E. Müller-Mertens, *Regnum Teutonicum* (Leipzig, 1970) pp. 145–327; H. Keller, 'Reichsstruktur und Herrschaftsauffassung in ottonisch-fränkischer Zeit', *Frühmittelalterliche Studien* 16 (1982), pp. 74–128 at p. 124.

[164] Widukind, *Rerum gestarum saxonicarum libri tres*, ed. P. Hirsch and H.-E. Lohmann, MGH SRG LX (Hanover, 1935), I, cc. 25, 39, pp. 33, 50; III, c. 49, p. 109.

[165] *Ordines coronationis Imperialis*, ed. R. Elze, MGH Fontes IX (Hanover, 1960) pp. 3–6: 'Benedictio ad ordinandum imperatorem secundum occidentales'. *Prospice* here, p. 4, and many subsequent appearances in imperial *ordines*.

the west.[166] Otto, legislating in Italy 'as a holy emperor' (*ut imperator sanctus*) gave colour to Liutprand's claim.[167] In the *Ottonianum*, he confirmed the privileges of the Roman Church under his imperial protectorship.

Otto's grandson Otto III, while using these themes, promoted a strikingly original conception of 'the renewal of the Roman Empire'.[168] His palace and court, based in Rome, were designed to replicate and supersede those of Constantinople. He created a rival version of the Byzantine family of kings:[169] he sent a crown to King Stephen of Hungary; according to Polish tradition a century later, he made the Polish duke Boleslaw 'brother and co-operator of the empire', briefly taking the imperial crown from his own head and placing it on Boleslaw's 'as a pledge of their friendship', and giving him 'instead of a triumphal standard, a nail from the cross of the Lord'.[170] The Poles could conceive of their land as autonomous within the *imperium christianum*. The language of brotherhood was appropriate for an emperor who called himself, as St Paul had done, 'the slave of Jesus Christ'. Otto transposed political and religious universalism. In his legislation he evoked Justinian.[171] Denouncing the Donation of Constantine as the product of papal arrogance,[172] Otto 'slave of the Apostles' stole the clothes of papal humility. Otto died young and his successor Henry II preferred to stay north of the Alps. But Otto's imperial vision never entirely faded. His successors perpetuated it in their symbols of state. Henry II's mantle, still to be seen at Bamberg, is embroidered with the stars of heaven in imitation of Byzantine imperial claims to cosmic authority.[173] More importantly, Otto had forged the bond between the *regnum* and the empire so strongly that it would not be broken even by rulers like Henry II with little interest in a Roman power-base. Conrad I, once elected king, was already an emperor-elect and the east Franish realm only one of the *regna* he would rule. His son Henry III immediately on Conrad's death took the title, no longer of 'king of the Franks' but 'king of the Romans'. When, later, there was a German kingdom, its ruler was never officially entitled 'king of the Germans'. German kingship had become inseparable from Roman emperorship.[174]

[166] Liutprand of Cremona, *Relatio de legatione constantinopolitana*, in: *Liutprandi opera*, ed. J. Becker, MGH SRG XLI (Hanover 1915), cc. 9. 10, 28; Eng. trans., F. A. Wright, *The Works of Liudprand of Cremona* (London, 1930) pp. 240–1, 251.

[167] Werner, 'L'Empire carolingien et le saint empire', pp. 160–1.

[168] *Renovatio imperii romanorum*: *Denkmale der deutschen Könige und Kaiser*, ed. P. E. Schramm and F. Mütherich 2nd edn (Munich, 1983), plate 101b and p. 199.

[169] See D. Nicol, 'Byzantine Political Thought', in: *The Cambridge History of Medieval Political Thought* ed. J. H. Burns (Cambridge, 1988) pp. 51–82 at pp. 57–8.

[170] Gallus Anonymus, *Chronica et gesta ducum siue principum polonorum*, ed. K. Maleczynski, Monumenta poloniae historica, Nova series II. ii (Cracow, 1952), I, c. 6, pp. 19–20; see also A. Vlasto, *The Entry of the Slavs into Christendom* (Cambridge, 1970) pp. 124–8.

[171] Werner, 'L'Empire carolingien', pp. 161–2.

[172] MGH Dip. regum et imperatorum germaniae II, no. 389, p. 819.

[173] Schramm and Mütherich, *Denkmale*, p. 163 and plate 130.

[174] Ullmann, *Growth of Papal Government*, pp. 413–14; see also Kern, *Gottesgnadentum*, pp. 97–8 and K. Leyser, 'The polemics of the papal revolution', in *Trends in Medieval Political Thought*, ed. B. Smalley (Oxford, 1965) pp. 42–65.

Select bibliography

Since the bibliography in the *Cambridge History of Medieval Political Thought* (1988) was produced, work on political ideas in the Carolingian and immediately post-Carolingian periods has highlighted (i) the ideology of the three orders (ii) the role of ritual in political action and in the containment of conflict (iii) the importance of bonds of lordship and aristocratic solidarity in the formation of kingdoms. This work has been incorporated into the present bibliography.

Primary sources

Adso of Montierender, *De ortu et tempore Antichristi*, ed. D. Verhelst, CCSL (CM) 45

Agobard of Lyons, *Epistolae*, ed. E. Dümmler, MGH Epp. V, pp. 150–239

Opera, PL 104, cols. 29–251; *Libri duo pro filiis et contra Iudith uxorem Ludovici Pii*, ed. G. Waitz, MGH SS XV, pp. 274–9;

Alcuin, *The Bishops, Kings and Saints of York*, ed. and trans. P. Godman, (Oxford, 1982)

Amalarius, *Epistolae*, ed. E. Dümmler, MGH Epp. V, pp. 240–74

Angilbert, *Carmina*, ed. E. Dümmler, MGH Poet. I, pp. 355–81

Annales Bertiniani, ed. G. Waitz, MGH SRG VII, and F. Grat, J. Vielliard and S. Clémencet (Paris, 1964); Eng. trans. J. L. Nelson, *The Annals of St Bertin* (Manchester 1991)

Annales Fuldenses, ed. F. Jurze, MGH, SRG VII; Eng. trans. T. Reuter, *The Annals of Fulda* (Manchester, 1992)

Annales Laureshamenses, MGH SS I, pp. 19–39

Annales regni francorum inde ab a. 741 usque ad a. 829 qui dicuntur Annales Laurissenses Maiores et Einhardi, ed. F. Kurze, MGH SRG VI; Eng. trans. B. Scholz, *Carolingian Chronicles* (Ann Arbor, 1970)

Benedictionals of Freising, ed. R. Amiet, Henry Bradshaw Society 88 (Maidstone, 1974)

Capitularia regum francorum, ed. A. Boretius and V. Krause, MGH Legum sectio II, i and ii. Partial translation P. D. King, *Charlemagne. Translated Sources* (Kendal, 1986)

Chanson de Roland. The Song of Roland: A New Translation, Dorothy L. Sayers (Harmondsworth, 1957) (1969)

Clausula de Pippino rege, ed. B. Krusch, MGH SRM I, pp. 15–16 (Hanover, 1885)

Codex Carolinus, ed. W. Gundlach, MGH Epp. III (Hanover, 1892)

Constitutum Constantini, *Das Constitutum Constantini (Konstantinische Schenkung)*, MGH Fontes X, ed. H. Furhrmann (Hanover, 1968)

Decretales pseudo-Isidorianae. Decretales pseudo-Isidorianae et capitula Angilramni, ed. P. Hinschius (Leipzig, 1863)

Dhuoda, *Manuel pour mon fils*, ed. P. Riché, Sources chrétiennes, Paris; Eng. trans. Carol Neel, *A Handbook for William* (Nebraska, 1991)

Einhard, *Vita Karoli*, ed. O. Holder-Egger, MGH SRG XXV (Hanover, 1911); Eng. trans. L. Thorpe (Harmondsworth, 1969)

Erchanbert, *Breviarium regum francorum*, ed. G. Pertz, MGH SS II (Hanover, 1881) pp. 327–8

Ermold, *Carmen in honorem Pippini regis*, and *In honorem Hludowici*, in: *Poème sur Louis le Pieux et épîtres au roi Pépin*, ed. E. Faral (Paris, 1932)

Flodoard, *Historia remensis ecclesiae*, ed. I. Heller and G. Waitz, MGH SS XIII (Hanover, 1881)

Fredegar, *The Fourth Book of the Chronicle of Fredegar and its Continuations*, ed. J. M. Wallace-Hadrill (London, 1960)

Gelasian Sacramentary, ed. L. C. Mohlberg, *Liber sacramentorum romanae ecclesiae ordinis anni circuli* (Rerum ecclesiasticarum documenta, series maior, Fontes IV) (Rome 1958)

Hincmar of Rheims, *De regis persona et regio ministerio*, PL 125, cols. 833–56; *De divortio Lotharii regis et Tetbergae reginae*, PL 125, cols. 619–772; *De ordine palatii*, ed. T. Gross, and R. Schieffer, MGH Fontes III (Hanover, 1980), Eng. trans. D. Herlihy, *A History of Feudalism* (London, 1970)

Hraban Maur, *De clericorum institutione*, PL 107, cols. 293–420. *Epistolae*, MGH Epp. V (Hanover, 1899)

Jonas of Orleans, *De institutione laicali*, PL 106, cols. 121–78. *De institutione regia*, ed. J. Reviron (Paris, 1980); Eng. trans. R. W. Dyson, *A Ninth-Century Political Tract* (Smithtown, N.Y., 1983)

Lex Salica, 100-Titel Text, ed. K. A. Eckhardt, MGH Leges IV.ii (Hanover, 1969)

Liutprand of Cremona, *Relatio de legatione Constantinopolitana*, in: *Liutprandi opera*, ed. J. Becker, MGH SRG XLI (Hanover, 1915) pp. 115–212; Eng. trans. F. A. Wright, *The Works of Liudprand of Cremona* (London, 1930)

Missale francorum, ed. L. C. Mohlberg, Rerum ecclesiasticarum documenta, series maior, Fontes II (Rome, 1957)

T. E. Mommsen and K. F. Morrison, *Imperial Lives and Letters of the Eleventh Century*, Records of Civilisation: Texts and Studies 67 (New York, 1962)

Nithard, *Historiarum libri IV*, ed. with French trans., P. Lauer, *Histoire des fils de Louis le Pieux* (Paris, 1926), trans. B. Scholz, *Carolingian Chronicles* (Ann Arbor, 1970)

Notker the Stammerer, *Gesta Karoli*, ed. H. F. Kaefele, MGH SRG n.s. XIII; Eng. trans. L. Thorpe (Harmondsworth, 1959)

Ordines coronationis imperialis, ed. R. Elze, MGH Fontes IX (Hanover, 1960)

Pontificale romano-germanicum, ed. C. Vogel and R. Elze, 2 vols., Studi e testi 226, (Rome, 1963)

Regino of Prüm, *Chronicon*, MGH SS I (Hanover, 1826), pp. 537–612 (1890); *Chronicon*, ed. F. Kurze, MGH SS L

Richer, *Historiarum libri IV*, ed. G. Waitz, MGH SRG LI (Hanover 1877) and R. Latouche ed. with French trans, Richer, *Histoire de France (888–995)* (Paris, 1967)

Sedulius Scottus, *Liber de rectoribus christianis*, ed. S. Hellmann, Quellen und Untersuchungen zur lateinischen Philologie des Mittelalters 1, I (Munich, 1906); Eng. trans. E. G. Doyle, Sedulius Scottus, *On Christian Rulers and The Poems* (Binghampton, 1983)

Smaragdus, *Via regia*, PL 102, cols. 931–70

G. Tessier, *Recueil des actes de Charles II le Chauve*, 3 vols. (Paris, 1943–55)

Vita Lebuini antiqua, ed. A. Hofmeister, MGH SS XXX. ii (Hanover, 1934) pp. 789–95

Widukind, *Rerum gestarum saxonicarum libri tres*, ed. P. Hirsch and H.-E. Lohmann, MGH SRG LX (Hanover, 1935)

Wipo, *Gesta Chuonradi*, ed. H. Bresslau. MGH SRG LXI (Hanover, 1915) pp. 1–62

Secondary sources

W. Affeldt, 'Königserhebung Pippins und Unlösbarkeit des Eides im *Liber de unitate ecclesiae conservanda*', *DA* 25 (1969) pp. 313–46

G. Althoff, *Verwandte, Freunde und Getreue. Zum politischen Stellenwert der Gruppenbindungen im frühen Mittelalter* (Darmstadt, 1990)

A. Angenendt, 'Das geistliche Bundnis der Päpste mit den Karolingern', *Historisches Jahrbuch* 100 (1980) pp. 1–94

'*Rex et sacerdos.* Zur Genese der Königssalbung', in: *Tradition als Historische Kraft. Interdisziplinäre Forschungen zur Geschichte des früheren Mittelalters*, ed. N. Kamp and J. Wollasch (Berlin, 1982) pp. 100–118

'Taufe und Politik im frühen Mittelalter', *Frühmittelalterliche Studien* 7 (1973) pp. 43–68

H. H. Anton, *Fürstenspiegel und Herrscherethos in der Karolingerzeit*, Bonner Historische Forschungen 32 (Bonn, 1968)

'Zum politischen Konzept Karolingischer Synoden und zur Karolingischen Brudergemeinschaft', *Historisches Jahrbuch* 99 (1979) pp. 55–132

H. X. Arquillière, *L'Augustinisme politique* (Paris, 1955)

G. Barraclough, *The Mediaeval Empire, Ideal and Reality* (London, 1950)

M. Bloch, *Les Rois thaumaturges: Etude sur le caractère surnaturel attribué à la puissance royale particulièrement en France et en Angleterre*, (Strasbourg, 1924); Eng. trans. J. E. Anderson, *The Royal Touch: Sacred Monarchy and Scrofula in England and France* (London, 1973)

La Société féodale, vol. I: *La Formation des liens de dépendance*, vol. II: *Les Classes et le gouvernement des hommes* (Paris 1939–40); trans. L. Manyon, *Feudal Society* (London, 1961)

C. A. Bouman, *Sacring and Crowning. The Development of the Latin Ritual for the Anointing of Kings and the Coronation of an Emperor before the Eleventh Century* (Djarkarta, and Groningen, 1957)

C. Brühl, *Deutschland und Frankreich. Die Geburt zweier Völker. Die 'regna francorum' im 10 Jh.* (Cologne and Vienna, 1990)

H. Brunner, *Deutsche Rechtsgeschichte*, 2 vols., 2nd edn (Leipzig, 1928)

D. Bullough, '*Imagines regum* and their significance in the early medieval west', in: *Studies in Memory of David Talbot Rice*, ed. Giles Robertson and George Henderson (Edinburgh, 1975) pp. 223–76, reprinted in: D. Bullough, *Carolingian Renewal: Sources and Heritage* (Manchester, 1991)

H. Büttner, 'An den Anfangen des abendländischen Staatsgedankens: die Königserhebung Pippins' in: *Das Königtum*, Vorträge und Forschungen (Sigmaringen, 1956) pp. 155–67

P. Classen, 'Karl der Grosse und die Thronfolge im Frankenreich', in: *Festschrift für H. Heimpel*, II (Berlin, 1972) pp. 109–34

'*Romanum gubernans imperium*: zur Vorgeschichte der Kaisertitulatur Karls des Grossen', *DA* 9 (1951) pp. 103–21

'Die Verträge von Verdun und Coulaines 843 als politischen Grundlagen des westfränkischen Reiches', *Historische Zeitschrift* (1963) pp. 1–35

M. David, *La Souveraineté et les limites juridiques du pouvoir monarchique du IXe au XVe siècle* (Paris, 1954)

E. Delaruelle, 'Jonas d'Orléans et le moralisme carolingien', *Bulletin de la littérature ecclésiastique* 55 (1955) pp. 129–221

R. Deshman, '*Christus rex et magi reges*: kingship and Christology in Ottonian and Anglo-Saxon art', *Frühmittelalterliche Studien* 10 (1976) pp. 375–405

'The exalted servant: the ruler theology of the prayer book of Charles the Bald', *Viator* 11 (1980) pp. 385–417

J. Devisse, *Hincmar Archevêque de Reims 845–882*, 3 vols. (Geneva, 1975–6)

G. Duby, *Les Trois Ordres ou l'imaginaire du féodalisme* (Paris, 1978); Eng. trans. A. Goldhammer, *The Three Orders. Feudal Society imagined* (Chicago, 1980)

O. Eberhardt, *Via regia Der Fürstenspiegel Smaragds von St Mithiel und seine literarische Gattung*, Münstersche Mittelalterschriften 28 (Münster, 1977)

J. Ehlers, 'Karolingische Tradition und frühes Nationalbewusstsein in Frankreich', *Francia* 4 (1976) pp. 213–35

E. Ewig, 'Zum christlichen Königsgedanken im Frühmittelalter', in *Das Königtum*, Vorträge und Forschungen 3 (Sigmaringen, 1956) pp. 7–73

'Überlegungen zu den Merowingischen und Karolingischen Teilungen', *Settimane* 27 (1981) I, pp. 225–53

H. Fichtenau, *Arenga*, Mitteilungen des Instituts für Österreichische Geschichtsforschung, Erganzungsband 18 (Cologne and Vienna, 1957)

J. Fleckenstein, *Die Bildungsreform Karls des Grossen als Verwirklichung der 'norma rectitudinis'* (Munich, 1953)

J. Flood and D. N. Yeandle (eds.) *'mit regulu bituungan'. Neue Arbeiten zur althochdeutschen Poesie und Sprache*, (Göppingen, 1989)

R. Folz, *Le Couronnement impérial de Charlemagne* (Paris, 1974); English trans. J. E. Anderson. *The Coronation of Charlemagne*, (London, 1974)

P. J. Fouracre, 'The context of the OHG Ludwigslied', *Medium Aevum* 54 (1985) pp. 87–103

J. Fried, 'Der Karolingische Herrschaftsverband im 9. Jh. zwischen "Kirche" und "Königshaus"', *Historische Zeitschrift* 235 (1982) pp. 1–43

H. Fuhrmann, 'Konstantinische Schenkung und Sylvesterlegende in neuer Sicht', *DA* 15 (1959) pp. 523–40

F. L. Ganshof, *The Carolingians and the Frankish Monarchy* (London, 1971)

'L'Église et le pouvoir royal dans la monarchie franque sous Pépin III et Charlemagne', *Settimane* 7 (1960) pp. 95–141

The Imperial Coronation of Charlemagne. Theories and Facts, The David Murray Lecture, no. 16 (Glasgow, 1949)

The Middle Ages. A History of International Relations (London, 1970)

D. Ganz, 'The *Epitaphium Arsenii* and opposition to Louis the Pious', in: *Charlemagne's Heir*, pp. 537–50

J. B. Gillingham, *The Kingdom of Germany in the High Middle Ages* (London, 1971)

P. Godman and R. Collins (eds.) *Charlemagne's Heir. New Perspectives on the Reign of Louis the Pious*, (Oxford, 1990)

H.-W. Goetz, '*Regnum*: zum politischen Denken der Karolingerzeit', *Zeitschrift für Rechtsgechichte, Germ. Abt.* 104 (1987) pp. 110–89

D. Green, *The Carolingian Lord* (Cambridge, 1965)

O. Guillot, 'Une ordination méconnue: Le Capitulaire de 823–825', in: *Charlemagne's Heir*, pp. 455–86

S. L. Guterman, *From Personal to Territorial Law. Aspects of the History and Structure of the Western Legal-Constitutional Tradition* (New York, 1972)

D. Hägermann, 'Reichseinheit und Reichsteilung Bemerkungen zur *Divisio regnorum* von 806 und zur *Ordinatio imperii* von 817', *Historisches Jahrbuch* 95 (1975) pp. 278–307

J. Hannig, *Consensus fidelium. Frühfeudale Interpretationen des Verhältnisses von Königtum und Adel am Beispiel des Frankenreiches*, Monographien zur Geschichte des Mittelalters 27 (Stuttgart, 1982)

I. Haselbach, *Aufstieg und Herrschaft der Karlinger in der Darstellung der sogenannten Annales Mettenses Priores*, Historische Studien 412 (Hamburg, 1970)

D. Iogna-Prat, 'Le "Baptême" du schéma des trois ordres fonctionnels', *Annales ESC* 41 (1986) pp. 101–126

J. Jarnut, 'Wer hat Pippin 751 zum König gesalbt?', *Frühmittelalterliche Studien* 16 (1982) pp. 45–57

K.-U. Jäschke, *Burgenbau und Landesverteidigung um 900* (Sigmaringen, 1975)

M. Jones, '"Bons Bretons et bons Francoys": the language and meaning of treason in later medieval France', *TRHS* 5th series, 32 (1982) pp. 91–112

E. H. Kantorowicz, '*Deus per naturam, Deus per gratiam*: a note on mediaeval political theory', *Harvard Theological Review* 4 (1982) pp. 253–77

The King's Two Bodies. A Study in Medieval Political Theology (Princeton, 1957)

Laudes Regiae. A Study in Liturgical Acclamations and Medieval Ruler Worship, University of California Publications in History 33, 2nd edn (Berkeley, 1958)

H. Keller, 'Reichsstruktur und Herrschaftsauffassung in ottonisch-fränkischer Zeit', *Frühmittelalterliche Studien* 16 (1982) pp. 74–128

F. Kern, *Gottesgnadentum und Widerstandsrecht im früheren Mittelalter* 2nd rev. edn, R. Buchner (Cologne and Vienna, 1954) (1st edn 1914, trans., with Kern 1919, by S. B. Chrimes, *Kingship and Law in the Middle Ages* (Oxford, 1954)

'Recht und Verfassung im Mittelalter', *Historische Zeitschrift* 24 (1919) pp. 1–79

M. Lemosse, 'La Lèse-Majesté dans la monarchie franque', *Revue du Moyen Age Latin* 2 (1946) pp. 5–24

K. L. Leyser, *Medieval Germany and Its Neighbours, 900–1250* (London, 1982)

'Ottonian Government', *English Historical Review* 96 (1981) pp. 721–53

Rule and Conflict in an Early Medieval Society. Ottonian Saxony (London, 1979)

H. Loyn and J. Percival, *The Reign of Charlemagne* (London, 1975)

R. McKitterick, *The Frankish Church and the Carolingian Reforms, 789–895*, Royal Historical Society (London, 1977)

E. Magnou-Nortier, 'Fidélité et féodalité méridionales d'après les serments de fidélité (Xe–début XIIe siècle)', in: *Les Structures sociales de l'Aquitaine, du Languedoc et de l'Espagne au premier âge féodal*, Colloques Internationaux du CNRS, Sciences Humaines (Paris, 1968)

K. F. Morrison, *The Two Kingdoms. Ecclesiology in Carolingian Political Thought* (Princeton, 1964)

E. Müller-Mertens, *Regnum teutonicum* (Leipzig, 1970)

L. Nees, *A Tainted Mantle. Hercules and the Classical Tradition in the Carolingian Court* (Philadelphia, 1991)

J. L. Nelson, 'Carolingian royal ritual', in: *Rituals of Royalty. Power and Ceremonial in Traditional Societies*, ed. D. Cannadine and S. Price (Cambridge, 1987) pp. 137–80

'Inauguration rituals', in: *Early Medieval Kingship*, ed. I. Sawyer and I. N. Wood (Leeds, 1977) pp. 50–71

'Kingship, law and liturgy in the political thought of Hincmar of Rheims', *English Historical Review* 92 (1977) pp. 241–79

'Legislation and consensus in the reign of Charles the Bald', in: *Ideal and Reality in*

Frankish and Anglo-Saxon Society. Studies Presented to J. M. Wallace-Hadrill, ed. P. Wormald (Oxford, 1983) pp. 202–27

'The rites of the conqueror', *Proceedings of the Battle Conference* 4 (1982) pp. 117–32, 210–21

'Ritual and reality in the early medieval ordines', *Studies in Church History* 11 (1975) pp. 41–51 (many of the articles listed above are reprinted in: J. L. Nelson, *Politics and Ritual in Early Medieval Europe*, (London, 1986))

D. M. Nicol, 'Byzantine political thought', in: *The Cambridge History of Medieval Political Thought*, ed. J. H. Burns, pp. 51–79

T. F. X. Noble, 'The monastic ideal as a model for empire: the case of Louis the Pious', *Revue Bénédictine* 86 (1976) pp. 235–50

The Republic of St Peter. The Birth of the Papal State, 680–825 (Philadelphia, 1984)

C. E. Odegaard, 'Carolingian oaths of fidelity', *Speculum* 16 (1941), pp. 284–96

'The concept of royal power in Carolingian oaths of fidelity', *Speculum* 20 (1945) pp. 279–89

E. Ortigues, 'L'Élaboration de la théorie des trois ordres chez Haymon d'Auxerre', *Francia* 14 (1987) pp. 27–43

P. Ourliac, Review of Fuhrmann 1972–4, *Francia* 8 (1980) pp. 787–90

U. Penndorf, *Das Problem der 'Reichseinheitsidee' nach der Teilung von Verdun (843)* Münchner Beiträge zur Mediävistik und Renaisssance-Forschung 20 (Munich, 1974)

E. Peters, *The Shadow King. Rex Inutilis in Medieval Law and Literature, 751–1327* (New Haven, 1970)

H. Pirenne, *Mohammed and Charlemagne* Eng. trans. B. Miall (London, 1939)

F. Prinz, *Klerus und Krieg im früheren Mittelalter*, Monographien zur Geschichte des Mittelalters 2 (Stuttgart, 1971)

T. Reuter, *Germany in the Early Middle Ages, 800–1056* (London, 1991)

(ed.) *The Medieval Nobility* (Amsterdam, Oxford and New York, 1979)

S. Reynolds, *Kingdoms and Communities in Western Europe, 900–1300* (Oxford, 1984)

P. Riché, 'L'Enseignement et la culture des laics dans l'Occident pré-carolingien' *Settimane* 19 (Spoleto, 1972), I pp. 231–53

'Les Représentations du palais dans les textes littéraires du haut moyen âge', *Francia* 4 (1976) pp. 161–71

R. Schieffer, *Die Entstehung des päpstlichen Investiturverbots für den deutschen König* (MGH Schriften XXVIII) (Stuttgart, 1981)

'Ludwig "der Fromme". Zur Entstehung eines Karlingischen Herrscherbeinamens', *Frühmittelalterliche Studien* 16 (1982) pp. 58–73

'Zwei karolingische Texte über das Königtum', *DA* 46 (1990) pp. 1–17

B. Schneidmüller, *Karolingische Tradition und frühes französisches Königtum*, (Wiesbaden, 1979)

P. E. Schramm, *Kaiser, Könige und Päpste*, 4 vols. (Stuttgart, 1968)

Der König von Frankreich. Das Wesen der Monarchie vom 9. zum 16. Jahrhundert, 2nd edn, (Cologne and Vienna, 1960)

P. E. Schramm and F. Mütherich, *Denkmale der deutschen Könige und Kaiser* (Munich, 1962)

E. Sears, 'Louis the Pious as *Miles Christi*. The dedicatory image in Hrabanus Maurus's *De laudibus sanctae crucis*', in: *Charlemagne's Heir*, pp. 605–28

P. Stafford, 'The king's wife in Wessex 800–1066', *Past and Present* 91 (1981) pp. 3–27

Queens, Concubines, and Dowagers. The King's Wife in the Early Middle Ages (London, 1983)

N. Staubach, 'Germanisches Königtum und lateinische Literatur', *Frühmittelalterliche Studien* 17 (1983) pp. 1–54

G. Tellenbach, 'Römischer und christlicher Reichsgedanke in der Liturgie des frühen Mittelalters', Heidelberger Akademie der Wissenschaften, philosoph.–historische Klasse, Sitzungsberichte (Heidelberg, 1934–5)

W. Ullmann, *The Carolingian Renaissance and the Idea of Kingship.* (London, 1969)

A. Vlasto, *The Entry of the Slavs into Christendom* (Cambridge, 1970)

J. M. Wallace-Hadrill, *The Frankish Church* (Oxford, 1983)

'The *Via regia* of the Carolingian age', in: *Trends in Medieval Political Thought*, ed. B. Smalley (Oxford, 1965)

K. F. Werner, 'Bedeutende Adelsfamilien im Reich Karls des Grossen', in: *Karl der Grosse*, I, pp. 83–142; Eng. trans in: *The Medieval Nobility*, ed. T. Reuter (Oxford, New York and Amsterdam, 1979)

'L'Empire carolingien et le saint empire', in: *Le Concept d'empire*, ed. M. Duverger (Paris, 1980) pp. 151–98

'Gauzlin von Saint-Denis und die westfränkische Reichsteilung von Amiens (März 880)', *DA* 35 (1979) pp. 395–462

'La Genèse des duchés en France et en Allemagne', *Settimane* 27 (Spoleto 1987) pp. 175–207

'*Hludovicus Augustus.* Gouverner l'empire chrétien – idées et réalités', in: *Charlemagne's Heir*, pp. 3–123

'*Missus-marchio-comes.* Entre l'administration centrale et l'administration locale de l'empire carolingien', in: *Histoire comparée de l'administration (IVe-XVIIIe siècles)*, ed. W. Paravicini and K. F. Werner, Beihefte der Francia 9 (1980) pp. 191–239

'Le rôle de l'aristocratie dans la christianisation du Nord-Est de la Gaule', in: *La Christianisation des pays entre Loire et Rhin, IVe-VIIe siècles, Actes du collque de Nanterre, Revue d'Histoire de l'Église de France* 62 (1976) pp. 45–73

C. Wickham, *Early Medieval Italy. Central Power and Local Society 400–1000* (London, 1982)

D. N. Yeandle, 'The *Ludwigslied*: King, church and context', in: '*mit regulu bituungen*'. *Neue Arbeiten zur althochdeutschen Poesie und Sprache*, ed. J. Flood and D. N. Yeandle (Göppingen, 1989)

3

The study of grammar

Vivien Law

The pre-Carolingian background

As in other domains, it is all too commonly the case that Carolingian work in grammar is viewed against the backdrop of Classical Antiquity; the intervening period, conveniently dismissed as the 'Dark Ages', forms a suitably obscure counterfoil to the supposed clarity prevailing before and after. This has had the curious effect of focusing attention upon the least innovative aspect of Carolingian grammatical activity, namely, the transmission of the grammars of Late Antiquity. Vitally important though this work was, it formed but one part of the many-sided linguistic studies of the Carolingians. Indeed, if asked to sum up the essential difference between the Carolingian approach to grammar and that of the previous two centuries in a single word, one would have to say 'diversity'.

The conversion of Celtic and Germanic Europe to Christianity from the fourth century on brought with it a new linguistic challenge: Latin, the language of the Church and of communication amongst civilised nations, was to be acquired by a relatively large number of people who were native speakers of Old Welsh, Old Irish, Old English, Old High German, or some other Celtic or Germanic dialect, who had few opportunities for day-to-day contact with Latin speakers, and who were not yet literate in their own language. This formidable educational problem was tackled with all the resources at the disposal of the missionaries and their earliest pupils. Attendance at services provided the young oblate with a passive knowledge of the shapes of Latin words. Although the sense was no doubt quite unintelligible, the words of the liturgy, the Psalms, and to some extent the hymns and the rest of the Bible as well, would gradually have become familiar, furnishing the teacher with a great stock of examples upon which to draw, which to some extent compensated for the lack of contact with native speakers. The available teaching manuals, the grammars by late-imperial teachers of the fourth and fifth centuries – only a small selection of which were available at any centre – posed their own problems. Designed as they were for native speakers or advanced foreign students (as was the case with grammars by teachers in the Greek east such as Priscian), these works did not provide the concise but comprehensive introduction to Latin inflection which teachers needed. The information they offer is visibly slanted towards the needs of their sociolinguistic setting. They are of three principal types:

1. The *Schulgrammatik* provided a systematically structured introduction to such basic concepts as the parts of speech and their properties. The emphasis fell on semantic categories rather than on the forms of Latin (assumed to be known to native speakers), and consequently few works of this type offer more than a small sample of paradigms. This is the case even with the most famous beginners' grammar of Late Antiquity, the *Ars minor* by the Roman teacher Donatus (*ca* 350). Although he discusses each of the eight parts of speech (noun, pronoun, verb, adverb, participle, conjunction, preposition, interjection) in turn, Donatus concentrates on their properties (e.g. number, gender, case, tense, mood, person) rather than on their form. He gives examples of the inflection of only three of the five patterns of noun declension, and just one model verb. He offers if anything less information on form in his longer and more advanced work, the *Ars maior*; what interests him here are units of speech smaller than the word – letters, syllables, metrical feet – or larger units – rhetorical figures such as hyperbole, for example. Other works of *Schulgrammatik* type follow the same basic pattern, some (like Charisius, Diomedes, Consentius and Probus' *Instituta artium*) offering rather more information than Donatus, and others (Dositheus, Scaurus, Audax, Asper, Augustine's *Ars breviata*) the same amount or less.

2. The commentary, a genre originally restricted to literary texts such as the works of Vergil and Terence, or to the Bible, was extended to grammar on the appearance of Donatus' works. Telegraphically concise, they were felt to require considerable elucidation – explanation of technical terms, expansion of elliptical statements, justification of Donatus' assertions, further examples. From the generation of Donatus' pupils on, a large number of teachers devoted themselves to this task: Servius, Sergius, Cledonius, Pompeius, Sergius (pseudo-Cassiodorus) and Julian of Toledo, to name only the better known.

3. The *regulae* genre is a loose category which includes a number of works of disparate structure which have in common a focus on form, and in particular the analogical patterns (*regulae*, Greek *kanones*) of Latin inflection. Apparently intended less for systematic study than for reference, they seek to be comprehensive with respect to one particular phenomenon. Phocas, for instance, lists every ending with which a noun may terminate in the nominative singular – *a*, *e*, *o*, *u*, *al*, *el*, *il*, *ol*, *ul* and so on – and indicates what gender and declension is found with each termination. Eutyches deals similarly with verbs, listing the conjugations to

which verbs in *-bo*, *-co*, *-do* and so on may belong. Such works are helpful to the advanced learner who has already mastered the basic forms of the language; they do not provide enough information to enable the complete beginner to take his first steps in Latin. This is the case even with a work which was to become extremely influential, a brief text by Priscian (Constantinople, *ca* 500), the *Institutio de nomine et pronomine et verbo*. In this work Priscian sets out the formal framework for the description of noun inflection:

> All the nouns which Latin eloquence employs are inflected according to five declensions whose sequence is derived from that of the vowels which form the genitive case. The first declension is thus that of which the genitive ends in the diphthong *-ae*, as in *poeta*, genitive *poetae*; the second is that in which the aforesaid case ends in long *-i*, as in *doctus*, genitive *docti*; the third ends in short *-is*, as in *pater*, genitive *patris*; the fourth in long *-us*, as in *senatus*, genitive *senatus*; and the fifth in *-ei* (two separate syllables), as in *meridies*, genitive *meridiei*.[1]

He does not, however, give more than a few paradigms. Other authors of *regulae*-type grammars are pseudo-Palaemon, pseudo-Augustine, and Probus (*Catholica*).

Several writers produced grammars which combined aspects of *Schulgrammatik* and *regulae* types, including Consentius, Diomedes, and most notably Priscian, whose great *Institutiones grammaticae* in eighteen books (which cannibalised much of Donatus) provided so detailed a description of Latin forms that all but the most confident would drown in it.

Although these works were written with a very different audience in mind, early medieval teachers were reluctant, or unable, to jettison the inherited works entirely, for they had nothing else. Nonetheless, they began to experiment. Grammars of the seventh and eighth centuries show us three responses.[2]

1. Commentaries. Teachers could, if they wished, ignore the problem or attempt to deal with it by word of mouth alone, focusing in their written expositions on the text of Donatus as something to be mastered in the same manner as the *Aeneid* or the Bible. Only in this way do commentaries such as the *Ars Ambrosiana*, compiled in the seventh century at Bobbio, an Irish foundation in northern Italy, become comprehensible. This work makes no attempt to fill the many lacunae (from the point of view of a foreign student of Latin) in the *Ars maior*, instead concentrating on every detail of Donatus' text like a late-

[1] Omnia nomina, quibus latina utitur eloquentia, quinque declinationibus flectuntur, quae ordinem acceperunt ab ordine uocalium formantium genetiuos. Prima igitur declinatio est, cuius genetiuus in ae diphthongon desinit, ut hic poeta huius poetae; secunda, cuius in i productam supra dictus finitur casus, ut hic doctus huius docti. Tertia in is breuem, ut hic pater huius patris; quarta in us productam, ut hic senatus huius senatus; quinta in ei diuisas syllabas, ut hic meridies huius meridiei (*GL* III, p. 443, lines 3–9). Texts discussed in this chapter are cited either by author, or in the case of anonymous works, by short title. Full details of editions or manuscript sources can be found in the select bibliography at the end of this chapter, arranged in alphabetical order of author or (for anonymous works) of title.

[2] More detail will be found in V. Law, *The Insular Latin Grammarians* and 'Linguistics in the earlier Middle Ages: the Insular and Carolingian grammarians', *Transactions of the Philological Society* (1985), pp. 171–93.

antique commentary. No doubt it was intended for relatively advanced pupils,[3] but from what had they learnt their Latin?

2. *Declinationes nominum.* The most straightforward solution was to assemble the missing material separately. Paradigms of nouns and verbs were collected and furnished with lists of examples drawn from ecclesiastical vocabulary. The resulting little texts, usually called *Declinationes nominum* or *Coniugationes verborum*, offered plenty of scope for experimentation in their organisation. Most compilers were agreed in making declension the dominant criterion, but thereafter complete freedom reigned, gender, nominative termination, *qualitas* (proper/common), or even language of origin (Latin, Greek, Hebrew) being used as secondary ordering criteria. Such texts proliferated from the end of the seventh century onwards.

3. Insular elementary grammars. An alternative was to supplement Donatus' *Ars minor* or *Ars maior* with the missing material, thereby retaining their essential information on the nature and properties of the parts of speech whilst adding a collection of paradigms. The process of *ad hoc* supplementation is most clearly seen in the *Ars Asporii*, a late sixth-century work; by the time of the Insular elementary grammars, around 700, a standard formula had been adopted. These works – the grammars of Tatwine and Boniface, and the anonymous *Ars Ambianensis*, for example – initially follow Donatus fairly closely, abandoning him on reaching the noun paradigms. Instead of copying out Donatus' paradigms of the five genders, these works turn to Priscian's *Institutio de nomine* and use its opening lines to create a framework for the systematic description of Latin declension. Sometimes drawing directly on a *Declinationes nominum* tract, they added paradigm after paradigm, determined to exemplify every conceivable type of variation. Thus, the first (a-stem) declension, represented in modern textbooks by one or two paradigms, was exemplified with four to eight paradigms, while the more problematical third declension (i-stems and consonant stems) might be represented by anywhere up to seventy-two paradigms.

These works of the seventh and eighth centuries – commentaries, collections of paradigms, and elementary grammars – provided the Carolingians with more appropriate resources to assist them in teaching Latin grammar than had previously been available. That early Carolingian teachers found them useful is clear from the fact that most of the elementary grammars and *declinationes nominum* tracts have come down to us in manuscripts dating from the end of the eighth and first half of the ninth centuries. Had the Carolingians simply wished to continue along the same lines as previous generations, they would on this

[3] Evidence for the relatively advanced level of its intended users comes, for instance, from the discussion of the verb, where the author asks why Donatus bothered to add that the verb does not show case, given that we know that verbs do not have case ('Quae necessitas compellit, ut diceret "sine casu"? nouimus, quia casus uerbo non accidit', *Ars Ambrosiana*, ed. B. Löfstedt, CCSL 133C (Turnhout 1982), p. 92, lines 32–3).

basis have been assured of preserving a reasonable standard of Latinity.[4] The literary ambitions of those in Charlemagne's circle may well have contributed to their interest in a greater range of ancient works than had formerly been in use. The attitude of some teachers, at least, is apparent from this comment:

> Donatus' grammars have been so vitiated and corrupted by everyone's adding declensions, conjugations and other stuff of that sort just as he fancies, or cribbed from other authors, that they are hardly to be found as pure and whole as when they left his hand except in ancient manuscripts.[5]

In the first half of the ninth century the efforts of some scholars to unearth previously neglected ancient grammars become apparent. The longer Donatus commentaries – Pompeius, Sergius and Sergius (pseudo-Cassiodorus) – found little favour after about 825. Several shorter works of *Schulgrammatik* type enjoyed a brief surge in popularity – Augustine's *Ars breviata*, Asper, Dositheus, Scaurus – but failed to establish themselves. As for the *regulae* type, Eutyches and Phocas continued to attract students, and indeed became the focus of commentary themselves. The *Regulae* attributed to Palaemon and Augustine were copied several times. But without doubt the most important grammarian to enjoy a revival of popularity during the ninth century was Priscian, as we shall see below. In some cases the dissemination of a rare text may be traced back to the palace library.[6]

Viewed in their entirety, the grammatical source material available to Carolingian teachers was thus considerably more diverse than that available to their Insular predecessors, although we should bear in mind that only a limited range of texts was to be found in all but the best-stocked libraries. Nonetheless, no ancient grammar was appropriate as it stood for the needs of a late eighth- or ninth-century class. Carolingian teachers were as energetic as those of earlier generations in devising new solutions to old problems.

Elementary Pedagogy

The first generation of Carolingian teachers took up the Insular elementary grammars with enthusiasm, not only copying out the texts introduced by the Anglo-Saxon mission, but compiling their own works of the genre. Two Italian teachers at Charlemagne's court, Paul the Deacon and Peter of Pisa, composed grammars of this type.[7] Paul took as his starting-point an interpo-

[4] On Carolingian literacy see McKitterick, *Carolingians* esp. chapter 1 and the literature there cited.

[5] Artium Donati liber ita a plerisque uitiatus est et corruptus, dum unusquisque pro libitu suo, siue ex aliis auctoribus, quod ei uisum est addidit, siue declinationes aut coniugationes et caeterum huiusmodi inseruit, ut nisi in antiquis codicibus, uix purus et integer ut ab eo est editus, reperiatur (*Cunabula grammaticae artis Donati* PL 90, col. 613C).

[6] The seminal study is Bischoff, 'Die Hofbibliothek Karls des Grossen', in Bischoff, *MS* III, pp. 149–69. On the transmission of the grammars of Late Antiquity see V. Law, 'Late Latin grammars in the early Middle Ages: a typological history', *Historiographia Linguistica* 13 (1986) pp. 365–80.

[7] The question whether the genre was independently practised in Italy or whether Paul and Peter came into contact with it only on travelling north remains to be resolved.

lated version of the *Ars minor*, and inserted into it additional material (all of which is preserved separately), including a complete *Declinationes nominum* tract and a compendium of pronoun paradigms designed to supplement Donatus'. Only one copy of Paul's grammar is known to survive (Vat. pal. lat. 1746 [Lorsch, s.viii in.], fols. 20r–40r). According to Einhard, Charlemagne's biographer, Peter of Pisa (rather than Paulus or, more surprisingly, Alcuin) was the emperor's tutor in grammar (*Vita Karoli*, c. 25). Although his grammar in many ways harks back to the Insular elementary tradition, it incorporates features which point ahead to characteristically Carolingian developments. It has come down to us in two versions, the relationship of which has yet to be established.[8] It proceeds in leisurely fashion through the material normally covered by Donatus and his followers, treating of some subjects (such as the moods and forms of verbs) twice over, following different sources.[9] Noun declension is amply covered with paradigms and lists like those found in texts of *Declinationes nominum* type (but not identical with any existing text), and similarly Peter provides paradigms of all four verb conjugations and an irregular verb (*fero*). In one version there are occasional passages in which Peter chooses a particular word – *pater* 'father', for example – and poses questions about it: 'What is *pater*? A word. What word class does it belong to? It is a noun. How many properties does it have?' and so on. As we shall shortly see, this form of pedagogy was to become characteristic of the Carolingians, and indeed of the rest of the Middle Ages.

The Insular elementary grammar found imitators to the middle of the ninth century. The grammar attributed to Clemens Scottus belongs to this genre, as does the *Ars Bernensis*, an anonymous work which covers the ground of the *Ars maior* in great detail. But by mid-century new works of the type were no longer being produced, nor were many copies of the existing ones still being made. Instead, teachers were experimenting with a new genre, the parsing grammar.[10] Invariably in question-and-answer form, these grammars permit the teacher to adjust the level of the interrogation (along with the information imparted) to the need of the pupil. Although question-and-answer form was widely used in Antiquity (Donatus' *Ars minor* is the best-known grammatical example), it was less popular than straightforward exposition; and even when it was used, as in the *Ars minor*, the choice seems arbitrary. But here and there in Late Antiquity we catch a glimpse of a more direct style of questioning – brief snatches

[8] Peter's name is associated with the copy in Bern, Burgerbibliothek 522 (Reims, s.ix1/4), fols. 4r–68r; the same version is also found in Berne, Burgerbibliothek 207 (Fleury, s.viii4/4), fols. 148r–168r (150r–170r) and St Gall, Stiftsbibliothek 876 (St Gall, s.viii ex.–ix in.), pp. 33–85. The other occurs in Berne, Burgerbibliothek 207, fols. 113r–127r (115r–129r); Oxford, Bodleian Library, Addit. C. 144 (central Italy, s.xi in.), fols. 1r–19r; and in part in Berlin, Staatsbibliothek Preussischer Kulturbesitz, Diez B. Sant. 66 (Charlemagne's court just before 791), pp. 3–66.

[9] Amongst its sources – which still await investigation – is the rather odd grammar or collection of excerpts in Oxford, Bodleian Library, Junius 25 (Murbach, s.ix), fols. 152r–155r.

[10] 'Parsing' is the name given to a type of grammatical analysis still in use into the twentieth century in which the pupil is asked to identify the declension or conjugation and the properties (e.g. number, gender, case, mood, tense, person) of a Latin or Greek word.

embedded in Pompeius' commentary on Donatus[11] and at length in Priscian's *Partitiones duodecim versuum Aeneidos principalium*, a protracted analysis of each word in the first lines of each of the twelve books of the *Aeneid*. Priscian proceeds thus:

> *Regina* 'queen' is what part of speech? A noun. What is a noun? A part of speech etc. How many properties does a noun have? Six: quality (proper/common), derivational status, gender, number, simple/compound status, case. What is its derivational status? Derived. Tell me its base form. *Rex* 'king'. Where does *rex* come from? From the verb *rego* 'I rule'.[12]

Although this type of analysis may very well have been in use in the monastic classroom in the seventh and eighth centuries, it is not until the very end of the eighth that it makes its appearance in written form. The earliest datable specimen occurs embedded in Peter of Pisa's grammar.[13] Following the discussion of the noun, Peter continues:

> We should ask what *poeta* is. A word. What word class does it belong to? It is a noun. How many properties does this noun have? Five. What are they? Quality, gender, number, simple/compound status, case. What quality is *poeta*? Common.[14]

Similar analyses of several other nouns – *musa*, *doctus* and *pater* – follow, but Peter seems to have lost his enthusiasm for this type of addition thereafter. From the end of the eighth century on, innumerable little texts of this type begin to appear. (The possibility that some might turn out to be of late-antique origin cannot be excluded.) They vary considerably in scale. *Codex quae pars*, for example, is concise and business-like:

> What part of speech is *codex*? It is a noun. How do you know? Because it is something known to us and is inflected for case.
> Is it a proper noun or a common noun? Common. How so? Because there are many codices.[15]

Questions and answers are closely tied to the head-word, and no extraneous information is offered. Compare this example from *Ordo ad cognoscendi nomen*, where the head-word serves as the starting-point for a leisurely and comprehensive exploration of grammatical doctrine:

11 *GL* V, p. 142, line 35–p. 143, line 9.

12 Regina quae pars orationis est? Nomen. Quid est nomen? Pars orationis et cetera. Quot accidunt nomini? Sex, qualitas species genus numerus figura casus. Cuius est speciei? Deriuatiuae. Dic primitiuum. Rex. Hoc quoque unde nascitur? A rego uerbum (*GL* III, p. 478, lines 25–8).

13 Interestingly, it occurs in only one of the two versions, that in Berne 522, Berne 207 (fols. 113r–127r [115r–129r]), St Gall 876. This version is the one with which Peter's name is associated.

14 Interrogandum est quid est poeta. Oratio. Quae pars orationis est? Nomen est. Quot accidunt huic nomini? Quinque. Quae? Qualitas genus numerus figura casus. Cuius qualitatis est poeta? Appellatiuae (Berne 522, fol. 14r).

15 Codex quae pars orationis est? Nomen est. Unde hoc scis? Quia res nota est et per casus inflectitur. Cuius qualitatis nomen est? Appellatiuae. Quomodo? Quia multi codices sunt (Berne 207, fol. 17r), printed in *GL* VIII, p. xxi.

> What is *doctus* 'scholar'? It is an utterance. What is an utterance? An utterance is a collection of words making up a complete sense-unit. What part of speech is *doctus*? It is a noun. How do you know that it is a noun? Because it has the cases and declension-pattern of a noun and can be declined like a noun.
> How did the noun come to be so called? 'Noun' is so called from 'note' because it makes things known to us.[16]

This genre too attracted experimentation. In a text from somewhat later in the period, *Magnus quae uox*, the author adroitly combines parsing grammar and commentary, moving back and forth from the narrowly focused question-and-answer format to an expository style while never losing sight of the parsing framework. Usuard of Saint-Germain (who died some time between 869 and 877) attempted to combine a parsing grammar with a *Declinationes nominum* tract by the simple expedient of copying out a passage from one followed by a passage from the other: a parsing analysis of *poeta* introduces the first-declension paradigms, *beatus* the second-declension ones, and so on.

Parsing grammars enjoyed a rapid growth in popularity which they retained until the end of the Middle Ages and beyond.[17] Two of the most widely-circulating elementary texts of the later Middle Ages, *Dominus quae pars* and *Ianua* (alias *Poeta quae pars*) continue the time-honoured formula; portions of the *Ianua* were incorporated into Despauterius' frequently printed grammar.

Alcuin and the rediscovery of Priscian

Up until the end of the eighth century the work through which Priscian was best known was the *Institutio de nomine*; the great *Institutiones grammaticae* was known to only a very few scholars, while there is no sign at all of the *Partitiones*. The rediscovery of these two works is associated with Alcuin's stay on the continent. Of the late eighth- and early ninth-century copies of the *Institutiones* of known provenance, three are from Italy (a country in which the study of the *Institutiones* enjoyed an uninterrupted tradition), two from Irish-influenced and two from Anglo-Saxon-influenced centres on the continent, and seven from northern France, including three from Alcuin's monastery of Tours.[18] Alcuin's own writings on grammar reveal a lively interest in what Priscian had to offer.

16 IN(terrogatio). Quid est doctus? R(esponsio). Oratio est. In. Quid est oratio? R. Oratio est structura uerborum cum plena significatione sensus. IN. Que pars orationis est doctus? R. Nomen est. IN. Unde hoc scis quod nomen sit? R. Quia casus et declinationem nominis habet et declinare potest sicut et nomen. IN. Quare dictum est nomen? R. Nomen a notamine dictum est eo quod nobis res notas faciat (St Gall 876, p. 30).

17 One version (in Paris BN lat. 7570 [s.x^2], fols. 68r–108v) was clearly conceived as a teacher's manual or formulary: instead of beginning with a particular head-word, *poeta* or *pater* or *anima*, it opens 'que pars orationis est ista?', 'what part of speech is this?', and throughout offers the teacher various options. The discussion of declension, for instance, begins thus: 'Δ. Cuius declinationis est istud nomen? M. Primae aut secundae uel cuiuscumque' ('Pupil. What declension is this noun? Teacher. First or second or whatever').

18 V. Law, 'Linguistics in the earlier Middle Ages' p. 185 and n. 8.

His *Dialogus Franconis et Saxonis de octo partibus orationis*, an engaging conversation between a fourteen-year-old Frank and a Saxon a year older, with occasional interventions from their teacher, sets out a large amount of doctrine from the *Institutiones grammaticae* in easily digestible question-and-answer form. From time to time Alcuin confronts Priscian's teaching with Donatus':

> Frank: Don't forget that you said there were fifteen pronouns. Then why is it that Donatus included 'who', 'what sort', 'such', 'how many', 'so many', 'which (= how many)', 'so many' amongst the pronouns as well?
>
> Saxon: I remember saying that there were fifteen pronouns about which there was no doubt. As for the ones you mention, there is room for doubt as to whether they are pronouns or nouns. Priscian, that ornament of Latin eloquence, says that they are interrogative, relative or redditive nouns and says that they cannot be pronouns because they do not denote a definite person, which is one of the properties of the pronouns which have case.[19]

Alcuin also attempted to popularise Priscian's doctrine by compiling a collection of extracts from the *Institutiones grammaticae*, mostly on syntactic problems. This was far less widely read than the grammar, but was the forerunner of a large number of similar attempts to cut the vast bulk of the *Institutiones* down to a manageable size, such as the *Adbreuiatio* of Ursus of Beneventum. The *Excerptiones de Prisciano* used by Ælfric as the basis of his Latin grammar of Old English is an abbreviated version of substantial size in its own right. Another approach was adopted by Walahfrid Strabo, who experimented with various ways of fusing Donatus' brevity with Priscian's more sophisticated doctrine. In one work he supplemented Donatus' *Ars minor* with material from the *Institutiones*, and in another he selected bits of information from the *Institutiones* and added to it material from the *Ars maior*. Hraban Maur quarried the *Institutiones* for all the information he could find on prosody.[20] The Donatus commentaries of the *scotti peregrini* also made regular use of the *Institutiones*. The activity of glossators was largely pursued anonymously in the margins of ninth- and tenth-century copies of the *Institutiones grammaticae*. It offers copious and as yet barely touched resources to increase our understanding of the Carolingian interest in and grasp of Priscian.[21]

[19] Fr. Memor esto, dixisse te quindecim pronomina esse. Sed quid est quod Donatus inter pronomina posuit *quis, qualis, talis, quot, tot, quotus, totus?* – Saxo. Memini me dixisse quindecim esse pronomina, in quibus nulla dubitatio esset. De istis enim quae ponis, dubitatio est an sint pronomina an nomina. Priscianus latinae eloquentiae decus nomina interrogatiua uel relatiua uel redditiua ea omnino dicit, et pronomina negat esse posse, quia finitas personas non habent, quod proprium est pronominis cum casus iuncti (PL 101, col. 873C).

[20] Abbo of Fleury's *Questiones grammaticales* are similarly preoccupied with prosody.

[21] A glimpse of one Carolingian reader's activities is given by M. Gibson, 'Rāg. reads Priscian' in: *Charles the Bald: Court and Kingdom*, ed. M. T. Gibson and J. L. Nelson (2nd edn Aldershot, 1990) pp. 261–6.

Dialectic and grammar

Of the many Carolingian contributions to the study of grammar, that with the greatest theoretical implications was the revival of dialectic, discussed in chapter 6 below. Naturally the proximity of the concerns of dialectic to those of grammar did not escape Alcuin and his contemporaries, steeped as they were in the traditional grammarian's view of language. Where the grammarian was concerned with correct speech, the dialectician was anxious to use it accurately – to formulate precise definitions and logical arguments. Initially, however, it was not altogether obvious just how the newly revived discipline could come to the aid of its better-established counterpart. Alcuin, himself an eager practitioner of both disciplines, made no attempt to integrate the two approachaes, merely including definitions of the noun and the verb *secundum philosophiam* (taken from Aristotle's *De interpretatione*) in his grammar.[22] The study of Priscian provided teachers with an additional impetus to master the techniques of dialectic. In the *Institutiones grammaticae* Priscian is more methodologically explicit than most other Late Latin grammarians, often commenting upon definitions and technical terminology. The technical terms called for special attention, for some were borrowed from the Greek tradition and bore a deceptive resemblance to terms from the Latin philosophical tradition: *substantia*, the cause of many wrangles between dialecticians and grammarians in the eleventh and twelfth centuries, is a case in point. The resources offered by dialectic promised to clarify much that Carolingian teachers found puzzling in Priscian.

Definitions were their starting point. The fifteen types of definition catalogued by Marius Victorinus, Cassidorus and Isidore were reduced to six, summarised thus by Clemens:

> Pupil: How many types of definition are there according to grammarians?
> Teacher: Six. The first is based on the substance, e.g. 'a noun is a part of speech with case'; the second is based on the sound, e.g. 'a noun is so called from being, as it were, a note'; the third is specific, e.g. 'it signifies an object or a concept and is either proper or common'; the fourth is based on number, e.g. 'there are eight parts of speech'; the fifth is based on the properties, e.g. 'it has six properties'; the sixth is etymological, e.g. 'man (*homo*) from earth (*humo*); earth (*humus*) from moisture (*humore*)'.[23]

In practice most grammarians relied upon a still further truncated list containing just three types: *definitio substantiae*, *definitio soni* and *definitio numeri*. Not content with classifying the definitions, they analysed their elements using the tools

[22] It is significant that whereas the standard grammatical definition of these two parts of speech is put into the mouth of one of the pupils, the philosophical definitions are explicitly designated as coming from the teacher (*Dialogus de Franconis et Saxonis*, PL 101, cols. 859B, 874A).

[23] Δ Definitionis genera secundum grammaticos quot sunt? M. Sex etiam: prima substantialis, ut nomen est pars orationis cum casu; secunda etiam soni, ut nomen dictum est quasi notamen; tertia specialis, ut corpus aut rem proprie communiterve significans; quarta etiam numeralis, ut partes orationis sunt octo; quinta

given by Porphyry's *Isagoge*, the notions of *species*, *genus*, *differentia*, *proprietas* and *accidens*. Perhaps the earliest applications of these notions to grammar occurs in the grammar of Peter of Pisa, where they are applied to Donatus' definition of the verb, *verbum est pars orationis cum tempore et persona sine casu aut agere aliquid aut pati aut neutrum significans* ('a verb is a part of speech with tense and person, lacking case, which signifies acting or undergoing action or neither'):

> How many things must we look out for in this definition? Five. What are they? Species, genus, *communio*, *differentia*, *proprietas*. This is how these five things are identified. Specific is when it says 'a verb', for what is specific pertains to one individual, whereas what is generic pertains to many. 'Verb' is a specific noun because when this whole word class is mentioned in accordance with its nature it is a specific noun. Generic is when it says 'a part of speech' because there are other parts of speech as well. *Communio* is when it says 'with tense and person', for tenses and persons are common to the verb, the pronoun and the participle. The verb has persons in common with the pronoun and tenses with the participle. *Differentia* is when it says 'without case' because it differs from the noun, the pronoun and the participle in that these parts of speech have case while the verb does not. *Proprietas* is when it says 'acting or undergoing action or neither', because the other parts do not have this.[24]

Analysis along these lines was practised with particular enthusiasm by the *scotti peregrini* in their commentaries on Donatus and other grammarians. Gradually, as the ninth century progressed, scholars asked more sophisticated questions about the relationship of dialectic and grammar. One remarkable text connected with St Gall, a centre at which the study of dialectic was pursued with great energy, takes up the complex question of the relationship of Aristotle's ten categories to the noun classes set out by Priscian. It begins by distinguishing between the respective domains of the two disciplines, and establishes the temporal priority of dialectic:

> The eight parts of speech show clearly what words are in themselves. Aristotle's ten categories, which pertain to logic, show first what those parts of speech signify beyond themselves, and then what they are in themselves. Nature shows us this same sequence in children: they learn to understand what the word 'man' is predicated of before they learn the inflection of the form: *homo*, *hominis*, *homini*, *hominem*, *ab homine*. Ever since languages

accidentalis, ut accidunt sex; sexta etymologiae, ut homo ab humo; humus ab humore (25, 20–26; *Laur*. 10, 14–21; Sed. 64, 16–23).

24 In hac definitione quot requirenda sunt? Quinque. Quae? Species genus communio differentia proprietas. Haec quinque hic qualiter cognoscuntur. Species est cum dicit uerbum quia speciale est quod unius est, generale quod multorum. Ideo speciale nomen est uerbum, quia cum tota pars illa secundum suam naturam dicitur speciale nomen est. Genus cum dicitur pars orationis, quia sunt et aliae partes orationis. Communio est cum dicitur cum tempore et persona. Communia enim sunt tempora et communes personae uerbo pronomini et participio. Personas communes habet uerbum cum pronomine, tempora cum participio. Differentia est cum dicitur sine casu, quia differt a nomine et a pronomine et a participio eo quod istae partes casus habent, uerbum casus non habet. Proprietas est cum dicitur aut agere aliquid aut pati aut neutrum significans. Proprium est enim uerbo agere et pati, quod ceterae partes non habent (St Gall 876, p. 59).

> originated everyone has attempted to understand utterances; only later did a few people begin to investigate the form of the utterances.[25]

In mapping Priscian's types of common noun onto the ten categories, the author first explores the grammatical use of the term in question, and then goes on to investigate which category it relates to, as in the case of collective nouns:

> A collective noun is one which, although itself singular, denotes a multitude, e.g. 'people', 'populace', 'assembly'. Which category do such terms belong to? We must look to the definition for the answer. A people is a multitude of human beings gathered together into a single city; the populace is the inferior part of the people; while an assembly is a meeting of individuals to hear a speaker. 'Crowd', 'troop', 'regiment', 'council', 'army', 'chorus' and 'flock' are other examples. If they signified one thing, they would certainly come under the definition of a single category; but since they denote substance and multitude, and a multitude is of indefinite quantity and predicated of something, they are assigned to these two categories: substance and relation.[26]

Grammars and commentaries of the later ninth and tenth centuries offer many examples of the gradual assimilation of the concerns of dialectic into grammatical pedagogy; the results can be seen in works like the Priscian commentary *Septem ΠΟΡΙΟΧΑΙ*, in which dialectic is applied to the analysis of the text of the *Institutiones grammaticae* in a sophisticated manner. It is thus by no means correct to ascribe the penetration of grammar by dialectic to the years immediately preceding Petrus Helias (*ca* 1150); the seeds were sown by the scholars in Charlemagne's circle, and tended by generations of Carolingian teachers.

Christianity and grammar

The goal of grammar was an enhanced understanding of the Word of God as made manifest in the Latin scriptures.[27] Yet, despite the fundamental position of *grammatica*, the first and most basic of the Liberal Arts, reluctant pupils snatched

[25] Octo partes orationis in grammatica quales in se ipsis dictiones sint liquido ostendunt.. Decem uero Aristotilis cathegoriae quae ad logicam pertinent quid ipsae partes orationis extra se significent, deinde quales per se sint ipse. Hunc ordinem in pueris natura ostendit qui prius intellegunt ea uox que est homo unde predicaetur quam in ipsa uoce fieri discant hanc flexionem: homo hominis homini hominem ab homine. Et a prima origine linguarum omnes se ad intellectum solum sermonum ferebant, postea aliqui ceperunt de ipsa quoque uoce sermonum tractare (*Distributio*, lxxvi, 1–12).

[26] Collectiuum est quod in singulari numero multitudinem significat ut populus plebs concio. Cuius haec sunt cathegoriae? Hoc ex diffinitione considerandum est. Est enim populus multitudo hominum collecta in unam ciuitatem, plebs uero inferior pars populi est, contio conuenticulum est hominum ad audiendum aliquem qui concionator dicitur. Nam et turba et turma et cohors et concilium et exercitus et chorus et grex talia sunt. Haec si unam rem significarent unius predicamenti diffinitionem ad certum susciperent sed quia substantiam significant et multitudinem, multitudo autem infinitae quantitatis est et ad aliquid predicatur, ideo duobus his asignantur predicamentis aeque communia substantiae et relationi (*Distributio*, lxxxv, 16–30).

[27] J. J. Contreni, 'Carolingian biblical studies', in: *Carolingian Essays: Andrew W. Mellon Lectures in Early Christian Studies* ed. U.-R. Blumenthal (Washington, D.C. 1983) pp. 71–98. On a seventh-century case of the application of grammar to exegesis, see D. Poli, 'La "beatitudine" fra esegesi e grammatica nell'Irlanda altomedioevale', *Giornale italiano di filologia* 36 (1984) pp. 231–44.

at any excuse to avoid it. They flung words of criticism they found in the writings of the fathers of the Church at their teachers, challenging them to justify this pagan subject full of the 'wine of error'. Arguments and counter-arguments can be sampled in this little text known from two ninth-century manuscripts:[28]

> Tell me, since you consider yourself a Christian, why you want to read the grammar of that pagan man called Donatus, when St Jerome said 'I do not fear the ferules of the grammarians' and St Augustine said 'It seems to me ridiculous to bind the words of the celestial oracle with the rules of the gramarians.' This is how to reply to them. St Jerome was not talking about the rules of the grammarians, but about the practices of the gentiles, who pin their hopes exclusively on grammar. Nor did St Augustine reject grammar when he said 'I was all but put to the torture by philosophers and grammarians' and St Gregory said 'It is not the words of Vergil which we criticise, which are, as it were, a golden vessel, but the wine of error which lying teachers have poured out for us.'[29]

The case for grammar was put even more cogently by the grammarian Smaragdus, author of the devotional *Diadema monachorum*, in the prologue to his grammar, written around 805, shortly before he became abbot of Saint-Mihiel-sur-Meuse:

> Some people who are naive by nature, others hiding behind the pretext of sanctity, and others in the grip of laziness say that since God is neither discussed nor mentioned by name in grammar, and the only names and examples found there are those of pagans, grammar can quite well be spurned and ignored by them. They are evidently unaware that teaching a technical subject is quite a different matter from speaking of God. We, in contrast, understand that when the people of Israel went out from Egypt, they took their gold and silver vessels with them, and despoiled the Egyptians to adorn themselves; what they took from the rites of the pagans, they brought to the service of the Lord. Relying on his help, not in some figurative or obscure sense but carrying it out spiritually and in truth, we learn the art of grammar which was so well codified by the pagans and offer it joyfully to the Lord ... Far from basing my book on Vergil's or Cicero's authority, or that of any other pagan, I have adorned its pages with verses from the Holy Scriptures, with the intention of pouring out for my reader a

28 Barcelona, Archivo de la Corona de Aragón, Ripoll 59, fol. 257v; Paris, BN lat. 5600 (St Martial, Limoges, s.ix), fols. 130v–131r. Compare too the *Sententia Hieronymi de utilitate grammaticae* in Leiden, BPL 135, fol. 93v.

29 Dic mihi, tu qui christianus esse censeris, cur artem pagani hominis qui dicitur Donatus legere uis, dum dixit Hieronimus 'Non timeo ferulas grammaticorum' et sanctus Augustinus dixit 'Ridiculum mihi uidetur ut uerba caelestis oraculi sub regulam grammaticorum constringamus.' Quibus econtra respondendum est: non dixit sanctus Hieronimus regula grammaticorum sed obseruatione gentilium qui spem suam in ipsa tantummodo posuerunt. Nec sanctus Augustinus rennuit illam dum dicit 'Pene apud philosophos et grammaticos depunctus sum' et sanctus Gregorius dixit 'Non blasphemamus uerba Virgilii, que sunt uelut uasa aurea, sed uinum erroris quod nobis propinauerunt magistri mendaces' (Barcelona, Archivo de la Corona de Aragón, Ripoll 59 (Ripoll, s.xi), fol. 257v). By no means all the quotations are correctly attributed: Augustine's first, for example, in fact belongs to Gregory. Another version is to be found in Paris, BN lat. 5600 (St Martial, Limoges, s.ix), fols. 130v–131r.

> pleasant draught of the Liberal Arts and the Scriptures, so that he may come to grasp the discipline of grammar and the sense of the Holy Scriptures side by side.[30]

Smaragdus carries out his promise in full measure. His grammar contains approximately 750 biblical examples, of which about three-quarters come from the Old Testament. A few were already current among grammarians such as Julian of Toledo and Bede, but the vast majority seem to have been assembled by Smaragdus himself.[31]

But Smaragdus' attempt to integrate the technical discipline of grammar with its object, the scriptures, went far beyond the substitution of biblical examples for secular ones. At every turn one can see how he strove to create a thoroughly Christian art of grammar. For instance, at the very start of the work he explains why it is that there are eight parts of speech, no more and no fewer. The Irish teachers of the next generation – Murethach, Sedulius Scottus and others – looked to the parts of speech themselves in accounting for their number. In the words of Sedulius:

> There are no more human functions than eight: either we point out a creature using a noun, or we take its place with a pronoun; we indicate actions or receiving action with a verb, or clarify that action or suffering with an adverb, or show the action or suffering action with nominal endings using a participle, or we link up the parts of speech with a conjunction, or we put one before another using a preposition, or we reveal a state of mind with an interjection.[32]

Instead of seeking to link specific linguistic categories with particular human activities (themselves simply projected from the parts of speech), as the *scotti peregrini* did, Smaragdus saw the number eight itself as the significant element, and looked for scriptural examples of eightfoldness – the eight passengers of the Ark, the eight Beatitudes, the eight cubits of the porch of the gate in Ezechiel 40:9, David, the eighth son of Jesse, and the circumcision on the eighth day. To

[30] Sunt etenim aliqui naturali simplicitate praediti et alii sub praetextu sanctitatis occulti et alii tarditatis ignauia pressi, qui aiunt, quoniam 'in grammatica arte Deus non legitur nec nominatur, sed paganorum tantum ibi et nomina resonant et exempla, et ideo a nobis merito calcata dimittitur et neglecta', nescientes, quia aliud est de arte tractare, aliud de Deo loqui. Nos autem intellegentes, quia populus Israhel egrediens de Aegypto uasa aurea et argentea secum detulit, Aegyptum scilicet exspolians se uestiuit, et quod a paganorum abstulit ritu, Domino obtulit in obsequio. Quod nos eius ope fulciti non iam figuraliter aut umbratice ut illi, sed spiritaliter et ueraciter implentes, a paganis bene dispositum artis grammaticae discimus ingenium et libenter illud in Domini offerimus sacrificio . . . Quem libellum non Maronis aut Ciceronis uel etiam aliorum paganorum auctoritate fulciui, sed Diuinarum Scripturarum sententiis adornaui, ut lectorem meum iucundo pariter artium et iucundo Scripturarum poculo propinarem, ut grammaticae artis ingenium et Scripturarum Diuinarum pariter ualeat conprehendere sensum (p. 1, lines 21–2, 34; p. 1, lines 15–20).

[31] As Holtz remarks in the introduction to his edition, pp. XLVI–XLIX. He suggests that Smaragdus made use of a kind of card index in compiling his examples.

[32] Non plura sunt officia hominis quam octo: aut enim creaturam ostendimus per nomen, aut uice ipsius fungimur <per> pronomen; ostendimus actum uel passionem per uerbum, aut ipsum actum uel passionem explanamus per aduerbium, aut ostendimus actum uel passionem cum casu nominis per participium, aut coniungimus partes per coniunctionem, aut praeponimus unam alteri per praepositionem, aut ostendimus affectum mentis per interiectionem (Sedulius 60, 75–83; cf. Murethach 49, 94–3).

Smaragdus and his readers such parallels demonstrated that linguistic phenomena, far from being arbitrary and meaningless, the consequence of man's presumptuousness in building the Tower of Babel, corresponded to patterns and regularities which rested upon divine authority. Grammar, as the discipline through which these regularities were codified, found therein its true *raison d'être*.

The question of authority was one which confronted every medieval grammarian. In the case of conflicts between the pronouncements of the ancient grammarians and scriptural usage, which was to prevail? Smaragdus is in no doubt: the Bible is his guide. For instance, after explaining that many authorities maintain that there is no need to use the subject pronouns with the verb, since a verb form like *lego* means 'I read' with or without *ego* 'I', he continues:

> But we do not fear to say this, guided by many cases in the Holy Scriptures. After all, when Peter said to the Lord *tu es Christus, Filius Dei uiui* ('thou art the Christ, the son of the living God'), the Lord replied: *et ego dico tibi: tu es Petrus* ('and I say unto thee: thou art Peter') etc. ... And you will find innumerable such cases in Holy Scripture.[33]

Smaragdus took his brief to extend beyond the cataloguing of anomalous forms and usage to the explication of subtle matters of intention and sense. Whereas his grammarian colleagues left the classification of the shades of meaning which might be conveyed by a particular tense, mood or preposition to the exegetes, that is, the people who concerned themselves directly with the study of the text of the Bible, Smaragdus included information on such issues under the relevant heading in his grammar. For instance, he lists the different types of illocutionary force which may be conveyed by the pronoun *quis* 'who?':

> *Quis* is used in cases when the questioner is ignorant, or when he in fact denies the question, or when he wishes to affirm the proposition, or with humility, or with desire, or with indignation, and thereby reveals a mental state. For example, when the questioner is ignorant: 'Lord, who shall abide in thy tabernacle?' or 'Who is he, Lord, that I might believe on him?'; when he denies the question: 'Who is so great a God as our God?', where 'no one' is to be understood . . .[34]

In a passage on the interjection he shows himself to be remarkably sensitive to non-linguistic modes of expression:

> Properly speaking, an interjection is an incoherent noise emitted from the secret depths of the mind which is uttered in public solely in order to reveal clearly the inner state of the person. It shows the emotions of the inner mind

33 Sed nos, quos Diuinarum Scripturarum plura instruunt testimonia, haec dicere non formidamus. Dominus enim Petro confitenti ac dicenti 'Tu es Christus, Filius Dei uiui' respondens ait: 'Et ego dico tibi: Tu es Petrus' et cetera ... Et innumerabilia talia in Diuinis repperies Scripturis (112, 56–62).

34 Et aut cum ignorantia interrogantis aut cum interrogatione negantis aut cum adfirmatione pronuntiationis aut cum humilitate precantis aut cum desiderio optantis aut cum exclamatione reprobantis uocis et mentis ostendunt affectum. Cum ignorantia interrogantis: 'Domine, quis habitabit in tabernaculo tuo?'; et 'Quis est, Domine, ut credam in eum?'. Cum interrogatione negantis: 'Quis Deus magnus, sicut Deus noster?', et est subauditio negantis 'nemo' (92, 56–93, 63).

> clearly in the expression of a happy person, the guffaw of someone laughing, in clapping, shuffling, winking, clearing the throat, shaking the head, wagging the finger, an indignant expression, a contemptuous look, a warning noise, an amorous gesture, tears, or a new meaning given to a word; for the secrets of the mind within are not known to anyone but God unless some kind of utterance or sign is made. By making them known openly through a spoken sign one person comes to know the secret thoughts of another.[35]

Smaragdus' novel approach was evidently appreciated by his contemporaries. His grammar survives in some nineteen copies, twelve of the ninth century. It was still being copied as late as the thirteenth century. At least two other teachers, the authors of the 'teacher's manual' parsing grammar *Que pars orationis est ista* (Paris, BN lat. 7570 (s.x.), fols. 68r–108r) and of *anima quae pars* (Worcester Cathedral Library Q5 (Canterbury, s.x ex.), fols. 64v–68r), borrowed heavily from it, and it may well be that other tenth- and eleventh-century grammarians incorporated its insights into their works.[36]

How grammar might be applied to the Bible can be seen in Carolingian exegesis, most notably in the writings of John Scottus Eriugena and Gottschalk. Although neither wrote a grammar as such, Gottschalk resorted frequently and expertly to grammar to fortify his position in theological controversy, notably in connection with his well-known dispute with Hincmar of Rheims over the use of the expression *trina deitas*.[37]

Grammatical commentary: the *scotti peregrini* and Remigius of Auxerre

Whereas the grammars we have considered so far were independent works designed for study on their own, without reference to any other work, commentaries were closely linked to another text. They might be entered in the margins of a copy of the base text, or they might be copied out on their own. Scarcely comprehensible without reference to the base text, they comment upon every detail of its doctrine and wording.[38] Up to the middle of the ninth century

[35] Interiectio proprie dicitur uox confusa de mentis archano prolata, quae tantum ad hoc profertur in publicum, ut interioris hominis lucide demonstret affectum. Et aut laetantis uultu aut in ridentis cacinno aut in plausu manuum aut interiectione pedum aut in nutu oculorum aut in gutturis sono aut in capitis motu aut in digitorum motu aut in indignantis uultu aut in dispicientis affectu aut in deterrentis sono aut in amantis affectu aut in plorantis luctu aut in mutato articulatae uocis intellectu aperte demonstrat interioris animi motum, quoniam internae mentis occulta non sine uoce aut signo aliquo alteri, sed tantum Deo sunt cognita; attamen per apertam prolationis uocem alter alterius occulta cognoscit (233, 4–15).

[36] Very few grammars of this period have been studied or even edited.

[37] J. Jolivet, 'L'Enjeu de la grammaire pour Godescalc', in: *Jean Scot Erigène et l'histoire de la philosophie* (Paris, 1977) pp. 79–87 at pp. 83–6; G. R. Evans, 'The grammar of predestination in the ninth century', *Journal of Theological Studies* 33 (1982) pp. 134–45.

[38] The boundary between glossing and commentary is not easy to define. Commentary may be taken as differing from glossing in being conceived of as reasonably continuous, comprehensive, and in some sense having the status of a text in its own right, copied out by successive scribes with no more changes than one would expect in any other text, whereas no two sets of glosses are ever the same; they usually lack any claim to exhaustiveness, very often petering out after an enthusiastic start, and tend to be added to by successive

the only grammars that had received commentary were Donatus' *Ars minor* and *Ars maior*. Irish scholars, in particular, had developed this method of teaching to a high degree, applying the same techniques to the text of Donatus as they did to the Bible.[39] It seems to have been the Irish on the continent, the *scotti peregrini*, who introduced this type of pedagogy to Carolingian schools.

Several of their commentaries on the *Ars maior* survive – those by Murethach, active at Auxerre and Metz in the 840s; his contemporary Sedulius Scottus, who also wrote commentaries on Eutyches, Phocas and Priscian's *Institutiones grammaticae*; and the anonymous works known as the *Ars Laureshamensis* and *Ars Brugensis*. All four depend heavily upon a lost commentary thought to have originated in the first quarter of the ninth century, presumably in Ireland,[40] copying lengthy passages from it verbatim, paraphrasing others, and occasionally adding bits of their own. In contrast to the content-oriented approach of previous generations, these works are text-oriented to a remarkable degree. The focus of attention is not the grammatical doctrine per se, but the way in which Donatus chose to express it. For example, in examining Donatus' statement 'all Latin vowels may be either long or short', Murethach comments:

> Why did he say 'Latin'? Why didn't he just say 'all vowels may be either long or short'? He said 'Latin vowels' because, unlike Latin vowels, Greek vowels are shortened and lengthened.[41]

Here the reason was not far to seek. Once in a while he was defeated, concluding on one occasion that the reason Donatus failed to mention certain forms was 'because they had perhaps slipped his mind'.[42] His attention extends even to the metaphors underlying technical terminology. Donatus, talking about *i* and *u*, which in Latin have the function either of vowels or of consonants, depending upon their phonological environment, says this: 'Two of the vowels, *i* and *u*, cross over (*transeunt*) into the power of consonants.' Murethach reflects:

readers. Commentaries might of course be copied into a manuscript around the text they were meant to accompany, as in the case of Orleans, Bibliothèque Municipale 295 (248 bis), where the scribe added Murethach's commentary, entering remarks on the *littera* and *sensus* – in other words, those matters most closely connected with the literal meaning of the text – between the lines and reserving more lengthy discussion for the margins. (See L. Holtz, 'Grammairiens irlandais au temps de Jean Scot: quelques aspects de leur pédagogie' in: *Jean Scot Erigène*, ed. Roques, pp. 69–78 at p. 76 n.2.)

39 See B. Bischoff, 'Turning-points in the history of Latin exegesis in the early Irish Church: AD 650–800' in: *Biblical Studies: The Medieval Irish Contribution*, ed. M. McNamara (Dublin 1976), pp. 73–160 (German text in Bischoff, *MS* I, pp. 205–73); V. Law, *The Insular Latin Grammarians*, chapter 6.

40 L. Holtz, 'Sur trois commentaires irlandais de l'*Art majeur* de Donat au IXe siècle', *Revue d'histoire des textes* 2 (1972) pp. 45–72 at p. 71; *Murethach* p. lxii. There are grave chronological difficulties with the identification of BN lat. 11711 (Corbie, *ca* 800), fol. 40rv, with Sedulius' commentary (B. Löfstedt, 'Nochmals zu Sedulius Scottus's Kommentar zu Donatus maior', *Sacris Erudiri* 29 (1986) pp. 119–20): either the dating of the manuscript is too early, or the text is not that of Sedulius' grammar but of the lost parent or some other closely connected work.

41 Latinae uocales omnes et produci et corripi possunt. Quare addidit "latinae"? Cur non ait potius "omnes uocales et produci et corripi possunt" absolute? Ideo addidit "latinae uocales", quia grecae uocales non ita corripiuntur et producuntur sicut latinae (14, 18–22; *Laur.* 155, 15–21; cf. Sed. 11, 1–5).

42 Forsitan quia eius memoriae non occurrit (70, 30f.).

> We know that anyone who crosses over leaves one place, goes through another place, and arrives at a third place. One may then ask what these letters are leaving, or what place they are going through, and what place they arrive at. The answer is that they leave the power of vowels, cross over the frontier zone and immense gulf which separates vowels and consonants, and arrive at the region of the power of consonants.[43]

This meticulous analysis was naturally applied most painstakingly to definitions: their structure was subjected to close scrutiny. We have already seen how the earliest generation of Carolingians catalogued the types of definition and distinguished between *definitio substantiae*, 'definition of the essence', and *definitio soni*, 'definition of the sound'. The *scotti peregrini* take this further. Borrowing their categories (directly or more likely indirectly) from Porphyry's *Isagoge*, as did Peter of Pisa,[44] they ask what each part of speech has in common (*communio*) with the others, and what distinguishes it (*proprietas*). As Sedulius says:

> Note that anyone who gives a definition of anything should define it in such a way that he indicates what it has in common with other things, and singles out for mention its unique characteristics. Donatus observed this in the above definition [of the noun] . . . What it has in common is shown by his saying 'a noun is a part of speech', in that it shares this with all parts of speech. And then when he says 'with case', this is shared with some but not all – with the pronoun and participle only. When he says 'which signifies an object or concept and is either proper or common', this is its unique property.[45]

Although the rediscovery of dialectic is connected with Alcuin and his circle, and there are signs of its application to grammar already in Peter of Pisa's grammar, the common source used by the *scotti peregrini* seems to have been the first grammar to apply it in a thorough-going way. Future research may clarify the question of who borrowed from whom, or alternatively may reveal that it is a case of simultaneous independent development.

A generation later, the commentary found a rather different realisation at the hands of its best-known representative, Remigius of Auxerre (d. *ca* 908). His interests extended far more widely than those of most of his predecessors. The authors he commented upon range from Vergil and Persius to Martianus

[43] Scimus enim, quia omnis, qui transit, locum deserit et per locum uadit, et ad locum peruenit. Unde quaeritur, quid deserunt istae litterae, aut per quem locum transeunt et ad quem perueniunt. Ad quod dicendum, quia deserunt potestatem uocalium, transeunt autem per confinium et differentiam magnam, quae est inter uocales et consonantes, et perueniunt in locum consonantium postestatis (11, 26–32; cf. *Laur.* 153, 55–61). The old-fashioned term 'power' has been used in preference to 'sound-value' or the like in order to retain the play on the meanings of *potestas*.

[44] Cf. also Sedulius' commentary on the *Ars minor* of Donatus, 8, 4–9.

[45] Sed notandum est, quod qui definitionem alicuius rei definit, ita debet definire, ut dicat ipsam partem, quae communis est ei cum altera, et dicat specialem, quam propriam et quam solam habet. Hoc ergo obseruauit Donatus in praedicta definitione . . . Nam commune est in hoc quod dicit 'nomen est pars orationis'; est enim illi commune cum omnibus partibus. Rursus cum dicit 'cum casu', et hoc commune est illi cum quibusdam, non tamen cum omnibus; est enim illi commune cum pronomine et participio. Quod dicit 'corpus aut rem proprie communiterue significans', est enim proprietas illius (65, 49–60; cf. *Laur.* 11, 24–32; Mur. 53, 3–9).

Capella, Caelius Sedulius, Boethius and Bede. Not only Donatus' two grammars but those of Eutyches, Phocas and Priscian (the brief *Institutio de nomine* and the *Partitiones*) attracted his attention.[46] His preoccupations differ strikingly from those of the *scotti peregrini* despite his heavy dependence upon the Irish commentators. The structure of definitions, the *communio* and *proprietas* of the parts of speech, play little part, and the rationale underlying Donatus' choice of wording and sequence interests him only sporadically. The focus is less on understanding *why* Donatus said what he did, on justifying his statements, than on understanding *what* he said. The words themselves – their meaning, etymology and associations – are the focus of attention. His commentaries abound in digressions, as in his careful analysis of how *risus* and *visus* could be said to be the names of invisible things.[47] Where Priscian uses the example *sequester*, Remigius comments: '*sequester* means "mediator". A mediator is someone who brings peace to two parties in disagreement. Hence Moses was a *sequester* between God and human beings'; and later on, *tuber*, 'mushroom': 'a *tuber* is a kind of fungus, that is, a truffle, which is said to spring from thunder'.

Remigius' commentaries on Donatus were more widely read than his other grammatical works, no doubt due to the fact that the basic texts were themselves shortly to fall out of favour. His name became virtually synonymous with grammar in the later Middle Ages, and various works were unjustly ascribed to him, including a popular late medieval parsing grammar (*Dominus quae pars*).

Many scholars besides those known to us by name jotted their learning and insights on the margins of manuscripts of the *Ars maior* and the *Institutiones grammaticae*. It is high time that modern researchers began to investigate what they had to say.

Conclusion

Whereas the influence of seventh- and eighth-century grammarians on subsequent centuries was indirect rather than direct, mediated by the Carolingians, several Carolingian grammarians were still being copied into the twelfth and thirteenth centuries, notably Smaragdus, Remigius and the *Ars Laureshamensis*. The parsing grammar continued to be an enormously productive genre at the elementary level until the close of the Middle Ages. These achievements would be sufficient on their own to guarantee the Carolingians an honourable place in the history of medieval grammar; but to them we must add the rediscovery of Priscian's *Institutiones grammaticae* and the first attempts to apply the new questions and techniques derived from the study of dialectic to language. These were to become the cornerstone of speculative grammar in the thirteenth

46 Editions of the grammatical commentaries are underway by C. Jeudy.

47 Commentary on Priscian's *Institutio de nomine*, BL Cotton Domitian I (St Augustine's, Canterbury, s. x. med.), fol 43v.

century, which without the pioneering work of the Carolingians would have been impossible.

Select bibliography

General

B. Bischoff, 'Die Bibliothek im Dienste der Schule', in: Bischoff, MS III (Stuttgart, 1981) pp. 213–33

H. Gneuss, 'The study of language in Anglo-Saxon England', *Bulletin of the John Rylands University Library of Manchester* 72 (1990) pp. 3–32

M. Gibson, 'Milestones in the study of Priscian, circa 800–circa 1200', *Viator* 23 (1992) pp. 17–33

L. Holtz, *Donat et la tradition de l'enseignement grammatical: étude sur l'*Ars Donati *et sa diffusion (IVe–IXe siècle) et édition critique* (Paris, 1981)

'L'Enseignement de la grammaire au temps de Charles le Chauve' in *Giovanni Scoto nel suo tempo: l'organizzazione del sapere in età carolignia* (Spoleto, 1989) pp. 153–69

'Grammairiens irlandais au temps de Jean Scot: quelques aspects de leur pédagogie', in: *Jean Scot Erigène et l'histoire de la philosophie*, ed. R. Roques (Paris, 1977) pp. 69–78

'Les Innovations théoriques de la grammaire carolingienne: peu de chose. Pourquoi? in: *L'Héritage des grammairiens latins de l'Antiquité aux Lumières* ed. I. Rosier (Paris, 1988) pp. 133–45

'Les Nouvelles Tendances de la pedagogie grammaticale au Xe siècle', Mitellateinisches Jahrbuch 24/25 (1989/1990) pp. 163–73

'Sur trois commentaires irlandais de l'*Art majeur* de Donat au IXe siècle', *Revue d'histoire des textes* 2 (1972) pp. 45–72

V. Law, 'Carolingian grammarians and theoretical innovation', in: *Diversions of Galway. Papers on the History of Linguistics*, ed. A. Ahlqvist (Amsterdam, 1992) pp. 27–37

The Insular Latin Grammarians (Woodbridge, 1982)

'Late Latin grammars in the earlier Middle Ages: a typological history', *Historiographia Linguistica* 13 (1986) pp. 365–80

'Linguistics in the earlier Middle Ages; the Insular and Carolingian grammarians', *Transactions of the Philological Society* (1985) pp. 171–93

R. McKitterick, *The Carolingians and the Written Word* (Cambridge, 1989)

J. Marenbon, *Early Medieval Philosophy (480–1150): An Introduction* (London, 1983)

Texts

Most of the grammars of the Late Latin grammarians were edited by H. Keil, *Grammatici latini*, 8 vols. (Leipzig 1855–60). References to manuscripts and editions of pre-Carolingian grammarians may be found in V. Law, *The Insular Latin Grammarians*. In the list below works about a text are listed under details of the text itself.

Abbo of Fleury, *Questiones grammaticales*, ed. A. Guerreau-Jalabert (Paris, 1982)

Alcuin, *Dialogus Franconis et Saxonis de octo partibus orationis*, PL 101, cols. 854–902

J. Marenbon, *From the Circle of Alcuin to the School of Auxerre: Logic, Theology and Philosophy in the Early Middle Ages* (Cambridge, 1981)

J. R. O'Donnell, 'Alcuin's *Priscian*', in: *Latin Script and Letters A.D. 400–900*, ed. J. J. O'Meara and B. Naumann (Leiden, 1976) pp. 222–35

E. Vineis, 'Grammatica e filosofia del linguaggio in Alcuino', *Studi e saggi linguistici* 28 (1988) pp. 403–29

Ars Bernensis, *GL* 8, 62–142

Ars Brugensis: unedited text in Bruges, Bibliothèque de la ville, 537, fols. 19r–48v

Ars Laureshamensis, ed. B. Löfstedt, CCSL (CM) (Turnhout, 1977)

B. Löfstedt, 'Zwei weitere Handschriften mit der *Ars Laureshamensis*', *Latomus* 39 (1980) pp. 418–20

Clemens Scottus, ed. J. Tolkiehn, *Clementis Ars grammatica, Philologus Supplementband* 20.3 (Leipzig 1928), reviewed by K. Barwick in *Gnomon* 6 (1930) pp. 385–95

Codex quae pars, excerpt printed in *GL* 8, xxi. Found in Berne 207, fols. 17r–18v (19r–20v), and in Leiden Voss. lat. Q. 33, fol. 71rv

Cunabula grammaticae artis Donati, PL 90, cols. 613–32

Distributio omnium specierum nominum inter cathegorias Aristotilis, ed. P. Piper, *Die Schriften Notkers und seiner Schule I: Schriften philosophischen Inhalts*, lxxv–lxxxix (Freiburg, 1882), completed in his 'Zu Notkers Rhetorik', *Zeitschrift für deutsche Philologie* 22 (1890) pp. 277–86

Erchanbert, *Erchanberti Frisingensis Tractatus super Donatum*, ed. W. V. Clausen (Chicago, 1948)

Excerptiones de Prisciano: unedited text in Paris, BN n.a. lat. 586 and other MSS

V. Law, 'Anglo-Saxon England: Ælfric's *Excerptiones de arte grammatica anglice*', *Histoire epistémologie langage* 9 (1987) pp. 47–71, esp. pp. 51–4

Gottschalk, *Oeuvres théologiques et grammaticales de Godescalc d'Orbais*, ed. D. C. Lambot (Louvain, 1945) pp. 353–496

G. R. Evans, 'The grammar of predestination in the ninth century', *Journal of Theological Studies* 33 (1982) pp. 134–45

J. Jolivet, 'L'Enjeu de la grammaire pour Godescalc', in: R. Roques, ed., *Jean Scot Erigène et l'histoire de la philosophie* (Paris, 1977) pp. 79–87

Gottschalk d'Orbais et la Trinité: la méthode de la théologie à l'époque carolingienne (Paris 1958) esp. pp. 23–31, 47–52, 65–74, 178–84

Hildericus of Monte Cassino: partial edition by A. Lentini, *Ilderico e la sua grammatica* (Monte Cassino, 1975)

A. Lentini, 'L'*ars Hilderici* del codice Cassinese 299', *Benedictina* 7 (1953) pp. 191–217

'La Grammatica d'Ilderico documento dell'attività letteraria di Paolo Diacono', *Atti del 2° Congresso Internazionale di Studi sull'Alto Medioevo* (Spoleto, 1952) pp. 217–40

'Ilderico e la sua Grammatica contenuta nel codice Cassinese 299', *Bollettino dell'Istituto Storico Italiano ed Archivio Muratoriano* 47 (1932) pp. 167–72

These three articles reprinted in A. Lentini, *Medioevo Letterario Cassinese: Scritti vari*, Miscellanea Cassinese 57, ed. F. Avagliano (Monte Cassino, 1988)

Hraban Maur, *Excerptio de arte grammatica Prisciani*, PL 111, cols. 613–70
Magnus quae uox, unedited text in Clm 14737, fols. 157v–183v
Murethach, ed. L. Holtz, CCSL (CM) 40 (Turnhout, 1977)

B. Bischoff, 'Muridac doctissimus plebis, ein irischer Grammatiker des IX. Jahrhunderts', in: Bischoff, *MS* II (Stuttgart, 1967) pp. 51–6

C. Jeudy, 'Nouveaux fragments de textes grammaticaux', *Revue d'histoire des textes* 14–15 (1984–5) pp. 131–41

W. Neuhauser, 'Ein bisher unbekannter Textzeuge eines mittelalterlichen Donat-Kommentars (Murethach, 9. Jh.)', *Festschrift für R. Muth* (Innsbruck, 1985) pp. 251–78

Ordo ad cognoscendi nomen: unedited text in St Gall, Stiftsbibliothek, 876, pp. 30–32
Paul the Deacon, *Ars Donati quam Paulus Diaconus exposuit*, ed. A. M. Amelli (Monte Cassino 1899)
Peter of Pisa: excerpts printed in *GL* 8, 161–71

B. Bischoff (ed.) *Sammelhandschrift Diez B: Sant. 66: Grammatici latini et catalogus librorum* (Graz 1973), esp. pp. 27–30

Remigius, *In artem Donati minorem commentum*, ed. W. Fox (Leipzig 1902)
In artem maiorem Donati commentum, *GL* 8, 219–74, supplemented by J. P. Elder, 'The missing portions of the *Commentum Einsidlense* on Donatus' *Ars grammatica*', *Harvard Studies in Classical Philology* 56–57 (1947) pp. 129–60; and M. L. Coletti, 'Un'opera grammaticale di Remigio di Auxerre: il commento al *De barbarismo* di Donato', *Studi Medievali* 26 (1985) pp. 951–67
In Prisciani Institutionem de nomine commentum, ed. M. De Marco, 'Remigii inedita', *Aevum* 26 (1952) pp. 495–517, supplemented by R. B. C. Huygens, 'Remigiana I: Le Commentaire sur Priscien "De nomine"', *Aevum* 28 (1954) pp. 330–42

M. Glück, *Priscians Partitiones und ihre Stellung in der spätantiken Schule. Mit einer Beilage: Commentarii in Prisciani Partitiones in medio aevo compositi*, Spudasmata 12 (Hildesheim 1967)

C. Jeudy, L'*Ars de nomine et verbo* de Phocas: manuscrits et commentaires médiévaux', *Viator* 5 (1974) pp. 61–156

'L'Attitude de Rémi d'Auxerre face aux innovations linguistiques de Jean Scot' in: *Jean Scot écrivain*, ed. G.-H. Allard (Montreal, 1986) pp. 299–310

'L'*Institutio de nomine, pronomine et verbo* de Priscien: manuscrits et commentaires médiévaux', *Revue d'histore des textes* 2 (1972) pp. 73–144

'Israël le grammairien et la tradition manuscrite du commentaire de Remi d'Auxerre à l'*Ars minor* de Donat', *Studi medievali* 18 (1977) pp. 185–248

'Les manuscrits de l'*Ars de uerbo* de Eutychès et le commentaire de Rémi d'Auxerre', in: *Mélanges E.-R. Labande. Etudes de civilisation médiévale (IXe–XIIe siècles)* (Poitiers 1974), pp. 421–36

'Les tradition manuscrite des *Partitiones* de Priscien et la version longue du commentaire de Rémi d'Auxerre', *Revue d'histoire des textes* 1 (1971) pp. 123–43

Sedulius Scottus, ed. B. Löfstedt, CCSL (CM) 40B–C (Turnhout, 1977)

M. W. Haslam, 'On the Sedulius commentary on Donatus' *Ars maior*', *Revue d'histoire des textes* 18 (1988) pp. 243–56

B. Löfstedt, 'Nochmals zu Sedulius Scottus' Kommentar zu Donatus maior', *Sacris erudiri* 29 (1986) pp. 119–20

'Zu Sedulius Scottus' Kommentar zu Donatus Maior', *Sacris erudiri* 27 (1984) pp. 433–42

Septem ΠΟΡΙΟΧΑΙ (sic, for *ΠΕΡΙΟΧΑΙ*): unedited text in Barcelona, Archivo de la Corona de Aragón, Ripoll 59, fols. 257v–288v

Smaragdus, *Liber in partibus Donati*, ed. B. Löfstedt et al., CCSL (CM) 68 (Turnhout, 1986)

A. Dubreucq, 'Smaragde de Saint-Mihiel et son temps: enseignement et bibliothèques à l'époque carolingienne', *Mélanges de la Bibliothèque de la Sorbonne* 7 (1986) pp. 7–36

L. Holtz, 'La Tradition ancienne du *Liber in partibus Donati* de Smaragde de Saint-Mihiel', *Revue d'histoire des textes* 16 (1986) pp. 171–211

J. Leclercq, 'Smaragde et la grammaire chrétienne', *Revue du moyen âge latin* 4 (1948) pp. 15–22

Terminationes nominum, ed. V. Law, 'A French metamorphosis of an English grammatical genre: *declinationes* into *terminationes*', in: *France and the British Isles in the Middle Ages and Renaissance: Essays by Members of Girton College, Cambridge, in Memory of Ruth Morgan* ed. G. Jondorf and D. N. Dumville (Woodbridge 1991) 17–42

Ursus of Beneventum: excerpts printed by C. Morelli, 'I trattati di grammatica e retorica del cod. Casanatense 1086', *Rendiconti della Reale Accademia dei Lincei, Classe di scienze morali, storiche e filologiche*, 5th series 19 (1910) pp. 287–328

Usuard of Saint-Germain, ed. J. M. Casas Homs, 'Una gramàtica inèdita d'Usuard' in *Miscellanea Anselm M. Albareda* 2, Analecta Montserratensia 10 (1964) pp. 77–129

Walahfrid Strabo: unedited texts in St Gall, Stiftsbibliothek 878, pp. 5–18 and 50–69

B. Bischoff, 'Eine Sammelhandscrift Walahfrid Strabos (Cod. Sangall. 878),' in: Bischoff *MS* II (Stuttgart, 1967) pp. 34–51

4

The emergence of Carolingian Latin literature and the court of Charlemagne (780–814)

Mary Garrison

> Inter caenandum aut aliquod acroama aut lectorem audiebat. Legabantur ei historiae et antiquorum res gestae.[1]
>
> While dining he used to listen to some entertainment or to a reader; stories and the deeds of the ancients were read to him.

If history has traditionally belonged to those who tell the stories, or leave records, then literary history has, even more problematically, been the domain of those whose tales and poetry were written down and survived. For the early Middle Ages, the implications of this fact are far-reaching. Thus we learn about the enemies of the Carolingian Empire chiefly through Carolingian historical sources; the extant Carolingian literature records the concerns and diversions of a small elite. Other types of composition (such as songs and stories in the vernacular or texts expressing the viewpoint of the people conquered by Charlemagne) did not make the transition from oral circulation to parchment. Indeed, despite Charlemagne's interest in the *barbara et antiquissima carmina* which told of ancient kings' heroic exploits, no manuscripts preserving such tales survive which can be traced directly or indirectly to Charlemagne's initiative.[2] Latin compositions had better chances of survival since the Latin language was primarily the medium of literate men working in stable institutions, such as cathedrals and monasteries, where texts could be copied and preserved. Nonetheless, many Latin poems can be shown to have perished while others survive in unique manuscripts or fragments only.

The survival of a poem or manuscript from the ninth century to the twentieth therefore reflects the complex interaction of chance and intention.

[1] Einhard, *Vita Karoli*, c. 24, ed. O. Holder-Egger, MGH SRG (Hanover, 1911) p. 29, lines 6–8. The account of after dinner entertainment is ultimately inspired by a similar passage in c. 74 of Suetonius' biography of Augustus in his *Vitae Caesarum*, but Einhard has made several significant omissions which indicate that he is attempting to provide an accurate portrait of his subject.

[2] Einhard, c. 29, p. 33, lines 11–12. On Old High German literature, see chapter 5 below.

The original composition and copying, however, required not only intention, but also a significant investment of effort and material resources. Accordingly, any significant increase in the creation and copying of literature, particularly when it is associated with the wealth and power of a secular court, demands investigation. An increase in literary activity raises questions for the historian which extend beyond literary history to a more abstract level of speculation about the relationship between wealth and power on the one hand, and artistic creation and the ideology which it incorporates, on the other. One might wish to speculate on the way material, political and social circumstances foster the circulation and later transmission of literature and even how these same factors may influence the genre, contents and arguments of compositions. For example, what effect do kings and courts have on the production and preservation of literature? What are the respective roles of wealth, absolute power and personal charisma in inspiring literary creation? How do rulers elicit panegyric? Conversely, what factors limit the scope for expressions of dissent? When and by whom can a king be criticised? Finally, can the language and form of a poem offer clues about the audience or occasion for which it was written?[3] In this connection, it is important to know that Latin poetry written according to the classical rules of prosody, that is, where vowel length rather than stress determined the metrical pattern, was an increasingly artificial, backward-looking form, removed from the stress-patterns and rhythms of the language spoken every day.[4] Although speakers of the languages descended from Latin, which are usually called the emergent Romance vernaculars, might understand such verse fairly easily, rhythmical verse in fact corresponded more closely to the stress system of the spoken language and would probably have been both easier to compose and to understand.[5]

Some of these questions will be addressed in this chapter with reference to the first generation of writers associated with the court of Charlemagne. First, however, a brief characterisation of the Carolingian literary revival will be necessary. In order to explain the sudden emergence of a lively interest in verse-writing at Charlemagne's court from the 780s, I shall discuss the interplay between the literary inspiration derived from earlier poetry and from the poets' immediate circumstances – their careers, their other activities and the nature of their shared life at court. I shall then analyse their perception of themselves and their claims for the status of their craft. Finally, the representation of current events will be considered and the opportunities for literary expressions of dissent will be assessed.

From the time of Charlemagne onwards there is evidence both for a proliferation in the copying of classical and late-antique Latin literature and also for a dramatic increase in the composition of new texts, especially Latin verse, in an

3 On the audience of Carolingian Latin verse, see the discussion by McKitterick, *Carolingians*, pp. 227–32.

4 On the Latin/Romance debate, see the essays in *Latin and the Romance Languages in the Early Middle Ages*, ed. R. Wright (London, 1991).

5 On rhythmical verse, see D. Norberg, *La Poésie latine rythmique du haut moyen âge*, Studia Latina Holmiensia 2 (Stockholm, 1954).

unprecedented range of forms and genres. There are also signs of a new standard of correctness.[6] These developments can be witnessed most dramatically in the king's immediate entourage from the late 770s, although there is some scattered evidence for literary activity in the preceding decades.[7] This increase in the production and survival of verse is especially striking because the evidence for Latin verse-composition anywhere else in the immediately preceding period is sparse. In some areas, verse-composition may have almost died out; in others, the verse that was written simply did not survive. In Spain, for example, no verse survives from the eighth century.[8] For England, the situation is more favourable. Despite the renown of the school and library at York, however, only two or three of Alcuin's poems can be shown to have been written in England.[9] Extant verse from Francia in the first half of the eighth century is no more abundant. For all areas, the very low survival rates for pre-ninth-century manuscripts are partly to blame, although in Francia (and perhaps elsewhere) declining standards of education and Latinity are also implicated, as the low standard of Merovingian charters might seem to indicate. Although it is not possible to trace a continuous tradition of Latin poetry in any region, we can be sure that the skill retained its prestige and continued to be taught, for most of the foreign scholars who assembled at Charlemagne's court would have been trained to write verse in their homelands. The Carolingian achievement in Latin verse-composition therefore results from an increase in production as well as from a significant improvement in the chances for survival. The implementation of *De litteris colendis* and the *Admonitio generalis* must have contributed to the survival of verse by promoting the establishment of scriptoria (albeit for the multiplication of liturgical and doctrinal texts).

The scholars responsible for this verse are referred to as poets in accounts of the literature of the period, but in most cases, verse comprises only a small part of their surviving writings, and they would have thought of themselves primarily not as poets, but as ambassadors, teachers of grammar, experts on time-reckoning and biblical exegesis, advisers to the king or theologians. Thus when Charlemagne eventually rewarded these members of his entourage with bishoprics and abbacies, he did so for their political, administrative and educational services rather than for their verse. Indeed, most of the authors who belong to the first generation of Carolingian scholars wrote many other prose works, and apparently did not concern themselves with the compilation or

6 On book production and copying, see chapter 8 below.

7 M. Manitius, *Geschichte der lateinischen Literatur des Mittelalters* I (Munich, 1911) pp. 243–248; W. von den Steinen, 'Der Neubeginn', in: *Karl der Grosse* II, pp. 9–27; D. Bullough, *The Age of Charlemagne* (1965; reprinted London, 1973) pp. 99–101 and '*Aula Renovata*: the Carolingian court before the Aachen palace', *Proceedings of the British Academy* 71 (1985) pp. 267–301 at pp. 269–77, reprinted in D. Bullough *Carolingian Renewal: Sources and Heritage* (Manchester, 1991) pp. 123–60.

8 See R. Collins, 'Poetry in ninth century Spain', *Papers of the Liverpool Latin Seminar*, 4 (1983) pp. 181–95.

9 For a discussion of literary activity at York in the later eighth century, see M. Lapidge, 'Aedilulf and the School of York', in: *Lateinische Kultur im VIII. Jahrhundert. Traube-Gedenkschrift*, ed. A. Lehner and W. Berschin (St Ottilien, 1990) pp. 161–78, at pp. 163–5. Godman, *Poetry*, pp. 1–4.

publication of their poems after they had been performed or sent to an addressee.[10] In striking contrast to classical authors and to one of the best-known early medieval poets, Venantius Fortunatus, Carolingian poets did not issue collections of their verse.[11] (There are only two known exceptions: for the verse of two authors, Alcuin and Theodulf, such assemblages existed in a single manuscript, but were probably not authorial, and in both cases the manuscript disappeared after its use by a seventeenth-century editor.) In the Carolingian world, the ability to write verse in Latin according to the rules of classical prosody did not make a man a professional poet; that skill was seen simply as the final phase of a thorough education. The challenge of composing Latin verse was naturally greatest for native speakers of a Celtic or Germanic vernacular. Hence it was an Anglo-Saxon, Aldhelm (d. 709), who had created the first *gradus*, or metrical dictionary, to assist non-Latin speakers.[12] Even for native speakers of the languages closely related to Latin, however, special instruction was necessary and this training continued to be regarded as an important goal of Latin education. In other words, the art of writing quantitative Latin verse seems to have been regarded as a prestigious acquisition, but neither such competence nor the careers of the early Carolingian writers qualify them as professional poets. It is therefore all the more significant that they elaborated a discourse about the value of poetry and the importance of the poet – claims which are contradicted by their apparent disregard for the preservation of their verse and by their careers.

These claims, along with the expanded range of forms and genres of Carolingian verse, reflect the availability of influential literary models. Equally important as a stimulus to poetic activity were the new occasions (mainly provided by the court) where verse was required for communication, celebration, entertainment and display. Although few scholars would wish to argue for the enduring literary quality of most of the verse that resulted, all would agree that it emerged in a burst of energy and innovation. Of course, writers continued to turn out poems in the standard genres (such as inscriptions for churches, dedicatory poems and epitaphs – all in demand throughout the Middle Ages), but alongside this predictable trend, important new developments can be traced. Secular epic re-emerged, apparently for the first time in centuries. Similarly, pastoral poems were composed after a centuries-long gap, modelled on Vergil's Eclogues and on the works of the later pastoralists: Calpurnius and Nemesianus. (The latter two authors seem to have been unread

10 On evidence for the performance of Carolingian verse, see below, p. 135.

11 On the transmission of Carolingian verse, see below, nn. 104 and 105; P. Godman, 'Latin poetry under Charles the Bald and Carolingian poetry,' in: *Charles the Bald: Court and Kingdom*, BAR International Series 101, ed. M. T. Gibson and J. L. Nelson (London, 1981) pp. 293–309 at pp. 294–295 provides the most useful and incisive summary of the issues, but note that Modoin's *Egloga* survives in two manuscripts, not one: E. Dümmler, ed. 'Nasos (Modoins) Gedichte an Karl den Grossen,' *Neues Archiv* 11 (1896) pp. 77–91.

12 'Aldhelm's prose writings on metrics', translated by N. Wright, appendix to M. Lapidge and J. Rosier, *Aldhelm: The Poetic Works* (Woodbridge, 1985) pp. 181–219, at pp. 188–9.

for centuries.)[13] There was a new vogue for acrostic poems based, like the pastoral, on late-antique models. The importation of the works of Ennodius of Pavia (d. 521) inspired the use of epistolary adonics[14] and the reintroduction by Alcuin of Boethius' *De consolatione philosophiae* would stimulate new directions in poetry and speculative thought in writers of the ninth century.[15] Finally, perhaps for the first time since Classical Antiquity, there begins to be an appreciable number of poems evoking biographical circumstances and the inner life – homesickness, longing for absent friends, dismay at finding a welcome denied – with striking freshness and poignancy. Beast-fable also returns, but love-lyric is conspicuously absent.

Perhaps the most important single model for Carolingian poets was the life and work of Venantius Fortunatus (*ca* 530–*ca* 600).[16] A prolific writer of epitaphs, panegyrics, poems of consolation or congratulation and other *pièces d'occasion*, Fortunatus had been a true professional poet. He had been able to make his living as an itinerant poet and courtier at several Merovingian royal and episcopal courts before becoming bishop of Poitiers. The eleven-book collection of his verse circulated widely and was closely studied in the early Middle Ages.[17] It decisively influenced the diction and generic range of Carolingian poetry. And it was from their knowledge of Fortunatus that Carolingian writers adopted the conceits of the professional poet. If the first generation of Carolingian authors managed to invent literary personae for themselves as 'court poets', their success certainly owed at least as much to Fortunatus as it did to the example of any classical poet. For in contrast to poets in the ancient world and to Venantius Fortunatus, Carolingian writers of verse could not make a living with their verse and yet nonetheless adopted their predecessors' lofty notions about poetry and even wrote about themselves as if they were professional poets.[18]

Despite the importance of classical and late-antique literary models, the novelty,

[13] On the probable reintroduction of these two authors from Italy by Paul the Deacon see Manitius, pp. 270–1, n.5; see also K. Neff, *Die Gedichte des Paulus Diaconus, kritische und erklärende Ausgabe*, Quellen und Untersuchungen zur lateinischen Philologie des Mittelalters III (Munich, 1908) p. 92, poem 19 (note on lines 7–14).

[14] On the probable introduction of the works of Ennodius to the Carolingian court by Paul the Deacon, see M. Lapidge, 'The authorship of the Adonic verses "ad Fidolium" attributed to Columbanus', *Studi medievali* 3rd ser. 18 (1977) pp. 815–80, at p. 823.

[15] See M. Gibson, 'Boethius in the Carolingian schools', *TRHS* 5th ser. 32 (1982) pp. 43–56 and P. Courcelle, *La Consolation de philosophie dans la tradition littéraire: antécédents et posterité de Boèce* (Paris, 1967) p. 335 and chapter 2: 'Alcuin et la tradition littéraire du IXe au XIIe siècle sur philosophie', pp. 29–66.

[16] See Manitius, pp. 171–81 and P. Godman, *Poets and Emperors: Frankish Politics and Carolingian Poetry* (Oxford, 1987) pp. 1–37.

[17] On the manuscripts and circulation of Fortunatus see W. Meyer, 'Über Handschriften der Gedichte Fortunats', *Nachrichten von der kgl. Gesellschaft der Wissenschaften zu Göttingen, philol.-hist. Kl.* (1908) pp. 82–114; R. Koebner, *Venantius Fortunatus, Beiträge zur Kulturgeschichte des mittelalters und der Renaissance* 22 (Leipzig, 1915) pp. 125–43; G. Glauche, *Schüllekture im Mittelalter, Münchener Beiträge zur Mediävistik und Renaissance-Forschung* 5 (Munich, 1970) pp. 5–6; M. Lapidge, 'Appendix: knowledge of the poems in the earlier period', *Anglo-Saxon England* 8 (1979) pp. 287–95 at pp. 287–88 (including notes) and Godman, 'Latin poetry under Charles the Bald', p. 294.

[18] I have in preparation a study of the patronage of Carolingian verse.

profusion and survival of Carolingian verse are at least equally indebted to the role of Charlemagne's court in fostering poetic endeavour. Although various earlier medieval rulers had had learned men in attendance and received panegyrics, there are no obvious parallels to the number (and far-flung origins) of the scholars Charlemagne had gathered around him by the 780s.[19] For example, Theodoric the Ostrogoth had employed both Boethius and Cassiodorus in administrative capacities, but had eventually executed the former, while the latter's most important literary work was accomplished after he had given up his official duties for monastic retirement. The Merovingian king Chilperic (d. 584) was remembered as a writer of verse by Fortunatus and Gregory of Tours and, indeed, a single poem by him survives, a rhythmical hymn.[20] The Merovingian courts of Chlotar and Dagobert II had attracted literate men including St Audoin (Audoenus or Dado, bishop of Rouen), St Eligius (bishop of Noyon, d. 660) and St Desiderius (bishop of Cahors, d. 655); their correspondence after each had left court for his bishopric might lead one to suspect that they would have been engaged in some literary sport while in the royal entourage, but if they were, no evidence of it survives and none of these bishops is remembered as a writer of verse. Most significantly, the court of the Lombard kingdom in Pavia had maintained an impressive interest in Latin culture, grammar and secular history, but that tradition was fatally interrupted by the fall of the kingdom in 774 and then by the punishments for the revolt of 776. In Francia before the 770s, during the reign of Pippin and the first decade of Charlemagne's rule, the limited evidence for a concern with learning reflects practical and ecclesiastical needs exclusively; the manuscript evidence is legal, liturgical and grammatical,[21] and the associated dedicatory verses are undistinguished, and in one case, largely derivative.[22] In the decade following Charlemagne's conquest of the Lombard kingdom, however, poetry for entertainment and display is associated with the Carolingian court for the first time.

To understand how what had been a peripatetic warrior-court became the setting for the performance and exchange of poetry, we need to consider two developments. First, Charlemagne's itinerant court had become larger and increasingly sedentary. Between the late 770s and the time of the court's final settlement in Aachen in 794, Charlemagne usually spent the whole winter in a small group of favoured palaces – perhaps six.[23] This extended sojourn enabled the king to gather an enlarged retinue and to eat, drink and plan with it for an

19 On literature produced at courts, see R. R. Bezzola, *Les Origines et la formation de la littérature courtoise en Occident (500–1200)* i, Bibliothèque de l'École des Hautes Etudes 286 (Paris, 1944); P. Riché, 'Le Renouveau culturel à la cour de Pepin III', *Francia* 2 (1974) pp. 59–70 and G. Chiri, *Poesia cortese latina: profilo storico dal V al XII secolo* (Rome, 1954).

20 Norberg, *La Poésie latine rhythmique*, pp. 31–40.

21 MGH Poet. I, pp. 89–90; Bullough, *Age of Charlemagne*, p. 79; pp. 99–101; see also Bullough, '*Aula renovata*,' pp. 269–270 and Manitius, pp. 245–7.

22 MGH Poet. I, p. 97 with borrowings from Eugenius of Toledo.

23 J. Fleckenstein, 'Karl der Grosse und sein Hof', *Karl der Grosse* I, pp. 24–50 at pp. 29–30: Herstal, Worms, Quierzy, Thionville, Attigny, Nijmegen.

extended interval of up to four months. If these conditions hardly seem conducive to study and writing, they were nonetheless an improvement over the old routine of continuous movement from one residence to the next throughout the Frankish realm. In the palace, poetry provided entertainment and an outlet for competition, while for courtiers absent on official business, the composition of poetic epistles was one way to stay in touch.

The second and more important factor was the influx of scholars (and their books) from all corners of Europe; their arrival was a consequence of Charlemagne's conquests, administrative and ecclesiastical aspirations and ability to reward talent.[24] The overthrow of the Lombard kingdom brought at least four new men: the first to arrive were probably Fardulf (*ca* 774) and the grammarian Peter of Pisa (by 769). Fardulf came as a captive or hostage, but eventually transferred his allegiance to Charlemagne and was rewarded for exposing the conspiracy of 792 by being appointed to the abbacy of St Denis; he also served as a *missus*. Only four poems by him survive. Peter had been at the Lombard court and was remembered by Einhard as Charlemagne's teacher. He wrote several poetic epistles in Charlemagne's name; these and his other verse show a streak of mocking humour. At approximately the same time, Paulinus joined the court and remained there until 787 when he became patriarch of Aquileia. His works include a versified account of the Trinity, several rhythmical poems, and a book of moral advice for Eric of Friuli, for whom he later wrote a lament (799). Charlemagne rewarded Paulinus' loyalty during the 776 Lombard uprising by granting him land that had belonged to one of the rebels.

That rebellion also led to the arrival of Paul the Deacon, the last of the Lombard scholars to reach Francia. He came to Charlemagne in 782 as a suppliant, begging for the release of his brother who had been taken into captivity in Francia for his part in the uprising seven years earlier. Paul had been educated in Latin and some Greek at the Lombard court in Pavia. Unlike the other members of the court circle, a significant portion of his extant work, prose and verse, predates his move north. His early works give some idea of the range of his interests and the cultivation of his Lombard royal patrons, for they include verse-epitaphs and praise poems for members of the royal family, and in prose, an abbreviated and extended version of the Roman historian Eutropius. The pre-Carolingian corpus of Paul's verse also includes a hymn in praise of St Benedict, and a rhythmical poem relating the history of the world. Paul's poems and letters illustrate his accommodation to the circumstances of his troubled times: while a monk in Italy he complained that his muse disliked the limits of the cloister; from Charlemagne's court he wrote back to his abbot at Monte Cassino, homesick for the monastery, and protesting that no promise of gold, only physical weakness kept him abroad.[25] Charlemagne initially seems to have detained Paul at court by his refusal to release the captive brother. Gradually,

[24] See the discussion by G. Brown, chapter 1 above.
[25] K. Neff, *Die Gedichte des Paulus Diaconus*, pp. 71–2.

however, the conqueror of the Lombards won Paul's loyalty, as the sequence of riddling verse-epistles and greetings exchanged in the early 780s demonstrates (Peter served as Charlemagne's poetic amanuensis). Paul went on to write various works while in Francia: a history of the bishops of Metz (influential as a model for all subsequent episcopal histories and itself based on the *Liber pontificalis*),[26] epitaphs for members of the royal family, a grammatical work consisting of extracts from Pompeius Festus, and a commentary on the Benedictine Rule. Eventually Charlemagne permitted Paul to return to Monte Cassino (probably in 786 or 787). From there he remained in touch with the king by letter and assembled a homiliary at his request. Although Paul had at first been virtually a hostage because of his need to appease his brother's captor, by the time of his departure Charlemagne had clearly succeeded in inspiring him with enthusiasm for his projects.

The Anglo-Saxon Alcuin joined this group sometime after 782 and remained at court until 796 when he became abbot of Tours. Unlike the Lombards, he seems to have left his native land voluntarily, invited by Charlemagne after a meeting in 781 in Parma. On several occasions Alcuin would feel compelled to defend his decision to leave the community in York where he had been raised; to his friends there, he insisted that his service to the Church, rather than the rewards proffered by Charlemagne, were keeping him abroad; in a letter to a Frankish colleague he explained that a holy man with the gift of prophecy had foretold his continental mission.[27] Charlemagne's teacher in rhetoric, dialectic and astronomy, Alcuin was remembered by Einhard as the 'most learned man anywhere to be found'. A host of students followed Alcuin to the continent, and some, also to Tours, including Frithugils (Fredegisus), Joseph Scottus, Hwita (Candidus or in German, Wizo). Alcuin himself was a prolific poet as well as an outstanding teacher; in addition to his theological and didactic works, he wrote verse for every possible occasion. Through his letters one can trace his reactions to Charlemagne's activities and to the political turmoil in late eighth-century Northumbria; his loyalty to his native York and his need to remain in touch with his former colleagues and students are also evident.

Theodulf, a Goth from Spain, joined the royal entourage probably sometime in the early 780s after he had been forced from his homeland, perhaps through exile or banishment.[28] He experienced banishment again in 817 when he was suspected of complicity in the revolt against Louis the Pious led by Bernhard of Italy. During the intervening years, he served as a *missus* on a judicial investi-

[26] L. Duchesne (ed.), *Liber pontificalis* (2 vols. Paris, 1886–92; vol. 3 with Duchesne's corrections and additions, ed. C. Vogel, Paris, 1957); trans. Raymond Davis, *The Book of Pontiffs. Liber Pontificalis.* Translated Texts for Historians: Latin Series 5 (Liverpool, 1989) and 13 (Liverpool, 1992).

[27] MGH Epp. IV, Alcuin letters nos. 43, 47 and 200 (pp. 87–9; 91–2; 330–3).

[28] E. Dahlhaus-Berg, *Nova Antiquitas et Antiqua Novitas: typologische Exegese und Isidorianisches Geschichtsbild bei Theodulf von Orléans*, Kölner historische Abhandlungen 23 (Cologne, 1975); D. Schaller, 'Philologische Untersuchungen zu den Gedichten Theodulfs von Orléans', *DA* 18 (1962) pp. 13–91; K. Liersch, 'Die Gedichte Theodulfs, Bischofs von Orléans', diss. phil. Halle-Wittenberg (Halle, 1880); L. Nees, *The Tainted Mantle* (Philadelphia, 1991).

gation in the south of France in 798 and as bishop of Orleans from 800. As a poet, Theodulf was perhaps the most versatile and accomplished of his generation; his verse bears the stamp of his familiarity with Ovid and Prudentius, as well as of his satirical temperament and his penchant for literary feuds.

Although native Franks undoubtedly played an important role in Charlemagne's administration, the Frankish contribution to the literature of the 780s and 790s was small – in part, no doubt, because Charlemagne recruited his Frankish helpers primarily from among the laity, in part, perhaps, because educational standards in Francia had sunk to a low level, as the very earliest Carolingian dedicatory verses imply.[29] Angilbert, courtier, *missus*, emissary to Rome and later lay-abbot of Saint-Riquier, was educated at court and given the by-name Homer by Alcuin. Contemporaries (Modoin and Fiducia) praised his poetic skill, but only two significant poems by him survive. Less than half a dozen compositions can be securely attributed to him and another group of his poems was rewritten and passed off as the work of a late ninth-century bishop.[30] Angilbert's poems and prose letters together reveal a shaky grasp of grammar and prosody not up to the standards of his teachers. Another Frank, Einhard, was educated at the monastery of Fulda and sent to court by his abbot in, or shortly after, 794. Although contemporaries regarded him as an accomplished poet, not a line of his verse survives; instead, he is remembered for his biography of Charlemagne. The Frankish contribution to Carolingian Latin literature increased in later decades as students in monastic schools began to reap the fruits of the revived interest in learning and the newly advertised prestige of poetry.[31]

Charlemagne's court was international and the scholars there were animated by feuds and one-upmanship as well as by a sense of common purpose and an awareness of their status as a new elite. On the basis of surviving evidence, Alcuin was excluded from the literary sport of Peter and Paul although he and Paulinus got along well. Theodulf despised several Irish scholars and was never given a nickname by Alcuin, although the jocular tone of some of Alcuin's letters to him indicates that he did not remain an outsider. The shared life at court therefore provided all of these learned expatriates with opportunities for collaboration as well as rivalry, and even invective, and these possibilities are dramatised in some entertaining poems associated with the court, which range in date from the early 780s to the mid-790s.[32] These poems are the chief evidence for the mentality and diversions of a versatile and extraordinarily lively and energetic group. The designation 'coterie poetry' signals an important common

[29] MGH Poet. I, pp. 89–90.

[30] Manitius, pp. 545–6; L. Traube, 'karolingische Dichtungen', in *Schriften zur Germanischen Philologie* I, ed. M. Roediger (Berlin, 1888) pp. 46–109 at pp. 57–60.

[31] For an account of later developments, see P. Godman, 'Louis the Pious and his poets', *Frühmittelalterliche Studien* 19 (1985) pp. 239–89.

[32] See K. Liersch, *Die Gedichte Theodulfs Bischofs von Orleans* (Halle, 1880) p. 13; D. Schaller, 'Vortrags- und Zirkulardichtungen am Hof Karls des Grossen,' *Mittellateinisches Jahrbuch* 6 (1970) pp. 14–36 and his 'Poetic rivalries at the court of Charlemagne', in *Classical Influences on European Culture, 500–1500*, ed. R. R. Bolgar (Cambridge, 1973) pp. 151–7; Godman, *Poetry*, pp. 9–13.

feature: the compositions are destined for the amusement of a limited contemporary audience of the author's learned friends and colleagues. Accordingly, they are characterised by insider jokes, allusions to earlier verse, the use of by-names – all traits that indicate their shared literary and social background.

The earliest example in this category is a verse epistle composed by Alcuin and sent from England probably in 781, before Alcuin joined the royal entourage.[33] The poem uses the literary device of a personified letter which is instructed to bring greetings and even a supply of grammar books to Alcuin's scattered continental acquaintances, emigrés from England and contacts from Alcuin's own previous voyages abroad. Presumably the poem itself and the books would have been conveyed by a single messenger. When the letter reaches the court it is instructed to greet Charlemagne and some of his attendants in terms which demonstrate that the criticism of others' verse by members of the court was already a routine peril:

> Hic proceres patres fratres percurre, saluta
> Ante pedes regis totas expande camenas,
> Dicto multoties: 'Salve, rex optime, salve.
> Tu mihi protector, tutor, defensor adesto,
> Invida ne valeat me carpere lingua nocendo
> Paulini, Petri, Albrici, Samuelis, Ione,
> Vel quicumque velit mea rodere viscera mursu [sic];
> Te terrente procul fugiat, discedat inanis.'[34]

> Run round to the great men, fathers, and monks, and greet them;
> Before the feet of the king, sing out all the songs you know,
> Many times over say to him: 'Greetings best King, hail.
> Be a protector to me, a guardian, and stand by as my defender
> Lest someone's envious tongue should harm me with its carping –
> Paulinus' or Peter's, Alberic's, Samuel's or Jonas' –
> Or whoever else might want to bite me to the quick.
> With you to terrify them, let them run off and depart without
> accomplishing any harm.

Additional evidence for the censure of verse comes from a poem addressed to Angelram of Metz (d. 791) by an otherwise unidentifiable figure called 'Fiducia'. In this text, Fiducia claims that Charlemagne himself had corrected Fiducia's faulty composition. The personified poem concludes:

> Me tetigit Carulus dominus de cuspide pinnae
> Errore confect [a] scriptio nostra fuit.[35]

> Lord Charles touched me with the tip of his quill-pen
> For our composition was confected with error.

[33] Alcuin, poem 4, MGH Poet. I, pp. 220–23; trans. H. Waddell, *More Latin Lyrics from Vergil to Milton* (London, 1976) pp. 150–5. For the precise generic description, *Stationsgedicht*, see D. Schaller, 'Vortrags- und Zirkulardichtung', pp. 19–20. The poem survives in a manuscript copied at St Denis, the location of its final addressee (Schaller, p. 19, no. 18).

[34] MGH Poet. I, p. 222, Alcuin poem 4, lines 37–44.

[35] Neff, pp. 181–3 and MGH Poet. I, p. 77, poem 44, lines 21–2; I have emended *confectus* to *confecta*.

More competent poets also feared back-biting; thus Peter to Paul the Deacon:

> Dentibus egregium tu desine rodere fratrem
> Iratus regis qui numquam cernitur aula.[36]
>
> You, hold off from gnawing the good brother [Alcuin or Peter?] with your teeth,
> Who never is seen to be angry by the king's court.

Ermold to Pippin:

> Carmina nostra tuo, princeps, tutamine posco
> Ante tuos vultus sint recitata, pie;
> Quisquis cupit nostros molimine rodere versus,
> Audiat a vobis: 'Parce Nigellus abest.'[37]
>
> I beg, good king, that with your protection
> Our poems may be recited in your presence;
> Whoever wants to gnaw our poetry violently
> Let him hear from you: 'Hold off! Nigellus is not here.'

Modoin of Autun:

> Forsan et obiciet crimina lingua nocens,
> Livor edax tacito sic secum murmure dicat.[38]
>
> And perhaps a hurtful tongue will bring accusations
> Just as gnawing envy should mutter to himself under his breath.

Another early example of Carolingian coterie poetry consists of a spirited sequence of riddle poems and challenges exchanged between 782 and 786 by Peter of Pisa, Paul the Deacon and Charlemagne. Two poems in this group illustrate the tenor of their poetic sparring vividly. First Peter writes to Paul on Charlemagne's behalf, welcoming him to court and extravagantly praising his learning and knowledge of Greek.[39] Paul's crisp reply reveals that he knows Peter to be the author of the first poem. He rejects the outrageous praise but belies his assertions of modesty by appending a Latin translation of a Greek epigram.[40] Other poems in the series show Charlemagne challenging Paul to

[36] Neff, p. 86, poem 17, lines 29–30, with discussion in the notes about the identity of the *egregium fratrem*.

[37] Ermoldus to Pippin, lines 215–18 of '*Ad eundem Pippinum*', ed. with Fr. trans., E. Faral, *Ermold le Noir, poème sur Louis le Pieux et épîtres au Roi Pépin*, Classiques de l'histoire de France au moyen age 14, 2nd edn (Paris, 1964), pp. 218–33 at p. 232, lines 215–18.

[38] Modoin's *Ecloga*, prologue, lines 10–11; MGH Poet. I, pp. 384–91; the text was re-edited by Dümmler after the discovery of a new manuscript: 'Nasos (Modoins) Gedichte an Karl den Grossen', *Neues Archiv* 11 (1896), pp. 77–91; ed. R. P. H. Green, *Seven Versions of Carolingian Pastoral*, Reading University Medieval and Renaissance Latin Texts (Reading, 1979) pp. 14–20 and pp. 62–9; D. Korzeniewski, ed., trans., *Hirtengedichte aus Spätrömischer und Karolingischer Zeit: Marcus Aurelius Nemesianus, Severus Sanctus Endelechius, Modoinus, Hirtengedicht aus dem Codex Gaddianus* (Darmstadt, 1976) pp. 74–101. Quotation here from prologue, lines 10–11 and see Green, p. 69, for note on line 10. Subsequent references to citations from this poem will be given from the text of Dümmler's *Neues Archiv* edition (unless otherwise specified) in the form 'Ecloga, lines . . . ' Partial text and translation in Godman, *Poetry*, pp. 190–6.

[39] Neff, pp. 60–2, poem 12; Godman, *Poetry*, pp. 9–10 and pp. 82–6.

[40] Neff, pp. 64–8, poem 13; Schaller, 'Vortrags- und Zirkulardichtungen', Godman, *Poetry*, pp. 9–10 and pp. 86–9.

to figure out a riddle overnight, and Paul stalling for time by replying with additional riddles. One of the riddles indicates that Charlemagne had already begun to be referred to as David.[41]

Two slightly later ventures show how a similar spirit of competition and collaboration animated other members of the court. Although the 'coterie' provides the circumstantial background for these poems, they are not, strictly speaking, 'coterie poetry', but epitaphs and acrostic panegyrics. Both projects also illustrate the role of classical models and the rivalry between Theodulf on the one hand, and Alcuin and his students on the other.

The earlier example consists of a group of seven elaborate acrostic poems dedicated to Charlemagne and transmitted together in a ninth-century manuscript (s. ix[1] Bern Burgerbibliothek 212).[42] On the basis of internal evidence, the compositions can be dated to the decade 780–90. They contain acrostics, telestichs and mesostichs which form separate messages. For the Carolingian authors, as for their late antique model, acrostic poems (*carmina figurata*, they would have called them) are primarily a medium for visual display and pious commonplaces. Of the seven poems, one is by Theodulf, two are by Alcuin and four are by Joseph Scottus, one of Alcuin's Irish pupils. All seven poems are directly inspired by the similar compositions of Publilius Optatianus Porfyrius, a fourth-century court poet who wrote a series of such poems devoted to Christian themes and to the praise of the emperor Constantine. Dieter Schaller's exhaustive investigation of these Carolingian acrostic poems, the manuscript and the text history of Porfyrius suggests that it was Alcuin who brought the text of Porfyrius to the continent and assembled his imitations and Joseph's for presentation to Charlemagne in this order: poem by Alcuin–four poems by Joseph–another poem by Alcuin. Soon afterwards Theodulf was invited to take up the challenging assignment and his poem was appended to the group. Surprisingly for a poem in a form that is constraining and derivative, Theodulf includes a poignant autobiographical allusion which indicates that he had only recently arrived at court: 'Since I am an exile from catastrophes without measure . . .'[43] Alcuin prefaced the new compositions with a copy of the old Porfyrian models, revealing that he did not fear comparison. This compilation was subsequently recopied at Saint-Amand to produce the manuscript Bern Bürgerbibliothek 212, the sole surviving witness to these Carolingian experiments.

The contest to write an epitaph for Pope Hadrian had higher stakes.[44] After

41 Neff, p. 105, poem 22.

42 D. Schaller, 'Die karolingischen Figurengedichte des Cod. Bern. 212', in: *Medium Aevum Vivum, Festschrift für Walter Bulst*, ed. D. Schaller and H. R. Jauss (Heidelberg, 1960), pp. 22–47 and R. McKitterick, *The Frankish Kingdoms under the Carolingians* (London, 1983) pp. 212–13. On Alcuin's figure-poems, see also H. B. Meyer, 'Crux, Decus es Mundi: Alkuin's Kreuz- und Osterfrömmigkeit', in: *Paschatis Sollemnia: Studien zur Osterfeier und Osterfrömmigkeit*, ed. B. Fischer and J. Wagner (Freiburg, 1959) pp. 96–107.

43 *quia sum inmensis casibus exul:* MGH Poet. I, pp. 480–2, Theodulf, poem 23, line 28. As an additional example of parallel literary endeavour, note that Alcuin and Theodulf both also wrote versions of the fable of the cock and the fox: MGH Poet. I, p. 262 (Alcuin poem 49) and p. 550 (Theodulf, poem 50).

44 The epitaphs written for Hadrian are published in MGH Poet. I, pp. 489–90 and pp. 113–14. Schaller, 'Vortrags- und Zirkulardichtungen', p. 28 proposed the competition theory; Liersch discussed the two

Hadrian's death on Christmas Day 795, Charlemagne apparently wanted to offer a special commemoration to the pope who had been a personal friend, and so in 796 both Alcuin and Theodulf composed appropriate epitaphs. Eventually a magnificently inscribed marble slab was sent to Rome.[45] Its perfectly executed square capital lettering was inspired by classical models and qualifies as the finest epigraphy made north of the Alps for centuries. As it turned out, it was Alcuin's text, not Theodulf's which was chosen for this impressive monument.

There is some evidence for an earlier instance of poetic emulation connected with the writing of epitaphs, for two commemorative epitaphs of the sixth-century poet Venantius Fortunatus survive, one by Alcuin, and the other by Paul the Deacon.[46] Paul's poem was composed sometime before 786. Years later in the *Historia langobardorum* he would explain how, when he came to pray at the grave of Fortunatus, he had been invited to write an epitaph by the abbot of Saint-Hilarius, Poitiers.[47] The occasion which prompted Alcuin to supply an epitaph for his most influential poetic forebear is unknown, but the wording indicates that this epitaph, too, was intended for display near Fortunatus' burial place; moreover, tenuous but undeniable similarities of diction suggest that either Alcuin or Paul was familiar with the other's work before undertaking his own; unfortunately the direction of influence cannot be established.

The latest and most entertaining examples of true coterie poetry are known as *Zirkulardichtungen* or circulating verse epistles.[48] Most extant examples date from after the time of the court's settlement in Aachen. Internal evidence from these poems shows that they were sent to court by their absent authors; the text was passed around for private reading by a select group before a public recitation. Representatives of this genre supply incidental information about court hierarchy, ceremonial and diet, and combine worshipful greetings and panegyric to Charlemagne with humorous and even, in Theodulf's poems, aggressive allusions to other members of the court. In 794 or 795 Angilbert used this form to send his effusive greetings to Charlemagne, the royal family, and their attendants.[49] His poem includes several lofty-sounding refrains. The use of a refrain is indebted to the intercalary verses in Vergil's eighth eclogue; the words of the refrain, however, echo Psalm 107:3. Thus the poem begins with the line '*Surge, meo domno dulces fac, fistula, versus,*' ('Arise, shepherd's pipe, make

epitaphs and the Theodulf–Alcuin rivalry at pp. 21–2. See also L. Wallach, *Alcuin and Charlemagne* (Ithaca, N.Y., 1959), pp. 178–97.

45 For illustrations of the inscription, see D. Bullough, *The Age of Charlemagne* (1965; 2nd edn, London, 1973), plate 19, facing p. 67 and S. Morison, *Politics and Script: Aspects of Authority and Freedom in the Development of Graeco-Latin Script from the Sixth Century B.C. to the Twentieth Century A.D.* (The Lyell Lectures, Oxford, 1957) ed. N. Barker, (Oxford, 1972) pp. 143–4, pp. 170–2 and illustration at p. 172 (plate 104). The slab itself can still be seen in Rome.

46 Alcuin, MGH Poet. I, p. 326, poem 99 section 17 and Paulus, poem 29, Neff, pp. 121–2; also printed in MGH Poet. I, pp. 56–7, poem 19.

47 *Historia langobardorum*, ed. L. Bethmann and G. Waitz, MGH SRL (Hanover, 1878), section II.xiii, p. 80.

48 D. Schaller, 'Poetic rivalries at the court of Charlemagne', pp. 151–7 and 'Vortrags- und Zirkulardichtung', pp. 14–36; Liersch, pp. 34–46; Godman, *Poetry*, pp. 10–13 and trans. at pp. 118–21, pp. 112–19, and pp. 150–63.

49 MGH Poet. I, Angilbert poem 2, pp. 360–3; text, translation in Godman, *Poetry*, pp. 112–19.

sweet verses for my Lord'), and that line recurs, with variations, eight more times. In addition, the line '*David amat vates, vatorum est gloria David*' ('David [i.e. Charlemagne] loves poets, David is the glory of the poets') is repeated ten times in the space of 108-line poem, celebrating the close relationship between the king and his 'poets' and perpetuating the fiction that a king who never learned to write was a connoisseur of Latin verse.

In 796 Alcuin and Theodulf each sent poems of this genre to the court. Alcuin's poem, which is fragmentary, contains the elaborate greetings, hyperbolic praise of Charlemagne and catalogue of court personnel which one would expect, and also shares with Angilbert's poem a concern with the status of poetry. Alcuin's anxiety however is more practical than ideological, for he is writing to complain about the lack of proper instruction in poetry since his retirement from the court to Tours. His poem also contains two characteristically Alcuinian features. The first of these is a reference to porridge, apparently a favourite food:

> Ipse Menalca coquos nigra castiget in aula,
> Ut calidos habeat Flaccus per fercula pultes.[50]
>
> And let Menalcas reprove the cooks in the dark hall
> So that Flaccus can have his warm porridge in courses.

In an earlier poem, the circular letter of pre-781, Alcuin had fondly recalled a meal of porridge with butter and honey.[51]

The second Alcuinian element is some criticism of the curriculum of the school at Aachen, to which I shall refer later when discussing the literature of dissent. Alcuin protests that all the other branches of learning have their representatives at the palace, but not poetry:

> Quid Maro versificus solus peccavit in aula?
> Non fuit ille pater iam dignus habere magistrum,
> Qui daret egregias pueris per tecta camenas?
> Quid faciet Beleel Hiliacis doctus in odis?
> Cur, rogo, non tenuit scolam sub nomine patris?[52]
>
> Was Maro the poet the only one who committed some sin at court?
> Or did that father not deserve to have a teacher
> Who would give choice verses to the students at court?
> What will Besaleel [i.e. Einhard], who knows the Iliadic odes do?
> Why, I ask, did he not keep the school in place of his father [i.e.
> Alcuin]?

50 MGH Poet. I, Alcuin poem 26, pp. 245–6, lines 48–9. Porridge (or a poultice) as a medicinal preparation is also mentioned earlier in this poem, at line 14.

51 See discussion of this poem above, p. 120. MGH Poet. I, pp. 220–3, Alcuin poem 4, lines 9–10: *In Traiect mel compultim buturque ministrat: / Utpute non oeleum nec vinum Fresia fundit.*' 'In Utrecht he [Hadda] serves you honey with porridge and butter, / Since Frisia doesn't pour forth wine or oil.'

52 MGH Poet. I, p. 245, Alcuin poem 26, lines 18–22 – an excerpt which contradicts the view expressed in the *Vita Alcuini* and followed by some modern scholars that Alcuin grew hostile to secular verse in his old age.

Such open criticism of Charlemagne's policy is unparalleled in the verse of Alcuin's contemporaries.[53] Although the unwritten code of deference at court permitted poets to compete and even to carp at each other, praise and respectful familiarity were the only registers available for addressing or describing the king. These literary conventions may reflect the social and ceremonial conduct of the king's retinue.

Theodulf's verse-epistle to the court outdoes its precursors in several respects. The praise of Charlemagne is extravagant:

> Te totus laudesque tuas, rex, personat orbis[54]

> The entire world sounds forth your praises

> O facies, facies ter cocto clarior auro,
> Felix qui potis est semper adesse tibi[55]

> O countenance, countenance more splendid than thrice-purified gold,
> Blessed the one who can always be near you

The hyperbole continues: the king's intellect, strength and beauty are derived respectively from David, Solomon and Joseph. The magnitude of his cleverness and prudence exceed the size of the largest rivers in the world. In contrast to Angilbert and Alcuin who had provided static images of the other members of the royal family, Theodulf animates his catalogue by recounting how obediently the king's sons take their father's gloves and sword, how charmingly the daughters bring flowers and fruits and then entertain their father with conversation, jokes and laughter. For Theodulf's antagonists outside the royal family, however, there is satire. Alcuin is a target twice when his pedantic riddling sessions with Charlemagne and his meal of porridge accompanied by wine or beer – or both – are caricatured.[56] Then abruptly Theodulf interjects: 'Good riddance, porridge and heaps of curds!'[57] Theodulf's next victim, a fat and stupid warrior, is depicted in a comic interlude. This character, Wibod, is apparently unable to understand the poem. He reveals his irritation, cursing at the absent Theodulf. When the king calls to him he makes his loud and clumsy way across the hall.[58] His discontent is mild compared to the tantrum of Theodulf's arch-enemy, a short irascible and competitive Irishman.

> Haec ita dum fiunt, dum carmina nostra leguntur,
> Stet Scotellus ibi, res sine lege furens,
> Res dira, hostis atrox, hebes horror, pestis acerba.[59]

[53] P. Lehmann, 'Das literarische Bild Karls des Grossen vornehmlich im lateinsichen Schrifttum des Mittelalters', in P. Lehmann, *Erforschung des Mittelalters; ausgewählte Abhandlungen und Aufsätze*, vol. 1 (Stuttgart, 1959), pp. 154–207 at pp. 155–6, observes that absolutely all contemporary Latin historical and occasional poetry depicts Charlemagne panegyrically and that critical characterisation is entirely absent.

[54] MGH Poet. I, pp. 483–90, Theodulf poem 25, line 1; trans. Godman, *Poetry*, pp. 150–63.

[55] Ibid., lines 13–14.

[56] Ibid., lines 131–41 and 191–9.

[57] Ibid., line 197; on *Speisemetaphorik*, compare Schaller, 'Vortrags- und Zirkulardichtung', p. 29.

[58] MGH Poet. I, pp. 483–90, Theodulf poem 25, lines 205–12.

[59] Ibid., lines 213–15.

While these things are going on, while our poem is read aloud,
Let the Irish twerp stand there, a thing raging without law
A dire thing, a savage foe, a sluggish horror, a bitter plague.

Nunc gemitus tantum, nunc fera verba sonet,
Nunc ad lectorem, nunc se convertat ad omnes
Adstantes proceres nil ratione gerens.[60]

By turns he utters groans, by turns, uncultivated words,
Now let him face the reader, now, all the assembled magnates,
Behaving with no rhyme or reason.

The poem concludes with the end of the banquet and a much needed apology:

At tu posce pio reditum mea fistula regi,
Et cunctis veniam, quos ciet iste iocus.[61]

But you my pipe, ask the good king for your return
And beg indulgence from all whom this jest incited.

Despite the differences in their background and training and their potentially divisive rivalries, many authors of Carolingian court poetry share certain distinctive claims about the significance of their learned activities. Firstly, they make lofty-sounding statements about the value of poetry and the poet's craft and secondly, they articulate the perception that they are engaged in a renewal of Antiquity a number of times. Neither discourse can be taken at its face-value, but some discussion of each may be helpful in order to show what these claims reveal about the writers' self-awareness and their relationship to their literary heritage and contemporary circumstances.

Claims about the value of poetry are often associated with the representation of Charlemagne as a connoisseur of poetry and learning. Angilbert's poem on the court (discussed above, pp. 123–4) repeated the line 'David [i.e. Charlemagne] loves poets, David is the poets' glory' nine times in a poem barely over one hundred lines in length, simultaneously flattering the king and exalting the importance of poetry at court.[62] An Irish poet at Charlemagne's court (*Hibernicus Exul*) asked his muse what poetry was worth and composed a reply for the muse which linked poetry's eternity with royal magnificence:

Regumque obrizo candor dum fulminat auro,
Munera Musarum saeclis aeterna manebunt.
His regum veterum clarescunt inclita gesta,
Praesentum et saeclis narrantur facta futuris.[63]

60 Ibid., lines 224–5.
61 Ibid., lines 237–8, interpreting *reditum* as a discreet reference to patronage; I am grateful to Neil Wright for this point.
62 MGH Poet. I, pp. 360–3; Godman, *Poetry*, pp. 112–19.
63 MGH Poet. I, pp. 396–9, lines 32–5 with a debt to Vergil and Ovid in line 33; Godman, *Poetry*, pp. 174–9.

As long as the splendour of kings flashes out in pure gold,
The everlasting gifts of the Muses [i.e. poetry] will endure through the ages.
With verse, the glorious deeds of ancient kings are celebrated
And the accomplishments of men of the present age are related to future centuries.

Modoin, probably less than ten years later, composed a similar debate about the value of poetry; this time a young poet-narrator champions his own cause against the discouraging counsels of a grouchy old poet.

Spreta adeo domino non sunt mea carmina magno:
Ille solet calamo silvestri ludere saepe,
Nec vilem tantus iudex me iudicat esse.[64]

My songs [i.e. pastoral, low style] are not so despised by the great lord,
He has a habit of often playing the woodland flute,
Nor does that great judge deem me to be so vile

Crede, satis gratas dominis consistere Musas
Praecipuis meritis hinc esse memento poetas.[65]

Believe me, poetry remains pleasing to the masters,
Remember that there are poets with outstanding rewards for that.

Theodulf insisted that his poetry could influence, not just please:

. . . sonet Theodulfica Musa,
Quae foveat reges, mulceat et proceres.[66]

Let Theodulf's Muse sing,
In order to cheer kings and charm magnates.

What is the material basis for these claims? From the point of view of text-history, statements about the eternity of verse seem to be a literary conceit divorced from reality. The transmission of Carolingian verse is poor and unsystematic; poems often travel individually or in miscellanies, rather than in authorial compilations; they are often transmitted without attributions; many survive in one manuscript only, and it is not unusual to find poems crammed into left-over space in codices devoted to other topics.[67] For example, the statement by *Hibernicus Exul* quoted above, Alcuin's verse-epistle to his continental colleagues (above, p. 120) and the Rhythm on the Avars (discussed below, pp. 132–3) all survive in single manuscripts only. In short, even if we allow for the ravages of time, the manuscript transmission of Carolingian verse implies a nonchalance about the value of poetry and its survival directly

64 Modoin *Ecloga*, I, lines 45–7.
65 Ibid., lines 95–6.
66 MGH Poet. I, p. 488, Theodulf poem 25, lines 204–5; Godman, *Poetry*, pp. 160–2.
67 The transmission and circulation of Carolingian verse require further investigation. Some studies are: E. Dümmler, 'Die handschriftliche Ueberlieferung der lateinischen Dichtungen aus der Zeit der Karolinger', *Neues Archiv* 4 (1878/9) pp. 87–159; 239–322; 511–582; Traube, 'Karolingische Dichtungen', *Schriften zur Germanischen Philologie* I, ed. M. Roediger (Berlin, 1888); Godman, 'Latin poetry under Charles the Bald,' pp. 293–309 at pp. 294–5.

contradicted by certain of the poets' claims. Apparently verse was intended to address and entertain contemporaries, not posterity.[68]

The internal references to patronage do nothing to contradict the impression that court poetry was ephemeral and occasional; they also reveal the gradual emergence of a discourse about poetry as an autonomous activity of professionals. The first court poets make few assertions about the value of their verse and rarely mention rewards for verse overtly, although poetry and hospitality from the king may be part of an exchange and poetry may serve as a tribute gift to the king. Thus Paul the Deacon implies that poetry is no match for riches:

> Nulla mihi aut flaventis est metalli copia
> aut argenti sive opum, desunt et marsuppia.
> Vitam litteris ni emam, nihil est, quod tribaum.
>
> Pretiosa quaeque vobis dona ferant divites
> . . .
> meo pura tribuetur voluntas in munere.[69]
>
> I have no heap of golden metal
> Nor of silver, nor of riches; I do not even have any money-bags,
> Unless I buy my keep with letters, there is nothing I could give.
>
> Let wealthy men bring all sorts of precious gifts to you,
> . . .
> From me, pure (good) will is bestowed as a present.

In the early 780s, both Theodulf and Paul implied that their willingness to compose verse depended upon their happiness at court. That scholars received rewards is evident from Einhard's and Notker's stories about the king's willingness to support learning, but poetry does not seem to have held a special place. Both Alcuin and Paul the Deacon wrote letters to the monastic communities they had left, protesting that it was not Charlemagne's wealth which detained them in Francia – but with no specific reference to poetry.

The students of the first court poets, though still conscious of the novelty of their role, were less reticent; in their verse, explicit references to remuneration from verse, and to verse as an annual gift to the king emerge.[70] Thus Modoin's Eclogue triumphantly likens Carolingian patronage to the patronage system of the Roman world; after recalling the rewards received by Vergil, Lucan and Ennius, Modoin announces:

> . . . haec etiam nostro nunc tempore cerne:
> nam meus ecce solet magno facundus Homerus
> Carminibus Carolo studiosis sepe placere.

68 These observations apply primarily to occasional and historical verse rather than to compositions intended to be inscribed in stone.

69 Neff, poem 13, pp. 64–8, stanza 7 and stanza 8 (excerpted); text, trans., Godman, *Poetry*, pp. 88–9.

70 Contrast *Hibernicus Exul*'s claims for the golden splendour of verse with Joseph Scottus' *carmen figuratum* where the thing brighter than gold is the four virtues, *Sapientia*, *Spes*, *Fides*, *Veritas*: MGH Poet. I, p. 154, Joseph poem 4, acrostic verses.

Ni Flaccus calamo modulari carmina nosset,
Non tot praesentis teniusset premia vitae.
Theodulfus gracili iam dudum lusit avena:
Plurima cantando meruit commertia rerum.[71]

See once again things are thus even in our age today
For my eloquent Homer [i.e. Angilbert] is accustomed
To please great Charles often with accomplished songs;
If Flaccus [i.e. Alcuin] had not known how to play songs on his flute
He would not have had so many of the rewards of this present life;
Now for a long time Theodulf has played a graceful pipe,
By singing he has earned great gains of affairs.

The catalogue of poets rewarded is an established literary commonplace.[72] To graft the Carolingian poets on to a list comprising Lucan, Vergil and Ennius, as Modoin has done, is to assert the prestige of contemporary verse with extraordinary confidence, a confidence which other writers of verse seem to share. Verse is no longer a poor substitute for riches as it had been for Paul, but a possible tribute-gift in its own right. *Hibernicus Exul* in the Tassilo-poem[73] and later, the Irish Dicuil, in an extended astronomical work, both present their compositions as tribute-gifts to the king with none of the diffidence evinced earlier by Paul.[74] Together with the quotations above, their statements indicate that the verse-writers succeeded in promoting their notion of poetry (or panegyric at least) as a prestige commodity. Or, more cynically, taking the king's point of view, one might conclude that the Carolingian capacity to exact poetry is a literary corollary to their improved ability to monopolise the plunder gained in battle.[75]

Statements about the *renovatio* of learning and the revival of Antiquity occur in prose and verse alike and evoke an exuberant sense of possibility and new beginnings. The classical by-names of many members of the court seem to reflect their cultural aspirations most directly. Alcuin, apparently the originator of this custom, called himself Flaccus (after the poet Horace), and occasionally Publius Albinus; Angilbert was Homer and Audulf, the cup-bearer, Menalcas; Pippin was Julius, Riculf of Mainz, Flavius Damoetas; Charlemagne was addressed on one occasion as Flavius Anicius Carlus and had other designations as well. Although many of the original court poets had already dispersed by the

71 Modoin, *Ecloga* I, lines 84–90.

72 Green, p. 77, in a note on line 71 of Modoin's poem, cites Ovid, *Tristia* 4.10.41 and Venantius Fortunatus, *Vita Martini*, 1.14; to these I would add Ovid, *Amores* 1.15.9ff. and compare *Versus Fiduciae* (Neff, pp. 182–3), lines 16–19.

73 On Hibernicus Exul, see below, p. 132.

74 On Dicuil, see Manitius, pp. 647–53; and M. Esposito, 'An Irish teacher at the Carolingian court: Dicuil', *Studies* 3 (Dublin, 1914) pp. 651–76; 'An unpublished astronomical treatise by the Irish monk Dicuil', *Proc. Royal Irish Academy*, 26 C (1907) pp. 378–446 and 'A ninth-century astronomical treatise,' *Modern Philology* 18 (1920–21) pp. 177–188, with the reference to the annual tribute at p. 182. These articles have been reprinted in: *Irish Books and Learning in Mediaeval Europe* ed. M. Lapidge (Aldershot, 1990) as article VI, article VII (the text) and article VIII.

75 T. Reuter, 'Plunder and tribute in the Carolingian Empire', *TRHS* 5th ser., 35 (1985) pp. 75–94 at p. 79.

time of the court's transfer to Aachen in 794, the building activities there seem to have made a great impression on the writers who were present. In Modoin's poetic transformation, Charlemagne becomes Palaemon and Aachen a new Rome:

> Prospicit alta novae Romae meus arce Palemon
> Cuncta suo imperio consistere regna triumpho
> Rursus in antiquos mutata secula mores,
> Aurea Roma iterum renovata renascitur orbi.[76]
>
> From the high citadel of a new Rome my Palemon sees
> That all the regna are joined in his empire through victory,
> That the age has been changed back into the culture of Antiquity,
> Golden Rome is restored and reborn to the world.[77]

Similarly, in the anonymous text known as the Paderborn Epic (composed in or after 799),[78] Charlemagne is likened to Aeneas and a retrospective account of the building of Aachen likens it to Rome: 'second Rome', 'Rome-to-be', or just 'Rome' are the designations employed.[79] With more intellectual than architectural concerns, Alcuin wrote to Charlemagne in 799: 'For if many men pursue the excellent subject of your wish, perhaps a new Athens may be established in Francia – indeed, one better by far; for this one, ennobled by the teaching of the Lord Christ, surpasses all the wisdom of academic striving . . . '[80]

Finally in his prologue to Einhard's *Vita Karoli*, Walahfrid Strabo looked back nostalgically to the revival of learning sponsored by Charlemagne as a Golden Age:

> Of all kings, Charlemagne was the most eager in his search for wise men and in his determination to provide them with living conditions in which they could pursue knowledge in all reasonable comfort. In this way Charlemagne was able to offer to the cultureless, and I might say, almost completely unenlightened territory of the realm which God had entrusted to him, a new enthusiasm for all human knowledge. In its earlier state of barbarousness, his kingdom had hardly been touched by any such zeal, but now it had opened its eyes to God's illumination. In our own time the thirst for knowledge is disappearing again: the light of wisdom is less and less sought after and is now becoming rare again in most men's minds.[81]

76 Modoin, *Ecloga* I, lines 24–8.

77 Godman, *Poets and Emperors*, p. 85; the theme of new or restored Rome had been a commonplace in earlier panegyrics; see below, notes 83 and 84.

78 *The Paderborn Epic*, also known as 'Karolus Magnus et Leo Papa' has been edited by Dümmler, MGH Poet. I, pp. 366–79 and by H. Beumann, F. Brunhölzl, W. Winkelmann, *Karolus Magnus et Leo Papa, Ein Paderborner Epos vom Jahre 799* (Paderborn, 1966); partial text and translation in Godman, *Poetry*, pp. 197–207.

79 See O. Zwierlein, 'Karolus Magnus – alter Aeneas?' in *Literatur und Sprache im Europaische Mittelalter: Festschrift für Karl Langosch*, ed. A. Önnerfors, J. Rathofer, F. Wagner (Darmstadt, 1973) pp. 44–52.

80 MGH Epp. IV, p. 279, letter 170, lines 22–6, addressed to Charlemagne in 799: 'si, plurimis inclitum vestrae intentionis studium sequentibus, forsan Athenae nova perficeretur in Francia, immo multo excellentior. Quia haec Christi domini nobilitata magisterio omnem achademicae exercitationis superat sapientiam.'

81 Einhard, *Vita Karoli*, ed. O. Holder-Egger MGH SRG (Hanover, 1911); Walahfrid's pref. at pp. xxviii–xxix; Eng. trans. L. Thorpe, *Two Lives of Charlemagne* (Harmondsworth, 1969) pp. 49–50.

A critical evaluation of these statements about poetry and renewal shows that they are not part of a single coherent ideology, and are far less programmatic than one might assume. For example, the characteristic renaissance-claims only occur in poems and letters addressed to Charlemagne[82] and might be seen as a special idiom for the flattery of a cultivated king. The designation 'second Rome' had been used in earlier panegyric poetry (of Constantinople)[83] and the image of the rebirth of Rome had occurred in royal panegyrics by Venantius Fortunatus.[84] As for Aachen, the New Rome and Athens: no form of the names for Aachen current in the eighth century could be accommodated in a Latin hexameter. Furthermore, the proliferation of by-names introduced by Alcuin included far more nicknames derived from the Old Testament, the animal world, and early Christian times than from Classical Antiquity. The nicknaming, then was just one part of a search for models and images from the past intended not to recreate another era, but rather as part of a search for transhistorical models which would express otherwise unarticulated dimensions of present circumstances. Some scholars have suggested that the names were meant to add a tone of informality to the court and classroom and indeed, Alcuin himself stated that they were given for familiarity. At the same time, the names might also be seen as the trappings of a new elite.

These strictures on the interpretation of the examples suggest that the poets' claims must be taken with a grain of salt. In other words, their lofty pronouncements are significant, but do not articulate any unified theory of Rome, Poetry and Greatness. Nonetheless, even if we dismiss some statements as a special type of panegyric and reject the notion that the poets were consciously trying to revive Antiquity, the novelty of the Carolingian literary revival is striking and stands out all the more when viewed in historical perspective. As the brief survey of its antecedents should have demonstrated, the awareness of new beginnings was fully justified.

The poetry so far surveyed sheds light on poets' presentation of themselves, the court and their high claims for the status of poetry. Charlemagne was represented as learned, but genial, and even in Theodulf's circular poem on the court, intended for recitation after the victory over the Avars, the harsh realities of warfare were bypassed for a splendid imaginary scene of Charlemagne receiving tribute from as yet unconquered peoples. In other words, despite the literary feuds, coterie poetry offers a genteel dinner-party image of the court in which the fiercest disputes were personal or intellectual.

Some contemporary historical poems can offer an alternative perspective on

[82] H. Frederichs made this shrewd observation in *Die Gelehrtenkreis um Karl den Grossen in ihren Schriften, Briefen und Gedichten* (*Teildruck*) (printed extract of an otherwise unpublished Berlin dissertation) (Berlin, 1931) p. 36.

[83] W. Hammer, 'The concept of the New or Second Rome in the Middle Ages', *Speculum* 19 (1944) pp. 50–62; Corippus' use of the phrase in his *In laudem Justini* discussed at p. 52.

[84] Godman, *Poets and Emperors*, pp. 20 and 85.

current affairs and on Charlemagne's rulership. The most important of these are: a poem on the 777 conversion of the Saxons;[85] a fragment attributed to *Hibernicus Exul* on the overthrow of Tassilo of Bavaria in 787;[86] a rhythmical poem on Pippin's victory over the Avars in 796;[87] and finally, the *Paderborn Epic* (also known as *Karolus Magnus et Leo Papa*) which describes events of 799.[88]

Almost without exception, these texts present difficult problems of dating, attribution and generic classification. All share an astonishing lack of interest in historical specificity. For example, the background of Tassilo's revolt is nowhere explained and his disobedience is accounted for by diabolical intervention. The Avar Rhythm presents a dramatic, ballad-like account of the way the cowardly Avar Kagan, or king, is intimidated by someone on his own side into surrendering; Pippin's success is credited to the intervention of St Peter. Extravagant praise for the Franks and a concern to demonstrate the Christian legitimation of their conquests were more important to these authors than journalistic detail. In any case, if the intended audience consisted of participants in these various expeditions, they would not need to be told what they had done, but would want to hear a celebration of their achievement. So, for example, the poem on the conversion of the Saxons wanders into an extended series of epic similes devoid of concrete information when it evokes Charlemagne's forced baptism of these enemies: he has turned wolves into sheep, crows into doves and so on, providing the poet with a chance to display his zoological knowledge while glorifying the conversion.[89]

The Saxon poem and the Avar poem both offer grotesque accounts of non-Christian practices. The Saxons' holy offerings are described as sordid gifts, and they are said to sacrifice bulls on gore-covered altars; barbarous frenzy (*barbarica rabie*) is the motive for their devotions.[90] The Avars are accused of desecrating Christian holy places:

> Multa mala iam fecerunt ab antico tempore,
> fana dei destruxerunt atque monasteria,
> vasa aurea sacrata, argentea, fictilia.
>
> Vestem sanctam polluerunt de ara sacratissima,
> linteamina levitae et sanctaemonialium
> muliebris tradita suadente demone.[91]

85 Saxons: MGH Poet. I, pp. 380–1.

86 Tassilo: MGH Poet. I, pp. 396–9; partial trans., Godman, *Poetry*, pp. 174–9.

87 Avars: MGH Poet. I, pp. 116–17; text, trans., Godman, *Poetry*, pp. 187–91; trans., H. M. Jones in P. S. Allen, *The Romanesque Lyric: Studies in its Background and Development from Petronius to the Cambridge Songs* (New York, 1928), pp. 231–3.

88 Paderborn Epic: MGH Poet. I, pp. 366–79; *Karolus Magnus et Leo Papa, Ein Paderborner Epos vom Jahre 799*, ed., trans. H. Beumann, F. Brunhölzl, et. al. (Paderborn, 1966); partial text, trans. Godman, pp. 197–207 and contrast Alcuin poem 45 (MGH Poet. I, pp. 257–9) and Theodulf, poem 32 (MGH Poet. I, pp. 523–4) which concern the same events.

89 MGH Poet. I, p. 380, lines 48–54 – i.e. seven lines out of the poem's seventy-five.

90 Saxons: MGH Poet. I, p. 380, lines 30–4.

91 MGH Poet. I, p. 116, stanzas 2 and 3; Godman, *Poetry*, pp. 186–9. Following Godman's text, I have emended *tradata* to *tradita*.

From ancient times they have done many evil deeds,
they have destroyed the monasteries and shrines of God,
their holy vessels of gold, silver and clay.

They have fouled the holy cloth of the most sacred altars;
At the persuasion of the Devil, they have given over
The linen vestments of deacons and nuns to their women.

In three of the poems, the political use of terror is depicted, even glorified. In both the *Paderborn Epic* and the poem on the conversion of the Saxons, terror as an instrument of religious and political coercion is presented in heroic terms. Unlike Alcuin, who had expressed doubts about the efficacy of forced conversion, the author of the Paderborn Epic had no such qualms:

Quod mens laeva vetat suadendo animusque sinister,
Hoc saltim cupiant implere timore coacti;
Quod non sponte prius miseri fecere rebelles,
Exercere student avide instimulante timore.
Qui pius esse fero iam dudum more repugnat,
fitque timore pio pius impius ille coactus.[92]

What the contrary mind and perverse soul refuse to do with persuasion,
Let them leap to accomplish when compelled by fear,
What wretched rebels at first did not do of their own accord,
They eagerly rush to accomplish, with fright goading them.
The one who in savage fashion for a long time refused to be pious,
That impious one, is made pious when coerced by holy fear.

In the poem on the conversion of the Saxons, a scattering of phrases borrowed from the *Aeneid* adds epic colouring. Here again, victory is achieved through intimidation and divine favour:

Hanc Carolus princeps gentem fulgentibus armis
Fortiter adcinctus, galeis cristatus acutis,
Arbitri aeterni mira virtute iuvatus,
Per varios casus domuit, per mille triumphos,
Perque cruoriferos unbos, per tela duelli,
Per vim virtutum, per spicula lita cruore
Contrivit, sibimet gladio vibrante subegit.[93]

Charles the Chief [subdued] this nation with weapons glittering,
Stoutly armed, crested with sharp helmets,
Assisted by the miraculous strength of the Eternal Judge,
He subdued [them] with various destructions, with a thousand triumphs
With gore-spattered shields, with spears of combat,
With the might of virtues, with blood-smeared javelins,
He ground (them) down and subjugated (them) to himself with his sword
flashing.

92 MGH Poet. I, p. 367, lines 41–6; Godman, *Poetry*, pp. 200–201.
93 MGH Poet. I, p. 381, lines 40–6; with echo of *Aen.* I.204 in line 43.

Finally, in the Avar Rhythm, terror is the motive for all of the poem's limited action and the Avars are portrayed as laughable cowards. The Avar king's adviser is '*satis pavens*', 'panicking quite a lot'; and the king himself, '*undique perterritus*', thoroughly terrified.[94] If the celebration of might and terror seems sinister from our contemporary perspective, it may be worth stressing that the Carolingian writers were merely applying to Charlemagne an earthly version of the terror and majesty of some representations of God in the Old Testament.[95]

Alfred Ebenbauer's recent study of Carolingian historical poetry has suggested that these poems attempt in various ways to transpose secular Frankish history to the level of *Heilsgeschichte*.[96] (*Heilsgeschichte* is the one-word term which encapsulates the aims of much medieval historical writing: it means salvation history, the interpretation of history stressing God's saving grace.) Ebenbauer's suggestion is persuasive.[97] From a comparative perspective, however, it may also be illuminating to consider these poems as a type of 'frontier literature'. Just as the participants in the American westward expansion believed in 'Manifest Destiny' and their divine right to the land,[98] so too, the Franks, from the 750s onwards, had encountered and eventually espoused the notion that they were the Chosen People.[99] Both groups misunderstood the behaviour of the peoples whose land they were expanding into and demonised their adversaries in songs. And finally Western songs and stories about Daniel Boone, Davy Crockett, Kit Carson and other frontier heroes, like these Frankish texts, see the conflict between settlers and natives in unambiguously heroic dimensions: a complex historical process is distilled into a simple conflict between adversaries: heroes with supernatural attributes and enemies of exaggerated treachery and iniquity, whether Saxon or Native American. In both instances, 'frontier literature' transmits stories from the perspective of the victors only. Curiously, the conquering Franks and the North American homesteaders also expressed similar cultural aspirations: just as Aachen was a new Rome or

94 MGH Poet. I, p. 116–17, stanzas 6 and 10; Godman, *Poetry*, p. 188.

95 On the Carolingian appropriation of the Old Testament image of God as the terrifying Lord of Hosts, see E. Rieber, 'Die Bedeutung alttestamentlicher Vorstellungen für das Herrscherbild Karls des Grossen und seines Hof', unpublished Ph.D. dissertation (Tübingen, 1949), p. 105.

96 A. Ebenbauer, *Carmen Historicum: Untersuchungen zur historischen Dichtung im Karolingischen Europa* I, Philologica Germanica 4 (Vienna, 1978).

97 In a review of Ebenbauer's book, T. M. Andersson objected: 'Carolingian verse is chiefly remarkable as a burst of literary energy, not as an arm of sacred history', *Speculum* 55 (1980) p. 115.

98 For an attitude to land apparently similar to the American notion of 'Manifest Destiny', note that the author of the Tassilo-fragment refers to the Bavarian territory as if it was already Frankish: MGH Poet. I, p. 398, line 92: '*nostris arvis*.' Compare the sentiment expressed in Robert Frost's poem 'The Gift Outright' which begins: 'The land was ours before we were the land's / She was our land more than a hundred years / Before we were her people . . . ' and ends with the lines: 'But still unstoried, artless, unenhanced, / Such as she was, such as she would become', *The Poetry of Robert Frost*, ed. E. C. Lathem (1969; reprinted London, 1971) p. 348.

99 On the identification of the Franks with the Chosen People of the Old Testament, see H. H. Anton, *Fürstenspiegel und Herrscherethos in der Karolingerzeit*, Bonner Historische Forschungen 32 (Bonn, 1968) p. 419 and note 266. The comparison emerges in the papal letters of the *Codex Carolinus* and the prologue of the *Lex Salica*. See also J. L. Nelson, 'The Lord's anointed and the people's choice: Carolingian royal ritual', in: *Rituals of Royalty: Power and Ceremonial in Traditional Societies*, ed. D. Cannadine and S. Price (Cambridge, 1987) pp. 137–80 at p. 149.

Athens, so too, Americans in their westward expansion established numerous Troys, Athenses, and Spartas, Arcadias and Carthages, and even went one step farther than Alcuin's circle in using Seneca, Vergil, Homer and Euclid as first names, rather than merely as by-names.[100]

Because these Carolingian historical poems bear a superficial resemblance to battle and victory poems from other cultures, medieval and modern, their role may seem less alien than, say, the custom of reciting circular letters to the court after a feast. Nonetheless, it may be worth looking for more explicit testimonies about their original diffusion or performance. What was their function? The Tassilo-poem poet begins with a description of the annual tribute-giving ceremony[101]. The leading men of the world approach the king with great loads of gold and jewels; the poet, at a loss, asks his Muse what he can give and she suggests that he should sing poetry. To dispel his doubts, she makes grandiose claims for the eternity of poetry and its capacity to celebrate the deeds of ancient kings and to transmit the accomplishments of the present age to future centuries (a nice irony in a poem that has survived in one manuscript only).[102] From this reference and from the one by Dicuil mentioned earlier, we can assume that poems might be offered to the king and performed at great assemblies such as the one for the collection of tribute in May. These were occasions for the king to dramatise his special status by festive crown-wearing, and the recitation of a victory poem would certainly have been appropriate. There is no incontrovertible proof that any of these poems was performed, but most seem to have been intended for recitation. Recall Einhard's comments about Charlemagne's fondness for reading and story-telling at meals. The fact that Theodulf's court poem (discussed above, pp. 125–6) was intended for performance after the Avar victory and that it depicted the occurrence during a feast of an imaginary tribute-giving ceremony supports the theory. Moreover, the colloquial language of the Avar Rhythm suggests that it was destined for a wider audience than just the court scholars. Finally, some evidence for liturgical commemoration of Carolingian battles has been discovered in two calendars from the eighth and ninth centuries, but the extent and precise nature of this practice have yet to be elucidated before its possible relationship with the performance of these poems can be a subject of speculation.[103]

The probable function and performance of these historical poems make it likely that they would have been composed and declaimed not long after the

[100] Perhaps the significance of this is just that one harks back to origins at the beginning of any new undertaking. On the use of classical names for people and places during the westward expansion of the US, see W. A. Agard, 'Classics on the midwest frontier', in: *The Frontier in Perspective*, ed. W. D. Wyman and C. B. Kroeber (Madison, Wis., 1957) pp. 165–83 at pp. 166–72.

[101] MGH Poet. I, p. 396 and Godman, *Poetry*, pp. 174–7. See Reuter, 'Plunder and Tribute', and Nelson, 'The Lord's anointed', p. 166. Also M. Esposito, 'A ninth-century astronomical treatise', *Modern Philology* 18 (1920–1) pp. 177–88, with the reference to the annual tribute at p. 182.

[102] MGH Poet. I, p. 397, lines 34 to 40; Godman, *Poetry*, p. 178.

[103] M. McCormick, *Eternal Victory: Triumphal Rulership in Late Antiquity, Byzantium, and the Early Medieval West* (Cambridge, 1986) pp. 360–2. The manuscripts are Willibrord's Calendar (BN lat. 10837) from Echternach and a Lorsch calendar from the second half of the ninth century (Vat. pal. lat. 485).

events they recount, for they would lose their relevance if too many seasons (and other exploits) had elapsed. There would be no point in celebrating Charlemagne's third-to-last victory when the story of a more recent triumph was waiting to be told. And a poem on the glorious 777 conversion of the Saxons would not be welcome after the Saxons' subsequent uprisings. In whatever way the poems were performed, we might imagine that they had a function analogous to someone's slide show of a recent trip – an excuse for participants and their friends to recall their adventures while confirming the solidarity of the group.

To judge from their transmission, these compositions were of relatively little interest to others. The Tassilo poem survives in one manuscript only (s. x or xi); the Avar Rhythm is also transmitted in a single manuscript – the nearly contemporary grammatical compilation, Berlin, Staatsbibliothek Diez. B. Sant. 66, where the text is scrawled on an empty leaf.[104] *The Paderborn Epic* too exists today in one manuscript dated to the end of the ninth century; but it was evidently available for study at court since Ermold the Black made extensive use of it in a poem in honour of Louis the Pious. The poem on the conversion of the Saxons survives in two manuscripts only. Additional manuscript witnesses for these poems may have perished or may await discovery, but the overall impression to be gained from the text histories of these court-poems is unlikely to be significantly revised: they were apparently ephemeral compositions destined for performance on a particular occasion. In contrast, evidence from medieval library catalogues shows that more extensive circulation was possible for at least one Latin heroic poem on a theme of more general and enduring interest, since versions of another (probably) Carolingian poem, the secular heroic epic known as the *Waltharius*, can be shown to have been available in several monastic centres.[105] The *Waltharius* is based on legendary material which enjoyed an almost pan-European diffusion in the Middle Ages; it tells the story of the escape-journey of Walter of Aquitaine from the court of Attila and the fights that ensue. Walter travels with Hiltgunt, a Burgundian princess, who had also been a hostage at the court of Attila. The poem concludes with a series of bloody combats in a mountain pass; Walter is wounded but survives to marry Hiltgunt and rule his own people.

The historical poems surveyed, all in different ways, present a smug and exultant portrait of Charlemagne's activities, and the view of poetry promoted by writers associated with Charlemagne implies that verse is the appropriately

104 There is a facsimile of the manuscript edited by B. Bischoff: *Sammelhandschrift Diez B. Sant. 66, Grammatici latini et catalogus librorum*, Codices selecti phototypice impressi, vol. XLII (Graz, 1973); the Avar Rhythm occurs on fols. 127–8.

105 For the text of the poem: MGH Poet. VI, i, pp. 24–85; *Walter of Aquitaine, Materials for the Study of his Legend*, translations, F. P. Magoun and H. M. Smyser (New London, 1950) at pp. 5–37; also *Waltharius and Ruodlieb*, ed., trans. D. M. Kratz (London, 1984). On the poem's tradition, P. and U. Dronke, *Barbara et antiquissima carmina* (Barcelona, 1977). For the date, see P. Dronke, 'Waltharius and the "Vita Waltharii"', *Beiträge zur Geschichte der deutschen Sprache und Literatur* 106.3 (1984) pp. 390–402 and *Barbara et antiquissima carmina*, pp. 66–79.

ostentatious gold frame for the portrait. The quantity of hyberbolic praise in this literature combined with the scarcity of criticism suggests that perhaps it was Charlemagne's might which both inspired poetry and excluded the possibility for dissent.

To find any criticism of the Carolingians, we must look farther afield, to later generations, to prose, and to other genres.[106] Even though it is not always easy to specify the genre of medieval Latin texts, the occasions for which they were composed exerted a decisive influence on the contents. Disagreement was usually confined to prose, or to texts not, as far as we can determine, intended for public recitation. The genre of *Fürstenspiegel*, or 'Mirrors for princes', which enjoyed a vogue at this time was one place for moral instruction.[107] Writers of a later generation discovered that laments and allegory offered safe poetic channels for expressing discontent: hence the otherwise unknown poet Angelbert's grim account of the Battle of Fontenoy in 841, fought by the sons of Louis the Pious: Lothar I and Pippin II against Louis the German and Charles the Bald,[108] or Florus of Lyons' apocalyptic complaint, disguised in the form of a lament, on the ensuing division of the empire in the 840s.[109]

When we look for earlier evidence of dissent, Alcuin stands out immediately – not only for his threatening letters to contemporary kings of Northumbria, written when he was safely separated from them by sea, but also for his confidence in disagreeing with Charlemagne in discussion, as Notker reports, as well as in prose letters. Notker (chapter 9), who had never met Alcuin, reported that Alcuin alone dared disagree with the emperor. Alcuin's occasionally assertive tone in letters to Charlemagne corroborates the report. For example, Alcuin argued emphatically against imposing the tithe too soon on the newly converted Saxons and dared advise against an expedition into Benevento in 800–801.[110] His advice was cautiously but firmly phrased; he nonetheless felt compelled to justify his presumption: 'perhaps somebody (may) comment: "Why does that man meddle in other people's business?" But he does not know that nothing concerning your prosperity is foreign to me, which I declare that I prize above the health of my body or the length of my life.'[111] After his retirement to Tours, Alcuin had complained to Charlemagne about the

[106] On the universally positive depiction of Charlemagne by contemporaries, see Lehmann, 'Das literarische Bild Karls des Grossen vornehmlich im lateinischen Schrifttum des Mittelalters', pp. 155–6; on positive and negative literary depictions of Louis the Pious, see H. Siemes, 'Beiträge zum literarischen Bild Kaiser Ludwigs des Frommen in der Karolingerzeit', unpublished Ph.D. dissertation (Freiburg-in-Breisgau, 1966) and Godman, 'Louis the Pious and his Poets'.

[107] Anton, *Fürstenspiegel und Herrscherethos in der Karolingerzeit*; L. K. Born, 'The *specula principis* of the Carolingian Renaissance,' *Revue belge de philologie et d'histoire* 12 (1933) pp. 583–612.

[108] MGH Poet. II, pp. 138–9; trans. Godman, *Poetry*, pp. 262–4; H. Waddell, *Mediaeval Latin Lyrics* (1929; reprinted New York, 1948) pp. 102–5 and trans., H. M. Jones in P. S. Allen, *The Romanesque Lyric*, pp. 231–3.

[109] MGH Poet. II, p. 559–64; trans., Godman, *Poetry*, pp. 264–73.

[110] On the tithe, MGH Epp. IV, p. 289, letter 174; for Alcuin's disapproval of the expedition to Benevento, ibid., letter 211.

[111] MGH Epp. IV, p. 352, letter 211: 'Forte quislibet dicit: "Quid ille homo alienis se ingerit rebus"? Non agnoscit nihil mihi alienum vestrae prosperitatis esse debere; quam super salutem corporis mei vel vitae meae longaevitatem diligere me testor.'

curriculum at Aachen in both prose and verse. For Alcuin, then, the capacity to criticise the king seems to have been a result of personal standing. In the Carolingian verse of Paul the Deacon, who might have harboured real bitterness against a king who had crushed the Lombard kingdom and imprisoned his brother, anti-Frankish sentiment is absent – and not surprisingly, for Paul came to court as a suppliant. In a prose letter written from court to his former monastic community, and in his *Historia langobardorum* (written for an Italian audience) however, Paul's true feelings can be detected,[112] and the contrast between those two texts and his court poetry signals the ambivalence which could be evoked by Charlemagne's might and charisma.

If any of the authors discussed in this chapter could be invited to participate in the historiographical debate about the Carolingian Renaissance, they would surely defend the term. For as we have seen, the perception that these authors are participating in a renewal of Classical Antiquity was articulated a number of times in Carolingian poetry. Yet the emulation of classical models is neither the most important inspiration for the first generation of Carolingian poets, nor the source of what is most lively and distinctive about that verse, for its vitality results from the picture that emerges of strong personalities responding to the challenges of each other's verse, and to the stimulus of their unique historical situation – rather than from enduring literary quality. To be sure, some critics have found little enough to admire. As Laistner commented, 'the first impression made on the mind of the reader who peruses the four massive volumes of Carolingian poetry in the *Monumenta germaniae historica* is inevitably one of fatigued disappointment . . . '[113] But as a lens through which to view figures and events which we encounter otherwise only in prose and documentary sources, Carolingian verse can offer unique insights into the aspirations, self-understanding and squabbles of a talented, influential and international coterie, for the Carolingian verse that survives refracts their concerns into an extraordinarily vivid – if narrow – spectrum. At the same time, the emergence of this verse as well as its circulation and transmission to our own century – all must be explained as consequences of Charlemagne's wealth, absolute power and concern for religion and education.[114]

112 See D. Bullough, 'Ethnic history and the Carolingians: an alternative reading of Paul the Deacon's *Historia langobardorum*', in: *The Inheritance of Historiography 350–900*, ed. C. Holdsworth and T. P. Wiseman, Exeter Studies in History 12 (Exeter, 1986) pp. 85–105 at pp. 96–7, reprinted in D. Bullough, *Carolingian Renewal: Sources and Heritage* (Manchester, 1991) pp. 97–122.

113 M. L. W. Laistner, *Thought and Letters in Western Europe AD 500 to 900*, revised edition (London, 1957) p. 330. P. S. Allen was no more enthusiastic: 'I may not speak for another, but I believe the inevitable sensation which comes from first reading in the volumes of the *Poetae aevi Karolini* is one of bitter disappointment. It is perhaps as if one's hand had reached out half unconsciously for a book of poems and had picked up a table of logarithms instead . . . For the purpose of appreciative comment and aesthetic criticism, the poetry of AD 580–880 is still an insoluble mess.' P. S. Allen, *The Romanesque Lyric* (North Carolina, 1928) p. 214.

114 Acknowledgements: I should like to thank Julia Crick, Matthias Kahl, Michael Lapidge, Rosamond McKitterick, Andy Orchard, Julia Smith and Neil Wright for suggestions and criticisms; of course, I am responsible for all errors that remain. I am also deeply indebted to the work of Dieter Schaller.

Select bibliography

Reference works

D. Schaller and E. Könsgen, *Initia carminum latinorum saeculo undecimo antiquiorum* (Göttingen, 1977) – this gives an alphabetical list of the *incipits* of Latin verse written before the eleventh century; for each text there is bibliographical information about manuscripts, editions, translations and recent scholarly discussions. For fuller information about the lives, works, printed editions and textual transmission of individual authors, see the articles in *Die deutsche Literatur des Mittelalters: Verfasserlexikon*, ed. K. Ruh, et al. (Berlin, 1978–). Extremely brief, but also useful as a guide to editions and translations is the *Tusculum Lexikon griechischer und lateinischer Autoren des Altertums und des Mittelalters* ed. W. Buchwald, A. Hohlweg and O. Prinz (Munich, 1982). For a concise survey of Charlemagne in medieval Latin verse, see D. Schaller, 'Karl der Grosse in der Dichtung, i. Mittellateinische Literatur', in *Lexikon des Mittelalters* V (Munich, 1991) cols. 961–2.

Primary texts

Most Carolingian Latin verse can be found in the volumes of the MGH Poetae latini medii aevii series: MGH Poet. vols. I (1881) and II (1884), ed. E. Dümmler; vol. III (1886–96), ed. L. Traube, vol. IV.i (1899) ed. P. von Winterfeld; IV.ii (1914), ed. K. Strecker; IV.iii, (1923), ed. K. Strecker; *Nachträge zu den Poetae aevi carolini*, I (1951), ed. K. Strecker and O. Schumann; II (forthcoming), ed. G. Silagi and B. Bischoff. For some texts, more recent editions have superseded those of the MGH but the volumes of the MGH still provide the most convenient collection for browsing through the whole range of Carolingian Latin verse. Note however K. Neff, *Die Gedichte des Paulus Diaconus, kritische und erklärende Ausgabe*, Quellen und Untersuchungen zur lateinischen Philologie des Mittalalters, III (Munich, 1908) (with interpretation and German translations). For pastoral see: R. P. H. Green, *Seven Versions of Carolingian Pastoral*, Reading University Medieval and Renaissance Latin Texts (Reading, 1979), pp. 14–20, 62–69; also two books by D. Korzeniewski: ed., trans., *Hirtengedichte aus Spätrömischer und Karolingischer Zeit: Marcus Aurelius Nemesianus, Severus Sanctus Endelechius, Modoinus, Hirtengedicht aus dem Codex Gaddianus* (Darmstadt, 1976) and *Hirtengedichte aus Neronischer Zeit: Titus Calpurnius Siculus und die Einsiedler Gedichte* (Darmstadt, 1971).

Literary histories and guides

R. R. Bezzola, *Les Origines et la formation de la littérature courtoise en Occident (500–1200)*, I, Bibliothèque de l'Ecole des Hautes Etudes 286 (Paris, 1944)

F. Brunhölzl, *Geschichte der lateinischen Literatur des Mittelalters* I (Munich, 1975)

E. R. Curtius, *European Literature and the Latin Middle Ages*, Eng. trans. W. Trask (London, 1953)

K. Hauck, *Kirchengeschichte Deutschlands*, vol. II, 3rd/4th edn (Leipzig, 1912)

M. Hélin, *A History of Medieval Latin Literature*, revised edn trans. J. C. Snow (N.Y., 1949)

M. L. W. Laistner, *Thought and Letters in Western Europe AD 500–900* (1931, revised edn London, 1957)

M. Manitius, *Geschichte der lateinischen Literatur des Mittelalters*, vol. I (Munich, 1911)

M. R. P. McGuire and H. Dressler, *Introduction to Medieval Latin Studies: A Syllabus and Bibliographical Guide*, 2nd edn (Washington, 1977)

D. Norberg, *Manuel pratique de latin médiéval* (Paris, 1968)

F. J. E. Raby, *A History of Christian-Latin Poetry from the Beginnings to the Close of the Middle Ages*. 2nd edn (Oxford, 1953)

A History of Secular Latin Poetry in the Middle Ages, 2 vols, vol. I, 2nd edn (Oxford, 1967)

L. D. Reynolds, et al., *Texts and Transmission: A Survey of the Latin Classics*, 3rd edn (Oxford, 1991)

K. Strecker, *Introduction to Medieval Latin*, trans., revised by R. B. Palmer (Berlin, 1957)

H. Waddell, *The Wandering Scholars* (1927, revised, reprinted London, 1958)

Some Carolingian verse available in English translation

P. S. Allen, *The Romanesque Lyric*, with translations by H. M. Jones (1928, reprinted N.Y., 1969) [To be read with caution]

P. Godman, *Poetry of the Carolingian Renaissance* (London, 1985) [The fullest selection]

H. Waddell, *Mediaeval Latin Lyrics* (1929; reprinted N.Y., 1948)

More Latin Lyrics from Vergil to Milton (London, 1976)

Discussions

R. Collins, 'Poetry in ninth-century Spain', *Papers of the Liverpool Latin Seminar* 4 (ARCA Classical and Medieval Texts, Papers and Monographs, 11) pp. 181–95

H. Cooper, *Pastoral: Mediaeval into Renaissance* (Ipswich, 1972)

P. Dronke, *Women Writers of the Middle Ages: A Critical Study of Texts from Perpetua (d. 203) to Marguerite Porete (d. 1310)* (Cambridge, 1984)

P. and U. Dronke, *Barbara et antiquissima carmina* (Barcelona, 1977) [On *Waltharius*]

R. Folz, *Le Souvenir et la légende de Charlemagne dans l'empire germanique mediéval* (Paris, 1950)

P. Godman, 'Latin poetry under Charles the Bald and Carolingian poetry', in: *Charles the Bald: Court and Kingdom*, ed. M. T. Gibson and J. L. Nelson, BAR International Series 101 (London, 1981) pp. 293–309

'Louis the Pious and his Poets', *Frühmittelalterliche Studien* 19 (1985) pp. 239–89

Poets and Emperors: Frankish Politics and Carolingian Poetry (Oxford, 1987)

M. Lapidge, 'The authorship of the adonic verses "ad Fidolium" attributed to Columbanus', *Studi medievali* 3rd ser. 18 (1977) pp. 815–80

P. Lehmann, 'Das literarische Bild Karls des Grossen vornehmlich im lateinischen Schrifttum des Mittelalters', in his *Erforschung des Mittelalters: ausgewählte Abhandlungen und Aufsätze*, vol. I (Stuttgart, 1959) pp. 154–207

F. P. Magoun and H. M. Smyser (trans.), *Walter of Aquitaine, Materials for the Study of his Legend* (New London, 1950)

L. Nees, *The Tainted Mantle* (Philadelphia, 1991) [On Theodulf]

D. Schaller, 'Poetic Rivalries at the Court of Charlemagne', in: *Classical Influences on European Culture 500–1500*, ed. R. R. Bolgar (Cambridge, 1973)

5

German vernacular literature: a survey

Cyril Edwards

Comparatively little original literature has survived in the early German vernaculars, Old High German (OHG) and Old Saxon (OS), although a host of translations and translation-based texts has been preserved. While many discoveries of texts dating from the high Middle Ages have been made in recent years, few from the Carolingian period have resurfaced, suggesting that the corpus was never very much larger. There are two obvious and complementary reasons for this: the dominance of Latin, and the predominantly oral nature of German culture in this period. Many of the OHG texts that have survived are unique early examples of their genres. External and indirect evidence, in the form of allusions to vernacular literature by clerical writers, and the wealth of later cognate literature, suggests that these *unica* are isolated written reflections of what, to judge from the quality of what has survived, must have been a very rich and generically varied oral culture.

A third reason for the paucity of texts is to be sought in the Church's attitude to the German vernaculars. Here, the Carolingian Church may have been influenced by the ambivalence which characterised the treatment of classical secular literature in the earlier Middle Ages, fluctuating between appreciation and condemnation, acknowledging the practical value of the great Latin authors with regard to the teaching of *grammatica*, of the literary command of the language, but highly suspicious of the content of their works.[1] While the practical usefulness of the vernacular established itself rapidly, the pre-Christian or extra-Christian culture with which the vernacular was associated was vituperatively condemned. The monk from his cell heard the songs of the people, but for him the vernacular was redolent of 'the stench of dung and the sweat of the warrior'.[2] The immense prestige of Latin stood in obvious contrast to the

[1] Compare M. L. W. Laistner, *Thought and Letters in Western Europe AD 500 to 900*, 2nd edn (London, 1957) pp. 221–2, and Brown, chapter 1 above, pp. 35–40.

[2] Wolfgang Haubrichs, *Geschichte der deutschen Literatur von den Anfängen bis zum Beginn der Neuzeit. Band I: Von den Anfängen zum hohen Mittelalter. Teil 1: Die Anfänge: Versuche volkssprachiger Schriftlichkeit im frühen Mittelalter (ca 700–1050/60)* (Frankfurt-am-Main, 1988) p. 42.

unlearned nature of vernacular culture. Moreover, the vernacular was viewed as a pagan and therefore tainted idiom, an attitude epitomised by the frequent use of epithets such as *obscenus, inutilis, barbara, rustica, indisciplinabilis*. Otfrid of Weissenburg, author of the longest work in German in the period, speaks in derogatory fashion both of the language which is his medium, and the secular oral culture in conscious opposition to which he has composed his *Liber evangeliorum*. Contrasting the fledgling Frankish tongue with Latin, he describes it as 'a barbaric language ... uncultivated and undisciplined'. He describes his poetic undertaking as having been motivated by a specific occasion when monastic and secular culture came into collision, when 'the sound of superfluous matters battered the ears of most esteemed men and the obscene song of the laymen troubled their sanctity'. His intent is that the *cantus* of his Gospel harmony should drown the sounds of such secular voices.[3]

The vernacular was not always viewed with such hostility. On the most practical level, it was regarded as indispensable in legal texts such as the *Strasbourg Oaths* and the Hamelburg and Würzburg boundary descriptions. Equally practical, but more problematic in that it reveals a gulf between theory and practice, was the Church's transmission of magico-medical material in the form of charms, blessings and recipes. The fact that Latin was not a language that came naturally to the German-speaking parts of the Carolingian Empire meant that both in texts for the internal use of the monastery such as prayers and the Benedictine Rule, and in documents relating to the intercourse between the clergy and the laity such as the baptismal vow and the catechism, recourse had to be made to German. The reasons for this were obvious: the inadequate Latin of the youthful oblate, of the late entrant to the monastery, of the layman with whom the priest had to communicate.

These functions derive from the dominant position of the Church and, to a far lesser degree, in terms of the use of the vernacular, of the law. Viewed hierarchically, these are functions imposed upon the vernacular from above, by a literate superstructure. At the same time, the vernacular had cultural functions which had their origin in a non-literate society, but which found their way into literate expression. The heroic lay, the popularity of which is attested in contemporary allusions and cognate Anglo-Saxon and Old Norse literature, survives in the form of a single OHG text, the *Hildebrandslied*. The oral preservation of myth is attested by the *Second Merseburg Charm*, which derives, at however great a remove, from a pagan society. But, as other charms in their combination of material from apocryphal traditions with elements deriving from Germanic folklore show, the vertical model is deceptively simple, in that it exaggerates the gap between learned and popular culture in the Carolingian period.

In some instances the mode of transmission would appear to reflect a

[3] Otfrid von Weissenburg, *Ad Liutbertum*, lines 63–4; 5–7; 11–12. Compare Walter Haug, *Literaturtheorie im deutschen Mittelalter. Von den Anfängen bis zum Ende des 13. Jahrhunderts* (Darmstadt, 1985) pp. 25–44.

functional distinction between texts which had the official backing of the Church, ranging from practical prose to biblical poetry, and those emanating from oral culture, which have survived in a more or less fortuitous manner, written on blank pages, fly-leaves or in empty margins. Such 'accidental' survival is epitomised by the *Lorsch Bee Charm* (plate 3), written upside-down at the bottom of a page. Yet the *Muspilli* (plate 2), a didactic poem drawing on a wealth of eschatological lore, enjoys a similarly precarious survival, and exposes the limitations of drawing conclusions about function and audience of a text purely on the basis of transmission. The *Muspilli* is one of a number of texts which point to what, in view of the oft-stated hostility of the Church to the vernacular, is a surprising new development in the ninth century: a productive co-operation between vernacular traditions and monastic aims which led to the creation of a body of original vernacular literature.

To see translation from the Latin as the precursor of German original literature is to oversimplify, for the two co-existed throughout the period and beyond. On its most basic level, translation took the form of the glossary and the gloss. The oldest German glossaries were a natural extension of the Latin monastic thesaurus, and may, like their Latin–Latin model, have originally served as an aid to understanding the Bible. The transmission of the oldest glossary, known after its first word as the *Abrogans*, dates from the middle of the eighth century, and that of the shortened version, the *Samanunga uuorto* ('collection of words') from the early ninth century. A manuscript of the second half of the eighth century (St Gall, Stiftsbibliothek, Cod. 913), known as the *Vocabularius Sancti Galli*, combines Anglo-Saxon and OHG glosses and includes a 450-word encyclopaedic glossary, arranged by topics, based on a Greco-Latin model, the *Hermeneuta*. As the emphasis is on explaining German words, the manuscript is generally interpreted as being the handbook of an Anglo-Saxon missionary.

The early ninth-century *Kassel Glosses* combine word-lists with complete sentences. It is the latter which predominate in the late ninth-century *Paris Conversations*, a guide book for a visitor to Germany from a Romance-speaking area, possibly Orleans, consisting of questions, answers and commands, ranging from the practical to the obscene. The German phrase, in a heavily Romance-oriented orthography, is followed by its Latin equivalent: *Gueliche lande cumen ger? de qua patria?* ('Which country do you come from?'); *Vndes ars in tine naso. canis culum in tuo naso* ('A dog's arse up your nose'). The user of the guide-book is envisaged, not without humour, as an armed married man: *Guar is tin quenna? ubi est tua femina?* ('Where is your wife?'); *Gimmer min schelt. scutum.* ('Give me my shield'). Accustomed to giving orders, he does not always have sufficient time for higher concerns: *Quandi næ guarin ger za metina? quare non fuisti ad matutinas? En ualde. ego nolui. Ger ensclephen bit te uip in ore bette. tu iacuisti ad feminam in tuo lecto* ('Why did you not go to matins? I did not want to. You were asleep with your wife in your bed.')

Well over a thousand manuscripts containing OHG glosses are known. The precise function of the individual gloss is often difficult to determine, but the majority of the glosses served to aid the comprehension of a Latin original. Glosses in which German is identifiable as the target language are comparative rarities. The greater part of this immense amount of glossing activity was restricted in its purposes and interests to the schoolroom. The glosses may be categorised as marginal, interlinear, or contextual, directly following the Latin word in the same line. Of this third type are the glosses in the *Wessobrunn Prayer* manuscript (Munich, Clm 22053), written *ca* 790–815, relating to geography, weights and measures, botany and entomology. The glosses in the section *De mensuris* fols. 63v–64v, for example, adduce German words in amplification of the definitions of Isidore of Seville, like the *Abrogans* forming a natural extension of the monolingual dictionary. The interlinear technique could be employed not merely for isolated words, but for whole texts, such as the interlinear version of the Benedictine Rule which was written in an Alemannic monastery in the early ninth century (St Gall, Stiftsbibliothek, Cod. 916).

It is not possible to speak of a continuous development towards the free translation of complete texts. The three glossing techniques continued to be employed throughout the period, but, sporadically, the impulse towards freer translation flowered. The earliest example is the Rhenish Franconian 'Isidore-group' of translations dating from the late eighth century, consisting of fragments of a translation of Matthew's Gospel, part of Isidore of Seville's treatise *De fide catholica ex veteri et novo testamento contra Iudaeos*, and a late eighth-century treatise, *De vocatione gentium*. A parallel column technique is employed, as the extract below, which reproduces the original format, shows:

Si christus deus non est	Ibu christus auur got niuuari; dhemu in
Cui dicitur in psalmis.	psalmom chiquhedan uuard
Sedis tua deus in seculum	Dhiin sedhal got ist fona euuin
seculi uirga ęqui	ineuuin. rehtnissa garda
tatis. uirga reg	ist garde dhines rühhes
ni tui. Dilexisti	Dhu minnodos reht endi
iustitiam et odisti	hazssedos unreht. bidhiu
iniquitatem prop	auur chisalboda dhih got.
terea unxit te deus.	

De fide catholica, BN lat. 2326

(If Christ, however, were not God, of whom in / [the] Psalms [it] was said: / Your throne, God, will last from eternity / to eternity. [The] rod of righteousness / is [the] rod of your kingdom. / You loved justice and / hated injustice. Therefore / God anointed you.)

The translator's syntax breaks away from the word-by-word technique, for example placing *in psalmom* before the verb in lines 1–2, and achieves considerable fluency. The Isidore translator also evolved his own orthographic system. A link has been suggested between the Isidore translations and Einhard's praise of

Charlemagne as having begun 'a grammar of his native tongue'.[4] To posit such a patronage context is problematic in the absence of any explicit link between Einhard's statement of intent and the Isidore translations, which are not prefaced by any programmatic statement. This typifies the methodological difficulties in contextualising OHG literature. The fragmentary and isolated nature of what has survived invites hypotheses ever open to refutation.

In terms of the development of translating skills, the Fulda *Tatian* might, by comparison with the Isidore translations, be regarded as a retrograde step. The first of the three large-scale German works modelled on the *Diatessaron*, the Gospel harmony attributed to the Syrian or Greek author Tatian, it was written by six Fulda scribes in the first quarter of the ninth century. Again parallel columns are employed, but while the degree of translating skill appears to vary from scribe to scribe, the German prose remains for the most part bound by the Latin syntax, as one would more readily expect of an interlinear translation. The fluctuation between word-for-word technique and the occasional nod in the direction of vernacular syntax may be observed in the rendering of the opening of St John's Gospel:

In principio erat verbum	In anaginne uuas uuort
et uerbum erat apud deum;	Inti thaz uuort uuas mit gote,
et deus erat uerbum,	Inti got selbo uuas thaz uuort,
hoc erat In principio	thaz uuas In anaginne
apud deum. Omnia per Ipsum	mit gote. Alliu thuruh thaz
facta sunt; et sine Ipso	uurdun gitán; Inti uzzan sin
factum est nihil;	ni uuas uuiht gitánes;

St Gall, Stiftsbibliothek, Cod. 56 (original layout)

In the beginning was word / And the word was with God. / And God himself was the word. / That was in [the] beginning / with God. All [things] through that / were made; And without him / nothing was made.)

While Boniface's own copy of Victor of Capua's adaptation of the *Diatessaron* (Codex Fuldensis Bonifatius I) was a prized possession of the Fulda monks, the OHG text is based not on the Victor manuscript, but on an independent St Gall Latin version, indicating active collaboration between the two monasteries. The text was intended to aid the monks in their study of the gospels, as the appended concordance shows. Behind the work is thought to lie the creative impulse of Hraban Maur, abbot of Fulda, one of the dominant intellectual figures of the first half of the ninth century.

The Carolingian reforms of the Church, voiced in the *Admonitio generalis* of 789 and in a plethora of subsequent capitularies and synods, provide the obvious explanation for the large number of short functional Church texts that have survived from the ninth and early tenth centuries. The priest is constantly being

[4] Einhard *Vita Karoli*, ed. O. Holder-Egger, MGH SRG (Hanover and Leipzig, 1911), c. 28; Eng. trans. L. Thorpe, *Two Lives of Charlemagne* (Harmondsworth, 1969) p. 82.

reminded of his duty to understand the basic tenets of the faith and to make these understood to the layman. The vernacular baptismal vows, creeds, paternosters, confessions and prayers originate from a wide range of central and southern German monasteries. These translations or translation-based texts frequently incorporate alliterative formulæ, as when the Bavarian priest swears to be *kahorich enti kahengig*, 'obedient and subservient', to his bishop, or the *Frankish Prayer* implores God: *forgip mir gauuitzi indi gǒdan galaupun*, 'bestow upon me wisdom and good belief'. The alliteration confers upon the texts a formality which would be familiar to the hearer as part of the aesthetic of oral culture. In the OS Baptismal Vow and in the OS Confessional Formula the pragmatic nature of such texts is clearly observable, in that the formulation undergoes local variation to meet the needs of the newly converted populace. The Saxon catechumen swears: *end ec forsacho . . . Thunaer ende Uuoden ende Saxnote ende allum them unholdum the hira genotas sint*, 'and I renounce Thor and Oðin and Saxnot and all the demons who are their companions'. And in the OS confession, the penitent admits: *Ik gihorda hethininussia endi unhrenia sespilon*, 'I have listened to heathen and impure songs.' Again one sees vernacular and learned culture in collision.

The synods and capitularies of 813 instructed the priest not only to impress upon the laity the importance of paternoster and creed, but commended that model sermons be translated into Romance and German vernaculars: *in rusticam Romanam linguam aut Theotiscam*.[5] The transmission of only one early sermon in the vernacular suggests that this ideal was rarely fulfilled, and that the attempt to instruct the laity in the tenets of the faith through the use of the vernacular remained for the most part on the very basic level indicated by the shorter functional texts. The *exhortatio ad plebem christianam* does however survive in two Bavarian manuscripts of the first quarter of the ninth century (Kassel, Cod. Kassell theol. quart. 24; Munich Clm 6244 (plate 1)). It makes explicit reference to baptism, the Creed and the Lord's Prayer. The Latin is translated freely and idiomatically, and the clear, emphatic style is admirably suited to a sermon intended to be preached to the laity. The Munich text begins as follows (abbreviations in the original manuscript have been silently expanded):

Audite, filii, regulam fidei, quam in corde
memoriter habere debetis,
qui christianum nomen accepistis,
quod est uestre indicium christianitatis,
a domino inspiratum,
ab apostolis institutum;

Hloset ir, chindo liupostun, rihtida thera
galaupa, thé ir in herzin kahuctlicho
hapen sculut Ir den c^{h}ristanun namun
intfangan eigut, thaz ist chundida
iuuerera christanheiti, fona demo
truthine in man gaplasan, fona sin sel
pes iu^{n}giron kasezzit

(Hear, dearest children, the rule of the faith, which you are to hold memorised in your heart; you have received the Christian name, that is the sign of your Christianity, blown by the Lord into man, by his own apostles established.)

5 Synod of Tours, MGH Conc. II.i. c. 17, p. 288.; compare Haubrichs, *Geschichte*, pp. 305–6.

The vernacular made few early inroads into legal texts. The sixth-century *Lex Salica* incorporated in its eighth-century recensions Germanic words known as the *Malberg Glosses*; part of a translation into High German of the *Lex Salica* survives in an early ninth-century fragment.[6] In most early charters the extent of the vernacular is limited to personal and place names. The Hamelburg and Würzburg boundary-charters, both dating in origin from the reign of Charlemagne, go beyond this. Beginning in Latin, the charters drift into German in the most natural fashion, achieving a macaronic effect as they specify the minutiae of the localities to which they apply: *de Scuntra in Nendichenveld, deinde in thie teofûn gruoba* ('from Scuntra to Nendichenveld, thence into the deep pit', *inde in Ennesfirst then uuestaron* ('thence to Ennesfirst, then to the west'). The *Trier Capitulary*, which survives only in Brower's *Antiquitates Trevirenses* (1626), is an interlinear, very literal translation of a capitulary of Louis the Pious of 818 or 819, authorising *That ein iouuelīhc man frīer geuualt have, so uuār sōse er uuilit sachun sīnu ce gevene,* ('That every man should have free authority to dispose of his property as he wishes'). It is thought that the Moselle Franconian translation was not made until the middle of the tenth century, perhaps for private legal purposes, but the late transmission renders precise contextualisation difficult.

Despite these rare records of German as a legal language, it is clear from the wording of ninth-century diplomatic records that German was used orally in legal contexts. The alliance between Charles the Bald, Louis the German and Lothar II of the Middle Kingdom in 860 was sworn both in *romana lingua* and *lingua theodisca*, Romance and German vernaculars, but the written record was made in Latin. That such a relationship between Latin and the vernaculars may have been the norm is suggested by the *Strasbourg Oaths* of 842, a trilingual document recorded by Charles the Bald's historian Nithard, the text of which has survived in a late ninth-century manuscript. The oaths are sworn in *romana lingua*, the oldest surviving Old French text, and in *teudisca lingua*; they mark the alliance between Charles and Louis the German against Lothar. The German dialect is Rhenish Franconian.

In the early ninth century the evidence points to a movement away from the translation-based text towards a freer collaboration between the purposes of the Church and vernacular oral-derived culture. Written between *ca* 790 and *ca* 814, the *Wessobrunn Prayer* (Munich Clm 22053, fols. 65v–66r) begins with a description of the void before the moment of Creation. It states the presence of the Creator, then invokes, by a process of anamnesis similar to that found in the charms, the powers manifested in the act of Creation to aid the present-day supplicant.

Dat gafregin ih mit firahim / firi uuizzo meista.	This my questioning among men determined, greatest of wonders.
Dat eroni / uuas, noh ufhimil.	That there was neither earth nor heaven,
noh paum / noh pereg niuuas.	Nor tree, nor mountain was there,

6 Stadtbibliothek Trier, Althochdeutsche und mittelhochdeutsche Fragmente, Mappe Nr. 4.

ninohheinig / noh sunna nistein,	Nor anything, nor did the sun shine,
noh mano / niliuhta, noh der marȩo seo. /	Nor the moon beam, nor the glorious sea,
Do dar niuuiht niuuas enteo / ni uuenteo,	When there was nothing of ends nor turnings.
7 do uuas der eino / almahtico cot.	And then there was the one Almighty God,
manno miltisto. / 7 dar uuarunauh manake mit / inan	Kindest of men. And there were also many with him
cootlihhe geista. 7 cot / heilac.	Divine spirits. And God Holy.
Cot almahtico du / himil 7 erda ga uuorahtos. /	God Almighty, you who created heaven and earth,
7 du mannun so manac coot / forgapi.	And you who bestowed so many good things upon men,
for gipmir indino / ganada rehta galaupa. /	Bestow upon me in your grace true belief.
7 cotan uuilleon, uuistóm / enti spahida.	And good will, wisdom and intelligence,
7 craft, tiuflun / za uuidar stantanne.	And power to withstand devils,
7 arc / zapi uuisanne, 7 dinan uuil / leon za gauurchanne.	And to shun evil, and to work your will.

Parallels in Anglo-Saxon literature suggest that the *Wessobrunn Prayer* derives from a tradition of alliterative poetry concerning the Creation.[7] The final lines of the text, on the other hand, are reminiscent of liturgical formulae such as those in the German versions of the Lord's Prayer, or the *Frankish Prayer*. This has led to assumptions of multiple authorship, which seem to a certain extent justified on linguistic grounds. The dialect is fundamentally Bavarian, but discrepancies point to a provenance further north or to an older stratum of the language. The surviving text (Munich Clm 22053, fols. 65v – 66r) is a copy of an older exemplar; speculation concerning the nature, date and provenance of this exemplar will probably continue to flourish. The same applies to theories concerning the work's function. Ultimately the emphasis on the Creation in the Anglo-Saxon lays probably had a missionary function, but there is no evidence in the manuscript to suggest that such an intention informed the *Wessobrunn Prayer*, and by the time of its copying, Bavaria had long been Christian.

The Synod of Tours (813) recapitulated earlier admonitions that the laity should be instructed through sermons about the rewards awaiting the good and the punishments awaiting the evil in the afterlife, and about how these relate to one's deeds in this life. We possess no vernacular sermons which concentrate on this theme, but it forms the subject-matter of a second Bavarian lay, the *Muspilli* (plate 2). As with the *Wessobrunn Prayer*, a poetic tradition may have combined with the aims of the Frankish Church to create the lay. Bede's account of the peasant-turned-poet Caedmon tells how 'he also made many poems on the terrors of the Last Judgement, the horrible pains of Hell, and the joys of the Kingdom of Heaven. In addition to these, he composed several others on the

[7] Cyril Edwards, '*Tôhuwabohû*: The *Wessobrunner Gebet* and its analogues', *Medium Aevum* 53 (1984) pp. 263–81.

blessings and judgements of God, by which he sought to turn his hearers from delight in wickedness, and to inspire them to love and do good.'[8] The *Muspilli* draws on both biblical and apocryphal accounts of the apocalypse, and seems to have made extensive use of the Book of Esdras, a copy of which was made for Louis the Pious in 822. The beginning and end of the poem are missing, probably because they were written on lost fly-leaves; the surviving 103 lines are written on the empty pages and lower margins of Munich Clm 14098, a manuscript containing the pseudo-Augustinian sermon *De symbolo contra Judeos*, which was presented by Archbishop Adalram of Salzburg to Louis the German in the third or fourth decade of the ninth century. The hand of the *Muspilli* forms a startling contrast to the beautifully executed script of the sermon; among the German hands of the Carolingian period, it is uniquely unpractised and untidy. This makes it difficult to date, although it is unlikely to be much later than 850. Speculation about the identity of the inexpert scribe has scarcely progressed beyond the 'who would dare?' argument – someone unversed in writing, therefore, perhaps a woman, such as Louis the German's wife Hemma, or even Louis himself?

Variations in the poem's orthography, which may point to a dialect mix, the uneven handling of alliterative technique, and the absence of a clear narrative line, have led, as with the *Wessobrunn Prayer*, to theories of multiple authorship. The *Muspilli* intersperses its vision of the final terror with calls to *diu uuenaga sela*, 'the wretched soul', to repent and turn to good works. It has been suggested that the more overtly didactic parts of the text are later interpolations, but their effectiveness points to their being an integral part of the poet's purpose:

pidiu ist durft mihhil
allero manno uuelihemo,   daz in es sin muot kispane,
daz er kotes uuillun   kerno tuo
enti hella fuir   harto uuise,
pehhes pina: dar piutit der Satanasz altist
heizzan lauc.   so mac huckan za diu,
sorgen drato,   der sih suntigen uueiz.

lines 18–24

Therefore there is great need / that each and every man should be urged by his mind / to carry out God's will gladly / and steer well clear of hell-fire, / the torment of pitch: there Satan the most Ancient offers / hot flames. Therefore a man should think hard on this, / turn his thoughts directly to anxiety, / if he knows himself to be sinful.

Interest in matters eschatological was widespread in the first half of the ninth century.[9] The poet of the *Muspilli*, employing an almost stream-of-consciousness technique, moves freely from one biblical or apocryphal account of the end

[8] *Bede: A History of the English Church and People*. Translated and with an introduction by Leo Sherley-Price (Harmondsworth, 1955) p. 247.

[9] Compare Haubrichs, *Geschichte*, p. 389.

of the world to another, ignoring the repetitions and discrepancies they contain, and never losing sight of his didactic aim.

The scholarship concerned with the *Wessobrunn Prayer* and the *Muspilli*, perpetuating the literary nationalism of the nineteenth century, has tended to concentrate upon elements of vocabulary and literary motifs which might be regarded as evidence of survival of the Germanic, pre-Christian world. The search for the Germanic past in Carolingian survivals would seem to have greater justification with regard to the third great alliterative poem of the ninth century, the *Hildebrandslied*, as its background dates from the fifth century. Charlemagne, according to his biographer Einhard, gave orders for the preservation in writing of *barbara et antiquissima carmina*, ancient songs of the kings of the past and their wars.[10] It is conceivable that the survival of the *Hildebrandslied* depended ultimately upon such an enterprise, but the fortuitous nature of the text's transmission, as with the *Muspilli*, militates against linking the text with an act of royal patronage. The two leaves on which the sixty-eight lines are written were the covers of an early ninth-century Fulda manuscript (Kassel theol. fol. 54) containing biblical and exegetical texts; the lay was also written in Fulda, probably in the fourth decade of the ninth century.[11] The leaves have had an adventurous life, disappearing to America after 1945, and making the front page of *The Times* when they were reunited in Kassel in 1972.

The *Hildebrandslied* opens with a similar formula to that in the first line of the *Wessobrunn Prayer*, or that which introduces the battle between Elias and the Antichrist in the *Muspilli*: *Ik gihorta ðat seggen*, 'I heard tell', suggesting that an oral tradition lies behind the only surviving OHG heroic lay. The narrator tells of a meeting between two champions, Hiltibrant and Hadubrant, and the central theme of the poem is broached in the fourth line, when the relationship between the two is described by the unique compound noun *sunufatarungo*, 'son and father'. The narrator and audience share from the beginning the knowledge of the relationship between the two antagonists. The son's conflict is simpler; refusing to accept the indications of kinship with which Hiltibrant presents him, he only has to choose between fighting and accepting gifts, the armrings which he regards as a bribe. The father's conflict is more complex, for he is by the end of Hadubrant's speech in full possession of the facts, and has to make the more open choice, a genuine and tragic dilemma. The warrior ethos is in direct collision with the father–son tie. It is this collision which is the major interest of the poet, rather than the battle itself, of which only the beginning is described.

In symmetrically structured dialogue the father and son seek to establish each other's identity. Hadubrant says that his father fled with Theotrih from the wrath of Otacher. The evocation of the historical figures Odoacer, king of Italy (476–93), and his murderer and successor Theodoric the Great (455–526), reverses both historical roles and the geographical direction of events. The

10 Einhard *Vita Karoli* c. 29.

11 H. Fischer, *Schrifttafeln zum althochdeutschen Lesebuch* (Tübingen, 1966) p. 15*.

role-reversal of Odoacer and Theodoric is anticipated in Carolingian historiography, for example in the writings of Paul the Deacon. But the *Hildebrandslied* further complicates matters by introducing *Huneo truhtin*, 'the lord of the Huns', presumably Attila, who died in 454. These distortions are symptomatic of the way in which oral tradition reworks and telescopes events.

Hadubrant states his presumption that his father is dead. In the first of two exclamations to the heavens, Hiltibrant states the nature of their relationship in thinly veiled terms:

> 'wettu irmingot' [quad Hiltibrant] 'obana ab hevane,
> dat du neo dana halt mit sus sippan man
> dinc ni gileitos'
>
> ('I call to witness the great God' [said Hiltibrant] 'from heaven above, that truly you have never held parley with so closely related a man')

Hadubrant spurns his father's offer of arm-rings, calling him *alter Hun*, ('old Hun'), which may be an insult, or merely an assertion of the racial gulf he believes to exist between them; he restates his belief that his father is dead. Hiltibrant contrasts his son's fortunes with those of the exile far from home.

Hiltibrant's second appeal against fate is voiced in words which find echoes in Anglo-Saxon heroic poetry. Like his lord Ðeodric in the poem *Deor* he has spent thirty winters in exile; like the *Wanderer* and the *Seafarer* he is the plaything of *wyrd*, fate:

> 'welaga nu, waltant got' [quad Hiltibrant], 'wewurt skihit.
> ih wallota sumaro enti wintro   sehstic ur lante,
> dar man mih eo scerita   in folc sceotantero:
> so man mir at burc ęnigeru   banun ni gifasta,
> nu scal mih suasat chind   suertu hauwan,
> breton mit sinu billiu,   eddo ih imo ti banin werdan . . . '
>
> ('Alas now, potent God' [said Hiltibrant], 'a woeful fate is taking its course. / I wandered sixty summers and winters far from my native land, / and was always placed among the spearmen, / yet never in any city has death seized me; / now my own child is to hew me with his sword / beat his blade upon me, or I am to be his bane . . . ')

There is no suggestion that the protagonists are anything other than Christians, but, as in the Anglo-Saxon poems, a Boethian view of fate prevails. Hiltibrant acknowledges that it would be despicable or cowardly on his part to shirk the battle, and issues the challenge. Spears are cast, shields clash and splinter, and the poem ends. There was room for the scribe to write more at the bottom of the second leaf if he wished; perhaps he did so on a third page now lost to us, and what we possess is only a fragment. But it is entirely possible that what we possess is the entirety of the lay, that the outcome of the battle was too well known for the poet to need to tell his audience about it, or perhaps even a matter of indifference to him. The ending varies in the later analogues of the poem, Saxo Grammaticus' *Gesta Danorum*, the thirteenth-century Old Norse *Piðrekssaga*, the fourteenth-century Icelandic *Ásmundar Saga Kappabana*, the robust, humorous fifteenth-century folk-ballad known as the *Younger Hildebrandslied*, and the *Snjolvskvæði*, a Faroese ballad collected in 1819. The killing of close relatives becomes a duplicated motif, suggesting that the later analogues all derive – at various removes – from a poem not dissimilar to that which has survived in Kassel.

The phenomenon of dialect mix, a recurrent characteristic of OHG texts suggesting a divide between authorship and scribe in almost every instance, is seen at its most problematic in the *Hildebrandslied*. Basically High German morphology contrasts with phonological features, notably unshifted consonants, which are suggestive of a Low German or pre-OHG dialect. The precise motive behind the writing down of the text has led to almost as much speculation as its linguistic provenance. It has been suggested that it was intended as a cautionary tale, to warn monks against the folly of the heroic ethos. A more precise contextualisation has been attempted, linking it with the father–son conflict between Louis the Pious and Lothar. Or does the poem owe its survival to the historiographical interests of Charlemagne's court, in particular the interest shown by Charlemagne in the historical Theodoric? The poet of the *Hildebrandslied* is no historian; for him the conflict between two imprecisely identified armies is merely the backcloth for the exploration of an ethical issue. If the *Hildebrandslied* was conceived as an alternative form of historiography, then one would expect the historical data to be both more accurate and more extensive. The form of transmission suggests the fortuitous survival on parchment of a genre which is well attested by allusion and later, cognate heroic material such as the Middle High German Dietrich epics, but which tended to be heard outside the Carolingian monastery rather than written down within it.

The largest corpus of alliterative verse in the ninth century comes from Saxony, in the form of the *Heliand* and the *Genesis*. It is probably no freak of transmission that the German Gospel harmonies, evolving with the full blessing of the Church, have a more widespread manuscript transmission than the *Hildebrandslied* or the *Muspilli*. The *Heliand*, which extends Tatian's synopsis of the Gospels to the point of the ascension of Christ, survives in two manuscripts and three fragments. The text as reconstructed from the two manuscripts, C (British Library, Cotton Caligula A VII) and M (Munich Cgm. 25), while incomplete, amounts to nearly 6,000 lines.

The major source for a contextualisation of the *Heliand* ('The Saviour') is the *Praefatio in librum antiquum lingua Saxonica conscriptum*, which was published by M. Flacius Illyricus in 1562. The *Praefatio* refers to *Ludouuicus piissimus Augustus* as having commissioned 'a certain man of the Saxon people, who had the reputation amongst his own people of being no mean poet, to take pains to translate the Old and the New Testament into the Germanic language, in order that the sacred reading of the divine precepts might reach not merely the literate but also the illiterate'. This, in all probability, refers to the *Heliand*, perhaps also to the *Genesis*. As with the prefaces to Otfrid's *Liber evangeliorum*, the wealth of authorial information supplied by the *Praefatio* presents many problems. The Carolingian habit of bequeathing names means that we cannot even be certain whether Louis the Pious (emperor 814–40) or Louis the German (king of Germany 843–76) is meant. It is quite conceivable that the completion of such a huge task spanned more than one reign.

The *Praefatio* also contains tantalising hints as to the audience of the *Heliand*. It specifies reception by the *illiterati*, and indeed by 'all the people subject to Louis who speak the German language', but it also states that the biblical chapter-headings accorded to the work's fitts are intended to help the 'zealous reader'. Stress marks and neumes in the manuscripts suggest that the *Heliand* may have been chanted or sung. There would seem to be a dichotomy here: the desire to reach the whole of the populace by translating Holy Writ is very much in the spirit of the Carolingian Church reforms, but the chapter-headings point to use within the monastery, during divine office or for readings in the refectory. Perhaps only on those occasions when the laity were admitted to the Church did the *Heliand* reach a wider audience. To seek to identify a specific section of the laity, such as the noblemen of Louis the German's court circle, invites problems, in that it presumes a more limited and specific audience than that specified by the *Praefatio*.

The presence of the Victor manuscript of Tatian's *Diatessaron* in Fulda means that, inevitably, Hraban Maur has been seen as providing the initiative behind the *Heliand*. However, the palaeographic evidence points away from Fulda and towards the monastery of Werden, which ties in with Franconian elements identified in the Munich manuscript. There can be no certainty as to which of the manuscripts is closest to the language or the hand of the original.

The employing of the native idiom affected the way in which the content of the Gospels was presented in the *Heliand*, creating a frequently anachronistic impression. This is seen in the appellatives employed of Christ (*landes uuard*, 'guardian of the land'; *thiodo drohtin*, 'lord of the peoples'), of the Virgin Mary (*adalcnosles uuif*, 'woman of noble lineage'), even of Herod (*boggebo*, 'giver of rings', *folccuning*, 'king of the people'). The Germanisation extends to narrative detail such as the portrayal of feasts, the omission of the ass from the entry into the Jerusalem, the replacement of the shepherds by *ehuscalcos*, 'horseherds'. The purpose underlying this 'accommodation' of the Gospel, this introduction of local colour, has been the subject of much debate. It may have been intended to make the material more palatable to a warlike, newly converted people. Or it may have been a semi-conscious process, a natural consequence of the poetic use of the native idiom.

The surviving fragments of the OS *Genesis* are thought for stylistic reasons to be the work of a different author. There is less extensive use than in the *Heliand* of the *Hakenstil*, the interlocking of half-lines. Instead there is lively, dramatic employment of dialogue, as when Abraham and God discuss the plight of Sodom:

,, . . .   Muot ik thi frâgon nu,
sô thu mi thiu gramara ni sîs,   god heƀanriki?
ef thu thar fiðis fîftig   ferahtara manno,
liuƀigaro liodo,   muot thanna that land gisund,
uualdand, and thînum uuillean   giuuerid standan?"
Tho quam im eft tegegnes   godas anduuordi:
„Ef ik thar findo fîftig," quað he,   „ferahtara manno,
guodaro gumono,   thea te goda hebbian
fasto gifangan,   thanna uuilli ik im iro ferah fargeƀan
thuruh that ik thea hluttron man   haldan uuille."

789–98

('May I now ask you, / provided you will not be angry with me, God of the Heavenly Kingdom? / If you find there fifty God-fearing men, / willing people, may the land then, / Mighty One Be whole and preserved in accordance with your will?' / Then there came to him God's reply: / 'If I there find fifty,' said he, 'God-fearing men, / good people, who hold to God / in fast embrace, then I will grant them their lives, / for I wish to retain the men of pure spirit.'

Over a thousand lines survive of what must have been a project of some magnitude. These encompass the rise and fall of Satan, mankind being raised to the tenth choir of angels, the vengeance of Satan through the seduction of Adam and Eve, the Fall, the triumph of hell, Cain and Abel, and Sodom and Gomorrah. As in the *Muspilli*, both biblical and apocryphal sources are exploited, and two of the sections, the fall of the angels and the tale of Sodom, end on a didactic note. Lot's wife serves as an exemplum:

                                   thar siu standan scal
mannum te mârðu   oƀar middilgard
after te êuandage,   sô lango sô thius erða lêƀot.

921–3

(There she shall stand / miraculous sign to men on middle-earth / ever after in eternity, as long as this earth shall live.)

The third ninth-century reworking of the Gospels is the work of the first German poet we know by name, Otfrid of Weissenburg. The Latin and German prefaces and epilogue to the *Liber evangeliorum* supply us with an unaccustomed wealth of information concerning Otfrid and his literary purposes. He identifies himself as a monk and presbyter, a pupil of Hraban Maur. The prefaces further enable us to date the work, or rather its completion, to between 863 and 871. Otfrid is proud of the novelty of his undertaking, as emerges from the preface to his first book, *Cur scriptor hunc librum theotisce dictaverit* ('Why the writer composed this work in German'):

Nu es fílu manno inthíhit, in sína zungun scríbit,
joh ílit, er gigáhe, thaz sínaz io gihóhe:
Wánana sculun Fráncon éinon thaz biwánkon,
ni sie in frénkisgon bigínnen, sie gótes lób singen?

I,i, 31–4

(Now since many a man proceeds to write in his own tongue, / and is diligent and hastens to elevate his own: / Why should the Franks alone deviate, / and not begin in Frankish to sing God's praise?)

The relative chronology of the *Heliand* and Otfrid is likely to remain uncertain. It may be that Otfrid is making claims for Frankish as opposed to other German dialects, but the stress on the more general word *theotisce* in the title of this preface implies either that Otfrid is in ignorance of the translations and biblical poetry that have preceded his own, or, more probably, that this is a polemical justification of his endeavours. Otfrid, it emerges from the dedication to Archbishop Liutbert of Mainz, is a highly self-conscious poet and orthographer. He discusses the problems of adapting the Latin alphabet to German, though without making the fine distinctions of the *Isidore* translator, and proceeds to discuss differences in style, metre and gender between Latin and German. The relative prestige of the two languages is clear in Otfrid's mind; he regrets that he has had to change the number and gender of some nouns to suit the native idiom, but argues that God has conferred upon man the gift of language, however corrupt, in order to sing his praise.

Otfrid makes a break with what has gone before, and with what was happening perhaps at the same time further north, in that he eschews the native form of verse, alliteration, and opts for end-rhyme. The model for his choice has been the subject of much controversy, but the consensus prevails that it was the metre of Latin hymns, in particular of the Ambrosian strophe in its modified medieval form, that influenced him.

The second book of the *Liber evangeliorum* is introduced by the beginning of St John's Gospel. Contrasting Otfrid's rendering with the version in the Fulda *Tatian*, one observes the advances made by the translator and interpreter of biblical material in the first half of the ninth century, as well as Otfrid's tendency towards verbosity:

Er allen wóroltkreftin joh éngilo giscéftin,
so rúmo ouh so in áhton mán ni mag gidráhton,
Er sé joh himil wurti joh érda ouh so hérti,
ouh wíht in thiu gifúarit, thaz siu éllu thriu rúarit:
So was io wórt wonanti er állen zitin wórolti;
thaz wír nu sehen óffan, thaz was thanne úngiscafan.
Er alleru ánagifti theru drúhtines giscéfti,
so wés iz mit gilusti in theru drúhtines brústi.
Iz was mit drúhtine sar (ni brást imos ío thar),
joh ist ouh drúhtin ubar ál, wanta ér iz fon hérzen gibar,

Then ánagin ni fúarit, ouh énti ni birúarit,
  joh quam fon hímile óbana (waz mág ih sagen thánana?)

(Before all the powers of the world and the creation of the angels / in space and in thoughts to which man cannot penetrate, / Before sea and heaven existed, or the earth so hard, / and before anything entered into these that now moves them all three: / Then there was the Word dwelling before all the times of this world; / that which we now see openly, that was then uncreated. / Before all the gift of the Lord's creation, / it existed in delight in the breast of the Lord. / It was there from the beginning with the Lord (nor did it ever fail Him), / and the Lord is above all things, for He created it from His heart, / He whom the beginning does not bring forth nor the end move, / And came from heaven above (what may I say of that?)

While in Fulda, Otfrid would no doubt have become acquainted with the structure of the *Diatessaron*, but he chooses to approach the material differently. The structure is outlined in the dedication to Liutbert: the five books concern themselves with (i) the birth of Christ, proceeding to the baptism and preaching of John the Baptist; (ii) the calling of the disciples and Christ's teaching; (iii) Christ's miracles; his preaching to the Jews; (iv) the way to the Passion and the death of Christ; (v) the Resurrection, Christ's preaching to the apostles, the Ascension and the Last Judgement. The five divisions correspond to the five imperfect senses of man, in contrast to the perfection of the even number of Gospels. This authorial statement has led to attempts to find further numerical symbolism in the work, which, like similar approaches to the *Heliand*, remain controversial. Otfrid's poem differs from the *Heliand* in that its didactic intent is more clearly signalled; the narrative is frequently and consciously interwoven with exegetical commentary, the sources for which have been only partially identified.

The problems of identifying patronage and audience resemble those affecting the contextualisation of the *Heliand*. Otfrid begins by singing the praises of Louis the German, but his dedication constitutes no hard evidence of Louis' patronage, and indeed shows uncharacteristic diffidence:

Themo díhton ih thiz búah; oba er hábet iro rúah,
  ódo er thaz giwéizit, thaz er sa lésan heizi
Er híar in thesen rédion mag hóren evangélion,
  waz Kríst in then gibíete Fránkono thíet.

Ad Ludowicum, 87–90

(For him I write this book; if he takes heed of it, / Or so comes to know it, that he commands it to be read, / Then here in these discourses he can hear the gospel, / that which Christ enjoined upon the Frankish people.)

Two further stimuli to the work's inception are specified in the preface to Archbishop Liutbert: fellow monks, perhaps the St Gall monks Hartmut (d. 895) and Werinbert (d. between 880 and 890) to whom the epilogue is dedicated; and 'a certain venerable matron by the name of Judith'. Judith, like Louis, is a popular Carolingian name, the name of the second wife of Louis the Pious and of the daughter of Charles the Bald, but for the link with regal patronage we lack evidence outside the prefaces, which may, like many literary dedications, include a measure of wishful thinking.

The widespread transmission of Otfrid's text points to the official backing of the Church, if not of the monarchy. Two manuscripts date from the ninth century, one of which (Vienna Cod. 2687) has been identified as being in Otfrid's own hand; a further manuscript and fragment date from the tenth century. Otfrid's South Rhenish Franconian dialect dominates in three of the four manuscripts. Accents and neumes in the Heidelberg manuscript (Cod. Palatinus 52) indicate that the *Liber evangeliorum* was intended to be read or possibly sung aloud. The emphasis on exegesis and cross-references within the text make it clear, however, that the work was intended primarily for *sacra lectio*, to aid the study of the divine word.

The transition from alliteration to end-rhyme as the dominant form of verse appears to have taken place in the middle of the ninth century. It seems inherently unlikely that this was entirely because of Otfrid's influence. Uncertainties with regard to the dating of the anonymous texts of the late ninth and early tenth centuries make one wary of a monogenetical explanation. The smaller rhymed texts survive in ways which make any attempt to date them accurately problematic. The problems are acute with regard to the fragmentary *Cologne Inscription*:

> Hir maht thu lernan   Guld bewervan
> Welog inde wisduom   Sigi[lof inde ruom]
>
> (Here you can learn to acquire gold / Wealth and wisdom, the victor's praise and fame).

It survives on a sixteenth-century map of Cologne, and is thought to derive from an inscription found on a building, perhaps the cathedral library built by Bishop Gunthar in the middle of the ninth century. If the hypothetical ending is correct, then the lines form an ominous bridge between the warrior ethos, ninth-century respect for learning, and market forces.

Other isolated instances of the couplet survive, which point to its playing a role in popular culture independent of Otfrid. To take one example from the late ninth century, the *St Gall Spottvers* ('Lampoon') survives on the front flyleaf of a manuscript (Cod. 30) containing the Proverbs, Ecclesiastes and the Song of Songs:

> liubene ersazta sine grūz   unde kab sina tohter uz.
> to cham aber starzfidere,   prahta imo sina tohter uuidere.
>
> (Liubene prepared (?) his root-beer   and gave away his daughter.
> But then Starzfidere came along   and brought him his daughter back.)

The couplet refers to a botched marriage arrangement; the brewing of the bridal cup is in accordance with Germanic law. *Starzfidere* ('cockfeather'?) is probably an obscene name.[12]

The *Ludwigslied*, written some two decades after the *Liber Evangeliorum*, adopts the Otfridian couplet, though it often prefers 'strophes' of three lines to Otfrid's two. The poem is entered in a manuscript now in Valenciennes (cod. 150) by the same neat, late ninth-century hand as wrote the immediately preceding text, the saint's life known as the *Eulalia Sequence*, which is the oldest surviving Old French poem.

The fifty-nine lines of the poem are preceded by a title in rustic capitals: RITH MUS TEUTONICUS DE PIÆ MEMORIÆ HLUDUICO REGE / FILIO HLUDUICI ÆQUE REGIS ('a German poem concerning King Louis of pious memory, son of Louis, also a king'). The present and future tenses employed within the poem itself make it clear that the title derives from the scribe, not the poet, and that the Louis who is the subject of the poem was alive at the time it was written. He is generally identified as Louis III (879–82), son of Louis the Stammerer and grandson of Charles the Bald. The opening lines emphasise the personal relationship between the poet and the king who may well have been the poet's patron:

Einan kuning uueiz ih, Heizsit her Hluduīg,
  Ther gerno gode thionōt: Ih uueiz her imos lōnōt.
Kind uuarth her faterlōs. Thes uuarth imo sār buoz:
  Holōda inan truhtīn, Magaczogo uuarth her sīn.
Gab her imo dugidi, Frōnisc githigini,
  Stuol hier in Vrankōn. Sō brūche her es langō!
Thaz gideilder thanne Sār mit Karlemanne,
  Bruoder sīnemo, Thia czala uuunniōno

(I know a king, he is called Louis, / He gladly serves God: I know he rewards [or: will reward] him for it. / As a child [or: young man] he lost his father. He was immediately compensated for that: / The lord called him, He became his tutor. / He bestowed upon him virtues, pious [or: lordly] followers, / A throne here in Francia. May he enjoy it long! / This he then immediately divided with Carloman, / His brother, this abundance of delights.)

The difficulties in interpreting the above passage are compounded by the poet's apparent distortion of the truth as preserved for us in contemporary annals and letters. The poet/propagandist casts Louis in a central role throughout, and telescopes events, conferring a headlong tempo upon the poem. The adverb *sār* ('immediately') glosses over the lengthy negotiations concerning the division of the kingdom and Louis' delayed reaction to the Viking raids:

12 Stephen Sonderegger, 'St. Galler Spottverse', in: *Die deutsche Literatur des Mittelalters. Verfasserlexikon*, 2nd edn, ed. Kurt Ruh (Berlin, 1978–) (henceforth referred to as *Verfasserlexikon*), cols. 1051–3. Other isolated couplets and single lines are considered by Brian O. Murdoch, *Old High German Literature*. Twayne's World Authors Series (Boston, Mass., 1983) pp. 108–10; Haubrichs, *Geschichte*, pp. 93–104.

Hiez her Hluduīgan   Tharōt sār rītan: 22
'Hluduīg, kuning mīn,   Hilph mīnan liutin! . . . '
Thō nam her godes urlub,   Huob her gundfanon ūf, 27
Reit her thara in Vrankōn   Ingagan Northmannon.
Gode thancōdun   Thē sīn beidōdun,
Quādhun al 'frō mīn,   Sō lango beidōn uuir thīn.'

(He [God] bade Louis ride there straight away: / 'Louis, my king, help my people! . . . ' / Then he took leave of God, raised the battle standard, / He rode thither to Francia to meet the Vikings. / Those who awaited him thanked God, / They all said 'My Lord, we have been waiting for you so long.')

The invasion of the Vikings is seen, like the Old Testament afflictions imposed upon God's chosen people, as a test of Louis and as punishment for the transgressions of the Franks. This biblical perspective finds parallels in contemporary historiography and sermons.[13] Before the battle, Louis encourages his troops in Agincourt style, promising them rewards in either this or the next world. The battle is seen as part of a Holy War, anticipating the ethos of crusading poetry. The brief description of the battle itself may well have been influenced by oral heroic poetry in its lexis and its employment of ornamental alliteration. Here too, however, the emphasis is on Louis as a Christian king, who has his troops sing the *Kyrie* before the battle:

Ther kuning reit kuono,   Sang lioth frāno,
Ioh alle saman sungun   'Kyrrieleison'.
Sang uuas gisungan,   Uuīg uuas bigunnan . . .

lines 46–8

(The king rode boldly, sang a holy song, / And they all together sang 'Kyrie eleison'. / The song was sung, the battle was begun . . .)

Louis' personal prowess in the battle is stressed. The poem ends with praise of God, Louis and all the saints, and a pious wish that the Lord may preserve him. This hagiographical perspective contrasts sharply with the actual circumstances of Louis' death almost exactly a year after the battle of Saucourt, as recorded by the previously supportive annalist of St Vaast. In a fit of youthful exuberance Louis pursued a girl into her father's house, omitted to dismount, and crushed his shoulderblades between his saddle and the doorway.[14]

The generic isolation of the *Ludwigslied* has led to divergent attempts to trace the influences upon its language and content. The saint's life, the sermon, Latin battle lays, the processional chant, contemporary legal texts, Anglo-Saxon heroic poetry, the Old French *chanson de geste*, all have been adduced with

[13] Compare Werner Schwarz, 'The *Ludwigslied*: a ninth-century poem', *Modern Language Review* 42 (1947) pp. 469–72; Paul Fouracre, 'The Context of the OHG *Ludwigslied*', *Medium Aevum* 54 (1985) pp. 97–103; Haubrichs, *Geschichte*, pp. 174–5.

[14] *Annales Xantenses et Annales Vedastini*, MGH SRG (Hanover and Leipzig, 1909) p. 52.

greater or lesser plausibility as analogues or possible models.[15] The poem may have absorbed elements from any or all of these, but its effectiveness as propaganda and poetry resides in its lucid, dynamic portrayal of events.

While the poem is clearly intended to boost its hero's image, the precise propagandistic intent has also been the subject of much conflict, as have the poem's historical context, and the implications of its Rhenish-Franconian dialect, which suggests a provenance far to the south-east of Saucourt.[16] It is not inherently unlikely that Louis III should have had a German supporter at his court who chose to sing his king's praises in his native idiom. If so, it would be only natural for him to employ the newly fashionable verse form in which Otfrid had composed his eulogy of Louis the German. Otfrid had stressed the special relationship between Louis III's great-uncle – Louis the Younger's father – and God, in strikingly similar formulation:

Óba iz ward iowánne in not zi féhtanne,
so was er ío thero rédino mit gótes kreftin óboro.
Riat gót imo ofto in nótin, in suaren árabeitin;
gigiang er in zála wergin thár: druhtin hálf imo sár
In nótlichen wérkon, thes scal er góte thankon;
thes thánke ouh sin githígini jóh únsu smahu nídiri.

Otfrid, *Ad Ludowicum*, lines 21–6.

(If it ever happened that fighting was forced upon him, / Then he always rose above the situation with God's backing. / God often advised him in need, in grave troubles; / If he entered danger anywhere, the Lord immediately came to his aid / In dire extremity, for which he should thank God; / may his followers thank Him too, and we in our humility.)

Otfridian verse was employed for a variety of other functions, including two further essays in biblical translation. Early in the tenth century, a Bavarian translation of the 138th Psalm was written on the penultimate leaf of a manuscript from Freising or Regensburg (Vienna, Cod. 1609). McLintock regards the poetic technique as inferior to that of Otfrid and thinks it may attest a pre-Otfridian employment of rhyme.[17] As in the *Ludwigslied*, the 'strophes' vary between units of two and three lines. The text is a free paraphrase of the psalm, which sees David very much as a mounted warrior-king, engaged with the Lord in a mutual enterprise to defeat evil:

15 Compare Paul Fouracre, 'Using the background to the *Ludwigslied*: some methodological problems', in: *'mit regulu bithuungan'. Neue Arbeiten zur althochdeutschen Poesie und Sprache*, ed. John L. Flood and David N. Yeandle, GAG 500 (Göppingen, 1989) pp. 80–93 at pp. 91–2; in the same volume Raimund Kemper, 'Das *Ludwigslied* und die liturgischen Rechtstitel des westfränkischen Königtums', pp. 1–17; Haubrichs, *Geschichte*, pp. 175–8; Kurt Ostberg, 'The *Ludwigslied* in the context of communication between the continent and Anglo-Saxon England', *German Life and Letters*, 38 (1984/85) pp. 395–416.

16 Compare Ruth Harvey, 'The provenance of the Old High German *Ludwigslied*', *Medium Aevum*, 14 (1945), pp. 1–20; Schwarz, '*Ludwigslied*'; Fouracre, 'Background'; Rosamond McKitterick, *The Carolingians and the Written Word* (Cambridge, 1989) pp. 234–5; Yeandle, 'The *Ludwigslied*: king, church and context' in: *'mit regulu bithuungan'*, pp. 18–79.

17 David R. McLintock, *Verfasserlexikon* VII, cols. 876–8.

Nū uuillih mansleccun alle fone mir gituon,
alle die mir rieton den unrehton rīhtuom,
Alle die mir rietun den unrehton rīhtuom,
die sint fīenta dīn, mit den uuillih gifēh sīn;
De uuider dir uuellent tuon, de uuillih fasto nīdon,
alle durh dīnen ruom mir ze fīente tuon.

lines 16–21.

(Now I will put away from me all murderers, / all those who prompted me to false wealth; / All those who prompted me to false wealth, / those are your enemies, to those I will be hostile; / Those who wish to act against you I will hate fiercely, / make them all my enemies for the sake of your glory.)

The ideology has much in common with the *Ludwigslied* and with Otfrid's praise of David as *gotes thégane* ('God's warrior') in the dedication to Louis the German (*Ad Ludowicum*, 37–64).[18]

Much less ambitious in its treatment of its biblical exemplar is the fragment of *Christ and the Woman of Samaria*, written as a 'filler' at the end of the Lorsch annals (Vienna, Cod. 515). The script is of the middle of the tenth century, but the dialect mix of both Alemannic and Franconian features makes the precise language and date of the original difficult to determine. The thirty-one lines, comprising units of both two and three lines, adhere closely to John 4:4–20, in contrast to Otfrid's more verbose treatment of the same passage. The dialogue has a lively tempo, omitting, for the most part, the introductory formulae to the alternating speeches in the biblical model. Its natural ring is spiced by the ironic anachronism in line 8:

'Biuuaz kerōst thū, guot man, daz ih thir geba trinkan?
iā ne niezant, uuizze Christ, thie Iudon unsera uuist'.
'Uuīp, obe thū uuīs sīs, uuielīh gotes gift ist,
unte den ercantīs, mit themo du kōsōtis,
tū bātīs dir unnen sīnes kecprunnen.'

lines 7–11

('Why do you desire, good man, that I give you to drink? / Truly, Christ knows, the Jews do not partake of our food'. / 'Woman, if you knew what is God's gift / and recognised him with whom you speak, / you would ask to be given of his well of life.'

John 4:9–10: Then saith the woman of Samaria unto him, How is it that thou, being a Jew, askest drink of me, which am a woman of Samaria? for the Jews have no dealings with the Samaritans. Jesus answered and said unto her, If thou knewest the gift of God, and who it is that saith to thee, Give me to drink; thou wouldest have asked of him, and he would have given thee living water.)

[18] For Haubrichs this warlike emphasis points away from a devotional function and towards an aristocratic, court context, *Geschichte* p. 383.

The *Petruslied*, a neumed text written down in the early tenth century, confirms that Otfridian verse was, at least on occasion, intended for musical performance. Three two-line strophes end with the *Kyrie* as a refrain:

Unsar trohtin hat farsalt   sancte Petre giuualt
daz er mac ginerian   ze imo dingenten man.
  Kyrie eleyson,   Christe eleyson.
Er hapet ouh mit uuortun   himilriches portun
dar in mach er skerian   den er uuili nerian.
  Kyrie eleyson,   Christe eleyson.
Pittemes den gotes trut   alla samant uparlut,
daz er uns firtanen   giuuerdo ginaden.
  Kyrie eleyson,   Christe eleyson.

(Our Lord has transmitted authority to St Peter, / That he may save the man who places hope in him. / Lord have mercy, Christ have mercy. / He keeps guard by his words over the gates of heaven / and can place therein him whom he would save. / Let us beseech God's beloved, all together, in full voice, / that he may deign to have mercy on us sinners.)

The text is written on the last page of a Freising manuscript, a copy of Hraban Maur's commentary on Genesis. The dialect is Bavarian, but Franconian traces point to an older exemplar. The eighth line is identical with a line in the *Liber evangeliorum* (I,7,28), which has led to inconclusive arguments concerning the relative chronology of Otfrid and the *Petruslied*. Comparisons have been drawn with a Latin processional hymn to St Peter, but the precise liturgical function of the *Petruslied* remains the subject of speculation.[19]

Very similar in form, but without neumes, are a number of short prayers in Otfridian verse. The *Augsburg* or *Rhenish-Franconian Prayer* was written on the front cover page of a Lotharingian manuscript containing penitential and other liturgical material, dating from the last quarter of the ninth century (Munich, Clm 3851). The German text is an adaptation of the preceding Latin prose prayer. Two prayers traditionally called after the scribe Sigihart were added at the end of the Freising Otfrid manuscript (Munich, Cgm. 14) in a hand dating from the early tenth century:

Du himilisco trohtin,   Ginade uns mit mahtin
  In din selbes riche,   Sóso dir giliche.
Aliter
Trohtin Christ in himile,   Mit dines fater segane
  Gínáde uns in çuun,   Daz uuir nílfiden uuêuuún.

(You heavenly Lord, Grant us by your power / Entry into your own Kingdom, Like unto you.
Aliter:
Lord Christ in heaven, With your Father's blessing / Have mercy on us for all eternity, That we may not suffer the pangs of hell.)

19 Helmut Lomnitzer, *Verfasserlexikon*, cols. 521–5; Haubrichs, *Geschichte*, p. 398.

Aliter, 'as before', suggests repetition as part of a liturgical rite, perhaps even a musical performance. These minor religious texts, however sporadically transmitted, suggest that Otfridian verse came to fulfil to some extent the programme outlined by Otfrid in his preface *Cur scriptor*, that it came to be regarded as the fitting vehicle for a wide variety of Church functions in the late ninth century.

While the life of Christ provided the major stimulus for composition in German in the ninth century, the lives of the saints are attested in surprisingly few early vernacular Romance or German texts. The *Petruslied* and some of the charms invoke saints' names, and the *Ludwigslied* calls upon all saints, but the earliest German saints' lives are attested only in eleventh-century manuscripts. The *Galluslied*, a commemoration of the eponymous founder of St Gall, was composed in OHG verse in the last quarter of the ninth century by Ratpert, one of the monastery's teachers, but it survives in the Latin translation by Ekkehard IV, pupil of Notker Labeo of St Gall. Ekkehard also preserved the tune of the OHG text, although it cannot be determined whether the form of the Latin version, seventeen strophes consisting of five long lines with internal rhyme, also corresponds to that of the original. The *Georgslied* marks a similar break with the Otfridian pattern – or perhaps a refinement upon it; this fragment of ten strophes has been preserved in an early eleventh-century copy, on the last pages of the Heidelberg Otfrid manuscript. The lost original has been linked with the late ninth-century revival of the cult of St George. The scribe of the *Georgslied* was clearly puzzled by what he had before him, and his attempt at a transliteration renders problematic the reconstruction, dating and location of the original.

More than any other genre, the early medieval charm is poised between learned and popular culture, drawing indiscriminately from both. It is customary to explain the monastic preservation of the charms by drawing upon the Augustinian distinction between white and black magic, but there is no evidence that this distinction was actively observed in the Carolingian period. The Church councils and penitentials are most vehement in their condemnation of *maleficium*, black magic, but their brief extends to a wide range of pagan practices, including medicinal magic. The *Admonitio generalis* of 789 indeed prohibits all kinds of magic.[20] The surviving German charms – in contrast to, for example, the Irish and Scandinavian charms, – belong primarily to the province of white magic, but even within this small corpus there is at least one, the *First Merseburg Charm*, which does not appear to fall within this province.

Some of the charms, such as the charm against epilepsy, *Contra caducum morbum*,[21] and the Strasbourg and Bamberg charms for staunching bleeding, draw on apocryphal traditions of the early Church; others would appear to be *ad*

[20] MGH Cap. I, p. 58.

[21] Wilhelm Braune, *Althochdeutsches Lesebuch*, 15th. edn revised by Ernst A. Ebbinghaus (Tübingen, 1969) XXXI (section 8). The charms are cited according to Braune's edition except where otherwise stated.

hoc creations, composed by the magico-medic to suit the practical demands of his contemporary environment. When it comes to establishing the identity of this hypothetical magico-medic, we can only hazard the guess that he or she was a monastic leech. The penitentials tend to refer to magico-medical practice as the province of women, and women do occur within the texts of both OHG and Anglo-Saxon charms, but even where the charm is prefaced by a Latin rubric, the instructions to the sorcerer do not identify the sex of the practitioner. The penitentials reveal knowledge of magic practice outside the monastery, the charms reveal that this lore existed within the monastery, but the channels of communication and the degree of dependence upon an orally preserved popular culture remain obscure.

Stuart and Walla revive the hypothesis that the charms are preserved not because of their practical usefulness as magico-medical texts, but for antiquarian purposes.[22] However, the Trier charms, *Ad catarrum dic*, for staunching bleeding, and *Incantacio contra equorum egritudinem quam nos dicimus spurihalz*, 'for curing a disease of horses called *spurihalz*', are transmitted in a tenth-century compilation of medical lore (Stadtbibliothek Trier, MS 40), and the Paris charms, *Ad equum errę̧het* ('For a sprained horse') *and Gegen Fallsucht* ('Against Epilepsy'), are in a similar twelfth-century compilation (BN n.a. lat. 229), pointing strongly to a utilitarian reason for their transmission. The charms which were written down in the Carolingian period survive as 'fillers', on originally blank leaves, or in the margins or empty spaces of theological manuscripts, but here too the fact that the *Vienna Dog Charm* and *Contra vermes* ('Against Worms') are juxtaposed with Latin charms serving similar purposes, points to preservation for functional rather than antiquarian reasons.

Only occasionally is there any direct relationship between the proscriptions of the Church and the surviving charms. The Decretal of Burchard of Worms and the Arundel Penitential condemn the use of *incantationes* to steal bees or honey as *maleficium*.[23] The *Lorsch Bee Charm*, written in the late ninth or early tenth century, upside-down on the lower margin of a leaf of a sermon manuscript, makes no reference to theft, but is intended to control a swarm (plate 3):

> Kirst, imbi ist huc^{z}e. nu fliuc du uihu minaz. hera
> fridu frono. In munt godes gisunt heim zi comonne.
> sizisizi bina inbot dir scē maria hurolob ni habe du. ziholce
> ni fluc du. noh du mir nindrinnes. noh du mir nintuuin
> nest sizi uilu stillo vuirki godes uuillon.

(Christ, the bee-folk is out! Now fly, my cattle, back / In holy peace, in God's authority, so that you arrive home hale. / Alight, alight, bee: the Virgin Mary commanded you. May you have no leave: To the wood / flee

22 Heather Stuart and F. Walla, 'Die Überlieferung der mittelalterlichen Segen', *ZfdA* 116 (1987) pp. 53–79.

23 Cyrille Vogel, 'Pratiques superstitieuses au début du XIe siècle d'après le *Corrector sive medicus* de Burchard, évêque de Worms (965–1025)', in: *Études de civilisation médiévale (IXe–XIIe siècles) Mélanges offerts à E.-R. Labande*. (Poitiers 1974) pp. 751–61 at pp. 759–60.

not, nor escape me, nor deprive me of anything. / Sit quite still, work God's will.)[24]

In the closely related *Anglo-Saxon Bee Charm*, however, there is a suggestion that the charm is intended to ward off a thief, in that the speaker is instructed to put earth under his right foot as protection *wið pā micelan mannes tungan*, 'against the mighty tongue of man'. The bee is addressed as a female in an alliterative formula strongly reminiscent of the Lorsch charm:

'Sitte gē, sigewīf, sīgað tō eorþan!
nǣfre gē wilde tō wuda flēogan! . . . '

('Alight, victorious women, descend to earth! / Never go flying wild to the wood.')[25]

The German charm is much more overtly Christian in ethos, despite being a good century older. It may have come to Germany with the Anglo-Saxon missionaries, or both charms may be reflections of a common Germanic popular culture – or they may both derive from Latin bee-charms.[26]

The alliteration in the *Lorsch Bee Charm* may point to early origin, but this can never be a certain indication of antiquity. The charm *Pro Nessia* ('Against Worms') is often referred to as the oldest surviving German charm. It survives in two variants, a Bavarian version written on the bottom of a leaf in the middle third of the tenth century[27] and an OS version, *Contra vermes*, written on the last page of a Vienna manuscript (Cod. 751), probably in the early tenth century. The OS charm reads as follows:

Gang ût, nesso mid nigun nessiklinon.
ût fana themo marge an that ben. fan themo bene an that flesg.
ut fan themo flesgke an thia hud. ût fan thera hud an thesa strala.
Drohtin uuerthe so.

(Go forth, worm, with nine little worms, / out from the marrow to the bone, out from the bone to the flesh, / out from the flesh to the skin, out from the skin to this arrow. / Lord, may this be so.)

The assumption that the charm is old, Germanic and pagan is based on the presence of alliteration, the absence in the charm of a narrative or epic introduction, and the lack of any reference to a medicinal course of action. The majority of the surviving OHG charms depend for their effect upon the speaker invoking a situation in the past in which the magic has worked. The power is then applied anamnestically to the present in the second, conjuring part of the

24 Text according to the manuscript, Vat. pal. lat. 220, fol. 58r. See plate 3.

25 Cambridge, Corpus Christi College, MS 41. Text according to *Sweet's Anglo-Saxon Reader*, revised by Dorothy Whitelock (Oxford, 1967; reprinted 1970) p. 100.

26 For an example of a macaronic, Latin–German bee charm, see Bernhard Bischoff, *Anecdota Novissima. Texte des vierten bis sechszehnten Jahrhunderts*, Quellen und Untersuchungen zur lateinischen Philologie des Mittelalters 7 (Stuttgart, 1984) p. 258.

27 Munich, Clm. 18524b, from Tegernsee; compare Bernhard Bischoff, 'Paläographische Fragen deutscher Denkmäler der Karolingerzeit', *Frühmittelalterliche Studien*, 5 (1971), pp. 126–7; 130–1.

charm. The *Vienna Dog Charm*, the function of which is to protect sheepdogs against the threat of wolves or thieves, may serve as an illustration of the pattern:

> Christ uuart gaboren êr uuolf ode diob. do uuas s̄c̄ē marti christas hirti. der heiligo christ unta s̄c̄ē marti. der gauuerdo uualten hiuta dero hunto. dero zohono. daz in uuolf noh uulpa za scedin uuerdan ne megi. se uuara se geloufan uualdes ode uueges ode heido.
>
> Der heiligo christ unta s̄c̄ē marti de frumma mir sa hiuto alla hera heim gasunta.
>
> (Christ was born before wolf or thief. Then St Martin was Christ's shepherd.
> Holy Christ and St Martin, may he guard today this dog, this bitch, so that neither wolf nor she-wolf may harm them, wherever they run, in the wood or along the path or in open country.)

In the *Lorsch Bee Charm* the narrative element is confined to *inbot dir sancte maria*, 'Holy Mary commanded you', while in the worm charms it is totally absent. But to assume on this basis that the worm charms emanate from an older culture, which relied upon the power of the conjuring word alone, smacks of nineteenth-century Romanticism. The German charms are generally transmitted without a rubric specifying a course of action to accompany the spoken word, but this does not necessarily mean that actions did not accompany the magic words. The final line of the worm-charm, with its reference to a spear or arrow, implies that some form of action concluded the medical process, perhaps invoking the magical powers of iron, perhaps involving some form of surgery, as at the end of the Anglo-Saxon charm *Wið Færstice* ('Against a Sudden Stitch', Harley MS 585): *Nim þonne þæt seax, ādō on wǣtan* ('Take then the knife, put it into the water'). Two ninth-century Latin charms preserved in St Gall have been suggested as models for the German worm-charms,[28] but the idea of worms as the bringers of disease is very widespread, as is the step-by-step conjuration. This also occurs in *Wið Fǣrstice*:

> Gif ðū wǣre on fell scoten,   oððe wǣre on flǣsc scoten,
> oððe wǣre on blōd scoten,   [oððe wǣre on bān scoten],
> oððe wǣre on lið scoten,   nǣfre ne sȳ ðin līf ātǣsed!
>
> (If you were shot in the skin, / or were shot in the flesh, / or if you were shot in the blood, / [or were shot in the bone], / or were shot in the limb, / may your life never be harmed!)[29]

A similar formula concludes the *Second Merseburg Charm*:

> P^h^ol ende uuodan   uuorun zi holza.
> du uuart demo balderes uolon   sin uuoz birenkict.
> thu biguol en sinhtgunt.   sunna era suister:
> thu biguol en friia.   uolla era suister;

28 Rainer Reiche, 'Neues Material zu den altdeutschen Nesso-Sprüchen', *Archiv für Kulturgeschichte*, 59 (1977) pp. 1–24.

29 *Sweet's Anglo-Saxon Reader*, p. 101; the lacuna is filled by Grimm.

thu biguol en uuodan. so he uuola conda:
sose benrenki. sose bluotrenki.
sose lidirenki:
ben zi bena, bluot zi bluoda,
lid ze geliden, sose gelimida sin.

('P^{h}ol and Wodan went to the wood. / Then Balder's foal's foot was sprained. / Then Sinhtgunt charmed it, Sunna's sister [or: and Sunna, her sister]; / then Friia charmed it, Volla's sister [or: and Volla, her sister]; / Then Wodan charmed it, as he well knew how [or: as best he could]: / be it sprain of the bone, or sprain of the blood, / or sprain of the limb: / bone to bone, blood to blood, / limb to limbs, be they [as] stuck together.)[30]

The Merseburg charms have provoked a wealth of scholarly analysis, stimulated initially by the glimpse they apparently offer of pagan beliefs. Both the narrative introduction and the conjuring formula of the second charm have analogues in many languages, even outside the Indo-European family. Only this charm, however, records the accident to Balder's foal. The procession of the gods to the wood finds its closest parallel in Snorri Sturluson's thirteenth-century account in the prose *Edda* of the daily journey of the Æsir to their seat of judgement, the Yggdrasil, the ash tree at the centre of the world. Snorri's list of Æsir includes Odin, Freyia, Fulla, Sol and Balder. The two most problematic gods in the Merseburg charm are the goddess Sinhtgunt and P^{h}ol. The identity of P^{h}ol has led to a massive amount of speculation. The only one of the Æsir who might be regarded as being of equal stature to Odin is Thor, and it may be that P^{h}ol is a corruption of Thor. The two are often found together as a pair, for example as gods of the Saxons, together with other gods, in the *Saxon Baptismal Vow*.[31]

The *First Merseburg Charm* also has links with the Scandinavian north:

Eiris sazun idisi, sazun hera duoder.
suma hapt heptidun, suma heri lezidun,
suma clubodun umbi cuoniouuidi:
insprinc haptbandun, inuar uigandun. .H·

(Once women sat down [alighted?), sat here and there [?] / Some fettered the captive, some hampered the army, / some picked at the fetters: / leap forth from the bonds, escape from the warriors.)

The Old Norse *Hávamál*, the 'Sayings of Oðin', lists two charms intended to fetter or set free captives, and in the *Svipdagsmál* the hero is taught a similar charm by his deceased mother Gróa. A loosening charm is referred to in Bede's story of Imma (*Historia Ecclesiae*, IV, 22), and in the Anglo-Saxon translation of Bede such charms are written on runes. Whether the *First Merseburg Charm* was intended to free captives has been contested. Latin charms which serve to ease

30 Braune's text has been modified according to the manuscript, Merseburg Cathedral Archive, cod. 136.
31 Braune XVI, 2, II; see p. 146 above. This suggestion will be discussed more fully in a forthcoming article.

childbirth contain similar 'loosening' imagery. The *idisi* in the first line were identified by Grimm with Valkyries; in the *Sigrdrífumál* a Valkyrie teaches the hero a birth-charm.

The Merseburg Charms have been linked with Fulda on the basis of the Latin prayer written below them in a different hand, which is closely related to a prayer in the Fulda Sacramentary. However this prayer, part of the monastic mass, belongs to a much older and wider liturgical tradition. The language of the charms points to an area north of Fulda. A monastery existed in Merseburg in 962; Bischoff dates the hand to the first or second third of the tenth century.[32] Also in favour of Merseburg provenance is the reluctance of the Saxons, superficially converted by Charlemagne, to relinquish their pagan beliefs, attested as late as the eleventh century by Adam of Bremen and Thietmar of Merseburg.

The Old Saxon charm *De hoc quod spurihaz dicunt*, in the same Vienna manuscript as the worm-charm *Pro Nessia*, serves a similar function to the *Second Merseburg Charm*, but here the narrative element is entirely Christian, if apocryphal, and, as in many later charms, liturgical elements have been introduced into the magic process:

De hoc quod spurihaz dicunt.
Primum pater noster.

Visc flot aftar themo uuatare, uerbrustun sina uetherun: tho gihelida ina use druhtin. The seluo druhtin. thie thena uisc gihelda. thie gihele that hers thiru spurihelti. Amen

(Of that which they call *spurihaz*. / First a paternoster. / A fish swam along the water, its gills burst: then Our Lord healed it. That same Lord, who healed that fish, may he heal this horse of the *spurihalz*.)[33]

A second tenth-century Low German charm against *spurihalz* (Braune 9B.2.) begins with a Christianised variant of the epic introduction to the *Second Merseburg Charm*. Instead of Phol and Odin, the two riders in the first line are Christ and St Stephen, and St Stephen's horse is healed by Christ. The same Trier manuscript contains the oldest surviving German charm for staunching bleeding, which shows the bipartite structure at its simplest:

Ad catarrum dic:
Crist uuarth giuund: tho uuarth he hel gi ok gisund.
that bluod forstuod: so duo thu bluod
Amen ter. Paternoster ter.

(Say to the catarrh: / Christ was wounded: then he became hale and healthy. / The blood stopped flowing: do you likewise, blood.)

This is one of a huge international family of haemostatic charms which make use of apocryphal material for their epic introduction.

The OHG and OS charms, small though they be in number, reach backwards

32 Bischoff, *Paläographische Fragen*, p. 111.

33 The apocryphal healing of the fish is contained in a tenth-century southern French charm (Clermont-Ferrand, Bibl. Munic. 201). Compare Bischoff, *Anecdota novissima*, p. 261, section II.

in history to apocryphal legends, and forwards to the later Middle Ages and modern folklore. They attest beliefs which were widespread in ninth- and tenth-century Europe, as the geographical range of the variants and analogues shows. Such continuity can scarcely be claimed for the rest of German vernacular literature in the tenth century, nor is that century characterised by texts which achieved a wide transmission. The impetus of the early and mid ninth century, the broadening of the uses of the vernacular, inspired by missionary zeal, did not last. The tenth century creates an impression of fragmentation. Copies were still being made of Otfrid's gospel harmony, of the *Heliand*, and of other minor religious texts, but no new major work emerges. There is no discernible new literary impulse until towards the end of the century, with the flowering of academic German in the schoolroom of St Gall under Notker III (d. 1022). The dearth of texts of any magnitude in the tenth century points in its negative way to the consequences when vernacular literature lacked active official backing. Only when the strength of the throne and the Church was behind it, could the vernacular prosper to the point where it could compete with Latin. The lack of central patronage is clear from the fact that, after the deaths of Louis the German (876) and Louis the III (882), there is no evidence, however indirect, which might be employed to associate a Carolingian monarch with vernacular literature.[34] At the same time, the more or less fortuitous transmission of texts such as the charms, which in the Church's eyes were regarded as *inutilis* or worse, provides invaluable evidence of the continuation of a healthy oral culture, which finally makes the breakthrough into literature in the court culture of the twelfth century.

Select bibliography

The standard student edition of OHG texts is: *Althochdeutsches Lesebuch*, edited by Wilhelm Braune (15th edn revised by Ernest Ebbinghaus, Tübingen, 1969). Most texts quoted are in the slightly standardised form employed by Braune, although reference to the manuscripts has been made wherever possible. The other major scholarly editions are:

K. Müllenhoff and W. Scherer (eds.), *Denkmäler deutscher Poesie und Prosa aus dem VIII.–XII. Jahrhundert*, 3rd edn revised by E. von Steinmeyer (Berlin, 1892, reprinted Berlin/Zürich, 1964).

E. von Steinmeyer (ed.), *Die kleineren althochdeuschen Sprachdenkmäler* (Berlin 1916, reprinted Berlin/Zurich, 1963).

Facsimiles of many of the texts are contained in H. Fischer (ed.), *Schrifttafeln zum althochdeutschen Lesebuch* (Tübingen, 1966). The palaeography of the texts is discussed by B. Bischoff, 'Paläographische Fragen deutscher Denkmäler der Karolingerzeit',

[34] Compare Haubrichs, *Geschichte*, p. 438. Haubrichs perhaps goes too far in his emphasis on the personal role of Louis the German; the interest of successive kings from Charlemagne onwards exerted a cumulative effect in stimulating writing in the vernacular.

Frühmittelalterliche Studien 5 (1971) pp. 101–34, reprinted in: Bischoff, *MS* III, pp. 73–111.

The most comprehensive literary history of the OHG period, to which unashamedly frequent allusion has been made in this survey, is that of W. Haubrichs, in the series edited by J. Heinzle: *Geschichte der deutschen Literatur von den Anfängen bis zum Beginn der Neuzeit. Bd. I: Von den Anfängen zum hohen Mittelalter. Teil 1: Die Anfänge: Versuche volkssprachiger Schriftlichkeit im frühen Mittelalter (ca 700–1050/60)* (Frankfurt-am-Main, 1988). This survey is also heavily indebted to:

J. K. Bostock, *A Handbook on Old High German Literature*, 2nd edn revised by K. C. King and D. R. McLintock (Oxford, 1976)

B. O. Murdoch, *Old High German Literature* Twayne's World Authors Series (Boston, Mass., 1983).

A critical bibliography of most of the texts discussed is to be found in:

J. S. Groselclose and B. O. Murdoch, *Die althochdeutschen poetischen Denkmäler* (Stuttgart, 1976). For articles on individual texts and more recent bibliography see: *Die deutsche Literatur des Mittelalters. Verfasserlexikon*, 2nd edn revised by K. Ruh (Berlin/New York, in progress)

Many of the texts discussed here are translated in full in Bostock's *Handbook*. A useful annotated selection aimed at the English reader is that by C. C. Barber, *An Old High German Reader with Notes, List of Proper Names, and Vocabulary* (Oxford, 1951).

6

Carolingian thought

John Marenbon

Introduction

The description of the Carolingian period as a 'renaissance' is double-edged with regard to the thought of the time. Carolingian thinkers, it implies, were important, not because of what they thought themselves, but because of the rebirth of ancient ideas which they fostered. Most historians of medieval thought have been quick to adopt this view of the period: an age when many classical and patristic works were studied and assimilated, but without any distinctive thought of its own; when the distinctively 'scholastic' use of reason on matters of doctrine had not yet replaced an encyclopaedic ideal of learning dominated by authority rather than argument. One figure alone has been allowed to escape this general characterisation of Carolingian thought – John Scottus Eriugena, an Irishman who worked at the court of Charles the Bald. But, in recognising the power and originality of his ideas, historians have added that Eriugena was a man outside his time, misunderstood by his contemporaries and more closely linked to the Greek than to the Latin tradition.

The following pages will question this common assessment of Carolingian thought. Although Carolingian scholars were eager to make themselves familiar with ancient and patristic authors, they were active assimilators, not passive ones. Often old ideas were merely the starting points for new ones; and even where they did not obviously innovate, the Carolingians transformed what they borrowed, giving new meaning to the individual arguments and motifs which they repeated from their authorities.

References to primary sources are usually given in brackets within the text: in the case of ancient and patristic texts, reference is to the books and chapters of the works; in the case of medieval works, reference is to the pages and lines of the edition given in the Bibliography at the end of this chapter, or to the column number for works published in Migne's Patrologia Latina.

The organisation and classification of knowledge

In the Carolingian period, the most usual classification of secular knowledge was provided by the seven liberal arts: the three verbal arts of the 'trivium' (grammar, logic and rhetoric) and the four mathematical arts of the 'quadrivium' (arithmetic, geometry, music and astronomy). The liberal arts and their relation to the study of scripture are first discussed in the Middle Ages by Alcuin. Alcuin (*ca* 730–804) was a teacher from York whom Charlemagne invited in 781 to help revive learning in his kingdom. Among Alcuin's works are manuals on the arts of the trivium, which are prefaced by a little treatise in the form of a dialogue between a master and his pupils, *De uera philosophia* ('On the true philosophy' – but it is usually treated simply as the preface to Alcuin's *De grammatica*).

De uera philosophia is often discussed in a way which reflects the stereotype of Carolingian thinkers as rediscoverers rather than inventors. Alcuin is supposed to have revived the classical scheme of seven liberal arts, borrowing from the late-antique *Institutiones* of Cassiodorus (II – praefatio) the parallel between the liberal arts and Solomon's seven-pillared temple of Wisdom and enriching his discussion with reminiscences – the earliest in the Middle Ages – of Boethius' *De consolatione philosophiae* (*ca* 522).[1] But closer inspection reveals a far more original train of thought.

For a start, the scheme of seven liberal arts is not, as scholars once believed, a reflection of common educational practice in Late Antiquity. It is, rather, the result of Neoplatonic speculation about knowledge, first and most fully expounded in Augustine's *De ordine*.[2] In his *De ordine*, Augustine – probably drawing closely on a Platonic source – describes how reason, seeking the contemplation of divine things, ascended through mastery of the liberal arts. 'Lest it should fall from on high, it sought for steps (*gradus*) and worked out for itself a way and an order through its possessions' (II, xiv, 39). The Master in *De uera philosphia*, too, is concerned to show by which steps (*quibus gradibus*) his pupils can reach the mastery of *philosophia*, which 'alone among the riches of the world never leaves miserable those who possess it' (col. 849D). The response is an interpretation of a verse from *Proverbs* (9:1): 'Wisdom built herself a house; she put up seven columns.' 'Although', the Master says, 'this statement refers to divine wisdom, which built itself a house – that is, a body – in the Virgin's womb, and strengthened it with the seven gifts of the Holy Spirit; or the Church, which is the house of God and which he illumined with these gifts; wisdom is, however, strengthened, by the seven columns of liberal letters, nor

1 See F. Brunhölzl, 'Der Bildungsauftrage der Hofschule' in: *Karl der Grosse*, II, pp. 28–41 and P. Courcelle, *La consolation de pholosophie dans la tradition littéraire* (Paris, 1967), pp. 33–47. On Boethius' *De consolatione*, see below, pp. 177–9.

2 Augustine, *De ordine*, *PL* 32. See I. Hadot *Arts libéraux et philosophie dans la pensée antique* (Paris, 1984) esp. pp. 101–214. For earlier views, compare H. I. Marrou, 'Les Arts libéraux dans l'antiquité classique' in: *Arts libéraux et philosophie au moyen âge*, Actes du quatrième congrès international de philosophie médiévale (Montreal/Paris, 1969), pp. 5–27.

has it led anyone to perfect knowledge unless he has been raised up by these seven columns or steps' (Col. 853 BC).

Although the link with Solomon's temple may have been suggested by Cassiodorus, it is Alcuin who expands the allusion and recalls the traditional exegesis of 'the house of wisdom'.[3] As a result, he is able both to insist on the radical need for knowledge of the arts and yet also to place the secular wisdom they represent within a scheme of Christian wisdom deriving from Christ, who is himself Wisdom. Alcuin has not merely, as often noted, transformed the *Philosophia* of Boethius' *De consolatione* into the Christian figure of Wisdom (*Sapientia*). He has also Christianised Augustine's argument in *De ordine*. As in Augustine, the liberal arts reflect the underlying structure of true knowledge. However, this is now seen to be grasped, not by the workings of reason itself, but through the interpretation of scripture. The liberal arts, then, are not – as Augustine himself would suggest in later works, such as *De doctrina christiana* – bare techniques which happen, as a matter of fact, to be valuable for the faithful. Rather, they reflect reality as it is made accessible to Christians through revelation.

In the later ninth and tenth centuries, the favourite textbook of the liberal arts was the *De nuptiis Mercurii et Philologiae* (On the marriage of Mercury and Philology), by Martianus Capella, a mysterious African who probably wrote late in the fifth century.[4] The *De nuptiis* was, indeed, the only ancient work to provide a set of introductions to each of the seven subjects; and Martianus must be considered, along with Augustine, as a founder of the system of liberal arts. The commentary on *De nuptiis* by Remigius of Auxerre (written *ca* 900), which is based on the work of his Carolingian predecessors, gives a good indication of how ideas about the nature and purpose of the arts developed in the century after Alcuin's *De uera philosophia*.[5]

The first two books of *De nuptiis*, which preface the monographs on each of the arts, describe the allegorical marriage of Mercury and Philology. For Martianus, this allegorical marriage was an expression of his Neoplatonism: Mercury stood for divine reason, Philology the soul, and their marriage represented the philosophical ascent of the adept achieved with the aid of theurgy.[6] Remigius' view is very different. Philology, he says (following John Scottus Eriugena), stands for 'wisdom and reason', whilst Mercury represents 'facility of speech'. Both eloquence and sharpness of reason are necessary to the wise man; and this marriage of Mercury with Philology opens the way to the liberal arts (I, 66:22–9). Of course, the Carolingian interpreters should not be

[3] Compare Gregory the Great, *Moralia in Iob* XXXII xvi 32 and Bede *In Proverbia Salomonis* I viii 34.

[4] See D. Shanzer *A Philosophical and Literary Commentary on Martianus Capella's* De nuptiis Philologiae et Mercurii *Book 1* (Berkeley/Los Angeles/London, 1986), pp. 5–17.

[5] Remigius uses glosses by John Scottus Eriugena and another set of glosses, which have been variously attributed to Dunchad, Martin of Laon and Heiric of Auxerre. For a brief discussion of the question of attribution (with bibliography), see J. Marenbon *From the Circle of Alcuin to the School of Auxerre* (Cambridge, 1981), pp. 117–9.

[6] Compare Hadot, *Arts libéraux*, pp. 137–9; Shanzer, *Commentary*, pp. 65–7.

thought deliberately to have distorted Martianus' intentions, which would not have been evident without a good knowledge of pagan Neoplatonism. Rather, they succeeded unconsciously in assimilating his thought to the needs and suppositions of their own culture. Read in Remigius' way, Books I and II of *De nuptiis* become a harmless prelude to the textbooks which follow – a chance for the exegete to demonstrate his knowledge of pagan mythology without having to face the challenge of pagan religion.

However, the Carolingian commentaries on Martianus also offered a more abstract account of the nature of the liberal arts. It occurs in a gloss to Book IV, on logic. Martianus has mentioned the term 'accident' which, in logicians' usage, means an attribute of something which it could (at least in theory) lack. The liberal arts are accidents in this sense, since they are non-essential attributes of those who have mastered them. But an accident cannot exist on its own: it must always be in a subject (whiteness, for instance, must be the whiteness of a man, a sheet of paper, an igloo). In what subject, then – Remigius asks – was the art of rhetoric before it was in, for example, Cicero? After rejecting the suggestion that the arts, as well as being accidents, are substances which can exist in their own right, Remigius (II, 26:13–17) concludes that

> every natural art is placed within human nature and created along with it. And so it is the case that all men naturally have the natural arts, but as a punishment for Adam's sin they have become obscure in men's souls and wrapped in profound ignorance. When we learn, what we do is to recall these arts which are hidden in the depths of our memory into the presence of our understanding . . .

Like Alcuin's *De uera philosophia*, this comment Christianises the liberal arts; but with a different emphasis. Remigius stresses the universality of the arts within divinely created human nature and uses the doctrine of the Fall to explain why men none the less need in some sense to learn them. Although this idea may reflect the teaching of John Scottus Eriugena, its adoption by Remigius and other scholars indicates that it became the common property of Carolingian thought.

The revival of logic

The two liberal arts most eagerly studied by the Carolingians were grammar and logic. It is not surprising that grammar should have been so important. Latin was the language of administration, the Church and learning, and even for those who spoke a kind of Latin as their native language, instruction in the complexities of its grammar was necessary. By contrast, the importance accorded to logic was a Carolingian innovation. In the ancient schools, a training in rhetoric had been much more common than instruction in logic; and, aside from brief discussions by Cassiodorus (*Institutiones* II, iii) and Isidore

(*Etymologiae* II, xxii–xxxi), there is no evidence that logic was studied between the death of Boethius and the late eighth century.

The revival of logic can be traced back to the initiative of one man: Alcuin. It was he who first attributed the *Categoriae decem*, a Latin adaptation of Aristotle's *Categories*, to St Augustine, supplied it with a preface in verse and introduced it into general use. In his *De dialectica*, he provided medieval readers with an elementary introduction to logic. The earliest surviving manuscript collection of logical texts (Rome, Bibliotheca Padri Maristi A. II. 1, written before 814) belonged to Alcuin's associate Leidrad and contains material associated with Alcuin himself, including extracts from his *De dialectica*. The other contents of Leidrad's manuscript are similar to the sources Alcuin used for his *De dialectica*: Porphyry's *Isagoge*, the *Categoriae decem* itself, Apuleius' *Periermenias* and Boethius' first commentary to Aristotle's *De interpretatione*.[7]

These works give an idea of what the study of logic involved for an early Carolingian student. Porphyry's *Isagoge* analyses the five predicables (genus, species, differentia, property and accident) – so called, because they are predicated of a subject in a statement (e.g. 'Socrates is an animal' [species]; 'Socrates is wearing a coat' [accident]). The *Categoriae decem* sets out the distinction between primary substances (individual things – this man or that horse), secondary substances (species and genera) and nine sorts of accidental attributes (quantity, quality, relation, place, time, being-in-a-position, having, doing and being-affected). Apuleius' *Periermeneias* provides an introduction to the logic of argument.

Why did Alcuin attribute the *Categoriae decem* to Augustine? A possible answer, with interesting implications, is provided by a group of passages probably compiled by Candidus, one of Alcuin's favourite pupils.[8] The first passage is entitled 'On Augustine's ten categories' and it consists mostly of an extract from Augustine's *De trinitate*, which shows how only one of the ten categories, substance, applies to God. For Alcuin and his circle, the *De trinitate* indicated Augustine's special interest in the logic of the categories: it also made manifest the link between logic and the study of Christian doctrine. The composition of Candidus' collection provides further evidence of such a combination, since passages discussing the Trinity and the existence of God are side by side with ones purely logical in their content. Another example of the link made between logic and theology at the end of the eighth century is provided by Book IV, chapter 23 of the *Libri Carolini*, the official answer drawn up by Charlemagne to Byzantine views on the worship of images. This chapter ostentatiously uses the analysis of syllogistic arguments provided in Aristotle's *De interpretatione* and Boethius' first commentary on it. The principal author of the *Libri Carolini* is now generally agreed to have been Theodulf of Orleans. But a powerful argument has been made by one distinguished scholar that Alcuin was the influence

[7] See Marenbon, *From the Circle*, pp. 31, 42, 52–3 (with further bibliography).
[8] Ibid., pp. 33–62.

behind this particular chapter, which brings logic to bear on theology in a way which he had made possible for medieval scholars.[9]

In the ninth century, developments in the study of logic continued to be linked to their use in doctrinal discussion. To give just two examples. Early in the 860s, Ratramnus of Corbie wrote a treatise attacking the views of a certain, otherwise unknown Irish monk, Macarius. Apparently Macarius, on the basis of a passage from Augustine, had claimed that souls are many and yet are also united as one. Ratramnus argued against Macarius' interpretation of Augustine by insisting that, when Augustine refers to a single, universal soul, he means 'universal' in a logical sense: he is talking about the species to which individual souls belong (e.g. 28:6–9). Then, basing himself on Boethius, he explains that species have no real existence outside the mind. They are concepts which people form from the individuals they perceive (96:8–11).

A little later – probably in the 870s or 880s – scholars in the school of Auxerre began to gloss the *Categoriae decem*. In what is probably the earliest glossed manuscript of the text (Milan Ambrosiana B 71 sup.; text and glosses written *ca* 865–75, probably in Auxerre), the main concern of the exegete is not to expound the doctrine of the Categories, but rather to link the pseudo-Augustinian text with metaphysical and theological ideas developed by Eriugena in his *Periphyseon*.[10] And John Scottus, in a different and far more sophisticated sort of way, had himself been inclined to theologise the logic of the *Categoriae decem* (see below, pp. 188–9).

Not all ninth-century logicians, however, entered into theological discussion with such abandon. A manuscript of the *Categoriae decem* from St Gall (St Gall Stiftsbibliothek 274), glossed probably only a decade or two later than the Auxerre manuscript, shares some of the Eriugenian material, but also contains much more straightforward exegesis of the text (and a preface based on Boethius' commentary to the *Categories*). A letter also from St Gall, and probably also from the mid- to late ninth century, shows a similarly sober attitude to the connections between logic and theology.[11] The author begins by examining a passage in Boethius' second commentary on the *Isagoge* dealing with the threefold powers of the soul: vegetative, animal and rational. This division – as he explains at some length – is that of a genus into its species (for instance, animal into man, horse, cow etc.), not of a whole into its parts (a house into its walls, roof, floor and so on). But, the writer goes on, is the vegetative soul of trees mortal or immortal? The answer is based on scriptural rather than

9 See D. Bullough, 'Alcuin and the kingdom of heaven: liturgy, theology and the Carolingian age' in: *Carolingian Essays* ed. U.-R. Blumenthal (Washington, D. C., 1983), pp. 36–7 reprinted in D. Bullough, *Carolingian Renewal. Sources and Heritage* (Manchester, 1991), pp. 161–240. On the authorship of the *Libri Carolini*, see P. Meyvaert, 'The authorship of the *Libri Carolini*: observations prompted by a recent book', *Revue Bénédictine* 89 (1979) pp. 29–57.

10 See Marenbon, *From the Circle*, pp. 121–38.

11 Ed. in L. M. de Rijk, 'On the curriculum of the arts of the trivium at St. Gall from *ca* 850 – *ca* 1000', *Vivarium* 1 (1963) pp. 35–86, at pp. 75–80; according to de Rijk, the sender was probably Liutbert, once a master of St Gall who was Archbishop of Mainz from 863 to 889 and the recipient was Iso of St Gall (d. 871).

philosophical considerations: surely paradise (which consists of trees and other plants) is immortal. Yet even this argument is proposed in self-consciously syllogistic form.

For a straightforward application of logic to doctrinal problems, the Carolingian scholar in search of an authority could turn to Boethius' *Opuscula sacra*. Two of these five short treatises (I, II) draw on logical teaching to show that God's trinity, although in no sense demonstrable, can to a certain extent be made more comprehensible by rational analysis. In another of them (V), Boethius demonstrates that two heretical views about the nature of Christ are not merely contradicted by authority, but are inconsistent even with logical reasoning. Although the earliest surviving manuscript of the *Opuscula sacra* dates from *ca* 820, there is good evidence that the works were known to Alcuin's circle before this.[12] Ratramnus of Corbie used Treatise V as a source for his views on universals, and John Scottus Eriugena drew more widely on the works. But it was towards the end of the ninth century that scholars appear to have begun glossing the *Opuscula sacra* in detail, in a way which – despite some Eriugenian speculations – made them completely familar with Boethius' method of applying logic to problems of doctrine.[13]

The Carolingian period had no logicians of genius, like Anselm in the eleventh or Abelard in the twelfth century. So far as the content of logical theory is concerned, it was a time of assimilation, not innovation. Yet Alcuin and his successors in the ninth century were novel in the importance they gave to logic within the curriculum – an importance connected with the close links they made between logic and the discussion of Christian doctrine. Although they could look to Augustine and Boethius for precedents, they transformed what was merely a strand in late-antique thought into a regular framework for teaching and speculation. Medieval philosophy and theology were shaped by the consequences of this initiative.

Interpreting Boethius

The fact that the authors of some ancient logical texts had been pagans did not pose a problem for their early medieval readers. Whilst it might be used for doctrinal purposes, logic itself was neutral with respect to revelation. Although Porphyry had been, in his non-logical writings, a fervent opponent of Christianity, there was nothing in his *Isagoge* which need be rejected by the most

12 Compare M. Gibson, 'The *Opuscula sacra* in the Middle Ages' in: *Boethius: his Life, Thought and Influence*, ed. M. Gibson (Oxford, 1981), pp. 214–34 at pp. 215–16; Marenbon, *From the Circle*, p. 163 n. 6 and C. Ineichen-Eder, 'Theologisches und philosophisches Lehrmaterial aus dem Alcuin-Kreise' *DA* 34 (1978) pp. 192–201.

13 The tradition of these glosses is a little more complicated than M. Cappuyns, 'Le plus ancien commentaire des "Opuscula sacra" et son origine', *Recherches de théologie ancienne et médiévale* 3 (1931), pp. 237–72, believes. He argues that the glosses, in their fuller form, are by Remigius of Auxerre. However, the 'abbreviated version' in fact contains much additional material; and (as with the glosses to the *Categoriae decem*) there is considerable variation in the glosses from manuscript to manuscript.

pious member of the Church. By contrast, other parts of ancient philosophy contained much which Christian readers could not easily accept. Even Platonism, which Augustine had recognized as nearer than any other philosophy in its teachings to the faith, had among its fundamental tenets some quite contrary to the Church's teaching: the eternity of matter; the pre-existence and reincarnation of souls; and the existence of a world-soul animating the universe as the human soul animates the body.

Plato's *Timaeus* was available at the time of Charlemagne in Calcidius' incomplete Latin translation, but it was a great rarity.[14] Carolingian scholars were confronted with the unacceptable aspects of Platonism by a different work – one which, in fact, was written by a Christian. Imprisoned and awaiting execution on fabricated charges of treason, Boethius, the author of the *Opuscula sacra* and numerous logical commentaries and translations, wrote his *De consolatione philosophiae*, in which the figure of Philosophia, using rational argument alone, brings the character Boethius from his initial despair to an understanding of the inviolability of goodness and the justice of divine providence. Nothing in the *De consolatione* is explicitly Christian, and in Book III, metrum ix Boethius provides a verse-summary of the *Timaeus*, including the doctrines of the world-soul and the pre-existence of souls.

In his discussion of this passage, Remigius of Auxerre uses the same technique which he applies to Martianus, interpreting whatever he finds in a Christian sense. He begins immediately by identifying the 'perpetual reason' by which, according to Boethius, God governs the world with God's wisdom, that is to say the Word or the Son of God. In consonance with a tradition of Judaeo-Christian Platonism going back as far as Philo, the allusions to a Platonic world of ideas (which Remigius notes explicitly) are interpreted in terms of God's advance planning of his creation: 'for before the world existed, it was in the mind of God' (334). The passage about the world-soul does not trouble Remigius either. He begins by mentioning that the 'philosophers' called the sun the soul of the world, because just as the human soul gives heat to the body, so the sun gives life to all things by its heat. A dangerous doctrine thus becomes a harmless analogy. He goes on to interpret the rest of the passage in terms of the analogy between man – the microcosm – and the universe (336–7). A similar strategy is employed on other potentially troublesome phrases and Boethius' reference to the pre-existence of souls is ignored.

Bovo, a monk of Corvey, who probably wrote before the end of the ninth century, took a very different approach. He begins his commentary, devoted to Book III, metrum 9 alone, by expressing his surprise that Boethius, the author of the *Opuscula sacra*, should have written things in his *De consolatione* contrary to the faith (384:40–50). Remarks like this, and his dismissal of the Platonic account of the descent of souls into their earthly bodies as 'utterly vain fictions'

[14] See Marenbon, *From the Circle*, p. 57.

(397:411), cannot disguise Bovo's eagerness to uncover and explain the true, Platonic significance of Boethius' metrum. From the start, he claims that in the *De consolatione* Boethius 'did not discuss anything of Church doctrine, but wished to reveal the teachings of the philosophers, especially the Platonists, to his readers' (384:50–3). Making clever use of the Platonist sources at his disposal (especially Macrobius' commentary on Cicero's *Somnium scipionis*), Bovo interprets Boethius' Platonic allusions – the world-soul, the pre-existence of souls – with remarkable directness and none of Remigius' Christianising. Bovo may have been sincere in his claims to be helping his readers by warning them of the danger posed by these far from Christian doctrines (and the greater, because hidden, danger which lay beneath other passages, less obviously offensive to Christian ears). But there is no disguising the scholarly interest and intellectual enthusiasm he brings to bear on the ideas he excoriates.

Carolingian theology

No area of Carolingian intellectual life seems, at first sight, more clearly to show lack of original thought and subservience to authority than the treatment of scripture and Christian doctrine. Biblical commentaries tend to be made up of excerpts from the commentaries of the Church Fathers. One of the most prolific exegetes, Hraban Maur *ca* (780–856), writes explicitly of his methods. He says, about his commentary on Kings, that 'I have worked in order to collect together in one, for the convenience of my reader, all the remarks which the holy Fathers have made about this book, so that he will find what each of them said from place to place in various comments ... arranged by us in order together.'[15] Independent treatises are often equally derivative. For instance, Alcuin's *De fide sanctae trinitatis* is an abbreviation of Augustine's *De trinitate*. And even doctrinal controversy is usually conducted by means of lengthy citation from patristic texts. For all these purposes, Augustine was a particularly favoured authority, and Carolingian opinions of him can verge on idolatry. Claudius of Turin (d. 827) writes, for instance, of the 'most saintly Augustine, most beloved of the Lord, pen of the Trinity, tongue of the Holy Spirit, earthly man but heavenly angel ... once surrounded by corruptible flesh, but ever gazing on God in incorruptible, immortal and angelic sight'.[16] Eriugena alone has the reputation of having avoided the servile dependence on authority which apparently characterises Carolingian theology.

Yet such judgements are misleading. They are made by considering only the methods used by Carolingian scholars, rather than asking the purposes to which these methods were put. The Carolingians did indeed work by reference to authorities, especially in matters concerning the faith. But there were many areas of doctrine where different authorities presented different views. Not only

[15] MGH Epp. V, p. 402:24–7.
[16] MGH Epp. IV, p. 599:8–11.

did the Carolingian scholars have to choose one position or another: often, whilst ostensibly basing themselves on authoritative citations, they went beyond their authorities, working out perhaps a bolder view or perhaps a more complex one.

Take, for example, the question of grace and free will. All Christian authors agreed that grace is required for salvation and that, nevertheless, men are responsible for their actions; but there was no clear guidance about how, and with which emphasis, these two principles were to be combined. In the reign of Charles the Bald, this question provoked the famous controversy over predestination, fought out between Gottschalk, John Scottus Eriugena and other leading thinkers of the time. But, before examining this dispute, it is illuminating to see how already, in the reign of Charles' father, Louis, a different aspect of the same problem had stimulated theologians. To what extent were some people excluded entirely from the possibility of being saved, however they acted? In particular: was the faith necessary for salvation available before the coming of Christ?

The question arises explicitly in a letter addressed (*ca* 830) by Agobard of Lyons to Fredegisus. Fredegisus was one of Alcuin's pupils and closest followers who, some years earlier, had written in a philosophically speculative though unsophisticated manner on the nature of nothing (*De nihilo et tenebris*). His intellectual adventurousness seems not to have abated and, in writings which do not survive, he asserted the pre-existence of the soul and discussed the relationship between God and truth. It is easy to dismiss Agobard's response as the mindless disapproval of an unenquiring, conservative churchman.[17] Certainly, he resorts to ridicule – demanding, for instance, with perfect logic, that if Fredegisus believes that souls pre-exist, he should be able to say *where*: north or south, east or west (294:14–18). But his disagreement over salvation rests on an abstract argument. According to Fredegisus, 'it is most absurd that [the holy patriarchs, prophets, kings and priests of the Old Testament] should be called Christians, because they would be Christians before Christ.' Agobard disagrees and explains that Fredegisus is basing himself on a faulty view of Christ derived from a faulty reading of Augustine. Christ existed even before he became man, and so faith in him was possible even before the Incarnation and was enjoyed by the holy men of the Old Testament (295:26ff.).

Whereas Agobard argues his position explicitly and insists that his is the correct interpretation of the authoritative writings of Augustine, his contemporary, Hilduin, approaches the same problem more delicately yet, in a sense, more boldly, since he subtly alters his sources so as to present his own views. As abbot of St Denis, he had been asked by Louis the Pious to translate from the Greek a corpus of works which claimed to be by Dionysius, the Areopagite converted by St Paul and also, so legend had it, the apostle of the Franks, to

17 As is done in Marenbon, *From the Circle*, pp. 64–6.

whom Hilduin's monastery was dedicated. Hilduin also composed a *Passio* of St Dionysius. Here he adapts his sources to show that Christ was recognisable to a wise pagan such as Dionysius before his conversion. For instance, in the seventh of his letters (which forms part of the corpus translated by Hilduin), Dionysius describes how he witnessed the eclipse which took place when Christ was crucified and was told by his companion, Apollophanus, that it was 'the presage of divine revolutions'.[18] Only after he has become a Christian, when he writes the letter, does Dionysius recognise Christ as the cause of the miracle. By contrast, in Hilduin's account, Dionysius remarks to Apollophanus *at the time of the eclipse*: 'this darkness, which to our amazement and against the order of things has come down before our eyes, was the sign of the coming of the true light of the whole world, a serene and dignified announcement of God's shining forth for the human race' (27B). Even as a pagan, then, Dionysius was able, according to Hilduin, to recognise the coming of Christ. There is a similar change of emphasis in Hilduin's account of Dionysius' conversion. In Hilduin's source, the Acts of the Apostles (17:17–34), St Paul finds an altar in the Areopagus at Athens dedicated to 'the Unknown God' and declares to those around that 'this God whom you have worshipped in ignorance I announce to you.' The Areopagite is one of those who are converted by Paul's preaching and becomes a follower. In Hilduin's account, however, Dionysius is no longer a mere bystander. Paul asks him about the altar dedicated to 'the Unknown God'. Dionysius replies: 'This God has not yet been shown to be among the Gods, but he is unknown to us and will come in future times. For he is the God who will reign in earth and heaven and his kingdom will have no end.' Dionysius goes on to explain that this unknown deity is 'true God and true man, and he will renew the world . . .' So full is this wise pagan's knowledge already that it is only left for Paul to fill in a few details and confirm his existing beliefs (27 CD).

It was as the result of Gottschalk's polemics that this earlier interest in questions about grace was channelled into the mid-ninth-century controversy over predestination. Gottschalk (*ca* 803–867 or 869), originally a monk of Fulda, then of Orbais, started propounding his views on predestination in the 840s, and they quickly gave rise to argument. From his own point of view, the consequences were disastrous. In 848, Gottschalk was condemned by a council at Quierzy and confined for the rest of his life in the monastery of Hautvillers. But this did not prevent him from carrying on writing and arguing his case. Gottschalk was himself by no means an unsophisticated thinker (though one more deeply influenced by his studies in grammar that those in logic); but it is the rather crude version of his position which his opponents attributed to him which is of importance for the history of thought. Gottschalk propounded a theory of dual predestination: of the blessed to salvation and the wicked to damnation. Leading

[18] See Hilduin's translation of this passage: G. Théry, *Etudes dionysiennes* II (Paris, 1937), pp. 314–5.

churchmen of the time, such as Hraban Maur and Hincmar, archbishop of Rheims (*ca* 806–83), feared the practical consequences of such a doctrine, which seemed to make it impossible for men to influence their eternal destiny by acting well or badly. It was a matter of urgency to refute Gottschalk's arguments. But Gottschalk did not offer his views as a personal, idiosyncratic interpretation of scripture: he backed them up with a body of quotation from Augustine.

Hraban wrote his most detailed reply to Gottschalk in a letter to Noting, bishop of Verona, whilst Hincmar's first response took the form of a letter to his parishioners (*Ad reclusos et simplices*).[19] Both churchmen were subtler than is often recognised. Whilst they countered authoritative texts with authoritative texts, they did not cite the Fathers mindlessly or incoherently.[20] Both men were aware of the difficulty of their position. They too accepted the central Augustinian tenet on which Gottschalk's position was based: that fallen man, unaided by grace, cannot live a life sufficiently good to lead to his salvation. But they denied that this implies dual predestination. God, they said, *predestines* some – the blessed – to salvation; he also *foreknows* both which individuals he will predestine and which he will not (and so will go to hell); but he does not *predestine* anyone to hell. Hraban and Hincmar were aware that their position (like Gottschalk's) risked making God seem capricious.

Hincmar responded by suggesting that God withholds his grace from those whose future misuse of their free wills he has foreseen, and that the damned are those who refuse to accept the grace they are offered (e.g. 275, 269); Hraban preferred to emphasise God's incomprehensibility (1533A–C, 1547D–1553B). Perhaps because neither was fully convinced that such answers were satisfactory – and also because Gottschalk was succeeding in winning the support of many distinguished scholars – Hincmar turned to John Scottus, who was at that time a teacher at Charles the Bald's palace school.

The *De praedestinatione* which John produced aroused disapproval much more unanimous than ever met Gottschalk's views. Prudentius of Troyes and Florus of Lyons wrote treatises specifically designed to refute its errors and Hincmar, embarrassed by the results of his commission, claimed to know nothing about the work – not even for sure who had written it. The hostile reaction to John's work has usually been taken by modern historians as a sign of the intellectual gulf separating Eriugena from his contemporaries.[21] According to this view,

19 Hincmar also wrote two later works on the subject. No attempt is made in this chapter to survey the controversy as a whole and the many different contributions to it. For fuller details, see D. Ganz, 'The debate on predestination' in: *Charles the Bald. Court and Kingdom* ed. M. T. Gibson and J. L. Nelson (London, 2nd revised edn, 1990), pp. 283–302; M. Cappuyns, *Jean Scot Erigène: sa vie, son œuvre, sa pensée* (Louvain/Paris, 1933), pp. 102–27 and J. Devisse, *Hincmar, Archevêque de Reims, 845–882* (Geneva, 1975–6), I, pp. 115–279.

20 For a full discussion of this, and John Scottus' intervention, see J. Marenbon, 'John Scottus and Carolingian theology: from the *De praedestinatione*, its background and its critics, to the *Periphyseon*' in: *Charles the Bald*, ed. Gibson and Nelson, pp. 303–25 at pp. 303–11.

21 See, for example, Cappuyns, *Jean Scot*, p. 111 and G. Schrimpf, 'Der Beitrag des Johannes Scottus Eriugena zum Prädestinationsstreit', in: *Die Iren und Europa im früheren Mittelalter* ed. H. Löwe (Stuttgart, 1982) pp. 819–65, *passim*.

other ninth-century scholars, used to basing doctrinal discussion on the citation of authorities, were unable to grasp a work which began by declaring that ignorance of the liberal arts was a root cause of doctrinal error (110:2–4), and went on to make extensive use of logical techniques in proposing its arguments. However, the discussions above of thinkers such as Alcuin, Candidus and Ratramnus of Corbie have shown how this view underestimates the intellectual sophistication of the tradition within which Eriugena worked. Moreover, John Scottus' point of departure is exactly that provided for him by Hraban and Hincmar: God foreknows the destinies of everyone, but he predestines only to salvation. In the case of those who will be damned, God does not act, but rather fails to act. John simply takes this idea further – far further. When the damned are punished, it is not by God, but by themselves. All that God does is to frame just laws, which conflict with the desires of the wicked, including their ultimate desire to distance themselves so far from God, the source of all being, that they cease entirely to exist. Moreover, Eriugena insists that in sinners it is not the human nature made by God, redeemed by Christ and shared by all men alike, which is subject to this self-punishment, but only the evil will (which God did not create).

In expounding these views, Eriugena is no less keen than most of his contemporaries to show that he has patristic support. Indeed, his wish to be seen not to conflict with the authority of the Fathers leads him into some dubious interpretative practices, such as insisting that at times Augustine meant exactly the opposite of what he wrote. Incidents like this show, not an irreverence for Augustine, but rather an exaggerated respect, comparable to Claudius of Turin's. Even when he declares that 'true philosophy is true religion and true religion true philosophy' (5:16–8), John is not, as might appear, insisting on the use of philosophical methods in doctrinal discussion, but quoting Augustine (*De uera religione* I, 1) on the identity of theory and practice within Christianity.

John Scottus Eriugena's later work

In the sections above, John Scottus has already been seen as a commentator on Martianus Capella and the writer of a treatise directed against Gottschalk. Little more than this is known about the earlier period of his life. He is first mentioned in connection with the controversy on predestination, and he seems at this time to have been teaching the liberal arts at the palace school of Charles the Bald. The name 'Scottus' indicates that John was an Irishman (as does 'Eriugena' – a Graecising title which he made up himself); but what education he received in Ireland, and when he came to the continent, remain matters for speculation. Irishmen had won a special position for themselves in intellectual life ever since the time of Charlemagne. Their high level of culture has sometimes been attributed to the education they received in their homeland, which – so the theory went – had been the refuge of scholars fleeing the barbarian invasions of the disintegrating Roman Empire. It now seems much more probable that the migrant Irish scholars gained most of their learning on the continent, stimulated to achievement by contacts with each other and perhaps by their position as a group of strangers in a foreign land. Among Eriugena's near-contemporaries were the two Irishmen Sedulius, who worked in Liège, and Martin, a schoolmaster at Laon. Sedulius was a sophisticated Latin poet, a wide-ranging reader of the classics and author of a work of guidance for rulers which imitated the prosimetric form of Boethius' *De consolatione*. Martin's activities were more directly pedagogic. Both men also knew, not just Latin, but a considerable amount of Greek. Knowledge of Greek – a rarity in the west in any period of the Middle Ages – seems to have been a speciality of the Irish scholars on the continent: Eriugena too acquired a knowledge of Greek and, for him though not for his contemporaries, it was instrumental in changing his intellectual horizons.

The works of pseudo-Dionysius had already been translated into Latin by Hilduin. But Hilduin's version was so literal as to be nearly incomprehensible. Late in the 850s, Charles the Bald asked John Scottus to produce a new translation. The task not only made John improve his Greek; it also brought him into contact with the intellectual world of Greek Christian Neoplatonism. John went on to translate works by the seventh-century monk, Maximus the Confessor, which, he believed, helped to elucidate the 'very obscure' ideas of Dionysius; and to make contact with an earlier type of Greek patristic thought by putting into Latin a treatise on the creation of man by Gregory of Nyssa (*ca* 330–94).[22] In the 860s Eriugena went on to write a series of works deeply marked by his reading of the Greeks. The most accessible of these (and – pseudonymously – the most widely diffused) is a short homily on the prologue to the Gospel of St John; but by far the most important is the *Periphyseon* (864–8).

The *Periphyseon* takes the form of a dialogue between a master and pupil, divided into five books and extending to roughly 700 pages of modern print. The Greek title means 'about nature', and Eriugena begins by setting out the fourfold division of universal nature, around which the rest of the work is structured (hence the title given to the work in older editions: *De divisione naturae* – 'On the division of nature'). All things may be divided into (1) that which is not created and creates; (2) that which is created and creates; (3) that which is created and does not create; (4) that which is not created and does not create (I, 441B–442A).[23] The first division corresponds unproblematically to God. The second division corresponds to what Eriugena calls the 'primordial causes'. These primordial causes are like Platonic Ideas (and, in line with the

22 On John Scottus' knowledge of Greek and his translations, see E. Jeauneau, 'Jean Scot Erigène et le grec', *Archivum latinitatis medii aevi (Bulletin du Cange)* 41 (1979) pp. 5–50 (reprinted in his *Etudes érigéniennes* (Paris, 1987), pp. 85–132).

23 References to the *Periphyseon* will be to the number of the book and the column in PL since these column references are given in both in the new critical editions of Books I–IV and in the translation.

common patristic Christianisation of this theory, are said to be in the mind – that is the Wisdom or Son – of God), but they also have some of the characteristics of the Stoic 'seminal reasons', innate principles of things, about which John learned from Augustine's *De Genesi ad litteram*. The third division of nature corresponds to the rest of the universe, created by God through the intermediary of the primordial causes. The fourth division corresponds, like the first, to God himself. But how can God be described as 'not creating'? The paradox is explained by the fact that Eriugena intends to give, not a static set of divisions, but an account of the history of the universe from creation to final judgement. God is one and indivisible, but whereas the first division describes God in his role as creator, the fourth division depicts him as the God to whom all things will return at the end of time (IV, 860 BC).

In Book I, Eriugena examines the first division, or rather explains, using pseudo-Dionysius's concept of 'negative theology' (see below, p. 187) why God *cannot* be comprehended except negatively, or metaphorically through terms which apply to what he has created. Created nature – the second and third divisions – can be understood as a series of 'theophanies', more or less perfect manifestations of God which make comprehensible what, in itself, must always remain beyond the grasp of the intellect. Books II–IV deal with the second and third divisions by describing the creation of the universe and man. John's account is, of course, based on Genesis, but the interpretation, although worked out in close relation to the biblical text, is highly allegorical, in a manner favoured by writers in the Greek tradition but held suspect by Augustine. Eriugena argues that the story of paradise should not be understood literally: it was only after the Fall, as the result of sin, that man acquired a physical body and was divided into the two sexes. In Book V, Eriugena discusses the return of all things to God.

Faced with a work of such vast proportions, generality of scope and unaccustomed ideas, it is hardly surprising that historians have tended to regard its author in isolation even from the cleverest of his contemporaries, 'a voice in the wilderness'.[24] But, since Eriugena's system of thought is not one (like, for instance, Aristotle's or Descartes') which it seems possible to grasp entirely on its own terms in an historical vacuum, scholars have usually sought to find some other context in which to place the *Periphyseon*. By his reading of the Greek Christian writers, opines one of Eriugena's recent editors, he was brought 'as wholly within the Greek tradition as if he had been a Byzantine writing in Greek'.[25] Many valuable studies have been written which, on this principle, examine John's ideas within the context of the Platonic tradition, pagan and

24 D. Knowles, *The evolution of medieval thought* (London, 1988, 2nd edn revised by C. N. L. Brook and D. E. Luscombe) p. 70.

25 I. P. Sheldon-Williams in: *The Cambridge history of later Greek and early medieval philosophy* ed. A. H. Armstrong (Cambridge, 1979) p. 520.

Christian.[26] Other historians have preferred to place Eriugena within a broader tradition of idealist philosophy, stretching back to Plato and forward to Hegel and the German Idealists. Indeed, the most recent of these writers has argued that Eriugena transformed his Neoplatonic sources, changing their realism into an idealism which had few precedents before the nineteenth century.[27]

There is, nevertheless, reason to think that the best context for John Scottus is provided by the milieu in which he actually worked, so long as it is understood that a context does not restrict a thinker so much as provide him with a set of opportunities.

Despite its difference in size and scope, in form the *Periphyseon* is based on a variety of Carolingian models. Like many of Alcuin's didactic works, it is set as a dialogue between master and pupil, in which the pupil is allowed to be intelligently inquisitive, but never to dominate his teacher in argument. Although the work has five books – the same number, perhaps not coincidentally, as Boethius' *De consolatione* – it is made up of just two types of composition. Book I is in its outlines an examination of the ten categories in relation to God: a type of discussion used, in greatly shorter form, by earlier Carolingian scholars (see above, p. 175). Books II–V are an hexaëmeron – an exegesis of the opening of Genesis, discussing the work of creation and, often, the temptation and Fall. Eriugena even manages to work his account of the Return into this commentary, by interpreting Genesis 3:22 ('lest perhaps he should put forth his hand and take from the tree of life and eat and live for ever') as a prophecy of man's eternal destiny. The hexaëmeron was a form used by the Latin as well as the Greek fathers; and Eriugena's medieval predecessors such as Bede, Alcuin and Hraban Maur had included hexaemeral sections within their commentaries on Genesis.

Important aspects of the subject-matter of the *Periphyseon* are related to Carolingian controversies. This is especially clear in Book V, where Eriugena returned to the theme he had discussed in *De praedestinatione*: the nature of punishment in hell and of God's responsibility for it.[28] In the two works written by Florus of Lyons and Prudentius of Troyes specifically to refute the errors of *De praedestinatione*, John's pronouncements on these subjects had received particular vituperation. Eriugena now took the chance to restate his position, clarifying it and defending it against some of the objections his adversaries had made. At the Return, 'evil will come to an end and will remain in no nature, since divine goodness will operate and appear in all things' (918B). Punishment will continue eternally, but what will be punished are non-things. Here John takes up a telling point which Florus had made against him. In *De praedestinatione*, Eriugena had insisted that punishment, being an evil, is not a substance but a deficiency (63:41–66:155) and cannot therefore be inflicted by God. Florus

26 The fullest is S. Gersh, *From Iamblichus to Eriugena* (Leiden, 1978).
27 D. Moran, *The Philosophy of John Scottus Eriugena* (Cambridge, 1989).
28 See Marenbon, 'John Scottus', pp. 311–4, 319–21 for fuller discussion.

had responded cleverly, by pointing out that, whilst punishment itself is not a substance, it can be in a substance (the body or soul which is punished) and from a substance (such as a whip or sword).[29] In the *Periphyseon*, John takes up Florus' point but turns it to his own purposes. Just as the punishments are non-things which are in real substances, so the objects of punishment, too, are non-things in real substances (V, 939C–940D). Human nature created by God, cannot be punished (a point already made in *De praedestinatione*); nor can the human will itself, which is part of human nature: rather, the objects of punishment will be 'the perverse and irrational motions of the will' which 'are altogether not understood to exist in the nature of things' (V, 940B).

The *Periphyseon* does not show the extreme reverence towards the authority of Augustine, characteristic of Carolingian scholars and found in John's own *De praedestinatione*. And, near the end of Book I (512B–513C), Eriugena produces an argument which seems to make light of the need for any sort of authoritative support whatever. Whereas authority is prior to reason in time, reason is prior to authority by nature and so is of greater worth. In fact authority is simply 'truth discovered by the power of reason and put into writing by the Holy Fathers for the benefit of posterity'. John does not, however, follow out the consequences of this theory in his practice. He is as keen to show that he has patristic support for his views as his contemporaries and is happy to insert long quotations from the writings of the Fathers. But it is the Greek Fathers (pseudo-Dionysius, Gregory of Nyssa, Maximus the Confessor, Basil, Origen) to whom he looks for support. Some of Ambrose's more heavily Platonic exegesis is also used, but Augustine (although *implicitly* through his *De Genesi ad litteram* perhaps John's most important source) more often than not appears explicitly as an opponent of the views which Eriugena wishes to champion.

The way in which Eriugena treats his Greek authors is, in practice, similar to the way in which other leading Carolingian scholars treated their Latin authorities. Ideas are borrowed freely and explicit citations in support of an argument or position are common; and yet, behind this appearance of servility, a transformation has taken place. Like his contemporaries, Eriugena thinks *through* his sources.

For example, in Book I Eriugena explains the distinction between negative ('apophatic') and positive ('cataphatic') theology, which he clearly attributes to pseudo-Dionysius (458A ff; cf. 509 ff). And it is indeed from pseudo-Dionysius that Eriugena derived the basic idea that every description of God is literally true only when negated, and that even in the case of being (which Augustine had believed could be used as a term to describe God) it is truer to say that God is not, than that he is. But John develops this idea in a systematic manner not anticipated in pseudo-Dionysius. Before he explains his fourfold division of nature, Eriugena discusses a more fundamental division of all things: into those

[29] PL 119, 161C–162A.

which are and those which are not. In its most fundamental form, this distinction is one between 'those things which can be apprehended by the bodily senses or by the intellect' which are said to be, and those which 'because of the excellence of their nature elude not merely every sense but all intellect and reason' and so may be said not to be (I, 443AB). Pseudo-Dionysius' statement that God is not should be taken, therefore, to mean that God cannot be known; but this, for Eriugena, amounts to far more than a banal statement of human incapacity.[30] To know is to define, to circumscribe, to place within limits. God creates by knowing and, in the *Periphyseon*, this notion is extended downwards, so that all of lower nature is created in man by his action of knowing it (IV 763C–786A). But man cannot know himself, only God can know what he is (e.g. II, 585B; IV, 771B–D). As for God himself, than whom nothing is higher, he cannot be known *even by himself* (II, 585A–598C). Were he comprehensible, even to himself alone, he would be in some sense limited; his infinity and his unknowability in principle go together. Eriugena thus succeeds in giving a strong sense to the pseudo-Dionysian assertion of God's non-being, which he extends further in Book III when he discusses, with remarkable theological audacity, the relationship between the nothing from which God created the universe and the nothing which is God himself.

Eriugena performs a similar transformation of his source-material in the discussion of deification in Book V.[31] Where Latin thinkers talked of 'glorification', the Greek Fathers tended to speak of 'deification' (*theosis/deificatio*). Deification meant, not complete identity with the deity (which would have compromised his transcendence), but assimilation to him. It was possible for the sage even in this life, and pseudo-Dionysius described the ways towards it, through mystic contemplation and through the sacraments. Other fathers, such as Gregory of Nyssa, emphasised the universality of *theosis*: the whole of human nature had been taken by God in the incarnation and so the whole of human nature was deified. But another of John's favoured authors, Maximus the Confessor, had been alarmed that this view seemed to imply the heresy of universal salvation, and he insisted that deification was open only to the worthy. Eriugena takes elements of all these ideas, but combines them into something very much his own. Deification will take place, he believes, only at the end of time. When it does so, it will be *both* universal *and* yet limited to the elect, who have lived good lives, since human nature, whole and entire, will be deified yet sinners will continue to be punished, not by God but by themselves.

Despite his enthusiasm for the Greek tradition, Eriugena did not lose his characteristically Carolingian interest in the liberal arts and, especially, logic. John combines his logical analyses, however, with ideas learnt from the Greek Platonists in such a way as to produce a type of thinking unique to him. Late-antique logic, as inherited by the early medieval west through Boethius,

30 See Schrimpf, *Das Werk* for an extended interpretation of the *Periphyseon* along such lines.
31 See Marenbon, 'John Scottus', pp. 316–19.

had mainly been elaborated by Platonists. But, following Porphyry, these ancient writers had worked on the assumption that Aristotelian logic is valid in its own sphere, as an analysis of perceptible reality. They did not, therefore, usually try to apply Platonic principles to it. These were reserved for metaphysics. As a rule, medieval logic is built on the Aristotelian basis inherited from Antiquity, except that logic is no longer regarded as merely provisional in its grasp of the truth. The superstructure of Platonic metaphysics has disappeared – overlooked rather than discarded – and logic has become a universal tool and source of speculation. Eriugena is an exception. In the *Periphyseon* he looks at the logic he has learned from his Latin sources – the *Categoriae decem* above all – in the light of the Platonic metaphysics he has learned from the Greek fathers. This is especially obvious in his treatment of three of the categories, substance (or, by the Greek name he usually used, *ousia*), place and time. At times, like Aristotle, John means by an *ousia* an individual thing. But often, he speaks of something's *ousia* as that *by which* it exists and then influenced by his negative theology he speaks of *ousia* in this sense as indefinable and unknowable: 'if . . . you follow more perceptively the footsteps of St Gregory the Theologian (i.e. Gregory of Nazianzen) and his expositor, the most wise Maximus, you will find that in all things which are *ousia* is in itself entirely incomprehensible not only to the senses but also to the intellect . . .' (I, 471B). A little later (I, 474B ff), Eriugena argues vigorously that place is not to be confused with body. Initially, this is a straightforward, logical point: place is the circumscription of a body, not the body itself. But Eriugena goes on to identify place with definition, and then to link definition with bringing into being. Place and time cease to be Aristotle's common-sense categories (Where is Socrates? In the forum. When? Today) and become the necessary conditions for the existence of all creatures.

It was perhaps as well for the development of medieval logic, and the other branches of abstract thought which grew up under its influence, that Eriugena's experiment in logic was without influence. Even the ninth-century scholars who used Eriugenian ideas in their glosses to the *Categoriae decem* were doing something very different: seizing on tenuous links between the logical text and John's thought, not trying to re-think Aristotelian logic from the perspective of Christian Neoplatonism. Although it is easy to fault Eriugena's logic for its frequent want of clarity and occasional lack of coherence, the daring and originality of his ideas here, as elsewhere, is undeniable. Yet, paradoxically, John arrived at his approach to logic not from a wish to innovate, but out of the desire to remain true to two traditions which were opposed in their implications: the Carolingian logical tradition, based on Boethius and, ultimately, on late Greek Platonic scholasticism; and the Platonic metaphysics of the Greek Christian writers. Such innovation reached through the pursuit of tradition provides a fitting epitome of Eriugena's thought; just as his thought as a whole offers, not an exception to the patterns of Carolingian intellectual life but, as it were, a summary, in exaggerated form, of what Alcuin and his successors had made possible.

Select bibliography

Primary texts (and translations where available)

Agobard of Lyons, Works, ed. L. Van Acker, CCSL (CM) 52 (Turnhout, 1981); MGH Epp. V, pp. 210–21

Alcuin, Works, PL 100–1 (*De uera philosophia* is in vol. 101)

Anonymous, Glosses to *Categoriae decem* in: J. Marenbon, *From the Circle of Alcuin to the School of Auxerre. Logic Theology and Philosophy in the Early Middle Ages*, Cambridge Studies in Medieval Life and Thought, 3rd series 15 (Cambridge, 1981) pp. 185–206; glosses to Boethius, *Opuscula sacra* (sometimes attributed to Remigius of Auxerre) in E. K. Rand, *Johannes Scottus* (Munich, 1906)

Bovo of Corvey, Commentary on Book III, m. ix of Boethius, *De consolatione* in: R. B. C. Huygens, 'Mittelalterliche Kommentare zum *O qui perpetua*', *Sacris erudiri* 6 (1954) pp. 373–427

Candidus Wizo, Philosophical and theological passages in Marenbon, *From the Circle*, pp. 152–170

Fredegisus of Tours, *De substantia nihili et de tenebris*, MGH Epp. IV pp. 552–5

Gottschalk of Orbais, C. Lambot (ed.), *Œuvres théologiques et grammaticales de Godescalc d'Orbais* (Louvain, 1945)

Hilduin of St Denis, *Passio sanctissimi Dionysii* PL 106, cols 23–50

Hincmar of Rheims, *Ad reclusos et simplices*, ed. W. Gundlach, 'Zwei Schriften des Erzbischofs Hinkmar von Reims – 2', *Zeitschrift für Kirchengeschichte* 10 (1889) pp. 258–309

Hraban Maur, Letter to Bishop Noting, PL 112, cols. 1530–53

John Scottus (Eriugena), Commentary on Martianus, ed. C. Lutz (Cambridge, Mass., 1939) (a different version of Bk I is ed. by E. Jeauneau in: *Quatres thèmes érigéniens* (Montreal/Paris, 1978); *De praedestinatione*, ed. G. Madec (Turnhout, 1978) CCSL (CM) 50); *Periphyseon* I–III ed. I. P. Sheldon-Williams (with parallel translation) (Dublin, 1968–81), IV, ed. E. Jeauneau (with parallel translation) (Dublin, forthcoming), V, ed. H. Floss in *MPL* 122: Homily on the prologue to John, ed. E. Jeauneau, with parallel French translation (Paris, 1969). **Translations**: *Periphyseon*, trans. I. P. Sheldon-Williams, revised by J. O'Meara (Montreal/Washington, 1987); Homily – trans. in J. O'Meara, *Eriugena* (Oxford, 1988) pp. 158–76

Libri Carolini, ed. H. Bastgen, MGH Conc. II, Supplementum (Hanover/Leipzig, 1924)

Ratramnus of Corbie, *Liber de anima*, ed. D. C. Lambot (Namur/Lille, 1952)

Remigius of Auxerre, Commentary on Martianus Capella, ed. C. Lutz (Leiden, 1962–5); Commentary on Boethius' *De consolatione* (extracts), in E. T. Silk (ed.), *Saeculi noni auctoris in Boetii consolationem philosophiae commentarius*, Appendix (Rome, 1935)

Secondary works

Collections

B. Bischoff (ed.), *Karl der Grosse: Lebenswerk und Nachleben* II (Düsseldorf, 1965)

M. T. Gibson and J. L. Nelson (eds.), *Charles the Bald. Court and kingdom* (London, 2nd revised edn, 1990)

H. Löwe (ed.), *Die Iren und Europa im früheren Mittelalter* (Stuttgart 1982)

General

A. H. Armstrong (ed.) *The Cambridge History of Later Greek and Early Medieval Philosophy* (Cambridge, 1970)

J. Marenbon, *From the Circle of Alcuin to the School of Auxerre* (Cambridge, 1981)

Historiography

G. Schrimpf, 'Ursprünge und Anfänge: Vor- und Frühscholastik' in: *Philosophie im Mittelalter*, ed. J. P. Beckmann, L. Honnefelder, G. Schrimpf and G. Wieland (Hamburg, 1987) pp. 1–25

Alcuin

F. Brunhölzl, 'Der Bildungsauftrage der Hofschule' in: *Karl der Grosse* II, pp. 28–41

D. Bullough, 'Alcuin and the kingdom of heaven: liturgy, theology and the Carolingian age' in: *Carolingian Essays*, ed. U.-R. Blumenthal (Washington, D.C., 1983) pp. 1–69, reprinted in D. Bullough, *Carolingian Renewal: Sources and Heritage* (Manchester, 1991) pp. 161–240

Logic

L. M. de Rijk, 'On the curriculum of the arts of the trivium at St Gall from *ca* 850 – *ca* 1000', *Vivarium* 1 (1963) pp. 35–86

A. Van de Vyver, 'Les étapes du développement philosophique du haut moyen âge', *Revue belge de philologie et d'histoire* 8 (1929) pp. 425–53

Use of Boethius

M. Cappuyns, 'Le plus ancien commentaire "Opuscula sacra" et son origine', *Recherches de théologie ancienne et médiévale* 3 (1931) pp. 237–72

P. Courcelle, *La consolation de philosophie dans la tradition littéraire* (Paris, 1967)

M. Gibson (ed.) *Boethius: his life, thought and influence* (Oxford, 1981)

F. Troncarelli, *Tradizioni perduti* (Padua, 1981); *Boethiana aetas* (Alessandria, 1987)

The glossing of Martianus Capella

C. Leonardi, 'I codici di Marziano Capella', *Aevum* 33 (1959) pp. 443–89; 34 (1960) pp. 1–99, 411–524

The controversy over predestination

D. Ganz, 'The debate on predestination' in *Charles the Bald*, ed. Gibson and Nelson pp. 283–302

J. Marenbon, 'John Scottus and Carolingian theology: from the *De praedestinatione*, its background and its critics, to the *Periphyseon*', ibid., pp. 303–25

G. Schrimpf, 'Der Beitrag des Johannes Scottus Eriugena zum Prädestinationsstreit' in: *Die Iren*, ed. Löwe, pp. 819–65

John Scottus (Eriugena)

M. Cappuyns, *Jean Scot Erigène: sa vie, son œuvre, sa pensée* (Louvain/Paris, 1933)
S. Gersh, *From Iamblichus to Eriugena* (Leiden, 1978)
E. Jeauneau, *Etudes érigéniennes* (Paris, 1987)
D. Moran, *The philosophy of John Scottus Eriugena* (Cambridge, 1989)
G. Schrimpf, *Das Werk des Johannes Scottus im Rahmen des Wissenschaftsverständnisses seiner Zeit* (Münster, 1982)

Other individual schools and masters

J. P. Bouhot, *Ratramne de Corbie* (Paris, 1976)
J. J. Contreni, *The Cathedral School at Laon from 850 to 930* (Munich, 1978)
S. Hellmann, *Sedulius Scottus* (Munich, 1906)
D. Iogna-Prat, C. Jeudy, G. Lobrichon, *L'Ecole carolingienne d'Auxerre* (Paris, 1991)
J. Jolivet, *Godescalc d'Orbais et la trinité* (Paris, 1958)
G. Théry, *Etudes dionysiennes* I and II (Paris, 1932, 1937)

7

The writing of history

Matthew Innes and Rosamond McKitterick

Why does any society keep a record of its past actions and deeds? What is the human impulse that creates historical writing? What distinguishes the oral from the written modes of memory keeping?[1] More specifically, what motives are apparent in the historical works of the early Middle Ages and can the general problems of history writing be discussed in the context of the early Middle Ages and, in particular, the Carolingian period?

Such questions are crucial when we consider the historical writing produced by the Carolingians, for it amounts to an historical revolution in both the range and quantity of historical writing produced, and reflects a qualitative change, with the written word superseding memory as a definitive means by which society recalled and recorded its past. If we examine the written precedents for Carolingian historical writing, therefore, we may be able to expose what style and methods of interpreting the past were available to Carolingian writers and the degree to which Carolingian historical writing is a taught mode of organising memory in forms derived from Classical Antiquity and early Christianity. The writing of history in the early Middle Ages was not intended, however, to be simply a matter of keeping a record for posterity. It was also an effort to make the past comprehensible and to relate it in some way to the present, whether as support for contemporary political ideology or to explain God's purpose for humanity. A further consideration, moreover, is the extent to which the recording of a people's past acted as an expression of that people's identity.

The keeping of records generally is something with which historiography can in part be associated, but the collective memory could have been transcribed for posterity in far duller a form and one which would not constitute a distinct

[1] For comments on memory in the Middle Ages and for the consequences of literacy on the interpretation of the past see Mary Carruthers, *The Book of Memory. A Study of Memory in Medieval Culture* (Cambridge, 1990) and Jack Goody and Ian Watt, 'The consequences of literacy', in: *Literacy in Traditional Societies*, ed. Jack Goody (Cambridge, 1968) pp. 27–68 at pp. 44–9.

genre with conventions of its own. This is where Ruth Morse's ideas are so productive, with her examination of history as literature and the degree to which it sets out to portray a true record, or a selective and dramatic presentation of events for particular purposes, and thereby becomes, in her words, 'implicated in styles and methods of interpretation which were the province of rhetoric'.[2]

The three main influences on early medieval historiography were potentially the pagan histories of the classical and late-antique authors, Christian historiography, and the Bible. They can be briefly characterised as follows: the principal Greek historians, Herodotus and Thucydides, wrote about contemporary or near contemporary events. They told a story and analysed a political situation. Only Polybius, another Greek historian, wrote about a past he had not actually witnessed. He viewed the lessons of history as the best training for political life. All three Greek historians wrote about war and politics, and this was also the main concern of the principal Latin or Roman historians, Caesar, Sallust, Livy, Tacitus and Suetonius. The Roman historiographical tradition was derived from annals, that is, the noting of events for a particular year, but to it the Roman authors added all the superstructure of the rhetorical tradition, particularly when it came to putting invented speeches into the mouths of characters in history. Roman historians regarded history as having a political and moral function.[3]

Thus, for a classical writer, war and diplomacy were the main subject matters, culture, society, the economy and religion have little place and the religious beliefs of the classical historian had no influence on how he wrote his history. A particular image of society is presented to posterity and the past is used to make moral observations to and on the present. These histories can function, therefore, both as a record of the past and as the exploitation of a different world in order to make particular political or polemical points.

Classical historical theory generally thought the historian must seek out the truth and present it in a methodical manner. Cicero best expressed this ideal in his treatise *De oratore*, where he wrote that chronological arrangement, geographical precision, a clear narrative of doings and sayings, an exposition of causes and consequences, biographical details about the characters' lives and a notion of what the author approved was the ideal form of history. Later writers had their own views on the function of history. Eusebius, for example, writing in the fourth century, regarded history as useful, and edifying, and thought that it provided a narrative vehicle for knowledge. The Anglo-Saxon historian Bede was of the opinion that his history could provide good examples as well as a record of the deeds of wicked men to encourage the reader to avoid what was sinful or perverse; the Gallo-Roman bishop Gregory of Tours wrote his book

2 Ruth Morse, *Truth and Convention in the Middle Ages* (Cambridge, 1991) p. 87.

3 A. Momigliano, 'Pagan and Christian historiography in the fourth century', in: *The Conflict between Paganism and Christianity in the Fourth Century*, ed. A. Momigliano (Oxford, 1963) pp. 79–99.

'to keep alive the memory of those dead and gone, and to bring them to the notice of future generations'.[4] We can compare these with the motives for historical writing outlined in the sixth century by Cassiodorus in his *Institutiones*:

> Christian studies also possess narrators of history who, calm in their ecclesiastical gravity, recount the shifting movements of events and the unstable history of kingdoms with eloquent but very cautious splendour. Because they narrate ecclesiastical matters and describe changes which occur at various times they must always of necessity instruct the minds of readers in heavenly affairs, since they strive to assign nothing to chance, nothing to the weak power of gods, as pagans have done, but to assign all things truly to the will of the Creator.[5]

The development of Christian historiography can be seen as a direct challenge to the pagan view of the past. Its first and most influential exponent was Eusebius.[6] One has to imagine the new Christian in the fourth century, who, by allying himself with the Christian faith, made acquaintance for the first time with Jewish and Christian history. Conversion to Christianity meant the discovery of, and realignment with, a new past – from Adam and Eve and the age of the prophets – very different from that with which an educated pagan Roman would have been familiar, and with very different historical models and understanding of man's place in the working out of God's providence. Pagans had to be introduced to the Jewish version of God's providence revealing itself in history, they had to be disabused of the view that Christianity was new and had no history. Their own past had somehow to be included in that of the Jews and in the followers of Christ whose deeds are recorded in the Gospels and the Acts of the Apostles. Eusebius introduced an historical reckoning of the past from Abraham, thus explicitly adding Christian to Jewish history as part of one long scheme of redemption. In this the Bible also exerted a major influence, partly through the first Christian historians. It provided a wide range of historical examples and parallels. Jewish history was linear. It began at the Creation and will end with the coming of the Messiah. The Jewish view of history represented in the Old Testament, moreover, was that history was the manifestation of God's will; a Christian historian could see the entire history of the Jews, therefore, as a preparation for the coming of Christ.[7]

Whereas religion had been rarely considered in classical history, Eusebius replaced the pagan concentration on military and political events with an account of religious beliefs and practices, wars against persecution and heresy, struggles with evil and the devil, and the fortunes of the Church in which he

[4] Cicero, *De oratore*, XIX.66 and XXXIV.120, ed. and trans. H. M. Hubbel in: *Cicero, Brutus, orator*, ed. with Eng. trans. G. L. Henderson and H. M. Hubbell (Cambridge, Mass.) pp. 354 and 394

[5] Cassiodorus, *Institutiones* I.XVII, 'On Christian historians': in *Cassiodori senatoris institutiones* (Oxford, 1937) ed. R. A. B. Mynors, trans. L. W. Jones, *Cassiodorus senator, An Introduction to Divine and Human Readings* p. 115.

[6] See A. Momigliano, 'Pagan and Christian historiography', pp. 90–3.

[7] Compare Augustine, *De civitate dei*, XXII, c. 30.

incorporated many documents, imperial letters and synodal proceedings. Christian historiography thus made no attempt to reinterpret military, political and diplomatic history; the models for these remained secular.

Eusebius' example of basing his history on the study of contemporary documents, and his promotion of religion and ecclesiastical affairs to the centre of his concerns was followed by most medieval historical writers who read the Latin adaptation of his work made by Rufinus between 345 and 410.[8] That Eusebius regarded Christians as a people and thus wrote the history of a *gens* (people) is also of crucial importance for our understanding of the structure and premises of the histories written within the barbarian kingdoms; the histories of the *gentes* of these kingdoms in some respects were regarded as a continuation of the history of the Christians outlined by Eusebius.

Gregory of Tours, for example, appears to have written his history directly within the tradition of Christian historiography established by Eusebius. Not only did he start his history with the Creation, but, according to his preface, he viewed all events as the working out of God's purpose in history and of the struggle between the wicked and the righteous. There is, however, much in his history which is ecclesiastical – miracle stories, exploits of bishops, fortunes of the Church and the faith, the fate of sinners and enemies of the Church, and a remarkable blending of the material and spiritual world to enlighten his audience in ways they would understand.[9] Yet he attempts to see the Frankish rulers as embodiments of the ideal Christian king, the Franks become the new chosen people of God and heirs to Rome. But is this an oversimplification? Does this not assume an essentially modern perception of the Frankish place in history, as Rome's successors rather than as her continuators?

Walter Goffart has argued just this, exposing assumptions on the part of modern commentators concerning the historical writings of Bede, Paul the Deacon, Jordanes and Gregory of Tours as 'national' histories of the Germanic peoples.[10] Goffart asks whether the 'barbarians' really were a special group of peoples with their own distinctive narrators, and argues that this categorisation is simply dependent on chronological convenience, first imposed on the study of history by the self-important humanists of the Renaissance. A detailed discussion of these four authors demonstrates that none was really the author of a new kind of history. The historians in the various Germanic successor kingdoms of the Roman Empire are continuing practitioners of narrative history in Latin as redefined in Late Antiquity; in neither subject nor form do they present a contrast to earlier centuries.

Yet even if Goffart's interpretation of what these authors meant to say is

[8] See Caroline Bammel, 'Products of fifth-century scriptoria preserving conventions used by Rufinus of Aquileia', *Journal of Theological Studies* 35 (1984) pp. 347–93.

[9] See the sympathetic exposition of Gregory's historical imagination by Giselle de Nie, *Views from a Many-Windowed Tower. Studies of Imagination in the Works of Gregory of Tours* (Amsterdam, 1986).

[10] Walter Goffart, *The Narrators of Barbarian History: Jordanes, Bede, Gregory of Tours and Paul the Deacon* (Princeton, 1988) p. 3.

correct, how can we be sure that early medieval readers decoded and understood these works in the ways he suggests? Authorial intent can be inferred from the contents of an historical book itself, the ordering of events, the plot, or the theme. This, of course, assumes that early medieval historians were conscious of the possibilities of literary artifice, and, using history as literature, aimed to produce a certain reaction on the part of their readers. To investigate the ways in which a work might be read, its message received and interpreted, is more problematic. In this respect the codicological context and textual traditions of a work, and the ways in which a work was modified and used by later copyists and writers can be invoked.

Goffart's arguments alert us to the importance of the form of historical writing, an author's choice of a particular type allied him, or her, to a particular tradition and suggested he wrote for a particular purpose. Both Isidore of Seville (not considered by Goffart) and Bede illustrate in their work the ways in which the Christian Latin tradition could be transformed into national history. But in Merovingian Gaul no such synthesis ever quite emerged. Gregory never deployed a new form to match the new, Frankish, elements of his message. Indeed, the codicological context in which both Gregory and the other Merovingian contemporary histories, such as the chronicle of Fredegar, are found underlines how fully these works stood in the tradition of Eusebius and Jerome's chronicle. Fredegar, Gregory and abridgements of Gregory are often found as parts of composite works of world history drawing on earlier chronicles.[11] Fredegar and his continuators, moreover, often go out of their way to include distant information, from beyond the boundaries of Gaul and the Frankish kingdoms, into their accounts. Thus in Francia at least, a clear continuity in historical writing can be observed. Is it then in the Carolingian period, rather than in the sixth, seventh and early eighth centuries, that we get major new developments in historical writing?

One further point about the classical and early Christian writers is the chronological scheme they followed. They had no clear system of chronology to record the passing of time. Generations were often used; so was the Olympiad, a cycle of four years starting in 776 BC, or a reckoning from the foundation in Rome 753 BC. Alternatively, there was a rough reckoning by consulships and magistracies. In the fourth century the Indiction was used. This was a fifteen-year interval between the levying of taxes starting in AD 297.

It was not until the fifth century that the Christian era started to be accepted as a consequence of the liturgical necessity to calculate the date of Easter. Easter Sunday falls on the first Sunday after the first full moon after the vernal equinox, and is thus dependent on both lunar and solar cycles. A nineteen-year cycle was observed. The method of calculating Easter on this 19-year cycle was defended by Dionysius Exigius in the sixth century and it, with its further

[11] J. M. Wallace-Hadrill, *The Fourth Book of the Chronicle of Fredegar and its Continuations* (London, 1960) pp. xlvi–lvi.

popularisation by Bede in his treatises on time and in his *Historia ecclesiastica*, had the effect of making *anno domini*, the year of the birth of Christ, much more widely known. The Christian era replaced any other reckonings of time in the Carolingian period. How simple the year of the Incarnation could render dating is clear from an example of a letter from Pope Honorius I in which the date is given as follows: 'Given on 11th June in the 24th year of our most religious Emperor Heraclius and the 23rd year after his consulship, the 23rd year of his son Constantine and the 3rd Year after his consulship, and in the 3rd year of the most illustrious Caesar his son Heraclius, in the 7th indiction.' That is, AD 634. Simplicity was not the only outcome. There is also a distinct and observable shift in the perception of the past, with the acceptance of a world organised in relation to the birth of Christ rather than to a Roman administrative sequence. It is in the Carolingian period that the fullest acceptance of this new chronological framework is to be observed, for dating according to *anno domini* is the norm in both historical writing and legal records.

Literacy thus brought the Carolingians into contact with a different past. In the Bible, for example, they encountered a new perception of man's role in relation to God, a new sense of man's role in the whole scheme of things and a model or set of models for the presentation of the past. The books of the Old Testament in particular present a convention and a genre. Any author who attempted something different is therefore to be appreciated all the more for adding his own contemporary perceptions of the function of historical writing and attempting to accommodate it in new historical literary forms. It is against this background that the Carolingian contributions to the genre are to be appreciated.

Further, it is clear from the different approaches to history that we have described that it is necessary to distinguish between a record of the past and the use of the past for different purposes. This raises the question of the perceptions not only of the past, and its relevance to the society or the author presenting a picture of it of some kind, but also to the perception of the function of historical writing itself. In this respect, the role of precedents and models in the Carolingian perceptions of the past, given that we are obliged to study this entirely from written sources which themselves form part of a written tradition, is crucial.

Library catalogues and extant manuscripts provide invaluable evidence that the Carolingians knew of these precedents and could draw on them when writing their own history. Among the classical texts are Sallust, Justinus, Dares Phrygius, Livy, Caesar and Eutropius in the libraries of Reichenau, St Gall, Lorsch, St Riquier and Charlemagne,[12] while the extant manuscripts provided

12 G. Becker, *Catalogi bibliothecarum antiqui* (Bonn, 1885) is still, despite its many errors and imperfections, the most comprehensive collection of catalogue texts. For reliable editions of the Reichenau and St Gallen catalogues see *Mittelalterliche Bibliothekskataloge Deutschlands und der Schweiz I Die Diözesen Konstanz und Chur*, ed. P. Lehmann (Munich, 1918). For commentary and discussion of these library catalogues see also McKitterick, *Carolingians*, pp. 165–210.

an even richer harvest, with copies of the authors already mentioned as well as Ammianus Marcellinus, Quintus Curtius Rufus, Frontinus, the *Historia Augusta*, Suetonius, and Tacitus.[13] Indeed, the earliest surviving manuscript of nearly all these authors is a Carolingian one. This witnesses to an extraordinary, creative and arguably deliberate cultivation of an interest in Roman history and pagan historiography, despite the fact that Cassiodorus and other biblical aids recommended Christian authors only. The evidence for wide dissemination of the Old Testament history books, and of the Christian, ecclesiastical historians is no less striking. Josephus, Eusebius, Orosius, the *Historia tripartita* of Sozomen, Socrates and Theodoret in the translation commissioned by Cassiodorus are prominent in the library catalogues,[14] and ninth-century manuscripts play a particularly important role in the transmission of the texts.[15] Further, the same can be said for the 'national histories', that is, the works of Gregory of Tours, Jordanes, Paul the Deacon and Bede, and of the *Liber pontificalis* or history of the popes. There is no doubt, therefore, that the principal precedents for the writing of history – classical, biblical, early Christian and 'barbarian', were all available to the Franks and that the Carolingians themselves did much to disseminate knowledge of them.

Yet the received views on the writing of history available in the ninth century have to be set against what we can determine of the Carolingians' own perception of the past and of their interest in record keeping by means of the written word.[16] Are there different perceptions and uses of the past in the Carolingian period as compared with the preceding centuries? There are certainly new *forms* of historical writing appearing then, and we need to consider these briefly before going on to discuss their implications.

Christian history and its theology form the essential backdrop against which the development of a new form of historical writing, the annal, must be seen. In relating the annual cycle of events through which men lived to the date according to the Christian era, moreover, the Carolingian annal explicitly linked the present to the whole course of Christian history and the life of Christ Himself. It is usual to give what might be termed an 'heroic' version of the 'rise of the annal' as a self-evident process of progression from notes in Easter tables to lists of events on separate leaves in manuscripts containing other texts, and from thence to full-scale historical works and ultimately to world chronicles. But these accounts fail to consider why these new and different forms were adopted.[17] To

[13] *Texts and Transmission. A Survey of the Latin Classics*, ed. L. D. Reynolds (Oxford, 1983). For those with strong Carolingian representation in their manuscript tradition see under Ammianus Marcellinus, Caesar, Q. Curtius Rufus, Eutropius, Florus, Frontinus, Justinus, Livy, Lucan, Sallust, *Scriptores historiae Augustae*, Suetonius, Tacitus. A paper exploring the significance of Roman historical writing in the Carolingian period is in preparation by R. McKitterick.

[14] As for n.12.

[15] A paper documenting this more fully is in preparation by R. McKitterick.

[16] For aspects of this see McKitterick, *Carolingians*.

[17] Michael McCormick, *Les Annales du haut moyen âge*. Typologie des sources du moyen age, ed. L. Genicot (Turnhout, 1975).

understand fully the proliferation of annal writing, and the urge to annalistic narrative which cross-fertilised other historiographical genres, it is necessary to relate this development to a wider change in the interaction of Church and society. In many ways the Carolingian era witnessed the triumph of the saints' cult as the fundamental preoccupation of society. Local saints and the churches which controlled the cult of their memories increasingly became the foci of community action.[18] The fact that Carolingian annals began as marginal notes in the Easter tables, or, probably at Echternach at least, in the martyrology,[19] is thus of great significance. Further there is the obvious mental and emotional connection to be made between the necrologies which preserved the memory of the dead, the *Libri vitae* and *Libri memoriales* which provided such vital networks of association and memory over the entire Frankish realm, and the notes of major events in annalistic form entered in the very same books. The cult of the dead and a sense of history were inextricably entwined.

Further, the Easter tables, necrologies and martyrologies were the very texts by which the Church had, by the eighth century, Christianised the framework of time and space. By the Carolingian era chronological correctness in the dating of Church festivals gained impetus from the Church reforms aimed at uniformity, or at least unanimity, of practice and was championed by the Carolingians themselves. Thus the urge to write down recent events must be linked to new uses of literacy, manifest in part in an obsession with lists throughout society: lists of peasant labourers, lists of those for whom to pray, lists of estates, lists of possessions, lists of books, lists of the dead.[20] A list of dates and important events was just one aspect of this, and a necessary tool to ensure that the observance of anniversaries was correct according to the new, universal, written standards.

If these concerns explain the beginnings of this new genre, how is the development of these notes into free-standing texts to be explained? The Lorsch annals, for instance, were written up year by year. This implies a great deal of institutional organisation and a concern with keeping a written record of the extraordinary events in the yearly cycle, to record the collective memories of the Saint and his *familia*, and the local community which focused on the cult. The annals are above all inward-looking texts aimed at creating an institutional memory. The lengths to which late eighth- and ninth-century annalists went in order to acquire information on the period before their own time for inclusion in their works is significant: the memory is to be projected back into the Merovingian past, and thus to Antiquity, and to the historical place of origin of the saints the Carolingians venerated. Thus a community could acquire an

18 See, for example, T. Head, *Hagiography and the Cult of Saints* (Cambridge 1991).

19 For Echternach martyrology see Discussione on Ganshof, 'L'historiographie', *Settimane* 17 (1970) pp. 688–9.

20 On literacy, McKitterick, *Carolingians*; the list preoccupation is also noted by Nelson, 'Literacy in Charlemagne's government', in: *Uses of Literacy*, p. 296. On necrologies and *Libri memoriales* see N. Huggebaert, *Les Documents nécrologiques*, Typologie des sources du moyen âge occidentale (Turnhout, 1972) and G. Tellenbach, 'Der *Liber memorialis* von Remiremont. Zur kritischen Erforschung und zum Quellenwert liturgischer Gedenkbücher', *DA* 25 (1969) pp. 64–110.

historical identity and an historical anchorage. Yet, by the ninth century, this community need not be equated with the confines of a monastery or cathedral church. If annals are to be seen as collective memories in a narrative form, then it must be recognised that the collectivities whose memory they record overlapped, without necessarily being concurrent with, the local churches who ministered over saints and their cults.[21] In Abbo of St Germain des Prés' epic poem on the defence of Paris against the Vikings in 885–6 this social relationship found its literary expression. Abbo placed his verses in the mouth of St Germain, who was the patron of both Paris itself and Abbo. Thus the city, in the person of its saint, in a sense gives voice and speaks on behalf of the Neustrians, the people who participated in the heroic campaign and placed themselves under the protection of the saint.[22]

The annal as a literary form, moreover, was determined by the annual cycle which shaped the lives of these communities. Thus a cyclical sense of time, moulded by the yearly rota of ritual, the peripatetic rhythm of the royal court and the aristocratic household, itself determined by the seasons, could find a narrative means of expression. Even an imitator of classical historians like Nithard based his account on a narrative rather than an analytical scheme: narrative was the obvious way to avoid the creative anarchy into which an analytical approach can so easily appear to fall, as it did in Notker's *Gesta Karoli*. Narrative was not just easy, allowing a story to develop – it was the way it had happened, and more than this, the way God had made it happen. It allowed analysis of a profound kind in the suggestion of cause and effect, the delineation of Providence at work in this world, in a neat unobstructive way. It could cement the local and particular event in the universal, the unchanging, the perennial Christian time and space. Prudentius of Troyes and Hincmar of Rheims, for example, in the so-called Annals of St Bertin (a crucial source for Charles the Bald's reign) both went to great pains to include distant foreign events in their private continuations to the royal annals.[23]

What annals represent is the memory of a *familia*: the 'Fulda annals', for instance, are the product of the entourage of the archbishops of Mainz, and this entourage doubtless also included laymen, political actors and warriors. Löwe has argued that Gerward, the palace librarian of Louis the Pious, wrote the Xanten annals until his death in 860.[24] Here again there is the whiff of a memoir, addressed to all the great men's followers. In their prefaces, both Einhard and the Astronomer, biographers of Charlemagne and Louis the Pious respectively, pay lip service to this tradition, recording the memory of their

[21] St Gall charters ed. H. Wartmann, *Urkundenbuch der Abtei St Gallen 700–920* I, II (Zurich, 1863) and Weissenburg charters, ed. A. Doll (from the *Nachlass* of K. Glöckner, *Traditiones Wizenburgenses: die Urkunden des Klosters Weissenburg 661–864*, Arbeiten der Hessischen Historichen Kommission (Darmstadt, 1979) reflect the membership of such collectivities.

[22] Abbo, *Bella parisiacae urbis* ed. H. Wacquet, *Abbon. Le siège de Paris par les Normands* (Paris, 1964).

[23] J. L. Nelson, *The Annals of St. Bertin* (Manchester, 1991) Introduction.

[24] H. Löwe, 'Studien zu den Annales Xantenses', *DA* 8 (1951) pp. 59–99.

lord for his followers and in order to repay their debts to their decreased patron.

The *familia* or entourage is thus the initial context of Carolingian historical writing, the 'textual community' whose outlook is expressed and whose memory is recorded.[25] It is in this context, moreover, that the Carolingian histories of abbacies and bishoprics, of St Wandrille, Auxerre, Metz, Rheims, Le Mans and St Bertin, although closely related to what was no doubt their model, the *Liber pontificalis*, should be seen.[26] Notker the Stammerer's account of the deeds of Charlemagne, written in 885–6, refers constantly to the memories and views of such men as Eishere, the warrior who had fought with Charlemagne himself against the Avars, his friend Welinbert the monk and others. These are the contemporaries with whom Notker conferred when writing his book. In a sense they are both the co-authors and the initial audience, a circle centred but not wholly dependent on the monastery of St Gall where Notker taught. This was the innermost of a series of concentric circles which comprised different audiences for a text, received the text in different ways and reached different conclusions from reading it. Some works never reached an audience wider than the first of these circles – the manuscript tradition of Nithard's histories, for example, makes it clear that here was one work which was never received by a wider public than the political and social grouping whose actions it justified.[27]

In the Carolingian world, private and public histories were written concurrently in the same text, rather than 'memories' constituting a recognisable genre separable from contemporary history. Of course, in a sense every text contains a private history, in that an author reveals, when writing, something of his own literary identity and experience. But Carolingian historical writing is also public in that it is recording a collective, not an individual experience; authorial intent like individual action of any kind in this period was modulated through the immediate group of co-actors. Texts which never reached an audience wider than the initial text community were exclusive and inward looking but they were written for a social group with all its tensions and jealousies as well as solidarities and shared values. This can best be seen in Paschasius Radbert's *Epitaphium Arsenii*, composed at Corbie in the late 840s or early 850s.[28] An account of the life of Abbot Wala of Corbie, it deals with the political crises of the reign of Louis the Pious and the division of empire which followed in a highly allusive style and was aimed at a group centred on Corbie anxious to discuss Wala's heritage.[29]

Charlemagne is said to have enjoyed hearing the deeds of the ancients and

[25] The notion of 'textual community' is developed by B. Stock, *The Implications of Literacy. Written Language and Models of Interpretation in the Eleventh and Twelfth Centuries* (Princeton, 1983), pp. 89–92.

[26] For details see select bibliography at the end of this chapter.

[27] J. L. Nelson, 'Public histories and private history in the work of Nithard', *Speculum* 60 (1985) pp. 251–93, reprinted in Nelson, *Politics and Ritual in Early Medieval Europe* (London, 1986) pp. 195–238.

[28] Paschasius Radbertus, *Epitaphium Arsenii*, ed. E. Dümmler, *Abhandlungen der kaiserlichen Akademie der Wissenschiften zu Berlin, phil.-hist. Klasse* (Berlin, 1990); Eng. trans. A. Cabaniss, *Charlemagne's Cousins: Contemporary Lives of Adalhard and Wala* (New York, 1967).

[29] D. Ganz, 'The *Epitaphium Arsenii* and the opposition to Louis the Pious', in: *Charlemagne's Heir*, pp. 537–50.

historical books recited at public readings at court.[30] It is significant that when the Carolingians turned their hand to this kind of political polemic they drew on the classical tradition. On the one hand, this immediately helped in the self-definition of an audience acutely conscious that they formed a privileged social and intellectual elite, supplying a badge of status.[31] On the other hand, the classical tradition allowed the use of rhetoric and invention and thus polemic of an intensity which was not possible through the Christian or annalistic traditions. It allowed the author, therefore, to place argument before literal truth or full and accurate reporting, all the more so as in this context the audience was in principle as knowledgeable about the subject of the treatise as the author himself.

Thus we have the beginnings of a genre of political polemic, probably circulated like the court poetry. Lupus of Ferrières' first letter to Einhard, dated 829–30, shows exactly how such a text might be read or interpreted. Lupus had read a copy of Einhard's *Vita Karoli* at Fulda and understood Einhard's idealised picture of Charlemagne's scholarly court as an elderly man's nostalgic criticism of current practice at the court of Louis the Pious and as a plea for greater patronage of the liberal arts. Much of this is Lupus attempting to flatter Einhard, but Lupus is clear in his own mind that Einhard's work had a rhetorical purpose and should be read as such within the Ciceronian tradition.[32]

Although this kind of polemical work could include subtexts written with personal intent, it was not their primary purpose. On the contrary, the genre of polemic was essentially self-justificatory, aimed at cementing the unity of the group which actually produced it by providing written vindication of the actions and a manifesto of their views. This function helps explain why a genre proper with a set form never developed, but instead miscellaneous but broadly historiographical forms were used – biography, vision literature, epic poetry, classical histories and hagiography.

The most dramatic developments in Carolingian historiography were concentrated in the reign of Louis the Pious, a coincidence whose significance for the writing of history has not been sufficiently appreciated hitherto.[33] The creation of a particular record of the past, and the image making it involved, are closely linked with the political circumstances of Louis' reign. Nevertheless, one can see too the intellectual outcome of the previous decades of development, and how this was exploited for political and cultural ends to create historiography of lasting stature. It is, therefore, worth looking at these works in some detail.

Einhard's *Vita Karoli*, for example, was, as secular biography, one of the most

[30] Einhard, *Vita Karoli*, c. 24, ed. Holder-Egger.

[31] Nelson, 'Public histories and private history', pp. 282–4.

[32] L. Levillain, *Loup de Ferrières. Correspondance* (Paris, 1927) I, Ep. 1, pp. 2–7, Eng. trans. G. W. Regenos, *The Letters of Lupus of Ferrières* (The Hague, 1966), pp. 1–3.

[33] On its political significance, however, see W. Wehlen, *Geschichtsschreibung und Staatsauffassung im Zeitalter Ludwig des Frommen*, Historiche Studien 418 (Lübeck and Hamburg, 1970).

novel works of the Carolingian Renaissance; it exploited a classical model, Suetonius' *Lives of the Caesars*, to create a new kind of historical writing.[34] The work achieved a prompt circulation: ninth- and tenth-century library catalogues list copies at Reichenau, St Gall, Bobbio, Lorsch and Regensburg, and the extant manuscripts indicate further copies at Soissons, Rheims, St Amand, Utrecht and possibly Egmont, Trier and Pontigny. The letters of Lupus of Ferrières indicate that Fulda also had a copy.[35]

A number of crucial questions arise: was it Einhard's role as a palace official at the court of Charlemagne's heir, Louis the Pious, which allowed his work to reach such a wide audience? The *Vita Karoli* was certainly known at the court of Louis the Pious, for Gerward, the palace librarian, made an edition of it to which he appended a verse eulogy of Einhard. It is the dating of Einhard's composition of the *Vita Karoli*, however, that is of paramount importance in determining the exact relationship between this text and Louis' court, and our interpretation of its contents. Hitherto, the *Vita Karoli* has been dated quite late in Louis' reign. Discussion has focused negatively on reasons why it was written so relatively late in Louis' reign,[36] rather than on suggesting cogent reasons why it may have been written before 821 and what kind of contemporary political impact may have been intended.

Ganshof maintained that no more precise dating than '817–30' could be reached for Einhard's great work.[37] Certainly the latest possible dates, 829 or 830, supplied by the probable date of the letter of Lupus of Ferrières,[38] places the work's composition firmly in the period when Einhard was a key figure at Louis' court before his retirement to Seligenstadt. Yet there are many indications that the date of composition was considerably earlier than this. A Reichenau library catalogue dated 821 or 822 records a *Vita et gesta Karoli*, and this is generally accepted as a reference to Einhard's work and not the Royal Frankish annals. It has been argued, perhaps inevitably and somewhat perversely, that this entry could represent a later interpolation, but as the original manuscript is now lost, this cannot be demonstrated; it has to be said, furthermore, that no editor of the Reichenau catalogue has observed any indication that this entry was added later. If one allows time for Reichenau to hear of the work, and procure an exemplar or a copy then one may be able to put back the date of the composition to 821 or even earlier.

In fact the *Vita Karoli* can indeed be placed in a more precise chronological and political context. It is certainly possible that Einhard wrote in or shortly after 817, for the *Vita Karoli* contains references to two events which occurred in

34 For details of editions and translations see select bibliography at the end of this chapter.

35 Lupus Ep. 1, ed. Levillain, p. 6, Eng. trans. Regenos p. 2.

36 See for example, the ingenious arguments of Heinz Löwe, 'Die Entstehungszeit der *Vita Karoli* Einhards', *DA* 39 (1963), pp. 85–103, in favour, ultimately, of 827–9.

37 F. L. Ganshof, 'Einhard, biographer of Charlemagne', in: F. L. Ganshof, *The Carolingians and the Frankish Monarchy*, trans. Janet Sondheimer, pp. 1–16.

38 Löwe, 'Die Entstehungszeit', prefers 834 and thinks 831 is the earliest possible date for Lupus' letter.

this year: a revolt by the Abodrites and the collapse of a portico in the palace at Aachen.[39] But what arguments can be adduced in support of so early a date for the work? Einhard's inclusion and handling of these events suggest that he was referring to near-contemporary matters of immediate concern. In both cases he is anxious to absolve Louis from any adverse association with these events, even going so far as to see the damage to the Aachen palace as a divine comment on Charlemagne's death, rather than on Louis' rule.[40]

Einhard distorts his Suetonian model in the great stress he places on Charlemagne's last years and death, emphasised through both the organisation of the plot and the sheer length of discussion. The inclusion of the full text of Charlemagne's will, complete with witness list, is especially striking: it is apparently Einhard's one concession to the Christian historiographical tradition of including documentary evidence in the narrative, and supplies essential authenticity to the high moral purpose of Einhard's plot. The clue to what this was is provided in Einhard's final sentence: 'Charles' son Louis, who succeeded him by divine right, read this statement and acted upon it with complete scrupulousness as soon as he possibly could after the death of his father.'[41]

This may be disingenuous, for Louis appears not to have proceeded as the will laid down as far as Charlemagne's library was concerned.[42] Of the will's guarantors, Theodulf of Orleans rebelled in 817 or 818, Wala of Corbie and Angilbert of St Riquier fell from favour, and Count Meginhar belonged to a family opposed to Louis in that his son Reginhard was one of the ringleaders of the 818 revolt.[43] Surely Einhard, whose loyalty to Louis is not in question and who is associated with the confirmation of Louis as heir to the Empire in 813, is claiming the moral high ground for Louis, stressing both his legitimacy and the regularity of his succession, in accordance with the wishes of Louis' father Charlemagne at a time when it would have made sense? The will would have lost much of its impact after 818 with so many of the witnesses discredited. Such a moral claim for Louis is best seen as a pre-emptive move, as Louis defended his

[39] Einhard, *Vita Karoli*, cc. 14, 32, ed. Holder-Egger. Compare, however, the interpretation offered by Ganshof, 'Einhard', n.42. Defending Einhard's veracity against the criticisms of Louis Halphen, Ganshof argues that the collapsing gallery at Aachen reported in the *Vita Karoli* c. 32 is not a disingenuous reference to the calamity recorded in the revised royal annals (s.a. 817) on the grounds that the *Vita* implies that the gallery was heavy whereas the annals refer to the brittle material wasting away. This is hardly conclusive, and Ganshof failed to consider the rhetorical nature of the *Vita*. Given the contrived character of several other portents included in c. 32, and the close relationship between the *Vita* and the revised annals it is surely plausible to read the passage in question as a reference to the events of 817 rather than to postulate an otherwise unattested calamity in 'around 813'.

[40] Compare the *Visio Wettini*, where Charlemagne is seen in hell, ed. E. Dümmler, MGH Poet. II, pp. 301–33, lines 446–61; Eng. trans. David A. Traill, *Walahfrid Strabo's Visio Wettini: Text, Translation and Commentary*, Lateinische Sprache und Literatur des Mittealters 2 (Bern, 1974) pp. 55–6.

[41] Einhard, *Vita Karoli*, ed. Holder-Egger, c. 33 following Thorpe's translation.

[42] The will stipulated that the books were to be sold and the proceeds distributed among the poor and needy. Louis' library, however, contained some of the books associated with Charlemagne: see B. Bischoff, 'Die Hofbibliothek unter Ludwig dem Frommen', in: Bischoff, *MS* III, pp. 171–86. It is nevertheless conceivable that it was Louis who 'bought' the books, distributed the money and kept the books, thus observing the terms of the will.

[43] See Einhard, *Vita Karoli*, ed. Holder-Egger, c. 33.

position and asserted himself in 816 and 817, attempting to answer dissidents before open rebellion broke out. In 816, moreover, Einhard received the lay abbacies of St Wandrille and St Bavo's at Ghent. This grant, in gratitude for 'services' rendered, and associated with Einhard's political support in the years 813–14 could conceivably also be linked with Einhard receiving a commission to write the *Vita Karoli* for Louis and his supporters.[44]

Einhard provides, for instance, a lengthy account of Charlemagne's coronation of Louis as emperor in 813, stressing the consensus of the Franks and Louis' own stature. Charlemagne is acting 'with divine inspiration for the welfare of the state; the people greet Louis 'with great enthusiasm'; the neighbouring peoples are now 'terrified'. Einhard follows this with accounts of Charlemagne's death, and only thereafter, exploiting Suetonius to dramatic effect, of the portents that foretold it, 'that not only other people but [Charlemagne] himself could tell that [death] was near'. The word *princeps* faded from Charlemagne's inscription at Aachen but 'Charles took no notice at all of these portents; or at least he refused to admit that any of them could have any connection with his own doings'.[45] The deaths of Louis' elder brothers in 811 and 812, likewise included by Einhard, were also seen by Louis' supporters as God's will that Louis alone should rule the empire.[46] Einhard thus expanded on the dispute over the succession in a tone critical of Charlemagne. Using a commonplace, which contrasted pious moderate behaviour with pride, tyranny and an over-reliance on individual merits, Einhard appears to be arguing that in his last years Charlemagne lost his humility, proudly refused to bow to God's will and thus lost his claim to divinely conferred imperial status.

This is entirely consistent with Einhard's role as mediator between Louis, court and magnates in 814, recorded in, for example, Ermold the Black's verse biography of Louis and implied by the diplomata referred to above. The agenda for rulership implicit in the *Vita Karoli*, with its stress on consensus and Frankishness, is thus best seen as a manifesto in support of the settlement of 813–14 at a time when it would, together with the great reform endeavours of 816–17 and the *Ordinatio imperii* of 817, have the greatest political impact.[47]

Indeed, the *Vita Karoli* can also be read as an attempt to define just what the Carolingians' imperial name meant. Einhard presumably had Louis' two imperial coronations in mind; the first by his father in 813 and the second by the Pope in 815, especially as the papal coronation of 815 created a dangerous precedent, furnishing the papacy with a claim to be the one able to confer and confirm the imperial title. Hence Einhard's extreme taciturnity in dealing with the events of 800, and perhaps too his comment that the coronation was sprung

44 Compare also the series of imperial diplomata granting land to Einhard in the period 814–19: M. Bouquet, *Recueil des Historiens des Gaules et de la France* 6 (Paris, 1870), pp. 473, 479, 518.

45 Einhard, *Vita Karoli*, ed. Holder-Egger, c. 32.

46 K. F Werner, '*Hludovicus Augustus*: gouverner de l'Empire chrétein – idées et réalités', in *Charlemagne's Heir*, pp. 3–124.

47 Einhard, *Vita Karoli*, ed. Holder Egger, cc. 16, 212 and 23.

on a less-than-happy Charlemagne by the pope. Indeed, Einhard places far more stress on Louis' coronation of 813 than on Charlemagne's of 800. In his handling of the events of 813, it is possible that Einhard was implying that if there was a legally constitutive emperor-making rite, it was through divine favour expressed through the consensus of the Franks, and that from then on the Frankish ruler was *de facto* emperor. If St Peter and his successor were to be respected, as they were by Charlemagne, the Frankish ruler was to go no further. The twin questions of the imperial title and Franco-papal relations loomed large in Louis' mind between 815 and 818.[48] Einhard's *Vita* emerges, therefore, as a text to be ranged alongside the *Ordinatio imperii* of 817, with its explicit imperial ideal, and the pact Louis reached with the papacy in 816. Their emphasis is echoed, moreover, by Ermold the Black in his verse biography of Louis, with explicit parallels made in his description of the kings and heroes depicted on the walls of Louis' palace at Ingelheim.[49]

The other element in Einhard's agenda for emperorship, namely, expansion at the expense of the peripheral peoples of Carolingian Europe, also accords with the policies pursued by Louis in the first five years of his reign. Indeed, the summary of Charlemagne's campaigns in Book II of the *Vita Karoli* matches Louis' campaigns and efforts at self-assertion in the period so closely that it allowed Thegan, Louis' biographer, virtually to mirror Book II of Einhard in chapters 8 to 18 of his own work.[50]

Einhard's revival of imperial biography in the manner of Suetonius can be understood on another level as well. Suetonius provided the form for Einhard's highly political account. The use of a classical rather than Christian model allowed Einhard, in stark contrast to Thegan or Asser,[51] to keep God in the background. The resultant emphasis on moral character as a ruler is reminiscent of the classicising historians of Late Antiquity such as Ammianus Marcellinus or Procopius. Further, to those knowledgeable enough to have encountered Suetonius at first hand, Einhard's *Vita Karoli* was obviously making a statement about the imperial title and its relation to that of the Roman emperors, rather than drawing parallels with an Old Testament king such as David,[52] or a popular hero of Antiquity such as Alexander the Great.[53] It was learned imperial image-

48 T. F. X. Noble, *The Republic of St Peter: The Birth of the Papal State, 680–825* (Philadelphia, 1984)

49 Ermold, *In honorem Hludowici Pii*, ed. E. Faral, *Poème sur Louis le Pleux et épitres au roi Pépin* (Paris 1964) lines 2142–63; Eng. trans. Godman, *Poetry*, p. 255.

50 Thegan, *Gesta Hludowici imperatoris*, ed. G. H. Pertz, MGH SS II, pp. 590–604, reprinted with German trans. Rau, *Quellen* I.

51 Asser, ed. W. H. Stevenson, *Asser's Life of King Alfred* (Oxford, 1904); Eng. trans. S. Keynes and M. Lapidge, *Alfred the Great. Asser's Life of King Alfred and Other Contemporary Sources* (Harmondsworth, 1983).

52 David was used by Angilbert, Alcuin and Theodolf of Orleans, for example, with reference to Charlemagne: MGH Poet. I. pp. 360–3, pp. 245–6, and pp. 48–9 in their poems on the court; Eng. trans. Godman, *Poetry*, pp. 112–21 and 150–63.

53 Known from the novels on Apollonius of Tyre and Alexander the Great, *Historia Apollonii regis tyri*, ed. A. Riese (Leipzig, 1893) and Quintus Curtius Rufus, *The History of Alexander* ed. K. Müller, *Q. Curtius Rufus Geschichte Alexanders des Grossen* (Munich, 1954) with Eng. trans. John Yarley (Harmondsworth, 1984). One ninth-century manuscript of the history of Alexander, BN lat. 5716, was copied for a

making; the more extraordinary borrowings from Suetonius, such as the collapse of a bridge over the Rhine before the subject's death, and the very description of the Emperor himself, could thus be understood on at least two levels, even as 'in-jokes' to those 'in the know'. The *Vita Karoli* as a written text, moreover, staked a claim for Charlemagne to be ranked by posterity among those great rulers whose deeds were recorded in writing.

Einhard raises the issue of the extent to which he, writing contemporary history at court, drew on a Carolingian tradition of 'official' or 'public' historical writing. From the reign of Pippin III at least, the Carolingian house sponsored the production of contemporary history to justify its actions. The anonymous continuator of Fredegar's chronicle, for example, tells us that he is writing at the command of the counts Childebrand and Nibelung.[54] This may merely be the continuation of a Merovingian tradition: Fredegar's chronicle had had at least two other continuations before the ones at the behest of the Carolingians, and it is possible that the *Liber historiae francorum* was commissioned by a rival, Neustrian, political grouping in the first part of the eighth century.[55] Yet it is important not to overemphasise this tradition; there is no sign that the Continuations to Fredegar were understood to be 'official' history and they create the impression of *post hoc* lumps of memoir added to an already extant chronicle rather than true contemporary history, officially sponsored. Further, the Continuations were commissioned by a cadet branch of the Carolingian house not the court circle itself. This is a far cry from the production of the Royal Frankish Annals in the first three decades of the ninth century, when the keeping of an official record of political and public events appears to have been the responsibility of the archchaplain at the royal court.[56]

Indeed it is significant that it is only from 788 onwards that the Royal Frankish Annals were produced in this way, as an official record, in that it coincides with the creation by Charlemagne of a large public court focused on the new palace at Aachen, which outshone the *familia* of the average Frankish aristocrat.[57] If there was no attempt at public record-keeping before then, this is surely due to the court not being, until Charlemagne's later years, a public forum with a centripetal political force. It is in this context, therefore, that the evident royal interest in history is to be understood. It is manifest, for example, in the commissioning of the deeds of the bishops of Metz (*Gesta episcoporum*

Carolingian Count Conrad by a scribe called Haimo in the Loire region in return for borrowing the text of Hraban Maur's *Expositio in Ecclesiastes* in order to copy it.

54 Fredegar, Cont. 34, ed. J. M. Wallace-Hadrill, *The Fourth Book of the Chronicle of Fredegar and its Continuations* (London, 1960) pp. 102–3.

55 R. Gerberding, *The Rise of the Carolingians and the Liber Historiae Francorum* (Oxford, 1987) with an English translation of the *Liber* on pp. 173–81.

56 For a discussion of annals as genre see M. McCormick, *Les Annales du moyen age*, Typologie des sources du moyen âge (Turnhout, 1975) and R. McKitterick, *The Frankish Kingdoms under the Carolingians, 751–987* (London, 1983) pp. 1–8 and their references.

57 D. Bullough, '*Aula renovata*: the Carolingian court before the Aachen palace', *Proceedings of the British Academy* 71 (1985) pp. 267–301, reprinted in D. Bullough, *Charlemagne Renewal: Sources and Heritage* (Manchester, 1991) pp. 123–61.

Mettensium) from Paul the Deacon, a work concerned with the glorification of the Carolingian house and the special church of their progenitor, St Arnulf, and in the initiative which produced the Royal Frankish Annals. These involved research into local annalistic traditions to augment the earlier sections; it resembled the process by which Charlemagne consciously sought to collect rare, important or definitive works for his court library.[58]

Nonetheless, it is in the reign of Louis the Pious above all that court historiography played such a crucial role in deliberately enhancing the public and political image of the ruler. As well as in Einhard's *Vita Karoli*, associated, as we have seen, with the initial effort on Louis' part to consolidate his position as Charlemagne's heir, Louis arguably commissioned the revision of the Royal Frankish Annals which add so much illuminating detail, often critical of Charlemagne, to the laconic record of the primary version. It is no accident that more historiographical evidence, political literature and imperial image-building survives from Louis' reign than from that of any other Carolingian ruler, for it fell to Louis to define and reinforce the significance of the events of Christmas Day 800, his father's extraordinary career and his own power.

In the sphere of imperial biography, the first prose Life of Louis the Pious was written in 836 by the auxiliary bishop of Trier, Thegan.[59] Thegan's work in its first twenty chapters closely mirrors that of Einhard, with its replicas of military initiatives, submission of rebels, the patronage of architecture and the description of Louis' appearance, in order to demonstrate that Louis truly was Emperor by divine grace. Writing in the aftermath of the revolt of Louis' sons in 833–5, Thegan uses his literary artifice to promote a rapprochement between the newly restored Emperor and Louis the German. The real *bête noire* for Thegan is Archbishop Ebbo of Rheims, the mastermind behind Louis' deposition in 833, whom Thegan savages with a fine piece of polemical writing.[60] Thegan here voices the concerns of his friends and contacts, Rhenish churchmen and aristocrats who were important peace-brokers, such as Abbot Marcward of Prüm, Archbishop Hetti of Trier and Count Gebhard. Yet Thegan's contacts also included two high-ranking palace officials, Abbot Grimald of Weissenburg and the poet Walahfrid Strabo. Thus his book also supplied a highly plausible happy ending which accorded with the aspirations of Louis the Pious' immediate entourage in 835.[61]

The other prose life of Louis was written by an anonymous author usually known as the 'Astronomer' shortly after Louis' death in 840.[62] Although in

[58] On the royal library see B. Bischoff, 'Die Hofbibliothek Karls des Grossen', in: Bischoff, *MS* III, pp. 149–70.

[59] See n.50 above and Ernst Tremp, *Studien zu den Gesta Hludowici Imperatoris des Trier Chorbischofs Thegan*, Schriften der MGH 32 (Hanover, 1988) and 'Thegan und Astronomus, die beiden Geschichtsschreiber Ludwigs des Fromen', in *Charlemagne's Heir*, pp. 691–700.

[60] Thegan, ed. Pertz. c. 44.

[61] See Tremp, 'Thegan und Astronomus'.

[62] *Vita Hludowici*, ed. G. H. Pertz, MGH SS II, pp. 607–48, reprinted with Germ. trans., Rau, *Quellen* I; Eng. trans., A. Cabaniss, *Son of Charlemagne* (Syracuse, 1965).

terms of content and structure there is little debt owed by the 'Astronomer' to Einhard, the work can nevertheless be seen in the tradition of the *Vita Karoli*. The author had clearly been a high-ranking palace official under Louis the Pious and, although he voices private motives for recording Louis' deeds in his preface, there are various indications that the book had political rationale as a public text. The outspoken criticism of Louis' rebellious sons, and the whole-hearted support for Charles the Bald is comparable to that offered in Nithard's work, commissioned at a similar date by Charles the Bald himself from his own cousin and supporter as a means of self-justification. Rare sources are used, moreover, such as the now lost account of Louis in Aquitaine by the monk Ademar and possibly also a lost set of annals for the years 830–5. It would appear that the 'Astronomer' was working hastily from what remained of the palace archive.[63]

Above all, the manuscript tradition demonstrates that here was a public biography in the Einhard tradition, for the Astronomer's 'Life' has virtually no codicological existence independent of the *Vita Karoli* and many manuscripts also include the court-produced Royal Frankish Annals. This is paralleled by Thegan. Evidently, both Lives of Louis were copied, in the ninth century at least, as parts of works linking serial imperial biography to Carolingian house history and the story of the Franks. Walahfrid Strabo, for instance, created just such a work in editing both Einhard and Thegan in an identical manner, dividing them into chapters with headings and adding prefaces in praise of their respective authors.[64] This activity may have had political rationale, and may be related to the court of either Charles the Bald or Louis the German in the 840s. A similar work was created by an anonymous editor at Lorsch in the middle of the ninth century, amalgamating Einhard, Thegan and the Royal Frankish Annals into a composite text and prefacing it with Trojan history.[65] Charles the Bald's court library seems to have contained a manuscript combining Einhard, the 'Astronomer' and the Royal Frankish Annals, and possibly a complex house genealogy as well.[66]

63 The exact fate of the royal archive, library and liturgical books is not clear. Compare n. 46 above and the Astronomer's *Vita Hludowici*, c. 63, where Drogo of Metz divides 'treasure and books'. If the archive were divided could this account for Charles the Bald's staunch use of Ansegis thereafter, in that he no longer had access to earlier copies of capitularies? See McKitterick, 'Zur Herstellung von Kapitularien: die Arbeit des *Leges* Skriptoriums', *MIÖG* 101 (1993) pp. 1–14 and G. Schmitz, 'The capitulary legislation of Louis the Pious', in *Charlemagne's Heir*, pp. 425–36, a shorter version of an article originally published in German in *DA* 42 (1986) pp. 471–516.

64 See Tremp, *Thegan*, pp. 112–27 (Walahfrid as editor) and pp. 174–200 (transmission of Thegan including one branch transmitted through Walahfrid as serial biography).

65 Ibid., pp. 174–200, Vat. pal. lat. 243.

66 St Petersburg, F.v.IV.4 is thought to be a copy of a manuscript from Charles' library: see R.McKitterick, 'Charles the Bald (840–877) and his library the patronage of learning', *EHR* 95 (1980) p. 32 n.3. Vienna, Oesterreichische Nationalbibliothek 510, moreover, likewise contains Einhard and the 'Astronomer' and is thought to descend from a common exemplar: O. Holder-Egger, 'Zur Überlieferung Einhards *Vita Karoli Magni*', *Neues Archiv* 37 (1912) pp. 395–414, esp. p. 400. The St Petersburg manuscript (N. France, *ca* 869) also contains the royal annals, and the unique text of a royal genealogy known as the *Genealogia regum francorum*, MGH SS XIII, pp. 246–8. On this text see K.-U. Jaschke, 'Die Karolingergenealogien aus Metz

The Carolingian court, therefore, took an active role in producing contemporary histories, annals and house history which was fully appreciated in the succeeding decades. The fluidity of this kind of historiography is made clear if one considers the form in which the great interest in genealogy and aristocratic lineage was expressed. Count Gerald of Aurillac, for example, took great pride in tracing his lineage back over five centuries to Caesarius, the sixth-century bishop of Arles.[67] Angilbert's genealogy is recounted at length in the chronicle of St Riquier.[68] Among peoples in which there was no rule of inheritance according to primogeniture and in which great stress could be placed on relations through maternal kin, the sense of family was maintained from generation to generation.[69] Genealogy could provide a necessary focus for loyalties and these loyalties were crucial for family identity. Its identification with a family church, monastery, saint, relic or renowned progenitor enhanced a family's interest sense of its history. Yet among all the aristocratic families of the Franks, only the Carolingians appear to have fostered this interest in any really developed form.

Written genealogies were produced at court from at least the reign of Charlemagne, when Paul the Deacon incorporated such a text, looking back to St Arnulf of Metz, in his history of the bishops of Metz. By the ninth century, semi-legendary written genealogies link the Carolingians by marriage to their Merovingian predecessors, to the Romans, and, via Aeneas, to the Trojans too; the scope, content and scale of these works is surely suggestive of royal patronage.[70]

There is ample evidence for a widespread knowledge of Carolingian court histories and much more than a whiff of propaganda, with the court disseminating texts which argued for a pro-Carolingian interpretation of events. Yet the process by which such texts functioned as propaganda was neither so cold-blooded nor as simple as the use of such a term might imply. The court and its library could play an important role in providing exemplars of ancient histories, such as Sallust, or more recent Christian texts, such as Bede.[71] The court played a similar role in providing official contemporary history and genealogy. The court was, after all, the focus of a politically conscious nation, the place where the Frankish people and the *proceres*, the holders of power, met and acted as groups. Smaragdus of St Mihiel, indeed, commented, that 'No learned man

und Paulus Diaconus. Mit einem Exkurs über Karl den Kahlen', *Rheinisches Vierteljahrsblätter* 34 (1970), pp. 190–218 at pp. 199–201 and Tremp, *Thegan*, p. 42, n.170.

67 Odo of Cluny, *Vita Geraldi*, I.1, ed. PL 133, cols. 639–704; Eng. trans. O. Sitwell, *St Odo of Cluny* (London, 1958) p. 94.

68 Hariulf, *Chronicon Centulense*, ed. F. Lot, *Chronique de l'abbaye de Saint-Riquier* (Paris, 1894).

69 Compare, however, Dhuoda's manual for her son William, in which she appears always to mention her husband's kindred and never her own for example, VIII.14 and 15 (ed. P. Riché, *Dhuoda. Manuel pour mon fils* (Paris, 1975) pp. 318–22; Eng. trans., Carol Neel, *Handbook for William: A Carolingian Woman's Counsel for her Son* (Lincoln, Nebraska, 1991) pp. 87–8).

70 MGH SS II, pp. 308–12 (and compare pp. 312–13) and MGH SS XIII, pp. 250–1 (and compare pp. 251–6). See also Tremp, *Thegan*, pp. 26–44.

71 Bischoff, 'Die Hofbibliothek Karls des Grossen'.

doubts, I think, that is the most ancient practice, habitual for kings up to now, to have whatever things are done or happen to be written down for posterity to learn about.'[72] It is no surprise that it was to the court that political actors looked for a public record of their annual doings.

Yet, in that the account sponsored by the Carolingian rulers at court could hardly help but reflect a Carolingian viewpoint, the social dynamic which elevated the court into the historical memory of the Frankish *gens* was also a powerful mechanism by which the Carolingians could disseminate political propaganda, without necessarily being conscious of the fact. Social structure, political imperative and literary genre married well and created a possibility for consensus.

The texts produced at court were not confined to contemporary history. In Freculf of Lisieux's world chronicle they included a schoolbook on ancient history.[73] Indeed, it was perhaps Freculf's work which was the real 'best-seller' among the court histories; there is ample evidence of a wide interest in this work, with copies recorded at Reichenau and St Gall and the librarian of Freising noting that he wished to acquire it for the library. St Gall's copy, indeed, was a 'deluxe' edition. The first book of Freculf's chronicle, dealing with world history from the Creation to the birth of Christ, that is, the first five ages of the world, was commissioned by Louis' chancellor, Helisachar, specifically to delineate biblical and pagan history alongside one another and to offer exegetical comment on some of the more difficult historical episodes in the Old Testament.[74] Freculf was a protégé of Hraban Maur of Fulda, and his style of scholarship is reminiscent of Hraban's[75] in that he created a recognisably novel synthesis. Freculf offered an often idiosyncratic interpretation of world history which combines the history of the Christian faith with that of the ancient world in the tradition of Eusebius–Jerome. He also makes perhaps the first explicit synthesis of the tradition of the six ages of the world, inherited from Roman Antiquity via Augustine, with that of the four world monarchies, inherited from the Bible via Orosius. The first book of Freculf's chronicle can best be seen as linked to the great project of collective biblical exegesis, organised by Helisachar and in which Hraban Maur participated.[76] Thus the chronicle is an authorised history textbook commissioned by the reforming circle centred on the court. Only two ninth-century Freculf manuscripts survive,[77] but school-

72 Smaragdus, *Vita sancti Benedicti Anianensis*, MGS SS XV, p. 201; Eng. trans. J. L. Nelson, 'The Annals of St Bertin', in: *Charles the Bald: Court and Kingdom*, ed. J. L. Nelson and M. T. Gibson, 2nd revised edn (Aldershot, 1990) pp. 23–40 at p. 23.

73 PL 106, cols. 919–1258.

74 Freculph, preface, PL 106, cols. 917–20.

75 See Brown, chapter 1, above, pp. 42–3.

76 Discovered by Bischoff, 'Die Bibliothek im Dienste der Schule', MS III, pp. 213–33. Freculf made use of Hraban's exegesis on the Book of Genesis in his text. At Reichenau his work was copied alongside exegesis in the same manuscript: see Lehmann, *Mittelalterliche Bibliothekskataloge*, p. 34.

77 One is noted by C. A. Naturewicz, 'Freculphus of Lissieux, his chronicle and a Mont St Michel manuscript', in *Horae eruditae ad codices sancti Michaelis de periculo maris* (Mont St Michel, 1966) pp. 90–134.

books notoriously are precisely the kind of text which would easily wear out, to be replaced or lost. The manuscript tradition of the work, however, with its large number of textual families of Book I alone, does indicate a wide dissemination of the chronicle and initially rapid creation of exemplars, and suggests that it was just the kind of text book it was intended to be.[78]

Book II of Freculf's chronicle is an account of world history from the birth of Christ until the expulsion of the Romans from Europe in the time of Gregory the Great by the 'barbarian peoples', above all, the Franks and Lombards. It was commissioned by the Empress Judith for the education of the infant Charles the Bald. This second Book is thus especially interesting, comprising as it does a novel perspective on the place of the Frankish monarchy in world history. Freculf's plot presents the new idea of a unified barbarian entity with the Frankish monarch at its head as a successor to the Roman Empire. A fifth, divine-ordained, world monarchy is thus added as God's chosen historical vehicle. Freculf reinforced this by assuring Charles in his preface to Book II that he hoped Charles would be 'our king of a new age'.[79] Surely the young Charles was intended to conclude that the Carolingian Empire created by his father and his grandfather was the temporal manifestation of this fifth, and presumably final, world monarchy?

Walahfrid Strabo, Charles' personal tutor, certainly saw history as playing a central role in Charles' education, Walahfrid's personal collection of teaching texts includes a world chronicle up to the year 808 based on a book found at the palace.[80] His moralistic verse dialogue on the ancient hero, Apollonius of Tyre, shows how history could supply exempla on rulership, as does the versified contemplation on the statue of Theodoric the Ostrogoth at Aachen (*De imagine Tetrici*).[81] This poem, partly addressed to Charles, discussed tyranny and just rule. Such a view of Theodoric marries well with Freculf's world history, as does the motif of the Carolingians springing from a Romano-Frankish marriage, central to the Carolingians' house genealogies. The commissioning of Freculf's work, then, seems to be the outcome of a widely felt need to educate, by means of history, and to be central in the nurturing of a 'Carolingian Renaissance prince', destined from birth to be a Christian Frankish ruler.

In view of Charles the Bald's education, it is scarcely surprising that of all his house he was the most flamboyant and successful user of history. The work of Nithard, in particular, indicates the degree to which Charles the Bald maintained his father's interest in the power of history, an interest that may also

The other fragment, was discovered recently in a binding of a printed book in Peterborough Cathedral Library, housed in Cambridge University Library, and dated by Bernhard Bischoff to s.ix 3/4.

78 Details are provided by Naturewicz, as in n. 77.

79 MGH Epp. 3, XIV, pp. 319–20, trans. E. Ward, 'Caesar's wife', in: *Charlemagne's Heir*, p. 224.

80 Bernhard Bischoff, 'Eine Sammelhandschrift Walafrid Strabos', in: Bischoff, *MS* II, pp. 34–51.

81 MGH Poet. II, pp. 370–8. For an alternative edition see M. W. Herren, *The Journal of Medieval Latin* 1 (1991) pp. 118–39 and compare M. W. Herren, 'Walahfrid Strabo's *De imagine Tetrici*: an interpretation', in: *Latin Culture and Medieval Germanic Europe*, ed. R. North and T. Hofstra, Germania Latina I (Groningen, 1992) pp. 25–41.

account for his commissioning of epic poems on the Franks and the dissemination of a work of serial imperial biography and Carolingian house history to justify his political position.

Charles himself commissioned Nithard's work in 841. Its public element was concerned with justifying the sets of choices made by Charles and his closest followers, his *familia*, in the political crisis that ensued on the death of Louis the Pious; its audience was to be the very group whose actions it sought to justify.[82] But, as Janet Nelson has demonstrated, Nithard's private history intervenes in the course of his public histories; Nithard clearly lost everything he had, and his life, as a result of his fidelity to Charles. In the event, his work never reached a wide audience, but its content is entirely consistent with the emphases in Carolingian royal historiography outlined so far.

Charles the Bald, moreover, turned in the course of his reign to other, more public media in his uses of history. The classical Roman past was of primary importance in developing what came to be the standard medieval ruler imagery and symbolism.[83] The court school of artists produced a remarkable series of ruler portraits, replete with historical and political symbolism and a stress on the divinely ordained element in his rule. A streak of self-conscious classicism ran through his public actions and pronouncements. Charles enjoyed a reputation as an avid collector of classical books and drew extensively on Roman law in his own legislation. Through the great public occasions associated with the court, such as the annual assemblies of the Franks, the great holy festivals, or the celebrations which marked the *adventus* of his itinerant court, such ideas could be impressed upon the Frankish lay and ecclesiastical magnates. Yet, the historically conditioned and divinely ordained ideal of rule thus articulated was only one face of the image of rule propagated at such events; the other, merging with it, was consensual, with the king reaching decisions with and feasting among his hosts and his men.[84]

Indeed, this kind of gathering, at which a political collectivity was formed, was, throughout the early Middle Ages, not only a central agent in the creation of 'national' identities, but also the social context in which the germs of 'national' history can be detected.[85] The classic Carolingian statements of self-conscious Frankish 'national' history can be linked to similar assemblies of the Frankish people. An example is Pippin III's prologue to his redaction of the

[82] For a full discussion of Nithard and the significance of his history see the excellent interpretation offered by Nelson, 'Public *Histories* and private history'.

[83] R. McKitterick, 'Charles the Bald and the image of kingship in the early Middle Ages', *History Today* (June 1988); J. L. Nelson, 'Translating images of authority: the Christian Roman emperors in the Carolingian World', in: *Images of Authority. Studies Presented to Joyce Reynolds on the Occasion of her Seventieth Birthday*, ed. M. M. McKenzie and C. Roueché, Cambridge Philological Society, supplementary volume no. 16 (Cambridge, 1989) pp. 194–205.

[84] See J. L. Nelson, 'Carolingian royal ritual', in: *Rituals of Royalty*, ed. D. Cannadine and B. S. Price (Cambridge, 1987) pp. 137–80.

[85] Walter Goffart suggests that while in the fifth century there was no united barbarian identity, it can be observed in the ninth century, in: 'Rome, Constantinople and the barbarians', in: Walter Goffart, *Rome's Fall and After* (London, 1980) pp. 1–32.

Lex Salica in which the Franks are eulogised as divinely chosen vanquishers of the corrupt, persecuting Romans.

The notion that the Franks were a special people is implicit in the whole structure and content of Freculf's chronicle and it is arguably contact with Rome which led to the development of this novel perspective during the Carolingian Renaissance. That is, the acquisition of the title of Roman Emperor by the Frankish ruler forced contemporaries to consider just where they stood in relation to the glory which had been Rome. But above all it was the Carolingian reacquaintance with classical literature which led to this new sense of the place of the present in the history of the world. The whole shift in perspective is part of the process by which the Roman heritage ceased to be felt primarily on a practical, everyday level or as an unbroken, unconscious tradition; now Rome was a more distant object of curiosity, to be self-consciously renewed, relearnt and revived and from whose heritage deliberate selections could be made.

That early medieval interest in the so-called 'barbarian histories' was part of a wider interest in the histories of various peoples, Romans and Greeks as well as Goths and Franks,[86] does not, therefore, entirely accord with the Carolingian evidence. In the library catalogues historical works are listed together so that national histories, with their deeds of the English and the Franks are alongside those of the Romans and Trojans. Yet on the evidence of library catalogues and extant historical collections, the Frankish interest in history was not indiscriminate; it was confined for the most part to the three peoples, Trojans, Romans and Jews, whose history was seen to stand in direct continuity with that of the Franks. BN lat. 5018 and lat. 7906, for example, use the Aeneid and Dares Phrygius' account of Trojan history as the first part of a compilation which ends with an account of the deeds of the Franks; the libraries of both Eberhard of Friuli and Eccard of Mâcon included books of explicitly Frankish history.[87] It is thus clear that by the ninth century the Franks had learned to see themselves as God's Chosen People. Contemporary reactions to political crises, such as Nithard's shocked tone in his account of the betrayals of 840–3 and Angilbert's verses on the battle of Fontenoy owe much to this deep-rooted self-image.

Yet to write a history of the Franks as a regenerate people whose rulers were, by definition, God's right arm in this world was, politically speaking, clumsy. Bede himself, after all, had been forced by the exigencies of contemporary politics to concentrate on a past golden age. National history as contemporary history was a two-edged sword. If in the past the Frankish monarchy had been God's chosen vehicle, to offer intelligent comment on contemporary politics and make realistic judgements one had to put this fact firmly to the back of

[86] Compare Goffart, *Narrators of Barbarian History*, pp. 7–12.

[87] Texts ed. and discussed P. Riché, 'Les Bibliothèques de trois aristocrats laïcs carolingiens', *Le Moyen Age* 69 (1963) pp. 87–104 and McKitterick, *Carolingians*, pp. 245–50.

one's mind.[88] Simply to see the ruler as the head of a teleological process towards a national destiny undermined any chance of offering critical or constructive comment on his policies, or, indeed, of explaining any setbacks. Thus the interventionist God or the heavy-handed authorial interpretation so evident in the histories of the Frankish past were out of place in contemporary history. This remained in the form either of annals, in which the plot developed as events succeeded one another, or as political polemic.

This relationship, between a profoundly and explicitly Christian and teleological sense of the past, and an understanding of contemporary history which necessitated a temporary suspension of judgement, lay at the base of the Carolingian historiographical synthesis observed in the works discussed above. What was combined was the Christian historiographical tradition, with its general explanation of historical change, and an annalistic or classicising approach to contemporary history. In terms of the actual writing of history the consequence was a powerful marriage of classical rhetoric with a profoundly Christian world-view which aimed to elucidate God's truth. Yet this synthesis was between two traditions originally diametrically opposed to one another.

In the medium thus created, narrative was the essential principle of organisation, yet subtle analysis was possible through the use of anecdote, moral fable, symbolism and parallelism in the plot. All three Carolingian imperial biographers are able to evoke three-dimensional characters. Nithard, the 'Astronomer' and Paschasius are all able to offer differing but far from simplistic analyses of the political crisis of the 830s. What we are dealing with is a process of translation not unlike that whereby the relics of a Roman saint could acquire a wholly new meaning in a new cultural and historical setting in Carolingian Francia. Einhard, the 'translator' of saints Marcellinus and Petrus, was also the 'translator' of Suetonius, Cicero and classical historiography.[89] Such a 'translation' not only imported a whole tradition of how to write history, but also a whole set of texts could be seen in a new perspective.

In Carolingian historical writing, therefore, there is a sense of continuity provided by working within the Eusebian and Christian historiographical tradition as well as drawing on classical models. There is the development in the eighth century of a secular historiographical tradition, and of new kinds of history writing: biography, epic poem, annals. These are the Carolingian contribution to historiography. The chronicles, annals, epic poems, historical narratives and imperial biographies reveal a preoccupation with noting important facts and events in one literary form or another, and situating events in time within the Christian chronological framework. There is a keen sense both of the relevance of the past and the importance of providing a record for posterity.

88 Compare J. M. Wallace-Hadrill, 'History in the mind of Archbishop Hincmar', in: *The Writing of History in the Middle Ages*: ed. R. H. C. Davis and J. M. Wallace-Hadrill (Oxford, 1981) pp. 43–70.

89 Compare Simon Franklin, 'The reception of Byzantine culture by the Slavs', *The 17th International Byzantine Congress: Major papers* (New York, 1986) pp. 383–96, at pp. 386–3.

There is an urgent political purpose in the interpretation of contemporary events. History contains a strong didactic element and classical rhetoric is used to sway its audience. Whereas many of our sources were not actually intended by those who left them behind to act as information for posterity, these historical accounts were: their authors have shown us their own image of society and its events which we in our turn must attempt to understand.

Select bibliography

Sources

Annals, histories and biographies

Abbot of St Germain des Prés, *Bella Parisiacae urbis*, ed. with French trans., H. Wacquet, *Le Siège de Paris par les Normands* (Paris, 1964); Eng. trans. D. Bullough, *Abbo of St Germain's Siege of Paris* (Manchester, 1993)

Annales Fuldenses, ed. F. Kurze, MGH SRG (Hanover, 1891); reprinted with Germ. trans. Rau, *Quellen* III: Eng. trans. with excellent commentary, T. Reuter, *The Annals of Fulda* (Manchester, 1992)

Annales mettenses priores ed. B. von Simson, MGH SRG (Hanover and Leipzig, 1909); reprinted with Germ. trans. Rau, *Quellen* II

Annales regni francorum, ed. F. Kurze, MGH SRG (Hanover, and Leipzig, 1909 and 1950); Germ. trans. Rau, *Quellen* I; Eng. trans. Scholz, *Carolingian Chronicles* (Ann Arbor, 1970). For the revised version of the annals see *Annales qui dicuntur Einhardi*, ed. F. Kurze, MGH SRG (Hanover, 1895)

Annales sancti Berlini, ed. F. Grat, J. Vielliard and S. Clémencet, *Annales de Saint-Berlin* (Paris, 1964); ed. with Germ. trans. Rau, *Quellen* II; Eng. trans. with excellent commentary, J. L. Nelson, *The Annals of St Bertin* (Manchester, 1991)

Annales Vedastini, ed. B. von Simson, MGH SRG (Hanover and Leipzig, 1909); reprinted with Germ. trans. Rau, *Quellen* II

Annales Xantenses, ed. B. von Simson, MGH SRG (Hanover and Leipzig, 1909); reprinted with Germ. trans. Rau, *Quellen* II

'Astronomer', *Vita Hludowici*, ed. G. H. Pertz, MGH SS II, p. 607–48; reprinted with Germ. trans., Rau, *Quellen* I; Eng. trans. A. Cabaniss, *Son of Charlemagne* (Syracuse, 1965)

Einhard, *Vita Karoli*, ed. O. Holder-Egger, MGH SRG reprinted with Germ. trans. Rau, *Quellen* I; ed. with French trans. L. Halphen, *Eginhard, Vie de Charlemagne* (Paris, 1947); Eng. trans. Lewis Thorpe, *Two Lives of Charlemagne* (Harmondsworth, 1969)

Ermold the Black, *In honorem Hludowici Pii* ed. with French trans., E. Faral, *Poème sur Louis le Pieux et épîtres au roi Pépin* (Paris, 1964); excerpts in Eng. trans., P. Godman, *Poetry of the Carolingian Renaissance* (London, 1985)

Flodoard, *Annales*, ed. P. Lauer, *Les Annales de Flodoard* (Paris, 1905)

Freculf of Lisieux, *Chronicon*, PL 106, cols. 919–1258

Fredegar, *Chronicon*, ed. with Eng. trans., J. M. Wallace-Hadrill, *The Fourth Book of the Chronicle of Fredegar and its Continuations* (London, 1960)

Historia ecclesiae remensis, MGH SS XIII

Liber historiae francorum, ed. B. Krusch, MGH SRM II, pp. 215–328; Eng. trans. (1) B. Bachrach, *The Liber Historiae Francorum* (Kansas, 1973), (2) Richard Gerberding, *The Rise of the Carolingians* (Oxford, 1987) pp. 171–81

Nithard, *De dissensionibus filiorum hludowici Pii*, ed. with French trans., P. Lauer, *Histoire des fils de Louis le Pieux* (Paris, 1964); Eng. trans., B. W. Scholz, *Carolingian Chronicles* (Ann Arbor, 1970)

Notker Balbulus, *Gesta Karoli*, ed. H. Haefele, MGH SSG n.s. (Berlin, 1959); reprinted with Germ. trans. Rau, *Quellen* III; Eng. trans. Thorpe, *Two Lives of Charlemagne*

Paschasius Radbertus, *Epitaphium Arsenii*, ed with Eng. trans., A. Cabaniss, *Charlemagne's Cousins: Contemporary Lives of Adalhard and Wala* (New York, 1967)

Regino of Prüm, *Chronicon*, ed. F. Kurze, MGH SRG; reprinted with Germ. trans. Rau, *Quellen* III

Richer, *Historia francorum*, ed. with French trans. R. Latouche, *Richer, Histoire de France 888–995* (Paris, 1967)

Thegan, *Gesta Hludowici imperatoris*, ed. G. H. Pertz, MGH SS II, pp. 590–604; reprinted with Germ. trans. Rau, *Quellen* I

House histories

Paul the Deacon, *Gesta episcoporum Mettensium*, ed. G. Pertz, MGH SS II

Gesta sanctorum patrum Fontanellensis coenobii, ed. J. Laporte and F. Lohier (Paris and Rouen, 1936)

Histories for comparison with those of the Franks

Bede, *Historia ecclesiastica gentis anglorum*, ed. with Eng. trans., R.A.B. Mynors and B. Colgrave, *Bede's Ecclesiastical History of the English People* (Oxford, 1969)

Eusebius, *Ecclesiastical History*, ed. with Eng. trans., K. Lake (Cambridge, Mass., 1926)

Gregory of Tours, *Historiae*, ed. B. Krusch and W. Levison, MGH SRM I (Hanover, 1937–51) (Hanover 1951); Eng. trans. L. Thorpe, Gregory of Tours, *History of the Franks* (Harmondsworth, 1974)

Isidore of Seville, *Historiae*, ed. T. Mommsen, MGH AA II.ii; Eng. trans. G. Donini and G. B. Ford, *History of the Goths Sueves and Vandals* (Leiden, 1970)

Liber pontificalis, ed. L. Duchesne (Paris, 1886–92); Eng. trans. Raymond Davis, *The Book of the Pontiffs* (Liverpool, 1989) and *The History of the Popes in the Eighth Century* (Liverpool, 1992)

Paul the Deacon, *Historia langobardorum*, ed. G. Waitz, MGH SS rer. lang.; Eng. trans. W. D. Foulke, *Paul the Deacon's History of the Lombards* (Philadelphia, 1907)

Suetonius, ed. with Eng. trans. J. C. Rolfe, *The Lives of the Caesars* (Cambridge, Mass. 1957)

Secondary Comment

Background

Brian Croke (ed.), *History and Historians in Late Antiquity* (Sydney, 1989)

Giselle de Nie, *Views from a Many-Windowed Tower. Studies of Imagination in the Works of Gregory of Tours* (Amsterdam, 1986)

Richard Gerberding, *The Rise of the Carolingians* (Oxford, 1987)
Walter Goffart, *The Narrators of Barbarian History: Jordanes, Bede, Gregory of Tours and Paul the Deacon* (Princeton, 1988)
Rome's Fall and After (London, 1990)
Judith Herrin, *The Formation of Christendom* (London, 1985)
C. Holdsworth and T. P. Wiseman (eds.), *The Inheritance of Historiography, 350–900* (Exeter, 1986), especially the chapters by Wiseman, Ray and Bullough
R. A. Markus, *Bede and the Tradition of Ecclesiastical History*, Jarrow Lecture 1975, reprinted in *From Augustine to Gregory the Great* (London 1980)
John Matthews, *The World of Ammianus Marcellinus* (London, 1989)
Arnaldo Momigliano, 'Pagan and Christian historiography in the fourth century AD', in: *The Conflict between Paganism and Christianity in the Fourth Century*, ed. A. Momigliano (London, 1962) pp. 79–99
Janet L. Nelson, 'Perceptions du pouvoir chez les historiennes du haut moyen âge', in *Les Femmes au moyen âge*, ed. M. Rouche (Paris, 1990) pp. 77–85
R. Syme, *Ammianus Marcellinus and the Historia Augusta* (London, 1969)
John Michael Wallace-Hadrill, *Early Medieval History* (Oxford, 1975)
The Long-Haired Kings (London, 1962)
P. Wormald (ed.) *Ideal and Reality in Frankish and Anglo-Saxon Society* (Oxford, 1986) especially the chapters by Patrick Wormald and Judith McClure

Carolingian historiography

H. Beuman, *Ideengeschichtliche Studien zu Einhard und anderen Geschichtsschreibern des frühen Mittelalters* (Darmstadt, 1962)
Donald Bullough, '*Europae pater*: Charlemagne and his achievement in the light of recent scholarship', *EHR* 85 (1970) pp. 59–105 at pp. 59–69
F. L. Ganshof, 'Einhard, biographer of Charlemagne', in *The Carolingians and the Frankish Monarchy* (London, 1971) pp. 1–16
'L'Historiographie dans la monarchie franque sous les Mérovingiens et les Carolingians. Monarchie franque unitaire et Francie occidentale', *Settimane* 17 (Spoleto, 1970), pp. 631–85
D. Ganz, 'The *Epitaphium Arsenii* and the opposition to Louis the Pious', in *Charlemagne's Heir: New Perspectives on the Reign of Louis the Pious* (Oxford, 1990), pp. 537–50
Hans-Werner Goetz, *Strukturen der spätkarolingischen Epoche im Spiegel der Vorstellungen eines Zeitgenossichen Mönchs. Eine Interpretation der Gesta Karoli Notkers von Sankt Gallen* (Bonn, 1982)
I. Haselbach, *Aufstieg und Herrschaft der Karlinger und der Darstellung der sogenannten Annales Mettenses Priores*, Historische Studien 412 (Lübeck, 1970)
H. Hoffmann, *Untersuchungen zur Karolingischen Annalistik* Bonner historische Forschungen 10 (Bonn, 1958)
A. J. Kleinklausz, *Eginhard* (Paris, 1942)
H. Löwe, 'Geschichtsschreibung der ausgehenden Karolingerzeit', *DA* 23 (1967) pp. 1–30
'Das Karlbuch Notkers von St Gallen und sein zeitgeschichtliche Hintergrund', *Schweizerische Zeitschrift für Geschichte* 20 (1970) pp. 269–302
'Regino von Prüm und das historische Weltbild der Karolingerzeit', *Rheinische Vierteljahrsblätter* 17 (1952) p. 151–79

'Studien zu den Annales Xantenses', *DA* 8 (1950) pp. 59–99
M. McCormick, *Les Annales du haut moyen âge*, Typologie des sources du moyen âge (Turnhout, 1975)
McKitterick, *Carolingians*, especially chapter 6 and pp. 236–41
R. McKitterick, *The Frankish Kingdoms under the Carolingians 751–987* (London, 1983) pp. 1–8
J. L. Nelson, 'The Annals of St Bertin' in: *Charles the Bald: Court and Kingdom*, ed. J. L. Nelson and M. T. Gibson, BAR Int. Ser. 101 (London, 1981, 2nd edn London, 1990) pp. 23–40, reprinted in J. L. Nelson, *Politics and Ritual in Early Medieval Europe* (London, 1986) pp. 173–94
'Public *Histories* and private history in the work of Nithard', *Speculum* 60 (1985) pp. 251–93; reprinted in Nelson, *Politics and Ritual*, pp. 195–238
M. Sot, 'Historiographie épiscopale et modèle familial en occident au IXe siècle', *Annales ESC* 33 (1978) pp. 433–69
E. Tremp, *Studien zu den Gesta Hludowici Imperatoris des Trier Chorbischofs Thegan*, Schriften der MGH XXXII (Hanover, 1988)
'Thegan und Astronomus, die beiden Geschichtsschreiber Ludwigs des Frommen', in: *Charlemagnes Heir*, pp. 691–700
R. C. van Caenegem, *Guide to the Sources of Medieval History* (Oxford, Amsterdam and New York, 1978)
J. M. Wallace-Hadrill, 'History in the mind of Archbishop Hincmar', in: *The Writing of History in the Middle Ages: Essays Presented to Sir Richard William Southern*, ed. R. H. C. Davis and J. M. Wallace-Hadrill (Oxford, 1981) pp. 43–70
W. Wattenbach, W. Levison and H. Löwe, *Deutschlands Geschichtsquellen im Mittelalter* (Weimar, 1953–90)
W. Wehlen, *Geschichtsschreibung und Staatsauffassung im Zeitalter Ludwigs des Frommen* (Lübeck and Hamburg, 1970)
K. F. Werner, 'Zur Arbeitsweise des Regino von Prüm', *Welt als Geschichte* 2 (1959) pp. 96–116

8

Script and book production

Rosamond McKitterick

Books in the Carolingian period were the main channel by which knowledge was transmitted. In considering Carolingian book production, therefore, we are observing the actual creation and dissemination of knowledge for a society, a process central to that society's culture. Well over 7,000 Carolingian manuscripts are extant from the ninth century alone, let alone the number that was produced in the closing decades of the eighth century. If we look in detail at a small selection of these Carolingian manuscripts, many of the key questions involved in assessing the book production of the Carolingian period will become apparent. So, too, will a range of technical matters such as different types of script and methods of book production; these will be explained in the succeeding discussion. We shall be able to observe how technical innovations in book production were connected with, influenced, and were influenced by, intellectual developments.

In about 846, a magnificent Bible, BN lat. 1, was presented to the Frankish King Charles the Bald by the monastery of Tours and its lay abbot, Count Vivian.[1] The gift was expressive of the patronage Count Vivian had enjoyed from the king and the count's own patronage of the abbey; many monasteries, as we shall see below, enjoyed the patronage of lay and ecclesiastical magnates which enabled them, or required them, to produce fine books for use by the magnates. Because it contains the entire text of the Bible, the book given by Count Vivian is known as a pandect. It was written at Tours, with the full range of display capitals, uncial script and beautiful decorated initials to set out the text and provide headings. The main text of the Bible is written in a distinctive and uniform formal caroline minuscule associated with Tours.[2] It is in fact one of many such enormous, one-volume Bibles mass-produced, probably on commission, at Tours for export to other centres throughout the Carolingian world

[1] R. McKitterick, 'Charles the Bald (823–877) and his library: the patronage of learning', *EHR* 95 (1980) pp. 28–47.

[2] E. K. Rand, *The script of Tours* (Cambridge, Mass., 1929).

(no less than thirteen Bibles or fragments of once-complete Tours Bibles survive, quite apart from nearly twenty Gospel Books, a copy of the New Testament and a Psalter.[3] These Bibles were produced in a standard format of two columns of 50–2 lines each on large pages and with a written space of about 360mm × 260mm, with generous margins (usually about 435 folios in all). The presentation of the text was wholly didactic, with every effort made to ensure ease of reference. Summaries of each book are set out at the beginning in enlarged letters, different scripts were deployed to make certain portions of the text – *capitula*, prologues and headings – stand out; there are running titles at the head of each page so that one knows exactly where one is when reading the text,[4] and the text itself is clearly divided using large initials and what is known as a 'hierarchy of script', in which very formal capitals 'rank' higher than uncial, half-uncial and minuscule (see below for an explanation of these types of script). Such a hierarchy of scripts for setting a text out clearly is used extensively in most medieval manuscripts, though it was first fully developed by Carolingian scribes. There are also, in the Vivian Bible, a number of magnificent illustrations, not least a presentation portrait of King Charles himself, depicted enthroned and receiving the gift of this great pandect from Count Vivian and the brethren from Tours. Others among the Tours pandects have important sets of illustrations as well but one of the most suggestive for Carolingian methods of the dissemination of texts is again from the Vivian Bible. It depicts the making of the Vulgate translation by Jerome, its transcription by his scribes, and the dissemination of the codices to other places by monks. The text in the Vivian Bible and other Tours pandects and Gospel Books was the famous corrected Bible text of Tours inaugurated by Alcuin (d. 804) to which additions had been made during the reigns of Abbots Fridugisus (807–34) and Adalhard. The Tours text, part of a general effort to produce a correct text of the Bible in the early Carolingian period, was essentially a corrected and tidied-up text rather than an edition, with a particular sequence settled on for the books of the Old and New Testaments, and their chapter divisions.[5] Inflated claims have been made for the extent of the influence exerted by the 'Alcuin Bible' text.[6] Yet not only did Theodulf of Orleans produce an edition of the Bible from his scriptorium at St Mesmin, Micy,[7] other centres in the Carolingian world, in response to the *Admonitio generalis* of 789 which had identified the need to produce correct texts of the 'catholic books', were working to produce a correct Bible text. The royal

3 H. Kessler, *The Illustrated Bibles of Tours* (Princeton, 1977) and Wilhelm Koehler and Florentine Mütherich, *Die Karolingische Miniaturen* 5 vols. (Berlin, 1935–82).

4 Compare Innes and McKitterick, chapter 7 above, p. 210 for Walafrid Strabo's layout of the text of Einhard's *Vita Karoli*.

5 B. Fischer, 'Bibelreform im Karolingerreich', in: *Karl der Grosse, Lebenswerk und Nachleben*. II *Das Geistige Leben*, ed. B. Bischoff (Düsseldorf, 1965), pp. 156–216.

6 For a refutation of these claims see R. McKitterick, 'Carolingian Bible production: the Tours' anomaly', in: *The Bible in the Early Middle Ages: Production and Decoration*, ed. R. Gameson, Cambridge Studies in Palaeography and Codicology (Cambridge, 1993).

7 E. Dahlhaus-Berg, *Nova antiquitas et antiquita novitas. Typologische Exegese und isidorianisches Geschichtsbild bei Theodulf von Orleans* (Cologne and Vienna, 1975).

court itself promoted the production and dissemination of Gospel texts produced in ateliers patronised by the Carolingian rulers.[8] Despite its being a text so central to the concerns of the Carolingians, in that it produced models of kingship, government, warfare, historical writing, and interpretation, public praise and private devotion, and was the focus of Carolingian intellectual preoccupations, in both content and format there was a remarkable diversity of Bible text consulted, cited and produced throughout the Carolingian period.[9]

How central the Bible was in the intellectual activity of the Carolingian scholars is clear from the great volume of Carolingian exegetical treatises commenting on books of both the Old and New Testaments. An example is the work of Claudius of Turin who in fact worked in the Lyons region in the early ninth century and whose work survives in a small number of near contemporary manuscripts, such as a copy of his unpublished commentary on the Gospel of St Matthew. This has been doing the rounds of the sale rooms in recent years and at present is in the possession of H. P. Kraus of New York.[10] Of a large format (332mm × 235mm), and handsome, the manuscript was produced in northern Francia in the second quarter of the ninth century and was given to the cathedral library at Lyons by the *prepositus* Teutbertus in about 900. Claudius' work is organised as a *catena*, in which the views of various authorities, such as Augustine, Origen, Hilarius, Ambrose, Jerome, Rufinus, John Chrysostom, Fulgentius, Leo, Maximus, Gregory the Great and Bede, are gathered together in a long series of 355 chapters under successive subject headings comprising passages from the Gospel of St Matthew.[11] The source of each quotation or paraphrase is indicated in a preface and by the initial letter of his name being set out into the margin of the text. Large plain initials are used at the beginning and the end of sections and the first few words of the section (the *incipit*) are written out in small red uncial letters. Some running titles in rustic capitals are also provided. The main text is set out in two columns of thirty-five lines each and appears to have been carefully copied from an exemplar, though occasionally the scribes of our manuscript cram the text into too small a space.

Another example of a popular biblical commentator in the Carolingian period is Hraban Maur.[12] A copy of Hraban's commentary on Genesis was given by Hincmar, archbishop of Rheims, to the library of St Mary's in Rheims and is now Cambridge, Pembroke College MS 308.[13] Again the layout of the text is didactic, with sections, headings and chapters all clearly indicated by using

8 Koehler, *Karolingische Miniaturen* II and R. McKitterick, 'Royal patronage of culture in the Frankish Kingdoms under the Carolingian: motives and consequences' in *Settimane* 39 (1992) pp. 93–129.

9 For an example of diversity in other respects see, for chants and hymns, D. Bullough and Alice Harting-Correâ, 'Hymnody at the court of Louis the pious', in *Charlemagne's Heir*, pp. 489–508, reprinted in D. Bullough, *Carolingian Renewal: Sources and Heritage* (Manchester, 1992) pp. 241–71.

10 H. P. Kraus, *One Hundred Distinguished Manuscripts and Printed Books* (New York, 1990) pp. 8–10.

11 Compare Freculf discussed above, pp. 212–13.

12 See Brown, chapter 1 above, pp. 42–3.

13 J. Vezin, 'Le Rêpartition du travail dans les "scriptoria" carolingiennes', *Journal des Savants* 1973, pp. 212–27.

different grades of script. Indications of the patristic authors whose authority is invoked by Hraban Maur are, as in the Claudius of Turin manuscript, clearly provided in the margins. What is particularly interesting for our understanding of the process of production of this book, however, is that each gathering, or group of pages, is signed by the scribe responsible for its copying, so that we can document a large group of scribes collaborating on the copying of this book at Rheims in the second half of the ninth century.

Both Claudius of Turin and Hraban Maur made copious use of patristic writers. Carolingian manuscripts of such authors as Augustine, Jerome or Gregory the Great abound. At Lyons, a pair of manuscripts is of particular interest. Both contain the *City of God* by Augustine, one of which (Lyons 606) was copied in the ninth century by the deacon Florus of Lyons (d. 859 or 860) in caroline minuscule from the other, a sixth-century codex written in Merovingian half-uncial (Lyons 607).[14] In the half-uncial exemplar can be observed many suggestions for the layout of the later copy, such as a two-column format, running titles, and the opening of each new book written in red uncial. Augustine's own citations of earlier authorities, pagan and Christian, are indicated by different symbols in the margins. Throughout the book can be seen sixth- and seventh-century notes in Merovingian cursive script as well as the annotations of the famous Carolingian scholar Florus, whose notes can be found in a great many other sixth- and seventh-century codices at Lyons.

Continuous use over two or more centuries indicated by marginal notes, and the recopying of a manuscript in the Carolingian period, can also be observed in a pair of canon law manuscripts from the south of France. The large, handsome and heavily annotated (and thus well used) Toulouse 364 was written in a fine uncial at Albi before 666 or 667 by Perpetuus, a priest of the diocese, at the request of his bishop Dido of Albi, and the copy of it was made in the same region (now Albi 2).[15]

In the Bible and canon law can be seen part of the essential equipment of the Carolingian churches, but the third major category of essential texts for the clergy is that of liturgical and service books, such as Sacramentaries (books containing the text of the mass), antiphonaries, Gospel and Epistle lectionaries (with the Bible readings for the liturgical year set out in order) and Homiliaries (collections of sermons). With the production of Sacramentaries, not least the group associated with the monastery of St Amand, we appear to have working texts for use in diocesan or cathedral churches, produced for export to these other centres (just as the Tours Bibles were produced for export) and the text modified for use, with such things as the insertion of special prayers for patron saints, by the recipient. A St Amand Sacramentary such as BN lat. 2290, for

[14] C. Charlier, 'Les Manuscrits personnels de Florus de Lyons et son activité littéraire', *Mélanges E. Podechard* (Lyons, 1945) pp. 71–84 and L. Delisle, 'Notice sur plusieurs manuscrits de Lyon', *Notices et Extraits* 29 (Paris, 1891) pp. 383–403 at pp. 366–9 and 397–401.

[15] On canon law manuscripts see R. McKitterick, 'Knowledge of canon law in the Frankish kingdoms before 789: the manuscript evidence', *Journal of Theological Studies* 36 (1985) pp. 97–117.

example, is set out with great clarity to assist the priest celebrating mass in the church of St Denis. Text division is marked with the use of rustic capitals and marginal capitals, while the two central prayers of the mass, known by their first words as the *Vere dignum* and the *Te igitur* and constituting the climax of the ritual, are distinguished by large eight-line initials and uncial script. The association of particular writing centres in the production of liturgical books and other essential texts for the work of the clergy for particular dioceses can be observed in many parts of the Frankish realms. One especially productive group of scriptoria, for example, is the constellation of convents in the Seine river basin, comprising Chelles, Jouarre, Rebais and Faremoutiers, whose nuns appear to have copied liturgical and patristic works for use in the dioceses of at least Cologne, Paris and Meaux.[16] It is worth remembering, moreover, that Chelles at least enjoyed royal connections; no less a person than Charlemagne's sister was abbess there during her brother's reign and there is some indication that these centres were producing liturgical books in the middle of the eighth century which can be linked with Pippin III's promotion of liturgical reform.[17]

In resorting to patristic authority and composing their own works, Carolingian scholars were also able to draw on the work of early medieval writers on particular subjects. Bede's works on time, for example, were enormously popular and widely circulated; copies of it were made in a number of centres. A manuscript in Trier, for example (Stadtbibliothek 2500), contains Bede's *De natura rerum*, *De temporibus* and *De temporum ratione* (and other texts, such as some annals and cosmographical treatises and a wealth of scientific material). It was written by at least four principal scribes in north-west Francia, probably at Rheims or Laon, in the first half of the ninth century, in a small, clear, caroline minuscule. The text is set out with headings in elegant red uncial letters and a great many large initials. A further aid to the reader's understanding is provided by the twenty-four large or full-page diagrams and tables, including a map of the world, tables of planets and the signs of the zodiac and tables for calendar calculations.[18] Such a resort to diagrams to explain a text appears to have been a Carolingian innovation as a way of visualising and interpreting ideas diagrammatically as well as with words. It is thus of immense significance for our understanding of the Carolingian transmission of knowledge. It is also to be set beside the crucial developments in book decoration where pictures, illuminated letters and capitals, used as a form of punctuation, also comprise images which both complement and are subservient to the text.[19] The Trier Bede's many

[16] On Chelles, see B. Bischoff, 'Das Kölner Nonnenhandschriften und das Skriptorium von Chelles', in: Bischoff, *MS* I (Stuttgart, 1966) pp. 16–34, and on Chelles and Jouarre, R. McKitterick, 'The diffusion of Insular culture in Neustria between 650 and 850: the implications of the manuscript evidence', in *La Neustrie. Les pays au nord de la Loire de 650 à 850*, ed. H. Atsma, Beihefte der Francia 16/2 (Sigmaringen, 1989) pp. 395–432 and 'Nuns' scriptoria in England and Francia in the eighth century', *Francia* 19/1 (1992) pp. 1–35.

[17] I suggested this in 'Royal patronage of culture', pp. 99–103.

[18] R. Nolden, 'Werke Bedas in der Bibliothek von St. Maximin', *Stadtbibliothek Trier. Karolingische Beda-Handschrift aus St Maximin* (Trier, 1990) pp. 31–4.

[19] R. McKitterick, 'Text and image in the Carolingian world', in: *Uses of Literacy*, pp. 297–318.

additional notes document its movement from place to place, whether on loan or as part of an individual's personal property. It was, for example, in the cathedral library of Laon soon after 876. For a time it was in the hands of Manno, a teacher at the 'palace school' of Charles the Bald between 864 and 876, for Manno inserted his own autograph notes of his birthdate and ordination to the priesthood. In the tenth century, further additions indicate that the manuscript was in the library of St Maximin at Trier, and it was at Trier that the calendar was modified for Trier use in the tenth century and recorded in the library catalogue made at Trier *ca* 1100.

As well as biblical texts and commentaries, and the works of early Christian and medieval authors, the Carolingians had access to many of the works of Classical Antiquity. In nearly every case, the earliest manuscript of a classical author to survive is a Carolingian one. Some are very fine illustrated texts, such as the copy of Terence's plays now in Paris, or the illustrated *Physiologus* and astronomy manuscripts copied at such centres as Rheims and Metz, no doubt for wealthy patrons and probably actually from surviving late-antique manuscripts. Certainly work done on the layout and relationship between text and illustration in these Carolingian copies of classical works has suggested that much of the original appearance of the older exemplars was retained.

Other copies of the classics, such as Laon 468, were designed as school-books. The Laon manuscript, copied and used in the later ninth century at Laon itself by the Irish master at the cathedral school there, provides a guide for students to Vergil, the liberal arts and to the Christian poet Sedulius.[20] In the copying process, Martin of Laon checked what another scribe had copied, filled in words or even phrases the scribe had omitted, added punctuation to make the text clearer, and altered spelling and abbreviations to make it easier for the student to understand. To account for such a remarkable catalogue of difficulties manifestly experienced by the original scribe, it has been suggested that the exemplar was written in Tironian notes, a form of shorthand most commonly associated with legal notaries. Further work by John Contreni, moreover, has established that this exemplar came from Soissons. The content of the manuscript is wholly didactic, with masses of apparently useful information, lists of philosophers, poets, sibyls, magicians and pagan gods, notes on familial relationships, glosses on Vergil's poetry, a 'Life' of Vergil and glosses on the *Carmen paschale* of the Gallo-Roman poet Sedulius. Most of the lists are arranged in double columns while the more extended prefatory texts on the first seventeen folios are written in long lines, with new sentences clearly indicated with capital letters and names set out in rustic capitals. Most of these glosses and notes are thought to have been in the original exemplar in Tironian notes, also a school-book. They were certainly found helpful by subsequent students, for the book was in continuous use for almost sixty years after it was copied.

20 J. J. Contreni, *Codex Laudunenssis 468. A Ninth-Century Guide to Virgil, Sedulius, and the Liberal Arts*, Armarium Codicum Insignium 3 (Turnhout, 1984).

Other classical texts may have been copied for the exclusive use of particular scholars.[21] One example is the copy of Cicero's *De oratore* made by Lupus of Ferrières.[22] Lupus himself has left us many letters revealing his efforts to obtain exemplars from other centres in order to collate them with existing copies known to him, or else to make fresh copies for his own use.[23] Study of the Carolingian Cicero manuscripts indeed reveals the careful collating work Lupus wished to undertake and the provision of other copies of texts – many of them quite possibly late-antique manuscripts.

Another classical text copied for a scholar is a text of Plato's *Timaeus* in the translation of Chalcidius (with commentary), a remarkable account of the physical world and its creation, once in the possession of Hucbald (d. 930), master of the school of St Amand (Valenciennes 293).[24] The text transmission of the Chalcidian *Timaeus* manuscripts, however, can be worked out only from evidence provided by the manuscript itself, without contemporary letters to help such as we have for Lupus of Ferrières. Knowledge of the *Timaeus* in the Carolingian period was reliant not only on the translation of Chalcidius but also on one made by Cicero. The Cicero translation survives as a fragment only; its transmission in the ninth century is associated with the monastery of Corbie and, as with other works by Cicero, with Lupus of Ferrières. The earliest manuscript of Chalcidius' translation, on the other hand, is from north-east Francia and datable to *ca* 800 (BN lat. 2164). It has a textual twin in a Lyons book (Lyons 324), and both can be associated with the royal library of Charlemagne.

The acquisition of such rare texts by Charlemagne's court library could be part of the outcome of efforts made by means of a letter, probably sent out in *ca* 780, calling for ancient or rare books; we have another witness to the success of this letter in the form of a remarkable list of books in Charlemagne's library identified by Bernhard Bischoff (Berlin, Diez B. Sant. 66).[25] These early Carolingian *Timaeus* books were presumably copied from a Merovingian, late-antique, Italian or insular exemplar.[26] They and the list of Charlemagne's library are a salutary warning to us not to underestimate the availability of texts and levels of intellectual interest in eighth-century Gaul. Two other surviving copies of the *Timaeus* are from the late ninth century. The origin of the

21 Compare Innes and McKitterick chapter 7 above, p. 198–9.

22 For a facsimile and commentary see C. H. Beeson, *Lupus of Ferrières as Scribe and Text Critic* (Cambridge, Mass., 1930).

23 Lupus of Ferrières, Epp. 1, 4, 5, 7, 8, 21, 35, 53, 65, 69, 77, 87, 88, 95, 100, 101, 104, 106, 108, 110, 113, 122, 133, ed. L. Levillain, *Loup de Ferrières. Correspondance* (Paris, 1968); trans. G. W. Regenos, *The Letters of Lupus of Ferrières* (The Hague, 1966).

24 I discuss this in 'Knowledge of Plato's *Timaeus* in the ninth century and the implications of Valenciennes, Bibliothèque Municipale MS 293' in: *From Athens to Chartres. Neoplatonism and Medieval Thought. Studies in honour of Edouard Jeauneau* ed. Haijo J. Westra (Leiden, 1992) pp. 85–95.

25 Bernhard Bischoff, 'Die Hofbibliothek Karls des Grossen', in: Bischoff, *MS* III, pp. 149–69, postulated this letter and discussed the list of Charlemagne's books.

26 T. Julian Brown, 'A historical introduction to the use of classical Latin authors in the British Isles from the fifth to the eleventh century', *Settimane* 22 (1975) pp. 237–93, and *Texts and Transmission. A Survey of the Latin Classics*, ed. L. D. Reynolds (Oxford, 1983) with full details arranged alphabetically by author.

Valenciennes copy can be located to Rheims; it was probably acquired by Hucbald of St Amand while he was still teaching at the school of Rheims (until 900) and subsequently used at St Amand in the tenth and eleventh centuries. This link with Rheims is echoed by a number of other important works of Classical and Late Antiquity copied there in the first half of the ninth century, so that in Rheims as well as the royal court of Charlemagne we appear to have one major centre for the maintenance of a continuity in learning from the fifth century into the Carolingian period.

A further point is to be made about the Carolingian *Timaeus* manuscripts. The many diagrams are for the most part set into the text. There is a good sense of the relationship between text and diagram and directions are given as to where to find the relevant portion of explanatory text. Many later Carolingian manuscripts of scientific or quasi-scientific works, not least the Bede collection discussed above, show a similar aptitude for arranging text and diagram harmoniously. As I suggested in describing the Bede codex, we may be observing a layout devised by intelligent Carolingian scribes rather than one present in the examplar from which these manuscripts were copied. Carolingian scribes are thus making a crucial contribution to the presentation and understanding of the text.

So far I have considered examples of types of book produced in the monasteries and cathedrals for use in churches, for reading, and for teaching. To find evidence of legal shorthand or Tironian notes in any of these, as we did in the Laon school-book explaining the works of Vergil, is comparatively unusual. Some law books, on the other hand, appear to have been produced for practical purposes, such as the administration of justice. A group of them, containing either whole texts of capitularies, charters in Tironian notes or extensive shorthand annotations, can be shown to have been produced not merely in a secular context, but by a group of scribes associated with the chancery of the emperor Louis the Pious himself.[27] Most contain copies of the *Lex Salica* and other *leges*. Warsaw quart. 480, for example, contains not only the *Lex Salica* and the *Breviary of Alaric* (a digest of the Theodosian code) but also the *Formulary of Tours*, which was a collection of model documents, charters and letters for use by a notary. There are many annotations in Tironian notes. Extensive production of this type of law collection is indicated by the other members of this group of manuscripts, not least Berlin lat. quart. 150, which is virtually a replica of the Warsaw book.

Legal documents, on the other hand, were sometimes preserved in registers, or cartularies as well as in individual documents. A striking example of a book which contained many texts to do with a community's members and possessions, and thus its identity, is the *Liber memorialis* from the convent of Remire-

[27] McKitterick, *Carolingians*, pp. 57–9 and 'Zur Herstellung von Kapitularien: die Arbeit des *leges* Scriptoriums', *MIÖG* 101 (1993) pp. 1–14.

mont, now MS 10 in the Biblioteca Angelica in Rome.[28] It is one of seven such commemorative books surviving from the Carolingian period. It was primarily designed to include the names of the living and the dead members of the community of Remiremont, as well as its donors and benefactors and names were added to it in both long lists and single entries from time to time. In addition, lists of names from other communities of monks and nuns were procured and copied or bound into the volume. There are over 11,500 names entered in the book altogether. Notes of charters recording gifts to the convent, a description of the estates and many notices of the deaths of people connected with the convent, or important in the secular world, were included. It was a memorial book for daily liturgical use, but it demonstrates also the contributions of no less than fifty-eight scribes who made more than five entries and a further eighty or so whose hands can be distinguished making occasional entries. Its witness to the levels of literacy in this monastery alone is of immense significance.

Within this group of Carolingian manuscripts many matters for consideration have emerged which are typical of the issues raised by the entire book production of the Carolingian period, in all its diversity and range of text. Firstly there are those which concern the technical aspects of book production, such as the codex format common to them all, the layout and the scripts deployed for the texts. All these link Carolingian books to their late Roman and early Christian predecessors in a way that needs to be more precisely defined.

In Antiquity, texts were published in the form of rolls, long strips of writing material usually only written on one side, rolled around a spindle. Yet during the fourth century the codex became the predominant form for the book and is closely linked with the expansion of Christianity, though how closely is still a matter of dispute.[29] The book in codex form was thus 'of Roman descent; its sponsors were the Church and the law; it was nourished in the hard times of the third century and came of age in the changed world of the fourth'.[30] It is clear from the surviving evidence, moreover, that the codex was the Christian's preferred format for the book. Of the 172 recorded items of Christian literature dating from before the fifth century, 158 are, or are from, codices, and 14 from rolls. From the same period there are 17 non-Christian codices and 857 rolls. The old link of papyrus with the roll and parchment with the codex has now been forcefully severed; that eleven of the 1,158 codices containing Christian writings date from the second century and are written on papyrus is certainly

[28] Text and facsimile, MGH Lib. Mem. I *Liber Memorialis von Remiremont*, ed. E. Hlawitschka, K. Schmid und G. Tellenbach (Munich, 1981) and on Remiremont and the *Liber memorialis* see R. McKitterick, 'Frauen und Schriftlichkeit im Frühmittelalter', in: *Weibliche Lebensgestaltung im früheren Mittelalter*, ed. H. W. Goetz (Cologne and Vienna, 1991) pp. 65–118 at pp. 79–86.

[29] C. H. Roberts and T. C. Skeat, *The Birth of the Codex* (Oxford, 1978).

[30] Earlier conclusion of Roberts and Skeat, 'The Codex', *Proceedings of the British Academy* 40 (1954) pp. 169–204.

sufficient warning not to associate papyrus exclusively with the roll and parchment with the codex. There is no evidence to indicate whether the change from papyrus to parchment influenced the change in the form of the book, and much to suggest that they were totally unrelated issues. The distribution of the evidence, moreover, gives rise to a number of other considerations. Most of our earliest codices, rolls and fragments, are written on papyrus and come from Egypt. The finds from Oxyrynchus, Antinoë and other provincial settlements in Egypt represent the material evidence for book production methods in the Roman world, and for the book trade in Egypt. The survivals, among which parchment books and books in codex form become increasingly predominant, may not reflect a change in Egyptian book-production techniques so much as the fact that a greater proportion of the book trade was now in books imported from parchment- and codex-producing countries elsewhere in the empire where these practices were becoming increasingly predominant in the course of the fourth century. While for durability, flexibility and cost Roberts and Skeat have established that there is not much to choose between parchment and papyrus, the great advantage of the former was that it could be produced outside Egypt. Parchment making, simple in principle, is a highly skilled art and in Egypt it appears to have taken a long time to establish itself sufficiently to challenge the manufacture of papyrus. A parallel can be made here with the length of time it took the paper-making industry to establish itself in western Europe in the later Middle Ages.

Yet the Christians produced their books in codex form almost exclusively. Why did they choose it, if, as the evidence suggests, it was indeed a deliberate development rather than a slow evolution? The practical advantages of the codex – its compactness, convenience of use, ease of reference, economy of writing material and above all its superior writing capacity – cannot be shown to have been the overriding considerations in the second and third centuries. All, however, may well have been factors in the growing popularity of the codex. Roberts and Skeat have put forward two hypotheses to explain the apparently deliberate selection of the codex form of the book: first, it is conceivable that the papyrus codex was a development from the compilation of St Mark's Gospel from St Peter's reminiscences into a notebook which went from Rome to Alexandria. The codex form of this Gospel could thus have acquired symbolic value and Alexandria could have set the new fashion in this method of book production.

The other possibility is that there may be a connection between the development of the *nomina sacra* (the ways in which the holy names of God, Christ and others were abbreviated by scribes in Late Antiquity and the Middle Ages)[31] and the codex. That is, both may have been introduced deliberately to differentiate Christian from both Jewish and pagan books. Both *nomina sacra* and codex

31 L. Traube, *Nomina sacra* (Munich, 1911).

format, therefore, witness to a degree of organisation hitherto unsuspected among early Christians. Within the early Church, the two Christian strongholds with sufficient authority to devise such innovation were Jerusalem and Antioch and it is on Antioch that the hypothesis of the origin of the codex is focused. Antioch was the earliest Christian missionary centre to the Gentiles, a milieu in which books were needed. There is support for this hypothesis from later contexts, where book production is closely linked with missionary enterprise and the establishment of the Christian Church in Anglo-Saxon England and in the east Frankish or German regions in the eighth century. Roberts and Skeat suggest, therefore, that the first work to be written in a codex was a Gospel. From the fourth century, therefore, books are codices, made up of gatherings of eight to ten leaves, sewn together into bindings which vary from a floppy parchment cover much like our modern paperback, wooden boards, leather-covered wooden boards, to 'treasure bindings' of ivory, gold and jewels. The format for the Gospels was thus a conscious choice and one which determined the form of the medieval Bible.

With the codex form established, scribes now had a completely different writing space to exploit, so that with the emergence of the page and of the double-page opening, new challenges are presented to the scribe for the organisation of the text being copied or composed. So much is obvious, but there are further matters to be considered in the layout or *mise-en-page* of a text in early medieval books.[32] In effect, the presentation of words on a page is a process of seduction and persuasion, and an essential component of literacy. The use of letters of different shapes and sizes arrests and directs the reader's attention; the deployment of illustrations essentially related to the text, the separation of words (an early medieval innovation) and the arrangement of spacing, columns and margins to achieve clarity as well as aesthetic satisfaction, are all designed to convey the meaning of the words more effectively. Page layout, in other words, cannot be taken for granted, for it has a purpose and a function. Further, the methods and conventions of the layout of the written word have been notably consistent from the early Middle Ages to the present day.[33] Our own visual and aesthetic comprehension of most of the texts of classical, Christian and Jewish Antiquity has been shaped by the scribes of the Carolingian period, for all these texts depend on copies made in the ninth century. They, in their turn, provided models for written compositions in both Latin and the new vernaculars of western Europe and determined the appearance of our own books now. Format could not only be determined by any conventions that a scribe might have had to know when copying a particular text, such as a law book or a Bible; there are also the requirements of individual patrons and customers, and the relationship between the text and its exemplar (the text from which a copy is made), its author, its glosses and its illustrations to be taken into account (plate 4).

[32] H. J. Martin and Jean Vezin, *Mise-en-page et mise-en-text du livre manuscrits* (Paris, 1988).
[33] For many examples illustrated see ibid., passim.

Medieval manuscripts reveal extraordinary continuities in the presentation of a text, complemented by remarkable versatility within the codex format in which the letter forms and the disposition on the page play an essential role. Not the least of the problems posed by such apparent continuities, however, is the fact that our earliest manuscripts of many texts are hundreds of years removed from the date of their composition. With whose cultural presuppositions are we dealing when we read a text of Cicero, or Augustine as set out by a scribe in the Carolingian period?

In comparison with some of the extant books from the fifth to the eighth centuries, however, it is clear that the Carolingian scribes did indeed make many innovations in text format. In the books discussed at the beginning of this chapter, for example, we noted the essentially didactic layout of the Carolingian Bibles, and the use of diagrams to elucidate scientific treatises. Where it is possible to compare exemplar and copy, as in the *City of God* and canon law manuscripts from Lyons and Albi respectively, referred to above, a different approach to the organisation of the text is clearly in evidence.

It was not only in format that the Christians opted for a distinctive outward appearance that was universally adopted by producers of the early medieval book. In script also, judging from the scripts used in extant Christian texts from the fourth and fifth centuries, it would appear that uncial letters rather than the rustic capitals of classical literary manuscripts were the Christians' preferred letter forms. Both uncial and capital letters were, however, part of a 'Roman script system',[34] that is, the scripts used in the Roman world for both books and documents, between the first and the fifth centuries AD. The main types of script in this system, with their own clearly defined functions and statuses, can be divided into two categories, book hand and documentary hand (cursive), and the types comprise square capitals and rustic capitals, early Roman cursive, late Roman cursive, uncial and half-uncial scripts. These scripts provided the fundamental base from which all other scripts in the Middle Ages were derived, though the most influential for both book hands and documents in the early Middle Ages and Germanic kingdoms proved to be the later Roman cursive and half-uncial scripts. These scripts of the Roman script system were written in the first six centuries of the Christian era. Uncial and half-uncial scripts, the preferred letter forms for Christian texts, began to replace rustic capitals in the fourth century.

Subsequently, new scripts for both books and documents developed in the various kingdoms of western Europe in the early Middle Ages. Yet the scripts of the Roman system were retained, to be used primarily for display purposes, for headings, titles, colophons (plates 6 and 7).[35] Uncial script, moreover, continued

34 The best introduction to the history of script is B. Bischoff. *Latin Palaeography. Antiquity and the Middle Ages*, trans. D. Ganz and D. Ó Cróinín (Cambridge, 1990).

35 See R. McKitterick, 'The scriptoria of Merovingian Gaul: a survey of the evidence', in: *Columbanus and Merovingian Monasticism*, ed. H. Clarke and M. Brennan, BAR Int. Series 113 (Oxford, 1981) pp. 173–207.

to be developed into distinctive English, Frankish and Carolingian forms and was used extensively in grand liturgical and biblical books as a text script as late as the eleventh century. It also lent a few of its letter shapes, notably those for 'a', 's' and 't' to the new caroline minuscule.[36] Half-uncial, on the other hand, more or less died out as a main book hand except for restricted purposes at Tours, and was replaced by a new script, caroline minuscule.

Essentially, caroline minuscule was an evolved form of script.[37] Transitional forms before then can be observed in manuscripts from the Lyons area in the sixth and seventh centuries. From Burgundy in the seventh and eighth centuries we see a deliberate calligraphical experiment in the formation of a distinctive script at Luxeuil, the 'Luxeuil minuscule' based on Merovingian cursive script, though uncial was retained for headings.[38] Lastly, from the Paris Basin in the first half of the eighth century we have manuscripts produced in Frankish uncial and half-uncial script and with the occasional use of a distinctive minuscule 'b-minuscule' with some connections with Merovingian cursive.[39] Caroline minuscule first appeared in its perfected form in the 780s in manuscripts from Corbie under the abbacy of Maurdramnus, and from the 'court school of scribes' (possibly based at Trier) of Charlemagne. Thereafter it emerges or is adopted over the whole Carolingian Empire (plates 4, 5 and 6). Rather than being used for the bulk of the texts copied, as was the case in Merovingian manuscripts, capitals, uncial, half-uncial and cursive adaptations are relegated to headings, prefaces or notes, and caroline minuscule takes over as the principal book hand. Because humanist scholars in the fifteenth century found caroline minuscule very attractive, they developed a new humanistic version. It was this humanistic script which formed the basis of the Roman type developed by printers, and it is one reason why we, our eyes and aesthetic sensibilities long accustomed to its forms, find it so much easier to read than many other scripts. As I have warned elsewhere, however, the features of caroline minuscule that are always stressed – its uniformity, consistency, regularity and clarity – are criteria for any successful book script.[40] In view of the fact that caroline minuscule was superseded for many centuries, we have to be careful not to assign too great an importance to its legibility as far as we are concerned; legibility to a very considerable degree is determined by what one is accustomed to reading. It may not be the actual letter shapes themselves which were so novel and attractive, though the possibility that the Franks adopted caroline minuscule so whole-

[36] R. McKitterick, 'Frankish uncial: a new perspective on the Echternach scriptorium', in *Willibrord. Zijn wereld en zijn werk*, ed. A. S. Weiler and P. Bange (Nijmegen, 1990), pp. 374–88 and 'Carolingian uncial: a new context for the Lother Psalter', *The British Library Journal* 16/1 (1990) pp. 1–15.

[37] Bischoff, *Latin Palaeography*. See also the stimulating assessment by D. Ganz, 'The preconditions for caroline minuscule', *Viator* 19 (1989) pp. 23–44.

[38] E. A. Lowe, 'The script of Luxeuil: a title vindicated', *Palaeographical Papers*, ed. L. Bieler, 2 vols. (Oxford, 1972) pp. 389–98.

[39] McKitterick, 'Diffusion of Insular culture' and 'Nuns scriptoria'.

[40] R. McKitterick, 'Carolingian book production: some problems', *The Library* sixth series 12 (1990) pp. 1–33.

heartedly was indeed because they too found it far more legible than the scripts to which they had been accustomed hitherto. What may have been more important was, first of all, the degree to which Carolingian scribes were able to reach agreement concerning text layout, punctuation, form and type of script and individual letter forms to achieve such remarkable consistency, discipline and regularity throughout the Carolingian world; a book written in Le Mans was like one written in Regensburg or Aachen. Secondly, the degree to which it was easier and quicker to write this script, because of the fewer pen strokes required for each letter, in comparison with earlier or other contemporary types.[41]

Caroline minuscule's rapid diffusion had much to do with the promotion of education and culture initiated by Charlemagne.[42] Further, it is possible to see the script which emerges in the 780s as the perfected caroline minuscule type evolving slowly in the course of the previous three hundred years. Caroline minuscule was the triumph of a disciplined harmonious and orderly script in which individual letters had developed from half-uncial and cursive forms. Uncial and rustic capital as high-ranking scripts within the script system were retained. Cursive was gradually adapted in various ways and used as a documentary hand in royal and 'private' diplomas. Caroline minuscule itself was nevertheless capable of great individuality and diversity within the basic script type. Within the accepted set of letter forms in this general type of script there was, therefore, room for sufficient local and individual variation for palaeographers (those who study ancient writing) to be able in many cases to determine not only in what part of Europe a book was written but even the actual writing centre which produced it. It should also be noted that in due course caroline minuscule was adopted as a book hand in Italy (plate 4), England and Spain.

From the examples cited at the beginning of this chapter, it might appear that the Carolingians had revived Roman methods of book production and that their approach to layout and use of caroline minuscule in some way represents a major break with the past. But the survival of late Roman and Christian methods of book production in Merovingian Gaul, the development of monastic book production, and crucial developments in the formation of script are all in fact apparent in extant manuscripts from the Frankish regions dating from the sixth to the eighth century. Even if we can be certain that the Carolingians do introduce many important innovations of their own, and develop methods and techniques of book production very considerably, they were drawing nevertheless on a continuous line of development, and even a tradition of experiment, within Gaul and Italy in the preceding three centuries. Indeed, the production of

41 For further discussion see S. Morison, *Politics and Script. Aspects of Authority and Freedom in the Development of Graeco-Latin Script from the Sixth Century BC to the Twentieth Century AD* ed. and completed by Nicolas Barker (Oxford, 1972) and Ganz, 'Preconditions'. See also D. Ganz, 'Book production in the Carolingian Empire and the spread of caroline minuscule' in: *The New Cambridge Medieval History* II ed. R. McKitterick (Cambridge, forthcoming).

42 See Brown, chapter 1 above, pp. 19–22 and his references.

books, annotations in them which are contemporary or later than the date of the text (such as I mentioned above in relation to the canon law text from Toulouse and Albi and the copies of Augustine's *City of God* in Lyons), a steady development in the style of book decoration and in the form of the letters in any period, argues for the existence of centres which could produce books, sufficient interest in their contents to do so, and people who could reward them.

When we come to Merovingian Gaul we find that despite the difficulty of survival from such an early period, there are about 300 MSS or fragments which can be assigned to Frankish Gaul between the fifth and the middle of the eighth centuries. As the total number of Latin manuscripts surviving from all regions of Europe and the Roman Empire is nearly two thousand before 800, this is a very fair proportion of the total. These surviving manuscripts in fact provide supplementary information concerning the transition from a Gallo-Roman to a Frankish and Christian culture. Some of the Merovingian books can be grouped according to a region, such as Lyons. Some we can even locate to a particular centre, such as Luxeuil, which had a flourishing scriptorium from the second half of the seventh century. Others remain isolated examples. The books produced during this period include pagan authors (a small minority and most are in palimpsest, that is, on parchment whose original texts have been erased and the new one written on top of it, often with some of the original script still visible), biblical and liturgical books, the works of the Christian fathers such as Augustine, Jerome, and those of later Christian writers such as Gregory the Great. There are also copies of the Theodosian code of Roman law and works by local authors such as Hilary of Poitiers, Avitus of Vienne and Faustus of Riez.

Thus, the manuscript evidence indicates that book production never actually ceased in Gaul. Owing to the destruction of the south by the armies of Charles Martel and Pippin III, when Aquitaine, Provence and Burgundy were subject to ruthless attacks year after year, the cultural pre-eminence the region had enjoyed in the Gallo-Roman period was lost. But it is possible to trace the production of manuscripts from the south (Roman Gaul) and east in the region round Lyons in the sixth century into Burgundy and thereafter to new centres in the north and north-west such as Laon, Chelles, Soissons, Corbie. This geographical shift was chronological as well. By the eighth century, the main centres of book production are north of the Loire. These centres, moreover, are for the most part the monasteries. Many Frankish monasteries were producing books by the end of the eighth century and the number of active scriptoria increased rapidly in the course of the ninth century.

As I mentioned earlier, individual or corporate traits retained within caroline minuscule make it possible to identify distinct local and regional types. The identification of such types has also given rise to the notion of 'house style', that is, a style of writing cultivated by a particular group of scribes within a centre which will so subordinate individuality as to make their work recognisable as the work of that particular centre. David Ganz has also made the point that a script demanding strict discipline can also be explained in relation to the discipline and obedience required by a monastic rule.[43] He was referring only to the discipline required by Columbanus at Luxeuil but the link between scribal and monastic discipline can surely be generally observed.

There are, nevertheless, distinct difficulties with the notion of 'house style' that it is as well to rehearse. I have argued elsewhere that we may need to think in terms of a 'house style' being a notion reserved for a high-grade script to mark out books as the product of one scriptorium for a particular purpose. We first encounter such a common style in the books of Luxeuil in the late seventh and early eighth centuries. What it is impossible to establish from the extant manuscripts is whether such notions were also current in the Roman world or whether it is an idea peculiar to the monastic production of books. The earlier material is too sparse and too varied in origin to enable us to be precise in the way we describe the organisation of book production and motives for the formation of different categories of script.

In the Carolingian period, on the other hand, the evidence is both more abundant and more specific.[44] At St Amand in the ninth century, for example, the high-grade house style seems to have been reserved for commissioned books for export to other centres. Thus a house style functioned as an 'export quality' script. St Amand was clearly not the only monastic or cathedral scriptorium to develop such a calligraphic distinction. Yet, in the script in Carolingian manuscripts we appear to be dealing not only with high-grade house styles but also with local and regional script types. One writing centre could have scribes who were accomplished in both grades of script. The wider dissemination of caroline minuscule had as a consequence a lessening of local differences. The conscious cultivation of a 'house style' became increasingly rare, and was for specific purposes.

It used to be thought that the monks in the monasteries had the monopoly of book production in the early Middle Ages, but there are some indications that the ability to copy books was not confined to monks but included nuns, cathedral clerics, lay craftsmen and notaries functioning as professional scribes. Within the religious context it does appear possible to identify coherent groups of scribes collaborating in the production of a text. Research on the extant manuscripts of the early Middle Ages, whether in Gaul, the newer Christian regions of Bavaria and Franconia, Italy or Spain, has established that many of them can be associated together as the work of a group of scribes who had, apparently, received very similar training and who were striving to create some kind of uniformity in their production.[45] The cooperation of scribes in the

43 D. Ganz, 'The Luxeuil prophets and Merovingian missionary strategies', *Yale University Library Gazette* 66 (1991) pp. 105–17 at p. 109.

44 I discuss this in detail in 'Carolingian book production'.

45 See in particular the work of B. Bischoff, *Lorsch im Spiegel seiner Handschriften*, Münchener Beiträge zur Mediävistik und Renaissance Forschung. Beiheft (Munich, 1974), idem, *Die südostdeutschen Schreibschulen*

production of books can be observed in the great majority of extant manuscripts. The notion of 'scriptorium' has been used to embody such cooperation; the word at least has an impeccable ancestry from the tenth century. It is used by Ekkehard of St Gall in his *Casus sancti Galli* and by Thankmar in his 'Life' of Bernward of Hildesheim.[46] That there was a place where scribes worked together is also indicated on the monastic plan of St Gall dated *ca* 820 where in one room beneath the *bibliotheca* are the *sedes scribentium* for the scribes.[47] Such scribes could in principle write in their own way, much as a lecture room full of undergraduates will write their own particular style of hand with their own individual traits. In the early Middle Ages, in order, apparently, both to achieve aesthetic unity and to enhance monastic discipline, scribes cooperated in the production of books and also wrote in a similar way. 'Scriptorium' thus has both a neutral meaning as a place where writing is done and a more specialised meaning, extensively deployed in studies of Carolingian and later manuscripts, as a producer, within a religious institution, of books written in distinctive homogeneous styles where scribes subordinate their individuality to a sufficient extent to make their own hands resemble those of their colleagues.

A productive scriptorium had many contacts, not only in terms of borrowed books written in other styles, but also from visitors. No scriptorium could remain entirely cut off from its fellows and thus maintenance of a highly distinctive style may simply not have been feasible except for special commissions. That said, the evidence of the manuscripts gives us abundant knowledge of the division of labour among scribes and the process of copying. Some manuscripts, such as Cambridge, Pembroke College 308 or Cologne Dombibliothek 63, 65 and 67, actually indicate the scribal portions by recording the name of the scribe who wrote each section.[48] In some cases there might be one scribe responsible for the production of an entire book such as Agambertus, scribe of Valenciennes, Bibliothèque Municipale 59, a copy of commentaries by Jerome, who tells us it took him thirty-four days to copy the book, an average of eleven pages per day between 1 July and 4 August, 806; in other cases as many as twenty scribes might collaborate in order to produce a book. Many Tours monks, for example, joined together to produce the great Tours pandects, and probably as many as fourteen nuns collaborated to produce the fine eighth-century copy of Augustine's *De trinitate*, now Oxford, Bodleian Library Laud. misc. 126. The nuns were assigned the work for the most part in quire divisions, that is, according to the sets of leaves or gatherings of pieces of parchment, usually four double leaves making eight folios or sixteen pages, which make up a

und Bibliotheken in der Karolingerzeit I *Die Bayerischen Diözesen* (3rd edn Wiesbaden, 1974) II *Die Vorwiegend Österreichischen Diözesen* (Wiesbaden, 1980) and B. Bischoff and J. Hofmann, *Libri Sancti Kyliani. Die Würzburger Schreibschule und die Bibliothek im VIII und IX Jahrhundert* (Würzburg, 1952).

46 Ekkehard IV, *Casus sancti galli*, c. 36, ed. with Germ. trans. H. F. Haefele (Darmstadt, 1980) pp. 80–2 (c. 3 MGH SS II, p. 95) and Thankmar, *Vita Bernwardi*, c. 6, ed. G. Pertz, reprinted with Germ. trans. by Hatto Kallfelz, *Vitae quorundam episcoporum seculorum X,XI,XII* (Darmstadt, 1973) p. 282.

47 Plan facs. W. Horn and E. Born, *The Plan of St Gall*, 3 vols. (Berkeley, 1978).

48 See above, p. 223.

codex. Quire divisions with changes of scribe correspond to divisions in the text. The scribes varied considerably in competence but all wrote very similar basic script types of Frankish uncial and half-uncial. In such cases it is likely that one person within the community maintaining the scriptorium would act as 'master' of the scriptorium or at least supervise the copying of a manuscript and ensure that it was checked and corrected. The main and most expert scribe in the Laud *De Trinitate* manuscript mentioned above, for instance, acted in this capacity, with her corrections manifest throughout the book. The monastery of St Gall provides important evidence in this respect in the person, among others, of Notker Balbulus who worked on many manuscripts personally, and made important contributions to the library catalogue of St Gall in order to ensure that his monastery had good and correct copies of all suitable Christian literature. The copying, conservation and study of books were Notker's central concerns.[49]

Even so, we are remarkably ignorant about the physical setting and provision of materials for the production of books in the early Middle Ages. We are obliged to piece together what we can from analogies with later information and pictorial representations of the process as well as from what can be deduced from the appearance of the extant manuscripts themselves. This is particularly true as far as methods for the supply of parchment for writing purposes are concerned.

Parchment is a generic term though strictly speaking it refers only to sheep skin, with vellum being the word used for calf skin and no special word being reserved for any other type such as goat, pig, or, later in the Middle Ages, rabbit and perhaps other small mammals.[50] The preparation of parchment even in modern times continues the old methods, and it is this, and the existence of later medieval descriptions, which enable us to know how it was done. Thus, parchment is prepared for writing in a process that is simple to describe but which nevertheless requires great skill and accuracy, particularly in the final stages. The skin, still with its hair or wool on it, is steeped in a lime solution for some days to loosen both hair and fat. It is then squeezed and wrung, and superfluous pieces of hair and skin are scraped off. While still wet it is stretched on a frame to dry. The stretching and drying process brings about a change in the physical molecular structure of the skin to render it supple and pliable. When dry and fully stretched the skin is then scraped with a half-moon-shaped knife. It is here that great skill is required, for the slightest alteration in pressure will result in nicked or even holed skins. Thereafter the skin can be trimmed to the correct size and stored for use. Generally the quality of parchment varies enormously according not only to the skill of the parchment makers but also to the quality and freshness of the skins being used. Modern parchment makers

49 Susan Rankin, 'Ego itaque Notker scripsi', *Revue bénédictine* 101 (1991) pp. 267–98.

50 *Pergament. Geschichte, Struktur, Restaurierung, Herstellung*, ed. P. Ruck, Historische Hilfswissenschaften 2 (Sigmaringen, 1991) and R. Reed, *Ancient Skins, Parchments and Leathers* (London and New York, 1972).

store their skins in salt which keeps them wet and from rotting. If salt, a precious commodity in the early Middle Ages, were spared for this purpose it would have made it possible to store skins for later use. Otherwise, quick access to an abattoir or large estates where animals were routinely slaughtered for food would be the only means of ensuring a supply of sufficiently fresh skins. This is where our information is deficient. That many monasteries had access to supplies of parchment, both new and second-hand, is clear, but how many of these writing centres produced their own parchment and how many procured it from a professional parchment supplier it is impossible to say. Corbie in the early ninth century, at least, appears to have processed its own skins, for the statutes of Adalhard of Corbie, dated 822, include a reference to one (lay) parchment maker.[51] Certainly, monasteries, with their estates and livestock, had the means for supplying the necessary skins and it does not take much imagination to realise how much wealth a parchment could represent, let alone a codex made up of many animal skins.[52]

Similarly, with writing implements (goose feathers and reed pens, and iron styli for use on wax tablets) and pigments used for painting, we judge early medieval practice almost solely from the results. Many pictures of scribes with writing implements exist, however, and there is an account, with recipes, of some pigments in a late eighth-century manuscript from Lucca (Biblioteca Capitolare MS 490). It is clear that many of the pigments used in early medieval manuscript illumination came from far-away places in Europe, the Mediterranean and even further to the east; they thus indicate access on the part of the wealthy to the early medieval trading network.[53]

Only the manuscripts themselves, moreover, tell us anything about the process by which a scribe was taught to write. There is in fact very little indication in surviving codices of the learning process. This is understandable, for there was surely little reason to preserve apprentice efforts at bookmaking; it was accomplished work and correct copies, by and large, that were preserved in the monastic libraries. Pen trials in manuscripts and occasional instances of a master scribe quite clearly directing the work of a less expert scribe have been discerned, but the initial process of learning a particular set of letter forms is only dimly understood.[54] That it is not easy to learn caroline book hand is suggested by Einhard's account of the pathetic attempts Charlemagne made to write in the

51 *Consuetudines Corbeienses*, c. 3, ed. J. Semmler, *Corpus consuetudinum monasticarum* I 9, (1963) pp. 364–418 at p. 367 trans. L. W. Jones, in W. Horn and E. Born, *The Plan of St Gall. A Study of the Architecture and Economy of, and Life in, a Paradigmatic Carolingian Monastery* III (Berkeley, Los Angeles and London, 1979) p. 103.

52 On the economics of book production see McKitterick, *Carolingians*, pp. 135–64. Further considerations on the cost of parchment production in early Anglo-Saxon England are provided by Richard Gameson, 'The cost of the *Codex Amiatinus*', *Notes and Queries* (March 1992) pp. 2–9.

53 McKitterick, *Carolingians*, pp. 141–6.

54 B. Bischoff, 'Elementarunterricht und *Probationes Pennae* in der ersten Hälfte des Mittelalters', in: Bischoff, *MS* I (Stuttgart, 1966) pp. 74–87, and A. Petrucci, 'Alfabetismo ed educazione grafica degli scribi altomedievali (secc. VII–IX)', in: *The Role of the Book in Medieval Culture*, ed. P. Ganz, Bibliologia. Elementa ad librorum pertinentia 3 (Turnhout, 1986) pp. 109–32.

night when he could not sleep.[55] Yet there were, undoubtedly, living teachers of script, as at St Gall where their students have left notes about the process of copying under the direction of the master scribe. In a group of ninth-century charters from Rankweil, moreover, it is possible to see how the priest Andreas had trained younger men to write who eventually succeeded him in his function as local scribe and notary.[56] Further sources of guidance were exemplars of texts, which themselves acted as teachers of script. In setting up a new monastery or convent and requiring it to be as self-sufficient as possible, guidance, and probably exemplars of essential texts were no doubt provided by those most interested in the initial foundation. Herrad Spilling, for example, has shown how this might have been the case at Fulda in the later eighth and early ninth centuries.[57] In some centres, such as Laon or Essen, it is clear from surviving books associated with these religious communities, that their members did not at first organise a scriptorium to build up a library or serve the needs of a school but acquired their books from elsewhere, by exchange, purchase or gift.[58] Subsequently, scribes were trained and the centre was able in time to produce its own books. Certainly the copying of books, whether for their own use or for that of a neighbouring or commissioning community, became standard. Nevertheless, it is important to distinguish between houses which possessed an organised scriptorium for the systematic production of books and those which appear simply to have had among their members scribes accomplished enough to make their own notes, write letters, or draw up charters.

Reference has been made several times to exemplars, and to the fact that books were copied, and books procured for copying. We need to consider what the mechanics for the provision of exemplars were. That is, how was the choice of what to copy made, how was knowledge of the whereabouts of copies of particular texts determined and how were exemplars procured? Two sources are of particular value in answering these questions, the first being the letters of Lupus of Ferrières, already mentioned above with reference to the procuring of classical texts. Lupus gives us a precious indication of the process by which particular texts might be obtained, copied or collated with other copies. As noted earlier, Lupus exchanged a number of letters with friends and acquaintances concerning books he wished to borrow so that he might copy them. He urges Orsmar, archbishop of Tours, for example, to obtain the Commentaries

55 Einhard, *Vita Karoli*, c. 25, ed. G. Waitz, reprinted with Germ. trans. Rau, *Quellen*, p. 196; Eng. trans. L. Thorpe, *Einhard and Notker the Stammerer, Two Lives of Charlemagne* (Harmondsworth, 1969) p. 79.

56 McKitterick, *Carolingians*, pp. 109–11.

57 H. Spilling, 'Angelsächsischen Schrift in Fulda', in: *Von der Klosterbibliothek zur Landesbibliothek*, ed. A. Brall (Fulda, 1978) pp. 47–98.

58 On Essen see G. Karpp, 'Bemerkungenn zum Bücherbesitz des Essener Damenstifts um 900', in *Octegenario. Dankesgabe für Heinrich Karpp überreicht von Schülern, Verwandten und Bekannten*, ed. J. Honscheid and Gerhard Karpp (Düsseldorf, 1988) pp. 51–115 and R. McKitterick, 'Frauen und Schriftlichkeit', pp. 87–90. On Laon, see J. J. Contreni, *The Cathedral School of Laon from 850–930. Its Manuscripts and Masters*, Münchener Beiträge zur Mediävistik und Renaissance Forschung 29 (Munich, 1978).

of Boethius on the *Topica* of Cicero in a papyrus manuscript which is in the library of St Martin of Tours, and asks Orsmar to send him the book with this courier 'whom we sent to you for this purpose'. In a letter to Einhard, the biographer of Charlemagne, Lupus explains that he would have sent him the Aulus Gellius, *Noctes Atticae* (which Lupus had earlier borrowed from Einhard) if Abbot Hraban Maur of Fulda (where Lupus was at the time of writing the letter) had not kept it, complaining that a copy had not yet been made for him. Hraban apparently had undertaken to write to Einhard himself in order to explain that he took the book away from Lupus and prevented him from returning it to Einhard. Lupus goes on to say that he will, nevertheless, return the book in due course, together with all the others which Einhard has lent him. It is Lupus' exchanges with Einhard, above all, that give some inkling of the means by which books were borrowed, and more importantly how information about who had particular books was gained. Lupus refers to a list of Einhard's books that appears to have been generally available.[59] As I have argued elsewhere, library catalogues listing the contents of various monastic libraries were also circulated, so that librarians might check the list against their own holdings and make arrangements for borrowing exemplars and making new copies as they wished.[60] We can see the librarian at Murbach in the mid-ninth century, for example, making lists of the books the library still needed in the catalogue. Notker Balbulus, whom we saw earlier so active in the copying of books, not only made qualitative comments on the books listed in the St Gall catalogue but appears also to have devoted himself to filling in gaps in the library's books of Scripture and patristic authors as well as to supervising the copying of more recent works by Carolingian writers such as Florus of Lyons, Ado of Vienne and Hraban Maur.[61]

Choosing which titles and authors to copy from available books, and ascertaining where they might be and making arrangements, such as special couriers, in order to borrow them, is, of course, only half the story. It is still necessary to know how the choice of what to copy and to write was made in the first place and how the Franks decided which books should go into their libraries. It is here that a combination of the extant manuscript evidence and the few surviving ninth-century library catalogues can be so revealing, for they indicate the key role played by the monasteries in the formation of a canon of essential texts.[62]

In the pre-Carolingian period a number of guides for a basic Christian library had been compiled, such as the *Institutiones* of Cassiodorus (which was basically an annotated bibliography of both pagan and Christian authors), Jerome-Gennadius, *De viris illustribus* (a list of approved Christian authors) and a Frankish text compiled *ca* 700 called the *De libris recipiendis et non recipiendis*.

[59] Lupus, Ep. 1 ed. Levillain; Eng. trans. Regenos.

[60] R. McKitterick, *The Frankish Kingdoms under the Carolingians, 751–987* (London, 1983) pp. 210–13 and McKitterick, *Carolingians*, pp. 165–210.

[61] Rankin, 'Ego itaque Notker'.

[62] For details and references for what follows see McKitterick, *Carolingians*, pp. 200–10.

These guides had made the Bible and commentaries on it by such church fathers as Jerome, Augustine, Ambrose and Gregory the Great, paramount. In the Carolingian period the guides to approved authors and their works were disseminated in compilations which I have described as bibliographical handbooks. They were clearly drawn on by those in charge of the scriptoria and libraries; a canon of approved knowledge emerges very clearly from such library catalogues as those from Lorsch, Reichenau, St Gall, Murbach and St Riquier in particular, where there is an array of Old and New Testament texts in newly corrected versions, patristic biblical exegesis and theology, treatises for use in the schools, guides to ascetic discipline and the religious life, liturgical books, practical manuals, legal compilations, philosophy, histories, pagan and Christian poetry and the works of early medieval authors from England, Spain, Italy and Gaul, among whom a number of Carolingians authors, notably Alcuin and Hraban Maur, were gradually included. Thus a model for an appropriately stocked library was created which prevailed for the rest of the Middle Ages. Both library catalogues and bibliographical handbooks represent a systematisation of the written word and an organisation of knowledge within which literate skills were to be exercised. There is, furthermore, a preoccupation with authority, orthodoxy and correctness which is also a prevailing characteristic of Carolingian scholarship.

With the ideal of a well-balanced range of available knowledge before them, it needs to be considered whether every scriptorium set out to supply all those needs. It is probably the case that some scriptoria, such as Murbach, St Gallen, Reichenau and Lorsch, did do so, and thus that their scriptoria for the most part produced books in order to fulfil the needs of the monastery's school and library. Some scriptoria, on the other hand, appear, from the evidence of extant manuscripts, to have specialised in the production, for export and on commission, of particular kinds of text in order to supply the needs of centres other than their own. Two factors may have played a role in this. The first is the availability of exemplars. This may originally have come about either by chance survival of a concentration of a particular kind of text in one region or as a result of the efforts of an individual to procure exemplars of certain types of text such as we observed with Lupus of Ferrières and his interest in the Latin classics. The second factor is the Carolingian production of edited, corrected and approved texts of the Gospels and the Bible, mass books, law and many others for wider dissemination and use within the Frankish realms. It would make much better logistic sense if the production of special categories of text were concentrated.

This is precisely what happened.[63] We have, for example, the official production of law books containing the laws of the Franks, Burgundians, Alemans, Bavarians and the digest of Roman law known as the Breviary of Alaric by the *leges* scriptorium associated with the court of Louis the Pious and referred to at

63 I elaborate this argument in 'Carolingian book production'.

the beginning of this chapter. No fewer than thirteen books survive produced by this group of scribes associated with the *leges* scriptorium. Two further houses concentrated their text output: Tours on the export of Bibles (again, mentioned at the beginning of this chapter) and copies of the *Vita sancti Martini*, and St Amand on the export of Mass Books (plate 6). In both cases, moreover, the scribes developed a calligraphic distinction between books produced for export and those for internal use, in that they perfected a high grade 'export quality' script, a 'house style' in every sense of the word, for use in these books.[64] We find St Amand Mass Books exported to Le Mans, Chelles, Tournai, St Denis, Rheims, St Germain des Prés and Sens. Tours Bibles are found in abundance associated with many different episcopal and monastic centres, and in a few cases, with lay owners, not least, as noted with the gift from Count Vivian, King Charles the Bald himself. Further, there are no less than ten surviving copies of the *Martinellus*, (the Tours compilation of texts relating to St Martin), clearly disseminated from Tours and some of them written in Tours' export-quality script. Other centres specialised on a lower level, concentrating their copying in particular subject areas, such as at Lyons with its predominance of codices containing Augustinian theology and the concentration of classical texts produced in the Loire valley monasteries of Fleury and Auxerre. This does not mean that other centres did not also produce these types of books. It is certainly the case, however, that in each of the instances I have cited the scriptorium in question dominated production and provided a model for production as well as a particular version of a text to follow.

Authors, moreover, depended on their home monasteries for help in disseminating a text. This has been charted with great verve by Malcolm Parkes as far as the publication of the works of Bede from Wearmouth-Jarrow was concerned,[65] but it can also be observed in Fulda's output of the commentaries of Hraban Maur.[66] Thus there is diversified production in some centres and specialised production in others. There is a ready exchange of exemplars, and a response to the political, religious, legal and intellectual needs of the day. Above all, there is an extraordinary degree of coordination, cooperation, organisation and discipline involved in Carolingian book production.

In all the examples of books commissioned so far, it has been clear that institutions, both monastic and episcopal, as well as individuals, members of the royal family, laymen and laywomen, monks, nuns and clerics alike, wanted or received books. These books served a great variety of purposes. There were practical manuals on estate management, warfare, medicine, mathematics, cos-

[64] See above, p. 235–6 and see also the comments by Frederick Paxton, *Christianizing Death. The Creation of a Ritual Process in Early Medieval Europe* (Ithaca, 1990) pp. 169–84.

[65] M. Parkes, *The Scriptorium of Wearmouth-Jarrow*, Jarrow Lecture (Jarrow, 1982) reprinted in M. B. Parkes, *Scribes, Scripts and Readers. Studies in the Communication, Presentation and Dissemination of Medieval Texts* (London, 1991) pp. 93–120.

[66] Philippe Le Maître, 'Les Méthodes exégétiques de Raban Maur', in *Haut Moyen-Age. Culture, Éducation et Société. Études offertes à Pierre Riché*, ed. Michel Sot (Paris, 1990) pp. 343–52.

mography, music, building, geography, astronomy, law and agriculture. There were commentaries to elucidate holy scripture and theological treatises to deepen understanding of the Christian faith. There were treatises designed to encourage a Christian way of life among both the laity and clerics. There were liturgical books, Psalters and prayer-books to enhance and provide the means of expressing piety and religious devotion. There were stories and poems to move, to delight and to entertain, histories to anchor the Franks to their present with a full knowledge of their past. Writing was also used for administration, communication by letter, and to record legal transactions and the settlement of disputes. Even if indirectly, no aspect of Carolingian society was left untouched by the written word. It was a written word, moreover, whose form and power were determined by Carolingian scribes.

Select bibliography

On palaeography

T. J. Brown, 'E. A. Lowe and *Codices latini antiquiores*', *Scrittura è civilta* 1 (1977) pp. 177–97

'Latin palaeography since Traube', *TCBS* 3 (1959–63) pp. 361–81. Reprinted in *Codicologia* I *Théories et principes* (Leiden 1976), part of the series *Litterae textuales*, ed. J. P. Gumbert, M. J. M. de Haan and A. Gruys

D. Knowles, 'Jean Mabillon' in D. Knowles, *The Historian and Character and Other Essays* (Cambridge, 1963) pp. 213–39

Format and layout

C. H. Roberts and T. C. Skeat, *The Birth of the Codex* (Oxford, 1983)

J. Vezin and H. J. Martin (eds.), *Mise-en-page et mise-en-texte dans les manuscrits du moyen âge* (Paris, 1990)

K. Weitzmann, *Illustration in Roll and Codex* (Princeton, 1970)

Development of script

B. Bischoff, *Latin Palaeography. Antiquity and the Middle Ages*, translated from the German edition of 1986 by D. Ganz and D. O. Croinin (Cambridge, 1990) [An essential book for all aspects of the history of the book in the Middle Ages, and with an extensive bibliography]

B. Bischoff and V. Brown, 'Addenda to CLA', *Medieval Studies* 47 (1985) pp. 317–66

E. Chatelain, *Paléographie des classiques latins* (Paris, 1884–1900)

Uncialis scriptura (Paris, 1901–2)

James J. John, 'Latin palaeography' in *Medieval Studies: An Introduction*, ed. J. Powell (Syracuse, N.Y., 1976) pp. 1–68

E. A. Lowe, *Codices latini antiquiores* vols. I–XI and Supplement (Oxford, 1935–1971)

Handwriting. Our Medieval Legacy (Rome, 1960)

Palaeographical Papers, ed. Ludwig Bieler, 2 vols. (Oxford, 1972)

J. Mallon, R. Marichal and C. Perrat, *L'écriture latine de la capitale romaine à la minuscule* (Paris, 1939)

B. L. Ullmann, *Ancient Writing and its Influence* 2nd edn (New York, 1969)

Manuals with collections of plates

Rutherford Aris, *Explicatio formarum litterarum* (Madison, 1990)

J. Kirchner, *Scriptura latina libraria* (Munich, 1970)

F. Steffens, *Lateinische Paläographie* 2nd edn (Trier, 1909)

Bibliographical guide

In addition to James John and Bernhard Bischoff above:

Leonard E. Boyle, *Medieval Latin Palaeography. A Bibliographical Introduction* (Toronto, 1984)

Cultural setting

In addition to Bernhard Bischoff above:

R. McKitterick, *The Carolingians and the Written Word* (Cambridge, 1989)
The Uses of Literacy in Early Mediaeval Europe (Cambridge, 1990)

S. Morison, *Politics and Script* (Oxford, 1972)

Scribal techniques

E. Chatelain, *Introduction à la lecture des notes tironiennes* (Paris, 1900)

D. Ganz, 'On the history of Tironian notes', in *Tironian Notes*, ed. P. Ganz (Wiesbaden, 1990) pp. 35–51

W. M. Lindsay, *Notae latinae* with a Supplement by D. Bains (1936, with reprint by Olms, Hildesheim, 1965)

Ludwig Traube, *Nomina sacra* (Munich, 1907)

C. H. Turner, 'The *nomina sacra* in early Christian Latin manuscripts', *Studi e Testi* 40 (= *Miscellanea Francesco Ehrle* IV) (Rome, 1924)

Studies of particular scripts and scriptoria

Insular

T. J. Brown, 'The Irish element in the Insular system of scripts', in: *Die Iren und Europa*, ed. H. Löwe (1982) pp. 101–19
'Northumbria and the Book of Kells', *Anglo-Saxon England* 1
'The oldest Irish manuscripts and their late antique background', in: *Irland und Europa*, ed. M. Richter and P. Ní Catháin (1984) pp. 311–27

R. McKitterick, 'The Anglo-Saxon missionaries in Germany: reflections on the manuscript evidence', *TCBS* 9 (1989), pp. 291–329

M. B. Parkes, *The scriptorium of Wearmouth Jarrow*, Jarrow lecture (1982)

D. H. Wright, 'Some notes on English uncial', *Traditio* XVII (1961), pp. 441–56

Italy

V. Brown (ed.), *The Beneventan Script* (Rome, 1980) 2nd edn of E. A. Lowe, *The Beneventan Script* (Oxford, 1914)

A. Petrucci, 'L'onciale Romana. Origini, sviluppo e diffusione di una stillizzazione graffica altomedievali (sec. VI–IX)', *Studi Medievali* ser. 3 XII (1971) pp. 75–134

'Scrittura e libro nell'Italia alto medievale', *Studi Medievali* ser. 3 X (1969), XIV (1973) pp. 961–1002

L. Schiaparelli, *Il codice 490 della Biblioteca capitolare di Lucca e la scuola scrittoria Lucchese (sec. VIII–IX)*, Studi e Testi 36 (Rome, 1924)

Spain

See the articles by E. A. Lowe on 'Visigothic Symptoms' in his *Palaeographical Papers* (Oxford, 1972). See also Plates etc. in John Williams, *Early Spanish Manuscript Illumination* (London, 1977)

Frankish Gaul

E. A. Lowe, 'The script of Luxeuil: a title vindicated', reprinted in his *Paleographical Papers* (Oxford, 1972) II, pp. 389–98

R. McKitterick, 'The diffusion of Insular culture in Neustria between 650 and 850: the implications of the manuscript evidence', in: *La Neustrie*, ed. H. Atsma, Beihefte der Francia 16/2 (Sigmaringen, 1989) pp. 392–435

'The scriptoria of Merovingian Gaul: a survey of the evidence', in: *Columbanus and Merovingian Monasticism*, ed. H. Clarke and M. Brennan, BAR International series 113 (Oxford, 1981) (with Bibliog.) pp. 173–207

L. Nees, *The Gundohinus Gospels* (Cambridge, Mass., 1987)

General considerations

B. Bischoff, *Latin Palaeography*, pp. 179–238

D. Ganz, 'The preconditions for caroline minuscule', *Viator* 18 (1987) pp. 23–44

R. McKitterick, 'Carolingian book production: some problems', *The Library* 6th ser., vol. 12 no. 1 (1900) pp. 1–33 [with full bibliographical references about other Carolingian scriptoria]

'Carolingian uncial: a context for the Lothar Psalter', *The British Library Journal* 16 (1990) pp. 1–15

'Text and image in the Carolingian world', in: *Uses of Literacy*, pp. 297–318

Carolingian scriptoria

B. Bischoff, 'Panorama der Handschriftenüberlieferung aus der Zeit Karls de Grossen', B. Bischoff, *MS* III, pp. 5–38 for all areas under Frankish rule in the period 768 to *ca* 814

Auxerre: *L'École carolingienne d'Auxerre de Murethach à Remi 830–908. Entretiens d'Auxerre 1989*, ed. D. Iogna-Prat, C. Jeudy and G. Lobrichon (Auxerre, 1991) pp. 57–130

Bavarian centres (Regensburg, Augsburg, Freising, Tegernsee, Salzburg etc.): B. Bischoff, *Die südostdeutschen Schreibschulen und Bibliotheken*, I *Die Bayrischen Diözesen* 3rd edn (Wiesbaden, 1974), II *Die vorwiegend österreichische Diözesen* (Wiesbaden, 1980)

Cologne: L. K. Jones, *The Script of Cologne from Hildebold to Hermann* (Cambridge, Mass., 1929)

Corbie: D. Ganz, *Corbie and the Carolingian Renaissance* (Sigmaringen, 1990)

Fleury: Marco Mostert, *The Library of Fleury. A Provisional List of Manuscripts* (Hilversum, 1989)

Fulda: Herrad Spilling, 'Angelsächsische Schrift in Fulda' in: *Von der Klosterbibliothek zur Landesbibliothek*, ed. A. Brall (Fulda, 1978) pp. 47–98

Laon: J. J. Contreni, *The Cathedral School of Laon: Its Manuscripts and Masters*, Münchener Beiträge zur Mediävistik und Renaissance Forschung (Munich, 1976)

Lorsch: B. Bischoff, *Lorsch im Spiegel seiner Handschriften*, Münchener Beiträge zur Mediävistik und Renaissance Forschung. Beiheft (Munich, 1974)

Reichenau: No synthesis has been produced but many sections of Bernhard Bischoff's works, collected in *MS* I–III, provide comments on Reichenau manuscripts in the ninth century

Rheims: F. L. Carey, 'The scriptorium of Rheims during the Archbishopric of Hincmar (845–882)' in: *Classical and Medieval Studies in Honor of E. K. Rand* (New York, 1938) pp. 41–60

St Amand: A. Boutémy, 'Le Scriptorium et la bibliothèque de Saint-Amand', *Scriptorium* 1 (1946) pp. 6–16

St Denis, J. Vezin, 'Les Relations entre Saint Denis et d'autres scriptoria', in: *The Role of the Book in Medieval Culture*, ed. P. Ganz. Bibliogia. Elementa ad librorum studium pertinentia 3 (Turnhout, 1986) pp. 17–40 and 'Les Manuscrits copiés à Saint Denis en France pendant l'époque carolingienne' in: *Paris et Île de France, Mémoires publiés par la Fédération des sociétés historiques et archéologique de Paris et l'Île de France* 32 (1981) pp. 273–87

St Germain des Pres: *Der Stuttgarter Bilderpsalter*, 2 vols., ed. B. Bischoff (Stuttgart, 1965)

Swiss monasteries: A. Bruckner, *Scriptoria medii aevi helvetica. Denkmäler Schweizerischer Schreibkunst des Mittelalters* (Geneva, 1935–78)

Tours: E. K. Rand, *A Survey of the manuscripts of Tours. Studies in the Script of Tours* 2 vols. (Cambridge, Mass., 1929)

Würzburg: B. Bischoff and J. Hoffmann, *Libri Sancti Kyliani. Die Würzburger Schreibschule und die Dombibliothek im VIII. und IX. Jahrhundert* (Würzburg, 1952)

9

Emulation and invention in Carolingian art

George Henderson

It is customary to say that Carolingian art appeared *ex nihilo*, among a people with no native tradition of figurative representation.[1] However, since precious metalwork was the leading art form in the Middle Ages up until at least the thirteenth century, and since so much of Carolingian art comprises essentially a political statement, emphasising power and splendour, a solid groundwork for subsequent Carolingian achievements can be seen to have been laid by earlier jewellers and goldsmiths. Frankish sword mounts, armlets and fibulae with their fantastic silhouettes, monumental forms, fastidious technique and sumptuous combination of crimson and gold, visually and aesthetically anticipate the best efforts of the designers of the illuminated letters in Carolingian Psalters and Gospel Books.[2]

In the high art of the Franks, as with the Carolingians, there is no segregation of the secular from the sacred. Royal regalia and saints' shrines or holy vessels are decorated in exactly the same fashion, using the technique of cloison cells arranged in a wonderful variety of ladder or cobweb patterns, fitted with flat garnets or mounted with cabochon gems and pearls. The leading exponent of this art was Eligius, bishop of Noyon (*ca* 590–660), who executed the shrines of the great saints of France, St Lucian of Beauvais, St Geneviève of Paris, St Martin of Tours and, above all, a complex set of precious structures marking the burial place of St Denis. Fragments only survive to show Eligius' legendary skill.[3] Perhaps attributable to him is the disc of gold and garnets which is now

1 For example J. Porcher, 'Book painting', in: J. Hubert, J. Porcher, W. F. Volbach, *Carolingian Art* (London, 1970) p. 71; C. R. Dodwell, *Painting in Europe 800 to 1200* (Harmondsworth, 1971), p. 15.

2 B. Arrhenius, *Merovingian Garnet Jewellery: Emergence and Social Implications* (Stockholm, 1985); for illustrations see also *Trésors romains–Trésors barbares: Industrie d'art à la fin de l'Antiquité et au début du Moyen Age*, Exhibition of material from the Römisch-Germanisches Museum, Cologne (Brussels, 1979); H. Roth, *Kunst der Völkerwanderungszeit*, Propyläen Kunstgeschichte, Supplementband IV (Oldenburg, 1979).

3 H. Vierck, 'Werke des Eligius', *Studien zur Vor- und Frühgeschichtlichen Archaeologie, Festschrift für Joachim Werner*, Münchner Beiträge zur Vor- und Frühgeschichte, Ergänzungsband, 11 (1974), pp. 309–80; C. Davis-Weyer, *Early Medieval Art 300–1150*, Sources and Documents (Toronto, 1986; first published Prentice Hall Inc. 1971) pp. 69–70.

attached to one end of the later shrine of the sandal straps of St Andrew at Trier. The minute rhythmically arranged T-shaped garnets are bravura examples of stone-cutting, very similar to those on the royal regalia from the Anglo-Saxon Sutton Hoo ship burial; the resemblance suggests luxury trading links between Germany and England in the early seventh century.[4]

Such expert shaping of precious stones may in fact represent continuity from Roman times, when Trier (plate 8) was a great centre of manufacture of precious and ornamental stonework. A giant agate handled bowl or tray of the fourth century, now in Vienna, is signed by a Trier artist.[5] The late-antique world is certainly evoked by the Frankish disc on St Andrew's shrine, since fixed at its centre is a gold medallion of the Emperor Justinian. In evaluating the antecedents of the Carolingian Renaissance, Frankish appreciation of distinguished antique works provides important evidence of cultural continuity. A deep brown and grey-blue agate vase at St Maurice d'Agaune, carved with figures placed in solemn confrontation, perhaps illustrating the story of Phaedra, is mounted on a brilliantly polychrome base, again perhaps by Eligius.[6] The quantity and quality of antique artefacts known to the Franks, and sadly lost to us, is tantalisingly recorded in the *Gesta pontificum* of Auxerre, listing by weight and by engraved or embossed subject-matter a treasure of massive silver gilt cups and dishes, bequeathed to his cathedral by Bishop Desiderius in the first quarter of the seventh century. Various of these vessels were decorated with 'the story of the sun', 'the history of Aeneas', 'a rider with a snake at his feet', 'a centaur', 'an Ethiopian'.[7] As well as precious plate, ivory carvings of late-antique origin were admired and preserved in the churches of Francia. In the twelfth century Suger, abbot of St Denis, reports that he took out of his stores, and repaired, ivory panels 'admirable for the most delicate and nowadays irreplaceable sculpture, with depictions of antique stories (*antiquarum historiarum descriptione*)'.[8] The reliefs which Suger rehabilitated as an ambo for reading the Gospels, no doubt in conscious rivalry of the great ambo at imperial Aachen,[9] need not have reached St Denis only through the munificence of Charles the Bald. A grand sixth-century ivory diptych, now in the Louvre, shows Justinian on horseback, triumphing over his enemies and receiving the tribute of his subjects.[10] Its heroic

[4] R. L. S. Bruce-Mitford, *Aspects of Anglo-Saxon Archaeology* (London, 1974) pp. 31–2, 273–5; Arrhenius, *Merovingian Garnet Jewellery*, pp. 157–60, 162–87. See also E. James, *The Franks* (Oxford, 1988) pp. 204–6, and plate 41. For the history of Trier, see E. M. Wightman, *Roman Trier and the Treveri* (London, 1970).

[5] H. P. Bühler, *Antike Gefässe aus Edelsteinen* (Mainz, 1973), no. 83, p. 70; *Trier: Kaiserresidenz und Bischofssitz*, Exhibition Catalogue, Rheinisches Landesmuseum, Trier (Mainz, 1984), no. 35, p. 118.

[6] Vierck, 'Werke des Eligius', pp. 333, 335–7, and plate 6; also J.-M. Theurillat, *Le Trésor de St-Maurice*, 2nd edn (St-Maurice, 1982) colour plate opp. p. 14.

[7] Davis-Weyer, *Early Medieval Art 300–1150*, pp. 66–9.

[8] Suger, *De administratione*, XXXIV, in E. Panofsky, *Abbot Suger on the Abbey Church of St-Denis and its Art Treasures* (Princeton, 1948) p. 72.

[9] For the late-antique ivories on the Aachen ambo see W. F. Volbach, *Elfenbeinarbeiten der Spätantike und des frühen Mittelalters* (Mainz, 1952) nos. 72–7, pp. 45–6 and plates 24, 25.

[10] *Age of Spirituality*, Catalogue of Exhibition at the Metropolitan Museum of Art, New York, ed. K. Weitzmann (New York, 1979) no. 28, pp. 33–5.

imagery has many echoes in Carolingian art,[11] but it was already available in Francia, in the seventh century, since, true to the function of such ivory diptychs as writing tablets, it carries on its reverse a list of the seventh-century bishops of Trier. Similarly a carved memorial of the appointment to consular office of Anastasius, from early sixth-century Constantinople, showing the consul sitting, in official dress, presiding over a theatrical performance, has on the back a seventh-century list of Liège saints.[12]

Ecclesiastical use of early ivories, and probable continuity of ownership in Francia, is vouched for by a series of sixth-century ivory panels, now scattered among museum collections in New York, Brussels, Tongres and Cambridge. They represent not pagan or secular subjects but instead scenes from the Gospels, and heavily built bearded figures of Evangelists and Apostles, placed frontally between elaborate grooved or fluted columns, supporting Corinthian capitals and shell niches (plate 9).[13] These large flat panels are pierced for mounting on a complex structure. The Cambridge panels are reported to have come from a monastery dedicated to St Maximin at Trier, and the whole series of figures, though by no means uniform in their handling of physiognomy and costume, has been identified as the remains of a grand episcopal throne or *cathedra*; similar standing figures and figure groups survive on the ivory throne presented to Bishop Maximian of Ravenna by the Emperor Justinian in the 540s.[14]

The existence from early-Christian times, and continued use in Francia, of such prestigious ecclesiastical furniture is supported by an event recorded in the *Vita sancti Wilfridi*, the seventh-century English monastic founder and bishop. St Wilfrid was a determined opponent of local customs and observances that might impair the unity of Christendom. To make certain that his own consecration as bishop would be valid he turned to colleagues in Francia to carry out the ceremony. Fourteen bishops met in Compiègne to receive his profession of faith, and after his consecration nine bishops carried him seated on a golden throne into the sanctuary of the church.[15] In this incident is encapsulated the formidable material culture of the Church in Francia. St Wilfrid was a friend of Agilbert, bishop of Paris. Part of Agilbert's monastery at Jouarre has survived as a crypt below later buildings, and contains stone sarcophagi impressively decorated with relief sculpture.[16] It is no long step from the apocalyptic imagery of Christ and his Evangelists on the alabaster throne presented to the bishop of Grado by the Emperor Heraclius in the early seventh century[17] to the sacred

[11] For celebrations of Charlemagne's victories, see the verses by Theodulf of Orleans, *Ad Carolum regem*; Eng. trans. Godman, *Poetry*, p. 152; see also ivory panels in Florence, A. Goldschmidt, *Die Elfenbeinskulpturen aus der Zeit der Karolingischen und Sächsischen Kaiser* (Berlin, 1914) I, no. 10, p. 12.

[12] *Age of Spirituality*, ed. Weitzmann, no. 88, pp. 97–8.

[13] Ibid., nos. 486, 487, pp. 540–3. See also Volbach, *Elfenbeinarbeiten*, nos. 152, 153, 154, 155, pp. 74–5 and plates 49–50.

[14] W. F. Volbach, *Early Christian Art* (London, 1961), plates 226–35 and p. 356.

[15] B. Colgrave, *The Life of Bishop Wilfrid by Eddius Stephanus* (Cambridge, 1927) c. XII, pp. 24–7.

[16] J. Hubert, J. Porcher, W. F. Volbach, *L'Europe des invasions* (Paris, 1967) pp. 64–78, plates 80–90.

[17] *The Treasury of San Marco, Venice*, Catalogue of an Exhibition at the British Museum, ed. D. Buckton (Milan, 1984), pp. 98–105.

scenes boldly displayed on the end and front of Agilbert's own sarcophagus at Jouarre. Equally illustrative of Francia's international contacts and unbroken technical expertise are the details of the building itself. Coloured marble columns are crowned by handsome foliated capitals. Particularly suggestive of Roman continuity is the chequer or network pattern, called by Vitruvius *opus reticulatum*, on one of the side walls of the Jouarre crypt. This looks exactly like the crisp ornamental stonework of the Roman walls of Colonia, Cologne on the Rhine.[18] We learn from Bede's *Lives of the Abbots of Wearmouth and Jarrow* that Francia was a source of the civilised techniques and manpower needed by the recently established Anglo-Saxon Church. Benedict Biscop hired stone masons to build his monastery of dressed stone according to Roman methods, *iuxta Romanorum morem*.[19]

The mention of St Wilfrid and Benedict Biscop leads us to the third precondition of the Carolingian Renaissance in art. As well as the aesthetic distinction of Frankish metalwork and an inheritance of treasure and skills from the Christian Roman Empire, Francia in the seventh and eighth centuries benefited from stimulating contact with English and Irish missionaries and scholars. How deeply entrenched the Insular presence was in Francia is nicely summed up by a small bone disc excavated in the amphitheatre at Trier inscribed with an intercession to the Trinity and the name of a nun, *Rotsvintda ancella Christi*, written in Insular capitals like those of the Lindisfarne Gospels. The disc is pierced for suspension and will have been part of a book cover, cross or some larger object. Its designer could have been influenced by the late fourth-century wooden coffin of St Paulinus, still preserved in Trier, which carries metal appliqués including an open-work disc bearing the name of a woman donor, Eleuthera.[20] The foundation of a monastery at Echternach in 698 brought the new vigour of Anglo-Irish Christianity and art to bear upon the long-established religious life of Trier and its environs.[21] The wooden fabric of St Paulinus' coffin is an important and suggestive parallel for the wooden coffin made on Lindisfarne to enshrine the body of St Cuthbert in 698. This coffin is incised with an early-Christian youthful beardless type of Christ; also with rare but presumably early-Christian full-length images of the Evangelist symbols, as well as images of angels and of the Virgin and Child.[22] It is one of a large body

18 See Hubert, Porcher, Volbach, *L'Europe des invasions*, plate 79. For Cologne, see V. H. Elbern, *Das Erste Jahrtausend: Kultur und Kunst im Werdenden Abendland an Rhein und Ruhr* (Düsseldorf, 1962), plate 5. Vitruvius, *De architectura* 2, c. 8, Loeb Classical Library, trans. F. Granger (Harvard, 1962), p. 110.

19 Bede, *Historia abbatum* in: *Venerabilis Baedae opera historica*, ed. C. Plummer (Oxford, 1896) p. 368. On the character of Frankish churches see James, *The Franks*, pp. 148–52.

20 For St Paulinus' coffin see Trier: *Kaiserresidenz und Bischofssitz*, no. 127, pp. 239–40.

21 For the Anglo-Saxon foundation of Echternach see T. D. Kendrick, T. J. Brown, R. L. S. Bruce-Mitford, *Evangeliorum quattuor Codex Lindisfarnensis* II (Olten and Lausanne, 1960) pp. 103–4. For the interest of the bishop of Trier in the Echternach foundation see McKitterick, *Carolingians*, p. 132. See also A. H. Anton, *Trier im frühen Mittelalter*, Quellen und Forschungen aus dem Gebiet der Geschichte N.F. 9 (Paderborn, Munich, Vienna and Zurich, 1987).

22 E. Kitzinger, 'The coffin reliquary', in *The Relics of St Cuthbert*, ed. C. F. Battiscombe (Oxford, 1956) pp. 202–304 and plates IV–XI.

of Insular works of art, directly responding to imported exemplars of the sixth century onwards.

No account of Carolingian art can afford to marginalise Insular art. It provides evidence for the availability in western Europe in the seventh and eighth centuries of a wealth of distinguished inconographic exemplars, costly pigments, and sophisticated techniques. The sound economic basis of Insular art patronage is again suggested by the career of St Wilfrid. He was no mere provincial spectator of the splendour of Frankish material culture. In 676 he backed a coup d'état by the supporters of the exiled west Frankish King Dagobert II, and despatched him to Francia equipped *magnifice*, with an armed escort.[23] Unusual ability to pay for the costs of manufacture will account for Wilfrid's being able to provide his foundation at Ripon with silk hangings and purple vestments, and above all with the copy of the Gospels written in gold letters on empurpled vellum.[24] A recent writer on art in the reign of Louis the Pious calls purple parchment 'a late antique artistic technique revived in Carolingian times',[25] but it was patronised by an Englishman in the seventh century. In the Lorsch Gospels, one of a series of 'royal' Gospel Books dating to around 800, the preface to St Matthew's Gospel is illustrated with a miniature showing crowds surrounding portrait icons of Christ's ancestors, Abraham, David and Jechonias.[26] An icon of Christ himself was carried by the clergy who arrived from Rome in 598 to preach the Gospel at Thanet in Kent.[27]

Among the books sent by Pope Gregory I, *ca* 600, to assist the work of the English mission one very probably survives – an Italian sixth-century copy of the Gospels which belonged to St Augustine's Canterbury in the Middle Ages. Opposite the first page of St Luke's Gospel is a miniature of the Evangelist, with his symbol, the winged bull, in the arch above, their relationship explained by a line of verse quoted from the late fifth-century Christian poet Sedulius' *Carmen paschale*.[28] Narrative illustration, and formalised late-antique naturalistic representation were introduced into England by gift or advantaged purchase throughout the seventh century. The educational ideas and artistic tastes pursued by Cassiodorus Senator at Vivarium in the sixth century were genuinely able to be transplanted to Northumbria.

Around 700 the scriptorium at Jarrow-Wearmouth was working on a

[23] Colgrave, *The Life of Bishop Wilfrid* c.XXVIII, pp. 54–5. See also D. Ó'Cróinín, 'Merovingian politics and Insular calligraphy', *Ireland and Insular Art AD 500–1200*, ed. M. Ryan, Royal Irish Academy (Dublin, 1987), pp. 40–1.

[24] ... *indumenta purpureaque et serica* ... *in membranis depurpuratis* ... Colgrave, *The Life of Bishop Wilfred*, c. LV, pp. 120–1; c.XVII, pp. 34–7.

[25] E. Sears, 'Louis the Pious as *Miles Christi*: the dedicatory image in Hrabanus Maurus's *De laudibus sanctae crucis*', *Charlemagne's Heir*, p. 625.

[26] Bucharest, National Library. See W. Koehler, *Die Karolingischen Miniaturen*, II, *Die Hofschule Karls des Grossen* (Berlin, 1958), pp. 92–3, and plate 104b.

[27] *Historia ecclesiastica gentis anglorum*, I, c. 25, in: *Venerabilis Bedae opera historica*, ed. C. Plummer (Oxford, 1896), p. 46.

[28] F. Wormald, *The Miniatures in the Gospels of St Augustine: Corpus Christi College MS 286* (Cambridge, 1954) especially pp. 3–6.

complete edition of the Bible, the *Codex Amiatinus*, prefaced by a facsimile of a complex series of diagrams and pictures designed originally for Cassiodorus' own *Codex grandior*.[29] The often-emphasised Insular aptitude for radical combinations or conflations of older imagery, or for wholly original invention, should not blind us to the culturally equally important fact that Insular scholar-artists of the seventh and eighth centuries felt the duty and interest of accurately reproducing important pictorial exemplars, a striking and indeed characteristic feature of ninth-century Carolingian art. Exactly the type of book that the Emperors Charlemagne, Louis the Pious and Lothar, or the Archbishops Ebbo of Rheims and Drogo of Metz would have been pleased to possess, comes before us in Bede's reference to a 'volume of the cosmographers', *mirandi operis*, bought by Benedict Biscop in Rome and afterwards sold for a grant of land to the learned Northumbrian King Aldfrith. Around 770, on the threshold of the Carolingian Renaissance, Bishop Lull of Mainz made efforts to obtain from York *Libros cosmografiorum*, perhaps Biscop's sixth-century codex itself, or an Insular copy.[30]

Apart from the remarkable accuracy in style and technique of the *Codex Amiatinus*' reproduction of its lost exemplars, a fair impression of Insular facsimile making is to be had from the manuscript, now in the Plantin Moretus Museum in Antwerp, of Sedulius' *Carmen paschale*.[31] By its script this manuscript has been assigned by Bischoff to the cathedral scriptorium of Liège, early in the ninth century, but on fol. 68v it appears to reproduce a note marking the end of a book belonging to, or written by, a man with an English name, Cutwine. Levison associated this name with the bishop of Dunwich whom Bede mentions as having brought from Rome an illustrated copy of the *Life and Labours of St Paul*.[32] Thus the Antwerp Sedulius may represent a Carolingian copy of an English copy of a late fifth-century exemplar. The unframed rectangular illustrations, in line drawing and cool bright colour-wash, intersperse the text. The figures wear mantles with appliqué stripes similar to figures in Ravenna mosaics. The exotic head-dress of Daniel in the lions' den (plate 10) is like the crown of Pharaoh in a scene from the story of Joseph carved on the ivory throne of Archbishop Maximian.[33] When Sedulius describes Judas' betrayal of Christ, he employs the imagery of a wolf and a lamb, but the literal illustration on fol. 33 of the Antwerp manuscript, of Judas and Christ in animal

[29] R. L. S. Bruce-Mitford, 'The Art of the Codex Amiatinus', *The Journal of the British Archaeological Association* 32 (1969) pp. 1–25; G. Henderson, 'Cassiodorus and Eadfrith Once Again', *The Age of Migrating Ideas, Proceedings of the Second International Conference on Insular Art, Edinburgh, 1991*, ed. J. Higgitt and M. Spearman, (Edinburgh, 1993) pp. 82–91.

[30] W. Levison, *England and the Continent in the Eighth Century* (Oxford, 1946) p. 42. For the meaning of 'Cosmographers' see Cassiodorus, *Institutiones*, ed. R. A. B. Mynors, *Cassiodori Senatoris Institutiones* (Oxford, 1937), I, XXV, p. 66.

[31] Antwerp, Museum Plantin-Moretus MS M.17.4, for which see J. J. G. Alexander, *Insular Manuscripts 6th to the 9th Century* (London, 1978), no. 65, p. 83.

[32] Levison, *England and the Continent* pp. 133–4; G. Henderson, *Bede and the Visual Arts* (Jarrow Lecture, 1980) p. 7.

[33] Volbach, *Early Christian Art*, plate 234.

form seems to carry us back to a very early stage of Christian iconography, to the symbolic art of the catacombs.[34] If an English intermediary did play its part in the transmission of these images it has not interfered at all with their late-antique character.

Thus we can reasonably see many of the products of Insular art as a 'trial-run' for later Carolingian productions. In its own right, however, Insular art exercised a profound effect on Carolingian decorative design, especially in the early Carolingian period, the last quarter of the eighth century. In the wake of the Irish and English missions to France and Germany quite mature types of book decoration were exported to the continent. An example of this is a copy of the Gospels now in Vienna, signed by a scribe with an English name, Cutbercht, working probably at Salzburg in Bavaria.[35] The large initial letters of the Cutbercht Gospel *incipits*, with interlace, scroll and animal ornament, and various other features in the gradation of script, closely parallel those in the south English 'Book of Cerne'. Both the English 'Cerne' manuscript and the Bavarian Cutbercht Gospels have features which seem to derive from a probably Northumbrian Gospel Book now in Rome.[36] This remarkable book not only handles Insular traditional motifs with tongue-in-cheek facility, but also outshines even the Lindisfarne Gospels in the Ravennate manner in which it treats the Evangelists. The Cutbercht Gospels likewise grapples with Italian models in its Evangelist portraits. The cultural mix promoted in Tassilo's duchy of Bavaria, before his overthrow in 788, comprises another 'trial run', as it were, for the art styles of the Carolingian Renaissance.[37] Stolid naturalistic figures of Christ and the psalmist David, framed in columns and arches filled with elegant Insular strap work, occur in a small Psalter, probably made for a member of Duke Tassilo's family and brought to Notre-Dame at Soissons after his fall.[38]

Italianate figures, framed by Insular key patterns or interlace occur in other media besides books. Two open-work ivory panels, carrying figure scenes elaborately framed, from St Martin's Church at Genoels-Elderen, now at Brussels, have been ascribed to England, or to Tassilo's Bavaria.[39] They once formed the covers of a book, either a Gospels or a Psalter. On one side we see the Annunication and the Visitation; on the other a youthful beardless Christ, accompanied by angels, triumphs over four beasts, in literal illustration of Psalm

34 J. Stevenson, *The Catacombs: Rediscovered Monuments of Early Christianity* (London, 1978) pp. 80–1, and plate 57.

35 Vienna, Österreichische Nationalbibliothek Cod. 1224; Alexander, *Insular Manuscripts*, no. 37, pp. 62–3.

36 Cambridge, University Library, MS Ll.1.10, and Rome, Vat. Barberini lat. 570, for which see Alexander, *Insular Manuscripts*, no. 66, pp. 84–5, and no. 36, pp. 61–2.

37 See D. H. Wright, 'The *Codex Millenarius* and its model', *Münchner Jahrbuch der bildenden Kunst*, 3rd series, 15 (1964) pp. 37–54.

38 Montpellier, Bibliothèque de l'Université, MS 409, for which see *Karl der Grosse*, Catalogue of Council of Europe Exhibition, Aachen 1965, ed. W. Braunfels (Düsseldorf, 1965) no. 450, pp. 272–3.

39 D. H. Wright, 'The Italian stimulus on English art around 700', *Stil und Überlieferung in der Kunst des Abendlandes*, Akten des 21. Internationalen Kongresses für Kunstgeschichte in Bonn 1964, I, ed. H. von Einem (Berlin, 1967) p. 91; J. Beckwith, *Ivory Carving in Early Medieval England* (London, 1972) no. 3, p. 118 and plates 14–15; C. L. Neuman de Vegvar, 'The origin of the Genoels-Elderen ivories', *Gesta* XXIX/1 (1990) pp. 8–24.

90:13. 'Thou shalt walk upon the asp and the basilisk: and thou shalt trample under foot the lion and the dragon'. A case might be made for Liège as the place of manufacture of the Genoels-Elderen panels. The ivory figures wear appliqué bands on their clothes, and reach out with preternaturally long arms, exactly like the figures in the Antwerp Sedulius manuscript. But that, as we have noted, may essentially preserve the appearance of an Insular model.

Perhaps the most thoroughly Insular of all early Carolingian manuscripts is the Psalter from Corbie, now in Amiens, Bibliothèque Municipale.[40] The initial letters of each psalm are made up of confronted and entangled beasts, or actually contain figures, in some way representing the 'subject-matter' of the psalm. Psalm 126, *Nisi Dominus*, for example, forms its initial letters out of three slim racehound-like creatures, with interlaced tongues and ears, purely Insular in design; they are closely paralleled in the Pictish eighth-century silver hoard from St Ninian's Isle, Shetland.[41] A splendid Psalter, made in Canterbury in the eighth century, now BL Cotton MS Vespasian A.I, provides precedents for the unusual narrative or 'historiated' content of the Corbie Psalter initials.[42] Psalm 114, *Dilexi quoniam*, in the Corbie Psalter imaginatively elaborates on the words of verse 8, 'He hath delivered ... my eyes from tears', with an image of Mary Magdalene at the feet of the risen Christ, interpreting the sense of the Psalms Christologically, as later they memorably are in a central work of the Carolingian Renaissance, the Stuttgart Psalter.[43] The heavy draperies, with zig-zag hems, in the Corbie Psalter initials, are familiar in eighth-century Insular sculpture, for example at Rothbury, of the Jarrow-Wearmouth school.[44]

The first manuscript that can certainly be associated with Charlemagne himself was written by the scribe Godescalc between 781 and 783.[45] It is a Gospel lectionary, for use in the liturgy throughout the Christian year. It features, however, some handsome initial letters, emulating Insular Gospel *incipits*, and fol. 48 contains a bird pecking grapes which might have been drawn by the designer of the Rothbury or Ruthwell Crosses. An English dimension can even be perceived in the splendid colour of the text pages. On fol. 125 Godescalc notes that he has painted his book *colore rosarum, munera martyri*. Bede, commenting on the purple textiles used in the ancient Jewish tabernacle, equated that colour with blood and the death of the saints.[46] Godescalc's use of gold writing on crimson vellum has a precedent in the extant mid-eighth-century

[40] Amiens, Bibliothèque Municipale, MS 18, for which see J. Porcher, 'L'Evangéliaire de Charlemagne et le Psautier d'Amiens', *La revue des arts*, VII (1957), pp. 51–8; O. Pächt, 'The pre-Carolingian roots of early Romanesque art', *Romanesque and Gothic Art: Studies in Western Art*, Acts of the Twentieth International Congress of the History of Art, I ed. M. Meiss (Princeton, 1963) pp. 67–75.

[41] A. Small, C. Thomas, and D. M. Wilson, *St Ninian's Isle and its Treasure* (Oxford, 1973), vol. 2, plate XVIII.

[42] See D. H. Wright, *The Vespasian Psalter*, Early English Manuscripts in Facsimilie XIV (Copenhagen, 1967).

[43] See below, pp. 265–6 and note 107.

[44] R. Cramp, *Corpus of Anglo-Saxon Stone Sculpture* I *County of Durham and Northumberland* (Oxford, 1984) part 1, pp. 217–22; part 2, plates 211–15.

[45] BN MS Nouv.acq.lat.1203; Koehler, II, *Die Hofschule Karls des Grossen*, pp. 22–9, and plates 1–12.

[46] Bede, *De Tabernaculo*, ed. D. Hurst, CCSL CXIXA (Turnhout, 1969), pp. 45–6, 99.

Canterbury Gospels now in Stockholm[47] as well as in the lost seventh-century Gospels of St Wilfrid.

But Godescalc's Gospel lectionary also asserts its independent Italian connections. As well as Insular decorative motifs it frames its text with sumptuous scroll or fern patterns, dimensional ribbons, and patterns like the striations or fossils in polished marble. The pairs of pages have a tall narrow format, like the hinged panels of consular diptychs. This resemblance might even be deliberate, since Godescalc's dedicatory verses commemorate Charlemagne's fourteen years of office as consul since his accession in 768. There is as yet no overt royal portraiture in the book, but it symbolically illustrates a significant state event, the baptism of Charlemagne's second son Pippin by Pope Hadrian I at St John Lateran in 781. The Baptistry font, sublimated into an image of the Fountain of Life, set in an ideal landscape, is the first Carolingian essay in classical architectural forms and illusionary depth in painting. The other prefatory illustrations consist of a portrait of Christ, and in turn the four Evangelists, vigorously and rather broadly painted as if from a panel painting model. Subsequent Evangelists in this particular sequence of Carolingian book illustrations put on more state, and have more complex seats and settings, whose antecedents lie in late-antique mosaics and ivory carvings.[48]

Closely allied to the Godescalc Gospels is the Dagulf Psalter, designed as a gift for Pope Hadrian.[49] It is a very formal book, with no pictures and fanciful or expository initials like the Corbie Psalter. The Dagulf Psalter text, with its sequence of canticles at the end, was put together to establish and publicise a new scholarly standard. A grand prefatory inscription opposite the text of the first psalm affirms the Carolingian's preference for Jerome's translation of the Psalms based on the Septuagint, that is, the Gallican or Vulgate version, as opposed to the Romanum favoured in Rome and in England. This concentration on the sacred authority of the Psalter text is given careful pictorial expression on the ivory covers of the Psalter.[50] On one side David is shown twice, once dictating the text of the Psalms (his writing desk is exactly like that of the Godescalc Evangelists), and then performing them in company with other musicians and dancers. This scene closely resembles the prefatory picture in the Canterbury Vespasian Psalter, and no doubt was likewise dependent on a sixth-century Italian model. The other side celebrates Jerome's work as translator and editor. The frames around the main scenes are crowded with meaning. On the David side angels and the Evangelist symbols accompanying the Holy Lamb, and on the Jerome side saints and cherubim accompanying an

47 Stockholm, Royal Library MS A.135; Alexander, *Insular Manuscripts*, no. 30, pp. 56–7; also C. Nordenfalk, 'A note on the Stockholm *Codex Aureus*', *Nordisk Tidskrift för Bokoch Biblioteksväsen* 38 (1951), pp. 145–55.

48 E. Rosenbaum, 'The evangelist portraits of the Ada School and their models', *The Art Bulletin*, 38 (1956), pp. 81–90.

49 Vienna, Österreichische Nationalbibliothek Cod 1861. K. Holter, *Dagulf Psalter* (Graz, 1970; also P. E. Schramm and F. Mütherich, *Denkmale der deutschen Könige und Kaiser* (Munich, 1962), no. 11, pp. 117–18.

50 Goldschmidt, *Die Elfenbeinskulpturen*, nos. 3, 4, pp. 9–10.

upraised right hand. According to Bede the Lamb symbolises Christ's humanity, while his divinity is symbolised by his being the *dextera patris*.[51] This remained a favourite Carolingian image; for example, it appears memorably as a preface to St John in the last great Carolingian Gospel Book, the *Codex aureus* of Charles the Bald.[52] The fact that a book not illustrated with pictures nonetheless displays narrative and symbolical images on its covers, as part of the whole organism of the book, undermines the belief that Charlemagne himself was somehow wary of Christian imagery.[53] It is true that the *Libri Carolini*,[54] the Frankish Church's official response issued in Charlemagne's name to the recent rehabilitation of images by the Greek Church, adopts a censorious tone towards the representational arts, seeking to set strict limits on both subject-matter and intellectual scope. But all that carefully mapped-out forbidden territory is exactly where Carolingian artists were to be most active. Even around the time of the promulgation of the *Libri Carolini*, in 794, the carved covers and complex figurative initials of the 'royal' Gospel Books, not to speak of the grand Apocalypse mosaic on the vault of the chapel at Aachen, themselves provided a positive challenge to the idea that artists could not represent the revelatory words of the Prophets and Apostles.

Carolingian commitment to narrative art and to textual illustration is demonstrated also in the ivory cover of a Gospel Book from Chelles, now in Oxford.[55] The cover is contrived like a five-part diptych, such as the diptych of Justinian triumphant from Trier. Heavy frames, ornamented with classical 'egg and dart', divide up a chronologically coherent series of scenes from the early life, and miracles, of Christ. In composition six of these scenes closely follow, though on a much reduced scale, ivory carvings made in Rome around 400, although the plain noble style of the late-antique exemplars was to be better understood by later Carolingian ivory carvers, at Metz. The large central panel of the Oxford book cover represents a single large figure of Christ, with florid draperies and carrying a ceremonial cross, similar to a mosaic of the martyr St Laurence in the fifth-century mausoleum of Galla Placidia in Ravenna.[56] In the specific context of the small Gospel scenes on the Oxford cover, the central panel might signify the Temptation of Christ, a subject which attracted some of the finest artistry of the Carolingian period, but if so it is elliptically expressed, by means of the imagery of Psalm 90:13, where the Saviour triumphantly treads *super aspidem, basiliscum, leonem, draconem*.

51 'Christus, enim qui in humanitate Agnus, ipse in Deitate dextera Patris est.' Bede, *Explanatio apocalypsis*, c. v, in PL 93, col. 146.

52 Munich Clm. 14000, fol. 97v; W. Koehler and F. Mütherich, *Die Karolingischen Miniaturen*, V, *Die Hofschule Karls des Kahlen* (Berlin, 1982) pp. 176, 196, and plate 66.

53 See for example, P. Harbison, 'The Carolingian contribution to Irish sculpture', *Ireland and Insular Art AD 500–1200*, ed. Ryan, pp. 105–6.

54 See A. Freeman, 'Theodulf of Orleans and the *Libri Carolini*', Speculum 32 (1957), pp. 663–705; 'Further studies in the *Libri Carolini*, I and II', Speculum 40 (1965) pp. 203–89; 'Further studies in the *Libri Carolini*, III', Speculum 46 (1971) pp. 597–612; also E. Dahlhaus-Berg, *Nova antiquitas et antiqua novitas*, Kölner Historische Abhandlungen 23 (Cologne, 1975), pp. 169–216.

55 Goldschmidt, *Die Elfenbeinskulpturen*, no. 5, p. 10; Volbach, *Elfenbeinarbeiten*, no. 221, pp. 95–6, plate 61.

56 Volbach, *Early Christian Art*, plate 146 and pp. 339–40.

The Oxford cover in fact illustrates the same passage from Psalm 90 as the perhaps earlier, certainly more 'archaic', Genoels-Elderen book cover. There is, however, an interesting difference between the two versions, which is nothing to do with style. The four different beasts required by any of Jerome's translations of the psalm, Romanum, Gallican, or Hebraicum, are picturesquely represented in the Genoels-Elderen panel. But on the Oxford cover, in spite of the inscription *sup(er) asp(idem)* on the book which Christ holds, he does not tread on any asp or viper: the fourth beast is another quadruped, like the maned lion above it. Two possible explanations are open to us. Either this Oxford scene was directly copied from an early fifth-century exemplar which illustrated the pre-Jerome Psalter text, the 'Old Latin', which reads 'leam', lioness, instead of 'aspidem';[57] or we see here the result of direct study of the original Hebrew text of the Psalms, such as Theodulf of Orleans was actively promoting at around this time, *ca* 800.[58] The Hebrew text speaks of 'a lion, and a young lion'. Either way we see that the visual arts in the Carolingian period were consciously literate.

The range of art motifs available, and the receptivity of Carolingian artists in the immediate aftermath of the Godescalc Gospels is demonstrated in a series of full Gospel Books which have all the hallmarks of official patronage. One of them was presented by Louis the Pious to Soissons in 827, and might have belonged to him as a boy.[59] It was certainly a book that meant a great deal to Louis' son Charles the Bald, who had some of its imagery directly transcribed into his own *Codex Aureus*.[60] Another of the 'royal' Gospel Books, now at Abbeville, Bibliothèque Municipale, was given by Charlemagne's son-in-law Angilbert to his church at St Riquier; written in gold script on purple vellum, it is St Riquier' equivalent of the Ripon Gospels, and like the earlier English book it too had a precious cover. It was even provided with a silver folding chair on which to be displayed.[61] A gilt bronze folding chair, provided with lions' heads and feet like a consul's throne in a consular diptych, was preserved at St Denis, the so-called throne of Dagobert.[62] It might have doubled for the Carolingian ruler himself or for the display of the holy scriptures, since Christ is King, and sits at the right hand of the Father. The Gospels in the Stadtsbibliothek at Trier is associated with *Ada ancilla dei*, who is recorded in the later necrology of St

57 For these various texts see *Biblia Sacra iuxta Vulgatum versionem*, ed. B. Fischer, R. Weber (Stuttgart, 1969); R. Weber, *Le Psautier Romain* (Rome, 1953); H. de Sainte-Marie, *Sancti Hieronymi psalterium iuxta Hebraeos* (Rome, 1954); A. Amelli, *Liber psalmorum iuxta antiquissimam latinam versionem* (Rome, 1912).

58 See E. Power, 'Corrections from the Hebrew in the Theodulfian MSS of the Vulgate', *Biblica* 5 (1924) pp. 233–58; Dahlhaus-Berg, p. 44.

59 BN Lat. 8850; Koehler, II, *Die Hofschule Karls des Grossen*, pp. 70–81.

60 F. Mütherich, 'Book illumination at the court of Louis the Pious', in *Charlemagne's Heir*, p. 594. Compare fol. 11 of the Soissons Gospels with fol. 11 of the *Codex Aureus* of St Emmeram, for which see Koehler II, *Die Hofschule Karls des Grossen*, plate 77; and Koehler and Mütherich, V, *Die Hofschule Karls des Kahlen*, plate 54.

61 Abbeville, Bibliothèque Muncipale, MS 4; Koehler, II, *Hofschule Karls des Grossen*, pp. 49–55, plates 33–41. See also C. Davis-Weyer, *Early Medieval Art 300–1150*, p. 96.

62 Elbern, *Das erste Jahrtausend*, no. 197, p. 49; *Le Trésor de Saint-Denis*, Catalogue of Exhibition, Paris, Musée du Louvre (1991), no. 5, pp. 63–8.

Maximin at Trier. It carried on its cover a great sardonyx cameo representing the Emperor Constantine and his family.[63] The two imperial eagles on the cameo provided exemplars for later artists, working at Metz, when they painted the constellation Aquila in a fine copy of an astronomical treatise, and carved the eagle symbol of St John for a book cover (plate 11), under the patronage of Charlemagne's son Drogo.[64]

As the programme of the 'royal' Gospel Books evolved, the Gospel concordances, the canon tables, soon dispensed with the interlaced or flat step bases, anvil-shaped capitals and abstract ornamental infill shared with, or derived from, Insular Gospel Books[65], and represent rich and showy architectural motifs, seen in perspective, columns fluted or coiled like barley sugar, to evoke the exotic form of the ciborium at the east end of Old St Peter's. This is a topographical reference, like the reference to the Lateran Baptistry which occurred in the Godescalc Gospels and was repeated in the Soissons Gospels.[66]

Beautiful and splendid as the visual images in the 'royal' Gospels are, their designers seem deliberately to have striven to emphasise an interaction of their images with the words of holy scripture. They are not content, like later Tours artists, following a late-antique exemplar like the St Augustine's Gospels at Canterbury, merely to define the relationship of the Evangelist and his superimposed symbol by borrowing a convenient caption from the *Carmen paschale*.[67] In the Soissons Gospels, and the closely allied Harley Gospels, the symbols have the task of displaying the Gospel *incipits* but the Evangelists themselves hold up for scrutiny very specific texts picked from the body of the Gospels. A few are passages already selected in Godescalc's Gospel lectionary, but quite a number read like admonitions of a master to servants, or a father to sons. Some also are significant pointers to pictorial imagery. The jewelled splendour of the St Matthew page in the Soissons Gospels, studded with fictive gold and peals and cameos, adds depth to the passage selected from Matthew 6:20: *thesaurizate autem vobis thesauros in caelo*. The text quoted by St John in the Soissons Gospels comes from the end of chapter 3, Christ's interview with Nicodemus, the subject of the little scene inset on the *In principio* page. In the Harley Gospels St John quotes chapter 4:38. The occasion when Christ pronounced these words is the probable subject of the little picture inset at the top right of the Soissons

63 Trier, Stadtbibliothek Cod. 22; Koehler, II, *Die Hofschule Karls des Grossen*, pp. 34–41. For the cameo, see Elbern, *Das erste Jahrtausend*, no. 112; also *Trier: Kaiserresidenz und Bischofssitz*, no. 34, pp. 117–18 and frontispiece.

64 Madrid, Biblioteca Nacional Cod. 3307, fol. 60; W. Koehler, *Die Karolingischen Miniaturen*, III, (i) *Die Gruppe des Wiener Kronungs-Evangeliars*, (ii) *Metzer Handschriften* (Berlin, 1960), plate 57c; Goldschmidt, *Die Elfenbeinskulpturen*, no. 34, pp. 20–1, and plate XVI.

65 Compare the canon tables in Paris, Arsenal MS 599, in Koehler, II, *Die Hofschule Karls des Grossen*, plates 16, 17, 18, with canon tables in two fragmentary Insular Gospel Books in the Trésor, St Catherine's Church, Maeseyck, in Alexander, *Insular Manuscripts*, nos. 22, 23, plates 90–107.

66 E. Rosenbaum, 'The vine columns of Old St Peter's in Carolingian canon tables', *Journal of the Warburg and Courtauld Institutes*, 18 (1955), pp. 1–15; P. A. Underwood, 'The fountain of life in manuscripts of the Gospels', *Dumbarton Oaks Papers*, 5 (Harvard, 1950), pp. 41–138.

67 See for example Stuttgart Landesbibl. II 40 and London, BL Add.MS 11848, illustrated in W. Koehler, *Die Karolingischen Miniaturen*, I, *Die Schule von Tours* (Berlin, 1930), plates 21, 22, 24, 25.

portrait of St John. The small inset illustrations in the 'royal' Gospels represent not visual reticence, but simply an original experiment in how to decorate the Gospel *incipit* pages.[68] That the same artists were ready, in a manuscript destined for a different, more studious or devotional function, to intersperse the Gospel texts with illustrations, on the pattern of the Antwerp *Carmen paschale*, is suggested by the picture of the angel's annunciation to Zacharias, fortunately preserved as a later paste-in in BL Cotton MS Claudius B.V.[69]

When Theodulf describes Charlemagne raising his eyes piously to heaven in his great new church at Aachen, and then returning accompanied by his sons and daughters to the palace,[70] we can reasonably assume that the series of 'royal' Gospel Books were in these people's hands. The grandiloquent architectural forms painted in these books became reality in the huge spaces of the Aachen octagon, with its gallery and tribune articulated with polished marble columns.[71] In the new building programme, inspired by the plan, scale, and soaring arches of San Vitale, and with precious old materials requisitioned for the task, Charlemagne may have been influenced by the references preserved in Cassiodorus' *Variae* to Theodoric rehabilitating the buildings of his capital with *spolia* in just this way.[72] Charlemagne commandeered from Ravenna a gilt bronze equestrian statue of Theodoric himself, armed heroically with a shield and lance.[73] If the massive gates, indicated by the gaping mortices in the stonework of Theodoric's mausoleum, were still extant, we might be able to recognise detailed Ravennate connections in the design of the bronze doors of the church at Aachen.[74] Although bronze doors once stood in Carolingian St Denis,[75] the Aachen examples alone survive. In their *gravitas*, scale, and technical efficiency, they comprise the single most impressive achievement of the Carolingian Renaissance. The sober geometry of the doors is animated by the lion handles, each individually modelled and cast (plate 12).[76] Early Christian ivories show lion-head handles projecting from the doors of Christ's sepulchre.[77] For the scale of the Aachen lions, locally preserved antique models suggest them-

68 For these pictures and texts, see Koehler, II, *Die Hofschule Karls des Grossen*, pp. 61–6 and plates 54–60; pp. 75–9 and plates 81–8; see also R. M. Walker, 'Illustrations to the Priscillian Prologues', *The Art Bulletin* 30 (1948) pp. 1–10.

69 W. Koehler, 'An illustrated evangelistary of the Ada School', *Journal of the Warburg and Courtauld Institutes*, 15 (1952) pp. 48–66.

70 See Godman, *Poetry*, p. 152.

71 Felix Kreusch, 'Kirche, Atrium und Portikus der Aachener Pfalz', in: *Karl der Grosse* III, pp. 463–533.

72 B. Brent, 'Spolia from Constantine to Charlemagne: aesthetics versus ideology' in: *Studies on Art and Archaeology in Honor of E. Kitzinger*, ed. W. Tronzo, I. Lavin, *Dumbarton Oaks Papers* XLI (Washington, D.C., 1987) pp. 102–9; Cassiodorus, *Variarum Libri* XII ed., Å. J. Fridh, CCSL XCVI (Turnhout, 1973) pp. 104–5.

73 D. Bullough, *The Age of Charlemagne* (London, 1965) p. 149.

74 R. Heidenreich and H. Johannes, *Das Grabmal Theoderichs zu Ravenna* (Wiesbaden, 1971), plate 29 and reconstructions on pp. 123, 125, 127, 128.

75 Suger, *De administratione* XXVII, in Panofsky, *Abbot Suger on the Abbey Church of St-Denis*, p. 46 and pp. 160–2.

76 Schramm and Mütherich, *Denkmale der deutschen Könige und Kaiser*, no. 4, p. 115 and plates on pp. 206–7.

77 For example an early-fifth-century ivory panel in the British Museum, for which see Volbach, *Elfenbeinarbeiten*, no. 116, p. 60 and plate 35.

selves: the shaggy maned lion masks on the hubs of Roman waggon wheels, or the pair of smooth plump-faced lion heads, carved in fourth-century Trier from rock crystal, perhaps for some spectacular throne.[78]

The mastery of Carolingian metalworking is seen at Aachen also in the variously patterned bronze grills that enclose the gallery where the emperor and his courtiers assembled.[79] The lamps and vessels of gold and silver given to Aachen by Charlemagne[80] are lost, but their quality and design can be judged from the grand gold and enamelled ewer studded with pale blue sapphires and edged with lush acanthus leaves, in the treasury of St Maurice d'Agaune.[81] The designer of all these works seems likely to have been Einhard, called Besaleel in the Carolingian court, after the 'wise-hearted' maker of the ornaments of the Jewish tabernacle.[82] Einhard's name is inscribed as donor and designer on the *tabula ansata* at the front of a miniature antique triumphal arch, cast and engraved in silver, which he presented to a church at Maastricht.[83] The horseman treading on a serpent from the description of Bishop Desiderius' treasure lives again on the flanks of Einhard's arch, together with images, perhaps embossed, perhaps in metal inlay, of Christ and the Apostles and Evangelists. The technical expertise and classical taste of Einhard were passed on to later artists at Metz; a miniature equestrian statue, formerly at Metz, may derive its motivation from the life-sized statue of Theodoric to be seen at Aachen, but its scale and detailing accords well with the prancing horse of Justinian in the Trier diptych. The Metz rider, however, strictly disavows the rhetorical pose and military dress of antique horsemen. He is clothed much as Charlemagne was accustomed to be, according to Einhard's eye-witness report in his biography of Charlemagne.[84]

Einhard also records the partition under Charlemagne's will of books and valuables stored in the palace treasury.[85] He refers tantalisingly to three grand works of art whose loss is especially to be regretted. We cannot tell if these were actual antique treasures, or masterpieces by Einhard himself. A square silver table, which Louis the Pious as his father's executor sent to St Peter's, Rome, represented *descriptionem urbis Constantinopolitanae*, evidently a visual survey or plan of the city. A second silver table, of round format, sent to Ravenna, was embellished with *effigie Romanae urbis*, evidently a figure personifying the city. A

[78] *Age of Spirituality* ed. Weitzmann, no. 330, pp. 346–7.

[79] W. Braunfels, 'Karls des Grossen Bronzewerkstatt', in: *Karl der Grosse* III, pp. 168–202. Compare the grills represented on the north face of the Arch of Constantine, for which see *Age of Spirituality*, ed. Weitzmann, plate on p. 68; also the grills represented on the Theodosian obelisk, ibid., plate on p. 108.

[80] Einhard, *Vita Karoli* c. 26, ed. O. Holder-Egger, MGH SRG XXV (Hanover, 1911, reprint 1922) p. 30.

[81] P. Lasko, *Ars sacra 800–1200* (Harmondsworth, 1972) pp. 23–4 and plate 22.

[82] See Alcuin, poem on the Court, in Godman, *Poetry*, p. 120; for Besaleel see Exodus 31:2–11; 35:30–39.

[83] B. de Montesquiou-Fezensac, 'L'Arc de triomphe d'Einhardus', *Cahiers archéologiques* 4 (1949), pp. 79–103; H. Belting, 'Der Einhardsbogen', *Zeitschrift für Kunstgeschichte* 36 (1973), pp. 93–121.

[84] Schramm and Mütherich, *Denkmale* no. 58, p. 137, and plate on p. 267; Lasko, *Ars sacra 800–1200*, pp. 18–20.

[85] Einhard, *Vita Karoli*, c. 33, ed. Holder-Egger, pp. 37–41.

third table outshone the other two in its weight and the beauty of its workmanship. It displayed a design of three concentric circles, or three shield-shaped segments interlocked, depicting the earth and the heavens, including the courses of the planets. This wonderful work was bought by Louis the Pious out of love for his father, its cost being added to the charitable alms collected in the sale.[86] The iconography of each of the tables can be understood in terms of pictures in books known to the Carolingians. The representation of cities is paralleled by fifteenth- and sixteenth-century copies of a lost Carolingian manuscript, once in the cathedral library at Speyer, itself a copy of the fifth-century *Notitia dignitatum* and other documents, a record of armaments, official regalia, personifications of cities and bird's eye views of towns and provinces of the later Roman Empire.[87] In one of the late copies of the *Notitia* Constantinople is a city view and Rome a personification, exactly as on Charlemagne's tables.[88]

Another book which was evidently preserved in the imperial library and the subject of a Carolingian facsimile, is now known only from seventeenth-century engravings after its pages. It was a picture calendar, to be dated to 354 judging from the list of prefects and consuls of Rome which it contains.[89] The inclusion of Trier, personified as a vigorous Amazon, as one of the four leading cities of the Roman Empire, must have specially attracted the Calendar's Carolingian owners and copyists. The convention of the personified city was of course familiar to the Carolingians from many antique works of art, notably ivories. A diptych now in Vienna featuring two majestic women, mural crowned or helmeted as Rome and Constantinople, carries on the reverse a Carolingian inscription hopefully, or ironically, characterising them as Temperance and Chastity.[90] But the scrupulously executed work of reproducing the Calendar of 354 will have refined Carolingian feeling for the personification mode.

A whole gamut of derivatives from the Calendar show invention and adaptation, as well as the intelligent capacity to comprehend and reproduce, for example the Calendar's illustration of the Emperor Constantius II distributing *largitio* to the public is absorbed into a picture of St Matthew in a Gospel Book from Saint-Vaast, now in Prague, in which the Evangelist casts away a shower of gold coins as he quits his counting house at Christ's command.[91] The personified figures of the months from the Calendar of 354 were adapted for use by a Carolingian artist to surround a great map of the heavens placed as an appendix to a ninth-century copy of Aratus' treatise on the stars, now in

86 F. N. Estey, 'Charlemagne's silver celestial table', *Speculum* 18 (1943) pp. 112–17.

87 J. J. G. Alexander, 'The illustrated manuscripts of the *Notitia dignitatum*', *Aspects of the Notitia Dignitatum*, ed. R. Goodburn and P. Bartholomew, *BAR* Supplementary Series 15 (Oxford, 1976), pp. 11–25.

88 Alexander, ibid., p. 15, argues however that the city view of Constantinople in Oxford, Bodleian MS Canon. Misc. 378 is an invention and addition by the fifteenth-century artist.

89 H. Stern, *Le Calendrier de 354. Étude de son texte et ses illustrations* (Paris, 1953).

90 *Age of Spirituality*, ed. Weitzmann, no. 153, pp. 173–5.

91 Prague, Kapitulni Knihovna, Cim.2, fol. 23v; F. Mütherich and J. E. Gaehde, *Carolingian Painting* (London, 1977), plate 39.

Leiden.[92] This map is just the kind of thing that Charlemagne's third table will have depicted. Louis the Pious evidently particularly associated his father with that table. Einhard records among other scholarly interests of Charlemagne that 'he traced the courses of the stars with great attention'.[93] The rational man who is the subject of the second poem in Boethius' *De consolatione philosophiae* does just that.[94] Observation of the stars also played its part in the calculation of the moveable feasts of the Christian year, and Charlemagne was concerned with the reform and standardisation of the calendar.[95]

Nonetheless the great antique exemplars of Aratus' treatise known to us now only in Carolingian copies were of no practical value for stargazing.[96] They represented the casual grandeur of books on secular topics prepared in the late-antique period for a connoisseurs' market. That their physical beauty survives so patently in the Carolingian copies is a tribute to Carolingian sophistication, whether in Aachen in Charlemagne's own day, or later, in the reigns of Louis the Pious and his son Lothar.[97] The copy of the Aratus in Leiden, in Germanicus Caesar's translation, represents the heroic figures of gods and constellations, plastically realised and vividly coloured, in framed pictures. The translation of Aratus by Cicero, now in London, in the Harleian collection, in part makes up the corporeality of the images with explanatory texts written in exquisitely accomplished rustic capitals, graded and aligned like the rippling patterns of precious alabaster or agate (plate 13). The painted portions of the designs have a startling authenticity. All the linear subterfuges of post-classical art are swept away. The art of Roman frescoists seems to live again on these broad parchment pages.[98]

I have already referred to the critical acquisitiveness of Carolingian artists. They absorb as well as reproduce. The signs of the zodiac pass into the visual, even the decorative vocabulary of Carolingian artists, as in the great initial 'D' to St Jerome's prologue to the Pentateuch in the Vivian Bible, presented by the clergy of Tours to Charles the Bald in 846.[99] The signs of the zodiac even appear in an illustration in a Carolingian Psalter, now in Utrecht, oddly arranged in an anticlockwise position that exactly matches the sky map attached to the Leiden Aratus.[100] The Leiden map re-used the figures of the months from the Calendar

92 See Stern, *Le Calendrier de 354*, p. 27; Leiden, Universiteitsbibliotheek Voss. Lat.Q.79, fol. 93v; W. Koehler and F. Mütherich, *Karolingischen Miniaturen*, IV, *Einzelhandschriften aus Lotharingien*, plate 94.

93 Einhard, *Vita Karoli* c. 25, ed. Holder-Egger, p. 30: ... *et intentione sagaci siderum cursum curiosissime rimabatur*.

94 Boethius, *The Consolation of Philosophy*, Eng. trans. S. J. Tester, Loeb Classical Library (Harvard, 1973), p. 136.

95 P. McGurk, 'Carolingian astrological manuscripts', in *Charles the Bald: Court and Kingdom*, ed. M. Gibson, J. L. Nelson, *BAR* International Series 101 (Oxford, 1981), pp. 320–1.

96 Ibid., p. 322.

97 F. Mütherich, 'Book illumination at the court of Louis the Pious' in *Charlemagne's Heir*, pp. 596–600.

98 Koehler and Mütherich, IV, *Einzelhandschriften aus Lotharingien*, pp. 108–16 and plates 75–96 for the Leiden MS: pp. 101–7 and plates 62–74 for Harley MS 647.

99 BN Lat.1, fol. 8. See Koehler, I, *Die Schule von Tours*, plate 79.

100 Utrecht Psalter, Utrecht, Universiteitsbibl. 32, fol. 36; E. T. De Wald, *The Illustrations of the Utrecht Psalter* (Princeton, 1933); J. H. A. Engelbregt, *Utrecht-Psalter: vollständige Faksimile – Ausgabe im Originalformat der Handschrift 32 aus dem Besitz der Bibliothek der Rijksuniversiteit te Utrecht*, Codices selecti 75 (Graz, 1982–4).

of 354, and so is certainly a Carolingian compilation or pastiche. In the Leiden map the months proceed clockwise, absurdly out of alignment with their corresponding zodiac signs. In the Utrecht Psalter, however, the anticlockwise zodiac shows us, suitably, God's outside view of his creation.[101] This particular motif is only one of hundreds in the Utrecht Psalter but the fact that it has its own contextual coherence and stability, when the Leiden Aratus has merely misapplied it, should at least introduce caution when we consider the vexed question of the origin of the Utrecht Psalter. The Psalter has initials of Insular decorative design. It is a Gallican Psalter, and conforms to the arrangement of the canticles first published in the Dagulf Psalter. To that extent it belongs to the Carolingian period. In its nervously dashing calligraphy it shares the character of the Evangelist portraits painted in a Gospel Book made at Hautvillers for Ebbo archbishop of Rheims. Given Ebbo's previous experience as imperial librarian, and taking into account also the sale and scattering of the Aachen library ordained by Charlemagne's will, the illustrations of the Utrecht Psalter have come to be generally regarded as an enormous essay in source research, the very type of Carolingian visual compilation and pastiche, masterminded by Archbishop Ebbo.[102]

Sedulius wrote his *Carmen paschale* to give late fifth-century Christians some poetry to read rather than Vergil. The Utrecht Psalter resembles the stateliest surviving late-antique copies of the *Aeneid*, written like them in rustic capitals, and interspersed with rectangular illustrations.[103] The *Aeneid* however is an historical narrative, whereas the Psalms are hymns and prayers. The various figures cannot be easily captioned for they represent states of mind, the whole gamut of metaphor used by the sacred poet. In the Utrecht Psalter the visual language is resolutely classical. The landscape is scattered with aqueducts, gates and city walls; river gods pour out their urns, and giant demon faces glower from the sky. The strong man who runs the race in Psalm 18 is recognisably Heracles wrapped in the skin of the Nemean lion. If the illustrations in the Utrecht Psalter had first been drafted in the reign of Justinian, or even of Theodosius, the triumphal horseman of Psalms 9–10, or the King of Glory approaching his city gates in Psalm 23 would not have been out of place.

In Psalm 41 the Psalmist says that his soul thirsts after God as the hart thirsts after the springs of water. A fifth-century mosaicist in Galla Placidia's mausoleum literally illustrated these animals drinking at the pool. The principle was

101 Oddly enough, in the Eadwine Psalter, Cambridge, Trinity College MS R.17.1, a twelfth-century English copy of the Utrecht Psalter, the signs of the zodiac represented in the illustration to Psalm 64 appear in the conventional clockwise order as viewed from the earth.

102 For a clear statement of this interpretation of the origin of the Utrecht Psalter, see F. Wormald, 'The Utrecht Psalter', in: *Collected Writings*, I (London, 1984) pp. 36–45. See also S. Dufrenne, *Les Illustrations du Psautier d'Utrecht*, Association des Publications près les Universités de Strasbourg, fasc. 161 (Paris, 1978).

103 K. Weitzmann, *Late Antique and Early Christian Book Illumination* (London, 1977) plates 2, 4; *Age of Spirituality*, ed. Weitzmann, no. 203, p. 227 and no. 224, p. 247. See also CLA III p. 7, no**296, Florence, Laurenziana XXXIX, 1.

no doubt extended in other early cycles of the Psalms.[104] In the Utrecht Psalter the provision of visual equivalents for the words of the Psalms is total; for example in Psalm 149 the Psalmist speaks of the binding of enemy kings *in compedibus* and their nobles *in manicis ferreis*, and so, precisely, the kings in the illustration sit with their feet in the stocks, while the nobles alongside have their wrists bound.[105] A consequence of such close attention to the words to be illustrated is that we can trace in the iconography of the Utrecht Psalter the influence of translations of the Psalms differing from the Gallican Psalter text written out beneath each picture, although a pre-St Jerome dimension, such as is perhaps suggested by the psalm illustration on the Oxford ivory cover is not indicated.[106] In fact the illustrations offer to their learned observer an alternative 'text', a 'translation' into pictures.

The historical assessment of the Utrecht Psalter cannot be separated from the assessment of some other Carolingian Psalters. A Psalter in Stuttgart attributed by Bischoff on palaeographical grounds to St Germain des Prés in Paris, around 820–30, is illustrated with brightly coloured pictures, not monochrome line drawings as in Utrecht.[107] The Psalms are interspersed with pictures illustrating a verse here, and a verse there. The contrast with Utrecht is seen, for example, in the illustration of the great Passion Psalm 21, where the bulls, the dogs, the casting of lots, are illustrated solidly and separately, not in the flickering multi-image manner of Utrecht; but of course the similarity is equally striking in that we are dealing with literal illustration.[108] Quite often the very same pictorial motif is employed in Stuttgart and Utrecht, for example the boats swept away by the storm in Psalm 47, even though the artistic style is quite different.[109] As with the illustrations in the Antwerp *Carmen paschale*, details of dress or iconography on Stuttgart appear directly to reflect an earlier phase of art. The daughter of Babylon in Psalm 136 wears a mural crown as if to the manner born.[110] In Psalm 48 (plate 14) the man who 'when he was in honour, is become like a senseless beast', is portrayed like the popular hero of a Roman chariot race, in a surviving fourth-century memento of such a event.[111] The broken bows, shields and swords of Psalm 75:3, look like the armaments and honorary regalia in the *Notitia dignitatum*.[112] The drift from one version of the psalm's text to another, of which we are conscious in the illustrations in the

[104] G. Bovini, *Ravenna Mosaics* (London, 1957), plate 4. See G. R. Benson, 'The Latin tradition and the Reims style in the Utrecht Psalter' part I of G. R. Benson and D. T. Tselos, 'New light on the origin of the Utrecht Psalter', *The Art Bulletin*, 13 (1931) p. 43.

[105] Utrecht Psalter, fol. 83.

[106] D. Panofsky, 'The textual basis of the Utrecht Psalter illustrations', *The Art Bulletin* 25 (1943) pp. 50–8.

[107] J. Eschweiler, F. Mütherich, *Der Stuttgarter-Bilderpsalter* (Stuttgart, 1965–6).

[108] Utrecht Psalter, fol. 12; Stuttgart Psalter, fols 25v, 26, 26v, 27. On the Stuttgart illustration of Psalm 21 on fol. 27, see J. O'Reilly, 'Early medieval text and image: the wounded and exalted Christ', *Peritia* 6–7 (1987–8) pp. 94–5.

[109] Utrecht Psalter fol. 27v; Stuttgart Psalter, fol. 60.

[110] Stuttgart Psalter, fol. 152v.

[111] Stuttgart Psalter, fol. 61; Compare *Age of Spirituality*, ed. Weitzmann, no. 95, p. 104.

[112] See, for example, the *Insignia magistri officiorum* in the Norwich Castle copy, illustrated in Alexander, 'Illustrated manuscripts of the *Notitia dignitatum*', plate VI.

Utrecht Psalter, happens also in the Stuttgart Psalter, but in the Stuttgart Psalter Romanum inscriptions actually within the pictures give support to the idea that a comprehensive pre-Carolingian exemplar was available.[113]

Yet another Psalter, Douce MS 59 in Oxford, although it provides pictures to only two of its Psalms, 51 and 101, makes a strong bid to hold the exact middle ground iconographically between the Utrecht and Stuttgart Psalters, yet in its painterly style it cannot be derived from either of these.[114] The Douce Psalter is written in gold on tawny red vellum, and its loose confident short-hand manner of painting utilises the effect of highlighting on a dark ground (plate 15).[115] The most elaborate versions of this style appear in the monumental Evangelist portraits in the Coronation Gospels in Vienna and in the picture of the four Evangelists seated in a romantic dawn-lit landscape, in the Gospels now in Aachen.[116] It is often stated that towards the end of Charlemagne's reign the style of these particular books ousted from favour the sumptuous descriptive style represented by the series of 'royal' Gospel Books.[117] However it is wrong to read the development of Carolingian art as a chronological stylistic sequence. The technique of the Coronation Gospels looks more spontaneous, and may have had a more personal devotional function. Aspects of the style of the Coronation Gospels and Aachen Gospels have antecedents in the portraits of the physicians in the early sixth-century Dioscorides manuscript now in Vienna,[118] but also earlier in the elegant fluid forms of the figures on a silver casket sent by Jerome's patron, Pope Damasus, to Milan,[119] and similar figures on a fourth-century ivory pyx from Trier.[120] All these are the kindred also of the svelte and impressionistic figures in the Utrecht Psalter. As remarked above, a contemporary work that resembles the Utrecht Psalter is the Ebbo Gospels, but the initiative of Ebbo in respect of the Psalter is not proven. If anything is truly original, that is, Carolingian, about the illustrations in the Utrecht Psalter it may be their line drawing technique, capturing the spirit but cutting out the labour

113 Psalm 18, on fol. 23. The inscription in the picture reads *Lex domini inreprehensibilis*, and the text of the Psalm itself reads *Lex domini immaculata*. See J. Eschweiler, 'Illustrationen zu altlateinischen Texten im Stuttgarter Bilderpsalter', *Colligere Fragmenta: Festschrift Alban Dold* (Beuron, 1952), pp. 49–51. R. Weber in his edition of the Romanum Psalter, p. 36 gives *inreprehensibilis* as the Romanum reading of Psalm 18, verse 8.

114 All three versions illustrate Psalm 101, verse 7, *Vigilavi et factus sum sicut passer solitarius in tecto*; on the relationship of Douce 59 and the Utrecht Psalter see D. Tselos, 'Defensive addenda to the problem of the Utrecht Psalter', *The Art Bulletin*, 49 (1967), pp. 334–49.

115 For Douce MS 59, see also O. Pächt and J. J. G. Alexander, *Illuminated Manuscripts in the Bodleian Library Oxford*, I (Oxford, 1966), no. 416, p. 32, plate XXXIV; Hubert, Porcher and Volbach, *Carolingian Art*, p. 105, plates 90–1.

116 Koehler, III, *Die Gruppe des Wiener Kronungs-Evangeliars*; and plates 1–27; 28–35. Schramm and Mütherich, *Denkmale*, nos. 13, 14, pp. 118–19; H. Swarzenski, 'The Xanten purple leaf and the Carolingian Renaissance', *The Art Bulletin*, 22 (1940) pp. 7–24.

117 For example, C. Nordenfalk, in: *Karl der Grosse* III, pp. 225–6.

118 Vienna, Nationalbibliothek Cod.med.gr. 1, fol. 3v, for which see K. Weitzmann, *Late Antique and Early Christian Book Illumination* (London, 1977), plate 16.

119 Milan Cathedral Treasury, silver reliquary casket from San Nazaro Maggiore, for which see Volbach, *Early Christian Art*, plates 110–15 and p. 332.

120 Volbach, *Elfenbeinarbeiten*, no. 162, pp. 77–8, and plate 53; see also the pyx in Berlin, from a site on the Mosel, ibid., no. 161, p. 77 and plate 53.

and cost of reproducing a great sixth- or seventh-century painted exemplar, now lost.

In the middle years of the ninth century two notable patrons really were able to pull together the various strands in Carolingian art, and produce a synthesis original in tone and content. The first of these is Drogo, whose see of Metz I have referred to already in respect of several important works. A Gospel Book in Paris[121], written on purple leaves in gold rustic capitals, follows the Aachen Gospels in the simple classical forms of its architectural canon tables, with the same odd short pediments and arches rising above the architrave, like ventilation shafts. The metallic crests and plumage-like tufts on the earlier canon tables develop, however, into marvellous swathed and coiling foliate ornament, in the masterly manner of the acanthus friezes on the Aachen Minster gallery grilles. A new and charming festive note is added in a second Gospel Book[122] by the pairs of little men who tie up garlands under the arches of Canon II. The zoomorphic capital letters of the *incipits* of the Gospels draw on the tradition of the Corbie Psalter, but now the letters are formed of the Evangelist symbols themselves, a motif first hinted at in a close relation of Cutbercht's Gospels, the *Codex millenarius* from Duke Tassilo's foundation at Kremsmünster.[123] Drogo's Evangelist symbols are like creatures designed by Tenniel: they have a sophisticated drollery difficult to parallel in early or high medieval art.

In Drogo's Sacramentary also in Paris[124] the gold acanthus-festooned capital letters are historiated with clever water-colour sketches of scenes from Christ's life, evidently based on excellent early Christian models,[125] but also original and imaginative, as in Christ's Temptation where the tempter is no easily dismissable black imp or demon but instead a strange beggar man.[126] The central scene of an ivory book cover from Metz, now in Frankfurt, also tackles the story of the Temptation. The tempter this time is more senatorial, but the easy naturalism and humanity of the scene, emphasised by a correct relative scale of the figures to the tree under which they stand, clearly answer the demand of a patron of the greatest intelligence and sensibility.[127] The pierced ivory covers of Drogo's Sacramentary are even more remarkable in the history of narrative representations. They follow through the performance of the mass and other liturgical rites, in a series of scenes that are like camera 'stills'. The figures are crowded together, interacting and on the alert, in well-realised space. The spontaneity

121 BN lat. 9383; Koehler, III(ii) *Metzer Handschriften*, pp. 128–33 and plates 61–4.

122 BN lat. 9388; ibid., pp. 134–42, and plates 66–75.

123 W. Neumueller and K. Holter, *Der Codex millenarius*, Codices selecti 45 (Graz, 1974).

124 BN lat. 9428; W. Koehler, *Drogo-Sakramentar*, Codices selecti 49, 49* (Graz, 1974).

125 Compare the historiated initial of the Ascension on fol. 71v of the Drogo Sacramentary with the Ascension in a fifth-century ivory in Munich illustrated in *Age of Spirituality*, ed. Weitzmann, fig. 67 on p. 455.

126 On fol. 41 of the Drogo Sacramentary; see also the impressive, theologically precise image of the sending out of the Holy Spirit jointly by the Father and the Son in the Pentecost initial on fol. 78 of the Sacramentary.

127 G. Schiller, *Iconography of Christian Art*, I (London, 1971) plate 391; see also Lasko, *Ars sacra*, p. 44.

and realism of these little ivory scenes, as well as their subject matter, are highly unusual.[128]

Technical prowess in ivory carving, but a very different pictorial ideal, is seen in the covers of two books made for Charles the Bald, his Prayer Book and his Psalter. Each of the four panels illustrates a psalm text, evidently chosen for their humble intercessory tone, in the literal tradition of the Utrecht Psalter.[129] The crowded agitated actions of the participants and the undulating landscapes of the Utrecht Psalter are ably reproduced in ivory. However, the scenes are framed by broad bands of acanthus, a treatment more reminiscent of the Douce Psalter; although for want of an alternative the Utrecht Psalter is normally recognised as the specific model used by the sculptors, there are curious discrepancies, not only in layout, which is understandable, but in details of iconography and content, for example a peacock is added to the illustration to Psalm 26,[130] and in Psalm 50 Uriah the Hittite's dead body is naked, not clothed. At the very least, however, Charles the Bald's book covers show that his artists were able to draw upon the formidable visual repertoire already employed in the Utrecht Psalter.

An ivory book cover preserved until the French Revolution at St Denis, a church which Charles the Bald provided with many treasures, illustrates not a psalm but an event reported in the Second Book of Kings, when the armies of Joab and Abner sit down in apparent amity at the pool of Gibeon. The wind that sends the sailing boat scudding across the pool is like the *spiritus vehemens* of Utrecht's Psalm 47, but there is a fine extra motif in the flying birds.[131] A prefatory picture in Charles the Bald's Prayer Book also shows knowledge of the Utrecht Psalter's repertoire. The figure of the king, kneeling before a crucifix, is closely matched by the figure of King Hezekiah blessed by God with long life in Psalm 60.[132] The broad painting technique of King Charles' portrait, however, is close to that of the Douce Psalter, and the wide gold acanthus frames to the texts equally clearly relate to the frames of the Psalter pictures in Douce. The prefatory pictures in Charles the Bald's Psalter, including a portrait of the king enthroned with God's right hand open in formal approval above his head are in another style, that of Drogo's Gospels and Sacramentary, painted in a bright deft water-colour technique, with sturdy well-modelled figures, and with pretty decorative drapery swags and gold foliate scrolls. These particular manuscripts belong to the private, devotional stratification of Charles the Bald's patronage. Both as recipient and patron, however, he was also officially

[128] R. E. Reynolds, 'A visual epitome of the Eucharistic *ordo* from the era of Charles the Bald: the ivory Mass cover of the Drogo Sacramentary', *Charles the Bald: Court and Kingdom*, ed. M. T. Gibson and J. L. Nelson. 2nd revised edn (Aldershot, 1990) pp. 241–60.

[129] The covers of the Prayer Book (Munich, Schatzkammer der Residenz) are in Zürich, Landesmuseum. The Psalter and its covers are in Paris, BN lat. 1152. See Goldschmidt, *Die Elfenbeinskulpturen*, nos. 40, 42, 43, pp. 23–7 and plates XIX, XXI.

[130] Among other similes, Cassiodorus compares the Psalter to a beautiful peacock, its tail full of eyes; see Cassiodorus, *Institutiones*, ed. Mynors, Bk I, IIII, p. 21.

[131] *Le Trésor de Saint-Denis*, Exhibition Catalogue, no. 15b, pp. 109–11.

[132] For the illustrations in the Prayer Book, and also for its ivory covers, see R. Deshman, 'The exalted servant: the ruler theology of the Prayerbook of Charles the Bald', *Viator*, 11 (1980), pp. 385–417.

involved with a much more ambitious series of books, editions of the whole Bible.

Bible production had been a priority of the scriptorium of St Martin at Tours since Alcuin's time; the earliest Tours manuscripts derive their decoration rather crudely from Insular models[133], but quite other exemplars and standards of design were promoted by Alcuin's successors, Fridugisus, Adalhard and Vivian. Tours Bibles were now provided with pictorial prefaces to various biblical books[134], a scheme of which the *Codex Amiatinus* from Jarrow-Wearmouth marks the tentative beginning. In the Vivian Bible the ceremony of the presentation of the book to King Charles is represented. The tall figure of the king, swathed in a splendid mantle, seated on a high round-backed throne, accompanied in a straight line by courtiers and guards, and with allegorical figures beckoning from the spandrels above, shows that the conventions of late-antique ruler portraits, such as in the great silver Missorium of the Emperor Theodosius, were familiar to official Carolingian artists.[135] The clergy of St Martin's stand in front, in a great semi-circle, elaborating on the idea of a crowd of figures in a circular space hinted at in the David and his musicians miniature in the eighth-century English Vespasian Psalter. In the Vivian Bible's own preface to the Psalter a quite different model has been employed. David and his fellow musicians have been raised to a timeless sphere; wearing strange clothes, they stand out against a deep blue disk, as physical and exotic as the gods and constellations of the Leiden Aratus. Roman thoughts too have struck the designer of the preface to the Apocalypse in the Vivian Bible. The picture represents the coming of the Lamb to open the sealed book in Revelation 4–5. Another persona of Christ, the Lion of Judah, is also represented, and yet another, the victorious rider on the white horse, of Revelation 19, is displayed above the altar, like a votive offering such as the bronze horseman from Metz may have been, but in the miniature the horseman wears Roman dress, and his horse rears, clearly copied from the Justinian diptych from Trier. Other pictures represent the creation and fall of man, with big emphatic figures set in a narrow landscape; and a history of Jerome's journeys and labours as editor–translator of the Bible, an extended version of the two scenes designed for the Dagulf Psalter. These clearly depicted narratives, involving rows of figures in different zones, inscribed and identified, may give us some impression of the appearance of the monumental histories, secular and sacred, reported to have been painted on the walls of the palace and church at Ingelheim.[136]

I referred earlier to a large decorated initial in the Vivian Bible. It represents a curious convention favoured by certain Tours artists, sometimes even used in narrative illustrations, whereby small figures are painted in silver or gold and

[133] See Koehler, I, *Die Schule von Tours*, plates 1–11.

[134] *Ibid.* I[2] (Berlin, 1933), pp. 27–64; plates 69–76. See also H. L. Kessler. *The Illustrated Bibles from Tours*, (Princeton, 1977).

[135] *Age of Spirituality*, ed. Weitzmann, no. 64, pp. 74–6.

[136] Davis-Weyer, *Early Medieval Art 300–1150*, pp. 84–8.

silhouetted against the ivory white vellum.[137] The source of this visual effect would seem to be metal intarsio work, a technique known in Late Antiquity, for example in a fourth-century bronze plaque with silver inlay, at Princeton, representing Heracles killing the Hydra.[138] That the Carolingians made use of it themselves is proved by the *Cathedra Petri*. The ivory throne, on a wooden core, is now generally accepted as having been brought to Rome by Charles the Bald for his coronation as Emperor in 875, and left behind as a pious donation, like his presentation of the last and grandest Bible in the Tours tradition to San Paolo-fuori-le-mura.[139] Various aspects of Carolingian art and design are summed up in the *Cathedra Petri*. Its top pediment has the stolid classical plainness of the architecture of the Coronation Gospels and the Drogo Sacramentary, and like the Sacramentary the plain architecture is enriched with friezes of busily swirling acanthus foliage. This foliage is inhabited by various mythical creatures, whose shape-shifting has something of the drollery that characterises Metz work. Embedded in the central frieze, is a bust-length portrait of Charles the Bald, guarded by angels. The front of the throne looks very different. It consists of square blocks of ivory, stacked up as if for some exotic lottery. These blocks are decorated with the Labours of Heracles, in a technique partly engraved, partly of gold inlay, the precious metal being mostly now lost. As Weitzmann has suggested, the imagery of Charlemagne's tables, especially the third, cosmological table, would have been clear to read if it was in this metal inlay technique.[140]

Weitzmann's suggestion that an Insular tendency has survived into the late Carolingian art of the throne is tempting. He senses constriction, entanglement, as Heracles takes on his opponents.[141] However the compositions of the Labours of Heracles on the *Cathedra Petri* seem less likely to be the result of a backward glance at such Insular monuments as the Rothbury Cross than of the need to secure in separate short sections the gold that was to make up Heracles' body. More acceptable is Weitzmann's observation that the drawing style, for example of the trees, relates to the Utrecht Psalter.[142] We have seen that Heracles takes the role of the strong man in Psalm 18. The formal contrast between the upper part, and the front, of the *Cathedra Petri* is not more striking than the contrast between the pictures in Charles the Bald's Prayer Book and Psalter, and their Utrecht Psalter-derived ivory covers. The range of styles and techniques that Carolingian artists had at their command was very wide, and

137 See for example Bamberg, Staatliche Bibliothek Misc. bibl. I, and Autun, Bibl. de la Ville MS 19, in Koehler I, *Die Schule von Tours*, plates 56, 63.

138 *Age of Spirituality*, ed. Weitzmann, no. 137, pp. 160–1 and colour plate III.

139 *La Cattedra lignea di S. Pietro in Vaticano, Atti della Pontificia Accademia Romana di Archeologia* ser. III, Memorie X (Vatican, 1971); K. Weitzmann, 'The Heracles plaques of St Peter's Cathedra', *The Art Bulletin*, 55 (1973) pp. 1–37; L. Nees, *A Tainted Mantle: Hercules and the Classical Tradition at the Carolingian Court* (Philadelphia, 1991).

140 Weitzmann, 'The Heracles plaques', p. 25.

141 Ibid., p. 14.

142 Ibid., p. 32.

uniformity was not an objective. As in the case of Charlemagne's *observatio astrorum*, a poem by Boethius in the *De consolatione philosophiae* helps us to understand what educated Carolingian opinion of Heracles would have been. For Boethius the Labours of Heracles represented man's struggle against odds, the hero's progress.[143] But this display of classical legend in such sumptuous materials, ivory and gold, underscores the debt that Carolingian art owed to the late-antique past of north-western Europe itself. Scholars who resisted the idea that the *Cathedra Petri* was entirely of Carolingian manufacture saw the front as a propagandist artefact made in the late third century for the tetrarch Maximianus Herculeus.[144] In Trier as it evolved under Constantine and his successors, a majestic throne of that kind might have stood in the *Aula Palatina*. Charles the Bald's throne in Rome reads almost like a bid to claim Gallo-Roman ancestry for the Carolingian royal house.[145]

As we have seen, even in the pre-Carolingian period treasures of the early Christian world were being imported to north-west Europe or were being confronted *in situ* by perceptive new observers. When Italy became part of the Carolingian empire, conditions were right for a renewal of official Christian art, on a scale and with an expenditure not paralleled in the west since the fourth century. The problem of Carolingian works of art such as the Utrecht Psalter – whether they are originals or copies – stems from this situation. Together with traditional Mediterranean images and techniques, Carolingian artists adopted and exploited many aspects of Insular design and ornament. Carolingian artists were gifted compilers. But the range of materials which they had at their disposal stretched their imaginations, and produced wholly new visual effects. In its final stages the elegance and dignity of Carolingian art clearly represents the first 'court style' of medieval Europe.

Select bibliography

Surveys

A. Boinet, *La Miniature carolingienne* (Paris, 1913)

W. Braunfels, *Die Welt der Karolinger und ihre Kunst* (Munich, 1968)

W. Braunfels, (ed.) *Charlemagne/Karl der Grosse*, Catalogue of Council of Europe Exhibition, Aachen, 1965 (Düsseldorf, 1965)

143 Boethius, *The Consolation of Philosophy*, Trans. S. J. Tester, Loeb Classical Library (Harvard, 1973), pp. 380–2.

144 See M. Guarducci, 'Gli Avori Erculei della Cattedra di San Pietro', *Atti della accademia dei Lincei, Anno CCCLXVIII*, 1971. *Memorie Classe di Scienze morali, storiche e filologiche*, ser. VIII, XVI fasc. 5 (Rome, 1972) pp. 263–350. See also K. Weitzmann, 'An addendum to "The Heracles plaques of St Peter's Cathedra"', *The Art Bulletin*, 56, (1974), pp. 248–252.

145 For Carolingian interest in genealogy and the history of the royal house see E. Hlawitschka, 'Die Vorfahren Karls des Grossen, in *Karl der Grosse* I, pp. 51–82; W. Kienast, *Studien über die französischen Volksstämme der Frümittelalters*, Pariser Historische Studien 7 (Stuttgart, 1968), p. 55 and also R. McKitterick, *The Frankish Kingdoms under the Carolingians, 751–987* (London, 1983) p. 24.

W. Braunfels, H. Schnitzler (eds.), *Karl der Grosse* III, *Karolingische Kunst* (Düsseldorf, 1966)

J. Hubert, J. Porcher, W. F. Volbach, *L'Empire carolingien* (Paris, 1968)
Carolingian Art (London, 1970)

W. Koehler, *Die karolingischen Miniaturen*, continued by F. Mütherich (Berlin, 1933–82)

P. Lasko, *Ars sacra 800–1200* (Harmondsworth, 1972)

R. McKitterick, 'Text and image in the Carolingian world', in: *Uses of Literacy*, pp. 297–318

B. de Montesquiou-Fezensac, D. Gaborit-Chopin, *Le Trésor de Saint-Denis* (Paris, 1977)

Early monuments

A. Haseloff, *Der Tassilo Kelch* (Munich, 1950)

W. Koehler, 'Die Denkmäler der karolingischen Kunst in Belgien', *Belgische Kunstdenkmäler*, ed. P. Clemen (Munich, 1923) (for Antwerp Sedulius) pp. 7–9

W. Neumueller and K. Holter, *Der Codex millenarius* (Graz, 1959)
Der Codex millenarius, Codices seleci 45 (Graz, 1974)

J. Porcher, 'Psautier d'Amiens', *La Revue des arts* 7 (1957) pp. 51–8

D. H. Wright, 'The *Codex millenarius* and its model', *Münchner Jahrbuch der bildenden Kunst*, 3rd series, 15 (1964) pp. 17–54

Trierer Apocalypse, commentary by R. Laufner, P. Klein (Graz, 1972)

Gospel Books

A. Boeckler, 'Die Evangelistenbilder des Adagruppe', *Münchner Jahrbuch der bildenden Kunst*, 3rd series, 3/4 (1952–3)

W. Braunfels, *The Lorsch Gospels* (New York, 1967)

W. Koehler, 'An illustrated evangelistary of the Ada School', *Journal of the Warburg and Courtauld Institutes*, 15 (1952) pp. 48–66

E. Rosenbaum, 'Evangelist portraits of the Ada School and their models', *The Art Bulletin* 38 (1956) pp. 81–90
'The Vine Columns of Old St Peters in Carolingian Canon Tables', *Journal of the Warburg and Courtauld Institutes* 18 (1955) pp. 1–15

P. A. Underwood, 'The fountain of life in manuscripts of the Gospels', *Dumbarton Oaks Papers* 5 (Harvard, 1950), pp 41–138

R. M. Walker, 'Illustrations to the Priscillian Prologues', *The Art Bulletin* 30 (1948) pp. 1–10

Psalters

E. T. De Wald, *The Illustrations of the Utrecht Psalter* (Princeton, 1933)

S. Dufrenne, 'Les Copies anglaises du Psautier d'Utrecht', *Scriptorium* 18 (1964) pp. 185–97
Les Illustrations du Psautier d'Utrecht (Paris, 1978)

J. H. A. Engelbregt, *Utrecht-Psalter* (Graz, 1982–84)

J. Eschweiler, F. Mütherich, *Der Stuttgarter-Bilderpsalter*, (Stuttgart, 1965–6); review by E. Kitzinger, *The Art Bulletin* 51 (1969) pp. 393–7

K. Holter, *Dagulf Psalter* (Graz, 1970)

D. Panofsky, 'The textual basis of the Utrecht Psalter illustrations', *The Art Bulletin* 25 (1943) pp. 50–8
D. Tselos, 'Defensive addenda to the problem of the Utrecht Psalter', *The Art Bulletin* 49 (1967) pp. 334–49
F. Wormald, 'The Utrecht Psalter', in: *Collected Writings*, I (London, 1984)

Antique revival 'facsimiles'

J. J. G. Alexander, 'The illustrated manuscripts of the *Notitia dignitatum*', *Aspects of the Notitia Dignitatum*, ed. R. Goodburn and P. Bartholomew, BAR Supplementary Series 15 (1976) pp. 11–25
L. W. Jones, C. R. Morey, *The Miniatures of the Manuscripts of Terence* (Princeton, 1931)
P. McGurk, 'Carolingian astrological manuscripts', in *Charles the Bald: Court and Kingdom*, ed. M. Gibson, J. L. Nelson, BAR International Series, 101 (Oxford, 1979)
Physiologus Bernensis, commentary by C. Steiger, O. Homburger (Basle, 1964)
H. Stern, *Le Calendrier de 354. Étude de son texte et ses illustrations* (Paris, 1953)
H. Swarzenski, 'The Xanten purple leaf', *The Art Bulletin* 22 (1940) pp. 7–24

Ivories

H. Fillitz, 'Elfenbeinreliefs vom Hofe Kaiser Karls des Kahlen', in *Beiträge zur Kunst des Mittelalters, Festschrift für Hans Wentzel*, ed. R. Becksmann (Berlin, 1975), pp. 41–51
A. Goldschmidt, *Die Elfenbeinskulpturen* (Berlin, 1914, 1918)
S. Lewis, 'A Byzantine "Virgo Militans" at Charlemagne's court', *Viator* 11 (1980) pp. 71–93
K. Weitzmann, 'The Heracles plaques of St Peter's Cathedra', *The Art Bulletin* 55 (1973) pp. 1–37; 56 (1974) pp. 248–252
'The iconography of the Carolingian ivories of the throne', in: *La Cattedra Lignea di S. Pietro in Vaticano*, ed. M. Maccarrone (Rome, 1971)

Metalwork

H. Belting, 'Der Einhardsbogen', *Zeitschrift für Kunstgeschichte* 36 (1973) pp. 93–121
V. H. Elbern, *Die karolingische Goldalter von Mailand* (Bonn, 1952)
F. N. Estey, 'Charlemagne's silver celestial table', *Speculum* 18 (1943) pp. 112–17
B. de Montesquiou-Fezensac, 'L'Arc de Triomphe d'Einhardus', *Cahiers archéologiques* 4 (1949) pp. 79–103

Late monuments

R. Deshman, 'The exalted servant: the ruler theology of the Prayerbook of Charles the Bald', *Viator* 11 (1980) pp. 385–417
J. Gaehde, 'Pictorial sources of the illustrations to the Book of Kings ... in the Carolingian Bible of San Paolo fuori le mura in Rome', *Frühmittelalterliche Studien* 9 (1975) pp. 359–89
H. L. Kessler, *The Illustrated Bibles from Tours* (Princeton, 1977)
W. Koehler, *Drogo-Sacramentar* (Graz, 1974)
Sakramentar von Metz, commentary by F. Mütherich (Graz, 1972)

10

Carolingian music

Susan Rankin

An intricately carved ivory panel made in northern Europe in the late ninth century represents the earliest known portrayal of choral singing in the West (plate 17): in the centre stands an archbishop and behind him five elaborately dressed priests holding *rotuli*.[1] In the lower part of the panel, with their backs to the onlooker, stand seven figures who, with arms held high, hands outstretched and mouths open, are singing. With his right hand the archbishop makes a sign to the singers; in his left he holds a book. Here are inscribed the words: 'Ad te l[e]vavi anima[m] mea[m] deus meus in te confido non erubescam [neq]ue inrideant me inimici mei etenim universi qui te expectant non confunden[tur]' (plate 16). These words pinpoint the exact moment portrayed both in the daily liturgical ritual and in the cycle of the whole liturgical year: *Ad te levavi* is the text which appears at the very beginning of books of mass chants, often with a highly decorated 'A'. The singers are performing the Introit of the mass for the first Sunday in Advent, the beginning of a Christian year. The celebrant raises his hand, not to 'conduct' the singers, but to indicate that he is ready, and that they may bring the Introit to a close.[2]

From the smallest details of this scene up to its overall organisation, dominated by a large central figure, there can be no mistaking what the onlooker is intended to understand; this is certainly not a narrative composition, to be understood in the reading, but a straightforward, forceful, statement. The scene represented is a performance of the *Roman* mass, its music sung by a group of specially designated singers. Central to the conception of the whole is not only

[1] Cambridge, Fitzwilliam Museum, McClean bequest M.12/1904. The ivory is one of a group of three probably by the same artist; see A. Goldschmidt, *Die Elfenbeinskulpturen aus der Zeit der karolingischen und sächsischen Kaiser*, I (Berlin, 1914), On the dating see C. Nordenfalk, 'Karolingisch oder ottonisch? Zur Datierung und Localisierung der Elfenbeine Goldschmidt I, 120–31', in: *Kolloquium über spätantike und frühmittelalterliche Skulptur, Heidelberg 1972*, III (Mainz, 1974), pp. 45–58 and plates 23–32, and *Zu Gast in der Kunstkammer, Eine Ausstellung anlässlich des einhundertjährigen Bestehens des Kunsthistorischen Museums Wien* (Vienna, 1991) pp. 10–45.

[2] The ritual on which this scene is based described in T. Klauser, *A Short History of the Western Liturgy* (Oxford, 1969) pp. 60ff.

the act of choral singing, but also what is sung in the Frankish Church, the Introit *Ad te levavi* standing not just at the head of the repertory, but as a paradigm of the Roman chant. Even in the niceties of the text version inscribed in the archbishop's book can the message of the ivory be followed. For here, in the opening words of Psalm 24, the artist has copied the text *not* from a Bible, but directly from a chantbook: sung as an Introit, this text omits the biblical *domine* ('Ad te *domine* levavi animam meam'), and later follows the Roman Psalter rather than the Gallican in the phrase 'etenim universi qui te expectant' instead of 'etenim universi sustinent te'.

Music as political programme

The Roman chant as sung by the Franks – what we know today as 'Gregorian chant' – inevitably dominates any study of music in the Carolingian world; this orientation is determined not only by the close relation between the Church and economic power (the Church having the means to preserve its music by the training of scribes and access to costly writing materials), but also, significantly, by the high degree of interest taken by those in the seat of power in ecclesiastical chant. Besides what is conveyed in the historical writings of Einhard, Walahfrid Strabo, John the Deacon and Notker,[3] concern on the part of Pippin III and Charlemagne is evident in a series of official documents,[4] most notably the *Admonitio generalis* of 789 (c. 80): 'To all the clergy. That they are to learn the Roman chant thoroughly and that it is to be employed throughout the office, night and day, in the correct form, in conformity with what our father of blessed memory, king Pippin, strove to bring to pass when he abolished the Gallican chant for the sake of unanimity with the apostolic see and the peaceful harmony of God's holy church.'[5]

The process of romanisation of the ecclesiastical chant and of the liturgy in which it was embedded had been launched in the Frankish realm long before Charlemagne's edict of 789. Writing in the middle of the ninth century, Walahfrid Strabo associated the initiation of this process with the meeting in France in 754 between the pope (Stephen II) and Pippin III; in reality the many contacts between northern Christians and the Church in Rome had, even before this, engendered some degree of influence.[6] From the middle of the eighth century on, official documents of the Frankish administration testify to the

[3] Einhard, *Vita Karoli*, in Rau, *Quellen* I, pp. 162–211; Walahfrid Strabo, *Liber de exordiis et incrementis quarundam in observationis ecclesiasticis rerum*, ed. A. Knoepfler (Munich, 1890); Johannes Diaconis, *Vita sancti Gregorii magni*, in: PL, cols. 63–242, esp. 90ff.; Notker, *Gesta Karoli*, in: Rau, *Quellen* III, pp. 321–427.

[4] C. Vogel, *Introduction aux sources de l'histoire du culte chrétien au moyen âge* (Spoleto, 1981) pp. 118ff.

[5] 'Omni clero: Ut cantum Romanum pleniter discant, et ordinabiliter per nocturnale vel graduale officium peragatur, secundum quod beatae memoriae genitor noster Pippinus rex decertavit ut fieret, quando Gallicanum tulit ob unanimitatem apostolicae sedis et sanctae dei aeclesiae pacificam concordiam.' A. Boret, *Capitularia regum Francorum* I, MGH Leges nat. germ. II (Hanover, 1883), no. 22; trans. from P. D. King, *Charlemagne: Translated Sources* (Kendal, 1987), p. 218.

[6] Vogel, *Introduction*, pp. 117–18.

efforts made by the Carolingians to provide the necessary support for the establishment of Roman liturgy, especially in this initial period by the acquisition from Rome of liturgical books and their being made available in the northern countries. An appreciation of the motives which lay behind this long-nurtured campaign must have a decisive impact on any interpretation of surviving traces of Carolingian music and assessment of the musical culture of the period 750–900.

'To be Roman' lay at the heart of the Carolingian political programme.[7] On the one hand, as their sphere of political influence widened, successive Carolingian rulers sought to subdue and control groups more used to self-governance (and often pagan) through the imposition of a religion which came complete with moral code, a highly sophisticated ritual, and priests to act as interpreters of its theology. On the other hand, their ambitions were more grandiose than mere territorial control: nothing less than dynastic legitimacy – the recognition that these were the true heirs to the glorious Roman Empire – would satisfy. To this end, it mattered that elements of Roman culture should re-emerge; music, as a central part of the liturgical ritual, as a vehicle of poetic expression, and as one of the seven *artes liberales*, occupied a pivotal place in this cultural programme.

Yet the initiative to sing Roman music and to study the musical thinking of classical writers was not only politically motivated, as Walahfrid's linking of the introduction of Roman chant with a meeting between the Frankish king and the Roman pope *in Francia* implies. Officials of the Church themselves had an interest in the import of the Roman musical repertory and skills. Foremost among these was Bishop Chrodegang of Metz, sent to Rome by Pippin in 753, and responsible for introducing the *cantilena romana* and Roman *ordo* to the church in Metz. From this time, Metz became the most famous Carolingian centre for the cultivation of Roman music, even giving its name to certain melodies composed by the Franks.[8] The Christian mission undertaken by Pippin III, Charlemagne, Louis the Pious and Charles the Bald had as its objective more than control of a powerful aristocracy and unification of diverse peoples: theirs was a religious duty, carried through as an aspect of their own faith in the Christian, Roman (thus *western*), Church. The relation of the Carolingian kings and aristocracy to Rome was much more dialectical than dependent: when Charlemagne in the *Admonitio generalis* titled himself 'king and rector of the Franks and devout defender and humble adjuvant of the holy church',[9] it was precisely this combination of power lent to, and authority deriving from, the Roman Church, which he expressed. This aspect of exchange underlies the

7 See J. L. Nelson, chapter 2, above.

8 The sequences *Metensis maior* and *Metensis minor*; on such melodies see the fourth part of this study, 'Musical creativity'.

9 'rex et rector regni francorum et devotus sanctae ecclesiae defensor humilisque adiutor'; Boret, *Capitularia* 22; trans. King, *Charlemagne* p. 209.

whole history of the development of a Franco-Roman liturgy and liturgical music in the Carolingian period.

It is in this context that the various elements of a legend attributing the composition of Roman chant to Pope Gregory I (the Great, 594–604) materialised. Venerated especially by the Anglo-Saxons, responsibility for his prominence in the Carolingian world must lie in part with the Insular churchmen Boniface and Alcuin (and the writings of Bede as well as the first *Vita*, composed by a monk of Whitby).[10] A book of homilies made *ca* 800 contains author-portraits of Ambrose, Jerome, Augustine and Gregory; made for Egino, monk of Reichenau and bishop of Verona, this represents the first depiction of Gregory as one of the four Latin doctors.[11] Long before the appearance of the familiar iconographic scheme showing Gregory with dove perched on his shoulder dictating chant to a monk provided with writing materials,[12] the first tangible sign of a perceived connection between Gregory and Roman chant is a text – which begins in hexameters – used as a preface to three of the four earliest Frankish books of mass chants (which record texts but lack musical notation), copied in the late eighth to early ninth centuries:[13]

> Gregorius praesul meritis et nomine dignus
> unde genus ducit summum conscendit honorem
> qui renovans monumenta patrumque priorum
> tum composuit hunc libellum musicae artis
> scolae cantorum in nomine dei summi.
>
> Gregory, worthy in merits and in name, bishop
> whence his family leads, enters into the highest honour,
> who, renewing the monuments of the fathers and the ancients,
> then composed this little book of musical art
> for the school of cantors in the name of the highest God.[14]

These five lines are simply packed with political statement: drawing the most direct relation possible between the famous Roman pope and a liturgical book – 'he *composed* this' (the significance of the description 'a book of musical art' will concern us later) – Gregory's importance is stretched out in all directions: worthy through his own deeds, through family lineage, through name (a pun on Latin *grex*, meaning flock; Gregory's most widely known work was the *Liber regulae pastoralis*), and as holder of the highest honour (in the place 'whence his

10 *The Earliest Life of Gregory the Great by an Anonymous Monk of Whitby*, ed. and trans. B. Colgrave (Cambridge, 1985).

11 Berlin, Staatsbibliothek Phillips MS 1676.

12 On this iconographic tradition see J. Croquison, 'Les origines de l'iconographie grégorienne', *Cahiers archéologiques* 12 (1962) pp. 249–62, and L. Treitler, 'Homer and Gregory: the transmission of epic poetry and plainchant', *The Musical Quarterly* 60 (1974) pp. 333–72.

13 The three sources are Lucca, Biblioteca capitolare 490 fols. 30–1 (fragment); Monza, Tesoro della Basilica S. Giovanni CIX; Brussels, Bibliothèque Royale 10127–44. The version quoted here is from the Monza source: B. Stäblein, '"Gregorius Praesul", der Prolog zum römischen Antiphonale', in: *Musik und Verlag. Karl Vötterle zum 65. Geburtstag* (Kassel, 1968) p. 544.

14 For this translation and for guidance on the interpretation of the hexameters I am indebted to Dr David Howlett; further translations quoted below are also by Dr Howlett if not otherwise attributed.

family leads', thus Rome). All this prefaces the vital message, based around the word 'monumenta' (the central word of the whole), that Gregory renewed the monuments of the fathers (of the church) and the ancients (those pre-Christian writers whose works were valued and could therefore be re-interpreted in a Christian light). Thus the authority of the liturgical books to which this preface is attached derives not only from Gregory's own stature, but from his being a representative – or better a 'transmitter' to the modern situation – of the older Christian classical world. In the face of such powerful arguments, the legitimacy of Roman chant, as contained in such books, could hardly be called into question.

But why, if Pippin, Charlemagne and their ministers could evangelise amongst the heathen and ensure that everyone throughout the kingdom worshipped the Christian God, whose church was based in Rome, should anyone try to go further? Why should those many well-established Christian communities closer to the heartland of the Carolingian kingdom *change* their long-established patterns of worship? Once again, the answer lies in the relation of Christian–political motives to the situation pertaining. While writer after writer was to underline the significance of choral singing,[15] singing *together* (as portrayed in the ivory shown in plate 17) for the harmonious concordance and unanimity of the Christian community,[16] the actual situation out there in the near and far reaches of Carolingian Europe was one of considerable diversity and freedom of practice. Besides the variations between liturgical practice in large regions of Merovingian Gaul, as well as areas on the edges (Septimania, Brittany, Milan), it was always possible for individual officials of the Church to introduce changes on their own initiative. In particular, before Pippin's meeting with the pope in 754, there was already well under way a kind of creeping romanisation: generations of pilgrims and visitors to Rome inevitably returned home with new ideas and, in many cases, books.[17] Nevertheless, the crucial point of change in official Frankish thinking on liturgical uniformity came in the middle of the eighth century: whereas in 742 Carloman (brother of Pippin III) was able to sanction the order that every priest should answer to his bishop for the 'ratio et ordo ministerii sui', by Pippin's death in 768 the order that all the Gauls should follow the tradition of the Roman Church in singing had gone out to 'all the churches of the Gauls'.[18]

In focusing on liturgical singing as a symbol of social unity, the early Carolingians set an entirely new value on uniformity and standardisation of

[15] Among them Augustine, Alcuin and Amalarius; see R. McKitterick, *The Frankish Church and the Carolingian Reforms, 789–895* (London, 1977), esp. chapter 4, 'The liturgy', and A. Ekenberg, *Cur cantatur? Die Funktionen des liturgischen Gesanges nach den Autoren der Karolingerzeit* (Stockholm, 1987), *passim*.

[16] On the specific aspect of concordance, a term introduced into the discussion of music in connection with the practice of polyphony, see K. F. Morrison, '"Know thyself": music in the Carolingian Renaissance', in: *Committenti e produzione artistico-letteraria nell'alto medioevo occidentale*, *Settimane* 30 (Spoleto, 1992), pp. 379ff.

[17] Vogel, *Introduction*, pp. 117–19.

[18] As reported in Charlemagne's *Epistola generalis*; trans. King, *Charlemagne*, p. 208.

musical practice. For the first time, it became important that at each individual church, as well as from one church to another anywhere in the kingdom, the liturgical chant should be sung in the same way each day of the year. And this in turn produced a widespread demand, directed towards the centre of policy-making, first and foremost for knowledge of Roman singing, but also, in the wake of this, for mechanisms which would support consistency of practice; in a culture whose means of passing on musical knowledge and expertise was essentially oral, the ability to formulate melodies in relation to their texts always in the same way each time repeated, and the regulation of patterns of recitation so that in specific melodic contexts these would be clearly determined, had to be achieved.

The way in which answers to these problems were found, a process on which Carolingian attitudes to the Latin language and to Latin texts had a profound influence, forms the central thread of the history of music in the Carolingian period. It is hardly too high a claim to state that the century between roughly 770 and 870 was the most intensive period of musical development of the whole Middle Ages; to this age belonged the invention of a detailed system of musical notation (some of the essential elements of which have remained in the western notational system ever since), the systematisation of modal behaviour (literally the grammar of relationships between individual tones and groups of tones), the final shaping of a characteristic melodic dialect for an enormous melodic repertory (the 'Gregorian' chant), and the setting down in textual form of a theory of modes.

These were the results, but as to how they were brought about, we have only an imperfect picture. The invention of notation has fascinated many, and produced much controversy, as has also the question of how Charlemagne's agents and their successors disseminated Roman chant, producing an astonishing degree of unanimity in the earliest extant notated examples of melodies for the Roman mass. Many questions remain to be answered, and yet a striking paradox of this musical culture for which the term 'renaissance' seems insufficient is on all sides evident: whereas the Carolingians expended a good deal of energy in looking backwards to an older civilisation, and in attempting to *conserve* the traditions and values of the Christian ancestors, their underlying motivation was essentially progressive, and what they actually produced was far from 'old-fashioned', nor limited by the boundaries of what had gone before. In making Roman and, above all, Latin techniques their own, they inaugurated a long period of musical creativity, the fruits of which may be found in the extant notated music of the late ninth, tenth and eleventh centuries.

Music and language: music as language

The story of the introduction of the Roman chant into the north was told many times in the Middle Ages, its tradition beginning already in the capitularies of

Charlemagne (referring to the actions of his father) and continuing in the ninth century in historical accounts penned by Walahfrid Strabo (of Reichenau), John the Deacon (of Rome) and Notker Balbulus (of St Gallen).[19] Leaving aside its chronological inaccuracies, Notker's version is the spiciest:

> Charlemagne, who enjoyed divine service so much that he never wearied of it, prided himself that he had achieved his object of making all possible progress in the study of the humanities. He was, however, greatly grieved by the fact that all his provinces, and indeed his cities and even the smaller localities, continued to differ in the way they worshipped God, and particularly in the rhythm of their chanting. He therefore asked Pope Stephen III . . . to send him some monks who were highly skilled in church singing. The Pope . . . dispatched to him . . . from his own apostolic see, a dozen monks well trained in chanting . . . When the time came for these monks to set out from Rome . . . they plotted among themselves to see how they could vary the ways of singing and so prevent the Franks . . . from ever achieving uniformity. When they reported to Charlemagne they were received with honour, and they were apportioned out to a number of very famous places. Each in his own appointed locality began to chant with as much variation and as incorrectly as he knew how, and did all he could to teach others to do the same. Charlemagne, who was certainly no fool, celebrated the Feast of the Nativity and of the Coming of Christ at Trier or at Metz one year, and with great insight and attention to detail came to follow and understand the style of singing there; and the following year he took part in similar solemnities at Paris or at Tours, and there listened to singing which was completely different from what he had heard twelve months before at the other places mentioned. In the same way he discovered, as time went on, that the monks whom he had dispatched to the other cities were all different from each other in their singing . . . [The story continues with the return of these monks to Rome, their disgrace, and the subsequent dispatch of 'two of the most intelligent monks' from Charlemagne's own entourage to Rome; it was, according to Notker, their teaching which 'spread throughout all the land of the Franks'.][20]

The move from Gallican to Roman singing was not an easy one: it could not be achieved in one simple step, nor did the Roman cantors cooperate, if Notker is to be believed. Keywords in this narrative are uniformity and variation: it comes as no surprise to find Charlemagne dissatisfied with singing which he observed to be 'completely different' from one major centre to another. Aside from the task of learning the words which made up the texts and the notes which made up the melodies of the Roman chants, the Frankish singers needed to learn the correct way of singing these: Notker's account returns four times to this issue.

19 Text sources as n.3 above; these reports and the contradictions between them are discussed in R. van Doren, *Étude sur l'influence musicale de l'abbaye de Saint-Gall (VIIIe au XIe siècle)* (Louvain, 1925) pp. 45ff.; S. J. P. van Dijk, 'Papal schola *versus* Charlemagne', in: *Organicae voces: Festschrift Joseph Smits van Waesberghe* (Amsterdam, 1963) pp. 121–30; S. Rankin, 'Ways of telling stories', *From Rome to the Passing of the Gothic. In Honor of David G. Hughes*, Isham Library Papers 4 (Harvard, forthcoming).

20 Notker, *Gesta Karoli*, I:10; this translation is from *Einhard and Notker the Stammerer: Two lives of Charlemagne*, trans. L. Thorpe (Harmondsworth, 1969) pp. 102–4.

The implication is that there were certain principles for the *delivery* of these chants to which the Carolingian cantors were expected to adhere.

No more explicit textual description of the difficulties encountered by these singers is known, nor, without the exercise of a great deal of imagination, do we have any way of reconstructing the difference between a good, correct, performance of chant in the late eighth century and a bad, incorrect, performance. Nevertheless, much can be inferred from the actual musical records: even though these only begin from *ca* 900, the 'Gregorian' melodies written down in far-distant centres, using distinct notational systems, are extremely close in their readings, both of pitch pattern and of rhythmic and expressive nuance, suggesting that earlier efforts to achieve uniformity were effective and successful.

If there is no reason to suppose that the notated melodies of *ca* 900 were divergent from those sung *ca* 800, we can use those later notations as the basis of a discussion of the nature of the music so highly esteemed by Charlemagne and his advisers. As an example, the Introit *Ad te levavi* 'sung' in the ivory shown in plates 16 and 17 will serve: it is presented in example 1 in a notation which uses modern clefs and unstemmed note-heads (thus without rhythmic significance) and, for convenience of reference, each syllable and note-group is numbered.

Leaving aside those elements in the act of listening which are to do with non-rational response – what St Augustine meant when he described sacred chants as 'beguiling'[21] – we might divide the process of understanding this chant as it unfolds in time into several levels: comprehension of the words of the text, recognition of patterns, short- and long-term, in the melody, and reaction to the interaction of text and melody. In the discussion of this chant which follows some instances of behaviour relating to each of these levels will be brought forward, so that the typical mechanisms and objectives of Gregorian chant will become clear. This is not, however, intended as an exhaustive critical analysis.

In the succession of single pitches and arrangement of pitches in groups, patterns are built up, and followed through or left without further substantiation. For example, in the passage from note-groups 25 to 37, we hear first an emphasis on **c** (including one note-group which repeats **c** four times), falling then to **a** (27); in 28–9 this same fall is repeated (filled by the intermediate tone **b**); then another emphasised **c** (30) is followed not by **a** but by the next lower tone, **G**; after repetition of this single tone (32–3), the melody moves back up to **c** (34), not by leap (as the melody fell) but by step; then the falling pattern is resumed with a descent through **a** to the tone below **G**, **F** (35–7). The whole passage is thus shaped by the descending zigzag **c** – **a** – **c** – **G** – **c** – **F**. In the passage immediately following (38–49), the descending movement is reversed, in a pattern built up in small stepwise gestures: first **F** moves to **G** through **a** (.·. , 38–40); then **G** moves to **a** through **b** (41–3), falling back to **G** (44–6); then **a** moves to **b** through **c** (47), and **b** to **c** through **d** (48); this is the highest

[21] St Augustine, *Confessions*, trans. W. Watts (1631; reprinted London, 1919), Bk 10, chapter xxxiii (pp. 165–9); 'sed delectatio carnis meae . . . saepe me fallit'.

Example 1

I To you I have lifted up my soul:
II my God in you I trust, I shall not blush for shame
III nor may my enemies mock me:
IV and, moreover, all those who wait for you will not be confounded
V Point out to me Lord, your ways, and teach me your paths.

point aimed for, and the passage concludes with a fall to **a** (49). (All Gregorian melodies 'cadence' through falling movement, like the Latin language.) These are examples of procedures which determine short-term melodic behaviour, and which can be altered and exchanged as a way of keeping momentum going. A dynamic which controls melodic behaviour on a larger scale is the tension between the principal high note used for recitation (**c**) and the principal low note, on which the melody finally cadences (**G**). The ways in which the tones **a** and **F** can be used to intensify the pull of **c** (set in a chain of thirds, **F** – **a** – **c**) and be balanced against **G**, or joined to **G**, shape much of the design of the whole. But these relationships are perceived, learnt, deepened, as the melody is heard, rather than known in advance. They represent the working out of a potential of this tonal system, and the interest of any individual melody is the way in which it seizes this potential. Of course, the possibility exists to make a melodic movement and to leave it 'unsubstantiated'; if an emphatic melodic gesture is not returned to, it may stand out all the more starkly. The fact that the dramatic fall of a sixth between 14 and 15 is never repeated in *Ad te levavi* helps to explain what is intended: nowhere else does the tone **d** connect with **F**, either by leap or in a scalic fall. We might say then that the two are not 'joined' here either, but heard as far apart – **d** heard as the end of a melodic rising pattern (established since the beginning), and **F** as the beginning of another. The significance of such a reading is revealed once the fabric of music combined with text is realised.

The text can be divided into syntactical phrases, into shorter groups of words, into single words, into single syllables. Through word order, syntax and sound, the text will, like the melody, develop internal patterns. The Roman numerals I–IV in example 1 indicate the four principal syntactical units. Sound patterns include all the rhymes, and other kinds of repetition: *meam* (10, end of I) /*erubescam* 24, end of II); *non erubescam* (20, leading to end of II), *non confundentur* (50, leading to the end of IV); *non erubescam/neque irrideant* (20–30) are some of the most prominent.

Example 2

Example 3

The interaction of text and melody in *Ad te levavi* should be first considered at the level of individual words: the melodic pattern for most words will follow an arch shape, falling at the end, except where the word comes at the beginning of a melodic phrase, where it is necessary for the melody to intone, or move upwards. In addition to this, the accented syllable of a word will usually be emphasised, by number of notes and/or higher pitch (example 2). This is the standard arrangement in this chant; but sometimes, particularly at the beginning or end of phrases, the text accent is noticed in the music in exactly the opposite fashion (example 3).

At the next level up, the melody will tend to associate or dissociate words. For example, the melodic patterns sung to single words may not sound complete in themselves, and may require the next parts of a pitch pattern to complete the melodic syntax (example 4).

Example 4

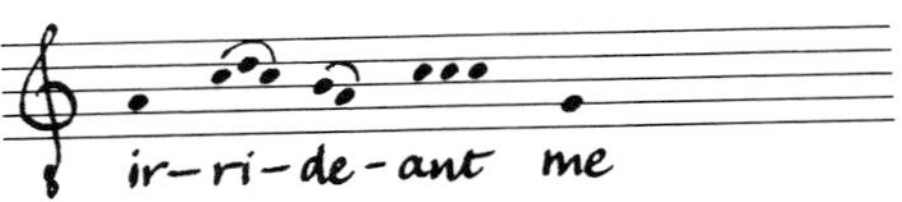

Or the next part of the melody may pick up what has happened immediately before and continue without any caesura (example 5).

Example 5

A special case of this is in phrase III (38–46): here, through the repetition of one pitch as a single note ('recitation') a whole series of words is linked.

As this last example demonstrates, larger numbers of words may be articulated by more long-term strategies. The sense of the melodic patterns in the passages 25–37 (the descending zigzag) and 38–49 (the three-note ascending pattern) becomes apparent when considered with the text. The descending zigzag brings the five words of the text phrase II together in one discrete melodic movement. Then the next five words are joined by a sequential melodic pattern, whose rising pitch takes the melody in the opposite direction to the preceding passage. In the Gregorian Introits it is common for the two halves of a psalm verse to be joined (37 ends on **F**, 38 begins from **F**) and contrasted (downwards movement towards 37, upwards movement from 38) in this way.

Turning to the opposite procedure, dissociation, the passage at the beginning of II provides a classic example: as discussed above, the fall between 14 and 15 creates a sense of caesura. Just before this a major text division has been marked by a fall to the lowest pitch, **F**; at the beginning of II, the melody intones upwards again. The continual pushing upwards from 11 to 14, followed by a melodic caesura, allows those two words 'deus meus' to be heard as exclamation, the climax of a movement upwards since the beginning of I (here the chain of thirds **F** – **a** – **c** allows a join across the textual phrase division).

With the setting of 'deus meus' we confront a procedure through which particular words have been highlighted. Emphasis is achieved elsewhere in less dramatic ways: the stress, through intensification, of the negative pair *non–neque* (example 6), the underlining of the text's large-scale structure through antecedent–consequent endings for I and II (example 7), and rhyming endings for II and IV (example 8), and, perhaps most interesting – given that this is the first chant for mass on Advent Sunday, when a period of waiting is announced – the prominence given to the word 'expectant' (47–9), set as the climax of a melodic pattern begun at 'etenim', given two of the sequential moves in a pattern built of four, and given as many notes for three syllables as the preceding seven syllables (example 9).

Example 6

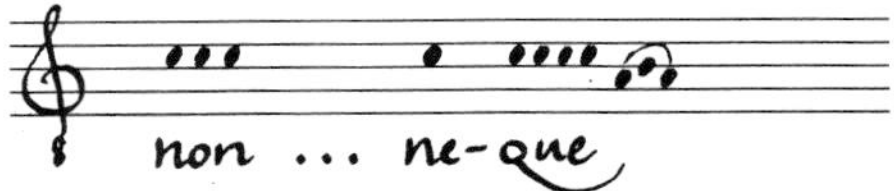

Example 7

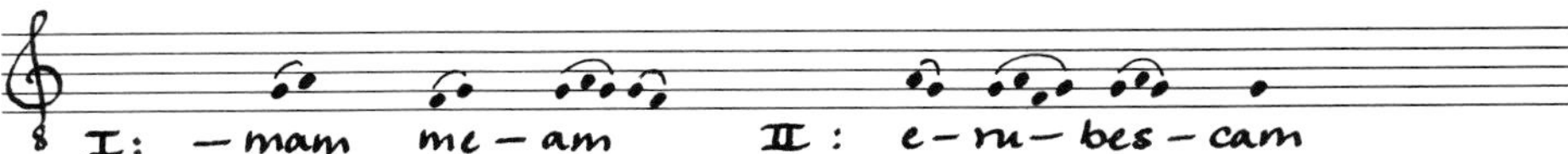

Example 8

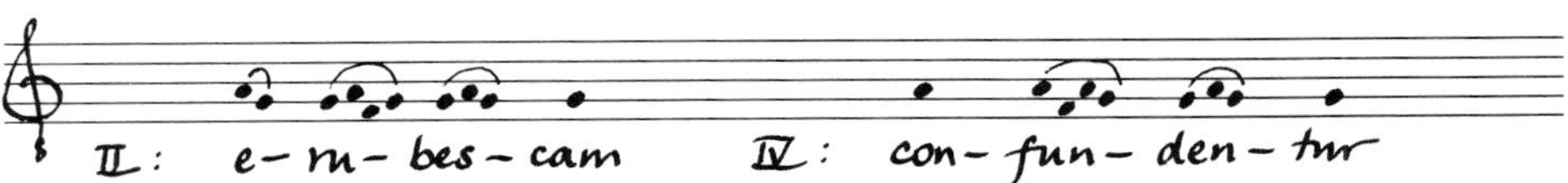

Example 9

It is one of the most impressive aspects of the Gregorian melodic art that it has this ability to pinpoint, emphasise, repeat, divide, move quickly past, round off, pause, literally 'read' the text (but with dimensions of colour and rhythm that the spoken text rarely matches), and thus shape its meaning. The most basic rule observed by this Introit melody is articulation of the syntactical structure of the text. At the same time, through attention to word accent, and through constant variation from one syllable to the next, so that each successive syllable is heard discretely with a different musical sound (except where a recitation pattern is deliberately chosen), the melody 'projects' the sound of the text. Some of these qualities are to do with rhythm, but whether Charlemagne's distress when confronted by the different rhythm of chanting of 'all his provinces' was related to ornamented melody of this kind, or to the more simple recitations of, for example, psalms in the offices, is impossible to tell. The third level of melodic reading is the subtlest: the balancing, linking, contrasting and separating of individual words and longer phrases. As an art, this is music which possesses much more than sensual (for which read 'spiritual' if preferred) power: it is a profoundly interpretative medium – a declamatory discipline capable of extraordinary nuance.

It would be a mistake, however, to infer from all this weight of argument that the only objective of Gregorian chant as sung by Carolingian cantors was to produce subtle performances of texts; so much chant, especially the highly elaborate repertories of the Graduals, Alleluias, Tracts and Offertories, allows much greater melodic freedom. And, taken out of a tight symbiotic relation to the text, the interaction between the two sound mediums is inevitably less intense. A melody such as that for the Easter Day Alleluia with verse *Pascha nostrum* (example 10) calls attention to itself through sheer virtuosity of expression, without being too necessarily connected with text interpretation (beyond the impact of such elaborate presentation).

Example 10

GRADUALE TRIPLEX p.197

Nevertheless, the use of an Introit as example demonstrates a critical aspect of the Gregorian repertory: it is not only the melody which reads the text, but also the text which reads the melody. The relation of syllable and note or note-group determines rhythmic patterns in the melody, determining which notes and patterns are to be heard as opening, continuing and closing gestures.

We have seen in *Ad te levavi* how tight can be the control of the succession of specific tones, and of their functional significance. Were a second example to be introduced, we would be able to see the same concept at work, but, of course, the ways of joining tones together and their relative weight within the melodic structure might be quite different. That the Carolingians regarded music as a kind of language is not in doubt: a first indication of this is the *topos* shared by a whole series of ninth-century treatises setting out the parallels between parts of text and parts of melodic structures. The *Musica enchiriadis*, composed towards the end of the ninth century in northern France, opens with one of the most worked-out statements of this kind:

> As the elementary and individual parts for the speaking voice are letters – syllables composed of them form nouns and verbs and they [in turn] the text of complete speech – so *phthongi*, which are called *soni* ['sounds'] in Latin, are the bases of the singing voice: and the content of the whole of music comes down to them in the final analysis. From the coupling of *soni* [are formed] *diastemata* [= Latin *intervalla*], and from *diastemata* are formed *systemata* [= Latin *constitutiones*]. But *soni* are the first foundations of the chant.[22]

Later in the same treatise, the parallel is carried on into longer structural units:

> Their lesser parts [i.e. of melodies] are the *cola* and *commata* of singing, which mark off the song at its endings. But *cola* are made by two or more *commata* coming together, although there are cases where *comma* or *colon* can be said interchangeably. And the *commata* are made by *arsis* and *thesis*, that is, rising and falling. But sometimes the voice falls in *arsis* and *thesis* just once in a *comma*, at other times more often.[23]

Such lucid and thorough expression of the text music analogy surely displays the results of a century of grammatically biased thinking. Yet the essence of this approach (which can be traced back to a classical Latin, and before that, to a Greek source)[24] is already manifest in a short passage on music composed by none other than Alcuin. The *Musica Albini* begins with an explanation which treats music firmly as part of the liberal arts curriculum:

> A musician ought to know that eight tones exist together in music, through which every modulation ('inflexion of tones') is seen to adhere to itself as if with a kind of glue. A tone is the least part of the rule of music. Just as the least part of grammar [is] a letter so the least part of arithmetic [is] unity. And as speech from letters [and] a cluster of numbers multiplied by unities rises and is raised up, in the same way also every song is modulated (tonally inflected) from a line of sounds and tones. It is defined thus: a tone is the distinctive feature (lit. 'what is taken away', the essential means of reckon-

22 The trans. from H. S. Powers, 'Language models and musical analysis', *Ethnomusicology* 24 (1980) pp. 1–60 at p. 49. 'Sicut vocis articulatae elementariae atque individuae partes sunt litterae, ex quibus compositae syllabae rursus componunt verba et nomina eaque perfectae orationis textum, sic canorae vocis ptongi, qui Latine dicuntur soni, origines sunt et totius musicae continentia in eorum ultimam resolutionem desinit. Ex sonorum copulatione diastemata, porro ex diastematibus concrescunt systemata; soni vero prima sunt fundamenta cantus; *Musica et Scolica enchiriadis*, ed. H. Schmid (Munich, 1981) p. 3.

23 Powers, 'Language models', p. 49. 'Particulae sunt sua cantionis cola vel commata, quae suis finibus cantum distingunt. Sed cola fiunt coeuntibus apte commatibus duobus pluribusve, quamvis interdum est, ubi indiscrete comma sive colon dici potest. At ipsa commata per arsin et thesin fiunt, id est levationem et positionem. Sed alias simplici arsi et thesi vox in commate semel erigitur ac deponitur, alias sepius', *Musica enchiriadis*, p. 22.

24 M. Bielitz, *Musik und Grammatik: Studien zur mittelalterlichen Musiktheorie* (Munich and Salzburg, 1977) pp. 30–1.

ing) of every harmonic arrangement and the specific amount which consists (lit. 'exists together') in an intonation or timbre of voice.[25]

A second indication of the language-orientated approach in Carolingian music is the control exercised in an example like *Ad te levavi* over the functional significance of specific tones and the ways in which individual tones may or may not be allowed to follow others. Our awareness of just how tight was this control is heightened through knowledge of a Roman version of the same melody (example 11).

Example 11

Although this was written down only in the eleventh century – Roman cantors having sustained an entirely oral musical tradition until much later than in the north – it evidently transmits melodic formulations which go back to the common origins of both the Frankish practice and one based continuously in Rome. In this sense the Roman version can be considered as bearing character-

[25] '[O]cto tonos in musica consistere musicus scire debet, per quos omnis modulatio quasi quodam glutino sibi adherere videtur. Tonus est minima pars musicae regulae. Tamen sicut minima pars grammaticae littera sic minima pars arithmeticae unitas. Et quomodo litteris oratio, unitatibus acervus multiplicatus numerorum surgit et erigitur, eomodo et sonorum tonorumque linea omnis cantilena modulatur. Diffinitur autem ita: Tonus est totius constitutionis armonicae differentia, et quantitas quae in vocis accentu sive tenore consistit', from H. Möller, 'Zur Frage der musikgeschichtlichen Bedeutung der Akademie Karls des Grossen: Die *Musica Albini*', in *Akademie und Musik*, ed. W. Frobenius, N. Schwindt-Gross and T. Sick, Saarbrucken Studien zur Musikwissenschaft 13 (Saarbrucken, forthcoming). I am grateful to Dr Möller for allowing me to read his study before publication.

istic traits of what the northern cantors of the late eighth century heard the Romans sing (the repertory is known to musicologists as 'Old Roman').

What the Gregorian and Old Roman melodies conspicuously share is a melodic dialect, strategies for putting notes together and for building patterns. But the actual patterns which they build are not always similar, and often lead to different structural designs. As an example, phrase III is instructive: the descending zigzag of the Gregorian formulation is present also in the Roman, worked through in full twice, and in condensed form several times: the pattern **c** – **a** – **c** – **G** – **c** – **F** is expressed from 26–31 and again (less clearly etched, and now as **a** – **c** – **G** – **c** – **F**) from 32–6. The fall from **c** to **F** is also present in the melisma heard at 30 and again at 36, here falling by step rather than zigzag. Both these melodic versions emphasise a pattern which falls from a high point of reference to the lowest pitch boundary; in the Roman reading, this melodic idea is insisted on through repetition, where in the Gregorian reading, it is stressed through being extremely sharply etched.

Up to now, we hardly appreciate the musical language of Old Roman chant in the same way as that of the Gregorian: a comparison of these versions of one chant needs to be set in the context of better knowledge of techniques of melodic process employed in the Old Roman repertory. Nevertheless, it is evident that the critical difference between the Gregorian and Roman formulations is not in the melodic ideas used, but in the way these are related to the text, and, in consequence, in the way these project a reading of the text. In the Gregorian, the text phrase 'neque irrideant me inimici mei' has to be heard as a unit – both because of the unfolding of the zigzag pattern through its whole length, and because of the joining of words, each new one beginning on the same pitch as that preceding ended – whereas the Roman version neither distinguishes so clearly between this text phrase and what had gone before nor holds the conclusion of the musical process for the conclusion of the textual.

Overall, it is not only that the Old Roman text reading is dissimilar to the Gregorian (for example, in IV, where it is the word 'universi' – all Christian peoples – rather than 'expectant' which receives musical emphasis), but also that it does not work quite so hard on this aspect: little is made of opportunities like 'deus meus', 'non–neque', even the 'non erubescam–non confundentur' rhyme becomes part of a more generally elaborate **G**-cadence behaviour heard also at 'irrideant me'. Above all, articulation of the major syntactical units of the text does not display the same qualities of fine shading and balance as the Gregorian.

This evidence of care and control in the manipulation of musical sounds in Carolingian melody has its counterpart in Carolingian music theory. Beside the music–text *topos* and evidence of a syntactical approach in the Frankish recension of Roman chant, the system of eight modes conceived in the late eighth century and gradually developed in the writings of ninth-century theorists forms a third aspect in the treatment of music as language. For the modal system, in both practical application and theoretical modelling, is nothing other than a set of grammatical rules for ordering the melodic behaviour of a vast, orally-transmitted, repertory.

The early Carolingian goal of musical unification (and its necessary corollary, standardisation) must have been, in large part, achieved through this conceptualisation of the tonal system underlying the Roman chant. Each one of the eight modes represents all of those chants, drawn from different genres, which share a set of tonal characteristics; the modes were not genre-specific (even though some genres use particular modes much more than others). From an analytical viewpoint, these modes can be reduced to scales, differentiated in the relation of each successive tone to that below (either a tone or a semitone). But the Carolingian system was much less reductive than this, and more directly based on melodic families and models. Apart from the *Musica Albini* which, following the passage on the parts of music quoted above, explains why the modes are named as they are (Protus, Deuterus, Tritus, Tetrardus, each in two positions), the earliest documentation of the modal system is a list of chants included at the end of a book containing the Gallican Psalter. The 'Psalter of Charlemagne' (BN lat. 13159) was probably copied to be presented by the king to the Abbey of St Riquier on the occasion of his visit there in the year 800. This earliest exemplar of a 'tonary', a type of document which later became a standard element in the library of any ecclesiastical institution, simply lists under the heading for each of the first five modes (the rest is lost) a series of mass chants in generic order (Introits, Graduals, Alleluias, Offertories, Communions).[26] Such a list would have provided a cantor with a written record of labels (text *incipits*) attached in his memory to particular melodic patterns. In its broadest sense, then, the business of classifying chants into one mode or another ensured the preservation of the correct tonal configurations in individual melodies, *without* the support of musical notation or abstracted explanations of these tonal schemes. At another level, of immediate practical value, the modal system guaranteed the use of a standardised set of melodic recitations for the singing of whole psalms in the office and psalm verses attached to the antiphonal chants of the mass (Introit and Communion, an example being the psalm verse of *Ad te levavi*).

As one of the seven liberal arts, music held a central place in the educational programme promoted by Charlemagne and Alcuin (described by Einhard as 'the most learned man anywhere to be found'), and thence taken over into the monastic and cathedral schools. Primary sources for this branch of learning were the *De musica* of Augustine, the *Institutiones* of Cassiodorus and the *Etymologiae* of Isidore of Seville. All were easily available to the Carolingians. The text which was destined to have the most widespread influence on Carolingian music theory, however, may not have reached the north before the first decades of the

[26] The text of the tonary edited in M. Huglo, *Les Tonaires* (Paris, 1971) pp. 25–9.

ninth century: the earliest extant copy of Boethius' *De institutione musica* (BN lat. 7201) was copied in the first half of the ninth century at a monastic centre in northern France, probably St Amand.[27] A second index of knowledge of Boethius' musical work is the entry in a Reichenau catalogue, made by Reginbert between 835 and 842.[28] Ten sources of the middle or late ninth century and an array of excerpts and glosses suggest an explosion of interest, especially in northern France; nine of the ten sources originated there, and only one in the east, at Freising.[29]

Boethius' work influenced the writings of every Carolingian music theorist, from Aurelian of Réôme, a penitent monk writing in the second quarter of the ninth century,[30] through Hucbald of St Amand and the anonymous French treatises, *Musica* and *Scolica enchiriadis*, the early portions of *Alia musica*, to Regino of Prüm, writing *ca* 900. While there is little in the way of shared new thinking to link these treatises, they are all concerned with the music of the Church and apply themselves in greater or lesser proportion to expounding (and thereby developing) understanding of the system of eight modes,[31] often trying to bring together Boethian theory and chant. Hucbald's *De harmonica institutione* and the *Musica enchiriadis* are the most notable in this respect.

In the Greek and Latin classical worlds the study of music had been concerned primarily with number; it was as a transmitter of this highly sophisticated knowledge that Boethius held a position of such significance in the intellectual life of the later Carolingians. And it was as one of the four disciplines of the quadrivium (arithmetic, geometry, music, astronomy) that Alcuin acknowledged music in a poem addressed to Charlemagne which names (using classical and biblical pseudonyms) some of the scholars and other educated men at court:

> Instituit pueros Idithun modulamine sacro,
> Utque sonos dulces decantent voce sonora.
> Quot pedibus, numeris, rithmo stat musica discant.
> Noctibus inspiciat caeli mea filia stellas
> Adsuescatque deum semper laudare potentem . . .[32]

> Idithun taught boys with sacred *modulamen*
> that they might sing sweet sounds with sonorous voice,
> that they might learn in how many feet, numbers, and rhythm music consists.
> Let my daughter look at the stars of heaven in the nights
> and may she grow accustomed always to praise the powerful God . . .

27 Boethius, *Fundamentals of Music*, trans. C. M. Bower (New Haven and London, 1989) p. xli.

28 M. Bernhard, Überlieferung und Fortleben der antiken lateinischen Musiktheorie im Mittelalter', in: *Geschichte der Musiktheorie* 3, *Rezeption des antiken Fachs im Mittelalter*, ed. F. Zaminer (Darmstadt, 1990) p. 24.

29 Lists of these sources in *Fundamentals*, ed. Bower, pp. xl–xliii, and Bernhard, 'Überlieferung', p. 25.

30 Aureliani Reomensis, *Musica disciplina*, ed. L. Gushee, Corpus Scriptorum de Musica 21 (American Institute of Musicology, 1975); Gushee there proposed the dates 840–9 for the compilation of the treatise. In a recent unpublished study he has revised this to 'the first quarter of the ninth century'.

31 R. Crocker, 'Frankish music theory', in *The Early Middle Ages to 1300*, ed. R. Crocker and D. Hiley, The New Oxford History of Music 2 (2nd edn, Oxford, 1990) pp. 278–83.

32 Alcuin, *Carmen* 26, MGH Poet. I (reprinted Munich, 1978) pp. 246–7.

All of this makes the rapprochement in Carolingian thinking, beginning with Alcuin, between music and the disciplines of the trivium (grammar, rhetoric, dialectic) stand out in greater prominence. Yet what can be read in their musical studies, steeped in a grammatical approach which represents the progressive dimension of musical learning of this period, can also be appreciated in their music. In combining art and learning with theological purpose, they shaped in the 'Gregorian' chant a powerful rhetorical language.[33]

Musical literacy

Musical notations make their first appearance in the west in manuscripts of the ninth century copied in the northern realms of the Carolingian kingdoms.[34] Although, where it is evident that a critical percentage of original material has vanished, the assessment of surviving documents must be approached with circumspection, it is nevertheless difficult to believe that any fairly precise notational system was in widespread use before the Carolingian revival of classical learning was well underway. Not only are there simply no examples of notation datable before (including 'which might be dated before') 820,[35] but in addition the impulses to create and use musical notation can be discovered as *the* central elements in Carolingian policy about, and conception of, music: on the one hand, standardisation, so that the authoritative Roman chant would be correctly sung, on the other, music as a medium which could be handled as a language and which possessed an internal grammar.

The link between such principles and the use of literate modes is hardly specific to Carolingian treatment of music, but relates directly to the use and functions of 'the spoken and the written word' in Carolingian society.[36] For the Franks, 'possession and use of writing were the keys to faith, knowledge and power'.[37] And the intimate association of ecclesiastical chant with the Latin language brought music into the specific linguistic domain most easily and immediately linked with literate traditions.[38] But, while the analogy of music and text leads to many insights about the invention and nature of musical notations, there are two significant areas of divergence in the history of the writing of words and of notes, both related to Carolingian endeavours. In the first place, the Carolingians inherited a Roman-Christian tradition which was

[33] On the persuasive power of music and its analogy to rhetoric in this age, see Morrison, '"Know thyself"', pp. 395–8.

[34] The most recent attempt to compile a list of ninth-century sources, with discussion of previous studies, is in S. Corbin, *Die Neumen*, Palaeographie der Musik I:3, ed. W. Arlt (Cologne, 1977) pp. 3.21–41.

[35] This is the earliest margin of the period suggested by B. Bischoff for the *Psalle modulamina* entry made by the scribe Engyldeo in Munich Clm 9543; see H. Möller, 'Die Prosula "Psalle modulamina" (Mü 9543) und ihre musikhistorische Bedeutung', in: *La tradizione dei Tropi liturgici*, ed. C. Leonardi and E. Menesto (Spoleto, 1990) p. 280.

[36] As described in McKitterick, *Carolingians*.

[37] Ibid., p. 4.

[38] Ibid., p. 21.

already highly literate: stated baldly, they already knew how to write text down (and had but to adapt the methods to their own needs and teach the art of writing more widely). For the writing down of music, however, they had no models (apart from the indirect models available through the association with text reading – metrical signs and punctuation marks), and had to invent *ab initio* ways to do this. Second: while Frankish society in the Carolingian period can be said to have been 'transformed into one largely dependent on the written word for its religion, law, government and learning',[39] the same cannot truly be said of musical notation – the majority of Carolingian notations acted as support of an oral practice, rather than vice versa.

Even in their most sophisticated forms, none of the diverse examples of Carolingian musical notation attempted to convey anything approaching all that was needed in order to sing a melody from knowledge of its written form alone. It would be a misunderstanding to read into this any substantial degree of insufficiency on the part of the notational creators and writers. Undoubtedly, through the hundred years from 800 to 900 processes of discovery and development led to greater refinement in the notation of pitch patterns, inflection, rhythmic nuance and expressive detail; at the same time, however, musical notation can only be understood as formed in response to demands made of it, and those demands, although multiple in the overall picture, were clearly more focused in specific situations. Here it is not so much the variety of ways of writing music down as the variety in the nature of what is written down, both in terms of genre and in terms of quality of information, which comes to mind. The notation made in any individual source is conditioned both by the wish and ability on the part of the notator to record detail and nuance, and by the type of book and user to whom the notation is directed.

The segment of Carolingian society concerned with writing music down, and with reading from it, was hardly as broad as that for which the writing of text became essential. The categories of sources into which musical notation was entered include music theory texts, liturgical collections for celebrants reciting ecclesiastical readings and prayers, liturgical books for the use of cantor and schola, and collections of texts for school use, such as the songs in Boethius' *De consolatione philosophiae*; this implies that many more than professional musicians could be confronted by musical notation, but limits its use to ecclesiastical circles, and to particular elements within them. Though relatively small in the scheme of things, however, the music writers – as we could call them – were at one and the same time spread over a large geographical/cultural area *and* brought into contact with others, through the interaction of royal courts, monasteries, cathedrals, and their schools. Thus the mixed and richly chaotic impression conveyed by surviving sources can in part be explained by the ubiquitousness of the impulse to create and refine ways of notating music. No

39 Ibid., p. 2.

matter which way they may be divided (of which more below), the varieties of notations made in the ninth century indicate that the invention of notation cannot be traced to a single, centrally determined, enterprise (although such a step may have played a part), but to multiple initiatives.

The process of building up funds of notational possibilities, and stylisation of ways of writing notational signs – both characteristic of progressive ecclesiastical centres, led in the tenth century to the establishment of classicised notational types, recognisable as different scripts. These were mainly regionally disposed: Lotharingian, Breton, Aquitainian, central French, German, Anglo-Saxon, Beneventan, and a plethora of northern Italian types. But it is only with difficulty that the 'school' model can be made to fit and interpret the ninth- and early tenth-century sources.[40] Scattered and fragmentary as they may seem, the extant examples of musical notation made in this first century of its appearance speak resoundingly of experimentation, of individual enterprise, of the fast transference of new ideas, and of the extreme skill of select music scribes.

The earliest extant examples of fully-notated chant books – our earliest substantial records of musical notation – belong to this stage of change-over from development and experimentation to established and stylised procedures. Two monuments of notational art, one of 'French', the other of 'German' origin, date from *ca* 900 or shortly after. Both books were intended for the use of professional musicians (the cantor and members of the schola), and contain melodies for the Proper of the mass. Laon, Bibliothèque Municipale 230 (Laon) has all the Proper material (Introit, Gradual, Alleluia or Tract, Offertory, Communion) for each feast;[41] St Gallen, Stiftsbibliothek 359 (SG) has notations for Proper items sung by soloists (Gradual, Alleluia, Tract).[42] Though made a long way apart, and using different music scripts, their notations exhibit a high degree of agreement in melodic patterns, the ways in which these are segmented, inflection and rhythmic detail. Plates 18 and 19 show their notations for the Easter Day Alleluia, with the verse *Pascha nostrum*; in example 12, these are laid out above a version written on staves, which elucidates the pitch pattern of the melody, but contains no rhythmic information.

Though differing in the way they combine straight lines, curves, dots, squiggles and letters, these two notations both set out to show the correspondence between specific musical gestures and syllables of the text; one can easily recognise here the conceptual analogy made in the *Musica enchiriadis* – individual sounds: letters, combining of sounds to make intervals: syllables, combining of

40 W. Arlt, 'Anschaulichkeit und analytischer Charakter: Kriterien der Beschreibung und Analyse früher Neumenschriften', in: *Musicologie médiévale. Notations et séquences*, ed. M. Huglo (Paris, 1987) p. 31.

41 Antiphonale missarum Sancti Gregorii IXe–Xe siècle: codex 239 de la Bibliothèque de Laon, Paléographie musicale 10, ed. A. Mocquereau (Tournai, 1909); this includes a facsimile and study of the manuscript, notably 'Aperçu sur la notation du manuscrit 239 de Laon. Sa concordance avec les "codices" rythmiques sangalliens' by A. Ménager, pp. 177–211.

42 *Cantatorium IXe siècle no. 359 de la Bibliothèque de Saint-Gall*, Paléographie musicale 2nd ser. 2 (Tournai, 1924); on St Gall notation see E. Cardine, *Sémiologie grégorienne* (Solesmes, 1970).

Example 12

LAON

groups of intervals: the text of a complete discourse (with the qualification that an individual syllable may be sung to a single note, to a group of notes, or to a series of groups).[43] Within each note group, and sometimes in the relation between them, both notations convey something of the intervallic content of the melody: thus, for the third syllable (*–lu–*), the Laon notation shows a group of three notes (in example 13, notes 1–3), each successively higher in the vertical writing space, then a group of two rising notes (4–5), the first shown vertically below the last of the previous group, and finally a single note (6), again beginning below the level of the last of the preceding group, moving as it finishes towards the beginning of *–ia*. The content of the St Gall notation is similar, if less precise about pitch and more concerned with continuity within note groups: the six notes are here written in two rather than three gestures, without indication of the intervallic content between the two groups (example 13). In neither case was it the primary object of the notation to indicate precise pitch: a properly trained cantor had the melodic pattern fixed in his memory, and could use such notation as a reminder of the detail of its behaviour, and of its coupling with the text.

43 For the *Musica enchiriadis* passage, see above p. 287.

Example 13

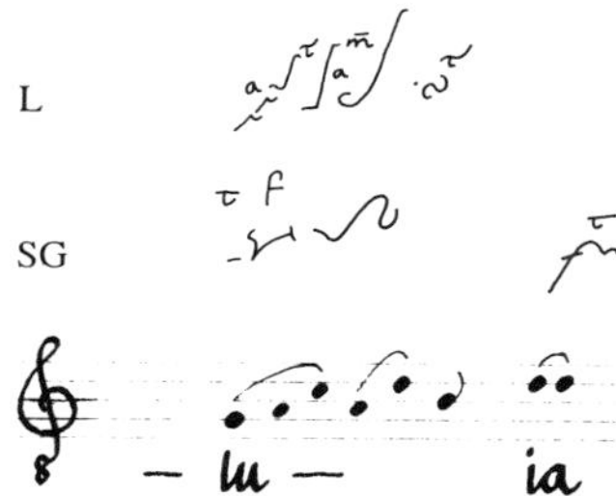

Beyond the recording of melodic gestures, linked to units of text, these notations set out to fix in writing details of inflection (such as the movement on the last note of the *–lu–* melisma), of expression (such as the indication 'f', 'ut cum fragore seu frendore feriatur efflagitat', 'demands insistently that it be struck with clashing or gnashing'),[44] and of rhythmic nuance (such as the holding of certain notes longer than others, indicated by the letter 't', 'trahere' or 'tenere', or the addition – in eastern notations – of a tiny horizontal or diagonal stroke to the basic neume). Considerable effort was invested in this part of the enterprise, and it is only with conscientious study of the semiology of each notator's work that such detail can be fully recognised and, in part, interpreted. The comparison of two passages from the Easter Alleluia of almost identical pitch content illustrates the fundamental orientation of these notations towards subtlety of expression (rather than the precise recording of a pitch pattern). The excerpts α and β shown in example 14 share a melodic pattern which moves up

Example 14

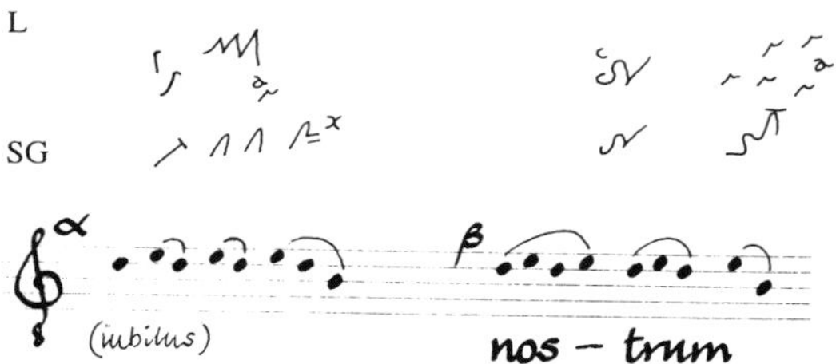

and down between the notes **d** and **e**. In α, the final fall moves from **e** through **d** to **b**; in β, which is one note shorter, the fall is directly from **e** to **b**.

In each of the two notations, the representation of these passages is dissimilar.

[44] The principal source of information on the meaning of these letters is a text attributed to Notker: see J. Froger, 'L'Épître de Notker sur les "lettres significatives". Édition critique', *Études grégoriennes* 5 (1962) pp. 23–71; for translations of many of Notker's instructions see S. Rankin, 'The Song School of St Gall in the later ninth century', Washington Symposium, *The Arts and Letters at St Gall* (1993).

In α, SG divides the notes into 1 + 2 + 2 + (2 + 1);[45] Laon is related to this with 1 + (6 + 1). Both versions contain the 'rhythmic' information that the first note is lengthened (in SG by the modification of to , in Laon by the writing of rather than), that the penultimate note also is more significant than those preceding (in SG by the modification of to in Laon by the fact that this is where the joined-up pattern breaks), and that the last note again receives a separate emphasis (in SG by the use of rather than). Whether the SG x ('exspectare') and the Laon a ('augete') refer to the lengthening of notes or to the greater interval between the last two notes (a third, instead of a second as before), is unclear.

In passage β, both notations divide the notes into 4 + 5; here, far from being emphasised, the first **d** is to be sung 'celeriter' (quickly, lightly – the opposite of the indication 't') according to Laon. In the second note group, where in α the Laon notator had represented a similar succession of pitches with one joined-up neume, he now wrote a series of single notes, thus asking for emphasis of each. The SG notator (who was much less willing to break up neumes into single signs) conveyed an element of emphasis through the addition of an episema to the second neume.

To do justice to the sensitivity of these two notators would take a great deal longer. In both cases we are dealing with high points in the history of local scriptoria at the end of a period of intense experimental activity; some of the results of this activity were picked up by later generations while others were abandoned. Richard Crocker has suggested that this early appearance of sophisticated notations is the direct outcome of the demands made on Frankish cantors: 'it is clear why the earliest neumatic notations [that is, notations of the kind in the Laon and SG books] were the most specific and rich in nuance of inflection and ornamentations; precisely because these were the parameters hardest to remember, most ephemeral'.[46]

The earliest neumatic notations – it would be fair to say those probably made before 850 – appear in situations which connect their use not with the most specialised musical act, the singing of the Propers of the Roman mass, but with the musical functions performed by priests and deacons (liturgical recitations), schoolteachers (recitation of poetry), possibly even cantors (the recording of more ephemeral material – such as new songs). It is only from the last quarter of the ninth century that we have examples of the highly nuanced neumatic scripts which translate onto parchment the detail of the cantor's art, and only from the end of the ninth century that we can follow in extant sources the notation, using such scripts, of the Gregorian melodies.

So careful and detailed are the notations in the Laon and SG books that they can only have been made by skilled singers. Both notators incorporated into

45 The use of brackets here indicates a relation between neumes written in separate strokes.

46 R. Crocker, 'Frankish classification of antiphons', *The Early Middle Ages to 1300* (2nd edn) p. 166.

their work many layers of information of a kind which could easily have been corrupted if copied by less musically sensitive scribes (and the control for which is the agreement between these two manuscripts, and between them and others).[47] In this sense, the notations in the two books can be understood as 'documentations of a performance practice' made by individuals who could build on the experience of some decades of notational experimentation, whether or not their notations represent copies made one or more copying generations removed from earlier notated sources; the task of copying such heavily weighted sign series from an exemplar would have demanded total comprehension of their semiology on the part of the scribe, and thus the ability to recall intricacies of melodic design and relate these to written signs. Paradoxically, it is the high degree of sensitivity of these notations which underlines the strength of the oral tradition passed from cantor to cantor.

It must have been notations of this kind which Hucbald of St Amand had in mind as 'customary notes' (*consuetudinariae notae*) when he compared them with 'more scientific signs' (*artificiales notae*):[48]

> Yet the customary notes are not wholly unnecessary, since they are deemed quite serviceable in showing the slowness or speed of the melody, and where the sound demands a tremulous voice, or how the sounds are grouped together or separated from each other, also where a cadence is made upon them, lower or higher, according to the sense of certain letters – things of which these more scientific signs [letters denoting pitch] can show nothing whatsoever. Therefore if these little letters which we accept as a musical notation are placed above or near the customary notes [neumes], sound by sound, there will clearly be on view a full and flawless record of the truth, the one set of signs indicating how much higher or lower each tone is placed, the other informing one about the afore-mentioned varieties of performance, without which valid melody is not created.[49]

Hucbald's comparison brings to the fore a tension felt by notators from the very beginning, the erratic progress towards a resolution of which (losing the detail of the neumes described by Hucbald) constitutes one of the most significant threads in the history of notation. This was the pull between ways of writing music which intended to provide as exact information as possible (within their limits) of the intended pitch pattern, and other ways of writing which subordinated this task to the indication of qualitative aspects of performance. There are examples of the former above all in music theory treatises of the

[47] See the study by A. Ménager, 'Étude sur la notation du manuscrit 47 de Chartres. Sa concordance avec les codices rythmiques sangalliens et messins' in: *Antiphonale missarum Sancti Gregorii Xe siècle: codex 47 de la Bibliothèque de Chartres*, Paléographie musicale 11 (1912) pp. 41–131. The manuscript, made in the late ninth or early tenth century and destroyed in 1944, was notated in 'Breton' neumes.

[48] Despite the use of palaeofrankish notation at the Abbey of St Amand (see below), it is likely that Hucbald became aware of other notation types while teaching elsewhere; that he had a strong interest in methods of notation is made abundantly clear in his writing.

[49] Hucbald, *De harmonica institutione*, trans. W. Babb, ed. C. V. Palisca, *Hucbald, Guido, and John on Music* (New Haven and London, 1978) p. 37; for the Latin text see Hucbald von Saint-Amand, *De harmonica institutione*, ed. A. Traub in: *Beiträge zur Gregorianik* 7 (1989) pp. 3–101.

ninth century: in Hucbald's *De harmonica institutione* a letter system derived from the teaching of Boethius, and in the *Musica enchiriadis* two systems (used together), one based on a series of signs, each of which signifies a pitch (Daseian notation) and one very like the later stave system, where the syllables of the words sung are arranged in different vertical positions, their height an indication of their pitch. Plate 20 shows an example from a copy of the *Musica enchiriadis* made at Christ Church, Canterbury in the later tenth century (Cambridge, Corpus Christi College 260). The potential of a range of vertical positions in open space ('in campo aperto') to represent pitches was also exploited in notations more closely linked with musical practice, although with much less consistency and precision. Plate 21 shows entries in a long list of mass Proper chants included in the Sacramentary BN lat. 2291 (made at St Amand for St Germain des Prés *ca* 870);[50] the notations above two incipits which both begin *Exaudi* were made so that the user could be reminded of their different melodic patterns (see example 15 (a) and (b)).

Example 15

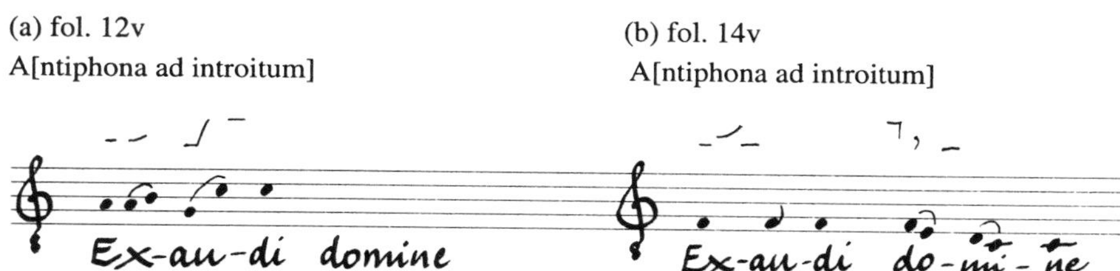

The first follows the unfolding pitch pattern especially closely. These notations appear in a book intended for a priest. A third category of source – the cantors' books which survive from the early tenth century on – also showed tendencies in this direction. Example 16 shows the notation in Laon 239 of a passage from the Palm Sunday Tract *Deus, deus meus*; because of the restricted range of the melody at this point, the notator was able to convey (with sporadic breaks) precise pitch information.

Example 16

[50] On this see J. Deshusses, 'Chronologie des grands sacramentaires de Saint-Amand', *Revue bénédictine* 87 (1977) pp. 230–7.

Such an example represents an extreme in this kind of source. Until the middle of the eleventh century, the balance in these cantors' books between 'diastematy' (heightening to indicate pitch) and qualitative aspects was more often towards the latter.

In all three source categories – the theory treatises, the books for priests and deacons, and cantors' books – the examples chosen have illustrated the aptness of notational design to a specific task, the ability of notation to communicate or remind the user of precisely what he needed to know. This was not always the case: there are plenty of examples, beginning from the *Psalle modulamina* notation of *ca* 820, and including such notations as those provided for Boethius' songs in a ninth-century St Gallen source[51] and for the song of the nightingale, *Sum noctis socia* in a ninth-century Fleury source,[52] which were much less satisfactory. Where the notated melody had no place in the Roman chant, and therefore no support in the form of recorded modal classification nor roots in a widely preserved oral tradition, the use of non- or semi-diastematic neumes left the uninitiated singer with no idea how to sing the notated melody. As Hucbald put it

> the signs which custom has handed down to us and which in various regions are given no less various shapes, although they are of some help as an aid to one's memory . . . the markings by which they guide the reader are always indefinite . . . you cannot even detect how this [the intervallic pattern of the melody] was prescribed by the composer unless you get it by ear from someone.[53]

*

While it is easy to perceive the relation between the sheer variety of notational methods available in parts of the Carolingian realm within a relatively short space of time and the widespread move towards literate modes in the fields of education and religion under the Carolingian kings, it is much less easy to identify points of origin, to distinguish between beginnings and developments, to understand the intellectual procedures which led particular individuals to conceive specific sign systems in the way they did. On this last, a whole series of backgrounds have been sketched out, this question claiming the attention of more early studies of neumes than any other. In a period of scholarship on Gregorian chant dominated by the (in many areas unsurpassed) studies of Peter Wagner, his promotion of the theory that neumes were derived from the Alexandrian prosodic accents used by Roman grammarians gained wide acceptance.[54] More recent studies have moved away from this explanation, recognising its historical attractions as illusory and little in accordance with the earliest

51 Naples, Biblioteca nazionale IV.G.68; for a description of the MS see C. Leonardi, 'I codici di Marziano Capella', *Aevum* 34 (1960) pp. 412–4.

52 Berne, Burgerbibliothek 36, vol. 139v; facs. of this page in W. Frei, 'Ein weltliches Neumen-Dokument aus dem 9. Jahrhundert in Codex 36 der Burgerbibliothek Bern', *Schweizerische Musikzeitung* 105 (1965) pp. 7–10.

53 Hucbald, *De harmonica institutione*, trans. Babb, p. 36.

54 P. Wagner, *Einführung in die Gregorianische Melodien* II: *Neumenkunde* (Leipzig, 1912).

layers of evidence.[55] That has left two principal hypotheses about the resources drawn on by the neume inventors: 'cheironomy', the explanation that 'musical neumes were written counterparts of choirmasters' hand-gestures, tracing melodic trajectories during performance',[56] and punctuation signs, a system developed principally by northern French scribes in the late eighth century which aided the reader in the correct delivery of the text. Since cheironomy belongs to the act of singing (without reading from notation) and the punctuation signs to the business of writing, we can imagine the conceptual leap from one to the other as the primary force which shaped the invention of neumes.

The association of and analogies between punctuation signs and neumes lead us back to the plain or more flowery accounts of Einhard and Notker, both of whom speak of Charlemagne's interest in the correct reading of lessons and chanting of psalms in the same breath. This provides at least circumstantial evidence in support of Treitler's claim that 'the early music-writing technology itself is ... dependent, in semiotic principle and paleographic form, on the Carolingian system of punctuation', from which he argues that 'the institution of [punctuation] in centres of Carolingian writing toward the end of the 8th century would mark some sort of *terminus ante quem non* for the invention of the neumes'.[57] Discussion of the period when neumes were invented, and the relation between types of use, development of neumatic systems and chronology is even more troubled by cross currents of historical belief than that of how the signs were invented. Not only is there great opportunity for confusion in the interpretation of the evidence – in that the surviving sources of notation are few, often brief, sometimes fragmentary, and difficult to date (how can neumes added by a hand which is not the text hand be dated?) – but there is a significant disagreement as to whether those sources which do survive represent early uses and types of notation in a manner proportionally true to what must once have existed.[58]

All of this is relevant to the question of how the Roman chant was learnt by the Frankish cantors: whether, as Levy has argued, 'an authoritative noted archetype of the Frankish–Gregorian Propers',[59] a book containing full notation for the Roman chants to be sung through the Carolingian realm was in circulation before 800. Against this stands the weight of direct evidence (the notations which do survive, and which do not until the later ninth century deal with Gregorian Propers) and the likelihood that oral transmission lasted longest and most successfully in those parts of the community best trained to depend on it, that is, the professional cantors.

55 See, principally, the discussion in L. Treitler, 'Reading and singing: on the genesis of Occidental music-writing', *Early Music History* 4 (1984) pp. 151–4.

56 K. Levy, 'On the origin of neumes', *Early Music History* 7 (1987) p. 63; this study includes a useful summary of previous theories on the origin of neumes.

57 L. Treitler, 'Communication', *Journal of the American Musicological Society* 41 (1988) p. 566.

58 The main arguments are set out in K. Levy, 'Charlemagne's archetype of Gregorian chant', *Journal of the American Musicological Society* 40 (1987) pp. 1–30 and Treitler, 'Communication'.

59 Levy, 'On the origin' p. 61.

Central to the unravelling of the complex of problems surrounding the origin and early uses of neumes must be consideration of the dichotomy between shared content and disparate ways of recording that content. And that in turn implies reflection on the nature of the disparity between notations which look different, but which are based on similar conceptions of how to write music down, and notations which, in translating sound into sign, are conceptually unalike. It now seems clear that the premise that notations which often use separate signs for one melodic gesture (in Laon for) and the notations which tend to write the gesture in one symbol (in SG for the same) stem from separate conceptions of notation is incorrect.[60] As was evident in the Laon example discussed above, the 'point notation' usually had the option of writing the same melodic gesture in joined-up form (in Laon or for); the insistence on individual signs represents a relatively late development inspired by the attempt to provide more rhythmic information (the individual signs implying greater rhythmic emphasis). This does not itself argue for the sharing of a common 'primitive' set of notations (of the Gregorian chant), but for the sharing of a pool of ideas about how to make notation. From that pool individual scribes developed strategies of notating[61] which formed the basis of regional practice. And the different script types are already apparent in notations of the first half of the ninth century, well before the point at which we encounter their stylised, practised, use.

The metaphor of a 'pool of strategies' proposed by Arlt has to allow for disparity also in the whole conception of how a line or curve drawn on parchment represents melodic behaviour. For there are two distinct approaches in the ninth-century survivals. The fundamental premise of the system which came to dominate, and to which both the Laon and St Gall notations belong, was that individual notes could be shown in two ways: (St Gall), (Laon), with an implied pitch difference between the two. Other neumes could be built up, thus could be written as (St Gall), and as (St Gall), as (Laon). The other approach, characteristic of the neumes named 'palaeofrankish' by Handschin,[62] has no such fundamental signs, but instead the principle of joining positions in space which represent notes: means (rather than a single note), and . Symptomatic of this most extreme iconic (i.e. based on resemblance)[63] approach is this notation's lack of consciousness of a sign system.[64] In the earliest example (the notation for part of a Greek Gloria in the St Amand Sacramentary BN lat. 2291), the notator used six different ways of expressing the melodic pattern within the space of twelve short lines of notation ( ).[65]

60 Ibid., pp. 65ff; Arlt, 'Anschaulichkeit und analytischer Charakter' pp. 37ff.

61 This model is Arlt's, ibid.

62 J. Handschin, 'Eine alte Neumenschrift', *Acta musicologica* 22 (1950) pp. 69–97.

63 The terms 'iconic' and 'symbolic' were introduced into the discussion of early notations in L. Treitler, 'The Early history of music writing in the west', *Journal of the American Musicological Society* 35 (1982) pp. 237–78.

64 This is more true of the earlier than the later examples; as the notation became more established so it became more systematic.

65 Handschin, 'Eine alte Neumenschrift', p. 77; this includes a facsimile.

The palaeofrankish neumes belonged in the very heart of the Carolingian realm, associated above all with St Amand, but found also on the eastern side at Corvey. That they could co-exist alongside the other developing scripts is only another mark of the Carolingians' inventive, highly experimental attitude towards musical notation. Any attempt to refine a chronological model of the emergence of musical notations beyond that which we already have (which is unable to link specific notational techniques with specific periods before 900) will have to admit heterogeneous chaos as a fundamental characteristic of the situation throughout the period of Carolingian rule.

Musical creativity

The Roman chant had been imposed on the Frankish cantors from above: now the Franks acted under the constraint of a centrally disseminated authoritative liturgy. Yet any word or sense of limitation produced by this is noticeably absent from writings of the period (composed, it must be admitted, by those in positions of established authority). The freedom for individual and communal expression in local liturgical practice (which had always been allowed by the Roman Church) was not diminished so much as deflected. As in other artistic spheres, the instilling of new force into what was presented by authority as a renewal brought its own dynamic to musical composition. Much of the new composition is 'elucidatory' in nature, prompted by the Franks' need to make the Roman repertory their own. However, while the friction between Frankish and Roman practices had significant influence on Carolingian musical culture, the aspect of continuity, of the perpetuation of older creative modes and their re-interpretation in the new conditions of an educated Christian society, is equally important.

The cross-currents and interaction of the older and the newer musical stimuli produced an abundance of diverse compositional types, such that any attempt to order them generically can hardly succeed. There are plenty of compositions of traditional kinds (some with new stylistic features), including those related to standard liturgical requirements such as hymns and offices for newly established feasts, and settings of Latin poetry, sometimes classical, sometimes newly composed for religious or courtly purposes. But in addition to these, ninth-century sources preserve in smaller or larger numbers other liturgically orientated compositions of less established nature. Many of the compositions transmitted in tenth- and eleventh-century sources represent Carolingian invention, but the more settled procedures and terminology reflected by these later sources cannot be projected backwards, since they pick up and exploit certain Carolingian initiatives and abandon others.

> *Sing to him a new song, sing to him well.* Every man asks how he should sing to God. Sing to him, but do not sing badly . . . This is how he gives you a way of singing: do not seek for words, as though you could explain what God

> delights in. Sing in jubilation . . . What is singing in jubilation? Understanding, but being unable to explain in words, what is sung in the heart . . . for the ineffable is he of whom you cannot speak. And if you cannot speak of him, and ought not to keep silent, what remains but that you utter a *jubilus*? That the heart should rejoice without words, and that the limitless expanse of joy should not bear the constraint of syllables.[66]

In Augustine's commentary on the psalm verse 'Cantate domino canticum novum' (32:3), we seem to touch on one of the most widespread musical practices of the western Church;[67] Augustine's commentary did not seek to justify a new kind of musical expression, but to provide a Christian theological basis for an old one. Several centuries later, evidence of free musical expression, without words, can be discovered in various parts of the Old Roman and Ambrosian rites, as well as the Gregorian.[68] The standard manner of incorporating such expression into the Gregorian mass was within the third Proper chant, the Alleluia: between the 'Alleluia' itself and the verse was sung an untexted melisma, known as the 'iubilus'. But there were other ways in which musicians fashioned new compositions from old, exploiting the opportunity given official sanction by commentaries such as Augustine's: by the further extension of Alleluia chants with longer closing melismas, by the addition of melismas to the responsories of the office (the most elaborate of the office chants, and, like the Gradual and Alleluia of the mass, sung by soloists), by the interpolation of elaborate melismas between psalm verse and Introit antiphon.

Such added or interpolated melodies could be extraordinarily long, but they were not necessarily so. Nor did their pitch range and melodic formulation of itself call for virtuosity (in the same manner as, for example, the verses of the Roman Graduals); many of these added melodies were composed as harmonious extensions of that which they elaborated. Nevertheless, the Frankish melodies *can* sound rather different from those of the Gregorian repertory. In the melody named *Fulgida* in a French source of *ca* 900 (the melody possibly composed long before),[69] constant repetition of the falling pattern **cbaaG** or **caaG**, the use of the rising pattern **DG ac** in conjunction with a **G**-final melody, and the swooping scalic behaviour of the third phrase pair, all set the idiom apart from the Rome-based chant (example 17).

Fulgida is one of a small repertory of examples notated in the ninth century, or close to it, which were probably intended to be sung at mass following the Alleluia. The new melisma would replace the second singing of Alleluia and

66 Augustine, *Enarrationes in Psalmos*, trans. Cattin, *Music of the Middle Ages* pp. 162–3.

67 B. Stäblein, 'Modes of underlaying a text to melismas: trope, sequence and other forms', in: *Report of the English Congress of the International Musicological Society New York 1961*, ed. J. LaRue (Kassel etc., 1961) pp. 12–29.

68 Ibid.

69 Autun, Bibliothèque municipale 28S, p. 64; facs. and study in B. Stäblein, 'Zur Frühgeschichte der Sequenz', *Archiv für Musikwissenschaft* 18 (1961) pp. 1–33. The transcription shown here represents a reconstruction based on heighted versions of the melody, adapted to the information of the non-diastematic neumes.

Example 17

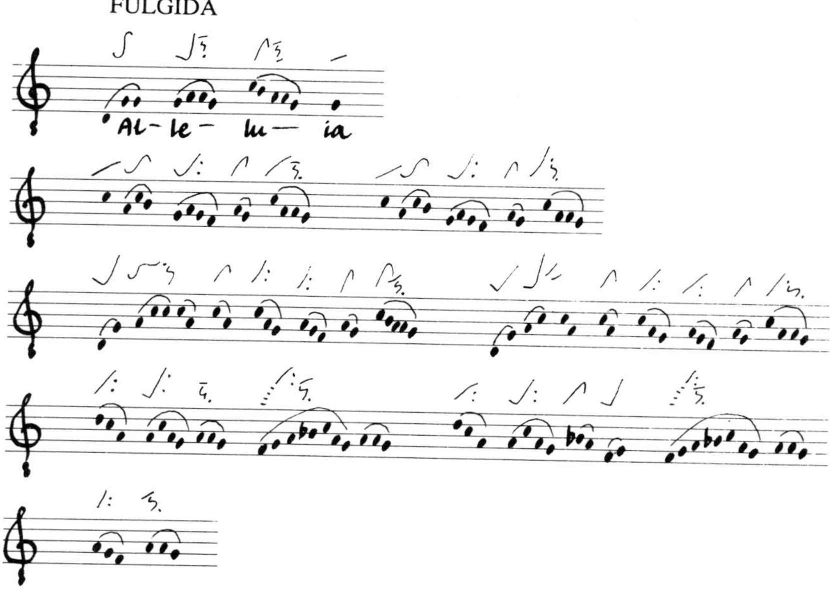

iubilus in the scheme Alleluia, *iubilus*, verse, Alleluia, *iubilus*.[70] This practice was described by the liturgist Amalarius in a manner noticeably dependent on Augustine's psalm commentary:

> The verse 'Alleluia' touches the cantor inwardly so that he may think in what way he ought to praise the Lord and in what way to rejoice. The jubilation, which cantors call a 'sequence' (a following) brings that condition to our mind when the uttering of words will not be necessary, but by thinking alone mind will show to mind what it holds within itself.[71]

Amalarius had already been given responsibility under Charlemagne; his *Liber officialis* was written before 823, probably at Aachen. This and his study of the office liturgy demonstrate a wide knowledge of the details of both Roman and Frankish practice. Specifically in relation to the addition of melismas to liturgical melodies, Amalarius' remarks can be read as implying that there is nothing new or unusual about the practice,[72] and that is an impression upheld by the source material.

The significance of the Alleluia chant as an expression of praise, very much in

[70] R. Crocker, 'The sequence', in: *Gattungen der Musik in Einzeldarstellungen: Gedenkschrift Leo Schrade*, ed. W. Arlt, E. Lichtenhahn and H. Oesch (Bern and Munich, 1973) p. 275.

[71] 'Versus alleluia tangit cantorem interius, ut cogitet in quo debeat laudare Dominum aut in quo laetari. Haec iubilatio, quam cantores sequentiam vocant, illum statum ad mentem nostram ducit, quando non erit necessaria locutio verborum, sed sola cogitatione mens menti monstrabit quod retinet in se.' Amalarius, *Liber officialis*, III: De officio missae xiii–xiiii in: J-M. Hanssens, *Amalarii episcopi opera liturgica omnia* II, Spicilegium Friburgense 139 (Rome, 1948) p. 304.

[72] J. Handschin, 'Trope, sequence, conductus', in: *Early Medieval Music up to 1300*, ed. Dom A. Hughes, The New Oxford History of Music 2 (1st edition, Oxford, 1954) p. 124.

accord with the Augustinian description of jubilation, and the recognised place for an untexted melisma within the Gregorian Alleluia allowed this part of the mass to act as the focus for much of this purely musical creative expression. But the survival of substantial repertories of melismatic interpolations (melismatic 'tropes') for Introit chants in the books of eastern Frankish monasteries, most prominently those at Mainz and St Gall, indicates that the practice of melodic extension was not restricted to the Alleluia alone.[73] As an example, the Introit for the feast of Holy Innocents, *Ex ore infantium*, is shown here with the interpolations recorded in a mid-tenth-century St Gall book (Stiftsbibliothek 484); every phrase which lacks text constitutes an addition to the Gregorian structure (example 18).

Example 18

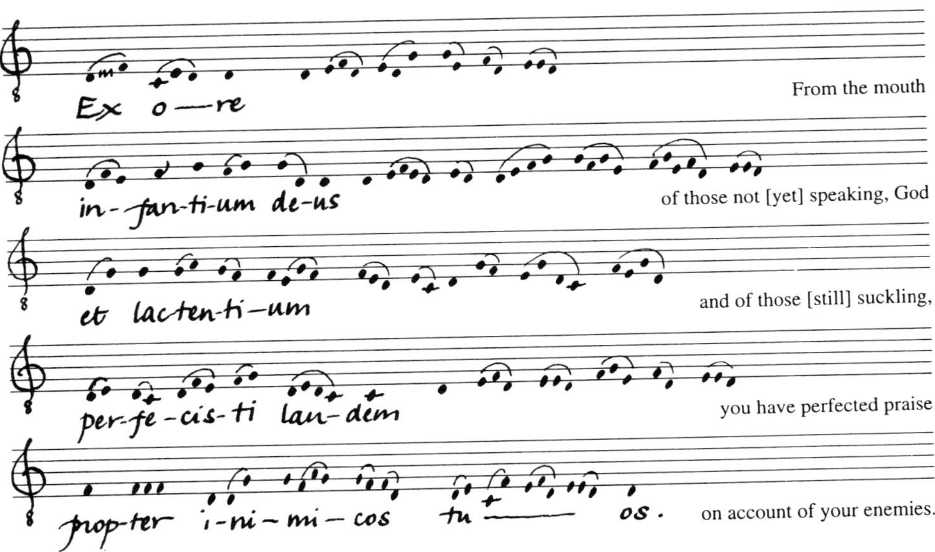
Ex o—re
From the mouth
in-fan-ti-um de-us
of those not [yet] speaking, God
et lacten-ti—um
and of those [still] suckling,
per-fe-cis-ti lau-dem
you have perfected praise
propter i-ni-mi-cos tu— os.
on account of your enemies.

One can easily believe that these new melodic phrases represent home St Gall composition, so much do they remain close to the idiom of the base chant and preserve its melodic syntax (excepting between the fourth and fifth phrases); the desire to uphold 'Roman' traditions is writ loud in this period of the Abbey's history.

Smaller repertories of such melismatic tropes appear in a few late tenth- and early eleventh-century books from south-west France, showing that this manner of building up the Introit was not limited to the east.[74] But it was already on the wane in that period from which the extant written sources

73 See A. Haug, 'Das ostfränkische Repertoire der meloformen Introitustropen', *International Musicological Society Study Group Cantus Planus: Papers read at the Fourth Meeting Pécs, Hungary 1990* (Budapest, 1992).

74 M. Huglo, 'Aux origines des tropes d'interpolation: le trope méloforme d'introït', *Revue de Musicologie* 64 (1978) pp. 5–54.

survive in some number. Such additions to the Roman chant were probably as much an art of performance as of recorded composition, and it is likely that what survives in written form represents only a fraction of what was actually sung; if the written sources of the tenth century present a reasonably true picture of liturgical practice, the interpolation of melismas had by then been displaced by the more popular texted trope (see below). The practice of weaving new melodies between the phrases of the Roman Introit is itself certainly Carolingian; remnants such as the *Ex ore infantium* melismas from St Gall illustrate one of many ways in which an active synthesis of Roman and Frankish music was achieved in the late Carolingian period.

Example 19

Words over the staves in capitals show the Alleluia text; slurs show note grouping in the melismatic chant. The new prosula text is under the staves.

Synthesis of a different kind had given rise to numerous experiments much earlier. The pervasive Carolingian interest in the Latin language had led to the texting of much of this melismatic material. If older chants could be elaborated with new melodies, why not the reverse – the elaboration of older melodies with new texts? An early example illustrates how this process of texting could work: in the 'prosula' *Psalle modulamina*, each note of a Gregorian alleluia is given one syllable of text (example 19).[75] The choice and order of words is related to the original arrangement of note-groups in the Alleluia, and the sound and placing of words reflects the original text arrangement:

Al- le- lu- ia. Christus resurgens . . .
Psal-le . . . dul-cia . . . Christus eripuit nos . . . resurgens . . .

Thus the new text has absorbed rather than replaced the older material.[76] Moreover, the syntax of the melody has been used as a model for that of the text, *and* the formulation of the text itself has produced a more exacting reading of the melody.

Yet another cross-breed is the 'partially-texted sequence', a kind of piece related to the long melismas which concluded alleluias, but which also had some texted sections. Although some have seen in these pieces an evolutionary stage between free untexted melody and the full texting of such melody, the most detailed investigation of this small repertory has led to a different conclusion: that the texted sections may themselves be relics of an older Gallican tradition, around which melismas were later woven.[77]

Far more dominant in the overall picture than either the prosula or these partially texted pieces, however, are two types of composition both quintessentially Carolingian, and both taken up as the main avenues for new musical composition in the succeeding centuries. Both involve a synthesis of Roman and Frankish material, although one appears to have shed its Roman skin at quite an early stage.

Most prominent among the new forms of the ninth century is the poetico-musical form now called 'sequence' or 'prose'. In its classic form, apparent in sources of the late ninth and tenth centuries, the sequence consisted of a text set syllabically to a melody arranged in a series of couplets, i.e. two successive lines set to the same melody, then another two lines sung to another melody; the first and last lines were often singles. This produced the form a bb cc dd . . . αα β. Within this framework, poet-musicians fashioned some of the freshest and most artful compositions of the age, with the *Liber ymnorum* of Notker Balbulus (literally, the 'stammerer') of St Gall standing as one of the great monuments of Carolingian creation. Notker's ability to compose lyrical

75 The transcription given here is based on that in B. Stäblein, 'Zwei Textierungen des Alleluia Christus resurgens in St. Emmeram-Regensburg', in: *Organicae Voces: Festschrift Joseph Smits van Waesberghe* (Amsterdam, 1963) pp. 157–67.

76 Crocker, 'New Frankish forms', *The Early Middle Ages to 1300* (2nd edn) p. 246.

77 W. von den Steinen, 'Die Anfänge der Sequenzendichtung', *Zeitschrift für Schweizerische Kirchengeschichte* 40 (1946) pp. 208–10; Stäblein, 'Zur Frühgeschichte', p. 30.

texts laden with imagery into shapes largely controlled by musical design was hardly equalled elsewhere. But the new art-form was a western as well as an eastern Frankish phenomenon, and the sequences of the west are often more rhapsodic and musically interesting. A stunning example of poetic and musical art, full of metaphorical and liturgical allusions, and yet with immediately

Example 20

Clangam, filii, ploratione una

A-li-tis cy-gni qui trans-fre-ta-vit ae-quo-ra.
O quam a-ma-re la-men-ta-ba-tur, a-ri-da

Se de-re-li-quis-se flo-ri-ge-ra et pe-tis-se al-ta ma-ri-a,
a-iens: In-fe-lix sum a-vi-cu-la, Heu mi-hi, quid agam mi-se-ra?

Pen-nis so-lu-ta in-ni-ti lu-ci-da non po-te-ro hic in-stil-la.
Un-dis qua-ti-or pro-cel-lis hinc in-de nunc al-li-dor ex-su-la-ta.

An-gor in-ter ar-ta gur-gi-tum ca-cu-mi-na, →
Cer-nens co-pi-o-sa pis-ci-um le-gu-mi-na, →

ge-mens a-la-ti-zo in-tu-ens mor-ti-fe-ra non con-scendens su-pe-ra.
non que-o in den-so gur-gi-tum as-su-me-re a-li-men-ta op-ti-ma.

Or-tus oc-ca-sus pla-gae po-li ad-mi-ni-stra-te lu-ci-da si-de-ra.
Suf-fla-gi-ta-te O-ri-o-na, ef-fu-gi-tan-tes nubes oc-ci-du-as.

Dum haec co-gi-ta-ret ta-ci-ta, ve-nit ru-ti-la ad-mi-ni-cu-la au-ro-ra.
Op-pi-tu-la-ta af-fla-mi-ne coe-pit vi-ri-um re-cu-pe-ra-re for-ti-a.

O-va-ti-zans iam a-ge-ba-tur in-ter al-ta →
Hi-la-ra-ta ac iu-cun-da-ta nimis fac-ta, →

et con-su-e-ta nu-bi-um si-de-ra.
pe-ne-tra-ba-tur ma-ri-um flu-mi-na.

Dul-ci-mo-de can-ti-tans vo-li-ta-vit ad a-moe-na a-ri-da.
Con-cur-ri-te om-ni-a a-li-tum et con-cla-ma-te ag-mi-na:

Re-gi ma-gno sit glo-ri-a. A-men.

affective impact, is the 'Planctus cigni' (Lament of the swan), composed somewhere in France in the late ninth or early tenth century (example 20).[78] Neither the melodic idiom nor the constantly syllabic text-music relation of this bears any relation to the Gregorian chant. The melody has no recitation patterns, and its tonal structure is made up of a series of statements which share tiny motifs, but do not work for coherence or cross-reference within a unified whole so much as for an increase in tension. This builds with the story; but, as the words slowly bring the swan back to safety, the high pitch and winding contours of the melody are transformed to mellifluous expression (example 21):

Example 21

In the preface to his *Liber ymnorum*, Notker had justified his new compositions with the explanation that they represented textings of the long melodies of chant which he had difficulty remembering in his youth.[79] His models had come from northern France, written underneath alleluia melismas in a book brought to St Gall by a monk of Jumièges fleeing from the Norse invaders. The explanation is typically Notkerian – fascinating in its narrative details but with some historical content, humble in tone, as befits a Christian monk and artist – but probably limited to only a small part even of Notker's experience, let alone the larger historical situation onto which it is often projected. Among the forty compositions in the *Liber ymnorum*, two rather different formal types can be distinguished (those made in couplets, and those not), and a substantial number cannot be formally related to any surviving alleluia melisma.[80] And, as with the *Planctus cigni*, some of the oldest sequence melodies (including some of those used by Notker) are so different from Gregorian melody that no connection could be imagined; these could, of course, represent textings of the Frankish melismas described by Amalarius. Again, as with all else of this time, the early sources encourage a sense of active development: there are many antecedents to what emerged as 'the sequence' with a place following the alleluia in the liturgy, by the time the Carolingians had lost power.

The other major Frankish invention of the ninth century was the fully texted trope, a kind of composition which has its roots in the same techniques of

[78] See B. Stäblein, 'Die Schwanenklage. Zum Problem Lai – Planctus – Sequenz', in: *Festschrift K. G. Fellerer* (Regensburg, 1962) p. 491–4; the transcription here is based on the two notations of the melody in Paris, BN lat. 1121 (fols. 67v, 196v–197r), with the text as edited in D. Norberg, *Manuel pratique de latin médiéval* (Paris, 1968) pp. 174–6. A translation of the sequence appears in Godman, *Poetry* pp. 322–5.

[79] Ed. in W. von den Steinen, *Notker der Dichter und seine geistige Welt*, 2 vols. (Bern, 1948), II pp. 8–10.

[80] R. Crocker, *The Early Medieval Sequence* (Berkeley, Los Angeles and London, 1977) pp. 11ff., 395ff.

elaboration as the sequence, but which – through its function – remained more closely allied to Gregorian chant. Like the sequence, possible antecedents of the text tropes are the untexted melodies added and interepolated into Gregorian structures, such as those for the Introit *Ex ore infantium* shown above. But the extant sources are too late and fragmentary for it to be possible to establish a chronology for each individual trope – some of which began life as melismatic tropes and were subsequently texted, and some of which were first composed with text, but also performed without. Tropes were made for all the chants of the Proper and Ordinary, the greatest number being for the Introit, followed by the Offertory, Communion, Kyrie and Gloria chants. All of these categories are represented in sources of the late ninth and first half of the tenth century.

The purpose of these compositions was both to enhance and to elucidate parts of the Roman liturgy. Most significant in this respect is the new liturgical function of the Introit chant: where, in Rome, this had been sung by a special choir (the schola cantorum), accompanying the procession into the church of the pope and his clerics, now in the Frankish monasteries it became the opening *communal* statement in the major daily liturgical service.[81] This had far-reaching consequences for the developing practice of troping, giving it a place within that important moment of communal expression, and encouraging the composition by individual cantors of new songs made for the communities they served. So there grew up, during the tenth and eleventh centuries, large locally based and regionally divided repertories of tropes.

It is possible in the case of a small number of tropes represented in the oldest extant 'tropers' to look back to the oldest layers of this kind of composition, traceable back to the last decades of the ninth century. That some of these are represented in books from both east and west points to the communication from one centre to another of such new compositions at an early stage (it is less common with later material). These oldest text tropes are far from uniform in character or form: some simply invite all present to sing, some work out the theological implications of the chant text in a more expansive way, some overshadow the chant by presenting around it a text which creates a new narrative for the whole; some are in prose, some in verse (including hexameters), some are long, some short. There is really no principle of composition beyond the provision of a new context for an older liturgical song. In the east, Notker's friend and fellow monk Tuotilo composed for the Easter Offertory a celebratory introduction – calling on the monastic community to rejoice and sing (the text of the Offertory chant is shown here in capitals to distinguish it from the added trope):[82]

[81] W. Arlt, 'Zu einigen Fragen der Funktion, Interpretation und Edition der Introitustropen', in: *Liturgische Tropen*, ed. Silagi, pp. 132–4.

[82] A hypothetical reconstruction of the melody for this trope (based on the unheightened St Gall neumes) is given in S. Rankin, 'Notker und Tuotilo: Schöpferische Gestalter in einer neuen Zeit', *Schweizer Jahrbuch fur Musikwissenschaft* 11 (1991) p. 24.

Gaudete et cantate
quia hodie surrexit dominus de sepulchro:
TERRA TREMUIT ET QUIEVIT
DUM RESURGERET IN IUDICIO DEUS
ALLELUIA.

Be joyful and sing
for today the Lord has risen from the sepulchre:
THE EARTH TREMBLED AND WAS STILL
WHEN GOD WAS RISING AGAIN IN JUDGMENT
ALLELUIA.

Psalm 75: 9–10

In stark contrast to this is a composition probably from the northern area between Seine and Rhine. For the same Easter Offertory chant, this set of trope elements refers to the (apocryphal) story of Christ's release of the souls of the dead before his resurrection, thus providing a whole new Christian narrative setting for the Old Testament psalm verse:[83]

Ab increpatione et ira furoris domini
TERRA TREMUIT ET QUIEVIT
Monumenta aperta sunt
et multa corpora sanctorum surrexerunt
DUM RESURGERET IN IUDICIO DEUS
Christus surrexit ex mortuis
venite adoremus eum una voce dicentes
ALLELUIA.

By the reproof and wrath of the fury of the Lord
THE EARTH TREMBLED AND WAS STILL.
The tombs were opened
and many bodies of saints arose,
WHEN GOD WAS RISING AGAIN IN JUDGMENT.
Christ has risen from the dead.
Come let us worship him with one voice proclaiming:
ALLELUIA.

One of the most outstanding tropes of absolutely certain ninth-century origin is Tuotilo's *Hodie cantandus est nobis puer*.[84] Composed as an introduction to the Christmas Introit *Puer natus est nobis*, this adopts a unique dialogue form, a structure which allowed the composer to place the Gregorian Introit as the resolution of the Advent expectations richly focused by the trope. Tuotilo's text

[83] On this set of tropes see G. Björkvall, 'The Last Judgment: the apocalyptic theme in the Easter offertory trope *Ab increpatione et ira*', in: *Feste und Feiern im Mittelalter*, ed. D. Altenburg, J. Jarnut and H.-H. Steinhoff (Sigmaringen, 1991) pp. 255–68, from which the translation given here is taken. For the music see A. Haug, 'Zur Musik der ältesten Ostertropen', in *Feste und Feiern im Mittelalter*, pp. 269–81, and Rankin, 'Notker and Tuotilo', pp. 22–3.

[84] The text ed. in K. Young, *The Drama of the Medieval Church*, 2 vols. (Oxford, 1933) I, p. 195; also in Von den Steinen, *Notker* I, pp. 46ff.; for the music see S. Rankin, 'The Song School of St Gallen'.

and music vibrate with a living sense of the arrival of a boy who (in the words of Isaiah and the Introit) 'shall be called "angel of great counsel"'. In such a composition, the ideals of linguistic expression of the early Carolingians have come to full fruition: here the music and text of a Frankish song moulded around a Roman nucleus have become dynamically paired elements in a highly effective rhetorical statement. This Carolingian synthesis of words and music created a language which had the ability to articulate the message of Latin words more eloquently than pure speech.

Select bibliography

(Many entries in this list relate to more than one of the three subheadings, but are only cited once.)

Gregorian chant

W. Arlt, 'Funktion, Gattung und Form im liturgischen Gesang des frühen und hohen Mittelalters – eine Einführung', *Schweizer Jahrbuch für Musikwissenschaft* n.s. 2 (1982) pp. 13–26

Aureliani Reomensis, *Musica disciplina*, ed. L. Gushee, Corpus Scriptorum de Musica 21 (American Institute of Musicology, 1975)

M. Bielitz, *Musik und Grammatik: Studien zur mittelalterlichen Musiktheorie* (Munich and Salzburg, 1977)

G. Cattin, *Music of the Middle Ages* I (Cambridge, 1984)

R. Crocker and D. Hiley (eds.), *The Early Middle Ages to 1300*, The New Oxford History of Music II (2nd edn, Oxford, 1990)

S. J. P. van Dijk, 'Papal schola *versus* Charlemagne', in: *Organicae voces: Festschrift Joseph Smits van Waesberghe* (Amsterdam, 1963)

A. Ekenberg, *Cur cantatur? Die Funktionen des liturgischen Gesanges nach den Autoren der Karolingerzeit* (Stockholm, 1987)

Graduale triplex (Solesmes, 1979)

H. Hucke, 'Toward a new historical view of Gregorian chant', *Journal of the American Musicological Society* 33 (1980) pp. 437–67

M. Huglo, *Les Tonaires* (Paris, 1971)

K. Levy, 'Charlemagne's archetype of Gregorian chant', *Journal of the American Musicological Society* 40 (1987) pp. 1–30

K. Levy and J. Emerson, 'Plainchant', *The New Grove Dictionary of Music and Musicians*, ed. S. Sadie, 20 vols. (London, 1980), XIV pp. 800–45

J. McKinnon, 'The emergence of Gregorian chant in the Carolingian era', in: *Antiquity and the Middle Ages: From Ancient Greece to the 15th Century*, ed. J. McKinnon (London, 1990) pp. 88–119

H. Möller, 'Zur Frage der musikgeschichtlichen Bedeutung der Akademie Karls des Grossen: Die *Musica Albini*', in: *Akademie und Musik*, ed. W. Frobenius, N. Schwindt-Gross and T. Sick, Saarbrucken Studien zur Musikwissenschaft 13 (Saarbrucken, forthcoming)

H. Möller and R. Stephan (eds.), *Die Musik des Mittelalters*, Neues Handbuch der Musikwissenschaft 2 (Laaber, 1991)

K. F. Morrison, '"Know thyself": music in the Carolingian Renaissance', in: *Committenti e produzione artistico-letteraria nell'alto medioevo occidentale, Settimane* 39 (Spoleto, 1992) pp. 369–479

Musica et scolica enchiriadis, ed. H. Schmid (Munich, 1981)

N. Phillips, 'Classical and Late Latin sources for ninth-century treatises on music', *Music Theory and Its Sources: Antiquity and the Middle Ages*, ed. A. Barbera (Indiana, 1990) pp. 100–35

H. S. Powers, 'Language models and musical analysis', *Ethnomusicology* 24 (1980) pp. 1–60

'Mode', *The New Grove*, XII, pp. 376–84, 447–8

F. Reckow, 'Zur Formung einer europäischen musikalischen Kultur im Mittelalter. Kriterien und Faktoren ihrer Geschichtlichkeit', *Bericht über den internationalen musikwissenchaftlichen Kongress Bayreuth 1981*, ed. C-H. Mahling and S. Wiesmann (Kassel etc., 1984) pp. 12–29

B. Stäblein, 'Die Entstehung des gregorianischer Chorals', *Die Musikforschung* 27 (1974) pp. 5–17

Die Gesänge des altrömische Graduale, Monumenta Monodica Medi Aevi 2 (Kassel, 1979)

'"Gregorius Praesul", der Prolog zum römischen Antiphonale', in: *Musik und Verlag. Karl Vötterle zum 65. Geburtstag* (Kassel, 1968) pp. 537–61

H. van der Werf, *The Emergence of Gregorian Chant*, 2 vols. (Rochester, 1983)

P. Wagner, *Einführung in die gregorianischer Melodien*, 3 vols. (Leipzig, 1895–1921)

Transmission, notation, semiology

W. Arlt, 'Anschaulichkeit und analytischer Charakter: Kriterien der Beschreibung und Analyse früher Neumenschriften', in: *Musicologie médiévale. Notations et Séquences*, ed. M. Huglo (Paris, 1987) pp. 29–55

E. Cardine, 'Sémiologie grégorienne', *Études grégoriennes* 11 (1970) pp. 1–58

S. Corbin, *Die Neumen*, Palaeographie der Musik I:3, ed. W. Arlt (Cologne, 1977)

J. Froger, 'L'Épître de Notker sur les "lettres significatives". Édition critique', *Études grégoriennes* 5 (1962) pp. 23–71

J. Handschin, 'Eine alte Neumenschrift', *Acta musicologia* 22 (1950) pp. 69–97

J. Hourlier and M. Huglo, 'Notation paléofranque', *Études grégoriennes* 2 (1957) pp. 212–19

Hucbald, *De harmonica institutione*, trans. W. Babb, ed. C. V. Palisca, *Hucbald, Guido, and John on Music* (New Haven and London, 1978)

D. Hughes, 'Evidence for the traditional view of the transmission of Gregorian chant', *Journal of the American Musicological Society* 40 (1987) pp. 377–404

E. Jammers, 'Die Entstehung der Neumenschrift', in: *Schrift, Ordnung, Gestalt: Gesammelte Aufsätze zur älteren Musikgeschichte*, Neue Heidelberger Studien zur Musikwissenschaft 1 (Bern and Munich, 1969) pp. 70–87

Tafeln zur Neumenschrift (Tutzing, 1965)

K. Levy, 'On Gregorian orality', *Journal of the American Musicological Society* 43 (1990) pp. 185–227

'On the origin of neumes', *Early Music History* 7 (1987) pp. 59–90
'Toledo, Rome and the legacy of Gaul', *Early Music History* 4 (1984) pp. 49–99
Paléographie musicale including:
Antiphonale missarum sancti Gregorii IXe–Xe siècle: codex 239 de la Bibliothèque de Laon, ed. A. Mocquereau, Paléographie musicale 10 (Tournai, 1909)
Antiphonale missarum sancti Gregorii Xe siècle: codex 47 de la Bibliothèque de Chartres, ed. A. Mocquereau, Paléographie musicale 11 (Tournai, 1912)
Cantatorium IXe siècle no. 359 de la Bibliothèque de Saint-Gall, ed. A. Mocquereau, Paléographie musicale 2nd ser. 2 (Tournai, 1924)
B. Stäblein, *Schriftbild der einstimmigen Musik*, Musikgeschichte in Bildern III:4 (Leipzig, 1975)
L. Treitler, 'Communication', *Journal of the American Musicological Society* 41 (1988) pp. 566–75
'The early history of the music writing in the west', *Journal of the American Musicological Society* 35 (1982) pp. 237–78
'Homer and Gregory: the transmission of epic poetry and plainchant', *The Musical Quarterly* 60 (1974) pp. 333–72
'Oral, written and literate process in the transmission of medieval music', *Speculum* 56 (1981) pp. 471–91
'Reading and singing: on the genesis of Occidental music-writing', *Early Music History* 4 (1984) pp. 135–208

New composition

W. Arlt and G. Björkvall (eds.), *Recherches nouvelles sur les tropes liturgiques*, Corpus Troporum, Studia Latina Stockholmiensia 35 (Stockholm, forthcoming)
Corpus troporum, Acta Universitatis Stockholmiensis: Studia Latina Stockholmiensia (1975)
R. Crocker, *The Early Medieval Sequence* (Berkeley, Los Angeles and London, 1977)
'The sequence', in: *Gattungen der Musik in Einzeldarstellungen: Gedenkschrift Leo Schrade*, ed. W. Arlt, E. Lichtenhahn and H. Oesch (Bern and Munich, 1973) pp. 269–322
J. Handschin, 'Trope, sequence, conductus', in: *Early Medieval Music up to 1300*, ed. Dom A. Hughes, The New Oxford History of Music 2 (1st edn, Oxford, 1954) pp. 128–74
A. Haug, 'Neue Ansätze im 9. Jahrhundert', in: *Die Musik des Mittelalters*, ed. Möller pp. 94–128
D. Hiley, 'Plainchant transfigured: innovation and reformation through the ages', in: *Antiquity and the Middle Ages*, ed. McKinnon, pp. 120–42
G. Iverson (ed.), *Research on Tropes*, Kungl. Vitterhets Historie och Antikvitets Akademien Konferenser 8 (Stockholm, 1983)
R. Jacobsson and L. Treitler, 'Tropes and the concept of genre', in *Pax et Sapientia. Studies in Text and Music of Liturgical Tropes and Sequences in Memory of Gordon Anderson*, ed. R. Jacobsson (Stockholm, 1986) pp. 59–89
R. Jonsson and L. Treitler, 'Medieval music and language: a reconsideration of the relationship', in: *Music and Language*, Studies in the History of Music 1 (New York, 1983) pp. 1–23

C. Leonardi and E. Menesto (eds.), *La tradizione dei tropi liturgici* (Spoleto, 1990)

G. Silagi (ed.), *Liturgische Tropen*, Münchener Beiträge zur Mediävistik und Renaissance-Forschung 36 (Munich, 1985)

B. Stäblein, 'Modes of underlaying a text to melismas: trope, sequence and other forms', in: *Report of the English Congress of the International Musicological Society New York 1961*, ed. J. LaRue (Kassel etc., 1961) pp. 12–29

'Zur Frühgeschichte der Sequenz', *Archiv für Musikwissenschaft* 18 (1961) pp. 1–33

W. von den Steinen, 'Die Anfänge der Sequenzendichtung', *Zeitschrift für Schweizerische Kirchengeschichte* 40 (1946) pp. 190–212, 241–68; 41 (1947) pp. 19–48, 122–62

Notker der Dichter und seine geistige Welt, 2 vols. (Berne, 1948)

Two books of significance to chant studies have appeared since this chapter was written – unfortunately too late for their conclusions to be taken into account in the discussion:

D. Hiley, *Western Plainchant: A Handbook* (Oxford, 1993)

P. Jeffery, *Re-envisioning Past Musical Cultures: Ethnomusicology in the Study of Gregorian Chant* (Chicago, 1992)

11

The legacy of the Carolingians

Rosamond McKitterick

There was a time when the tenth century was regarded as a *saeculum ferreum*, an era after the glories of the Carolingian Renaissance when life was even more nasty, brutish and short than ever before and cultural activity was at a low ebb. The essays in this volume, however, have made it clear that culture was not turned off like a tap in 900 AD. Such an arbitary cut-off date simply makes no sense and is entirely irrelevant in many regions of western Europe. Not one of the essays in this book has indicated any complete break at all. On the contrary, in every respect – education, thought and logic, book production, the writing of history, hagiography, political ideas, theology, literature and particularly in music – there is not only continuity into the tenth century but indisputable evidence of firm foundations built and the inauguration of a long period of intellectual, artistic and musical creativity. In spheres it was not possible to cover in this volume, notably science (such as knowledge of the physical world, astronomy, medicine, mathematics and geography) and law (both secular and ecclesiastical) the same can be said.

Certainly the Carolingians drew fruitfully in many respects on a still older heritage. They often looked back to a past which they endeavoured to emulate. In their work can be seen a highly creative culture in which the interaction of royal courts, monasteries, cathedrals and their schools is most striking. It was a culture unafraid of experimentation and innovation. It provided for individual enterprise to a remarkable degree. In every sphere we can observe the speedy communication, exchange and transference of new ideas, and the skill and devotion of scholars and practitioners of the various arts. The essays in this book have each demonstrated extraordinary diversity. Yet in the different areas of cultural activity they discuss, Carolingian culture was far from being fragmented, disparate or unconnected; there is sufficient similarity of response and coherence to suggest that this richly variegated culture can be understood as a coherent whole. It was a literate culture dependent on the written word in many respects, but, as Susan Rankin has stressed in her exposition of the extraordinary concurrence of developments in music, in relation to texts, language and writing, with those in other spheres in the Carolingian world, it was also a culture that was still highly dependent on, as well as able to support, oral practice. It did so to such an extent that written and oral modes were interdependent, with writing harnessed in ways most useful to the Franks.

A constant and striking theme of the essays in this book has been the strength of the Romano-Christian tradition inherited by the Franks and the strength of the attachment to Rome or, at least, what was perceived and understood to be Roman. It was far from being a simple or single idea of Rome that might be invoked. Different weight was accorded by various individuals to the classical tradition, Roman imperial ideas (both pagan and Christian), and papal Rome and the pope as the prime source of religious authority and leadership. The Franks were indeed Rome's heirs; they made Roman, Christian and Latin ideas and techniques of art and scholarship their own. In this the role of the Christian Church was no less crucial, not only for the spiritual and moral framework it provided for much of the Carolingian achievement, but also for its specific liturgical and educational needs.

Every apparent manifestation of debt to Rome, however, requires careful distinctions to be drawn and a precise understanding of what this potentially multi-faceted concept of 'Rome' meant in any one context. In particular, the transmission of specific ideas, methods of thinking, learning, teaching and writing, genres, and texts have been highlighted by all the chapters in this book. Janet Nelson demonstrated the evocation and utilisation of the idea of Rome and Roman imperial power in her chapter on political thought. Vivien Law explained how the art of the Latin grammarians was mediated through the Carolingians and how parsing grammar continued to be an enormously productive genre until the fifteenth century. Carolingian scholars made the first attempts to apply the new questions and techniques derived from the study of dialectic to language. Mary Garrison elucidated the theme of 'Rome's heirs' in terms of different poetic metres and literary genres. The emulation of classical models and the expression of a sense of the participation in a renewal of Classical Antiquity, however, is but one aspect of the vitality of Carolingian literature, with, in Garrison's words: 'strong personalities responding to the challenges of each other's verse, and to the stimulus of their unique historical situation'. Old High German and Old Saxon texts also reflect this, and many of the Old High German texts that survive, as Cyril Edwards has pointed out, are unique early examples of their genre. John Marenbon showed how much the Carolingian scholars drew on past methods of thought and how innovation was achieved through the pursuit of tradition. In the writing of history, too, the sense of continuity created by working within the Eusebian and Christian historiographical tradition as well as drawing on classical models is balanced by many new kinds of secular history writing – imperial biography of a distinctive kind, epic poem and annals. Caroline minuscule emerged from the Roman script system in use in the preceding eight centuries and in its turn provided the basis for all subsequent developments of book and documentary script. In all aspects of art, as George Henderson has demonstrated, emulation and invention are again the keys to understanding the various forms of Carolingian artistic expression; we can see how much of an inspiration was provided by the Roman classical heritage as well as how much the Carolingians were able to draw on other, Germanic and Insular, sources of inspiration and weld them together to produce wholly new visual effects. Much of what we observe in Carolingian music was entirely new, but even here, the Roman ecclesiastical musical heritage and sense of a Roman past played a crucial role, and classical musical theory had its place in the musical treatises of such authors as Hucbald of St Amand and Aurelian of Réomé.

Thus Carolingian scholars, authors, scribes and artists provided a bedrock so firm that it could support and direct the shape of many new developments. A symbol of this bedrock is the vehicle for knowledge, the book, the evolution of caroline minuscule and the creation of musical script. Methods of book production, script, layout, decoration and illustration were received and further refined by the Carolingian scribes. So too were the means of exchanging and storing knowledge in libraries, transmitting texts and ensuring their availability for future generations. Knowledge was organised and classified, in the sphere of secular knowledge and thought discussed by John Marenbon, as well as more generally. Frankish creators of libraries and monasteries and masters of scriptoria had a clear and inherited sense of what a well-equipped library should contain. The preservation of some late-antique educational traditions in Gallo-Roman and Merovingian Gaul, and the dissemination of various texts, not least Cassiodorus' *Institutiones*, had helped to create the cast of mind and customary frame of reference, in the sense of particular authors and texts, within which to organise knowledge. Yet it was in the Carolingian period that we see this systematised and disseminated ever more widely as new monasteries, such as Fulda, Lorsch, Reichenau, St Gall, Würzburg and Corvey were founded in the course of the eighth and ninth centuries. Older monasteries such as St Denis, St Amand, Echternach, Corbie, St Martin at Tours and St Germain des Prés came, or continued to flourish, under royal protection, and many acquired the necessary surplus of wealth to apportion some of their endowment towards the promotion of culture.

To Carolingian monasteries we owe the definition of a canon of approved knowledge which remained the basis for education and intellectual endeavour throughout the Middle Ages. It took the form of an array of Old and New Testament texts in newly corrected versions, patristic biblical exegesis and theology, treatises for use in the schools, guides to ascetic discipline and the religious life, liturgical books, practical manuals, legal compilations, philosophy, histories, pagan and Christian poetry and the works of medieval authors from England, Spain, Italy and Gaul, among whom those of a number of Carolingian scholars were gradually and increasingly included. The Carolingians transmitted to their contemporaries and successors a model for an appropriately stocked library for the safeguarding of Christian learning. It was within the Carolingian ecclesiastical centres that there developed the prescriptive codification of this approved canon of knowledge in the form, firstly, of bibliographical handbooks, based on such texts as Jerome-Gennadius, *De viris illustribus*, pseudo-Gelasius, *De libris recipiendis et non recipiendis* and Cassiodorus, *Institutiones*, and, secondly, the library catalogues of which we have surviving examples from such houses as St Riquier, Lorsch, Murbach, Reichenau and St Gallen.[1] How fundamental this legacy was can easily be recognised in the structure and content of libraries of eleventh- and twelfth-century European monasteries and concentrations of book production such as can be seen at St Amand, Corbie, Zwiefalten or Monte Cassino.[2]

The classical late-antique and early Christian heritage of the Carolingians with respect to texts and transmitted learning is very clear. The Franks nevertheless grafted onto that heritage a growing body of new authors and new works, such as the exegesis of scripture, poetry, encyclopaedic compendia, philosophical discussions and didactic treatises of the Insular scholars Bede, Alcuin, Dicuil, John Scottus Eriugena, Martin of Laon and Sedulius Scottus, of the Visigoths, Theodulf of Orleans and Claudius of Turin, and of the Franks, Hraban Maur of Fulda, Walahfrid Strabo of Reichenau, Jonas of Orleans, Magnus of Sens, Lupus of Ferrières, Heiric of Auxerre, Angelomus of Luxeuil, Freculf of Lisieux, Agobard of Lyons, Gottschalk of Orbais, Hincmar of Rheims, Hucbald of St Amand, Notker of St Gall, Smaragdus of St Mihiel and many more who have been discussed in the preceding pages. Thereby they created a distinctive culture and intellectual tradition in its own right as well as defining it and delimiting it for their successors.

Important questions that remain to be explored are the endurance of the Carolingian efforts to create some semblance of unity of purpose and coherence, if not actual unity and uniformity, in different aspects of cultural life elucidated in the first chapter of this book by Giles Brown. If they endured, was this despite, or because of, political and economic reorientations on a massive scale? Further, can the many intellectual and cultural achievements of the Carolingian Renaissance be understood in any sense as comprising a culture that remained common to the whole of Europe? Was Carolingian culture a binding force in the development of western European civilisation in ways that can be specified in terms of precise examples?

The acceleration of Viking raids from the second half of the ninth century,

[1] McKitterick, *Carolingians*, pp. 165–210.

[2] On twelfth-century French libraries see Leopold Delisle, *Le Cabinet des manuscrits de la bibliothèque impériale*, 3 vols (Paris, 1868–81) especially II, pp. 427–550. On Zwiefalten in southern Germany see Sigrid von Borries Schulten, *Die Romanischen Handschriften der Württembergischen Landesbibliothek Stuttgart* I *Provenienz Zwiefalten* (Stuttgart, 1987). On Monte Cassino in Central Italy see Herbert Bloch, *Monte Cassino in the Middle Ages* 3 vols. (Cambridge, Mass., 1986).

the replacement of the Carolingian rulers in the west and east Frankish kingdoms in the course of the tenth century, and the major changes in political authority in the whole of western Europe that can be observed in the course of the tenth and eleventh centuries certainly contributed to the redistribution of patronage, the prominence of new centres such as Liège and Trier, and the relative obscurity of others, such as Tours.[3] Political and economic developments also arguably altered intellectual and cultural priorities. It is clear, for example, that the Ottonian rulers of the Saxon kingdom in the tenth century did not emulate the Carolingians in taking a lead in cultural affairs. Unlike the Carolingian rulers of the ninth century, there is no evidence of the Ottonian rulers' systematic patronage of particular centres, no group of schools associated with the court, no royal role in the dissemination of particular texts, no direction or impetus provided for the cultivation of contemporary scholarship, no court atelier for the production of fine books for use by the royal family, and little sign of even occasional sponsorship of individual scholars or craftsmen.[4]

Yet cultural activity did not cease in Ottonian Germany. Far from it. It was episcopal, rather than royal, patronage which was the deciding factor in the degree of literacy and educational achievement in Ottonian Germany. This can be observed in the accounts given of the schools of Augsburg, Würzburg, Cologne, Liège, Metz, Toul, St Gall, Mainz, Magdeburg, Hildesheim, Reichenau and many more.[5] Certainly episcopal schools appear to have eclipsed monastic schools east of the Rhine, but the extent to which this is the case in the tenth-century west Frankish region has still to be determined.

It should be noted that the bishops presiding over these schools were originally monks from some of the 'reformed' centres of Lotharingia and elsewhere. Indeed, it is somewhat surprising that the conjunction of the monastic reform movement with the supposed dearth of culture in the tenth century should not have acted as a warning sooner than it did to be wary of underestimating either what was being produced in the various monasteries and episcopal sees of western Europe in the course of the tenth century, or the degree to which these were a natural outcome of developments in the ninth century. The expansion of Christianity into northern and eastern Europe in the tenth and eleventh centuries also ensured the continuation of Frankish Christian Latin culture, and much of this went hand in hand with either conquest or the assertion of political roles of dominance, alliance or agreed coexistence.

The wealth of recent work on intellectual and cultural creativity in the tenth and early eleventh centuries, and the agenda for future research together suggest,

3 On political and cultural developments in the tenth century see most recently *Il secolo de Ferro. Mito e realtà del secolo X. Settimane* 38 (Spoleto, 1991).

4 See R. McKitterick, 'Ottonian intellectual culture in the tenth century and the role of Theophanu', *Early Medieval Europe* 2 (1993) pp. 53–74. For a richly illustrated interpretation of Ottonian artistic culture and its context see Henry Mayr-Harting, *Ottonian Book Illumination. An Historical Study*, 2 vols. (London, 1991).

5 A useful synthesis is Pierre Riché, *Écoles et enseignement dans le Haut Moyen Age de la fin du Ve siècle au milieu du XIe siècle* (Paris, 1979).

moreover, that common assumptions of a major watershed in European culture around the year 1000 may also be totally inappropriate. Discussions of tenth-century Latin culture in particular, while acknowledging that the creativity of the tenth century was not as spectacular as those of the ninth or twelfth centuries, nevertheless makes it clear how much was going on in France, Germany, Italy, Spain and England, and how Latin culture together with Christianity expanded to embrace Denmark, Sweden, Norway, Iceland, Bohemia, Poland and Hungary in the course of the tenth century.[6] Particular individuals, such as Gerbert of Rheims, Letald of Micy, Widukind of Corvey, Hrotsvita of Gandersheim, Odo of Cluny, Liutprand of Cremona and Rather of Verona made their own distinctive contributions. There was a wealth of hagiography and accounts of the translations of relics. A lack of much new theology was amply compensated for by a creative liturgy, with liturgical poetry, tropes, sequences, offices and other new musical compositions. Important new literary works were composed, in both Latin and the various vernaculars. Innovations were made in teaching methods, especially of grammar. Aspects of both classical and contemporary Greek culture played an increasingly influential role in western culture.[7] Book production continued in many centres in Germany, northern Italy, Spain and France in the best traditions established by the Carolingian scriptoria. Common to all was the maintenance of the Latin language as the means of formal communication and conduct of intellectual life even though, as we have seen, the German vernaculars became increasingly effective instruments of communication and Notker Labeo, among others, taught in German with German translations of Latin texts at St Gall. If one thing only were to be highlighted as a fundamental legacy of the Carolingians to western culture, it would be the consolidation of the position of Latin, the secure access thereby provided to the classical world and knowledge of Antiquity, and the provision of a common tongue, especially for intellectual discourse, for the whole of western Europe for centuries to come.

Nevertheless, knowledge of the tenth century itself, still less the ways in which the foundations of eleventh- and twelfth-century culture are to be specifically identified in the eighth, ninth and tenth centuries (as distinct from vague theories of cultural continuity) are not yet ready for a full-scale analysis. It is essential to recognise the impossibility of generalisation at this stage. Not only is there enormous regional variation, so that what may be true of western France may be totally at odds with what we know of south-eastern Germany, central Italy or the Rhineland. There is also the fact that many studies have focused on very specific texts or centres without considering them in a wider context. Although the regional diversification in the late ninth and tenth centuries is

[6] *Lateinische Kultur im X. Jahrhundert. Akten des I. Internationalen Mittellateinerkongresses Heidelberg, 12–15.IX.1988*, ed. Walter Berschin (Stuttgart, 1991) = *Mittellateinisches Jahrbuch* 24/25 (1989/90).

[7] Walter Berschin, *Griechisch-lateinsiches Mittalalter. Vom Hieronymus zu Nikolaus von Kues* (Bern and Munich, 1980); Eng. trans. by J. C. Frakes and revised and expanded edition, *Greek Letters and the Latin Middle Ages* (Washington D.C., 1988).

undoubted, change and reorganisation in the political sphere, for instance, is not necessarily an indication of discontinuities in the cultural sphere. The indications so far, indeed, are that Carolingian culture had sufficient strength and energy to endure despite the fragmentation of the political and social context within which it had flourished. Much more work remains to be done, not least on the manuscript evidence from west of the Rhine and Rhône-Saône rivers in the tenth and early eleventh centuries, on the lines of Hoffmann's monumental and masterly survey of Ottonian book production.[8]

Full assessment of the Carolingian legacy, both in its impact and in its ramifications, therefore, is still something for the future. It will need to be conducted on very precise lines, both in terms of specific centres and regions, and in those of particular manifestations of cultural activity within their own social and political contexts. Nevertheless, even our present and partial understanding of Carolingian culture is of a diverse legacy of great power and an outstanding contribution to the continuity of creative endeavour within human society. The Carolingians imparted to future generations with their emulation and invention in all aspects of culture, the conviction that the past not only mattered but was a priceless hoard of treasure to be guarded, conserved, augmented, enriched and passed on.

[8] Hartmut Hoffman, *Buchkunst und Königtum im ottonischen und frühsalischen Reich*, 2 vols., MGH Schriften 30 (Stuttgart, 1986).

Index of manuscripts

General index

Manuscripts known by a name, for example, Coronation Gospels, are listed with a cross reference to the Manuscripts Index. Works by authors are listed under the relevant author, except in the case of anonymous works, which are listed by title. Only those modern authors referred to by name in the text (rather than the footnotes) have been included in the index.